Jeffrey Richards is Professor of Cultural History at Lancaster University. His books include *Sir Henry Irving: A Victorian Actor and His World, John Ruskin and the Victorian Theatre* and *The Ancient World on the Victorian and Edwardian Stage*. He is General Editor of I.B.Tauris's *Cinema and Society* series and he is a regular broadcaster on BBC radio.

'I rejoice at Jeffrey Richards' achievement: the first thorough and gratifyingly detailed study of London's pantomimes from the 1830s through to *c.*1900 which quietly blends immaculate scholarship, close analysis and archival work with entertaining readability. So doing, he has produced a work entirely free from whimsy, mawkish nostalgia and enforced rapture that so disfigure earlier attempts to describe this major English theatrical genre.'

David Mayer,
Emeritus Professor of Drama, Manchester University

'An insightful and passionate study of the pantomime written by one of Britain's leading cultural historians. Jeffrey Richards is able to bring the Victorian panto back to life, show its vibrancy and popularity, and the extraordinary detail with which it was discussed in the print media. Richards almost made me want to go back in time to witness these spectacles firsthand.'

Anselm Heinrich,
Head of Theatre Studies, University of Glasgow

THE GOLDEN AGE OF PANTOMIME

SLAPSTICK, SPECTACLE AND SUBVERSION IN VICTORIAN ENGLAND

Jeffrey Richards

I.B. TAURIS

LONDON · NEW YORK

First published in 2015 by I.B.Tauris & Co Ltd
6 Salem Road, London W2 4BU
175 Fifth Avenue, New York NY 10010
www.ibtauris.com

Distributed in the United States and Canada Exclusively by Palgrave Macmillan
175 Fifth Avenue, New York NY 10010

Copyright © 2015 Jeffrey Richards

ISBN: 978 1 78076 293 7
eISBN: 978 0 85773 587 4

A full CIP record for this book is available from the British Library
A full CIP record is available from the Library of Congress

Library of Congress Catalog Card Number: available

Typeset by Data Standards Ltd, Frome, Somerset, BA11 2RY
Printed and bound in Sweden by ScandBook AB

For Jennie Bisset and Michael Kilgarriff

Table of Contents

List of Illustrations

D.N.B.   *Dictionary of National Biography*

I.L.N.   *Illustrated London News*

I.S.D.N. *Illustrated Sporting and Dramatic News*

Introduction and Acknowledgements

I have always loved Christmas, taking a Dickensian delight in everything to do with the festive season – cards and carols, turkey and Christmas pudding, presents and family gatherings and, of course, the pantomime. Little suspecting the direction in which my future research would take me, I was fortunate to see at Birmingham's theatres in the 1960s and 1970s many of the giants of the music hall in the pantomime: Ken Dodd in *Dick Whittington*, Arthur Askey in *Jack and the Beanstalk*, John Inman in *Mother Goose*, Les Dawson in *Babes in the Wood* and Frankie Howerd and Tommy Trinder in *Robinson Crusoe*. Every year from 1990 until 2002 I went to the much-missed Players Theatre at Charing Cross to see one of the Victorian extravaganzas by writers such as J.R. Planché and H.J. Byron. All these experiences prepared me perfectly to study the Victorian pantomime. For the essence of pantomime is performance and it was invaluable experience to have seen both pantomime and extravaganza live and in action. All that remains of the Victorian pantomime is the often incredibly detailed reviews and the evocative engravings in the new illustrated magazines. I have drawn extensively on these sources to try and recreate for the modern reader something of the nature and experience of the Victorian pantomime. The present book is one of the three intended outcomes of a three-year Arts and Humanities Council-funded project, *A Cultural History of Pantomime, 1837–1901*. The other two outcomes will be a single-authored monograph by my research partner, Kate Newey, and an edited volume of essays based on contributions to the three conferences staged as part of the project. So thanks are due first to the A.H.R.C. for funding the project and the conferences. My principal debt is to my research partner, Professor Kate Newey, and to our invaluable and indefatigable research associate, Dr Peter Yeandle, for their assistance, inspiration and creative cooperation. I also learned much from the many scholars who participated in and contributed to the three conferences and the symposium that were integral to our research programme. The staffs of the British Library, Bristol University Theatre Collection, the Theatre Museum, Blyth House, the

Victoria and Albert Museum, the Newspaper Library at Colindale, Lancaster University Library and the Garrick Club proved ever-helpful. I am grateful to Linda Persson and Lauren Kenright for their word-processing expertise. I also owe a special and particular debt to Michael Kilgarriff, literally a giant of pantomime, who presented me with Dan Leno's own annotated script to the 1896 Drury Lane *Aladdin*, and Jennie Bisset who placed at my disposal her entire research on the career of Dykwynkyn. This book is dedicated to them in recognition of their extraordinary generosity of spirit. My thanks are also due to Kate Reeves for her copy-editing and to Zoe Ross for compiling the index.

Preface

The pantomime as we know it today developed in the 1840s from a merger of three distinct genres: the harlequinade, the largely dialogue-less comic knockabout of Clown, Harlequin and Pantaloon; the extravaganza, the elegant and witty satire of modern life in comic versions of classical myths and fairy tales; and the burlesque, the irreverent send-up of everything the Victorians customarily took seriously, such as English history, grand opera and Shakespeare. This book will seek to show how this merger took place and how the pantomime continually evolved over the rest of the nineteenth century into something that would be recognizable in the twenty-first century. It will examine how the pantomime directly embodied the dominant spirit of the age and how it reflected changes in that spirit. It will analyse the regular ingredients of the pantomime: spectacle, slapstick, gender role reversal and topical allusion. One of the enduring values of pantomime is its role as a cultural barometer for its times, directly reflecting current attitudes, beliefs and preoccupations, fads and fashions. The book will highlight the vital contribution to the evolution of the genre made by four titanic figures: the writers J.R. Planché and E.L. Blanchard, the scene-painter W.R. Beverley and the producer Sir Augustus Harris. The second half of the book will concentrate on the Theatre Royal, Drury Lane, and by analysing every Christmas pantomime staged there up to 1901 will demonstrate how this most popular of genres changed and developed.

1

Transformations

Of all the theatrical genres most prized by the Victorians, the pantomime is perhaps the most recognizable in the twenty-first century. It remains true that it constitutes the first theatrical experience of most children and now, just as in the nineteenth century, a successful pantomime season is the key to a profitable year's work in most theatres.[1] What explains the enduring success of this strange hybrid combination of slapstick and spectacle, comedy and art?

Firstly, pantomime had a universal appeal. Everyone went to the pantomime in Victorian England. From the Queen and the royal family to the humblest of her subjects. It appealed to West End and East End audiences, to London and the provinces, to both sexes and all ages. The first play Queen Victoria saw after her coronation was the Drury Lane pantomime, *Harlequin and Jack Frost*, which she visited on 10 January 1839. In December 1860, to entertain the royal children, there was a command performance of *Babes in the Wood* at Windsor Castle. The royal children even performed their own pantomime-type play *Red Riding Hood* for their parents, an event captured in a charming canvas by E.H. Corbould, which Prince Albert commissioned and presented to his wife on her thirty-sixth birthday, 24 May 1855.[2] Many of the luminaries of the Victorian Age, among them John Ruskin, Lewis Carroll, Charles Dickens, Matthew Arnold and W.E. Gladstone, were devotees of the pantomime. But ordinary people also queued for hours to get into the pantomime all over the country. Illustrated magazines regularly published pictures of the queues and the packed galleries.

The magical escapist appeal of pantomime was put into words by theatre-mad Charles Dickens in his account of David Copperfield's visit to Covent Garden to see the pantomime:

> The mingled reality and mystery of the whole show, the influence upon me of the poetry, the lights, the music, the company, the smooth stupendous changes of glittering and brilliant scenery, were so dazzling and opened up such illimitable regions of delight, that

when I came out into the rainy street, at twelve o'clock at night, I felt as if I had come from the clouds, where I had been leading a romantic life for ages, to a bawling, splashing, link-lighted, umbrella-struggling, hackney-coach-jostling, patten-clinking, muddy, miserable world.[3]

Secondly, pantomime was never static as a form but was continually evolving. In 1881, the eminent critic Dutton Cook, surveying the history of pantomime wrote:

Some eighty years ago John Kemble, addressing his scene-painter in reference to a forthcoming pantomime, wrote: 'It must be *very short, very laughable* and *very cheap*'. If the great actor-manager's requirements were fairly met, it is certain that the entertainment in question was a kind very different to the pantomime of our day – a production that is invariably very long, rarely laughable and always of exceeding costliness ... In modern pantomime it may be said that the opening is everything and that the harlequinade is deferred as long as possible.[4]

How had this come about? Through a series of transformations, in which the key figures were James Robinson Planché (1796–1880), William Roxby Beverley (c.1810–89), Edward Leman Blanchard (1820–89) and Sir Augustus Harris (1852–96). All of these changes were contested and there was a continual battle for the soul of the pantomime. A recurrent refrain from theatre critics throughout the nineteenth century is 'the pantomime is not what it was.' This is declared, for instance, by Leigh Hunt in 1831, by Andrew Halliday in 1863, by W. Davenport Adams in 1882 and by Max Beerbohm in 1898.[5] In fact it was never what it was but was always being refreshed and reinvigorated.

In the Regency period, the harlequinade was everything and the 'opening', a handful of scenes with a fairy story or nursery rhyme narrative, was as short as possible. In the celebrated production *Mother Goose* (1806–7), which ran for ninety-two performances, made Grimaldi a star and defined the nature of the Regency pantomime, there were four opening scenes and fifteen of the harlequinade. The harlequinade was essentially dialogue-less and centred on physical action, slapstick, knockabout and comic songs, a form dictated by the 1737 Licensing Act which gave the monopoly of the spoken word on stage to the patent theatres, Drury Lane and Covent Garden.

The passing of the Theatre Regulation Act of 1843 signalled a major shift in the nature of the genre. The act abolished the patent theatres' monopoly of the spoken word and opened up the use of dialogue to all theatres. This had a direct effect on the pantomime opening, which got steadily longer and longer, revelling in the linguistic freedom allowed by rhyming couplets, the ability to pun and the chance to comment on current events. It was now directly affected by another form which had emerged to beat the dialogue ban – the extravaganza or burlesque. These forms emerged from the *burletta*, 'by which description' Planché reported:

> after much controversy both in and out of court, we were desired to understand dramas containing not less than five pieces of vocal music in each act, and which were also, with one or two exceptions not to be found in the *repertoire* of the patent houses.[6]

The Olympic and Adelphi Theatres were specially licensed for burlettas and James Robinson Planché perfected the extravaganza form, first seen at the Olympic in *Olympic Revels* in 1831. There is no doubt that the extravaganza and burlesque were different animals and a whole scholarly industry has grown up seeking to define and distinguish between them.[7] In fact we can do no better than refer to Planché who wrote that the term extravaganza distinguished 'the whimsical treatment of a poetic subject from the broad caricature of a tragedy or serious opera which was correctly described as a burlesque.'[8] The problem for the learned academics agonizing over precise descriptions is that in their characteristically expansive way the Victorians used the terms interchangeably throughout the century. W. Davenport Adams, for instance, in his 1891 history *A Book of Burlesque* announced that he would not be covering extravaganza but then claimed that Planché had been the pioneer of 'the classical or fairy burlesque'.[9] Planché, who prided himself in writing extravaganzas, rather than burlesques, would have been furious.

From 1831 to 1856 Planché provided extravaganzas for a succession of theatres, culminating in the series at the Lyceum which was deemed to represent the peak period of the form. Dutton Cook, like Davenport Adams equating extravaganza and burlesque, wrote:

> Without doubt the modern pantomime opening owes much of its form to modern burlesque and extravaganza, of which the late Mr Planché may be regarded as the inventor … Gradually he created a school of burlesque writers indeed; but his scholars at last rebelled against him and 'barred him out', a fate to which schoolmasters have often been liable. Still burlesque in the worthy Planché form, and of the spuriously imitative form, which copied, and at the same time degraded him, grew and throve and at last invaded the domains of pantomime. 'Openings' fell into the hands of burlesque-writers … punning rhymes, parodies and comic dances, delayed the entrance of clown and harlequin, till at last their significance and occupation seem almost to have gone from them.[10]

The 1850s and 1860s were the heyday of the burlesque and extravaganza. The stage, liberated by the 1843 Theatre Regulation Act, revelled in wordplay. The particular appeal of burlesque lay in puns, parodies both musical and literary, topical allusions and contemporary slang. Certain theatres, notably the Olympic, the Adelphi, the Strand and later in the century the Gaiety, came to specialize in burlesque and a group of talented writers provided an unending flow of scripts: Frank Talfourd, H.J. Byron, Frank Burnand and the Brough Brothers, Robert and William, among them. But as Richard Schoch points out, none of the great actor-managers of the nineteenth century, Macready, Phelps, Charles Kean, Irving or Tree, ever staged a burlesque, though Macready did memorably produce a Planché extravaganza.[11] Everything was fair game for burlesquing: classical myths, fairy tales, popular melodrama, English history, Arthurian legend, Arabian Nights tales, grand opera, Shakespeare, Scott, Ainsworth and Dickens. A breed of burlesque performers developed who attracted devoted followings: Madame Vestris, Marie Wilton, Nellie Farren, James Bland and Fred Leslie among them. This all had an unquestionable effect on the pantomime.

The success on the stage of extravaganza and burlesque led the *I.L.N.* (2 January 1847) only four years after the Act was passed to comment: 'Every season convinces us more and more that [pantomimes] have had their day; and that, with the exception of their mere physical jokes, none can elicit from an audience those peals of laughter and applause which accompany the progress of a burlesque.' The physical jokes which elicited the laughter the critic enumerated:

> There are ludicrous associations connected with putting a sweep in a milk-pail, or knocking over an image-man; and an assault upon any of the recognised authorities (especially policemen) is sure to be hailed with shouts from the gallery. But when these are over, the insipidity of the attempts at comicality, and want of sustaining interest in the action, become very tedious.

The critic complained that the pantomime had fallen way behind other theatrical forms, had not changed or developed in twenty years, that the harlequinade was now just meaningless knockabout and that there was no link between it and the opening:

> It is generally acknowledged ... that amusement is only to be found in the openings of pantomimes; and that the dreariness begins as soon as the characters are changed. We think that a great hit might be made by producing a pantomime all opening. Let us have all the funny big heads, the imps and fairies as at present; but work all the tricks into the action, abolishing the Clown and his companions altogether ... and the hits at the day might all be worked in mechanically, as they are in the dialogue of the burlesques; and the greater the anachronism the greater the entertainment.

This is exactly what did happen, but not for forty years. The conclusion was that:

> Burlesque has entirely superseded pantomime, as at present constructed; and we expect that the latter will, in a year or two, go out altogether, and rank with the Mysteries and other dramatic productions of the past, unless some entirely new elements are introduced.

What happened was not the disappearance of pantomime but the merger of the pantomime opening and the extravaganza, ensuring the continued life of the pantomime. *The London Dispatch* (1 January 1837) reported:

> The general characteristics of pantomime have been changed of late years. We have less humour and innocent satire, but more of scenic effects, blue fire and magic. Harlequin has less occasion to be piquant and active, when the eye of the spectator is to be pleased and not his mind; and the Clown and Pantaloon need not be satirical and humourous, when a rope-dancer is the chief attraction of the evening. Sufficient, however, is still left to make us laugh heartily; and we do not find that the children of the present day are less amused than those of our younger year.

John Bull (27 December 1841) attributed the change in the nature of pantomime to its transformation into a show aimed specifically at children:

> A few years ago all ranks flocked to see the pantomime. The question was then put with a confident smile, when your opinion was inquired, as certain you had witnessed the favourite and national pastime. Now young men have a pride not to see such amusements, which are thought to be specially devoted to children.

Now the humour had been watered down so much that neither adults nor children were likely to be amused by pantomimes: 'They are losses to the management and unprofitable to the spectators.' Like the *I.L.N.* critic, the *John Bull* critic predicted the demise of the form. The young men he mentions had, it seems, transferred their patronage to the burlesques which were aimed at an adult audience.

Reviewing the classical burlesque, *The Paphian Bower* at the Olympic, *The Athenaeum* (29 December 1832) praised it at the expense of the pantomime:

> The time for this species of entertainment is nearly gone by. They had reached their high point of attraction some twenty years ago, and have been declining ever since.

This critic attributed this decline in pantomime's appeal to rising educational standards.

The critic in *The Morning Chronicle* (27 December 1845) assessing Planché's *The Bee and the Orange Tree*, the Christmas extravaganza at the Haymarket, began his review by saying:

> Pantomimes are vanishing from the stage as fast as stage coaches from the country road. On this side the water there are but two legitimate pantomimes, the other Christmas pieces being extravaganzas and fairy tales which, indeed, are more suited to the stage than the pantomime, from the facility with which they can be made the medium of conveying instruction in an amusing manner and effectively ridiculing any prevailing mania or quackery, political or social.

In the same issue of the same newspaper the critic reviewing *Harlequin Gulliver* at
Drury Lane took an entirely different and in retrospect much more accurate view of
the development of pantomime:

> In former days, the opening business was a very solemn and serious affair, and audiences
> had to wait for the transformations before their laughter could be legitimately provoked
> ... Now the tumbling and buffoonery are but a very secondary consideration – the fun
> begins at once, for the contortions of a Clown, the whirling of the Harlequin, the
> decrepitude of the Pantaloon, and the dancing of a Columbine, are confined within very
> narrow circles. With GRIMALDI, indeed, died the unctuous humour of pantomimes.
> His successor T. MATTHEWS, gives us, it is true, the traditions; but the rich laugh, the
> merry voice, the irresistible drollery, and ludicrous satire of the great original cannot be
> forgotten by the present generation of playgoers. The scene-painters have also made
> great havoc with orthodox pantomime. STANFIELD and THE GRIEVES, with the
> brush, have eclipsed the harlequin's wand. But at the same time we must express our
> conviction that the decay of pantomimes, according to the common saying of the day, is
> purely visionary; they have simply taken a new *direction*, and the incidents have now a
> greater satirical relation to every-day events than in the olden time. The absurdities, the
> weaknesses, the follies, the drolleries of human life, are now portrayed in animated
> action. Thumps and bumps, larcenies and changes, must have a point for the audience to
> enjoy unalloyed merriment. There must be application in the mechanism, and method in
> the mummers; the past year must stand in review before the pantomimic public; wisdom
> must go hand-in-hand with mirth, ... Last night upward of a dozen pantomimes were
> produced in London, independently of burlesque spectacles, which are, in point of fact,
> only *speaking* pantomimes ... The fall of pantomime, indeed! Monstrous is the
> supposition.[12]

Although Planché did provide some pantomime openings, it was Edward Leman
Blanchard who most successfully ensured the fusing of the pantomime opening
and the extravaganza. Blanchard's theatrical output consisted of farces, burlesques
and dramas until 1846 when he embarked on the sequence of pantomimes that
was to dominate the rest of his career. He became by common consent, 'the King
of Pantomime writers'. He furnished the annual Drury Lane pantomime from 1852
to 1888 and in 1852 alone had five different pantomimes playing at different
theatres. Modern pantomime historian Gerald Frow has written: 'He was one of
the most prolific, the most literary, the most consistently inventive of pantomime
writers and his work stands as a monument to the charm, grace, prettiness and true
delights of Victorian pantomimes.'[13] The classic Blanchard pantomime combined a
book of inventive rhyming couplets, the imaginative telling and sometimes
interweaving of fairy tales, folk tales and nursery rhymes, lengthy and elaborate
ballet sequences, beautiful scene-painting and moral lessons. This came to be seen

as the required form of the pantomime and Blanchard would become the hero of those who valued the 'traditional pantomime' and resisted changes in the model he had perfected.

The merger of the pantomime opening and the extravaganza was well underway by the 1850s and the emergence of the new pantomime consisting of an extravaganza opening and the traditional harlequinade was recognized by the press. In 1855 the Adelphi put on *Jack and the Beanstalk*, and *The Times* (27 December 1855) described it as 'a decided novelty in its kind, being a mixture of the burlesque spectacle and the pantomime proper.' This was emphasized in the prologue in which Mother Goose and the Spirit of Burlesque reviewed the elements of recent Adelphi triumphs, complete with puns, points and topical allusions, but then called in aid the Spirit of Old Adelphi Pantomime to produce a new kind of Christmas show. The *I.L.N.* (29 December 1855) found the combination 'ingenious'. *The Era* (23 December 1855) thought this new merger would give the Adelphi an advantage over its opponents: 'All the elements of attraction ... are included in the development of this Burlesque-Pantomime, or Pantomimical-Burlesque, whichever title the public may receive it under.' The following year the Adelphi staged *Mother Shipton's Wager or Harlequin Knight of Love. The Times* (27 December 1856) described the show as being 'of a composite order, happily combining the rich fancy and delicate conceit of the modern extravaganza with the hearty humour and practical drollery of the ancient pantomime.' Also in 1856 the Lyceum, the recognized home of extravaganza, now also presented a hybrid, *Conrad and Medora or Harlequin Corsair and the Little Fairy at the Bottom of the Sea*, which merged a burlesque of Byron's poem *The Corsair* and the harlequinade. *The Era* (28 December 1856) called it 'a capital Burlesque and a very good pantomime'.

In a hard-hitting article published in 1861 in *Temple Bar* magazine, Planché, admitting that he had invented the extravaganza, declined to accept responsibility for what others had done to the form, in particular the vulgarization of the dialogue. He made it clear that he had lofty aims for this theatrical form, his stated ambition being to create a new kind of satirical comedy. Instead it had been used to enrich and reinforce the pantomime opening. Planché lamented the fact that 'Extravaganza had been patched onto pantomime, to the serious injury of both.'[14] He expanded on this in his memoirs:

> Instead of the two or three simple scenes which previously formed the opening of the pantomime, a long burlesque, the characters in which have nothing to do with those in the harlequinade, occupies an hour – sometimes much more – of the evening, and terminates in one of those elaborate and gorgeous displays which have acquired the name of 'transformation scenes', are made the great feature of the evening; and consequently, after which the best part of the audience quit the theatre, and what is by

courtesy called the 'comic business' is run through by the pantomimists in three or four ordinary street or chamber scenes ... the 'transformation scene' is, however, declared every year to be unparalleled. That is the object of attraction, and all the rest is 'inexplicable dumb show and noise'.[15]

He regretted the demise of the traditional pantomime and the acting, particularly that of Grimaldi, which it had inspired.

At the same time as the extravaganza was being merged with the harlequinade, a third transformation occurred, similarly inspired by the extravaganza – the rise of spectacle. Dutton Cook explained:

> The custom of interrupting the harlequinade by the exhibition of dioramic views, at one time contrived annually by Clarkson Stanfield, expired about thirty years ago; as a substitute for them came the gorgeous transformation scenes, traceable to the grand displays which were wont to conclude Mr Planché's extravaganzas at the Lyceum, when under the management of Madame Vestris.[16]

The appetite for spectacle was central to Victorian culture. As Kate Flint has rightly observed: 'The Victorians were fascinated with the act of seeing, with the question of reliability – or otherwise – of the human eye and with the problems of interpreting what they saw.'[17] This included observations both of the natural world and the human environment and works of art of all kinds. So the Victorian world was dominated by the visual image at every level. The Victorians were literalists. They liked their paintings to tell a story and to tell it in strong visual terms. So artists frequently turned to literature for inspiration and produced a host of pictures based on scenes from, for instance, Shakespeare and Scott.[18] The Victorians also had a taste for the epic in painting both of the empires and apocalypses of the ancient world (John Martin, David Roberts, Francis Danby) and of the more familiar scenes of the modern world, captured in the teeming canvases of W.P. Frith (*Derby Day, The Railroad Station, Ramsgate Sands*) and George Elgar Hicks (*The General Post Office, Billingsgate Fish Market*). People queued up to see them and bought engravings of the most popular to put on their walls. The pictures accompanying the text in popular novels such as those of Dickens, Thackeray and Ainsworth were frequently as important as the words. Dante's *Divine Comedy*, Cervantes' *Don Quixote* and even the Bible reached ever wider audiences, thanks to the vivid illustrated versions by Gustave Doré.

Technological developments considerably enhanced the ready availability of imagery. There was an explosion of illustrated papers following the launch of the *Illustrated London News* in 1843, followed by *The Illustrated Times* in 1853, *The Graphic* in 1869, and *Illustrated Sporting and Dramatic News* in 1874. From the 1820s panoramas and dioramas recreated the sights and sounds of foreign travel for the stay-at-homes. Museums and galleries were founded up and down the land to display the latest specimens of visual art. The art of photography developed apace. By 1900 there were 256 photography clubs and an estimated 4 million amateur photographers in Britain. Even before photography developed, devices such as the magic lantern, the kaleidoscope, stereoscope and zoetrope were bringing pictures into the home. The introduction of gaslight and plate-glass made the shop windows in the big cities a visual attraction. Posters and advertisements covered every available wall-space. Victorian society was in short, as Michael Booth puts it 'a world ... saturated in pictures.'[19]

In this regard, theatre merely reflected popular taste and on the stage, spectacle became an indispensable part of opera, melodrama, Shakespeare, historical drama and pantomime. However much the opponents of stage spectacle might complain at the swamping of the drama by the visuals, audiences loved it. As Booth says, the taste was:

> not in origin exclusively East End or West End, working or lower middle class on the one hand or upper middle class and fashionable on the other. It was a homogeneous, a ubiquitous taste and had nothing to do with income levels, employment, living conditions, or class positions.[20]

The staging of spectacle was facilitated by technological changes. As Booth pointed out:

> All through the century ... technological change was occurring. The theatre passed from lighting by candle and oil lamp to lighting by electricity in two generations, and new trapdoors, new fabrics, and new kinds of special effects were regularly introduced from the early years of the century.[21]

William Roxby Beverley was, according to the D.N.B., 'after Clarkson Stanfield ... the most distinguished scene-painter of the nineteenth century'.[22] In 1847 he joined the Vestris-Mathews regime at the Lyceum where he became the third member of the triumvirate widely held responsible for the most memorable shows in London. He remained with the management until 1855 when Mathews relinquished his management on account both of his wife's illness and their bankruptcy. Beverley was snapped up by E.T. Smith at Drury Lane and from 1854 until 1887 when his eyesight failed and he was forced to retire, he was a fixture at the Theatre Royal, Drury Lane, painting the scenery both for Shakespeare and the pantomime. Planché acknowledged Beverley's ability, describing him as combining the pictorial talent of Clarkson Stanfield with the mechanical ingenuity of the machinist E.W. Bradwell. This did not stop him expressing his exasperation at the overshadowing of his texts by Beverley's scene-painting.[23] This was because Beverley had perfected the transformation scene, the often spectacular sequence linking the opening and the harlequinade. Contemporary reviews regularly reported that when the curtain rose on a Beverley scene, audiences demanded that he appear and take a bow, sometimes more than one. They almost never called for the author. However, Planché was not alone in his concerns. An equally prolific wordsmith, H.J. Byron in an article in *The Theatre* declared, 'splendour has gone a great way to obliterate the actual *fun* of pantomime there can be no doubt.' Like Planché, he blamed Beverley and in particular the great hit show *The Island of Jewels*:

> 'The transformation scene' became an immediate institution. Just at the very time when the author has wound up his story and tied his threads together, he is horrified by a stage-managerial announcement that 'at least a quarter of an hour more is required to set the 'Transformation Scene' ... As one who has suffered from 'Transformation Scenes', I protest against their undue importance, and I believe that nine-tenths of the audience would rather go to the 'fun' of the comic scenes a good deal sooner.[24]

This judgement is not borne out by the enthusiasm of the audiences for the transformation scenes, the box office returns and the gradual withering of the 'comic scenes' (i.e., harlequinade) due to lack of interest.

In a rare interview published in *The Sunday Times* (8 March 1885) Beverley recalled more positively:

> My relations with Charles Mathews, Planché and Madame Vestris are very pleasant reminiscences. We all worked well together, and the finale of the acts in Planché's extravaganzas were as a rule, left up to me to invent ... those were the days when imagination in scenic art was valued.

Blanchard did not share Planché's exasperation. An altogether more modest and retiring figure, he did not emulate Planché in for instance authorizing publication of a spectacular six-volume set of his extravaganzas as a permanent reminder of his talent. He valued Beverley's contribution to the success of their shows, dedicating the published script of his 1863 Princess' Theatre *Riquet with the Tuft*, to 'Mr William Beverley whose artistic ability and exquisite taste in embellishment for so many years have enabled the Wonders of Fairyland to be realised on the English stage which he has done so much to adorn by his pictorial skill and poetical fancy.'

Dutton Cook concluded his account of the progress of the pantomime succinctly by stating: 'The author ousted the mute; and now the author, in his turn, is overcome by the scene-painter, the machinist, and the upholsterer.'[25] But even as he wrote, a fourth transformation was underway, the so-called 'music hall invasion'. This was widely attributed to Sir Augustus Harris. The critic H.G. Hibbert summed up the general view when he wrote in 1920: 'Harris was ... greatly responsible for the vulgarising incursion of the music hall to the "Christmas annual" ... Harris' example was copied far and wide.'[26]

But this was only part of a general transformation overtaking the pantomime in the 1870s, with the role of the harlequinade increasingly curtailed, prose replacing rhyming couplets and most significantly the interjection of music hall acts into the pantomime. Augustus Harris Sr (1825–73), who for twenty-seven years was associated with the stage and general management of Covent Garden, was retrospectively accused of beginning the 'vulgarization' of the pantomime and specifically introducing music hall performers into West End pantomime. The key date was said to be 1871 when music hall star G.H. Macdermott appeared in *Bluebeard* at Covent Garden.[27] It was not long before other music hall comedians, among them James Fawn, Herbert Campbell and Harry Nicholls, were performing in pantomimes in both the East and West End. It was Harris' son, Augustus Harris Jr, who set the seal on this development when he took over Drury Lane in 1879. The Christmas pantomime now became a combination of music hall knockabout and costly and lavish spectacle, in particular long processions on such themes as the Kings and Queens of England, nursery rhyme characters and famous beauties of history. So from the 1870s battle was once again joined for the soul of pantomime, with critics such as John Ruskin, Charles Dickens Jr and W. Davenport Adams regularly denouncing the new developments and Oscar Barrett, first at the Crystal Palace and later at the Lyceum, mounting what came to be seen as traditional pantomimes in competition with Harris' new model.

Blanchard, still providing the scripts for Drury Lane, hated the Harris innovations. But with his health breaking down in the 1880s, he lacked the energy to resist. Harris was conscious of the publicity value the Blanchard name still carried. But Blanchard's diaries record his increasing distress at the way in which his scripts were distorted and adulterated. Hibbert recorded that Harris had 'ruthlessly edited his books, with the help of Harry Nicholls, and later Horace Lennard.'[28] Both Blanchard and William Beverley, who equally regretted the change in the nature of pantomimes, died in the same year, 1889.

The transformations in the pantomime are not just due to artistic, technological and legal changes, but also to wider societal changes. For there is no doubt that British society was undergoing a major transformation. The great social historian Harold Perkin summed it up as follows:

Between 1780 and 1850 the English ceased to be one of the most aggressive, brutal, rowdy, outspoken, riotous, cruel and bloodthirsty nations in the world, and became one of the most inhibited, polite, orderly, tender-minded, prudish and hypocritical.[29]

The American War of Independence ended with the surrender of British troops at Yorktown in 1781. The band played 'The World Turned Upside Down'. This is how it must have appeared to many in the last years of the eighteenth and the early years of the nineteenth century. For the early decades of the nineteenth century witnessed

The Transformers

Pantomime in the nineteenth century was transformed by the activities of four remarkable individuals.

1. James Robinson Planché – the creator of the extravaganza

2. Edward Leman Blanchard – 'the prince of pantomime writers'

THE LATE MR. W. R. BEVERLEY.

3. *William Roxby Beverley – the painter of fairyland*

4. *Sir Augustus Harris – master of spectacle*

the seismic effects of both the French and Industrial Revolutions, mass migration from countryside to town, the rise of a distinctively urban society and the creation of an urban proletariat packed into slums which were, in the words of G.M. Young, 'undrained, unpoliced, ungoverned and unschooled'.[30] There was perpetual fear of subversion, the French Revolution and the rise of Napoleon a permanent reminder of the instability of the old order and events such as the Cato Street Conspiracy, the Peterloo Massacre, the Luddite disturbances and the assassination of Prime Minister Spencer Perceval in the very House of Commons evidence of the dangerous thinness of the 'crust of civilization'.

The Grimaldian pantomime was a direct product of a Regency England which was characterized by binge drinking, sexual profligacy, political corruption, cruel animal sports, bare-knuckle prize fighting, public executions and reckless gambling. Grimaldi's Clown, dubbed by Jane Moody 'the Urban Anarchist', epitomizes the spirit of the age.[31] He was described by one pantomime arranger as 'a half-idiotic, crafty, shameless, incorrigible, emblem of gross sensuality', ready to defy authority, law and convention to fulfil his desire for immediate gratification.[32] Interestingly in 1801, Charles Lamb described London itself as 'a pantomime and a masquerade', evoking the bustle, variety and liveliness of the capital and eliding the boundary between the stage and reality.[33] At the same time as Grimaldi was flouting the law and public decorum for a popular audience, satirical prints by the likes of James Gillray, Thomas Rowlandson and George Cruikshank, witty, ingenious, vicious, subversive, gross, bawdy and scatological, were holding authority up to ridicule. As Vic Gatrell points out in his definitive study of the phenomenon, although consumed only by the middle and upper classes, these prints were 'invaluable cultural barometers' of the age.[34]

Gatrell points out too that there were limits to the apparent subversion of the prints. 'To constitution and hierarchy the print shops were steadfastly loyal.' They mocked the Prince of Wales but not the institution of monarchy, greedy lawyers but not gallows justice, gluttonous clergymen and canting dissenters but not the Christian faith itself. 'If they joked about London living, to its inequalities they turned blind eyes. No print overtly challenged privilege or ... conceded that the established order was threatened seriously.'[35]

Similarly, there were limits to the subversive possibilities of the theatre as the stage was subject to the constraints imposed by censorship. From 1737 to 1968 the stage functioned under the oversight of the Lord Chamberlain's office and had to conform to a strict set of regulations designed to preserve moral standards and the political, religious and social status quo. Plays could not be performed without the Lord Chamberlain's official imprimatur. This effectively meant the exclusion from the stage of explicit discussions of politics, religion and sex. The rules applied to pantomime scripts as much as to the legitimate drama and in many cases the only copies of pantomime scripts from the nineteenth century to survive are those in the Lord Chamberlain's collection. Dialogue was, however, not the only way of conveying a message to the audience. Gesture, costume and makeup could be used to make a point wordlessly, and to circumvent the letter of the regulations.[36]

The pantomime conforms to Mikhail Bakhtin's definition of the carnivalesque, a manifestation of folk culture, which assumes three forms, closely linked and interwoven: ritualized spectacle, comic verbal compositions, such as parodies, and various genres of billingsgate, such as curses and oaths. The harlequinade consisted of ritualized mayhem, endlessly repeated; the verbal humour of the mature pantomime depended heavily on puns and parodies; and curses and spells were regularly placed on the good characters in pantomime by the forces of darkness.[37]

Pantomime laughter similarly conforms to Bakhtin's definition of carnival laughter. It is festive, not an individual reaction to some isolated comic event. 'Carnival laughter is the laughter of all the people.' It is universal in scope, directed at everyone. 'The entire world is seen in its droll aspect.' Finally, it is ambivalent, being at the same time gay and triumphant and mocking and deriding.[38]

Images of the body are prominent in Rabelais and defined by Bakhtin as 'grotesque realism', wherein 'all that is bodily becomes grandiose, exaggerated, immeasurable.' This is a perfect description of the 'big heads' that were a feature of pantomime in its mid-Victorian heyday.[39] These were the grotesque papier-mâché masks, worn by the performers in the pantomime opening which allowed them to make the quick change into the characters of the harlequinade during the transformation. Once two different companies were used to perform in the opening and the harlequinade, the heads became unnecessary and their use was discontinued after the middle of the nineteenth century.

But how should the anarchic behaviour of the harlequinade be related to the jingoism of the early nineteenth-century patriotism which was also present in the shows? J.M. Golby and A.W. Purdue have an explanation. In *The Civilisation of the Crowd* they write: 'The audience was populist in its tastes and sympathies rather than radical and so were its entertainers.' They cite nineteenth-century showman Thomas Frost who in his 1881 book *The Old Showman and the Old London Fairs* described 'entertainers' as 'a class, loyal, under whatever dynasty or form of government they live, providing that it does not interfere with the exercise of their profession'. Golby and Purdue conclude that:

> There is, of course, always an element of the Lord of Misrule in popular culture, and pantomime certainly incorporated it. It is significant, however, that the humbling of the mighty and the elevation of the clown is in pantomime, as in carnival and other traditional festivals, a temporary affair that emphasises rather than questions the normal

order of things; in both pantomime and much of melodrama it is not authority *per se* which is derided but the *wicked* squire, the *pompous* mayor or the lord who in the final scene turns out to have no right to his title and estate and has to hand them back to the rightful owner, the hitherto humble hero.[40]

They thus echo Gatrell's interpretation of the nature and role of the satirical prints.

For all the elements of subversion and mayhem present there were forces at work seeking to purify and improve this society. Commentators were continually trying to define the 'spirit of the age'. In 1823 Lord Byron, with the libertine's presumption of moral hypocrisy in the pious, dubbed his era 'The Age of Cant'. Macaulay in the same year declared it the 'Age of Societies', 150 of them, mainly Evangelical in outlook, aimed at improving every aspect of society.[41] In 1829 Carlyle dubbed it 'The Mechanical Age' in recognition of the development of railways, canals, steamboats, the electric telegraph, gaslight and macadamized roads.[42] All this was summed up by Asa Briggs in his classic work *The Age of Improvement* (1959). Covering the years from 1783 to 1867 and arguing that 'The period was one of formative changes in the structure of the English economy, the shape of English society and the framework of English government', Briggs took as his text G.R. Porter's statement in *Progress of the Nation* (1836) that his lifetime had seen 'the greatest advances in civilization that can be found recorded in the annals of mankind' and Lord Macaulay's declaration in his *History of England* (1848, 1855, 1861) that the 'history of our country during the last hundred and sixty years is eminently the history of physical, of moral and of intellectual improvement.' The era saw the industrial and agrarian revolutions, the expansion of the British Empire, the rise of the middle classes, constitutional reform, an increase in material wealth, new technologies of steam and iron, an improvement in manners and morals and a new relationship between Man and Nature. The pre-eminent symbol of all this progress was the Great Exhibition of 1851.[43]

As the historian G.M. Young described it:

By the beginning of the nineteenth century, virtue was advancing on a broad invincible front ... The Evangelicals gave to the island a creed which was at once the basis of its morality and the justification of its wealth and power, and with the creed, the sense of being an Elect people, which, set to a more blatant tune, became a principal element in Late Victorian Imperialism. By about 1830 their work was done. They had driven the grosser kinds of cruelty, extravagance and profligacy underground. They had established a certain level of behaviour for all who wished to stand well with their fellows. In moralizing society they had made social disapproval a force which the boldest sinner might fear. By the beginning of the Victorian age the faith was already hardening into a code ... The Evangelical discipline, secularized as respectability, was the strongest binding force in a nation which without it might have broken up.[44]

The Evangelicals, characterized by an intense seriousness of purpose, immense industry and enthusiastic missionary spirit, censorious highmindedness and a puritanical abstention from worldly pleasures, mounted a full-scale and successful assault on every level and aspect of society, promoting philanthropy, religion, education, duty and hardwork, and attacking cruelty, frivolity and vice in all its forms.

It was Evangelical activists who ensured the civilizing of society by banning the slave trade and public executions, by outlawing cruel sports like bull-baiting, cock-fighting and bare-knuckle prizefighting, by restricting gambling and drinking, by abolishing the national lottery, by imposing a puritanical code of sexual conduct and inculcating the ideas of duty, service and conscience, thrift, sobriety and personal restraint.[45] The change was recognized at the time. Edward Bulwer-Lytton wrote in *England and the English* (1833): 'The English of the present day are not the English of twenty years ago.'[46]

The change was also commented on by amongst others, Francis Place, Leigh Hunt, William Wilberforce, Robert Southey and Henry Angelo.[47] The death of Grimaldi three months before the accession of Queen Victoria was almost symbolic of the passing of the Regency era and its values. Victoria's reign came to be regarded as the era of bourgeois respectability, with family life pre-eminent and childhood idealized. Similarly the pantomime came to be seen as the essential child-focused family entertainment, as *John Bull* (25 December 1837) acknowledged in an article written at the outset of the Victorian Age:

> We ask, what is the intent of the Christmas holydays? The merest child would give the correct answer – to eat plum-pudding, and see the pantomime … And, pray, what is a pantomime to us, unless rows of excited and happy little countenances are beaming around – frank, open countenances, fragrant with health – such as our own blessed land alone can show? How can we laugh at a pantomime, unless rows of excited and happy little countenances are chirruping on all sides? A pantomime without would be a worse punishment than seven years' transportation … One more argument, for we have set our hearts upon every little boy and girl spending a merry Christmas. This is a marked, an auspicious year in our annals, and we would have it made memorable to them. Let your little folks have it to say, we saw our first pantomime in the very year QUEEN VICTORIA came to the Throne.

The Victorian Age witnessed the continuing transformation of society, particularly in the 1850s, a decade of rising wages, cheaper food, better conditions of life, labour and leisure. Chartism peaked and labour unrest diminished. Levels of crime, poverty and drunkenness which had reached their highest point in 1842 dropped year by year. The mid-Victorian period witnessed the final emergence of a strongly structured and regulated society – orderly, law-abiding and deferential. There were a number of contributory factors: the growth of the factory system which instilled punctuality, regularity and discipline and of large-scale organizations like the railways and the Post Office which enforced military-style discipline and uniformed their employees; the work of the newly created police force and the courts; a general improvement in the quality of life (health, housing, transport, civic amenities); the socializing effects of schools and Sunday schools on the young, trade unions, adult education and temperance movements on their elders; and above all the pervasive power of the doctrine of respectability at all levels of society.

This did not happen overnight. It was a process not an event. But the key decades were the 1850s and 1860s, an era the historian W.L. Burn felicitously dubbed 'The Age of Equipoise' in which competing forces and interests were kept in balance – a workable balance between individualism and collectivism, the centralizing state versus local autonomy, freedom versus discipline, license versus authority, with various disciplines exerting a cohesive influence: the spectre of poverty, the pressure of respectability, the drive to philanthropy, the hierarchical role of the family and the force of religious beliefs and doctrines.[48] There is no better representative of the Age of Equipoise than the Blanchard pantomime, in which a moral, tasteful and genteelized opening was balanced by the harlequinade, but a harlequinade in which the pure anarchy of Grimaldi was diluted by the progressive introduction of a series of novelty turns (boy sopranos, dancing girls, acrobats, performing animals), which increasingly turned it into a variety show. If the Grimaldian harlequinade, with its gusto, bustle, instability and upheaval, embodied the spirit of the Regency period, the Blanchard pantomime reflected the more tranquil and affluent atmosphere of the mid-Victorian Age of Equipoise.

Donald Gray in his analysis of the varieties of laughter in Victorian England argues that humour became steadily more genteel:

Most of the critics, many of the creators, and presumably many of the patrons of comic entertainments tended to discourage the ... kind of laughter, in which it came close to saying something serious and unsettling about the people and attitudes which governed England, and to approve of amusements in which laughter came close to saying nothing at all. From the beginning of the century critics worried about the topics of laughter. Both Hazlitt and Lamb, for example complained in the 1820s of the burgeoning gentility which disapproved of the grossness of Restoration comedy and discouraged contemporary dramatists from playing with such base matter. By mid-century this gentility was pervasive, and critics are less likely to complain of it than they are to judge in its name. The Victorian commentary on laughter is full of reviews which regret the obscenity and gross physicality of Chaucer, Fielding, and Byron, of biographies which reprimand or patiently try to mitigate the penchant for rude practical jokes and personal abuse exhibited by such Regency wits as Theodore Hook ... More important than these attempts to suppress the traditional alliance between laughter and man's unelevated predilections were the frequent attempts to warn laughter away from some profoundly important topics. Religion, for example ... The way it turned out was that Dickens and a few other extraordinarily gifted writers continued to use laughter in their attempts to recreate and rehabilitate society, while a great many less talented, less self-confident, but nonetheless accomplished and energetic entertainers worked hard to amuse their contemporaries without disturbing them.[49]

Roger Henkle, in his study of English comic writing between 1820 and 1900, takes the same view and attributes it to changes in the social and cultural context, and in particular the emergence of the middle class and its influence on the tone and nature of popular culture. He notes:

Light, gentle humour set the comic tone of the mid-Victorian decade, the 1850s and 1860s. The magazines that sprang into being during the period were a far cry from the sensationalist journals of the 1830s and early 1840s. The sketches of boisterous London low life and high jinks on the road that dominated previous comic literature had virtually passed away. Replacing them were vignettes of social snobbery in St. James Park and wry observations on the types one meets in railway coaches. Political commentary tended to be arch in contrast to the slapdash ridicule of an earlier day, and instead of thinly disguised satires of prominent figures, that peculiar phenomenon of Victorian literature, the nonsense verse, appeared on the scene. The gentler tone and demure outlook of the mid-century periodicals reflected an evolution in the nineteenth-century reading public, a public grown larger and more affluent than ever, with all that that means in increased leisure time and greater enjoyment of its status.[50]

The nonsense verse of W.S. Gilbert, Edward Lear and Lewis Carroll thrived on whimsy as opposed to the savage satire of an earlier age. Comedy began to focus on domestic concerns, as reflected in the popularity of works such as *Mrs Caudle's Curtain Lectures* and *The Diary of a Nobody*. Henkle concludes that comic writers identifying with the middle class and finding humour in its domestic concerns reflected: 'English culture's ingrained assumption that it can tolerate and accomodate all manner of eccentricity, make room for all individualism (which) undoubtedly induces its writers toward less radical expression.'[51] This is the spirit of Blanchard's writing.

Victorian society was to see a final ideological transformation which would impinge directly on the pantomime. The last decades of the nineteenth century witnessed the triumph of imperialism when the two dominant ideologies of the mid-Victorian period, evangelicalism and a revived chivalry, merged to provide the justification for a world-wide empire that had been acquired initially for economic, strategic and political reasons. The Evangelical impulse, the desire to bring the heathen to the light of God, and the Calvinist idea of the Elect, the British as the greatest nation on earth being obliged to provide justice and good government for inferior races, intertwined with a chivalric vision of empire as a vehicle for young Englishmen to demonstrate the virtues that made them gentlemen.

Every aspect of popular culture contrived to instil pride in the British imperial achievement: the regular exhibitions highlighting the produce and artefacts of Empire; novels, stage melodramas and later feature films about gallant imperial heroes showing the flag and quelling rebellious natives in far-off dominions; genre paintings like those of Lady Butler and the illustrations in a raft of magazines, postcards, cigarette cards, and commercial packaging and advertising; daily newspapers like *The Daily Mail* and *The Daily Express* with an explicit commitment to Empire; popular biographies of imperial heroes; juvenile literature in the form of books and magazines that promoted a consistent line in imperialism. It was an image further inculcated at school via history textbooks, readers and geographies, by the uniformed youth movements like the Boy Scouts (originally to have been called the Young Knights of the Empire), and by a range of invented traditions and public rituals designed to promote Empire, culminating in the introduction in 1904 of Empire Day with its religious services, processions, concerts and imperial displays.

When it comes to the theatre, Bernard Porter has argued that, having consulted the list of play titles but not the texts in the Lord Chamberlain's collection, 'very few related to the Empire in any way.'[52] Consulting the same list together with the texts some years later, Marty Gould in his excellent new book, *Nineteenth-Century Theatre and the Imperial Encounter*, has identified 300 imperially themed plays, on such subjects as the Indian Mutiny, the Australian and South African Gold Rushes and the Boer War, not to mention 200 versions of the classic colonialist text *Robinson Crusoe*.[53]

If Grimaldi embodied the Spirit of the Regency Pantomime and Blanchard, the Age of Equipoise, the genius of imperial pantomime was Sir Augustus Harris. Augustus Harris was the supreme impresario and showman of his age. Lessee and manager of the Theatre Royal, Drury Lane, from 1879 until his death in 1896, Harris was the only Drury Lane lessee to die rich. Universally known as 'Gus', Harris delighted in his *Punch* nickname Augustus Druriolanus, a name implying empire. The actress Dame Geneviève Ward deemed it highly appropriate: 'In his nature, his power and the vast reach of his schemes he was truly of the imperial line' she wrote.[54] Veteran theatre historian Macqueen Pope called him 'a King of Pantomime, indeed an Emperor'.[55] Bearded, rotund and frock-coated, Harris famously looked like the Prince of Wales. Harris' fortune and success lay in giving people what they wanted: 'My constant aim has been to gauge the taste of the theatre-going public with the greatest possible accuracy, and to follow intelligently in the matter of dramatic entertainment the unerring law of supply and demand.'[56] So Harris based his theatrical regime at Drury Lane on a sensational autumn melodrama and a spectacular Christmas pantomime, both of them produced as lavishly as possible.

His shows cost between £5,000 and £6,000 to stage, 'unheard-of expenditure then', said Macqueen Pope.[57] His pantomimes employed between 700 and 800 people. Significantly his melodramas and pantomimes played not just at Drury Lane but elsewhere in the country as he sold the acting rights to other managements. Harris pantomimes could be seen in Manchester and Glasgow. His autumn melodramas were played everywhere, not least in the East End of London and south of the river where they could be seen in such venues as the Britannia, Hoxton and the Surrey, Lambeth.

Five of the autumn melodramas featured imperial campaigns and they were very much personal projects for Harris. He produced them, co-wrote them and in the early days acted in them. The first imperial melodrama, *Youth* (1881) had a hero Frank Darlington who is falsely accused of a crime and imprisoned in Dartmoor. He redeems his honour by enlisting in the army, serving in South Africa, rescuing his regiment from annihilation and winning the Victoria Cross. The play contained an episode inspired by the 1879 defence of Rorke's Drift in the Zulu War. *Freedom* (1883) took place entirely in Egypt and was directly based on recent events. In September 1881 a nationalist army revolt had broken out in Egypt, led by Colonel Ahmad Urabi Pasha, with the slogan 'Egypt for the Egyptians', aimed at ending foreign domination of the country. British fears for the security of the Suez Canal and riots in Alexandria leading to the deaths of fifty Europeans prompted a military response from Britain. The Royal Navy under Admiral Sir Beauchamp Seymour bombarded Alexandria and an army under General Sir Garnet Wolseley landed and defeated the Egyptian rebels at the Battle of Tel-el-Kebir (13 September 1882), securing British control of Egypt and peerages for Seymour and Wolseley. In *Freedom* Urabi Pasha is represented by Araf Bey who raises revolt in Egypt and attacks the British consulate in an unnamed Egyptian town (presumed to be Alexandria). The consulate is defended by the captain of a British gunboat. *Human Nature* (1885) focused on the expedition to the Sudan to relieve General Gordon. *A Life of Pleasure* (1893) saw two young men involved in the Third Burmese War of 1885 and featured another of those desperate military engagements with the outnumbered British trapped and rescued in the nick of time. *Cheer, Boys, Cheer* (1895) took place largely in South African diamond mine country but its climactic event was based on the massacre of Major Allan Wilson and the thirty-two-man Shangani River Patrol by the Matabele in 1893. In the play, they were rescued in the nick of time by the British cavalry, a scene, according to *The Theatre* (1 October 1895), 'certain to appeal to the heart and imagination of every Englishman'.

In seeking a descriptive metaphor for the nature of the Drury Lane pantomime *The Star* (27 December 1900) turned naturally to the Empire:

The Drury Lane pantomime, that national institution, is a symbol of our Empire. It is the biggest thing of its kind in the world, it is prodigal of money, of invention, of splendor, of men and women; but it is without the sense of beauty or the restraining influence of taste. It is impossible to sit in the theatre for five hours without being filled with weary admiration. Only a great nation could have done such a thing; only an undisciplined nation would have done it. The monstrous, glittering thing of pomp and humor is without order or design; it is a hotchpotch of everything that has been seen on any stage.

In his illuminating discussion of pantomime imperialism, Marty Gould highlights *Robinson Crusoe*. Quoting W. Davenport Adams, who in 1882 reported that *Robinson Crusoe* was second only to *Dick Whittington* in popularity among pantomime subjects, he provides the evidence. In each of the years 1876, 1877, 1882 and 1886, there were no fewer than seven *Crusoes* in production and in 1897 the Lord Chamberlain reviewed ten new versions. One of the stimuli for this, he identifies as being 'the reflecting of Britain's evolving overseas interests'. Daniel Defoe's original novel, with its lone English castaway, using his skills and tools to transform a desert island into an orderly and productive settlement and acquiring a faithful native servant in Friday has long been seen as celebration of colonization. But examining a variety of nineteenth-century pantomime texts, Gould concludes that during the course of the century:

> The paradigmatic colonial Crusoe in the narrative tradition was replaced by an imperial adventurer who has no time to construct or expand his settlement. Having shed his colonizing impulses, Crusoe began to take less interest in cultural reform and instead uses his time on the island to subdue a hostile native force and establish British political hegemony over the territory.

Gould identifies a transformation of Crusoe from 'colonist to conquistador' and traces an increase in the appearances of the British flag, British military valour and the process of imperial annexation.[58] This is not just a London phenomenon. *The Theatre* reported that *Robinson Crusoe* at the Grand Theatre, Leeds, in 1882 had Crusoe rescued by 'the military might of Great Britain' and 'the cannibal king is brought to England à la Cetewayo' referring to the Zulu King's visit to England in 1882 after the Zulus' defeat at Ulundi in 1879.[59]

There was sometimes a direct connection between the autumn melodrama, the Christmas pantomime and current imperial events. This occurred notably in 1882–3. Just as the melodrama *Freedom* (1883) was inspired by the bombardment of Alexandria and the suppression of the nationalist revolt in Egypt, so too was the 1882–3 pantomime *Sindbad the Sailor*, scripted by the veteran E.L. Blanchard and produced by Harris. *The Times* (27 December 1882) review encapsulated the way in which the Arabian Nights tale had been transformed by the injection of current events:

> To such an extent ... has the 'gorgeous East' been laid under contribution that the story is frequently lost sight of altogether, a great part of the action being taken up with the domestic and business arrangements of Kibosh Pasha, an Eastern slave-dealer, with whose niece Sindbad is in love, and with the experiences of the youthful Khedive of Egypt, who travels in search of adventure under the guidance of a rascally tutor.

To elaborate, the story is set in Egypt and one of the pantomime's villains is Kybosh (his full name significantly Kybosh Arabi Pasha). A bankrupt slave dealer, he is sold with his nieces to the young Khedive Kabob and his tutor Professor Hankipanki. Sindbad, who loves the niece Fatinitza, and his crew rescue the girls but they are pursued and captured by the Khedive. The girls, however, are taken over by Kabob's father, the sinister Padishah (also known as the Old Khedive). The Young Khedive enlists Sindbad's help to rescue them. Sindbad does so but Kabob and his tutor pursue them in a balloon. The Diamond Prince, however, explains to the Young Khedive that he should desist because Sindbad is a favourite in London. The Khedive and his tutor claim not to know where London is. So there ensues a procession at the Tower of London of the Kings and Queens of England from William the Conqueror to Queen Victoria, who parade to the strains of 'God Save the Queen', 'God Bless the Prince of Wales' and 'Rule Britannia'. Significantly the Victorian Age is represented by a parade of children dressed as policemen and by a review of juvenile soldiers representing the British and Indian troops, recently engaged in Egypt. It culminates in the appearance of Britannia singing a patriotic song.

The Khedive Kabob is depicted as young and amiable but weak-willed and under the thumb of others, exactly as Khedive Tawfik was described by the Earl of Cromer, British Agent and Consul-General in Egypt. His father, the Padishah or Old Khedive, who is the real villain of the pantomime, is based on Khedive Ismail Pasha, deposed at the instigation of the British in 1879 because of his extravagance and despotic rule. His 'sinister influence' was felt long after his deposition, according to Lord Cromer.[60] Ahmad Urabi Pasha is the bankrupt slave trader. Sindbad has the backing of Britain in rescuing the girls from the Egyptians. The spectacle included the bombardment of Alexandria and a parade of victorious troops.

Drury Lane was not alone in celebrating the bombardment of Alexandria and the victory at Tel-el-Kebir. *Cinderella* at the Pavilion managed to introduce the events of 1882 at the ball, where Prince Paragon welcomes and addresses guests made up to represent the Duke of Connaught and the Prince of Wales, the Khedive of Egypt, Sir Beauchamp Seymour and Sir Garnet Wolseley. Then a spectacle called 'The United Kingdom United' saw groups of men and women, 'brightly and picturesquely costumed' as Wales, Scotland, Ireland and England, who in turn sang 'The Men of Harlech', 'The Bonnets of Bonnie Dundee', 'The Minstrel Boy' and 'Rule Britannia'. It celebrated jointly the United Kingdom and the triumphant Egyptian campaign.

Sanger's Amphitheatre contrived to introduce the Egyptian campaign into its Christmas pantomime *Bluff King Hal or the Field of Cloth of Gold*, despite its ostensible sixteenth-century setting. The pageant of the *Field of Cloth of Gold* included a scene in which *The Era* (30 December 1882) said 'the enthusiasm of spectators is ... evoked by excellent counterfeits of Baron Alcester (the estimable Sir Beauchamp Seymour) and Lord Wolseley, standing on triumphal cars, being pushed on the stage by diminutive blue jackets and soldiers to the music of a patriotic song and chorus.' In *Bluebeard* at Liverpool's Alexandra Theatre, the pantomime included, according to *The Theatre*, 'some capital military scenes founded on episodes in the recent Egyptian war.' This included a tableau of the bombardment of Alexandria. In *Sindbad the Sailor* at the Theatre Royal Manchester, the transformation scene had Sindbad 'extending a welcome to our soldiers and our Queen.'[61]

The 1882 *Sindbad* was not Blanchard's first venture into imperial commentary. In 1875 he scripted the Crystal Palace pantomime, *Jack in Wonderland*, which was a variation on *Jack and the Beanstalk*, directly inspired by the Prince of Wales' visit to India. Climbing the beanstalk, Jack is transported to India, as *The Era* (27 December, 1875) reported, and to the front of a gorgeous palace:

> with a host of characters suggestive of the reception of the Prince of Wales. This happy idea is carried out in a manner worthy of the event itself. There is a grand Indian ballet, with dances by Nautch girls and a shawl dance, arranged with great taste and skill ... while as a contrast there are palm trees, elephants, camels etc. The Midget Hanlon *troupe* do excellent service in this scene. Made up as monkeys, they climb the tree with wonderful agility, leap from branch to branch, tumble over head and heels, and gambol in the most approved monkey fashion. A group of Ethiopian minstrels – Bernard's *troupe* of Christy's – sing and dance in this scene, the conclusion of which is really splendid, the stage being filled with gaily-dressed figures, a good notion being that a number of natives are carrying flags, inscribed with the words 'Tell mama we are happy!' – a significant message for the Prince of Wales to carry home to the Queen', and one which we trust would be echoed by the natives in reality.

So the evocation of India is an exotic composite of Nautch dancers, palm trees, elephants, monkeys and black-face minstrels but with richly dressed natives carrying a message of loyalty to the Queen.

One of the functions of the harlequinade in its heyday was to comment on the events of the past year. Topical allusions can tell us what the pantomime producers considered significant events and the reports of audience reaction can tell us about the popular attitude to these events. There was no more traumatic event in the history of the British Empire than the Indian Mutiny and it inevitably featured in the pantomimes of 1857–8 in both West End and East End and south of the river. In Drury Lane's *Little Jack Horner* by E.L. Blanchard, *The Era* (27 December 1857) tells us that 'allusions to the prevalent topics embrace almost every subject that has lately attained notoriety.' The topics received 'with the most relish' were the Sepoy Mutiny and 'the modern extravagance of dress'. At Astley's the pantomime *Don Quixote and his Mare Rosinante* was preceded by a re-enactment of the storming and capture of Delhi. Turning to the suburban theatres, at Sadler's Wells, *Harlequin Beauty and the Beast* introduced a scene in which a figure of justice in a sign-painter's establishment came to life and awarded a peerage and a pension to the Mutiny heroes General Havelock and Sir Colin Campbell. It was, said *The Era*, one of 'the great hits' of the harlequinade. At the Surrey, the pantomime *Queen Mab* had a scene in the harlequinade set in the United Services Club and the stage was filled with Union Jacks. Clown and Pantaloon played cribbage with giant playing cards, featuring contemporary figures. When General Havelock was played over Nana Sahib, the mutiny leader, there was 'enthusiastic applause'. The pictures of 'Wilson taking Delhi' and 'Florence Nightingale' also elicited applause. Then there was a gruesome scene in which a sepoy was killed by Clown, dressed in antique Grenadier's costume, stuffed into a mortar and fired at the butcher's shop where his disjointed body replaced the mutton and beef on the hooks. This reproduced in comic form the punishment being inflicted on captured mutineers. At the Marylebone Theatre, the pantomime *Joe Miller* included a view of Delhi 'with incidental allusion to late events' and this brought on 'the hearty and unrestrained applause of the house'. At the City of London Theatre, where *William the Second and the Fayre Maid of Honour* was the pantomime, the show included a scene of sepoys being captured before Delhi and Nana Sahib was blown from the mouth of a cannon into a thousand pieces, said *The Times* (28 December 1857), 'to the great satisfaction of the delighted audience'. At the Standard, Shoreditch, *Harlequin Georgey-Porgey Pudding and Pie* contained a realization of the celebrated *Punch* cartoon by Sir John Tenniel of the vengeance of the British Lion on the Bengal Tiger headed 'Caught at Last'. At the Grecian, *Peter Wilkins and the Flying Indians* had a scene in the harlequinade with British soldiers shelling sepoys and Nana Sahib, caught under an extinguisher, being labelled 'out of Luck-now'. At the Victoria, whose audience, according to *The Times*, comprised 'the very humblest ... class of the community', *Harlequin Prince Love-the-day and Queen Busy Bee* contained reference to Nana Sahib which was greeted with 'a shout of execration. So spontaneous and characteristic was this ebullition of popular feeling that one could have wished no higher retribution for this arch-ruffian than that he should have been given over ... to the fury of the crowd from whom it emanated.' The pantomimes present no evidence of anything but general support for the suppression of the Mutiny and for the most savage reprisals against those who have dared to challenge the might of the Raj.

The finale of the 1886–7 pantomime *The Forty Thieves* was a celebration of Queen Victoria's Golden Jubilee, depicted in imperial terms. The sequence begins in a ruined Indian temple where an act of *suttee* (widow-burning) is about to take place. Civilization (represented by a flying dancer Madame Aenea) flies to the rescue and English pioneers plant the flag of St George to symbolize the advent of British rule. The scene changes to a British warship where the children of Madame Katti Lanner's National School of Dance appear and perform English, Scottish, Welsh and Irish national dances. Finally in the temple of fame, where there is a statue of Queen Victoria, Britannia welcomes the colonies of the British Empire who arrive to pay tribute. England, Scotland, Ireland and Wales lead the way, followed by the knights of Malta, residents and natives of Cape Colony, Canadians dressed for wintry weather, Australian diggers bearing their nuggets of gold and with their rifle volunteers, who, reported *The Era* (1 January 1887) 'in remembrance of good service recently done, are welcomed with a special cheer', New Zealanders, Straits Settlements (Malaya) colonists and then 'all the gorgeousness of the East, in deputations from Burmah and Ceylon and India'. 'There are heraldic devices and banners in abundance, and, particularly in the case of the representatives of the three places last named, wondrous richness and variety in the way of costumes and trophies.'

It was not just Drury Lane that celebrated the Jubilee, but also the suburban and transpontine theatres. There were Golden Jubilee imperial tableaux in *Jack and the Beanstalk* at the Surrey Theatre, in *Cinderella* at Sanger's Theatre, in *The Goblin Bat* at the Britannia, Hoxton; in *Robinson Crusoe* at the Grand Theatre, Islington, in *Jack in the Box* at the Elephant and Castle and in *Jack and the Beanstalk* at Sadler's Wells.

There was a major transformation in the subject matter of the pantomimes. Journalist W. Davenport Adams argued in 1882 that one of the chief drawbacks of modern pantomimes was the limited number of subjects being treated. The prevailing subjects, in order of their popularity, were now *Dick Whittington, Robinson Crusoe, The Forty Thieves, Aladdin, Babes in the Wood, Little Bo-Peep, Jack the Giant Killer, Cinderella, Bluebeard, Sindbad the Sailor, Red Riding Hood, Jack and the Beanstalk, Beauty and the Beast* and *Goody Two-Shoes*. He drew attention to the fact that both Sheffield theatres and two of the three Glasgow theatres were performing *Dick Whittington* that year.[62]

In 1884, *The Era* (19 January 1884) published a pantomime census, revealing that nationwide, *Dick Whittington* was being played at eleven theatres, *Cinderella* and *Red Riding Hood* at ten each, *Sindbad* and *Aladdin* at nine, *Babes in the Wood* and

The Forty Thieves at seven, *Blue Beard* and *Robinson Crusoe* at six, *Little Bo-Peep* and *Jack and the Beanstalk* at four, *St. George and the Dragon, Beauty and the Beast* and *Jack the Giant Killer* at three, *Queen of Hearts, Jack and Jill* and *Goody Two-Shoes* at two, *Little Jack Horner, Humpty-Dumpty, Puss in Boots, Jack Frost, Queen Dodo* and *King Aboulifar* at one each.

By 1901, *The Stage* (26 December 1901) was reporting that the most popular title was *Babes in the Wood*, being played at fifteen theatres, *Aladdin* and *Cinderella* at fourteen, *Dick Whittington* and *Robinson Crusoe* at eleven. It also revealed that the most popular subjects over the previous decade had been *Aladdin* (1892–3 and 1893–4), *Babes in the Wood* (1894–5), *Dick Whittington* (1895–6), *Cinderella* (1896–7, 1897–8 and 1898–9), *Cinderella* and *Dick Whittington* joint first (1899–1900) and *Cinderella* (1900–1). The relative popularity of Orientalist subjects (*Aladdin, Sindbad, Ali Baba*) and the colonialist *Robinson Crusoe* may reflect the increasing prominence of matters imperial in the mass media.

Individual titles moved up and down in popularity but the basic stock of stories remained largely unchanged. This continues to be the case up to the present day. The pantomimes playing in the 2009–10 season, as listed in *The Stage* (7 January 2010), were *Cinderella* at twenty-four theatres, *Jack and the Beanstalk* and *Aladdin* at twelve, *Snow White and the Seven Dwarfs* at eleven, *Sleeping Beauty* at eight, *Mother Goose* and *Dick Whittington* at five, *Peter Pan* at four, *Beauty and the Beast* at three, *Robinson Crusoe* and *Robin Hood* at two, *Goldilocks and the Three Bears, Humpty Dumpty* and *Ali Baba and the Forty Thieves* at one each. *Snow White* and *Peter Pan* were twentieth-century additions to the repertoire and some once-popular titles (*Sindbad, Puss in Boots, Bluebeard*) have almost entirely disappeared. But the traditional favourites show remarkable staying power.

This state of affairs dated only as far back as the 1870s. Before that decade the pantomimes were remarkable for the variety and eclecticism of their subjects. For example at the outset of Queen Victoria's reign, the pantomimes on offer in the 1838–9 season included *Harlequin and Jack Frost* at Drury Lane, *Harlequin and Fair Rosamund* at Covent Garden, *Harlequin and the Silver Dove* at the Adelphi, *Harlequin and Little Tommy Tucker* at Sadler's Wells, *The Rose of Stepney or Harlequin and Old Father Thames* at the Pavilion, *Harlequin and the Enchanted Figs* at the Surrey, *Harlequin and the Sprite of the Elfin Glen* at the Victoria, *Marrow-Bones and Cleavers or Harlequin's Wedding Day* at the Marylebone and *Jane Shore or Harlequin and the Baker of Shoreditch* at the City of London.

The same degree of variety prevailed in the 1867–8 season, which saw productions of *Faw Fee Fo Fum; or, Harlequin Jack the Giant Killer* at Drury Lane, *Babes in the Wood or Harlequin Robin Hood and His Merry Men* at Covent Garden, *Harlequin Cock Robin and Jenny Wren* at the Lyceum, *Valentine and Orson or Harlequin and the Big Bear and the Little Fairy* at the Holborn, *Little Red Riding Hood or Harlequin*

Prince Hopeful, Baa Baa Black Sheep and the Cruel Wolf at Sadler's Wells, *Harlequin Nobody and Little Jack Horner, Goody Two-Shoes, Old Crosspatch, and Three Men in a Tub* at Astley's, *The Fair One with the Golden Locks or Harlequin and Davy Jones's Locker* at the Surrey, *Charles the Second and Pretty Nell Gwynne or Harlequin Oliver Cromwell and the Little Fairies of the Enchanted Oak* at the Victoria, *Harlequin Ric Rac, the Giant of the Mountains and the Goblin Gift and the Kingdoms Three* at the Grecian, *Oranges and Lemons said the Belles of St. Clements or Harlequin and the Good Fairy of the New Year* at the Standard, *Wat Tyler or Harlequin Love, War and Peace* at the City of London, *Harlequin Robin Hood and his Merry Men* at the New East London, *Robin Hood and His Merry Men or Ivanhoe, the Jewess and the Knight Templar* at the Pavilion, *Harlequin O'Clock and the Knight, the Minstrel and the Maiden* at the Oriental, *Little Bo-Peep Who Lost Her Sheep or Harlequin Jack and the Ogre of the Brazen Castle* at the Marylebone, *Don Quixote or Sancho Panza and his Wife Tereza* at the Britannia, *Little Giselle, the Dancing Belle, or Harlequin, the Demon Hunter and the Fairies of the Willi Lake* at the Alexandra and *Little Red Riding Hood or Harlequin Jack Horner and a Frog He Would a Wooing Go* at the Crystal Palace.

Nelson Lee (1806–72) was one of the most prolific of pantomime scriptwriters. A former actor, who had played Harlequin for seven successive years at the Surrey Theatre, he turned to management and successively ran the Marylebone, Pavilion, Standard and City of London theatres, where his pantomimes were always a highlight of the repertoire. He is estimated to have written over 100 pantomimes and he rarely repeated himself. His pantomimes included *Harlequin Grammar or Murray and A.E.I.OU.* (1843), *Auld Lang Syne or Morning, Noon and Night and Harlequin Jack O'Daylight* (1846), *Harlequin and Yankee Doodle who came to Town upon his Little Pony* (1849), *Knife, Fork and Spoon or Harlequin Breakfast, Dinner, Tea and Supper* (1850), *Red Rufus or Harlequin Fact, Fiction and Fancy* (1851), *King Emerald or Harlequin's Crystal Palace in Fairy Lane* (1852), *Romeo and Juliet or Harlequin Queen Mab and the World of Dreams* (1852), *Harlequin King Ugly Mug or My Lady Lee of Old London Bridge* (1853) and *Young Norval of the Grampian Hills or Harlequin Lord Ullin's Daughter* (1854).[63]

By 1874–5, however, there had been a total transformation. Gone were the folkloric, allegorical, literary and historical subjects and in were all the fairy stories that were to be the staples of the pantomime stage down to the present day. *Aladdin* was playing at Drury Lane, the Charing Cross and Sanger's, *Babes in the Wood* at Covent Garden and *The Children in the Wood* at the Adelphi, *Beauty and the Beast* at the Princess', *Whittington* at the Alhambra, *Sindbad the Sailor* at the Holborn, *Jack and Jill* at the Victoria, *The Forty Thieves* at the Surrey, *Robinson Crusoe* at the Standard, *Little Boy Blue* at the Marylebone, *Little Bo-Peep* at the Greenwich, *Sleeping Beauty* at the Albion, and *Cinderella* at the Pavilion and the Crystal Palace.

What explains this transformation? Davenport Adams suggested that:

Something of this is owing to the habit that obtains in the provinces of shifting about the same production from theatre to theatre – libretto, dresses, scenery, and appointments being bought bodily for the purpose. Still more, however, is owing to the unwillingness of entrepreneurs to advance, however so little, from the well-beaten track.[64]

The fact that the trend was for pantomimes to get longer and more and more spectacular, and therefore expensive to stage, would tend to confirm this. The merging of several nursery rhymes to create a single narrative in the 1867–8 list suggests that the meatier narratives of the familiar fairy stories provided better subject matter for the lengthier productions. Their recurrent success would confirm managers in their conservatism of choice.

There was another transformation that was a constant feature of pantomime, burlesque and extravaganza: the presence in the cast of the principal boy, a woman dressed in male attire, and the dame, a man dressed as an old woman. This cross-dressing tradition has given rise to considerable discussion about its cultural meaning. In a pioneering article, David Mayer advanced a Freudian interpretation of pantomime, arguing that it is a fantasy, 'a mechanism for dealing with real and immediate and acute anxieties in disguised form.' These anxieties are predominantly sexual. Referring in particular to the harlequinade, Mayer interprets the magic bat (or slapstick) which the boy Harlequin received from his mother as a symbol of the phallus as part of the transition to adulthood, always a fraught time emotionally and sexually. This transition concludes with Harlequin's embrace of adult heterosexuality, symbolized by his marriage to Columbine at the climax of the harlequinade.

If Mayer is correct, this strongly sexual element will have been continually diluted through the nineteenth century as the harlequinade became separated from the opening, often performed by a different cast, as it shrank in length and importance and as the addition of speciality acts turned it from a mythic or symbolic account of growing up to a prototype variety show.[65] However, a Jungian interpretation seems, if anything, more plausible. For the characters in the harlequinade, the extravaganza and the pantomime proper are classic archetypes, comical ones admittedly but archetypes nonetheless: the dashing hero, the innocent heroine, the pompous old man, the shrewish old woman, the sinister villain. They are pitted against each other in eternal conflict.

The principal boy is defined by David Pickering in the *Encyclopedia of Pantomime*:

The ostensibly male hero of pantomime plots, who is usually by convention played by an actress. Such actresses are most definitely not male impersonators and retain their femininity in the role, generally wearing flattering costumes showing off their legs – to which they draw enthusiastic attention by giving them an occasional hearty slap –

despite the fact that the character they play is generally of the strapping, undaunted, even chauvinistic, masculine variety. The principal boy is jaunty, unruly, unflinching in the business of vanquishing giants and demons and ultimately always successful in his love for the PRINCIPAL GIRL.[66]

Pickering similarly defines the dame:

The comic female character (usually the hero's mother) whose presence dominates the modern pantomime and provides much of the best of its humour. Irascible, irrepressible in the face of adversity, quick to take offence, vulgar, vain, and probably the best loved of all characters in the pantomime, she has long been the province of male comedians.[67]

The dame had been played by a man as long ago as 1731 when a male actor played the cook in *Dick Whittington*. Comic dames were entirely familiar by the time of the Regency pantomime. Similarly female principal boys became familiar after an appearance in *Harlequin and Fortunio* in 1815. The earliest principal boy known by name was Eliza Povey who played Jack in *Jack and the Beanstalk* at Drury Lane in 1819.

Interestingly there is no tradition of male dames in the extravaganzas of Planché. Only twice in the whole of Planché's *oeuvre* do men play female parts – both old women – Robert Roxby in *The Queen of the Frogs* and Frank Matthews in *Cymon and Iphigenia*. There are, on the other hand, twenty-two major roles with women playing men. The largest number was played by Madame Vestris who became associated with the 'breeches role'. It is worth considering why there was this distinction between extravaganza and pantomime, where the dame reigned supreme. The likelihood is that it lay in the audience. The extravaganza was directed at and appealed most to middle-class audiences and reflected their interests and values; the pantomime had a strong working-class appeal. For the middle classes the elegance and stylishness of the principal boy appealed more to middle-class taste and the caricatured shrewish harridan to established working-class stereotypes.

There was a long tradition of cross-dressing in the theatre. Boys had played all the female roles on the Elizabethan and Jacobean stage. But there was a fundamental difference between them and the principal boys of the nineteenth-century stage. Sixteenth- and seventeenth-century boy actors were expected to be believable women; nineteenth-century principal boys were not expected to be convincing males. Kathy Fletcher, having studied Planché's work in detail, concludes, 'nothing in the available evidence suggests a sustained, realistic attempt on the part of the extravaganza actress to recreate or mimic adult male behavior ... While endearing, boyish characteristics were appreciated ... it was important to retain certain feminine attributes.'[68] In his essay on cross-dressing, Laurence Senelick observed, 'the tradition of the breeches role on the English stage avoided a convincing

5. *The Pantomime Dame – Dan Leno as Mother Goose*

6. *The Principal Boy – Fanny Leslie as Robinson Crusoe*

7. *The Infant Prodigy – Percy Roselle, who may or may not have been a dwarf*

8. *The Pantomime Family – the Vokes Family who combined comedy and dance*

impersonation of the male' and as for the dame, 'Red-nosed comedians carried on as sex-starved harridans and slatterns ... Theatregoers were not confronted with a man playing a desirable woman or a woman playing a he-man.'[69] Similarly Peter Ackroyd in *Dressing Up* notes:

> the male impersonator is never anything more than what she pretends to be: a feminine, noble mind in a boy's body. It is a peculiarly sentimental and therefore harmless reversal ... The dame is never effeminate; she is never merely a drag artist, since she always retains her male identity. The performer is clearly a man dressed as an absurd and ugly woman, and much of the comedy is derived from the fact that he is burlesquing himself as a male actor.[70]

What is equally significant is that there is no record of principal girls ever being played by men. They remain in both role and performer ideals of femininity: pure, demure, pretty and sweet-natured.

Audiences were in no doubt as to why the hero was being played by women, and what the appeal was. This is highlighted by a joke in *The Entr'acte* magazine (25 June 1881), when a twelve-year-old girl asks her father: 'What is a burlesque? It is a take-off, isn't it?' And the father replies: 'Yes, it is a takeoff. Actresses take-off just as much as they dare.' Fred Willis, veteran observer of London life, recalling his Victorian boyhood, reported:

> From my youngest days I always knew the principal boy was a girl, and far from resenting it I revelled in it. I remember that the experiment of having a man for principal boy was tried once at Drury Lane with disastrous results. Nobody liked it. A principal boy has to be dashing and fairy-like. No man could do this in pantomime without being ridiculous, and to have a ridiculous principal boy is opposed to all tradition.[71]

The illustrator Ernest Shepard recalled, as a boy, seeing Marie Lloyd playing principal boy in *Humpty Dumpty* at Drury Lane:

> I did not think it possible that such feminine charms existed as were displayed by the Principal Boy. Ample-bosomed, small-waisted and with thighs – oh, such thighs! – thighs that shone and glittered in the different coloured tights in which she continually appeared. How she strode about the stage, proud and dominant, smacking those rounded limbs with a riding crop! At every smack, a fresh dart was shot into the heart of at least one young adorer.[72]

So how finally are we to interpret this phenomenon? Some commentators (Ackroyd, Mayer, Weltman) see it as a way of defusing sexual tensions and anxieties (the fear of dominant aggressive women or the dread of homosexuality). Others (Eigner, Golby and Purdue, Willis) see it as a temporary carnivalesque role reversal which merely serves to emphasize the natural and normal order of things. The latter seems more likely to me, given the continuing emphasis on heroic masculinity and grotesque femininity. But the debate will doubtless continue.[73]

The net result of all the transformations during the nineteenth century was that the pantomime was very different in 1900 from what it had been in 1800. But it was in 1900 recognizable as the precursor of the pantomime that still holds sway on the Christmas stages today.

2

Harlequinade

The classic Victorian pantomime was a fusion of the harlequinade and the extravaganza, the former essentially physical and the latter predominantly verbal in nature. The form owed its emergence to the Theatre Regulation Act of 1843 which ended the monopoly of the spoken word previously enjoyed by the Theatres Royal at Drury Lane and Covent Garden. This restriction led all the other theatres, the so-called minors, to seek ways round the regulation and in response new forms, melodrama, burletta and pantomime, were developed. Not primarily dependent on the spoken word, they deployed music, action and spectacle to tell their stories.

Pre-eminent among these forms was the pantomime or harlequinade. The English pantomime developed from the Italian *commedia dell'arte*, as refined and transformed into the harlequinade in the French theatre. This dramatic form, with its regular cast of characters, Harlequin, Columbine, Pantaloon, Pierrot and Scaramouche, and its standard plot (young lovers, aided by ingenious servants, thwarting the plans of father or guardian to marry the heroine to a wealthy older man) carried out in dumb-show, reached England in the late seventeenth century.

It was in the eighteenth century that John Rich, first at the Lincoln's Inn Fields Theatre and later at the newly built Theatre Royal, Covent Garden, transformed the continental model into a distinctively English form. Producing and devising the show as well as playing Harlequin, Rich linked the action of the harlequinade to an opening story derived from classical mythology, imbued his characters with magical powers and combined music, dance, mime, acrobatics, spectacle, special effects and topical allusions into an appealing and exciting whole.[1]

The harlequinade reached its apogee in the period 1806–28, the heyday of Joseph Grimaldi, the man *John Bull* (31 December 1820) called 'The Garrick of Clowns'. Grimaldi made the ingenious, outrageous Clown the central figure of the show and, according to David Mayer in his definitive account of this era, 'pantomime structure was cast in a more fixed form than previously and assumed conventions of characterisation, performance, and methods of production which made it unique at a time when innovation and novelty ... were endemic to the theatre.'[2]

With its form fixed but far from static, the pantomime was breathlessly topical, indiscriminately featuring the events, fads and sensations of the day. The pantomime parodied and burlesqued other popular theatrical forms: Gothic melodrama, aquatic spectacle, burletta and animal dramas. It satirized extravagant male fashions. It celebrated new technology and transport developments (steamboats, balloons, railways, tunnels and bridges). As David Worrall has shown, pantomime also became a vehicle for the representation of varieties of race and ethnicity and the transmission of early imperial ideology.[3] Mayer says that the pantomime 'by the very nature of its wide scope and satiric tone, was an unofficial and informal chronicle of the age' recording 'in often comically satiric terms ... events and attitudes, technical achievements and artistic movements, major political and social crises, and everyday trivia'.[4] It also took advantage of all the latest devices, tricks and mechanical developments to create eye-catching special effects.[5]

But at the heart of the show – and the source of its enduring appeal – was the comic mayhem perpetrated by the Clown. Grimaldi transformed Clown from a bumbling, addlepated country bumpkin in a smock into a versatile, dandified, brightly garbed madcap (the English equivalent of Scaramouche). Grimaldi's latest biographer sums up his impact:

> Grimaldi's clown was a Londoner in hyperbole: channelling its voracious consumerism and infusing his clowning with its manic energy, flamboyant theatricality and love of show. ... Grimaldi's clown was cunning, covetous and childlike in his wants, an uncensored mass of appetites and an embodied accumulation of unconscious desires. Everything tempted him, calling him forward and enticing him to touch, tinker and meddle, with an impetus that overrode all considerations, especially the law ... Londoners revelled in Grimaldi's lawlessness, watching him commit a litany of crimes that outside the theatre would have been rewarded with transportation or death. 'Robbery became a science in his hands', wrote one commentator, recalling with relish the way he would pilfer a leg of mutton and, with 'bewitching eagerness', extract handkerchiefs and pocket watches with 'such a devotion to the task' that he 'seemed imbued with the spirit of peculation'.[6]

There was, however, a limit to the irreverence. The censors forbade disrespectful depictions of monarchy, national politics and religion, although the London police force, incompetent and corrupt before Sir Robert Peel's creation in 1829 of the Metropolitan Police, came in for regular rough treatment in the harlequinade, to the delight of audiences. But along with the irreverence there went a belligerent and chauvinistic patriotism, particularly during the Napoleonic Wars, which saw the regular performing of patriotic songs and celebrations of British naval successes and Wellington's military victories.

The popularity of Clown raises the age-old question of the nature of comedy. Is it fundamentally subversive or conformist? Is it highlighting and satirizing social, political or even personal ills, with the aim of reforming or eliminating them or is it acting as a safety valve, providing a cathartic outlet for the audience's more disreputable urges and anti-social impulses, and in purging them, allowing society to proceed undisturbed on its appointed way? Or is it simply funny? Assuming that any given audience is a collection of individuals, each person may react differently – some finding the show subversive and others finding it cathartic.[7]

Andrew Halliday, himself a playwright and pantomime writer, in one of the earliest accounts of the English pantomime, *Comical Fellows* (1863) thought it was just funny:

Wise men of all ages have affirmed that laughter is a good thing. It clears the lungs, shakes up the diaphragm, and loosens the fetters of the brain. How, then, shall we get a good hearty laugh? Shall we apply to the wit for his subtle refinements, and caustic jokes? They but make us smile. Shall we seek the broader drolleries of the humorist? They only tickle us. If we want a good roar, if we want to make our lungs crow like chanticleer, we must go and see the Christmas pantomime. There is no fun like it after all.[8]

He lists the slapstick highlights traditional to the harlequinade:

What verbal joke that ever was uttered can equal the exquisite comicality of popping a red-hot poker into the palm of the Pantaloon when he innocently and trustingly holds out the hand of fellowship to the Clown? Where is the witticism that can compete with sitting on a baby, and flattening it to the shape of a pancake? ... Is there a more ludicrous object in the world than a policeman with his hat knocked over his eyes? ... Can you find us in the whole range of the drama a more telling situation than where the butterman slips down and hurts himself on the slide which the clown has made out of his own pound of butter? Pantomime has the power of giving a comic aspect to everything. It makes even crime amusing, and yet without conveying a bad moral. The clown cuts off the head of a dandy who is proud of his whiskers , and the children clap their hands with delight. There is a moral, d'ye see? He was inordinately proud of that figure-head of his, and he was punished. Serve him right. The clown is an arrant thief. He robs unwary tradespeople right and left, and their discomfiture is the greatest fun in the world. He is dreadfully cruel, and is forever burning Pantaloon with red-hot pokers, slapping him in the face, and shutting his head into boxes; but how we enjoy it all! We will not stop to inquire why cruelty is so exquisitely funny; but it is exquisitely funny; nothing more so. And, burning with pokers, and jamming fingers into doors, and stealing legs of mutton, and squashing babies, are such very good jokes, that we can bear to see them repeated year after year without feeling weary of them, or voting them stale and dull.[9]

In *A Curious Dance Round a Curious Tree* in *Household Words* (17 January 1852), Dickens wrote of the escapist nature of the humour in:

> the jocund world of Pantomime, where there is no affliction or calamity that leaves the least impression; where a man may tumble into the broken ice, or dive into the kitchen fire, and only be the droller for the accident; where babies may be knocked about and sat upon, or choked with gravy spoons, in the process of feeding, and yet no Coroner be wanted, nor anybody made uncomfortable; where workmen may fall from the top of a house to the bottom, or even from the bottom of a house to the top, and sustain no injury to the brain, need no hospital, leave no young children; where everyone, in short, is so superior to all the accounts of life, though encountering them at every turn, that I suspect this to be the secret ... of the general enjoyment which an audience of vulnerable spectators, liable to pain and sorrow, find in this class of entertainment.[10]

Grimaldi's breakthrough show had been *Harlequin and Mother Goose or The Golden Egg* (1806) which ran for ninety-two performances and was – unusually for pantomimes – set in England with scenes in a rural village, Vauxhall Gardens, St. Dunstan's Church and Golden Square. The opening had four scenes and the harlequinade fifteen. This set the pattern for future shows. But after Grimaldi's retirement the openings began to get longer and the producers particularly in the 1830s increased the amount of spectacle. This led to the beginning of what was to be a regular complaint for the rest of the century: 'The pantomime is not what it was.' Veteran pantomime producer Derek Salberg devoted an entire chapter of his affectionate history of the genre, *Once Upon a Pantomime* (1981) to a litany of complaints from the nineteenth and twentieth centuries about the decline of pantomime. They are drawn from a wide spectrum of sources with *The Times*, *Daily Telegraph*, *Chambers Journal*, *The Theatrical Inquisitor* and *The Illustrated London News* all chanting the same refrain.[11]

Leigh Hunt, who wrote enthusiastically of the Grimaldian pantomime in 1817 in *The Examiner* (15 January 1817), was lamenting by 1831 in *The Tatler* (28 December 1831):

> It is agreed on all hands that Pantomimes are not what they were. The story with which they used to set out, and which used to form merely a brief excuse for putting the Harlequinade in motion, now forms a considerable part of the performance; an innovation which we should hail with pleasure if it were always in such good taste as in some instances, but which is rarely apt to be so, and is followed by a set of tricks and transformations equally stinted and wanting in fancy, and a total departure from the old and genuine Harlequin plot, which consisted in the run-away vivacities of a couple of

lovers full of youth and spirits, the eternal hobbling after them of the decrepit Pantaloon, and the broad gluttony, selfishness, and mischief of his servant the Clown, all tending to one point. The Clown retains something of his character still, but the rest has become a mere mass of gratuitous absurdity without object. There is no real action going on … In short, Pantomimes seem to have become partakers of the serious spirit of the age, and to be waiting for the settlement of certain great questions and heavy national accounts, to know when they are to laugh and be merry again.[12]

In 1863 Andrew Halliday attributed the change directly to the absence of a true successor to Grimaldi:

> Playgoers of the old school would describe the period upon which we are now entering as marking 'the decline and fall of pantomime'. In Grimaldi's days the pantomime depended for its success upon the pantomimic powers of those who performed in it. It was the exquisite fooling of clown, pantaloon, harlequin, and columbine that drew crowded audiences and brought down the applause. But in the period that succeeded, when there were no worthy successors of Grimaldi and Bologna [the harlequin], it was found necessary to call in the aid of gorgeous dresses, magnificent scenery, and the most elaborate mechanical effects. We have seen that Joe Grimaldi could get on without these aids, and that his grimacing and filching, and kicking and slapping, were so comical in themselves that the public desired nothing else. True pantomime may therefore be said to have declined when there were no longer representatives of the various characters who could hold the attention of the public by their own unaided talents.[13]

This is not in fact true. There was only one Grimaldi but he did indeed have admired successors, Tom Matthews, Richard Flexmore, Robert Bradbury, Redigé Paulo, George Wieland and Harry Boleno among them, who kept the Grimaldian tradition going well into the Victorian Age. Pantomime as an institution not only survived, it evolved and went from strength to strength. *The Era* (19 January 1884) reported that for the 1883–4 season, there were pantomimes at 104 theatres in seventy-two British towns and cities: eleven in London, five in Liverpool, four in Glasgow, three in Manchester and Birmingham, two in Edinburgh, Yarmouth, Leeds, Newcastle, Oldham, Sheffield, Bristol and South Shields and one in each of sixty-two other towns.

It was the harlequinade element in the show that declined, as luminary after luminary in the Victorian theatre-world testified. Charles Dickens, whose works, it has been suggested, are steeped in the characters and attitudes of the pantomime, celebrated Grimaldi in a version of the great clown's memoirs which he edited and partly rewrote in 1838.[14] As late as 1899, the eminent critic Clement Scott, devoting a chapter in his history of nineteenth-century theatre to 'The Lost Art of Pantomime' was lauding the great clowns and lamenting:

The Harlequinade of our boyhood's day is, I fear, a pleasure lost for ever and denied to the generation of to-day. No more jolly old Clown, with the purloined sausages or red-hot poker, and the immortal Hot Codlins; no more spangled Harlequin; no more Joey the Pantaloon; no more Sprites; no more delightful Columbine with her white tarletan skirts. In our memories of the past we must not forget Tom Matthews, Flexmore, Harry Boleno, Harry Payne, or their brilliant predecessors George Wieland and Joey Grimaldi.[15]

Even the writers whose work was believed to have contributed to the decline of the harlequinade lamented its passing. During the 1880s E.L. Blanchard penned a celebration of Tom Ellar, a noted Harlequin of his boyhood:

Boys born sixty years ago had, at least, one source of delight which the children of a later generation will never know. In the days of the past, when we were taken to the theatre for our holiday-treat at Christmas, the true hero of our imagination was Harlequin. He was not reduced, as he is now, to a mere incident in a supplementary comic scene, coming at the end of an elaborate spectacular entertainment; but was the one object impatiently waited for by the younger folk when the slight fairy tale, represented in the dumb show, was brought to a swift conclusion. Harlequin would then perform his feats of transformation continuously through a long series of adventures, in which we were all greatly interested, by a steady succession of surprises of the most astonishing kind; and as every trick had a sort of political, or social, significance, a vast amount of information about passing events was concurrently imparted to the youthful spectator.[16]

The inventor of the extravaganza J.R. Planché similarly lamented the relegation of the harlequinade in his 1872 autobiography:

Instead of the two or three simple scenes which previously formed the opening of the pantomime, a long burlesque, the characters in which have nothing to do with those in the harlequinade, occupies an hour – sometimes much more – of the evening, and terminates with one of those elaborate and gorgeous displays which have acquired the name of 'transformation scenes', are made the great feature of the evening; and, consequently, after which the best part of the audience quit the theatre; and what is by courtesy called the 'comic business' is run through by the pantomimists in three or four ordinary street or chamber scenes. The usual number of curiously dressed people stream in and out of exhibitions or cross the stage; the usual number of policemen are bonneted; the steps are buttered; the redhot poker is exhibited; the real live pig let out of the basket; and then ... a portion of the transformation scene is suddenly discovered, sufficiently shorn of its beams to escape recognition by the two or three score of persons who have courageously sat out the performance, and are too much occupied in putting on their coats and shawls to think of anything but their beds or their suppers ... How different were the Christmas pantomimes of my younger days ... There was some congruity, some dramatic construction, in such pantomimes, and then the acting! For it was acting, and first-rate acting ... Grimaldi! – There is no describing the richness of his humour, the expression of his countenance, the variety of his resources, and his skill in their employment.[17]

Significantly all these commentators are waxing nostalgic about their lost boyhoods when the annual visit to the pantomime was a cherished highlight of what in retrospect has come to seem a lost and irrecoverably innocent and ideal world.

If we discount, as we should, the absence of talented clowns, what explains the decline of the harlequinade? The obvious theatrical answer is the passing in 1843 of the Act which ended the patent theatres' monopoly of the spoken word. This led to the major structural change by which the opening expanded and the harlequinade shrank. The extended opening demanded performers who could sing, dance and act and increasingly the situation developed in which, unlike the position in Grimaldi's day, the pantomime essentially became two shows in one, with the spectacular transformation scene marking the division. The two shows now had two separate casts, with the pantomimists who specialized in acrobatics and knockabout confined to the harlequinade. As the spectacle became more and more important in spectator appeal, so the slapstick of the harlequinade began to lose its appeal. With the length of pantomimes growing to three and four hours, the newspapers began to report people leaving before the harlequinade, which often did not begin before midnight.

There is a wider societal explanation. Leigh Hunt hinted at it when he suggested that pantomimes had become 'partakers of the serious spirit of the age'. Significantly Grimaldi, who embodied the spirit of the Regency pantomime, died three months before the accession to the throne of Queen Victoria, whose reign became indelibly associated with the values of respectable society. The family and family life, epitomized by the royal family, came to stand at the heart of respectable society. Christmas became the family festival *par excellence* and the exclusive association of the pantomime with the Christmas season became part of the elaboration of that festival. The Victorians did not, as some have claimed, invent Christmas, but they did elaborate it. Christmas cards, Christmas trees and Christmas shopping were all Victorian developments. There was a dramatic revival in the writing of Christmas carols. Charles Dickens in his eagerly awaited annual Christmas stories, most memorably *A Christmas Carol* (1843), enshrined Christmas in the culture as a time of happy family gatherings and goodwill to all men. Before the Victorian Age the pantomime had not been restricted to Christmas and had been seen as an entertainment for adults rather than children, even though children went. Pantomimes in the Regency period were performed four times a year, on December 26 and the weeks following, Easter Monday and Whit Monday and the weeks following, early July and the summer months and Lord Mayor's Day,

9 November, and the weeks following. But after 1843, the pantomime became essentially a Christmas family event, particularly aimed at children.[18]

Fashions changed and the spirit of the age changed. Interestingly D.J. Anderson, writing in *The Theatre* in 1879, denounced the harlequinade in terms which suggested that it no longer conformed to the spirit of the age. The harlequinade, he said, was atrophied, the comic business, stagnant ('for a long time past he [harlequin] has not ventured any new business') and the traditional situations, no longer funny. Partly tongue in cheek but also reflecting changed sensibilities, he says that when the clown sits on the baby, he can only think of the anguish of the infant's mother; when the leg of mutton is purloined, his sympathies are with the respectable family left dinnerless and when the old gentleman tumbles on the buttered slide, he feels for the old gentleman, and he dislikes seeing the police pelted with stale vegetables. The problem, as he sees it, is that 'all Clown's jokes are based on cruelty. He is a demon in baggy breeches, and laughs at the discomfiture of unoffending mankind', and is the product of an age 'when parsons got drunk, nobles gambled away their estates, and most of our national sports were dashed with cruelty.'[19] In other words, the harlequinade was an unwanted relic of the Regency, out of kilter with the more civilized, restrained and respectable society of Victorian England.

The *I.L.N.* (5 January 1861), reviewing the pantomime *Peter Wilkins* at Drury Lane, similarly found the demoralizing effect of the harlequinade offensive:

> There is a great moral in a pantomime ... Unfortunately, notwithstanding the fears of the Clown, and the trembling guilt of his clumsy accomplice, the Pantaloon, this moral is not brought so prominently forward in our modern pieces as it should be. We see indeed at the commencement ... that vice and virtue have their adequate reward. The tyrannical baron, the abominable uncle, the uxorious miser ... get punished – but how? By being changed into two fellows who enjoy themselves through every variety of scene, who annoy and rob everybody, who jump through laws and first floor windows, who pop down trapdoors and over ten commandments with perfect impunity and who end all this wicked life in a perfect blaze of triumph, promising, too, to continue their existence as long as the laughing audience like to see them ... Censor of the stage, can such things be?

The history of the harlequinade at Drury Lane is indicative of its fate more generally. At the start of the 1830s the harlequinade encompassed seven scenes as it had since the outset of the Victorian era, and the critics were still taking it seriously enough to devote a substantial part of their reviews to describing it. By the early 1860s the harlequinade had shrunk to four scenes and then in the 1880s to two scenes. Coverage in the newspapers diminished in proportion to its length.

The Drury Lane clowns were, for most of the Victorian Age, the recognized masters of the craft. Tom Matthews (1806–89) was the pupil and associate of Grimaldi. He had first played Clown in 1829. He became chief clown at Drury Lane, last performing it in the 1855–6 season. But he always also acted in the opening and continued to do so even after he ceased to appear in the harlequinade. Harry Boleno (d.1875) took over from Matthews as Clown in 1854–5. But in 1855–6 Drury Lane introduced the gimmick of a double harlequinade, with all the characters played by two different performers, presumably with the intention of doubling the fun. The first such pair were Boleno and Matthews. From 1856–7 to 1859–60 Boleno was joined by the celebrated Richard Flexmore (1825–60) as Clown, except for 1858–9 when Boleno was partnered by Delevanti. Boleno and Flexmore were highly regarded. *The Times* (27 December 1859) said of Boleno that he was 'one of the driest, and therefore, one of the best of modern clowns' and of Flexmore that he was 'decidedly the funniest, most original, and (in spite of his somewhat hoarse vocalization, quite perfect dancing and extraordinary agility), the most *clownish* of Clowns since the days of the truly inimitable Grimaldi.'

The 1860–1 and 1861–2 seasons saw the Clowns played by Messrs Huline and Power and then Messrs Huline and Forrest. Of the first pair, *The Times* (27 December 1860) said they were 'neither of them adequate substitutes for the lamented Mr Flexmore'. Flexmore had died and Boleno had decamped to Covent Garden to perform in *Bluebeard*. But the next year Boleno was back at Drury Lane and from 1862–3 to 1868–9 played Clown, partnered by Charles Lauri (1833–89). In 1869–70 Boleno made his final Drury Lane appearance, partnered by Rowella. From 1870–1 to 1880–1 the principal clown was Fred Evans, partnered first by W.H. Harvey (1870–4), then H. Wright (1875–6), Charles Lauri (1876–7 to 1878–9), Will Simpson (1879–80) and finally Rowella (1880–1). Once he took over at Drury Lane Augustus Harris reverted to the single harlequinade company for the 1880–1 season.

Harry Payne (1830–95), was the last of the great Drury Lane clowns. He played Clown from 1881–2 until his death in 1895. By then the Drury Lane harlequinade was, according to *The Times* (27 December 1894), 'the ghost of its former self'. *The Era* (29 December 1895) said the harlequinade was 'commendably brief'. In 1897 the reviewer in *The Stage* (30 December 1897) admitted that he had not bothered to stay for the harlequinade in view of the lateness of the hour. After Harry Payne, Clown was played by Tom Lovell in 1895–6 and Jimmy Huline in 1896–7. Whimsical Walker then took over for the rest of the century in a harlequinade, which lasted now for only ten minutes. It hung on into the twentieth century but Arthur Collins eventually killed it off.[20] After the harlequinade expired, Walker went on to play Clown at the annual Christmas circus at Olympia.

The continuing elements of the harlequinade were the contemporary urban settings – usually familiar London locales; the topical references which promoted a mutually knowing attitude that provided for instant bonding between performers and spectators; and the slapstick both traditional and innovative, often involving ingenious stage machinery. But as time wore on and the familiar tricks and stratagems seemed to some increasingly stale, more and more speciality acts were inserted so that in the end it looked more like a variety show than the traditional harlequinade familiar since the days of Grimaldi.

E.L. Blanchard's first Drury Lane pantomime, *Harlequin Hudibras* (1852–3) concluded with a harlequinade in which the performers from the opening assumed the roles of the familiar characters of Clown, Harlequin and the rest. This continued to be the case until 1859. 'The inimitable' Tom Matthews, who had played the title role in Hudibras, became Clown and, reported *The Era* (2 January 1853), 'was full of animal spirits and appeared quite at home in his old character.' The action took place against the familiar urban background of a row of shops, hairdressers, 'Life's Elixir' warehouse, dyers, booksellers, bill discounters, clock shop, tobacco emporium and light depot. It highlighted 'the topics and follies of the day', which included teetotalism and the sale of sarsaparilla; the *Uncle Tom's Cabin* mania, which had seen a host of dramatic adaptations following the sensational publishing success of Harriet Beecher Stowe's 1852 novel; Chancery reform; the Derby election; the inhabited house duty; the Beerbottle question; and the Australian Gold Rush. 'To gratify all tastes,' said *The Times* (28 December 1852) 'a squad of police are brought in and assaulted by the Clowns.' The 'Peelers' are discomfited 'to the frantic joy of the topmost tiers' of the gallery that is the working-class section of the audience, to whom the police were generally anathema. *The Morning Chronicle* (28 December 1852) preferred the harlequinade to the opening and particularly liked Tom Matthews' Clown – 'a good sample of the old legitimate Clown, with all the ancient tricks and conventional jokes, which make us laugh none the less that they are old.'

The following year, *King Humming Top* was the pantomime. This time *The Daily News* (27 December 1853) thought the harlequinade superior to the opening. Tom Matthews, who had played King Humming Top in the opening, was Clown again. *The Times* (27 December 1853) reported:

> The 'comic business' is chiefly based on the old principle of tumbling, knocking and kicking, which seems to amuse as much as ever when enlivened by such an obliging clown as Mr Tom Matthews, who can sing those national melodies of pantomime 'Hot Codlins' and 'Tippitywitch' with infinite good humour and gusto.

The Era (1 January 1854) expanded:

> The comic business is this year unusually lively and bustling, and the fun never flags for an instant. Tom Matthews is a capital Clown, thoroughly versed in all the art and mystery of Pantomimic action, and his various acts of petty larceny are so palpably committed for 'the fun of the thing' that the sternest judge would forgive the offender. Milano, as Harlequin, is indefatigably active, dancing with consummate grace, and taking leaps with

an agility in which he has scarcely a rival ... and the Columbine and Harlequina, Mdlle Annie Cushnie and Miss Marie Charles, are both exquisite dancers, and, with figures of faultless symmetry, exhibit a graceful combination of elegance and activity.

The Times, however, thought the best thing in the harlequinade was a remarkable series of transformations, with the dead wall of Farringdon Street turned into a market 'instinct with the life and bustle of a Saturday night', a 'fanciful' scene in which the different personalities of the harlequinade are seen in infancy and raised to the advanced stage of childhood by hothousing and with the usual comic business performed by a talented party of juveniles and 'a marvellous metamorphosis by which the Queen's Head Tavern is made a kind of Post Office Directory.'

The pantomime in 1854–5 was *Jack and Jill, Harlequin King Mustard and the Four and Twenty Blackbirds Baked in a Pie*. Harry Boleno, who had played King Mustard, was Clown, and according to *The Era* (31 December 1854), 'certainly one of the best, if not *the* best of Clowns, his movements not having the least approach to vulgarity, and his by-play quiet and easy.' The harlequinade contained scenes set at the Turk's Head public house, the Great American Baby Show ('affords a great deal of amusement'), the new wing of Somerset House where the civil list is reformed, and the magic kitchen of celebrity chef Alexis Soyer, in the news for providing kitchens for the troops in the Crimea where the war was raging. Too many cooks spoil the broth and Soyer ends up in his own soup. There were hits at the new 1854 Beer Act which closed drinking places for a large part of Sunday and a comic scene of a costermonger selling ginger beer from a barrow and his customers fighting over it. *The Times* (27 December 1854) had only one complaint, that 'the mouldy nuisance' of *Hot Codlins*, the song associated with the harlequinade since the days of Grimaldi, was forced on the audience by 'sundry of the gods' and the clown, Boleno, was compelled to sing it 'much against his will'. This says much about the conservatism and traditional expectations of the working-class section of the audience. There was a mishap one night when Clown brought on a basket of Watling's Pork Pies. A live pig escaped from it and ended up in a private box, to the astonishment of the barrister whose party was occupying it.

For *Hey Diddle Diddle or Harlequin King Nonsense and the Seven Ages of Man* (1855–6), Drury Lane introduced the double harlequinade. Tom Matthews and Harry Boleno, who had acted in the opening, became two Clowns. The events satirized included the shortage of accommodation at the Paris Exposition, which had run from 15 May to 15 November 1855. Clown and Pantaloon are reduced to engaging a bed in the coal hole and taking wrongful possession of a bedroom not their own where the bed rises twenty feet in the air and Clown seeks to sort out all the problems by setting about him with a warming pan. Another target – and according to *The Morning Chronicle* (27 December 1855), the hit of the harlequinade – was the satire on the betting mania in which Clown and Pantaloon set up a betting shop in empty premises between a pawnbroker's and a cheesemonger's and people flock to it until settling-up day when they abscond. They are then caught and handed over in chains to an indignant populace. There is a scene in a garden with a beehive which Clown puts on his head, causing it to swell up to twice its size. There are also hits at ladies' wheel-hats, the shoeblack brigade and the trend of using shop fronts for advertisements.

The doubling of the harlequinade was not universally welcomed. By the time of *Little Jack Horner* (1857–8), *The Era* (27 December 1857) found it made the harlequinade 'not only long but wearisome'. *The Times* (28 December 1857), however, for once preferred the harlequinade:

> on the whole, the liveliest, most amusing and varied that has been witnessed for years. So excellent is it, indeed, as not merely to warrant but to render advisable a very considerable abridgement of the far less diverting introduction, in order that no one may be deterred by late hours from remaining till the end.

The critic found 'Mrs Soapsud's Laundry and Drying-ground' a veritable 'side-splitter' and the 'tricks and transformations ... more ingenious and in more rapid alternation than of later years, and, considering this was the first performance, were attended for the most part with wonderful good-luck. The allusions to prevalent topics embrace almost every subject that has lately attained notoriety.' All that was required to ensure 'a long and prosperous "run"' was 'judicious use of the pruning-knife on the introductory burlesque.' The topics of the harlequinade included the Westminster Bell, the Siamese Ambassadors, the penny newspapers, the increasing popularity of telegrams (a term first substituted for the earlier 'telegraphic despatches' in 1855), and the mania for photography. But the topics received with 'the most relish', according to *The Era* (27 December 1857), were the Sepoy Mutiny and 'the modern extravagances of dress'.

In *Jack and the Beanstalk* (1859–60), of the performers in the opening, only Madame Boleno was carried on into the harlequinade, symptomatic of the increasing tendency to employ different casts for the opening and the harlequinade. The harlequinade, however, was more closely integrated with the opening than usual, as the whole pantomime was divided into twelve scenes each representing a different month. In the harlequinade, July was represented by a seaside scene and a marine parade, with the riflemen formed up to repel a French invasion. August was set in the village and mansion of the Marquis of Flowerdale and had a sequence of high days and holydays. September was a street in London, first seen in 1759 and then transformed into the same street in 1859, where everything is new and fast. October was set in the Kentish Hop Gardens and a well-known brewery, November had bonfire night and fog and December, Christmas. But there was plenty of knockabout and *The Era* (1 January 1860) particularly liked the scene in which Clown (Richard Flexmore) 'tortures his foppish master by the abundance of his pranks and the gratuitous exhibition of stupidity in a manner that kept the house in a continuous roar.'

By the 1860s and the reduction from seven to four scenes, *The Times* (28 December 1863), reviewing *Sindbad the Sailor* was declaring 'The time when the harlequinade ever approached the introduction in importance has long since passed away from the annals of pantomime.' The following year, reviewing *Hop O' My Thumb*, *The Times* (27 December 1864) again noted, 'as is universally the case with modern pantomime, the opening is more important than the motley supplement.'

Efforts were made to pep up the interest of the harlequinade. One was to increase the spectacular 'magical' transformations that were a regular feature. *The Era* (1 January 1865) reported of *Hop O' My Thumb* that Drury Lane observed 'certain desirable traditions of the old school' such as total changes of scene at Harlequin's command, noting that elsewhere 'that glittering, patchwork-covered individual has, of late years, been partially deprived of his power, the acrobatic element and other innovations having taken place of the old-fashioned mechanical tricks.' *Hop O' My Thumb* contained a series of transformations which seemed to celebrate progress and modernity: a villa and its grounds transformed into a railway station, a waggon into a steam threshing machine and a windmill and farmyard into a patent bread and biscuit factory. In *Number Nip* (1866–7) an omnibus turned into a greengrocer's shop, the statuary establishment Bird's Stone and Marble Gallery into a tavern, and a fancy fair stall turned into a doll's house from which the ballet girls emerged to do a dance of the dolls.

Some critics still appreciated the performance of the harlequinade company even when it was reduced to four scenes. In *Little King Pippin* (1865–6), the scenes were an alamode house, the high road to Trulyrural in the sporting season, a banker's and a house to let, and a fashionable hair-cutting saloon. The routine comprised acrobatics, dances, ballet and slapstick. *The Era* (31 December 1865) reported that 'a better double company could not be collected' and approvingly described the antics of Clown and Company:

Mr Boleno stands at the head of the acting Clowns of the day and Mr C. Lauri, as all the world knows, is a perfect wonder of agility and neatness. His springing into a large barrel as it is being carried across the stage is an extremely clever thing in its own way. Mr Boleno has a way of his own when attempting most things, and walks half way up the shop windows before taking the orthodox leaps in the coolest manner possible. Mr John Brougham's 'Bobolink Polka' is danced by Madame Boleno and Mr Cormack in the first scene, and the same couple give a very characteristic Jockey Dance in the second. Mr

Boleno deposes a respectable proprietor and boils down a human being for soup in a cookshop, besides behaving in his ordinarily impertinent manner to all the customers. … In the 'row' which ensues the ghosts of the boiled down individuals rise and complicate the facetious Boleno's distresses. Some good changes take place in the comic scenes, though nothing very remarkable as regards tricks. The usages and customs of Pantomime are, perhaps, undergoing a gradual change, for year by year the specimens of wholesale magic, as exemplified in the rapid transformation of whole scenes by the Harlequin, are less frequently met with. Much fun is produced by Messrs Boleno and Morris in a Village Scene, where sportsmen chase a church steeple, and where the Pantomimists, armed with guns, compel sundry unfortunates to disrobe, and shiver in the refreshing atmosphere of a village 'Cage'.

The Times (27 December 1865) preferred the ballet of twenty-four dancers carrying devices which eventually made up a Union Jack to any of the comic knockabout.

By the late 1860s, Drury Lane was peppering the harlequinade with variety acts and introducing sequences with child performers, which were always guaranteed to 'bring the house down.' In Faw, Fee, Fo, Fum (1867–8) there were three pantomime companies, two sets of adults and a further set of child performers as Clown, Harlequin, Pantaloon and the rest.

The Era (29 December 1867) reported that 'The Harlequinade is distinguished by several decidedly novel features':

The follies of the day are fired at on the wing and hit with unerring aim. The leading events of the year are passed under review by Field-Marshal Harlequin, and we have practical allusions to the grievances of the cabmen, to the high price of meat, and some sly hits at that new growth of trade competition, the Licensed Victuallers' Tea Association. One of the most striking scenes in the Harlequinade is a miniature picture of life in Paris, where every type of French character is represented by a little boy or girl, concluding with a review of French troops by the Emperor, the Empress and the Prince Imperial in miniature. This really charming scene reflects great credit upon the inventor, Mr Cormack. Another capital scene represents the Russian forest, where snow-balling and skating take place. The performance of Madame Fredrika and Mr Elliot, 'the champion skaters of the world', was exceedingly graceful, and gave great delight to the audience. The flambeaux dance was also very effective; but the scene which will give the liveliest satisfaction to the juveniles, and put a distinguishing mark upon the comic business of the Drury-lane Pantomime of 1867, will be, we predict, the miniature representation of life in Paris.

With Grimalkin the Great (1868–9) The Times (28 December 1868) noted of the harlequinade: 'Nowadays the nominal chiefs of pantomime have less to do than in the olden time, and the attractions of the harlequinade at Drury-lane consist chiefly

9. *Clown – from the heyday of Grimaldi, the clown was the principal attraction of the harlequinade*

10. *Anthropomorphic animals – these were always scene-stealers and some performers specialized in animal impersonation. The most popular was Puss in Boots, seen here in the pantomime* Grimalkin the Great

SCENE FROM THE LILIPUTIAN PANTOMIME AT THE ADELPHI THEATRE.

11. Child troupes – one of the most popular features of the pantomime was troupes of children – often several hundred of them – dancing, drilling or playing pixies, elves, squirrels and monkeys

of exhibitions in which Harlequin has no part.' Among them this time was a ballet by the 'girls of the period'; a troupe of performing dogs; a breakdown dance by an expert dancer, a 'nigger' or blackface dancer, a dance by a very small dancer (La Petite Annette); and a small horse (the smallest horse in the world) trained by a diminutive trainer. But most effective was the representation of the deck of a man-of-war, manned by 300 children. 'They go through a series of evolutions, terminating with the semblance of an engagement and a wave of the Union Jack as a signal of victory. This scene is admirably managed and is one of the best things in the entire pantomime.' *The Era* (31 December 1868) called it:

> a most interesting and animated scene, reflecting great credit on Mr Cormack [choreographer John Cormack], who must have had no end of trouble in drilling the youngsters, who perform the evolutions with remarkable precision, and at the same time with a hearty enjoyment of the work in which they are engaged. We may say … that this man-of-war scene is worth all the money.

The highlight of *Beauty and the Beast* (1869–70) was, thought *The Era* (1 January 1870), a recreation of W.P. Frith's celebrated painting *Ramsgate Sands* 'not quite in the order observed by Mr Frith in his great picture.' Against a background of pier, harbour and town, there was a dance for the ladies of the ballet who represented the Oxford and Harvard crews, each carrying an oar from which they pulled English and

American flags. The Tremont Minstrels did a blackface minstrel act. The Manly family did an acrobatic performance. Clown opened a photographic establishment ('quaintly handled by Mr Boleno') but also caused mayhem by throwing babies in the sea, falling in himself and then when a squall broke out, Harry Boleno as Clown and Paul Herring as Pantaloon floated out to sea on two bathing machines. In addition to this sequence, the Tyler Family formed 'the smallest brass band in the world', Professor Peterson introduced his performing dogs and John Cormack drilled 300 children to impersonate the Volunteer camp at Wimbledon.

These developments were not apparently being as successful as was hoped. *The Era* (1 January 1871) reported in its review of *The Dragon of Wantley* (1870–1) that the harlequinade was 'so good that it is to be hoped that the prevalent custom of leaving after the Transformation will be at once abolished.' The knockabout took place at a Baker's, Fishmonger's and Market-Inn, at a baby show and at a waxworks, with the usual repertoire of thefts, chases, policemen knocked over and the Clown baked in a pie. But there was also a succession of speciality acts: Master Rawlings, the clog dancer; Mr Sloman who imitated birds and beasts; Master Dassie, a child of five and a half, and Mr Lyon, 'a giant of nineteen' who sang together the 'Chickaleary Boy'; Mr Collard, 'the pocket Sims Reeves' who sang some of the great tenor's most popular songs; Miss Ada Peterson, 'the infant Paganini'; and La Patrie, 'the infant velocipedist'. John Cormack also devised a sequence of a Highland Games near Balmoral featuring 300 children.

For the harlequinade in *Tom Thumb the Great* (1871–2) the familiar knockabout took place in scenes of a pawnbroker's and butcher's shops, rival baker's shops and during a harvest home in a wheatfield in Cornwall. But *The Era* (31 December 1871) noted: 'As is the custom nowadays, the Harlequinade introduces entertainments most varied and original, and may be separated distinctly from the pantomime proper.' Among the individual items were the Almonte troupe of tumblers; a stilt dance by Mr Harry White; Mr Powell and his performing cats; Mr Sloman's 'very clever' imitations of birds and beasts, a skipping rope dance by Miss Leslie (much applauded); the 'Dolly Varden Polka' danced by the ladies of the *corps de ballet* and a 'pretty' jockey dance by thirty children. There was a scene of animated furniture in furnished apartments in Belgravia which *The Era* thought went on for rather too long. But the highlight of the harlequinade was a recreation of Frith's celebrated painting *Derby Day* 'which fairly astonished the house on account of the completeness of the representation.' The variety acts seem to have eclipsed the knockabout, if *The Daily News* (27 December 1871) is to be believed. The critic noted that the harlequinade was 'not remarkable for the novelty of tricks ... the practical jokes stand in need of refreshing.'

In *Jack in the Box* (1873–4), the harlequinade had slapstick scenes in a hairdresser's (complete with comic shaving scene), a farmyard, a laundry and a dairy.

But there was greater interest in the speciality acts, which included Piero the 'one legged dancer', acrobatics by the Brothers Ethair and Mr Levantine, 'the American Wonder' who lay on his back and balanced barrels on his feet. There was a skating sequence in the Arctic regions by the Neviers Sisters, described as 'Nubian'. There was a dance of dominoes and a 'pretty and picturesque' hop garland dance in the hopfields of Kent by the *corps de ballet*. A particular highlight was a Lilliputian brewery, with children as draymen, coopers and other employees ('a really pleasing and astonishing scene of industry').

The trade paper *The Era* (29 December 1873) was now one of the few journals to devote any detailed discussion to the harlequinade. *The Daily News* customarily dismissed it in three or four lines. But *The Times* (27 December 1876) reviewing *The Forty Thieves* (1876–7) unexpectedly came to the aid of the beleaguered harlequinade:

> The harlequinade must not be passed over with a few words. Formerly this was the pantomime itself, and we suspect that in the eyes of the rising and probably many of the older generation it is even now the most attractive part of the entertainment. To say nothing of harlequin and columbine, and pantaloon, now so thoroughly acclimatised to England, who does not experience more or less pleasure at hearing the cheery voice of the clown as he wishes us a happy new year, and who does not heartily condone his Jacobin-like disregard of order and the rights of property in consideration of his untiring pleasantry. He reminds us of those red-lettered days in our boyhood – our first visit to the theatre, and even when his practical and verbal jokes are somewhat hackneyed, he seems possessed of some mysterious power to amuse.

There was a double harlequinade, with the mayhem taking place in front of tradesmen's shops, the house of a spirit medium named Dr Slade (American spiritualist medium 'Doctor' Henry Slade had been exposed as a fraud in September 1876), at the gates of the Woolwich Arsenal, and in a kitchen. *The Era* (13 December 1876) thought 'some of the tricks [we]re marvellously ingenious', particularly Charles Lauri's burlesque of the 'Mysterious Cabinet' (one of the celebrated tricks of magician J.N. Maskelyne), and Fred Evans' doings as a Clown, with the head of a man and the limbs of a baby. *The Daily News* (27 December 1876) on the other hand reported: 'Of the harlequinade ... nothing need be reported beyond the fact that ... all went with the simple minds and hearty fun always associated with a Boxing night at Drury-lane.'

But with the pantomime of 1877–8, *The White Cat*, *The Times* (27 December 1877) was back to its perfunctory coverage, devoting two and half lines to it: 'The harlequinade was of the usual madcap and boisterous character, keeping the good-humoured audience in continual merriment.' The double harlequinade was headed by two Clowns, Charles Lauri and Fred Evans. *The Era* (30 December 1877) expanded on the contents:

> The Harlequinade ... is particularly calculated to afford enjoyment to the little folks ... Some of the tricks introduced in a scene representative of a mansion which is to be let and a florist's are exceedingly good. The illustration of how to make and sell umbrellas caused great hilarity, notwithstanding the fact that it presented Mr Clown as a very great rogue indeed. The Clown, at the end, desires to take the vacated mansion, but, by a wave of the Harlequin's wand, the interior being brought before his notice, he discovers that it is crowded with cradles and babies. The Clown rushes off in horror, and the spectators indulge in a hearty roar ... Mr Evans also has any number of ingenious tricks at his command, a ladder which cannot be mounted and a pair of steps which have a habit of running away from the feet that would touch them, being worthy of notice. Mr Evans also causes some excitement by the introduction of a 'box of foreign toys' from which he brings in succession capital effigies of the Czar, the Sultan and the Prime Minister. Mr Evans, it must be remembered is a Talking Clown. He has plenty to say for himself. He indulges in a stump speech, and this, too, is a very comical affair. The Harlequinade, regarded as a whole, is certainly one of the best, because one of the funniest, we remember having seen.

A sign of the times is that *The Times* (28 December 1874), reviewing *Aladdin* (1874–5), devoted just nine lines in a two column piece to the harlequinade, revealing that it included scenes representing a railway station and Ramsgate Sands, both realizing Frith paintings, and Temple Bar, with a Lord Mayor's procession in which 400 children took part. *The Era* (31 January 1875) thought the harlequinade 'a very bustling and a very merry affair, thanks especially to the energy of Mr Fred Evans, who is never still, and who even at the end makes his disappearance in anything but orthodox fashion – flying away suspended by the tail of a huge kite.' But there was also an elegant acrobatic display by Heinrich Schmidt and his three 'beautiful children' who performed 'incredible' feats greeted by a 'delighted and astonished' audience 'with the most enthusiastic plaudits'. Also featured were the gymnastics of Hector and Faust. *The Times* (28 December 1875) passed over the harlequinade in *Dick Whittington and His Cat* (1875–6) in three lines.

Cinderella (1878–9), the final pantomime of the Chatterton regime, boasted the usual double harlequinade, with Charles Lauri and Fred Evans as the Clowns. *The Times* (27 December 1878) noted that under the influence of the two clowns 'the fun ... became fast and furious', adding, 'The clever fooling was, of course, the occasion of much laughter, but there was in it little that was novel.' There were scenes in a police station and a restaurant. An Italian organgrinder was introduced. He was stripped of his outer garments and turned into a 'wild Irishman', his instrument being transformed into a jar labelled 'Italian sauce'. There was also much knockabout fun as wines and spirits were taken into the restaurant cellar. The next scene – Furnished Apartments – had Fred Evans and Company go through what *The Era* (29 December 1878) called 'the old but still amusing business, in which human beings are converted into articles of furniture.' There followed a scene in a Toy Repository featuring a dance of coins of the realm; a view of Kennington Oval; a Toxophilite dance; an entertainment by the expert Bale troupe; and finally the building of 'England's Exhibition' by 200 children, employed in a 'Brickfields near London'.

By the 1880s the newspapers' interest in the harlequinade was virtually nil. Of *Bluebeard* (1879–80) *The Era* (28 December 1879) said only that the Harlequinade 'shoots at the subjects of the day', dismissing it in one line. On *Mother Goose and the Enchanted Beauty* (1880–1), *The Times* (28 December 1880) merely noted 'a short harlequinade follows.' In its review of *Sindbad the Sailor* (1882–3) *The Times* (27 December 1882) devoted one line to the harlequinade: 'The harlequinade business was carried through with the usual spirit by Mr Harry Payne as clown.' *The Era* (30 December 1882) merely said: 'For those who are not tired and who are not above a little harmless fun settle down to revel in the practical jokes provided by Mr Harry Payne, who, as clown, is as comical and witty and hard-working as ever.' On *Cinderella* (1883–4) *The Times* (27 December 1883) reported: 'The harlequinade, is in the hands of Mr Harry Payne, who revives the best traditions of clown and pantaloon.' *The Era* (27 December 1884) reviewing *Whittington and His Cat* (1884–5) reported, 'in the harlequinade the popular Mr Harry Payne is again clown.' However talented the Clown, the whole business of the harlequinade had become a more or less irrelevant relic, a mere footnote to the main business of the show, not even deemed worthy of a detailed description.

What is perhaps surprising is not that the harlequinade disappeared but that it hung on as long as it did – further evidence of the innate conservatism of Victorian theatregoers. It was not until the 1880s that the word harlequin, once an essential part of the title or subtitle of the pantomime, began to vanish completely. By the 1890s it was rarely to be found. Even then the harlequinade did not disappear entirely. The knockabout routines of the harlequinade were captured on early short films, their essentially wordless action ideally suited to the needs of silent cinema. There was even one theatre which retained the harlequinade in a self-conscious act of theatrical preservation. This was the Lyceum, run from 1910 to 1939 by the Melville family. Almost every year until their deaths respectively in 1937 and 1938, the brothers Walter and Frederick Melville devised the annual pantomime. Writing in 1952, A.E. Wilson, who had first been taken to a pantomime at the age of three, recalled:

> The Lyceum pantomimes had a character peculiarly their own. They were dexterously designed to give pleasure to children and adults and were ample in all the good things that pantomime ought to provide, including a transformation scene of exceptional

gorgeousness ... And they even believed in retaining some vestige of the Harlequinade even if it was only five minutes of the ancient fun ... There never was any pantomime quite so good, so ample or so hearty. We have had nothing like them, alas, since Melvillian days![21]

They even preserved the now archaic tradition of writing their scripts in rhyming couplets. But it paid off. Wilson reported: 'The pantomimes rarely made an annual profit of less than £10,000 and often the figure was nearer £20,000 and £25,000'.[22] So perhaps harlequin had the last laugh after all.

3

Fairyland

At the end of J.M. Barrie's *Peter Pan* (1904), audiences were asked 'Do you believe in fairies? If you believe, clap your hands.' Audiences of all ages invariably thundered their assent. Although *Peter Pan* was a fairy play – part of a distinctive Edwardian cycle that included *Bluebell in Fairyland* (1901), *Pinkie and the Fairies* (1909) and *The Blue Bird* (1909) – and not a pantomime, it has since Barrie's time been coopted into the roll of pantomime subjects. It now appears regularly among the theatre's seasonal offerings, latterly as a vehicle for faded American television stars (David Hasselhoff, Henry Winkler) to cavort as Captain Hook. The same thing happened to *Snow White and the Seven Dwarfs* which after its original Walt Disney cartoon appearance in 1937 also joined the ranks of pantomime subjects. Travelling in the opposite direction, regular pantomime subjects *Cinderella* and *The Sleeping Beauty* became full-length Disney cartoons in the 1950s. What they all had in common was fairies.

There had been a belief in the existence of fairies since the earliest times. There was a variety of explanations for them. Some saw them as the souls of the dead, wandering between the overworld and the underworld. Others saw them as fallen angels. Yet more people saw them as a real race of invisible beings existing in a parallel universe. They could be human size or small, benign or malign.

The nineteenth century saw a massive upsurge of interest in fairies. As Diane Purkiss puts it: 'It is in Victorian England that fairyland ... undergoes a popular explosion. Fairies, elves, gnomes and small winged things of every kind multiply into swarms and infest writing and art and the minds of men and women.'[1] This belief continued on through the Edwardian period and into World War I. It is epitomized by the massive popularity of Estella Canziani's painting *The Piper of Dreams* (1914) in which a boy piping in a gloomy wood is surrounded by the ethereal images of fairies – it sold 250,000 copies in its first year – and the widespread belief in the transparently faked photographs of the Cottingley Fairies in 1917.[2]

It was a particular combination of cultural circumstances which inspired the explosion of interest in fairies and fairyland. Perhaps most significant was the dominance of romanticism in art and letters in Western Europe in the period 1750–1850. Romanticism was a violent reaction against the classical balance and rational common sense of the Age of Reason. Bold, individualistic, unconventional, it exalted the imagination, the emotions, dreams and fantasies. It had certain fascinations: the past, especially the medieval past, the cult of naturalism and spontaneity, and the occult. It produced the historical novel, the gothic tale, the lyric poem and the romantic melodrama; the poetry of Byron, Keats and Shelley; the music of Berlioz, Liszt and Wagner; the paintings of Delacroix, Turner and Goya. It also stimulated a great revival of interest in the fairy story.

The study of fairies was also part and parcel of the emerging discipline of folklore studies. The term folklore was only used for the first time in 1846; the Folklore Society was founded in 1878. Folklore studies as a discipline was strengthened and reinforced by the new Victorian social sciences of ethnology, archaeology and anthropology and validated by the Darwinian idea of evolutionary stages in the story of mankind. Fairy tales were seen as relics of pre-Christian religion or as a race memory of a primitive pygmy race which had preceded human beings. Works like Thomas Crofton Croker's *Fairy Legends and Traditions of the South of Ireland* (first published in 1825 and joined in 1828 by two further volumes covering Wales and England) and Thomas Keightley's *The Fairy Mythology* (published in 1828, revised and expanded in 1850) were constantly reissued throughout the nineteenth century. By the 1880s leading folklorists like Sabine Baring-Gould, Andrew Lang and Sir John Rhys were collecting oral evidence on the existence of fairies.

Victorian fascination with the supernatural – ghosts, vampires, poltergeists, angels and the like – was reinforced by the emergence of spiritualism and both were given added impetus by the rise of religious doubt, challenges to conventional religion and the search for alternatives to Christianity.

Spiritualism originated in the United States in 1848. It began with mysterious rappings experienced by the Fox family of Hydesville, New York, and led to séances, mediumship and communication with the spirits of the dead. Although many years later the Fox girls Kate and Maggie admitted that it had all been a hoax, it was by then too late to halt a movement which had spread rapidly through the United States and had reached Europe, as the bereaved sought to make contact with deceased loved ones. By the 1850s there were at least five spiritualist journals, countless books and pamphlets and an estimated 100 mediums in New York City alone. Within twenty years of the Hydesville rappings, there were some 11 million believers in the United States.[3]

Spiritualism arrived in Britain in 1853 and by the end of the century, there were over 200 organizations provincial and metropolitan and over a dozen journals and magazines had been founded. The Spiritualist National Federation was set up in

1891. Over the years the movement acquired many notable adherents, among them the naturalist Alfred Russel Wallace, the Socialist Robert Owen, the novelist Edward Bulwer-Lytton, the poet Elizabeth Barrett Browning, and later Sir Arthur Conan Doyle, the crusading journalist W.T. Stead and the physicist Sir Oliver Lodge.

From the first there were fierce opponents of spiritualism, among them the Calvinists, humanists and philosophers, and there were sceptics such as Charles Dickens and Robert Browning. But spiritualism in Britain received a powerful boost from the activities of the celebrity medium Daniel Dunglas Home. Born in Scotland, raised in the United States, he acquired a reputation as a medium by the age of seventeen. Coming to England, he gained a devoted following as he extended the spiritualist experience beyond mere communication with the dead to include physical materializations, levitations, ectoplasm, spirit music, phantom hands and the movement of heavy objects. Home was a trained magician and the Davenport Brothers, exposed as frauds in Liverpool in 1868, were skilled conjurers. Over the years other magicians, among them J.N. Maskelyne, Robert-Houdin and Harry Houdini systematically exposed these phenomena as tricks or illusions. Ruth Brandon notes that Home was 'the only medium of any note never either to confess or be exposed.'[4] But none of this succeeded in denting the faith of believers. George Bernard Shaw wrote of English society before 1914 that it was:

> addicted to table-rapping, materialization, séances, clairvoyance, palmistry, crystal-gazing, and the like to such an extent that it may be doubted whether before in the history of the world did soothsayers, astrologers, and unregistered therapeutic specialists of all sorts flourish as they did during this half century of the drift to the abyss.[5]

From the first, spiritualism appealed to both sexes, all classes and members of all professions. There was a form of Christian spiritualism preached by some Anglican clergymen, although the Church of England officially rejected it. But at the same time there was a strong anti-Christian spiritualist movement, linked to working-class Liberalism, Socialism and trade unionism.[6] The particular appeal of spiritualism lay in its combination of a form of religious commitment with the language of scientific progress and the firm belief that its central tenets had been proved by scientific investigation. Spiritualism received a powerful boost after World War I as the bereaved flocked to establish contact with lost loved ones and there developed a vogue for spirit photographs, which led in 1920 to Conan Doyle proclaiming the authenticity of the photographs of the Cottingley fairies, taken by two Yorkshire teenage girls. This scientific 'proof' of the existence of fairies eventually turned out to be illustrations to a poem by Alfred Noyes entitled 'A Spell for a Fairy' cut out and pinned to bushes. But the desire to believe in the fairies powerfully attests to the continuing fascination with the phenomenon that had haunted the Victorian imagination.

Just as in some quarters there was a reaction against traditional Christian piety and belief systems, so in others there was a reaction against the effects of industrialization and the cult of modernity, against materialism, the factory system and the exploitation and dehumanization of the workers. As Nicola Bown put it, 'fairies are consistently associated with nostalgic yearnings for golden ages, times of stability and simplicity ... Fairyland is a version of the pastoral, in other words, an Arcadia for the industrial age.'[7]

John Ruskin, whose *Storm Cloud of the Nineteenth Century* painted an apocalyptic picture of industrial pollution, thundered against the effects of industrialization in an 1884 lecture on Fairyland, describing the landscape of this arcadia:

> There are no railroads in it ... no tunnel or pit mouths ... no league-long viaducts – no blinkered iron bridges ... There are only winding brooks, wooden foot-bridges and grassy hills without any holes cut into them! ... And more wonderful still – there are no gas-works! no waterworks, no mowing machines, no sewing machines, no telegraph poles, no vestiges in fact, of science, civilization, economical arrangements, and commercial enterprise.[8]

According to Carole G. Silver, within the generalized interest in the supernatural, particular fairy phenomena tapped into deep-lying Victorian fears and apprehensions.[9] The fascination with changelings, she contends, represents a middle-class fear of the loss of security, power and fortune; swan maidens raised questions about female power and sexuality; dwarfs, goblins and gnomes embodied an imperial fear of racial degeneration and regression; and stories of the elfin horde evoked the spectre of the anarchic mob, seen in violent action during the French Revolution and the European revolutions of 1848.

The fairy tale as we now know it – the literary fairy tale – dates from the late seventeenth and early eighteenth centuries. Fairy tales derived from a tradition of oral folk tales, reaching back to medieval and even pre-medieval times; hence, their evocation of an agrarian society and a hierarchical community, peopled by kings and queens, princes and princesses, soldiers and peasants, animals and supernatural creatures of various kinds and in the background the ever-present deep, dark forest. It was a group of aristocratic French writers, notably Charles Perrault, Madame Marie-Catherine d'Aulnoy, Mademoiselle Marie-Jeanne L'héritier, Madame Jeanne-Marie Leprince de Beaumont and Mademoiselle Rose de la Force, writing initially for adults rather than children, who took up some of these oral tales and transformed them into what they called *contes de fées* (fairy tales). Fairy tales were not universal, timeless and ageless. They derived from specific social and cultural contexts and they changed to accommodate changes in value systems. They were institutionalized, according to Jack Zipes, the doyen of fairy story analysis, 'as an aesthetic and social means through which questions and issues of civilité, proper behaviour and demeanor in all types of situations, were mapped out as narrative strategies for literary socialization.'[10] The culmination of this development was *Le Cabinet des Fées*, 41 volumes of major literary fairy tales edited by Charles Joseph de Mayer and published in 1785–9. It was not until the late eighteenth century that literary fairy tales were being aimed specifically at children. For that purpose, they were carefully purged and sanitized with elements present in earlier folk tales (incest, cannibalism, bestiality, dismemberment, infanticide) systematically eliminated. For the child reader, fairy tales were about growing up, establishing an identity, developing talents, finding independence and success in society. The aim was to socialize the youthful readers just as much as the earlier literary tales had been to instruct their elders. The fairy tales were to be didactic, to teach correct behaviour and manners, approved gender and class roles and the values of a civilized society.

In an essay in *Household Words* in 1853, Charles Dickens lauded the didactic role of the fairy story:

> It would be hard to estimate the amount of gentleness and mercy that has made its way among us through these slight channels. Forbearance, courtesy, consideration for the poor and aged, kind treatment of animals, the love of nature, abhorrence of tyranny and brute force – many such good things have been first nourished in the child's heart by this powerful aid … In a utilitarian age, of all other times, it is a matter of grave importance that Fairy tales should be respected … To preserve them in their usefulness, they must be as much preserved in their simplicity, and purity and innocent extravagance, as if they were actual fact.'[11]

This became a widely accepted view. As Jack Zipes says of Perrault, who was responsible for many of the classic fairy tales (*Cinderella, Sleeping Beauty, Little Red Riding Hood, Bluebeard, Tom Thumb* and *Puss in Boots*), 'By examining the major features and behaviour of Perrault's male and female protagonists it becomes crystal clear that he sought to portray ideal types to reinforce the standard of the civilizing process set by upper-class French society.'[12] His heroes were ambitious, intelligent, brave and well-mannered and his heroines refined, dignified and self-disciplined. Madame d'Aulnoy's stories were principally directed at women and regularly reworked the 'beauty and the beast' motif. Zipes writes:

> All D'Aulnoy's fairy tales provide moral lessons, and the ones which involved 'beauty and the beast' reiterate the message of Perrault's tales. The woman must be constantly chastised for her curiosity, unreliability, and whimsy. True beauty depends on prudence and discretion which is figuratively depicted by the heroine either sacrificing herself to a male beast or submitting to his commands and wishes because he has a noble soul and civil manners. The hidden message in all these tales is a dictum which the women of

D'Aulnoy's time ... had to obey or else face degradation and ostracism: control your natural inclinations and submit to the fate which male social standards decree.[13]

If the eighteenth century was the century of the aristocracy, the nineteenth was the century of the bourgeoisie. This was directly reflected in the fairy tales of the nineteenth century, particularly those of the Brothers Grimm and Hans Christian Andersen.

The brothers Jakob and Wilhelm Grimm collected over 200 folk tales as part of a lifelong, systematic historical study of German language, literature and culture. They continually revised the stories and there were in the end seventeen successive editions of their fairy tale collection between 1812 and 1864. They made major changes in the stories. Jack Zipes summarizes them as follows:

They eliminated erotic and sexual elements that might be offensive to middle-class morality, added numerous Christian expressions and references, emphasised specific role models for male and female protagonists according to the dominant patriarchal code of that time, and endowed many of the tales with a 'homey' or *biedermeier* flavour by the use of diminutives, quaint expressions and cute descriptions.[14]

More generally, the brothers turned the stories into bourgeois morality tales showing how to use your powers to be accepted in society and stressing what values should be learned, values which were inevitably those of the Protestant middle class (thrift, industry, patience, obedience, etc.). Hans Christian Andersen, who wrote over 150 fairy tales, according to Zipes 'furthered bourgeois notions of the self-made man or the Horatio Alger myth, which was becoming popular in America and elsewhere, while reinforcing a belief in the existing power structure that meant domination and exploitation of the lower classes.'[15]

Whereas in France and Germany the literary fairy tale became a new art form and the expression of the new Romantic sensibility, in England it was discouraged by the forces of Puritanism. However, collections of classic fairy tales began to appear in English translation in the first decades of the nineteenth century. In 1823 and 1826 Edgar Taylor's translation of Grimms' fairy tales, *German Popular Stories* was published, illustrated by Cruikshank. It has been called 'the most important publication to stimulate an awakened interest in fairy tales by children and adults.'[16] In 1827 Thomas Carlyle published a selection of German fairy tales in two volumes, *German Romances*. In 1840 there was a new translation of tales from the *Arabian Nights* by Edwin Lane. In 1846 the first English translation of Hans Christian Andersen's fairy tales appeared. This literary development inspired noted English writers to pen new fairy tales, among them Dickens, Carlyle, Thackeray, Hood and Ruskin. But whereas the fairy tales of Perrault, the Brothers Grimm and Hans Christian Andersen validated courtly or bourgeois value systems, many of the

English fairy tales were allegorical critiques of modern industrial capitalism. The genre diverged from the 1860s onwards as the majority of fairy story writers (such as Mrs Craik, Andrew Lang and E. Nesbit) sought to reconcile their readers to the status quo, while a minority continued to question existing social structures and values (Lewis Carroll, George Macdonald, Oscar Wilde).

While many scholars have approached the analysis of the fairy tale from a sociological perspective, in the twentieth century fairy tales have provided a rich and fertile field of study for psychoanalysis. In *The Uses of Enchantment* (1976) Bruno Bettelheim provided the classic Freudian interpretation of the fairy tale. His position was that there was nothing in the whole of children's literature 'as enriching and satisfying to child and adult alike as the folk fairy tale.' He admitted that, having been created in a pre-industrial world, they taught little about the conditions of life in the modern world, but 'more can be learned from them about the inner problems of human beings, and of the right solutions to their predicaments in any society, than from any other type of story within a child's comprehension.'[17]

He saw fairy stories as carrying:

> important messages to the conscious, the preconscious, and the unconscious mind, on whatever level each is functioning at the time. By dealing with universal human problems, particularly those which preoccupy the child's mind, these stories speak to the budding ego and encourage its development while at the same time relieving preconscious and unconscious pressures.[18]

The child needed to master the psychological problems of growing up. Bettelheim lists these as 'overcoming narcissistic disappointments, oedipal dilemmas, sibling rivalry, becoming able to relinquish childhood dependencies; gaining a feeling of selfhood and of self-worth, and a sense of moral obligation.'[19] A child achieves this not by rational comprehension of the nature and content of his unconscious but by daydreaming. Fairy tales have 'unequalled value' because they provide form and structure to the daydreams through which the unconscious pressures can be comprehended and dealt with. They simplify all situations, provide characters as types rather than individuals and strictly polarize good and evil.[20] The fairy tale takes existential anxieties seriously and addresses them directly: 'The need to be loved and the fear that one is thought worthless; the love of life and the fear of death.' Bettelheim writes that the happy ending – 'they all lived happily ever after' – is not unrealistic wish-fulfilment but the confirmation that by forming true interpersonal relationships, the child escapes the 'separation anxiety' that haunts him. He/she can do this only by going out into the world and finding the person with whom to live happily, thus relinquishing infantile dependency. The child going out into the world is often helped by being in touch with primitive things – a tree, an animal, nature – and can thus establish a meaningful relationship with the world around him.

Bettelheim concludes that 'while it entertains the child, the fairy tale enlightens him about himself, and fosters his personality development.' But it is not the only meaning. Fairy tales make 'a unique contribution to the child's moral education'.[21]

The rival interpretation, the Jungian view, was advanced by Marie-Louise von Franz in *The Interpretation of Fairy Stories* (1970) in which she approached the stories as 'the purest and simplest expression of collective unconscious psychic processes'.[22] In Jungian theory, fairy stories, like myths, derive from a collective unconscious and deal in universal archetypes and the process of self-realization. The characters and the events in the stories are stylized and highly symbolic and provide the means to reach a higher consciousness.

At the same time as the native English fairy tale began to flourish, a strong tradition of fairy painting developed in Victorian England, as exemplified by the work of Richard Dadd, Joseph Noel Paton, Dicky Doyle, John Anster Fitzgerald (known as 'Fairy' Fitzgerald) and Arthur Rackham. As Charlotte Gere puts it: 'Fairy painting is the visual evidence of a spectrum of mid-nineteenth century preoccupations: nationalism, antiquarianism, exploration, anthropology, the dismantling of religious belief and crucially, the emergence of spiritualism.'[23] In the 1830s and 1840s at least one fairy painting was exhibited every year at the Royal Academy and British Institution exhibitions.[24] Shakespeare's *A Midsummer Night's Dream* inspired 135 paintings between 1750 and 1900, chiefly of the fairy scenes.[25] Some of the fairy painting was dark, sinister and disturbing, particularly the work of Dadd who went mad, murdered his father and spent the rest of his life in a lunatic asylum where he continued to paint fairyland.

John Ruskin was a powerful advocate of the school of fairy painting but he preferred the more wholesome and innocent creations of Kate Greenaway and Helen Allingham. He devoted one of his six lectures that made up *The Art of England* to fairyland. In it he claimed to have been brought up 'principally on fairy legends' and to entertain still a predilection for them.[26] He actually wrote a popular and much reprinted fairy story, *The King of the Golden River* (1850) and he persuaded the publisher J.C. Hotten to reissue Edgar Taylor's translation of Grimms' Fairy Tales in 1869, contributing an introductory essay to the collection. Although some sexualized imagery of fairies remained in circulation, in for instance Christina Rossetti's poem *Goblin Market* (1862), it is clear that Ruskin associated fairies directly with childhood innocence and fairyland with a beautiful and spiritual pre-industrial landscape, an ideal and idealized pre-lapsarian world. This became the majority view.

Despite the importance of fairy story books and the vogue for fairy painting, the place where fairyland came alive for most Victorians was the theatre. It was an article of faith in Victorian Britain that the fairy tale was one of the highest and purest forms of literature. This extended to its stage manifestations. Tracy Davis records:

In addition to the Shakespeare canon ... and W.S. Gilbert (the only Victorian dramatist of fairy fare that endures in popular memory), fairies appear in productions from every decade and in every genre ... To some people, fairies were commensurate with theatre and theatrical practice, indelible to the idea of theatre as a metonym of faith in magicality.[27]

It was Madame Vestris who restored Shakespeare's fairy play *A Midsummer Night's Dream* to the stage in her production at Covent Garden in 1840. The play had not been seen in its original form since the closing of the theatres in 1642. When it had been staged, it had been in the form of operatic adaptations like Purcell's *The Fairy Queen* (1692). Madame Vestris staged it as a fullblown fairy extravaganza, complete with Mendelssohn's celebrated overture, ballet sequences and sliding panoramic scenery. The critic Edward Dutton Cook complained that the play had been reduced 'almost to the level of a fairy spectacle of commonplace quality; the poetry of the subject lies hidden under stage carpentry.'[28] But he rather missed the point. This *was* the appeal of the play to Victorian audiences and is what inspired successive memorable productions across the century by Samuel Phelps, Charles Kean, Charles Calvert, Augustin Daly and Herbert Beerbohm Tree.[29]

There were notable fairy ballets: *Ondine, Giselle, Eoline* and *La Sylphide* in the 1830s and 1840s and later in the century Tchaikovsky's *Swan Lake, The Sleeping Beauty* and *The Nutcracker*. There were fairy operas such as Weber's *Oberon*, with libretto by J.R. Planché, and John Barnett's *The Mountain Sylph*, and fairy operettas (*Iolanthe, Fallen Fairies*). There were no fewer than eleven different operatic versions of *Cinderella* between the mid-eighteenth and the late-nineteenth centuries. But it was the pantomime which was the principal and continuing vehicle for the transmission of fairy lore in its most vivid and immediate form to an audience of both adults and children. Ironically, given the pre- and anti-industrial appeal of fairy tales, the theatre needed the full panoply of heavy backstage machinery and a large and low-paid labour force to create the magical stage illusion of fairyland.

4

James Robinson Planché
and the Classical Extravaganza

James Robinson Planché (1796–1880) was one of the most significant figures in the history of the nineteenth-century stage. Born in London, the descendant of Huguenot refugees, he was to become a prolific dramatist – some 180 pieces of all kinds – for the London stage. But more than this, he was directly responsible for the introduction of the 'antiquarian' approach to the staging of historical drama by insisting on historically accurate costumes, sets and accessories, an approach which became the accepted method of staging plays in Victorian England and led to the spectacular stage productions of Charles Kean, Henry Irving, Wilson Barrett and Herbert Beerbohm Tree. He argued from a position of authority as alongside his dramatic endeavours he became a leading historian of British costume and an expert on heraldry. He published his *History of British Costume from the Earliest Period to the Close of the Eighteenth Century* in 1834, and a two-volume *Cyclopaedia of Costume* in 1876–9. He was elected a Fellow of the Society of Antiquaries in 1829 and was a founder member of the British Archaeological Association in 1843, acting as its honorary secretary for twenty years. His expertise in heraldry led to his appointment in 1854 as Rouge Croix Pursuivant at the College of Arms, being promoted to Somerset Herald in 1866. His output of plays dramatically declined after 1855 as he devoted himself to scholarly pursuits. These pursuits resulted in nineteen volumes written, edited or revised by him and more than sixty articles in archaeological journals. But he remained the grand old man of English theatre, campaigning both for copyright protection for dramatists and the establishment of a national theatre.[1]

Not only did he change the nature of staging of plays, he also introduced two new dramatic forms to the English theatre – the extravaganza and the revue. Both were derived from the French stage, on which Planché, a fluent French speaker, was an expert, but they were thoroughly anglicized. It was the extravaganza that was to have a decisive effect on the form and nature of the pantomime.

Planché's first play, *Amoroso, King of Little Britain* (1818) was a burlesque, intended for amateur production but receiving a successful staging at Drury Lane. This launched him on his playwriting career. The peak of his career was perhaps achieved in his extravaganzas for the Lyceum in the 1850s. They were witnessed by the critic Clement Scott and the theatrical impresario John Hollingshead in their youth and they later paid tribute to them. Scott wrote: 'More graceful extravaganzas than those written for the Lyceum by Planché were never seen on any stage, the versification was always neat and admirable, the rhyming faultless and the puns of the best kind.'[2] Hollingshead wrote: 'He raised theatrical extravaganza and burlesque to the dignity of a fine art and wrote verses to be sung on stage which could be read with pleasure in the study.'[3]

Planché earned the plaudits of fellow playwrights both for his work and his character. Looking back from 1879 to the 1850s, Tom Taylor wrote:

> Planché then was the Lord and Master of Burlesque. We young hands looked up to him and loved him alike in his person and his work. I wish I could unload myself of my debt of gratitude to that kind, good man, and delightful writer; that I had room to express here my sense of the graceful and harmless amusement he has afforded to so many generations of play-goers, combining in one entertainment pretty story, humorous action, pointed and graceful dialogue, sweet music, beautiful scenery and tasteful costumes, as no man ever before combined them.[4]

J. Palgrave Simpson in a long and appreciative obituary called him 'One of the brightest and most genial writers that ever shed sunlight on the British drama' and declared:

> There can be no doubt that he exercised a considerable influence on the English stage. The two most characteristic qualities of his writings were taste and elegance ... His name must be always chiefly remembered in connection with his elegant and graceful 'extravaganzas' , as he called these freaks of pretty fancy. How he writhed, poor man, with indignation and annoyance if anyone spoke of them as 'burlesques'.

Simpson lamented their eclipse by later, more heavy-handed productions:

> Eminently successful and highly prized as these vivacious and witty effusions were, illustrated by the prettiest and most graceful melodies in vogue at the period, as well as by exquisite scenery and dresses, they ceased in time, even during their author's life, to maintain a hold on public favour. They grew to be old-fashioned. The graceful extravaganza was gradually elbowed off the stage by the modern burlesque, in which pun was set aside for jingle of words or distortion of syllables; 'breakdowns' [i.e. comic dances] became a necessary ingredient to catch the public fancy; and music-hall songs were substituted for popular Italian airs. Old playgoers lamented the loss of these bright

and delicate fairy-tales; and an attempt for a return to the old refinements of Planché's pleasant *féeries* was made from time to time. Managers revived, now and then, 'The Invisible Prince' or 'The King of the Peacocks', as refreshers to the popular taste of a more unrefined time. But their efforts were useless. Planché 'drew' no longer, spite of all his bright and sprightly grace. ... Those who would now appreciate Planché's style in this species of composition – his graceful sweetly flowing lyrics, his happy parodies, his witty turns of phrase, his fertile power of punning, ... must now revert to the collection of his noted extravaganzas, and read what they can no longer see, supplying all the brilliant scenic accessories of other times by the force of imagination.[5]

His work did not appeal to everyone, but the extent of Planché's pre-eminence in this period can be gauged by the references to him in a critical article by the poet and scholar W. E. Aytoun in *Blackwood's Magazine* in which, denouncing theatrical taste in London in 1845, he excoriated the theatres for 'their sheer and gross absurdity, which, without actual experience, is almost too monstrous for belief.' His particular bugbear seems to have been the extravaganzas:

Go into any of the London theatres now, and the following is your bill of fare. Fairies you have by scores in flesh-coloured tights, spangles, and paucity of petticoats; gnomes of every description, from the gigantic glittering demon beetle, to the grotesque and dusky tadpole. Epicene princes, whose taper limbs and swelling busts are well worth the scrutiny of the opera-glass-dragons vomiting at once red flames and witticisms about the fountains in Trafalgar Square ... and the Seven Champions of Christendom smoking cigars upon the parapet of Hungerford Bridge! All these things have I seen ... and cheered them to the echo, in company with some thousand cockneys, all agape at the glitter of tinselled pasteboard, and the glories of the Catherine-wheel. Such is the intellectual banquet which London, queen of literature, presents to her fastidious children.

The success of such spectacles had persuaded the public 'to cashier Shakespeare, who is now utterly out of date, and to install in his place a certain Mr. J. R. Planché as the leading swan of the Thames.'[6]

Indeed Richard Hengist Horne in his *The New Spirit of the Age* (1844) saw Planché as embodying the spirit of the age. He agreed that:

The Drama should be the concentrated spirit of the age. The stage should be the mirror over which every varying emotion of the period should pass. What is the Spirit of the Age as regards the Drama? Certainly the theatrical Spirit is the most undramatic that can be.

The real dramatic spirit, he thought, was to be found in literature in the published works of Dickens, Hood, Mrs Gore and Mrs Trollope and not on the legitimate stage. For plays which 'reflect the tone and temperament of the age', it was necessary to turn to the 'skilful little comedies and bright, racy Dramas' of Jerrold, Planché, Dance and others who wrote for the minor theatres and not the patent theatres, and who had 'lavished much wit, fancy and invention on their productions, doomed by the theatrical destinies to an ephemeral existence.'

Horne praised Planché because he:

> has a vivid notion of manners and depicts character as exemplified and modified by them admirably ... He has strong feeling for, and admiration of the artificial elegancies of life – considerable fancy – and a ready invention in character and situation, and a great skill in new adaptations; not much wit or repartee, but a genial and laughable humour, and the rare art of throwing a refining atmosphere round even the most unpromising subject.[7]

In 1861 Planché devoted an article in the magazine *Temple Bar* to refuting what, only partly tongue-in-cheek, he called the charges that had been levelled against him:

> The first count in the indictment ... charges me with creating, encouraging and abetting a vicious taste for spectacle, which has seriously affected the health of the highest order of the drama, and inflicted ruinous expense upon all classes of managers. The second, with having ... originated, written and represented, or caused to be written and represented, divers and sundry entertainments for the stage called burlesques or extravaganzas, to the grievous bodily harm of the minor drama, and the utter destruction of her Majesty's English ... The third count is almost the echo of the first, and sets forth that, not content with the injury done to the classical drama of the country by overlaying it with dresses and decorations, said defendant did annually... cause certain scenes, called 'last scenes' to be exhibited in said burlesques or extravaganzas, on which vast sums of money were wantonly, wastefully, and unnecessarily expended, to the great loss of the lessee, and encouragement of the said vicious taste for spectacle.

To these charges he pleaded not guilty. He readily conceded that he was responsible for the movement for historical accuracy in costume and accessories that had become a feature of the stage. It began in 1821 in his suggestion to Charles Kemble that his forthcoming revival of *King John* should utilize armour and costumes that were historically correct. He researched the subject 'without fee or reward' and produced a series of designs which when realized in the production led to audience applause and box office success. His motive, he insisted, was 'solely and purely... that love of the stage which has ever induced me to sacrifice all personal consideration to what I sincerely believed would tend to elevate as well as adorn it.' He was proud of his achievement in this regard but was not to be held responsible for the actions of those short-sighted managers who pushed accuracy towards extravagance and elevated mere accessories into the principal feature of their productions. Planché also admitted responsibility for the introduction of the extravaganza. 'The popularity of that peculiar class of entertainment, of which I am by no means ashamed to admit I was the originator in this country, naturally induced many of my brother authors to try their fortunes in that style of composition.'[8]

Although Planché rightly claimed responsibility for its creation, there remained considerable confusion in the minds of contemporaries about what to call this new breed of entertainment. Planché first launched his extravaganzas at the Olympic Theatre but the early ones were not called by this name. *Olympic Revels* (1831) was billed as a 'mythological allegorical burletta', *Olympic Devils* (1831) as an 'original mythological burlesque burletta', *The Paphian Bower* (1832) was 'a classical, musical, mythological, astronomical and tragic-comical burlesque burletta'. It was not until *High, Low, Jack and the Game* (1833) that the show was described as 'a most extravagant extravaganza'. The *Deep, Deep Sea* (1833) reverted to 'an original, mythological, aquatic, equestrian burletta'. *Telemachus* (1834) was 'a classical and mythological extravaganza'. But the first fairy extravaganzas *Riquet with the Tuft* (1836), *Puss in Boots* (1837) and *Bluebeard* (1839) were described respectively as 'a burlesque burletta', 'a fairy burletta' and a 'burlesque burletta'. It was when he moved to Covent Garden that Planché settled firmly on the term 'extravaganza' to describe *The Sleeping Beauty in the Wood* (1840), *Beauty and the Beast* (1841) and *The White Cat* (1842). But that we should regard the Olympic pieces as extravaganzas too is confirmed by their inclusion in the five volumes of Planché's collected extravaganzas, published in 1879.

Planché himself confirmed the significance of the move from a minor theatre – the Olympic – to a patent house – Covent Garden – in the matter of names:

> The extremely absurd laws which at that period tramelled the minor theatres not affecting the patent houses, the vague title of burletta was no longer necessary to describe the particular style of drama I had originated in England. 'The Sleeping Beauty' was therefore announced as an extravaganza – distinguishing the whimsical treatment of a poetical subject from the broad caricature of a tragedy or serious opera which was correctly described as a burlesque.[9]

The term burletta originated in Italian opera and was a comic interlude in the operatic programme, first used in England in the mid-eighteenth century. There was a major development in the form with Kane O'Hara's *Midas*, first seen in Dublin in 1762 and in London in 1764. *Midas* combined the ballad opera and the burlesque, introducing English humour and English characters, popular English and Irish tunes and satire on the contemporary legal system and the state of marriage, to produce an English-language equivalent of the burletta. It contained jokes, rhymed couplets and – crucially – recitative in place of spoken dialogue; crucially because legitimate or spoken drama was in London confined to the patent theaters, the Theatres Royal Covent Garden and Drury Lane (all the year round) and Haymarket (in the summer). The success of *Midas* at Covent Garden sparked off a fashion for burlettas at the patent theatres. But the minor theatres, denied the ability to perform legitimate drama, latched onto burletta as a viable alternative. It remained exclusively musical for the first ten to fifteen years of the nineteenth century. But then Charles Dibdin the Younger at Sadler's Wells began to alternate sung and spoken dialogue in his shows. He and other managers emulating him were deliberately pushing at the boundaries of what was legally permissible. The rebuilt Lyceum (1809) was specially licensed for the performance of English opera and musical drama. The Adelphi and the Olympic had the Lord Chamberlain's license for the performance of burlettas only, 'by which description', Planché reported, 'after much controversy both in and out of court, we were desired to understand dramas containing not less than five pieces of vocal music in each act, and which were also, with one or two exceptions, not to be found in the *repertoire* of the patent houses.'[10] But as Planché also pointed out the minor theatres 'had adopted the term "burletta" as a general and conveniently vague description of every variety of piece performed by them.'[11]

As P.T. Dirks has argued, Planché's burletta related directly to the eighteenth-century burletta tradition and bore little relationship to the many plays called burlettas just to avoid the restrictions of the theatrical monopoly.[12] But he evolved a distinct form when he insisted on faithful dramatizations of the original source story, a well-constructed plot, accurate and elegant sets and costumes and a moral at the conclusion. He began to mingle spoken dialogue with songs and arias in the manner of the ballad opera.

To ensure fidelity to the original sources, he produced his own new English translations of the French fairy tales of Madame D'Aulnoy (1855) and Charles Perrault (1858), his two principal sources. Originally written for adults and often containing adult themes, they were from the end of the eighteenth century aimed at children, having been suitably bowdlerized. Planché so admired Madame D'Aulnoy that he based fourteen of his own twenty-two fairy extravaganzas on her stories. Commentators at the time saw Planché's approach as positive. In his early history of pantomime *Comical Fellows* (1863), playwright Andrew Halliday headed his discussion of Planché 'Mr Planché's improvements' and claimed that after Grimaldi he was 'the great innovator of the period'.[13]

Planché was as critical of the necessity to include operatic arias as he was of the development of spectacle – anything which drew attention away from his carefully crafted and richly allusive scripts.

An extravaganza ... should depend upon its language, and not on its music, and that music should be, however good and classical, of a style that is easy of execution, and above all things that enables the audience to catch the words ... I always regretted being obliged to introduce grand Italian arias to which it was impossible to write anything readable.[14]

There was certainly a strong linguistic appeal about extravaganzas, which were an elaborate tissue of puns, parodies, contemporary slang and topical allusions. But there was another non-verbal appeal.

. One of the recurrent visual attractions was the scantily clad chorus girls, or coryphées as they were known. *Figaro in London* (2 February 1833), only partly tongue-in-cheek, complained of *The Paphian Bower* that the female cast members, 'selected only for (their) looks' were 'wearing such dresses as would warrant interference of the society for the suppression of vice' and calling on some moral member of parliament to bring in 'a bill for lengthening Madame Vestris' petticoats.' *The Satirist* (4 January 1835) reviewing *Telemachus* said 'Calypso's bevy of nymphs, in costume of the chase, is a pretty sight, and the display of feminine legs might tempt Saint Agnew, as an anchorite, to pleasurable meditations.'

The earliest extravaganzas from *Olympic Revels* in 1831 to *Bluebeard* in 1839 were co-written by Charles Dance, and Planché subsequently expressed his exasperation that the view had got about both in Britain and America 'that the fun was all Dance's and merely the stage carpentry mine',[15] whereas much of the comic wordplay and literary allusion were evidently Planché's. When, after *Bluebeard*, Dance married and retired temporarily from playwriting, Planché was able to claim sole authorship.

Planché declined to accept responsibility for what others had done to the form:

> If some have lavished a wealth of wit to which I could never pretend upon inferior structures, or suffered their racy spirits to ride rough-shod over the vulgar tongue, and plunge them into jungles of jingles and sloughs of slang, all I demand is not to be accused of having set the example. I deny the right of any one to call upon me to answer for the direction which has been given by others – for better or for worse – to a line laid down for myself, and have never departed from.

He made clear that he had lofty aims for his extravaganzas.

> They are greatly mistaken who imagine that I had no higher object in view than the mere amusement of the holiday audiences. I was impressed with the idea that I was opening a new stage-door, by the which the poet and the satirist could enter the theatre without the shackles imposed upon them by the laws of the regular drama ... my ambition was to lay the foundation for an Aristophanic drama, which the greatest minds would not consider it derogatory to contribute to.

However, his adaptation of 'one of the Athenian satirist's extravaganzas', *The Birds*, was a critical success but a box office failure. 'A celebrated foreign artiste pronounced it to be "too damned clever"', recalled Planché.[16]

The third charge he sought to refute was that the extravaganza had precipitated a trend towards ruinously expensive spectacle. Referring to his Lyceum extravaganzas, beginning with *The Golden Branch*, he wrote:

The beautiful scenery, by Mr. William Beverley, challenged and received its well-merited
share of approbation ... Year after year Mr. Beverley's powers were taxed to outdo his
former outdoings. The *last* scene became the *first*, in the estimation of the management.
The most complicated machinery, the most costly materials, were annually put into
requisition ... As to me, I was positively painted out. Nothing was considered brilliant
but the last scene.[17]

He made it clear that he did not regard scenic magnificence as essential to the
success of the extravaganza, pointing out that the shows he wrote for the Olympic
under Alfred Wigan's management triumphed because of the acting of Frederick
Robson: 'I once more had to rely upon acting rather that scene-painting.' He
expressed the hope that 'the mania for mere magnificence' would pass and declared,
'it has been too sadly proved, in many instances, that scenery, however beautiful,
cannot sustain a worthless drama, valuable as its assistance must always be to a
good one.'[18]

It was the success of the revival in 1825 of Kane O'Hara's *Midas* at the Haymarket
with Madame Vestris as Apollo, and a longstanding love of mythology that inspired
Planché to pen the one act *Prometheus and Pandora*, a similar classical burletta,
based on George Colman the Younger's *Tale of the Sun Poker*, 'a rather dull burlesque
poem based on the Prometheus story.'[19] No management, however, would touch it.
In 1830 Madame Vestris took over the management of the Olympic Theatre and
asked Planché if he had anything that was ready for immediate production. He dug
out *Prometheus and Pandora* and with the help of Charles Dance, revised it. It was
launched under the title *Olympic Revels* at the Olympic Theatre on 3 January 1831,
'the first of that long line of extravaganzas which for nearly thirty years have been,
without a single exception, honoured by the approbation of the public.'[20] He recalled
in his autobiography:

The extraordinary success of this experiment ... was due not only to the admirable
singing and piquante performance of that gifted lady [Madame Vestris], but also to the
charm of novelty imparted to it by the elegance and accuracy of the costume; it having
previously been the practice to dress a burlesque in the most *outré* and ridiculous
fashion. My suggestion to try the effect of persons picturesque attired speaking absurd
doggerel fortunately took the fancy of the fair lessee, and the alteration was highly
appreciated by the public.[21]

So accurate Greek costumes were employed (up to a point) in *Olympic Revels* but
due to 'haste and lack of funds' the scenery was limited to 'a few clouds, the interior
of a cottage, and a well-used modern London street'. However, for the next classical
piece, *Olympic Devils* the principle of authenticity was applied to the scenery as well
as the costumes:

We had a most infernal Tartarus, a very gloomy Styx, and a really beautiful Greek landscape with the portico of the Temple of Bacchus, the columns of which joined in the general dance ... to the great delight of the audience. The Bacchanalian procession, arranged by Oscar Byrne, considering the size of the stage and numbers employed, has never been surpassed for picture and animation.[22]

He concluded: 'The popularity of this class of entertainment was now fairly established and each succeeding Christmas witnessed the praiseworthy exertions of the management to sustain the reputation it had acquired for taste and accuracy in dress and decoration.'[23]

There was a hiatus in the partnership when in 1835–6 Planché left briefly to work for Alfred Bunn at Drury Lane and Charles Dance left over a dispute about payment of a fee. In their absence Samuel Lover provided the Christmas extravaganza *Cupid and Psyche*, but it was not a success and Planché returned to the Olympic for Christmas 1836 with a new development, the fairy extravaganza.

It was while in Paris on his honeymoon in 1821 that Planché had seen the *Folie Féerie*, *Riquet à la Houpe*. He was delighted with the 'whim, the delicate satire, the playful philosophy of the piece' and produced an English translation seeking to 'preserve the graceful badinage which abounded in it.'[24] As with *Prometheus and Pandora* no one would present it on stage until Christmas 1836 when he persuaded Madame Vestris to produce it and it achieved 'signal success'. Planché recalled: 'In this and the following Christmas pieces, *Puss in Boots* and *Bluebeard*, the same plan was pursued of rigidly adhering to truth and picture in costume and scenery (now medieval), while the dialogue was of course a tissue of anachronisms and absurdities.'[25]

In 1839 Madame Vestris took a lease on Covent Garden, bringing with her many of her production staff from the Olympic, machinist E.W. Bradwell, ballet master Oscar Byrne, chorus master James Tully and Planché as 'superintendent of the decorative department', while retaining Sir Henry Bishop as composer in residence and the Grieves, father and sons, as scene-painters. But here they found the harlequinade so well established at Christmas that the Planché extravaganza was staged at Easter. After Madame went bankrupt and lost the lease of Covent Garden in 1842, Planché transferred to the Haymarket and the management of Ben Webster, for whom he provided five Christmas extravaganzas. There he concentrated on language and performance rather than lavish spectacle.

In 1847 Madame Vestris and her husband Charles Mathews took the Lyceum Theatre, refurbished it handsomely and reassembled many of their old team with Planché again employed as 'superintendent of the decorations department' and once again to provide the Christmas and Easter extravaganzas. *The Era* (2 January 1848) called the refurbished theatre 'the most beautiful of its kind in Europe'. The

Christmas and Easter shows became in the words of Madame's biographer William Appleton 'the theatre's chief glory' as the talents of William Beverley were engaged to provide the visual splendour that made the shows so memorable and earned the ire of Planché.[26] *The Era* (26 December 1847), paying tribute to the Vestris management for its 'taste, tact and talent', welcomed the arrival of Planché with his 'wit and elegance' to provide the Christmas show, 'the great attraction' of the season:

> Mr Planché has a higher aim than that of creating a laugh. Nobody can create more merriment, but he never causes any at the expense of good taste; his jokes are never vulgar, and his puns, even when least pointed, have about them a degree of originality which do not belong to the class who commit any excess, for the sake of saying something comical or suggestive of a ridiculous thought. Although essentially capable of writing Burlesques, Mr Planché is not a Burlesque writer. He takes a higher ground, between broad ridicule and sheer satire, between utter absurdity and cold irony; and working up his artificial materials with artistic skill, he makes his fairy finery the medium for introducing pleasantry that is refined, wit that is harmless and censure that does not fail to reach its mark, because it is not rudely flung. He does more, he conveys a moral. In every one of his graceful extravaganzas which we have witnessed, there has been a moral conspicuously to be seen through the tinsel that surrounded it. These glittering fabrics of his cultivated fancy he makes the vehicles for introducing, not only smart sentences and happy jokes, but some special and timely hits at the follies of the day. He retains all that is desirable of fairy tales and discards the vulgar dross.

Planché provided ten extravaganzas for the Lyceum in the eight seasons that Vestris ran the theatre before ill-health forced her retirement in 1855; she died in 1856.

Planché was back at the Olympic for three Christmas extravaganzas in 1854 (*The Yellow Dwarf*), 1855 (*The Discreet Princess*) and 1856 (*Young and Handsome*), rejoicing in the fact that they depended on the acting talents of the remarkable Frederick Robson rather than the scene-painting, however good, of William Beverley.[27] His last extravaganza was *King Christmas*, written for the German Reeds' Gallery of Illustration in 1871, a return after nearly fifteen years to the form he had invented. Planché noted its 'gratifying reception ... by both the Press and the public', adding:

> my greatest pleasure was to perceive that the style of the dialogue and character of the songs had an attraction for the younger portion of the audience; and they found it was possible to derive some amusement from a piece written in passable English, having a rational object, and intelligently acted, with tasteful and appropriate scenery and dresses; but devoid of all the meretricious allurements which have latterly been supposed indispensible to the success of a holiday entertainment.[28]

One reason for Planché's success was his long-lasting association with Madame Vestris, in whom he found a most sympathetic coadjutor. Madame Vestris, born Lucia Elizabeth Bartolozzi in 1797, the daughter of an Italian father and a German mother, was one of the most influential figures in the theatre of the first half of the nineteenth century. She married in 1813 Armand Vestris, the celebrated premier danseur and later ballet-master of the King's Theatre, who was ten years her senior. An incorrigible philanderer, Vestris deserted her after three years of marriage. He died in 1825 and she subsequently married in 1838 Charles James Mathews, who became an accomplished light leading man. But she was always known as Madame Vestris.

She made her theatrical debut aged eighteen as a singer, served her theatrical apprenticeship in Paris and became a star in the London burlesque *Don Giovanni in London*, playing the lead, a 'breeches' role. She subsequently achieved triumphs in opera, light comedy and further 'breeches' roles, which became a particular speciality. The actor George Vandenhoff wrote of her in *An Actor's Notebook* (1859):

> She was the best soubrette *chantante* of her day; self-possession, archness, grace, coquetrie, seemed natural to her; these, with her charming voice, excellent taste in music, fine eyes and exquisite form, made her the most fascinating and, (joined to her *esprit d'intrigue*) the most dangerous actress of her time. Believe it, reader, no actress that we have now can give you an idea of the attractions, the fascinations, the witcheries of Madame Vestris in the hey-day of her charms.[29]

In 1830 she made history by becoming the first West End female actor-manager when she took the lease of the Olympic Theatre in Wych Street, a rundown 'cheap melodrama' house in a notably rough and disreputable area of central London. She had the theatre completely refurbished in the French Style, gained permission from the Lord Chamberlain to stage a programme of 'entertainment of music, dancing, burlettas, spectacle, pantomime and horsemanship'[30] and she succeeded in attracting patrons from fashionable society. *Bell's Life in London* (9 January 1831) reported that the opening of the Olympic 'excited a considerable sensation', fashionable society had booked all the boxes and aristocratic carriages blocked all the narrow streets up to Drury Lane.

She introduced French-style innovations: the use of traps to speed up the action; a curtain which parted in the middle and drew up to the side of the stage; ending performances at 11.00 p.m. rather than carrying on beyond midnight as was the practice in many theatres. Her productions like her acting became known for their elegance, charm and restraint; in short their continental sophistication. Moreover when she was not herself on stage, she watched her productions from her private box, noting and correcting anything slipshod in the performance. She regularly redressed her shows during their run so that they were 'as brilliant on the last as on the first night of their performance'.[31] She was also notable for paying salaries in advance, setting regular hours of work with appropriate rest periods and for demonstrating concern for the welfare of her staff. Her principal object, however, was to imbue her theatres with respectability both in terms of productions and audience. The very fact of the decision to stage Christmas extravaganzas rather than pantomimes confirms this, for the two forms were different and distinct.

The Athenaeum in 1843 expressly contrasted the two forms, underlining the class difference, and declaring of extravaganza:

> This pleasant sort of entertainment, which sends light laughter round the theatre, and keeps up a continual smile on the countenances of the audience, compared with the coarse exaggeration and vulgar buffoonery of pantomime, is what the raillery of polished wit in a drawing room is to the rude horse-play and ungainly gambols of rustic merry-making.[32]

At the end of her tenure of Covent Garden, *The Morning Post* (29 April 1842), paid a generous tribute to Madame Vestris' achievement:

> She has banished vulgarity, coarse manners, *double-entendre*, and impertinence from the boards over which she presided, and in their place has evoked the benefits that flow from a dramatic interpretation of polished manners, refinement and politeness. Her green-room was the resort of the learned, the witty and the wise, a miniature picture of polite and well-bred society whence a wholesome example spread itself on all within its influence. Once communicated to the stage, it became communicable to the public, and sure we are that a desirable tone of refinement both in manners and conversation has been extensively spread in private life by the lady-like deportment and acting of Madame Vestris. To art she gave an impulse of no mean importance. Witness the magnificent scenery, as appropriate as it was beautiful which her fine taste caused to be continually brought before the public. The *mise-en-scène* was never perfect until Madame Vestris taught her painters how to execute and the public how to appreciate her own pictorial conceptions, and to her judgement in this way the playgoing world has been indebted for much of its theatrical enjoyment.

Planché concurred in this appreciation of Madame, recording that when he went with her to Covent Garden: 'I had the pleasure of continuing my reform of the costume of the national drama ... with the additional advantage of the great taste and unbounded liberality of the manageress, whose heart was thoroughly in the cause, and spared neither time, trouble, nor money in promotion of it.'[33] Dedicating his play *The Two Figaros* to Madame in 1836 he proclaimed the Olympic 'not only one of the most popular and fashionable theatres London ever saw, but serv[ing] as a life-boat to the respectability of the stage, which was fast sinking in the general wreck.'

W. Davenport Adams noted in his pioneering 1891 history of the burlesque form: 'As Planché was, in effect, the Father of Classical Burlesque, so was he also, even more irrefragably, the Father of the Burlesque of Faerie – of the fairy tales of the nursery.'[34] In turning for inspiration to classical mythology and fairy lore, he was tapping into two of the cultural preoccupations of the nineteenth century. Both preoccupations can be seen at one level to be responses to the remorseless pace of change, the apparent heartlessness and materialism of the new industrial age, and to the power of modernity that was transforming society. Escape from it could be found in the idealization of a pre-industrial world, pastoral and Arcadian, in which older values – decency, honesty, compassion – prevailed.

There was a flood of novels, paintings and intermittently plays dealing with the Ancient World but from the 1830s to the 1870s, Ancient Greece was largely seen through the medium of the classical burlesque. Planché pointed out the irony that he was not:

> a classical scholar, and have been as much amused as surprised to find that I had as unconsciously as undeservedly acquired a reputation of being one in the estimation of some of the most erudite in our great universities and public schools, from the manner in which I treated mythological subjects.

He pointed out that he had barely mastered the Greek alphabet and derived his classical knowledge from the translations of the great poets, historians and dramatists of Greece and Italy plus Lemprière's Classical Dictionary, 'the best thumbed book in my own possession'.[35] While Planché was neither a classical scholar nor a University man, several notable authors of classical burlesques were. Frank Talfourd and Robert Reece were at Oxford and Frank Burnand at Cambridge.

Edith Hall and Fiona Macintosh, in their magisterial study of Greek tragedy on the English stage (calling the classical burlesque genre 'dazzling, cheeky and surprisingly erudite'), argue that it had universal appeal, transcending class boundaries; that the burlesques repudiated classical education by satirizing it yet at the same time appropriated the more pleasurable parts of its content for ordinary people; and that this testified to a widely disseminated classical knowledge. These conclusions are questionable.[36]

The fact that classical mythology was satirized did not mean that a classical education was being repudiated. The Victorians satirized everything and they were certainly not repudiating other notable burlesque subjects such as Shakespeare, English history or grand opera. Positing a cross-class audience for the burlesque flies in the face of the accepted wisdom of theatre historians, as expressed, for example, by Michael Booth who stated: 'Extravaganza and burlesque were almost entirely aimed at the relatively educated and the middle class.'[37] It is also contradicted by Richard Schoch who cites evidence that the sophisticated burlesque and extravaganza did not go down well with the working-class audiences of the so-called transpontine theatres. One unattributed newspaper clipping from December 1864 declared:

> Burlesques and extravaganzas have never been extremely popular on the south side of the river and the manager who would venture to place either of those innovations before a transpontine audience on Boxing Night would assuredly meet with the treatment that so daring an iconoclast would deserve.[38]

Christopher Stray has convincingly argued that an education in and knowledge of the classics served to consolidate and define the aristocratic-bourgeois elite and exclude the lower classes and uneducated.[39]

This leads to the question of how far audiences understood and appreciated what was being burlesqued. Schoch draws attention to this problem directly when he talks of competent and incompetent spectators:

> Competent spectators possessed sufficient knowledge of the burlesque's 'sources', whether plays, novels, poems, operas, fables, history books, or contemporary events. Such knowledge enabled them to appreciate not just the manifest amusement of the burlesque's catchy songs, dances, and 'gags', but also, and more importantly, the cut and thrust of its pointedly topical parody. By contrast, incompetent spectators – that is, those who lacked the requisite foreknowledge – would be unable to fully appreciate a burlesque *as* a burlesque ... The extent to which audiences met – or failed to meet – the various demands of 'knowingness' posed by Victorian burlesques remains unquantifiable. Yet logic alone tells us that no theatrical form can long survive if it attracts a predominantly incompetent audience. Burlesque's popularity throughout the nineteenth century indicates the continuing existence of a critical mass of knowledgeable spectators.[40]

Schoch seeks to qualify Booth's definition of the burlesque audience by arguing that given the fact that the burlesque did not set out to improve or educate its audience and satirized middle-class values and morals, it was not the whole middle class that attended burlesques but only a section – the young raffish Bohemian section.[41]

Some of the authors of the burlesques, notably Frank Talfourd and Robert Brough, could be characterized as racy Bohemians who lived fast and died young. But none of this applies to the ultra-respectable Planché. He prided himself in the fact that his extravaganzas had moral messages. He was regularly praised by the critics for his elegance, taste and refinement and his audiences for their decorum. So even if burlesques did appeal to Bohemian bachelors out on a spree, there was also evidently an appeal to a wider and more respectable family audience.

The weight of the evidence suggests that while the pantomime had genuine and enduring cross-class appeal and retained its hold on working-class as well as middle-class audiences, the extravaganza was aimed at and most appreciated by middle-class audiences, who were always Madame Vestris' target audience. This was recognized at the time. *The Morning Herald* (2 October 1849) declared: 'The spirit of gentility presides' wherever Madame Vestris is in management, 'The Lyceum is eminently an aristocratic theatre.'

The Era (29 December 1850) observed that where 'the gods' in other theatres were noisy and unruly, at the Lyceum they were 'orderly, patient and satisfied'. *The Times* (27 December 1849) reported: 'Boxing-night at the Lyceum is always truly respectable – the galleries quiet, the pit critical, the boxes fashionable ... Strange as it may appear, no apples or orange peels were projected from the gallery, and yet the people in the pit seemed as pleased as the gods with Boxing-night.' This was the audience for which Planché was writing. *The Era* (30 December 1849) confirmed this when it declared of Planché:

> He has evidently studied to produce unexceptionable language – eschewing slang and vulgarity ... Mr Planché has a difficult task – that of making an extravaganza exceedingly funny, and yet avoiding the broadest humour and extremest absurdity. We all know that coarsest jokes excite the loudest laughter, especially as the more vacant the mind the more noisy the cachinnation. But enjoyment is not always expressed by violent mirth, and Mr Planché caters for intelligent people, and a Lyceum audience is considered to be select. The characters then, speak with great propriety, and there is a polish about the couplets consistent with the getting up of the piece.

The recurrent terms used to describe Planché's writing are wit, taste and refinement. *The Morning Chronicle* (27 December 1850) reviewing *King Charming*, praised 'the wit, the taste and the refinement' characteristic of the author and the management. The same newspaper (27 December 1851) observed that:

> his burlesques do not betray the slightest leaven of vulgarity or impropriety. They are better adapted to the tastes of the dress circle than the gallery but though their humour is of a more subtle and polished kind than the writers of these whimsies care to adopt, their quaintness and pungency are nonetheless apparent.

Reviewing *The Seven Champions of Christendom*, *The Morning Chronicle* (10 April 1849) noted that Planché's humour was not of the slangy, pot-house order, but drawing room and boudoir-like – terse, elegant and scholarly. John Hamilton Reynolds, poet and critic, wrote appreciatively to Planché about the appeal of his extravaganzas:

> What I like about your fairy dramas is their truth in delicate humour, and the perfect understanding you shew of the nice art of Burlesque *in flower* ... You have run the veins of life into the little 'span-long elves' that flit, or strut, or skip, or coquet about Fairy-land.

You inform grown-up beings how they may be reflected in fairy mirrors ... You put with an elegant manner *our* household words into mouths, and our habits and foolish manners into persons and places I don't know how far off, or how *very* out of sight, and we laugh at, and enjoy ourselves, and our own delectable nonsenses, all because it pleased a French Countess to be a delicate fairy humourist, and you to be a man of a poetical mind who knew how to translate her into the rarest English Burlesque.[42]

Olympic Revels or Prometheus and Pandora, starring Madame Vestris as Pandora, opened on 3 January 1831. But it was only one part of the evening's dramatic entertainment which began with a play, *Mary, Queen of Scots*, based on incidents in Sir Walter Scott's novel *The Abbot*. It ended with two more pieces, *The Little Jockey* and *Clarissa Harlowe*. In between came *Olympic Revels*, which recounted the tales of Prometheus' theft of fire from the gods and Pandora's box but with a happy ending. Hope, emerging from the box, persuades Jupiter to pardon them both. *Bell's London Life* (9 January 1831) thought *Olympic Revels* the main attraction of the evening:

> a most exquisite little burletta of the *Midas* school, and, in our opinion, superior even to that popular production – and this is no mean praise. It was full, from the first to last, of the witty allusions, vocal parodies, and whips and cranks of all description; and the delightful singing, looks and acting of Vestris, as Pandora, carried it through with unabated spirit. We cannot dismiss the subject without mention of the very liberal and creditable manner in which it ... has been got up, as regards, scenery, dresses and properties.

The success of *Olympic Revels* led directly to a follow-up, *Olympic Devils or Orpheus and Eurydice*, first produced on 26 December 1831. Its success exceeded even that of *Olympic Revels*, as it ran for 131 nights. Madame Vestris had the 'breeches' role of Orpheus. It told the familiar story of Orpheus seeking to rescue Eurydice from the underworld but once again it provided a happy ending, reuniting them for six months of every year. Puns abounded. When Cerberus, the three-headed dog guarding the entrance to Hades, appears there is talk of him quoting doggerel, speaking dog-Latin and singing a bark-a-role.

The Christmas novelty of 1832 was *The Paphian Bower or Venus and Adonis*, which opened on 26 December 1832, with Madame Vestris as Venus. This reworking of the tale of Venus and Adonis was praised by *Bell's London Life* (30 December 1832) for its acting, scenery and music. But *The Age* (6 January 1833) and *Figaro in London* (2 February 1833) both thought it inferior to its two predecessors, and its sixty-six night run, compared to the 131 nights enjoyed by *Olympic Devils*, suggests that they may have been correct.

This was followed by *The Deep, Deep Sea*, which opened on 26 December 1833 and told the story of Perseus and Andromeda with Madame Vestris again in a breeches role, Perseus, in this version a half-pay officer, Captain Perseus of the Winged Horse. Neptune and his tritons all spoke like characters in a nautical melodrama ('Avast! Belay there! Stow your jawing gear, ye noisy swabs! Shiver me timbers!') and the novelty was that the classical monster in the story was replaced by the Great American Sea Serpent, 'half man, half horse and half alligator', cast up by the storm. He was given a drawling American accent, a long rifle and a theme tune to the strains of 'Yankee Doodle Dandy'. This derived from the regular press reports at this time of sea serpents spotted off the coast of America.

The Satirist (29 December 1833), reviewing *The Deep, Deep Sea*, interestingly suggests that burlesque was overtaking pantomime in popularity:

> Vestris eschews pantomime for entertainment of her holiday visitors, and wisely, too, considering what pantomimes are in these degenerate days. Another potent reason is, that she can give us something better, at least to our taste; for though we own to a relish for a good pantomime – that is, when there is lots of fun, an invaluable ingredient, but almost wholly omitted by our modern concoctors – yet somehow the glory of this species of entertainment has been gradually departing since intellect began to march. We, therefore, right merrily trusted our bark to *The Deep, Deep Sea* ... in full confidence that we should not be disappointed. Nor were we: the piece is good after its kind, stuffed full of puns, natural and artificial free and forced, queer conceits and absurdities, that cause laughter from their oddity, and ludicrous combinations of the grave and ridiculous, truth and fable. It is also set off by the jingle of rhyme, and popular music, prettily sung and executed.

The fifth Planché / Dance Christmas extravaganza was *Telemachus or the Island of Calypso*, which opened on 26 December 1834. It recounted the imaginary adventures of Telemachus, son of Ulysses as he made his way back to Ithaca after the Trojan War, accompanied by his tutor Mentor, who was in fact the goddess Minerva in disguise. It was based on the didactic novel *Télémaque* (1699), written by François de Salignac de la Mothe-Fénelon, Archbishop of Cambrai. Madame Vestris played Calypso. *The Times* (27 December 1834) thought it the best Christmas show so far. Most of the critics united in praising the acting, scenery, costumes and music.

Planché returned to classical mythology for the Easter 1848 Lyceum extravaganza, *Theseus and Ariadne or The Marriage of Bacchus*, first seen on 24 April 1848. *The Era* (30 April 1848) thought 'the dialogue is very smart, full of puns and jokes, and at times particularly effective' and *The Times* (25 April 1848) declared Planché 'unique'. But now William Beverley was also reaping superlatives for his scene-painting, a sign of things to come.

5

James Robinson Planché and the Fairy Extravaganza

The Olympic Christmas show of 1836 was *Riquet with the Tuft*. Opening on 26 December 1836, it was, Planché recalled, 'a turning point in the history of extravaganza'.[1] It marked the superseding of the classical burlesque by the fairy extravaganza. A variation on the 'Beauty and the Beast' theme, it starred Madame Vestris as Princess Emeralda and Charles Mathews, a new recruit to the company, as Riquet, a limping, grotesque hunchback with a noble soul who is at the end transformed into a handsome prince. Mathews was an instant hit, entrancing audiences with his natural elegance and gentlemanly manner. Victorian theatre historian H. Barton Baker wrote of him:

> It was the very perfection of Charles Mathews' art that made it look so much like nature … No English rival approached that combination of consummate ease, nonchalance, polished manner, and brilliant vivacity that marked his performances until he was nearly 70 years of age.[2]

Mathews married Madame Vestris in 1838.

From this point onwards Planché brought the world of faery to life on the London stage. *The Standard* (27 December 1850) described him as 'the Macaulay of fairy-dom'. Each Christmas and Easter for many years the theatres for which Planché worked were filled with fairies, wizards, witches, ogres, dragons, elves, dwarves, sprites, anthropomorphic animals, spells and transformations, magic rings and magic swords, enchanted trees and flowers. It was a theatre of reassurance as the fairies were always on hand to assist the ugly and despised, the poor and oppressed and lovers parted by circumstances. Young men and sometimes even young women disguised as men were set tests and quests to prove themselves and they invariably won through by use of their wits, strength, kindliness and often with supernatural aid. The dynastic problems of mythical kingdoms, succession disputes and arranged marriages, most notably, were resolved successfully. Family tensions involving jealous and spiteful brothers and sisters, wicked stepmothers and murderous uncles were satisfactorily sorted out.

Planché was careful to set *Riquet* in the context of fairy stories and to justify its dramatization. The extravaganza opens in fairyland where Queen Mab and the fairies sing the praises of fairy tales and fairy lore. But Mother Bunch, a folkloric figure to whom collections of English fairy tales were regularly attributed, rises up to complain that fairy stories are threatened by the advance of 'Useful Knowledge' and that her book of fairy stories 'is banished nursery and hall.' Queen Mab complains that she is too pessimistic and that 'on summer eves, and winter nights, and still in every clime, the fairy tale is told; and loved the fairy rhyme.' Queen Mab invites Mother Bunch to the fairy feast and she says she will come after she has seen to the needs of her godson, Prince Riquet. At the end, after Riquet has been united with Princess Emeralda, Mother Bunch takes them to the feast at Queen Mab's court where all the famous figures from fairy stories appear: Jack the Giant Killer, Cinderella, Little Red Riding Hood, Beauty and the Beast, Valentine and Orson, the White Cat, Puss in Boots and the Six Champions of Christendom. Queen Mab invites Riquet 'to join our band, Denizen of Fairy Land.' *The Times* (27 December 1836) having praised the acting, scenery, dresses and dialogue ('sparkling in the extreme, full of point and humour, and the jokes told right well'), concluded that it was 'unquestionably the very best thing of its kind that has ever been produced within the walls of this agreeable theatre.' This was the general verdict of the critics and audiences alike.

Encouraged by the success of *Riquet*, the Olympic management agreed to a second incursion into Fairyland, *Puss in Boots*, with Madame Vestris as the hero Ralph and Charles Mathews as Puss. *The Morning Chronicle* (27 December 1837) reported appreciatively:

> The dialogue is lively throughout, and abounds in well-placed puns and *double entendres* interspersed in three or four places, though by no means offensively, with a reference to the cant terms of the day ... the acting was very good throughout ... the scenery was well painted ... the dresses were appropriate and handsome.

But some critics were offended by the use of slang. *Figaro* (30 December 1837) was snobbishly withering:

> The Olympic Christmas piece is from the united pen of Dance and Planché. The senseless ribaldry with which it abounds ought to have ensured its '*deep damnation*'. Such coarse and disgusting rubbish as – 'Does your mother know you're out?', 'He's an out and outer!' and other slang fit only for St Giles's, should have been scouted from a stage which the elegant Vestris has brought to something like a state of refinement. We wonder she does not get out of the hands of these Siamese brothers, this duality of paint

pot and scissors workmen. How can an ex-patten maker be supposed to possess the education necessary to write for the stage, or for anything else? Surely if Mr Planché thought it expedient to give up the *patten* business, he might so far sink the shop as not to make himself a *clog* to the London Theatres. The taste of Vestris has done all that could be done for 'Puss in Boots' but we do not expect the existence of this thing will at all bear out the general rule as to the long retention of life by that useful domestic animal.

Bluebeard, opening on 2 January 1839, was the last collaboration of Dance and Planché. Madame Vestris played the female lead, Fleurette. Planché abandoned the Oriental setting the story had used since George Colman's melodramatic opera version (1798), and set it in fifteenth-century France, the period from which Charles Perrault derived his story. *The Morning Chronicle* (3 January 1839) pronounced it 'a genuine Christmas drollery, full of fun and frolic. It belongs to the most enjoyable species of burlesque.'

The Times (3 January 1839) was particularly impressed with the visuals. Referring to Planché's researches as having established the fifteenth century identity of Bluebeard, *The Times* said:

> The costume of that period has been most carefully preserved, and the most singular and picturesque effects are produced in the party coloured dresses and pointed shoes of that gallant time ... the scenes, particularly one representing a ball-room, were splendid and not merely splendid, but exhibiting a most artistical spirit, and a sedulous attention to antiquarian proprieties. Every shield that adorned the room was itself a little picture. The interior of the terrible 'blue chamber' was most whimsically conceived, and most ingeniously executed.

The scenery was by William Telbin and William Cuthbert. Of the script, *The Times* remarked: 'As usual the dialogue contained smart hits at the present times, and some of them produced unanimous laughter.'

By the Christmas of 1839, Madame Vestris and Charles Mathews had taken over the Theatre Royal, Covent Garden, where interestingly the audience demanded a traditional pantomime. As Planché put it, 'a harlequinade being unavoidable', the fairy extravaganza which had become an institution at the Olympic was postponed until Easter. Planché chose as his subject *The Sleeping Beauty in the Wood*, which opened on Easter Monday, 20 April 1840. It was now expanded to three acts and had the advantage of scene-painting by the Grieves, father and son. Madame Vestris played the Sleeping Beauty, Princess Isabelle. There was a chorus of praise from the critics, typified by *The Times* (21 April 1840), which called *Sleeping Beauty* 'as pretty a thing of this kind as we have ever seen ... all was very beautiful and fairylike and sparkling.' Acting, sets, singing and dancing all received praise, and of the graceful seventeenth and eighteenth century costumes, the critic noted: 'Mr Planché's taste for costume was abundantly displayed.' *Champion* (26 April 1840) said: 'As a fairy extravaganza it is unique in conception, pre-eminent in execution. The scenery is most superb.'

Planché provided the script for the pantomime demanded by the patrons of Covent Garden and chose Horace Walpole's romance, *The Castle of Otranto* as the basis of *The Castle of Otranto or Harlequin and the Giant Helmet*, which opened on 26 December 1840. The choice inspired the allegorical opening scene in which Romance appears in a ruined monastery by moonlight, surrounded by spirits, and summons her heroes to defend her against attack by her foe Burlesque. Her call is obeyed by figures from Romantic fiction: the Seven Champions of Christendom, Amadis of Gaul, the Scottish Chiefs, the Bleeding Nun, Ivanhoe, the Bravo of Venice and Doctor Faustus, to defend the castle of Otranto, home of Romance, against the assaults of Burlesque. But the Spirit of Burlesque is supported by Tom Thumb, Bombastes Furioso, Don Whiskerandos, Don Quixote and the Kings of Brentford and after a battle they seize the castle.

Thereafter Prince Manfred plays a series of tricks to get rid of his wife Hippolyta and keeps his ward, Lady Isabella, from her lover, the peasant Theodore until the rightful heir of the castle, the Marquis of Vicenza appears. The most notable features were the giant helmet and giant hand of the ghost of Alfonso, the murdered lord of Otranto, which were praised in *The Age* and *The Examiner*. The opening ends with the Spirit of Burlesque invoking the spirit of pantomime and introducing the harlequinade.

Most of the reviews devoted considerable space to the harlequinade which took place against a series of scenes of London. In the first scene at Strawberry Hill, Horace Walpole's house, Clown and Pantaloon are stuffed into a raspberry and a gooseberry and labelled 'raspberry fool' and 'gooseberry fool'. The importation of French capers mixed with English hops sets everyone and everything present dancing: policemen, Quakers, old women, eggs, fish and pigs. In the second scene the National Gallery is seen boarded up as workmen erect Nelson's column in Trafalgar Square. When the boards are removed the column springs up fully finished. The boards are covered with amusing advertisements, for instance the best brandy available at the British and Foreign Temperance Society, Exeter Hall, and hands wanted for Master Humphry's Clock by 'Boz'. Satirizing the vogue for promenade concerts and highlighting the dire state of the drama, Clown takes over the temple of drama and introduces promenade concerts with an imported French band, and similar concerts are advertised for Westminster Hall, Newgate and Brixton Treadmill. The statues of the dramatic poets are furnished with fiddles and Melpomene and Thalia, the muses of tragedy and comedy, are knocked off their pedestals. But the venture fails and Shakespeare takes the dominant position again, an appropriate outcome for a production in one of the patent theatres.

The Examiner (3 January 1841) complained about 'the dreary lack of comic invention' in the harlequinade, and *The Penny Satirist* (9 January 1841) called it 'infinitely more meagre in tricks, tomfoolery and grotesque than even the least of the minor theatres'. The show ended with a diorama beginning in St Helena from which the remains of Napoleon were in 1840 removed back to France, the taking of Tchusan and Tinghei by the Royal Navy as part of the Opium War with China and the bombardment of Acre by commodore Napier as part of the British intervention in Syria in support of the Sultan of Turkey's attempts to end Ibrahim Pasha's seizure of power in that country. It concluded with a patriotic tableau in which Britannia received the homage of Neptune, the arts and commerce and the Spirit of Justice and Liberty. *The Examiner* reported that after the tableau 'an enthusiast in the lower boxes' stood up and said 'Gentlemen and Englishmen, allow me to propose three cheers for Commodore Napier.' The audience responded either with 'bravo' or 'turn him out' but the three cheers were delivered. *The Era* (3 January 1841) found the bombardment scene 'magnificent' as did *The Penny Satirist*.

The Belle Assemblée (28 December 1840) declared the diorama scenes 'beautifully painted' and of the whole show:

> Improvement combined with Amusement is the avowed order of the day, and even a
> Christmas pantomime may be said to cultivate (though still not devoid of sober fun) the
> minds of the rising generation by giving practical illustrations of mechanics in its clever
> mechanical illusions and lessons on the fine arts by its exquisite scenery.

The Morning Chronicle (28 December 1840) – while praising the scene-painting, particularly 'a magnificent view of Canton beautifully painted, and with the gay junks and stately English vessels, forming a delightful picture' at the mouth of the Nankin River, 'an excellent piece of art, the vessels at anchor in the bright haze and the boats landing the soldiers are perfect' – found the effects of the storm at sea and the bombardment unconvincing.

The Age (3 January 1841) thought the opening the best part of the pantomime but 'what is theatrically speaking, called "the comic business" is the greatest failure it has been our lot to witness for years' and 'We have never seen a worse Clown or Pantaloon at any theatre.' 'Instead of "dumb show", we are inflicted with a noisy dialogue.'

> The scenery is the great feature of the pantomime, and those that pleased us most
> consist of the exterior of the Castle of Otranto, Trafalgar Square and the Temple of the
> Drama. The diorama concluded the piece and the subject selected by the Grieves is not
> the most happy one ... Nevertheless they have done their work well, and saved the
> pantomime; but the diorama of the present year will not stand the feat of comparison
> with Stansfield's last, which was exhibited during Mr Macready's management.

As if in acknowledgement of the fact that pantomime was not his forte, Planché did not write the script for the 1841–2 Christmas pantomime, *Guy, Earl of Warwick or Harlequin and the Dun Cow*, which, according to Vestris' biographer William Appleton was 'hailed as the best Christmas pantomime seen at that theatre in 20 years.'[3]

Planché was back with extravaganza for Easter 1841 and settled on *Beauty and the Beast*. He was told it was stale and hackneyed as a subject but he devised an entirely new treatment. It had usually been given an Oriental setting but Planché decided to set it in England, in no particular period and with no authenticated period costumes. Compared with the shows at the Olympic, those at Covent Garden were longer, more lavish and more elaborate. There were now lengthy ballet sequences as well as special visual effects and spectacular scene-painting.

The Times (13 April 1841) reported of *Beauty and the Beast*:

> The drama was completely overlaid with scenic decoration, and the fertile genius of this house has been fully employed in devising new effects and new machinery. The first scene, representing the Parliament of Roses, opened by their Queen in person, is a most singular piece of mechanism. The rose-bushes which stand round the stage open every one of their flowers, and a lady-face appears from each of them, while a larger rose in the centre unfolds itself, and discovers the Queen seated on a splendid throne. The closing scene of the piece in which a large transparent flower rises from a trap, adorned with a number of small roses, is an equally beautiful effect, differently worked out. These are merely mentioned as the most curious effects, in a mechanical point of view: in scenic beauty the piece is equal throughout.

The paper complained, however, that it was more like an opera than a burlesque and was signally lacking in humour. However, the critics noted the show was greeted by applause throughout and 'tumultuous approbation' following the descent of the curtain. *The Era* (18 April 1841) similarly noted 'a paucity of fun':

> The present adaptor, has, we think, failed in the grand object of burlesque, for such we presume to have been the mark of his intention. It lacks breadth and humour. The songs are not parodies, but new versions, and fall pointless on the ear … the musical selections, with but very few exceptions, are of too classical a character to carry even the lightweight of lyrical burlesque. The jokes are, unexceptionably well-bred; they never surprise, never act rudely on the cachinnatory muscles, and thus distort with vulgar grinnings, the placidity of the human face divine.

The White Cat, the final Planché extravaganza at Covent Garden, opened on Easter Monday, 28 March 1842. Planché recalled that its reception was 'fully as favourable as that which was accorded to its predecessors.' This once popular tale featured three princes in search of a little pet dog for their father and a beautiful princess as a wife. The White Cat who aids Prince Paragon turns out to be an enchanted princess, whom he marries. An advance was made in the ballet department (with Chinese and Moorish dancers featured) but:

> the special feature in the *mise en scène* was the very ingenious realisation of the description in the story of the attendance of hands without bodies. They appeared in all parts of the stage bearing flambeaux, moving chairs, and executing various other orders in the most natural and graceful manner without its being possible to detect the *modus operandi*. It was certainly the *chef d'oeuvre* of that unequalled machinist Mr. W. Bradwell and the effect was as picturesque as it was puzzling.[4]

Most critics liked it. *The Times* (29 March 1842) thought 'the whole affair was very amusing and likely to prove attractive' and praised 'the scenery and general "getting up"' as 'exceedingly tasteful and ingenious', especially the management of the hands. 'Tasteful' was an adjective that recurred in the reviews.

The next Easter extravaganza was *Fortunio and His Seven Gifted Servants*, based on Madame d'Aulnoy's *Belle-Belle ou le Chevalier Fortuné*. It was first performed at the Theatre Royal, Drury Lane on Easter Monday, 17 April 1843, and 'achieved a brilliant success' recalled Planché.[5] He attributed this to 'the excellence of the story, as well as to the admirable interpretation it received from a company, with one exception, entirely unaccustomed to this peculiar species of entertainment.' This was contrary to expectations. There had been dire predictions of failure. Madame Vestris was absent for the first time and this was considered potentially fatal. She and Mathews had lost control of Covent Garden and taken an engagement with the actor-manager W.C. Macready at Drury Lane and Planché had followed them. But they had quarrelled with Macready and decamped to the Haymarket Theatre to join Benjamin Webster. Webster invited Planché to join them there but he had committed himself to providing an Easter piece for Macready and honoured the commitment. So Easter 1843 saw the production of 'one of the most popular of my extravaganzas' and the first not to be associated with the name of Madame Vestris. He was fortunate in his young and untried cast, many of whom later became stars; notably Priscilla Horton. Macready supervised the rehearsals 'judiciously and energetically', threw himself into the spirit of the show, learned all the parts and acted them out, and it was performed as Planché always hoped it would be, with no-one trying to be funny. 'Taking their cue from the great tragedian who, like all the greatest tragedians I ever knew, might have been an almost greater comedian, everyone in the piece acted as they would have done in any ordinary comedy, melo-drama, or opera.' The result was 'one of the most triumphant successes I was ever gratified by.'[6] Planché gratefully dedicated the published version of *Fortunio* to the Drury Lane cast of the show.

The show was rapturously received by the critics. *The Era* (23 April 1843) reported:

> The story is the best that has been hitherto selected for dramatic elaboration, and most felicitously has Mr Planché effected his task. Its chief points are seized with a kindred spirit – the legendary abstractions are made instinct with humour – and the entire pageant moves forward amid an atmosphere of fun, spirited parody, sparkling wit, embodied burlesque, and ingenious machinery. The author never avails himself of his verbal pungency and Parthian words to inflict a wound – he has urgent good temper, and although he gives evidence of being, if occasion serve, a severe hitter, the punishment is scientifically administered and rendered innocuous, by the humane use of the gloves.

The critic sees evidence not just of poetic imagination but of worldly knowledge in the script.

The Times (18 April 1843) agreed:

> The fairy extravaganza of *Fortunio* ... is an exceedingly clever and amusing burlesque. The effects are novel and surprising; the dialogue is smart, and contains many fair 'hits' at the times. The music is well selected, and the manner in which the piece is put upon the stage is most complete. Although from the want of real interest dramas of the burlesque kind are apt above all others to fall into the tedious, there is no defect of the kind in this one. A spirit truly hilarious prevails throughout; a verbal joke is briskly followed by a lively song or a striking scenic effect, and thus the demon of weariness is kept aloof. Rarely have we seen a piece of this description received with such unalloyed satisfaction by an audience, with such an abundance of laughs, and with such a total absence of yawns.

At the close of the 1842–3 season, Planché's engagement with Macready was up and he accepted another to write exclusively for three and a half years for Benjamin Webster at the Haymarket Theatre. Vestris and Mathews had fled the country to avoid their creditors and were subsequently declared bankrupt. Planché's Christmas extravaganzas at the Haymarket were now one act in length and lacked the spectacular production values of Covent Garden and Drury Lane.

The Fair One with the Golden Locks was performed first on 26 December 1843. *The Times* (27 December 1843) praised the dialogue ('exceedingly smart and comical') and the acting ('The burlesque was as well acted as it could be'). But the critic noted the difference from the Drury Lane production:

> The piece is successful, but we think it will not have the 'run' of *Fortunio* and some of its predecessors. The Haymarket is not the theatre for spectacle, and although the dresses are very splendid, the author did not receive the assistance from decoration which was so serviceable at Drury-lane.

The Era (31 December 1843), however, praised Webster for avoiding 'gaudy and tricksy pantomimes' and turning to Planché who provided a show in which there was 'exquisite burlesque and pungent piercings at the follies of the day, strewed thick and almost incessant throughout the piece, with admirable parodies of favourite indigenous music, Italian airs and cadenzas and the wild notes of *Der Freischutz*.'

The show was revived in 1868 at Sadler's Wells as *Queen Lucidora, the Fair One with the Golden Locks, or Harlequin Prince Graceful, the Carp, the Crow and the Owl*. In a sign of the times, a harlequinade had been added to the extravaganza to turn it into a pantomime. *The Times* (28 December 1868) said: 'Mr Planché's clever lines come out wonderfully fresh and piquant and are fitted with new verses referring to current events and songs adapted to all the most popular tunes.' The transformation scene produced applause and the artist T. Evans and manageress Miss Hazlewood were summoned by the audience to take a bow. A smaller audience than usual was reported due to the weather but the pit and gallery were filled to overflowing, according to *The Daily News* (28 December 1868).

For Christmas 1844, the extravaganza at the Haymarket was *Graciosa and Percinet*. *The Times* (27 December 1844) reported that Planché had provided 'another of his elegant burlesques' which though it:

> may perhaps be inferior in point of broad fun to some of its predecessors, it yields to none either in the elegance and neatness of its dialogue, the tact with which it is constructed, or the taste shown in the getting up both as regards the dresses and the scenery. ... The burlesque in short was quite a hit, affording ample amusement as long as it lasted, and at the conclusion a shower of plaudits fully ratified the success.

The Era (29 December 1844) called it 'spirited, elegant and humorous', praised the costumes and scenery, the acting, 'the sparkling dialogue and profusion of repartee and fun' and the music, both vocal and instrumental, 'of a lively and animated character'. It also noted that 'the delight it imparted to the younger branches of the audience was evinced by the number of charmed and happy faces visible in all parts of the house.'

The Christmas extravaganza for 1845 was *The Bee and the Orange Tree*. *The Times* (29 December 1845) praised the adaptation as neat and tasteful and noted 'the language is neat, smart and appropriate, though the dialogue runs rather too much upon railways ... the songs are well selected, not too long, and not too numerous.' *The Morning Chronicle* (27 December 1845) said 'it is as full of good hits as a Christmas pudding is of raisins and currants, and with the good singing, acting, and stage arrangements, which gave it such good effect last night, it cannot fail to have a good run.' *The Standard* (27 December 1845) reported that the show gave 'universal satisfaction. It was admirably got up and the parts were well sustained. The dialogue possesses a full average degree of smartness, and the songs ... were very clever and elicited much laughter and approbation.'

Planché's final Haymarket extravaganza was *The Invisible Prince or the Island of Tranquil Delights*, which opened on 26 December 1846. Planché recalled that it was a huge success, running initially for seventy-six nights and being revived at the Haymarket in 1847 and 1848 and later at the Adelphi in 1859. The novelty here was the setting, the Kingdom of Allaquiz on the Spanish Main, where Spanish tyrant rulers, Queen Blousabella and her son the Infante Furibond, are contrasted with the Catspaw Indians and Aztec-type natives with names like Xquisitelittlepet and Itzaprettypetticoatl. Don Leander, descendant of the original native rulers of the land, is aided by the Fairy Gentilla to defeat Furibond and take over the kingdom, marrying the Princess of the Isle of Tranquil Delights. This seemed to be a thinly disguised version of current events in Spain where civil war had raged for several years between the main Bourbon line and the Carlist claimants to the throne, and where Queen Blousabella looked like a combination of the wayward Queen Isabella and her mother, Queen Maria Cristina who had caused a scandal by marrying an army sergeant-major after the death of King Ferdinand VII.

The Daily News (28 December 1846) called it:

> one of the prettiest of that series of extravaganzas which have for some years past attracted first the joyous expectation and then the lightsome steps of Christmas merry-makers to this agreeable theatre. The dialogue is racy and telling, 'full of wise saws and modern instances', and with its wonted *nice morality*, giving sharp raps over the knuckles of knavery in general, ... while for the simple follies of the day it has its laughing jest and jollity. The performances are all that Mr Planché or the public could desire. They enter throughout into the fun of the thing, and thus give each line, every word, its full effect ... the scenery is beautiful.

The Lady (2 January 1847), talking of 'its admirable wit, sublime drollery, and a *mise en scène* quite unparalleled', noted that 'the usual call for performers was responded to, and Mr Planché bowed from a private box. Strange as it may appear, this was the first time Mr Planché has ever been compelled to show himself in public.'

Planché rejoined the Mathews at the Lyceum in 1847 in the same capacity he had filled at Covent Garden. His first Christmas extravaganza there was *The Golden Branch*, based on Madame d'Aulnoy's 'Le Rameau D'Or'. The Golden Branch comes from the magic Tree of Entertaining Knowledge and if 'love or charity enough remain, to make of earth a fairyland again', the Branch will do its work. An eagle applies the Golden Branch to the deformed Prince Humpy and ugly Princess Dumpy, who have been imprisoned after refusing to marry. They are transformed into a beautiful shepherd and shepherdess in Arcadia. The evil spirits Humguffin and Mandragora plan to transform them into a toad and a butcher bird, but the Good

Fairy Pastorella changes them into a grasshopper and a cricket and when they are found in the trunk of the Fairy Tree of Entertaining Knowledge, back again into their beautiful human forms. There was something new and different about these Lyceum extravaganzas. The arrival of William Beverley took the scene-painting to a new level of excellence and the introduction of more and more dance sequences, choreographed by Oscar Byrne, led *The Times* (28 December 1847) to suggest that the piece 'gains more the character of a *ballet* than that of a burlesque.' Extraordinary parallels were being suggested, attesting to the ambitions of the Lyceum regime. *The Times* thought the transition from the enchanter's castle 'with its gloomy splendour' to the Arcadian landscape where the prince and princess are turned into shepherd and shepherdess 'produces a sensation which may be compared to that created by the transition from the tragic to the pastoral in *The Winter's Tale*.' *The Era* (2 January 1848) observed that the shepherds and shepherdesses were grouped in exact imitation of Watteau.

The *I.L.N.* (1 January 1848) said:

> We expected something very good at the Lyceum and we were not disappointed. That many others thought the same was evident from the fact of most of the leading critics of the papers being there in preference to the other houses ... Mr Planché's tact and delicate humour; Madame Vestris' taste and keen eye for effect and Mr W. Beverley's beautiful scenery were certain to produce a most perfect *ensemble*.

The Era (2 January 1848) was aware that something new was happening in *The Golden Branch*. Proclaiming it 'the piece of the season', the journal declared:

> The Golden Branch is no mere burlesque, it is an extravaganza – a distinction and a difference. Mr Planché has brought out some excellent things in this way, but he never mainly contributed to a production of greater merit, and one more successful. The marking out, and much of the filling up of the plot, and dialogue, are his; but Madame Vestris has called to his aid talent of a different nature to his own. The scene-painter, the mechanist, the decorator, the dancer, the musician, have one and all contributed, and exerted their various abilities to make the whole perfect. This is a fact which generally escapes the observer, but, in this instance, it is so manifest that we begin by calling attention to it. It is one which the talented author of the piece will be the first to subscribe to, and one which in no way takes from his own individual praise.

As dance became more and more prominent in the productions, the contributions of choreographer Oscar Byrne became more and more important, along with those of the resident machinist (H. Sloman) and composer-conductor (R. Hughes). The dances included a mazurka-polka, a pastoral gallopade, a gavotte and two *pas de deux* by a male and female pair. Particularly striking was one of the dances in which the ladies danced with crooks, each topped with a rose wreath, and they raised and moved them together to create what *The Era* called 'a very pretty effect'.

The King of the Peacocks was the Christmas extravaganza for 1848. It maintained the same formula as had brought success to *The Golden Branch* and ran for seventy-two nights. The story has Princess Rosetta determined to marry Argus, King of the Peacocks and travelling by Chinese junk to the Kingdom of Peacocks. The Princess' governess, Baroness Von Huggermugger, has Rosetta thrown overboard and replaced by her own daughter, the ugly Rumfizina. Rosetta is saved by the assistance of an Irish fisherman and her own green poodle Fretillon, and is eventually happily united with King Argus.

The Era (31 December 1848) declared *The King of the Peacocks*:

> the most gorgeous production of its kind that we ever remember to have seen ... The Lyceum itself, the most elegant little theatrical temple in Europe, with its drawing-room air and highly finished appearance, could not be more elaborately chaste than it is; and when the curtain is up and the brilliancy of costume and scenic beauty belonging to this piece are exhibited, the picture is remarkably splendid.

The critic thought it was justly termed an 'extravaganza', that Planché had kept strictly to the original story, 'unfolding it after his own approved and witty fashion.' He went on:

> The dialogue is humorous throughout, and sometimes exceedingly witty. There is no vulgarity belonging to it, but common phrases are introduced so as to bring no coarseness with them; and there is a finish about the jokes and puns peculiar to Mr Planché's composition. The piece is precisely after his own style; and that is well known and appreciated by the public.

The Times (27 December 1848) thought 'The tale does not afford such striking dramatic situations as some others in the collection ... Finding that the subject does not yield great variety of incident, he tries its capabilities for magnificence, and the result has been a spectacle gorgeous beyond comparison.' The inhabitants of the Verdant Valley are dressed in 'brilliant medieval costume' and the inhabitants of the land of peacocks in Chinese style, with peacock feathers being used in every scene. The final scene, 'an ingenious combination of brilliancy and elaborate mechanism, which process an effect entirely unique' was a giant peacock feather fan.

'The success was immense' concluded *The Times* and everybody was called:

> Nevertheless, we should recommend a lightening of some of the musical portions of the piece, especially towards the end of the first act. The dances by the *corps de ballet* were, on the other hand, highly valuable, the compound of hornpipe and quadrille, with which

the first act concludes being one of the most successful things of the kind ever seen on any stage.

This sequence, 'Royal Peacockian Navy Quadrille' was, said *The Era*, 'bewitchingly performed by some sixteen damsels, with the truly nautical steps and spirit.' But the length of the show and the large element of musical parody produced in some quarters expressions of discontent. *The Daily News* (27 December 1848) noted that the dialogue was:

> carried on in doggerel rhymes, full of puns, quibbles, Cockney slang, smart jokes and epigrammatic points and witticisms. This kind of language is rendered piquant by its contrast with the situations in which it is uttered; and it has a very telling effect from the unexpected and happy allusions and strokes of satire with which, in Mr Planché's piece, it abounds. But perpetual burlesque, long continued, becomes fatiguing; and it is found, in these pieces as in other things, that 'brevity is a soul of wit'. 'The King of the Peacocks' is as long as a regular play or a grand opera; and in the spirit of the writing, cleverness of the acting, and splendour of the spectacle, could not prevent a great deal of it from moving very heavily ... there is a great deal of singing in the piece; too much, indeed, for much of it was ineffective and heavy. There were a great many parodies of songs, duets, and even scenes, from 'Norma', 'Guillaume Tell', 'The Huguenots', 'Haydee' and other operas, which were but indifferently executed, and made no impression. The only portion of the music that pleased were two or three airs sung by Madame Vestris ... There was some excellent dancing, especially the hornpipe by a party of female sailors, which closed the first act and was more applauded than any other part of the performance ... there were long intervals of heaviness and silence, but the happier parts were warmly applauded; and if the management take the hint given by this reception and enliven the piece by abridging, they will certainly insure to it a long and profitable run.

John Bull (30 December 1848) made the same criticism.

The Island of Jewels, based on Madame d'Aulnoy's 'The Green Serpent', was an even greater success, running for 135 nights. A variation on the theme of 'Beauty and the Beast', this story has Princess Laidronetta sought in marriage by King Emerald. He turns out to be a green serpent, under a spell cast by an evil fairy. At first repulsed, she later demonstrates her love and the serpent is changed back into a prince.

The Daily News (27 December 1849) praised Planché's intention but found fault with his dialogue:

> Mr Planché continues to extract morals from the Countess D'Anois's stories. And a very pleasant means they are of telling people wholesome truths. This year he endeavours to impress the folly of listening to slanderous suggestions and the fatal effects of female curiosity ... Truth to tell, however (and we say this, with every affection of our old friend Planché), it was the dialogue that was mainly deficient. We remember few pieces by the

same author with so few 'points' or 'hits'. Except one hit at the 'Railway King' (rather a familiar topic), there were no allusions to the subjects of the day. Some of the new songs to old tunes were amusing ... but we remember very little else that occasioned a laugh, and we know that we came away ourselves with the entire conviction that every one had behaved with such extreme propriety, that one might fancy there was no such time as Christmas, no such night as boxing-night, and no use whatever for the Druidical plant called mistletoe.

Nevertheless, he argued that it must be seen: the scenery surpassed all previous efforts of the same artists; the costumes were admirable; the dancing skilfully arranged and rightly applauded; and Planché's pieces 'constitute a sort of era in dramatic art, and not to see one of them is to put one's self out of the pale.' On the other hand, The Examiner (29 December) thought it 'graced by much of Mr Planché's best writing and by excellent hits at the passing topics of the day.' But the visuals were as ever extravagantly praised. John Bull (29 December 1849) thought it a 'brilliant and gorgeous spectacle ... the piece was well received; though he did not excite much mirth, and is, perhaps too clever for Christmas week.' The Morning Chronicle (27 December) said, 'the piece was decidedly successful – the success depending not less upon the merits of the piece itself, and the finished character of the acting, than upon the extreme beauty of the scenery and appointments.' At the close of the extravaganza, the actors took their bows and 'there were loud and protracted calls for the author, which, however, were not responded to.' The Standard (27 December) thought 'there seems to be hardly as much point and variety in the dialogue as usual. But how exquisitely it is strengthened by Mr Beverly, whose scenes are as beautiful as can well be imagined. There is no artist who is publicly engaged upon labours of this ideal character who displays such adroit and attractive talent' and it attributed the success of the show chiefly to the final scene, this 'superb piece of scenic contrivance'.

The Easter piece for 1849 was The Seven Champions of Christendom, which was, according to Planché, more of 'a dramatic political allegory' than a comic extravaganza, and another of his periodic attempts to show that 'the mission of the dramatist was of a much higher nature than the catering of mere amusement for the million.' The background was the 1848 revolutions which had led to the overthrow of the French monarchy, the proclamation of a republic and a Communist uprising in Paris; war between Prussia and Denmark over Schleswig-Holstein; insurrections all over Italy; uprising in Hungary; disaffection and famine in Ireland; a major diplomatic breach between Britain and Spain. 'The only bright spot in the political horizon, so far as England was concerned was the satisfactory establishment of the overland route to India by the indefatigable exertions of Lieutenant Waghorn.' So Planché sought to retell the familiar stories of the Seven Champions attacking and destroying by intellectual progress and education Tyranny, Falsehood, Superstition, Ignorance and 'all the plagues of humanity' in the semblance of giant ogres, witches, sorcerers, demons, dragons and serpents, while commenting on current events. He recalled that it proved 'a brilliant success' and praised Madame Vestris for supporting such an innovative venture.[7] *The Morning Chronicle* noted that almost all the characters took a curtain call and 'the author bowed his thanks to the audience from his box.'

St George despatches the champions, St Denis of France, St Anthony of Italy, St James of Spain, St Andrew of Scotland, St David of Wales and St Patrick of Ireland to their native countries specifically to remedy the current political difficulties in each. St Denis proposes to break a lance against the philosophy advocated by the socialists in France ('all property is counted theft') and takes on as squire a French perruquier who declares himself 'tired of equality'. St James of Spain takes on Leporello who expatiates on the state of Spain:

> Spain seems more barbarous than Barbary,
> Kept by her own flies in perpetual blister,
> By turns Christino, Carlist, Progresista,

St Patrick expels the vermin from Ireland which are causing the potato blight.

Charles Mathews once again stole scenes as Charley Wag, taken on as St George's squire. Planché gave him a patter song lamenting the rise of alternative entertainments to the drama: dioramas, cosmoramas, cycloramas, panoramas, art collections with free admission, Italian opera, shilling concerts, poses plastiques, cider cellars, Ethiopian Serenaders, 'Infantine Precocities', and public houses with singing licenses. His final song expressed the hope that each nation will extinguish:

> Every sort of desire to kindle any fire
> Except that of a generous emulation

He ended with:

> I have only to request, as we really have all done our best
> To add to your amusement and edification,
> That when, as I mean, I change to the last scene,
> Which, I think, you will own is a gorgeous decoration,
> You'll be kind enough to say, in your usual good-natured way,
> That the scenery, by Mr Beverley,
> Has been painted very cleverly,
> And that the piece, taken altogether, meets with your full approbation

The Times (10 April 1849) said that 'his dialogue, while it is, as usual, neat and smoothly versified, is more pointed than in most of his productions.' *The Era* (15 April 1849) said:

It is more a spectacle than an extravaganza, and less a burlesque than either. Mr Planché has written a mixture of common sense and smart satire, sprinkled over with puns and *bon mots*, and with a smart dash of ridiculousness in it; but he has avoided burlesque. He has confined himself to the story of the Seven Champions, working it out after his own approved fashion, and so as to introduce remarks that refer to topics of the day. There is so much rationality in what he has written – so much that may be said by Seven Champions in a drama – and so much that hits off the follies of the age in sober seriousness, that the romance of the past and the reality of the present divide the spectators' thoughts; and it is not often that a broad joke or a slangy sentence creates a roar, but the enjoyment is the same. You have more wit than absurdity, and more pointed dialogue than ridiculous drollery. Mr Planché is desirous of elevating burlesque writing to epigrammatical composition, and he succeeds in doing it. His parodies are neatly struck off, and his allusions to 'nationalities', and subjects of public notoriety, are very happy. He goes so far as to moralize, applying his caustic delicately but unmistakeably to many evils, such as Chartism, Agitation, and the like, and he even touches upon national faults and failings. At all of this, the audience laughs goodnaturedly, or smiles in significant silence, broken by an occasional ejaculation or spontaneous clapping of hands.

The Morning Chronicle (10 April 1849) was similarly appreciative. Noting that the story had been told many times before on the stage, it went on:

But MR PLANCHÉ'S exquisite taste, and mingled style of piquancy and elegance, gave to the old materials a degree of novel lustre, which more than made up for their comparative antiquity on the boards. Sparklingly witty, and that wit, not of the slangy, pot-house order, but drawing-room and boudoir-like-terse, elegant and scholarly as all MR PLANCHÉ'S burlesques are – we think that the *Seven Champions* is entitled to take a very high rank, indeed, among its clever compeers. The heroes of the piece, as the representatives of European powers, permitted the introduction of many elegantly-turned allusions to continental politics, some of which rose quite to the level of brilliant epigram – while the idea of making the *Champions*, to a certain extent, the heroes and harbingers of enlightenment and civilization, and warring against ignorance and bigotry, in the form of foul enchanters and potent ogres – threw over the entire production a more elevated tone than we usually look for in pieces of the kind.

Of his 1850 Christmas offering *King Charming or the Blue Bird of Paradise* Planché recorded in 1879 that it could be performed today without alteration, for 'a pretty fairy drama with a regular plot, good situations, and opportunities for acting, will be available as long as a stage exists.'[8] He noted that it ran eighty-four nights, but Charles Mathews had to act King Charming for two months of the run, due to the severe indisposition of Madame Vestris. It was revived later in the season, running a total of 193 nights, but although Madame Vestris resumed the role, her appearances in it were 'erratic' and Charles Mathews often had to take over.

King Charming of the Fan-Sea Islands seeks the hand in marriage of Princess Florina, daughter of King Henpeckt the Hundredth of Cockaine. The King's second wife, Queen Tyrana, tricks Charming into eloping with her ugly daughter, Troutina. When Charming discovers the truth and refuses to marry Troutina, her evil fairy godmother turns Charming into the Blue Bird of Paradise. When the Blue Bird is badly injured, the evil fairy restores him to his normal shape on condition he marries Troutina. But Charming loses his reason and continues to behave like a bird. However, aided by Charming's fairy godmother and three magic swan's eggs, Florina reaches Charming, he recovers his reason and they are married.

The Times (27 December 1850) reported that *King Charming* 'for splendour of decoration and brilliancy of scenic effect, fully equals, if it does not surpass, anything that has yet been produced at this establishment, famous as it is for entertainments of this description.' Noting that Planché follows the original story as closely as 'scenic exigencies would admit', the reviewer praises the dialogue 'thrown into the light and sparkling form of versification, of which M. Planché is so great a master, and is made a vehicle for many humorous and satirical allusions to the prevailing topics of the day.' *The Era* (29 December 1850) also praised the script 'replete with clever allusions, odd yet striking similes, and crammed with puns, like the currants in a Christmas-pudding.'

The Great Exhibition of 1851 directly inspired a dance sequence in the second act. It contained, according to *The Times* (27 December 1850) 'a grand fairy quadrille, gallop, and every country dance – being an industrious exhibition of the steps of all nations.' During the performance a forest of banners, representing the principal nations of the world, was introduced and as each country's particular dance was performed, the corresponding banner was placed centre stage. *The Era* (29 December 1850) noted that the fairies danced the various dances 'with wonderful effect, perpetual variations and untiring energy'. The banners waved 'in delightful union, and were vociferously applauded.' It added that the choreographer Oscar Byrne 'deserves a niche in the Crystal Palace for this industrious Terpsichorean exhibit.'

The Daily News (27 December 1850) began its review by saying:

There are a crowd of people strong in the belief that Christmas would be a dull season without the aid of Mr Planché. What he 'would do this Christmas' has been a favourite enquiry round the fireside of theatre-goers during the past week; - and last night, a crowd that nearly took the check-takers by storm, thronged to the Lyceum to have their expectations satisfied. It may be observed by the way that crowd was, for the Lyceum, an extremely noisy crowd. There is usually so much decorum before the curtain in this house that one was really surprised last night to find a pit that stamped, and stormed, and groaned, and whistled, just as if every member of it had paid toll over the adjacent bridges. However, noisy thought it was, it was a good-humoured crowd. There was only one cry of 'turn him out' during the whole evening.

But *The Daily News* thought the show half an hour too long – suggesting cutting down the ballet, which lasted three quarters of an hour so 'despite excellent dancing, the audience grew quite weary.' Of the script, it said:

Mr Planché as a dramatic writer, is an artist, and this extravaganza is worked out with all his accustomed skill. But it has precisely the same weakness as his Christmas piece of last season, namely, a want of point and piquancy in dialogue. The applause was all awarded to the actors, to the music, the singing, the dancing, the costumes, and above all, the scenery; there were scarcely a dozen 'hits' throughout the piece that told, though the actors strove to point whatever appeared jocular, and the audience certainly did not seem obtuse. Of the construction of the piece, however, and of all that has been done to aid, it is impossible to speak too highly.

The Morning Chronicle (27 December 1850) noted that there were enthusiastic calls for performers and author at the end.

For Planché's final Easter piece for the Lyceum it was decided that in view of the approaching Great Exhibition, which would be attracting hordes of visitors to London:

a brilliantly got-up fairy spectacle, which would appeal to the eye rather than to the ear, would be more acceptable to foreigners than a *Revue* which must naturally be a running commentary on recent Metropolitan events, to which they were utter strangers, and therefore could neither comprehend the allusions to nor take the slightest interest in.

So he deliberately chose Madame d'Aulnoy's *La Grenouille Bienfaisante*, adapted as *The Queen of the Frogs*, which had an interesting but straightforward plot: 'A series of startling and exciting events, the action ... which required no verbal explanation, and numerous opportunities for scenic display and sumptuous decoration.'[9] Queen Dulcibella and Princess Carissima, wife and daughter of King Fulminoso, are captured by the evil fairy Leona. The fairy Grenouilletta, Queen of the Frogs, gives Fulminoso a magic ring to help him free his family. Fulminoso enlists the aid of the Dragon Fee-Fo-Fum with the ring and the Dragon performs the rescue but demands the Princess as his reward. Grenouilletta gives Prince Nonpareil the sword of sharpness, the cap of science, the coat of darkness and the shoes of speed and with the aid of these items, he kills the Dragon and rescues the Princess. Discussion of the visuals duly dominated the reviews. Typically *The Times* (22 April 1851) praised 'the point and neatness' of Planché's whimsical dialogue, his comic allusions and parodies, but added 'No one, however, who witnessed *The Queen of the Frogs* could conceal from himself the fact that the main success of the piece depended upon the scenery and decorations.'

The Christmas piece for 1851–2 was *The Prince of Happy Land or the Fawn in the Forest*, based on Madame d'Aulnoy's *La Biche au Bois*. Prince Felix of Happy Land falls in love with the portrait of Princess Desiderata. She has been kept in a closed tower for twenty years as a result of a spell, cast by the fairy Carabossa, in consequence of an imagined slight, and which will take effect if the light of day shines upon her. Eventually it does and the Princess turns into a white fawn, doomed to be hunted, but returned to normal each sunset. Prince Felix shoots her while out hunting. Carabossa agrees to lift the curse if Felix will marry Princess Nigretta of Ethiopia. Felix and Desiderata prefer to die together. The Fairy Pineapple appears, establishes a court to hear the case and appeals to the audience as the jury. They reunite the lovers. It ran for seventy-nine nights. *The Era* (28 December 1851), calling the show 'another triumph for the Lyceum', praised the script, the critic claiming 'his peculiar talent for this kind of composition has not abated, while his practice has increased' with the story merely a thread 'on which Mr Planché strings his smart jokes and very pleasant puns.' But – the sting in the tail for Planché – the play was 'the medium for introducing some of the most finished and really beautiful scenery that ever was exhibited upon any stage.' The songs, the dances and the finery were praised but the scenery rhapsodized over.

Planché's official connection with the Lyceum ended with the close of the 1851–2 season as he had arranged to live in Kent with his married daughter and her clergyman husband. But he provided the Christmas show, *The Good Woman in the Wood* based on the 'little known but amusing story, *La Bonne Femme* by Mdlle de la Force'. Madame Vestris at fifty-six had decided that 'breeches' roles were now beyond her but Planché fashioned an excellent dame role for her Dame Goldenheart, in a show that opened on 27 December 1852 and ran sixty-five nights. Dame Goldenheart is a noble widow, living in a rural cottage, who has rescued and raised as her own Prince Almond and Princess Olive, the children of King Philbert poisoned by his brother Bruin, and Princess Sylvia, Bruin's stepdaughter. The play consists of the attempts of King Bruin to eliminate the children and the successful efforts of Dame Goldenheart, aided by Fairy Fragrant and her magic, to protect the children.

It may have been an awareness of Planché's imminent departure that prompted some of the critics to deliver encomiums upon the author. *The Era* (2 January 1853) declared:

It is but fair to mention that this veteran punster and rhymester does more than provide the dialogue, for not only is the story prepared and the text set down by him but the scenes are imagined by and sketched from his fertile mind and comparatively but little is done by painter, machinist, decorator, dresser, dancer and musician without his suggestion and subsequent aid. We were among the first to solicit a fair share of applause for the unseen artists who required heads as well as hands for the production of those exquisite works which from time to time charmed the eye, and beguiled the imagination, with such scenes as we expect to find only in books and dreams; but in procuring for them their justly earned meed of praise, we would not deprive the originator of one iota of that to which he is entitled … his rhymes … are … graceful, and pointed, and appropriate, and sometimes witty in the extreme.

The Times (28 December 1852) took the same line:

The comic muse of Planché, easy, playful, and yet elegant, almost to classic grace as it is, would scarcely be appreciated without that perfection of stage embellishment which gives his pieces a home at the Lyceum. On the other hand, though scenic decoration and good acting can do much for a play, it is everything to explore the realms of fancy with one who treads there lightly and airily, whose creations are delicate and gay enough to ride on sunbeams, and who deals with good and evil genii as familiarly as if he had grown old among them … It is a rare gift which enables him to distinguish so nicely the exact boundary line between the ludicrous and the vulgar, which imparts to all his plays a refined expression that never ceases to exert its salutary influence upon the audience. And truly at Christmas time this is much needed, for then the popular craving for amusement is too prone to seek its gratification in the coarsest and broadest representations of the drama in displays that neither charm the fancy, nor engage the mind. It is good to give even the uneducated an opportunity of having something better on boxing night than 'Hot Codlings' and, thought we wish Clown and Pantaloon all the compliments of the season, we think a reasonable preference will be shown by all people of taste for such fairy extravaganzas, so written, so acted, and so put upon the stage as *The Good Woman in the Wood*.

The Examiner (1 January 1853) declared:

The burlesque at the Lyceum … as usual excels every other effort of the season as a spectacle to charm the fancy. It represents a pleasant fairy tale characterized by a great deal of quiet taste in the telling, spiced as usual with puns that are something perhaps below the author's average in pungency, but all very clever as well as very agreeable … Mr Beverley's scenes are beautiful in the extreme, the last being quite unique.

The Daily News (28 December 1852) noted:

Season after season we have had to commend Mr Planché as conspicuous among the
writers of the comic drama for ease and elegance – pleasantry and point. And in *The
Good Woman in the Wood* we have now no falling off to record ... he is still Mr Planché
– a jester upon affairs of the day, with a feeling for the picturesque and poetical, and an
undercurrent of scholarship and literature, which does not confound the gallery, while it
propitiates the boxes and stalls.

A dissident note was expressed by *The Morning Chronicle* (28 December 1853):

Entertainments of this nature have long been so hackneyed that they have ceased to
amuse the public, and the story being in itself flat enough, and devoid of any striking or
attractive features, the piece fell coldly and heavily on the ear of the spectators. The
excellent acting of Mr F. MATTHEWS, in the stock extravaganza character of a fiery-
faced tyrant, probably alone saved it from decisive condemnation.

This is not borne out by reports of the enthusiastic applause from a crowded house,
carried in the other reviews.

Although he had retired to the country and officially severed his connection with
the Lyceum, Planché was prevailed upon to provide one last extravaganza for
Christmas 1853 and wrote *Once Upon a Time There Were Two Kings*, based on
Madame d'Aulnoy's *La Princesse Carpillon*. The action centres on the ruthless
conquistador Brutus the Crooked, eldest son of King Periwigulus of Rumantica. He
conquers the Peaceful Islands and dethrones King Placid and Queen Dominanta,
who seek refuge as shepherds in Verdant Valley. He demands the hand of the
reluctant beauty Capillona, who flees to the Verdant Valley to escape him. There she
finds love with the foundling shepherd boy Corin. Capillona turns out to be the long-
lost daughter of Placid and Dominanta, Corin, the long lost younger son of
Periwigulus. They are all captured and sentenced to be burned at the stake by
Brutus. But the tables are turned with the aid of Fairy Amazona. Brutus is burned
instead, the lovers united and Placid and Dominanta restored to their throne.
Planché had intended to retain the D'Aulnoy title but the re-engagement of James
Bland, the so-called 'King of Extravaganza', who was a popular favourite, and the
engagement of Mr Wright, a comedian who had been obtaining success at the St
James' and the Adelphi Theatres, led Charles Mathews to suggest the new title to
which Planché agreed. Wright failed in the role and was rapidly replaced by Robert
Roxby. But the piece succeeded and ran eighty-seven nights, though Madame Vestris
was sometimes too ill to appear and was replaced by Mrs Frank Matthews, and the
following season Madame retired through ill-health, dying on 8 August 1856.
Planché records that this was the only one of his extravaganzas that he did not see.
    The Era (1 January 1854) reported:

Once Upon a Time There Were Two Kings will detract nothing from the character for profuse liberality and matured taste, discrimination, and judgment, which has distinguished the present management of this theatre. Former productions might be supposed to have exhausted the realms of fancy, and in matters of scenic and decorative brilliancy to have trenched upon the confines of the world of impossibility. But we must confess that, palled and jaded as the appetite may be, there is nothing here that cloys. All is fresh, all is brilliant and piquant, and, what is more, all is *apropos* and to a considerable extent novel. It boots little in the case of fairy extravaganzas to talk of the plot, and, truth to say, these plots are somewhat difficult of unravelment. Still, in this instance there is a plot, and a very appreciable one, which affords ample scope and a fair and legitimate vehicle for all the fun and fancy which hang upon it.

The Era reported:

The mere fable ... is nothing. The piece owes its success to the gorgeous and unequalled scenery, the magnificent and priceless mounting, the chaste, elegant, and classic writing of Planché, the admirable acting of everyone concerned, and the many clever parodies and musical imitations with which it abounds.

But once again it was Beverley's contribution that was lauded. Professor Henry Morley in *The Examiner* (31 December 1853) praised Planché for avoiding almost entirely political allusions:

for we cannot perceive any connection between corn laws, foreign wars, cab strikes and fairy land; and it is quite right that Mr Planché should deny practically their existence. Allusions to current events are the life of a pantomime, but they are the death of a fairy spectacle, presented in good, earnest fairy style.

The Morning Chronicle (27 December 1853) while praising the costumes, the acting and the scenery, complained about the length (two hours, which coming after the comedy *Bachelor of Arts* meant a midnight finish) and suggested cutting the ballet 'which is nothing but legs, muslin garlands and inanity' to shorten the running time. It also had harsh words for Planché's script:

There is no scope for acting. MR WRIGHT had not a comic situation – neither had anybody else; while the dialogue, though studded with artificial and ingenious puns, and written with MR PLANCHÉ'S accustomed elegance, could not support characters without interest, and incidents so old, threadbare and inevitable that the audience saw them with perfect indifference. There was not a 'hit' at passing matters – formerly the cream of a spectacle in two long acts – and not a dramatic situation from beginning to end.

12. *Making the masks and Big Heads for the performances in the opening*

13. *Scene-painting and set-building for the pantomime*

14. Dressing the Fairy

The Daily News (27 December 1853) took an entirely different view opening its review by praising Planché:

> who succeeds better than anyone else has ever done, in clothing the old, graceful fairy tales which he takes for his subject, with a dress at once quaint and elegant, and in preserving their romantic interest while mixing it up with grotesque extravagance ... *Once Upon a Time There Were Two Kings* ... is certainly one of the prettiest things of the kind that can be imagined – a delightful melange of amusing incident, dialogue sparkling with wit and humour, agreeable music, and brilliant and beautiful spectacle.

It noted perceptively:

> A piece of this kind requires as good acting as a regular drama. On the part of the performers there must be no appearance of intentional extravagance. To make burlesque really effective, it must have all the semblance of being entirely in earnest; and, to do justice to humour such as Mr Planché's, great refinement and discrimination are demanded. Of this the Lyceum actors seem fully aware – they have learned it by long experience.

The critic praised Frank Matthews, Madame Vestris, Mr Wright and Julia St George. The review ended: 'But after all, the most remarkable feature of this piece is probably its wonderful splendour and beauty as a spectacle.'

Departure from the Lyceum did not mean retirement from Christmas writing. Planché provided the 1853–4 pantomime *Harlequin and King Nutcracker or The*

World of Toys for the Strand Theatre. Critics commented on the fact that the narrow stage and limited space of the theatre, not apparently suitable for pantomime, had been overcome successfully with the help of the clown Flexmore and an expert harlequinade company. *The Standard* (29 December 1853) reported:

> The opening of the pantomime is by Planché, who has made an adaptation of a nursery tale by Hoffmann, which he entitles *King Nutcracker or The World of Toys*. The moral is sanitary. The spirit Malaria is one of the principal personages. The mischief occasioned by this popular demon is stayed by the Fairy Abernethia, who restores a sick child to health which has been periled by bad drains and worse ventilation, and transports him to Toyland … The arrival of King Nutcracker leads to some amusing parades of *infantry*, immediately prefacing the harlequinade, the precise connection of which with the extravaganza proem it would indeed be hard to discern. The latter, however, being by so dexterous a writer as Planché, is vastly superior to the ordinary run of such productions. Its allusions to the apathy of the authorities as regards sanitary measures are strokes of satire as neat as they are timely.

Timely it was, as 1853–4 saw London in the grip of a cholera epidemic which killed 11,661 Londoners. This was only the latest of a series of such epidemics, the results of the wholly inadequate drainage and sewerage systems, polluted water supply and the role of the River Thames as in effect an open sewer.

The Era (1 January 1854) thought that the pantomime's *raison d'être* was Richard Flexmore the Clown.

> The pantomime is … Flexmore, for upon him thenceforth everything depends. Never still for an instant; now spinning like a top, now bounding like a ball, or trundling himself along like a hoop, he is at once the personification of a whole world of toys. His imitation of the equestrian performances in the ring is very funny, and has the rare peculiarity of being entirely novel. The song and mimic reproductions of the Clown in the Grimaldi style, and the Clown who does the posturing, and Clown who exhibits trained animals, will also be found equally illustrative of his comic powers and wondrous versatility.

Bell's Life in London (1 January 1854) thought the opening lacked the essential ingredient, fun, and only became funny when Flexmore and the pantomimists took over. *The Morning Chronicle* (27 December 1853) elaborated on the plot. Dame Reinhold is nursing a sick child, young Reinhold. But the boy is visited by the Spirit Malaria who 'bestows some severe and well-merited sarcasms upon the negligence and apathy of the public and their rulers' in sanitation matters. The Fairy Abernethia, perpetual chairwoman of the Industry and Good Health Insurance Company, and guardian spirit of all good boys, rescues young Reinhold and transports him to Toyland. King Nutcracker pays a state visit to Toyland with his court, reviews his infantry and cavalry, 'who meet with a misfortune from the violence of the wind.' The artillery is summoned but being out on strike, only Monsieur Bonbon appears and at the King's command fires a gun loaded with lollipops and brandyballs at the juvenile inhabitants of Toyland, to their great joy. Fairy Abernethia calls forth the pantomimists to perform the harlequinade. They 'kept the audience in roars of laughter for a long period.' The critic declared:

> The dialogue of the introductory portion of the piece was sharply written, witty and effective, abounding with numerous political hits. It was well supported by the performers, whose acting, and the greater portion by far of them were children, drew forth loud and continuous praise from the audience. The pantomimic conclusion revealed a great falling off from the anticipations which the previous part had raised. It had nothing in itself, either novel or striking, to recommend it, and such, being the case, it was considerably too long.

The critic conceded, however, that it was well received by the audience mainly owing to the unrivalled dexterity of Flexmore. 'The scenery, which was well painted and appropriate, was magnificently got up.'

Planché meanwhile was providing the extravaganzas for Alfred Wigan at the Olympic and they gave him the satisfaction of not having to play second fiddle to the scene-painting. As he wrote of those one-act Olympic pieces:

> In all these pieces I had once more to rely upon acting rather than upon – scene – painting ... Mr Robson being my *deus ex machina* at the Olympic left me nothing to desire in his admirable impersonations of the Dwarf, Prince Richcraft, and Zephyr, in my last three fairy extravaganzas.[10]

He noted that in the travesties of *Macbeth* and *The Merchant of Venice* and as Desmarets in Tom Taylor's *Plot and Passion*, Robson had 'established himself in the front rank of the profession as an actor possessing the rare gifts of genius as well as natural humour and general histrionic ability. His premature decease was a serious loss to the stage, which can ill afford to lose a great and original artist.'[11]

Contemporary theatre historian Barton Baker wrote in 1889:

> Robson was a great genius; who that saw him when in the full possession of his powers can ever forget the strange-looking little man with the small body and the big head who played upon his audience as though they had been the keys of a piano, now convulsing them with laughter as he perpetrated some outrageous drollery, now hushing them into awe-struck silence by an electrical burst of passion or pathos, or holding them midway between terror and laughter as he performed some weirdly grotesque dance? The impression he conveyed in those moments of extreme tension was that of a man overwrought by excitement to the verge of madness; the wild, gleaming eyes, the nervous twitching of the marvellously plastic features, the utter abandon to the feeling of the

moment, whether it were tragic or grotesque, the instantaneous transition from the tragedian to the clown, were no stage tricks, but an inspiration, an irrepressible impulse.[12]

But 'morbidly timorous and nervous', a prey to chronic stage-fright and the haunting fear that his fall would be as rapid as his rise, he took to drink to fortify him for his appearances and died in 1864 at the early age of forty-three.

Robson had appeared while at the Queen's Theatre, Dublin, between 1850 and 1853 in productions of Planché's *Theseus and Ariadne*, *King Charming*, *The Sleeping Beauty in the Wood* and *The Prince of Happy Land*. Brought by William Farren to the Olympic, he had created a sensation in two Francis Talfourd burlesques, *Macbeth* and *Shylock or The Merchant of Venice Preserv'd*, playing Macbeth as a red-headed Scottish militia sergeant and Shylock as a Jewish old-clothes seller from Houndsditch. *The Observer* (1 May 1853) noted that his Macbeth was an 'original creation' and that Robson belonged to 'no recognised school of burlesque acting'. He remained at the Olympic when Alfred Wigan took over the management and triumphed in the straight role of the shabby little spy Desmarets in *Plot and Passion*.[13]

Planché turned again to Madame d'Aulnoy for *The Yellow Dwarf*, which the critics noted he had followed faithfully, apart from providing a happy ending in which the lovers, turned into a pair of palm trees, are brought back to life by the benevolent mermaid Syrena. Robson created a huge effect on his audience. As an 1854 oil painting confirms, his appearance was striking: he was the Yellow Dwarf to the life, his makeup reminding more than one critic of the malignant dwarf crouched over the swooning maiden in Fuseli's *The Nightmare* (1781), but there are also echoes of Blake's yellow demon in *The Ghost of a Flea* (1819–20).[14]

It was very much a star vehicle, *The Times* (27 December 1854) reporting:

Those striking situations which sometimes produce so much effect, and cause such wonder in a fairy extravaganza do not abound in the *Yellow Dwarf*; and hence there are some scenes so flat that, with respect to them, any amount of curtailment would be desirable. These are the scenes in which the dwarf himself does not appear, for whenever he was visible, the admirable acting of Mr F.W. Robson kept the audience in a tumult of delight. Accurately measuring the powers of that most peculiar and deservedly popular actor, Mr Planché has made the Yellow Dwarf a decidedly tragic part, in which fiendish malignity is contrasted with intensity of passion. Into this combination Mr Robson enters with all his heart and soul, and while his minute figure – yellow from head to foot – is that of a demon … the varieties of love, exultation and spite into which his countenance passes endow him with a human interest. … the verses with which he concluded the piece, to the tune of 'Villikins and his Dinah' brought down the curtain with a roar of applause, and this success on the part of the actor was the more valuable as some of the scenes in the piece had elicited a few sounds of disapprobation.

The introduction of the old ballad *Villikins* had been a masterstroke, for Robson had sung it as a down-at-heel musician Jem Bags in a revival of Henry Mayhew's farce *The Wandering Minstrel* in 1853 and it had brought the house down and had been in constant demand since. After Robson took his curtain call, there were cries of 'author' and Mr F. Vining had to appear to announce that Mr Planché was not present.

Doubtless Planché would have gained further satisfaction from the report in *The Times* that confirmed that text and performances had not been overwhelmed by the scenery:

> Without aiming at the decidedly grand spectacle, the manager of the Olympic has done a great deal for the Christmas entertainment. The costumes are gorgeous and fanciful throughout, the scenery is generally light and picturesque, and a transformation from the exterior of the dwarf's dwelling to the Royal Palace was executed with a degree of neatness and rapidity that excited universal applause.

The settings got little more mention in other reviews, the scene-painter was not named and the bulk of the reviews concentrated on story and performance.

The Era (31 December 1854) declared:

> The burlesque, which has the advantage of being in one act, is written with the same neatness and facility of versification by which all the author's previous productions have been so prominently distinguished. Here and there we may detect a pun more far-fetched than ordinary, or a joke more broadly elaborated than usual, but the skill of this eminent 'artist in words' is as clearly and as constantly perceptible as ever, and if the satire is less keen, or the wit less pungent than usual, we may fairly ascribe it to the paucity of topics on which to hang a comment, and the gradual exhaustion of those stores of puns which have been so mercilessly ransacked by our modern scribes.

The Examiner (30 December 1854) said:

> As a piece – on the score of literary merit – Mr Planché's *Yellow Dwarf* is more complete than any other holiday performance, and Mr Robson's Yellow Dwarf we should take to be the best specimen now to be seen of burlesque acting. The fairy drama has been set upon the stage, not indeed with the splendour of Lyceum scenery, but in a careful and agreeable way, with enough sparkle to please young people, and enough good taste to satisfy their elders.

The Daily News (27 December 1854) praised the script: '"The quality of joking was not strained" but all was fitness and genial humour. The house went along with the author heartily; not a point was missed.' *John Bull* (30 December 1854) similarly noted of Planché, 'his burlesque is full of grotesque humour, without the slightest tinge of vulgarity. The dialogue sparkles with true and polished wit; and the allusions are so pointed and happy that scarcely one of them was lost upon the audience' and that Robson's was 'a most artistic performance worthy of this extraordinary and original actor'. *The Yellow Dwarf* ran for five months and Robson later played it in Birmingham and Dublin.

The next year Planché turned to Charles Perrault for *The Discreet Princess or The Three Glass Distaffs* (1855–6). He acknowledged that in Robson he had the perfect actor for the embittered and deformed Prince Richcraft, geared the script to his particular talent and was rewarded with a run of 105 nights. The villainous Richcraft tries to carry off the three princesses confined to a tower by their father King Gander when he goes off to war. *The Times* (27 December 1855) reported:

> Mr Planché's version of this pleasant story is replete with points and parodies. Most of the leading incidents of the day are alluded to in a quaint and telling way, and many of the popular airs of the time are cleverly paraphrased. Music of a higher order is also plentifully interspersed and many of the most celebrated scenes of Shakespeare are admirably parodied. Messrs [John] Gray and [Hawes] Craven have produced much beautiful scenery, and the concluding scene in Fairy Land is of so gorgeous a character that it would be difficult to surpass it. The dresses and appointment are elegant and unique ... Mr Robson played the part of Prince Richcraft with marvellous skill, and displayed those powers of combined tragedy and comedy which he exhibited in so marked a degree in *The Yellow Dwarf*, and which have stamped him as an actor in this particular line as unapproachable and *sui generis* ... The piece met with unqualified approbation. The curtain rose a second time upon the last scene and Mr Robson and the author were loudly called for.

The Era (30 December 1855) reported of Robson that it was his character on which the interest of the piece depended:

> The marvellous acting of Mr Robson, to whom this part is allotted, must alone command success. His singing of a parody of the 'Ratcatcher's Daughter' convulsed the house with laughter. The travestie of Hamlet's ghost scene, and the pantomimic exit, after his interview ... with his brother, was one of the drollest achievements we ever witnessed. His raving soliloquies, after he has been rolled down a rock inside a barrel, and all the subsequent representations of a maddened brain, riveted the attention of the audience, and excited general bursts of laughter. The genuine broad humour of the clever actor was nevertheless toned down ... by the exercise of discretion. The part assigned to Mr Robson is in itself of a character out of the ordinary range of those which distinguish extravaganzas, and we may be permitted to doubt whether any other individual could delineate it with the same sterling effect.

Intriguingly *The Era* recorded: '"Boxing Night" audiences are proverbially noisy and turbulent, but on this occasion the company here was of a very different character – the stalls and boxes being filled with elegant company.' This is perhaps not surprising when you realize that Robson was a favourite of Queen Victoria who several times braved the mean streets in which the Olympic was situated to see his performances as well as summoning him to Windsor Castle for command performances.

Planché's last Olympic extravaganza was *Young and Handsome*, based on a story by the Countess de Murat, *Jeune et Belle*. The story has the jealous witch Mordicanta seeking to separate the lovers Princess Young and Handsome and the shepherd Alidor, first aided and then thwarted by the aery spirit Zephyr. Planché recalled:

> The wholesome lesson conveyed in the punishment of the thoughtless Zephyr, who, discontented with his happy, ethereal existence, desired to exchange it for that of a mortal, and having obtained his wish, finds himself burdened and tormented by all the perils and 'ills that flesh is heir to', has the special advantage of being so ingeniously told that though the subtlety of the satire may escape observation, the fun of the situation is broad enough to amuse the large majority of readers or spectators who are 'pleased, they know not why, and care not wherefore'. I consequently felt that I might indulge my constant desire to elevate the character of Extravaganza without running the risk of failure from a non-appreciation by the audience of the deeper meaning of the subject.

He was also keenly aware of the need to tailor it to Robson's abilities.

> In Mr Robson I had an actor whose drollery was irresistible, while his refined taste and keen sense of the poetic side of a composition rendered him the most valuable representative of the part that I could have found in the whole profession.

But sadly soon after the opening Robson 'was suddenly attacked by a serious complaint to which he was unfortunately subject, and compelled to give up the part; and though after a short period he resumed it, he was never again, during the season, equal to the exertion which the continual dancing required.'[15] So the piece was withdrawn after seventy nights.

The *I.L.N.* (3 January 1857) noted that 'the piece has not all the force, but it has more than the usual elegance, of Mr Planché's former extravaganzas and depends not so much on its appeals to our risibility as to our good taste.' This resulted from the decision to give the piece in costume and setting the appearance of a Watteau painting, an idea, according to *The Times* (27 December 1856) 'very gracefully carried out.' The *I.L.N.* thought 'the scenery is very exquisitely painted, and the costumes are some of the prettiest we ever witnessed.' But as before the reviews concentrated on Robson's performance. The *I.L.N.* noted that as Zephyr:

> Mr Robson appears in a new character ... in which there is no call on the actor's tragic extravagance but a peculiar lightness of manner is demanded, which, in the abundant comprehensiveness of his genius, this excellent performer is at no loss to supply. Both as

a sprite and a fop ... His *Zephyr* was throughout a piece of Watteau art, and fluttered through all the intricacies of pastoral courtship with infinite grace until, all perils past, the happy shepherd and his bride are united in the 'Porcelain Pavilion'.

The Times noted that the 'passionate abandonment' with which he danced a *pas de fascination* with Princess Young and Handsome 'could not be excelled, and well merited the hearty *encore* that it received.' At the end the star, though not the author, was called.

King Christmas (1871), Planché's last extravaganza, was something of an oddity. It originated in several pieces devised for private parlour performance. The first, 'The Compliments of the Season' was written at the request of Charles Mathews in 1867 for him and his stepson to perform for a gathering of friends at his house in Pelham Crescent, Brompton. Planché composed what he called a 'masque' in which he himself played the Old Year, Charles Mathews, Christmas and William Mathews, the New Year. On a visit to Cornwall in 1868 he amused himself writing two similar pieces, 'Stirring the Pudding' and 'The King of the Bean' and returning to London, published all three masques as 'Pieces of Pleasantry for Private Performance', dedicating them to Lady Molesworth, at whose country seat he had written them. Then in 1871, Mrs German Reed asked him to produce something for Christmas for the Gallery of Illustration, the establishment for genteel entertainments which she ran with her husband. So Planché amalgamated the three pieces as *King Christmas*, describing it as a 'fancy-full morality', and it was first performed at the Gallery of Illustration, Regent Street on 26 December 1871.

It is somehow symbolic that the final Planché extravaganza should have been staged at so quintessentially middle-class an institution as the Gallery of Illustration. Sir Frank Burnand who also wrote for it, recalled in his autobiography:

'The Gallery of Illustration' was at one time 'an institution'. Thither that considerable section of the public which loves theatricals and yet will not, on principle, set foot within a theatre, found the *via media* provided for them by Mr and Mrs German Reed's entertainment. It was a vastly clever idea.

German Reed, 'a thoroughly capable musician, a fair composer and excellent pianist, for some time conductor of orchestras in many of our principal theatres ... and a good businessman as well,' had married Priscilla Horton, an actress and singer who had starred in Planché's extravaganzas at the Haymarket Theatre in the 1840s.

This couple, breaking with the theatre, started the sort of 'entertainment' which would find enthusiastic and paying patrons among that non-theatre-going portion of the public which was becoming tired of scientific lectures, dissolving views, panoramas, and conjurers.

Essentially they provided 'pocket-musical-comedies' in an elegant drawing-room setting giving the idea 'that you were attending a meeting and nothing in any way resembling a theatre.'[16] The German Reed entertainments ran in a variety of locations – but most notably the Gallery of Illustration in Lower Regent Street – from 1855 to 1895. *The Daily News* (27 December 1871) reported: 'Those who omit to visit the Gallery of Illustration this season will have themselves to blame for missing an unusually clever and amusing entertainment.' The critic claimed that Planché was:

> really seen at his best. None of his extravaganzas at the Lyceum, in the famous Vestris days, were written with more delicacy, neatness, and point ... The charm of the work ... lies in its dialogue. Mr Planché is no mere punster. His lines embody something more than verbal conceits. There are ideas in them – ideas gracefully and wittily expressed, which would fly over the heads of many theatrical audiences, but which certainly meet with due appreciation at the Gallery of Illustration. Allusions to topics of the day, of course, abounded, and never missed their mark.

Bell's Life in London (30 December 1871) noted that 'the elegance of this graceful trifle makes itself felt in every line. The wit is without slang, the humour without coarseness and the action, small as it is, full of interest.'

The report in *The Era* (31 December 1871) makes it clear that it was above all a genial, genteel and nostalgic piece, which opened with Mrs German Reed in full evening dress as the 'Genius of the Drawing Room' ('the appointments surrounding her display her taste and judgement to the greatest advantage'). Home for the holiday, she wishes to make everyone as happy as possible ('a faculty which we need hardly say Mrs German Reed possesses to no common degree'). She also makes clear her nostalgia for the old Christmases:

> I'm an old-fashioned genius, I confess, –
> Although folk mightn't think so by my dress; –
> And like the genial, generous, hearty way,
> England kept Christmas in the olden day.
> When the boar's head was brought with garland crown'd,
> And the rich wassail bowl went gaily round.
> The bowl's bowl'd out – the fine old spirit fled,
> And left us but the bore without a head.
> Still, there are spirits whom I might invoke;
> Choice spirits, too – not too refined to joke;
> And it is just the witching time of night,
> When, at my bidding, many a tricksy sprite,
> A Christmas gambol would rejoice to play,
> And make with merry mortals holiday.

The spirits of Good Humour, Good Fun and Good Cheer all appear in full evening dress, apologizing that they are not in spangled tunics with gauze wings, blaming the current rage for realism in the theatre. 'The Genius of the Drawing Room' compliments them on maintaining the habits of gentlemen. They decide to mix the Christmas pudding and put in the ingredients in a parody of the witches' incantation from *Macbeth*. Care appears reminding the spirits that there are many with heavy bills to pay and no money; many others who are starving. The three spirits combine to sing 'Begone, dull care'. But King Christmas then appears, announcing that his mission is to cheer people up. Asked by Care why he comes but once a year, he replies:

> To set a good example which I'd fain
> All folks would follow till I come again.
> Tonight begins my brief reign of hilarity;
> But my chief mission and delight is charity!
> To feed the hungry – cause the hearts to glow
> Of those who shiver, houseless, in the snow;
> Find feuds forgotten, bid detraction cease,
> And all the world enjoy my Christmas *piece*

Christmas then sings 'Cheer, Boys, Cheer' including the lines:

> Revel, ye rich, but let your poorer brothers
> Share in the goods by Fortune on you thrown

The Old Year appears complaining that although he is only twelve months old he feels decrepit. Then the New Year appears jumping about excitedly, as 1872 is a leap year. Fancy appears and is asked to be the medium of communication with the spirits and they hold a séance to summon the spirit of Old Moore, the astrologer and Almanac compiler, and he predicts a series of comically ambiguous events for the coming year. Fancy then suggests winding up the season with private theatricals and a medieval masque 'Twelfth Night Years Ago'. The Lord of Misrule appears and sings a lengthy evocation of the old Christmas in Merrie England. Old England appears in Elizabethan costume accompanied by Young England in knickerbockers and velvet jacket smoking a cigar and Old England sings to the tune of 'A Fine Old English Gentleman' a song delivered with a mournful gravity, 'A Fine Young English Gentleman' gently mocking the young man's dedication to change and progress and use of modern slang. It was the hit of the show and encored at the audience's demand. The Christmas cake is cut up and Young England gets the bean and is crowned King of the Bean. Everyone drinks a toast to their next merry meeting.

The Era warmly welcomed Planché's return to the stage:

the name of Mr Planché carries us back to the 'good old times' of extravaganza, when, in conjunction with Madame Vestris, the Lyceum theatre became the very fairy home of refined burlesque, in which wit the most brilliant and fancy the most exquisite had full scope, being delivered in such a manner that no joke ever lost its point in the telling, and no fancy or whimsical conceit was ever clouded by the uncultivated brain or untutored tongue of its narrator. Mr Planché appeared to handle the innocent myths of childhood almost reverently, and so far from spoiling them his delicate manipulation frequently brought out their hidden charms, so that children lost nothing, and children of a larger growth frequently gained by the process. That Mr Planché has not lost his old faculty for writing graceful and polished metres might have been discovered by paying a visit on Tuesday to the Gallery of Illustration where *King Christmas* ... written by that gentleman for Mrs German Reed and her clever little company, was produced with the greatest success.

Throughout their existence as genres the extravaganza and burlesque were characterized by topical references – to products, personalities, shops, novelties, political developments, London landmarks and sensations of the day. *The Deep, Deep Sea* (1833) alluded to lithographs, a form of illustration, popular in the caricature magazines of the 1820s and 1830s, the Court of Chancery, Barclay's Double Stout, Cowes Regatta, Lemprière's Classical Dictionary and John Loudun Macadam (who 'macadamized' the roads). *Telemachus* (1834) referenced curry, India-rubber cloaks, penny magazines, temperance societies, hunting to hounds, the grammarian Lindley Murray and the drink sellers Hodge and Thompson. *The Invisible Prince* (1846) contained references to Lord Rosse's telescope, perfected in 1845; penny steamboats, first introduced in 1845; Captain Warner's long-range cannon; Madam Wharton's *poses plastiques* in Leicester Square (shows of semi-naked females in classical poses); Baring's and Rothschild's banks; martello towers; and steam-engines. *Fortunio and His Seven Gifted Servants* (1843) referred to Pickford's removal vans, Duff Gordon Sherry, Tariff (i.e., cheap imported) Beef, the Corn Laws, special trains, the writer Samuel Lover, Tattersalls the sporting club, Van Amburgh and Carter the lion-tamers. *The Fair One with the Golden Locks* (1843) referenced hansom cabs, Punch's Pocket Book, Allsop's Pale Ale and the celebrated auctioneer George Robins. *Graciosa and Percinet* (1844) referenced Rowland Hill and the penny post, introduced in 1839; the new Thames Tunnel, opened in 1843; Chubb's locks; the fashionable venue Almack's assembly rooms and Flint's West End emporium. One significant regular subject of reference was upmarket shops, another clue to the dress and interests of the audience. For example, *The Sleeping Beauty in the Wood* (1840) referenced the Bond Street Jewellers Storr and Mortimer and Rundell and Bridges, the makers of plate, and *The Fair One with the Gold Locks* (1843), Howell and James Regent Street Store.

The King of the Peacocks (1848) opened with a direct reference to the 1848 Revolution and the ousting of the French monarchy. Fairy Faithful and Fairy Fickle appeared in the Pleasure Gardens and Chateau de la Beauté in the Verdant Valley and Fairy Faithful reported that 'the silly Elves' demanded a constitution, King Oberon fought for 'Fancy's absolute dominion' but faced by revolution, backed by science, fled with Titania, leaving nothing but 'anarchy and wild confusion'.

> The Empire of the Fairies is no more –
> Reason has banished them from ev'ry shore;
> Steam has outstripped their dragons and their cars;
> Gas has eclipsed their glow-worms and their stars.
> Robbed of the legends of their golden age,
> Mortals make sport of them upon the stage;
> And all poetry of ancient times
> Profane by paltry puns and doggerel rhymes

But Fairy Fickle welcomes change and novelty.

> For musty codes I've not the least compassion;
> Let me be anything – but out of fashion ...
> I'm for the new lights of this wondrous age –
> No Fairy-land – except upon the stage!

Faithful replies:

> In my allegiance I will falter never!
> King Oberon and Fairy-land for ever!

In *The King of the Peacocks* the dialogue contains allusions to Bradshaw's Railway Guide first published in 1841, Dr Arnott's Water Bed, a Sea Serpent (who is off to dine with the First Lord of the Admiralty), the maritime heroine Grace Darling among other contemporary allusions. There is a comical French chef, Soyez Tranquille, made up to resemble the celebrated chef of the Reform Club, Alexis Soyer, and played by Charles Selby who specialized in comic Frenchmen. The use of the Chinese Junk was highly topical; the ship (the three-masted *Keying*) had arrived in England in March 1848, the first such vessel to round the Cape of Good Hope. Dickens reported on it in *The Examiner* (24 June 1848).[17] The *I.L.N.* (20 May 1848) reported that the Queen and Prince Albert had visited it, 'this promises to be one of the most popular exhibitions of our metropolis for some time to come; it is certainly one of the most rational objects of curiosity that has ever been brought to our shores.'

The Queen of the Frogs (1851) contains references to Alexis Soyer the chef, the Regent's Park Menagerie, Parr's Pills, Van Amburgh the lion-tamer, the Great Exhibition, Bow Church Steeple, the railways and the large-scale model of the globe in Leicester Square. The ferocity of reviews in *Blackwood's Magazine* was referred to in *Once Upon a Time There Were Two Kings* (1853). It is this immediacy of reference which made revivals so difficult and makes much of the content incomprehensible today.

Hall and Macintosh plausibly suggest that it was the mid-Victorian debate about divorce and child custody that inspired the sudden and dramatic upsurge in plays about Medea between the 1850s and the 1870s, plays of all kinds (tragedy, burlesque and spectacle). No single Greek tragedy had ever produced so many versions in the space of a few years at any other period between 1660 and 1914. While specifically focusing on the restrictive divorce legislation and the limited rights of women, in general these plays prefigure the 'New Woman' dramas of the late nineteenth century. Medea plays disappeared after the early 1880s when the law was properly reformed to extend the rights of divorced women.[18]

Planché's *The Golden Fleece* (1845) was the first important version. In part 1, Jason gains the Golden Fleece with the aid of Medea after overcoming wild bulls and a dragon. Part 2 finds Jason and Medea in Corinth where he is neglecting her and their children in favour of his new mistress Glauce. Medea sings a song describing her neglect in entirely contemporary terms:

> He leaves me to darn his stockings, and mope in the house all day,
> While he treats her to see 'Antigone', with a box at the Grecian play,
> Then he goes off to sup with Corinthian Tom, or whoever he meets by the way,
> And staggers home in a state of beer, like (I'm quite ashamed to say)
> A fine young Grecian gentleman,
> One of the classic time.
> Then his head aches all the next day, and he calls the children a plague and a curse
> And makes a jest of my misery, and says, 'I took him for better or worse;'
> And if I venture to grumble, he talks, as a matter of course,
> Of going to modern Athens, and getting a Scotch divorce.
> Like a base young Grecian gentleman,
> One of the classic time.

The Chorus declares: 'All decent people sure your side must be on.' But Creon appears with a new bill which will banish her. Jason proposes a deed of separation, promising to settle something handsome on the boys. Medea agrees but sends a ring and mantle to Creon and his daughter which burn them to ashes when they put them on. Rather than kill her children as she does in the Euripides play, she pretends to flog them and then flies off with them in a chariot drawn by two fiery dragons, intending to enrol the boys in a Greek grammar school. She and Jason then appeal to the audience as the jury as to whether they will be allowed to stay in the theatre.

One of the purposes of the extravaganzas was evidently to reconcile the audiences to the inexorable march of progress. In *Riquet with the Tuft*, Princess Emeralda hymns progress:

> The dream of other days has faded,
> Its misty clouds are past –
> My path too long by folly shaded,
> Is clear and bright at last!
> The sun of reason o'er it rising,
> Sheds forth its cheering rays,
> And my mind the new born splendour prizing,
> Makes light of other days!
> The world itself they say is bright'ning,
> An age of darkness flies,
> The torch of knowledge fast as light'ning,
> O'er earth and ocean hies!

Modern modes of transport figured regularly, their efficiency underlined by the incongruity of their presence in the Ancient World of the classical burlesques and the medieval setting of the fairy extravaganzas. In *Olympic Revels*, the goddess Juno is pressing for the introduction of a railway to Olympus to speed up deliveries. In *The Paphian Bower* the muses arrive to visit Venus by omnibus. In *Telemachus* the eponymous hero escapes from Calypso's island by iron-build Mediterranean steamer. *The Bee and the Orange Tree* (1845) is constructed entirely around the current 'Railway Mania'. The Ogre Ravagio is first seen hunting the moors for and devouring railway surveyors and engineers who are swarming over the country in large numbers. The hero Prince Amiable sings a song in praise of rail travel:

> Hurrah! The old slow coach is gone!
> Hurrah! For the engine's power,
> That along the rail will waft us soon
> At a thousand miles an hour!
> With eyes of fire see the monsters fleet
> Come panting through every vale,
> Whilst the whistle shrill afar we greet –
> Then hurrah! Hurrah for the rail!

But along with the satire on 'Railway Mania', there is some sharp social comment appropriate to the mood of 'The Hungry Forties'. Ravagio the Ogre enters singing a song – 'I am an Ogre I beg to say' – in which he claims to be no worse than those humans who exploit their fellow men:

Who lives on his neighbours is sure to live well,

What sharper, or swindler, or usurping Jew,

But lives much the same as the Ogres do.

He who plunders an orphan child,

Mightn't he just as well eat him *broiled*?

He who robs his neighbour of bread,

Had better have swallowed him whole instead.

The sempstress wasted by slow decay,

Has her bones picked in another way;

To the weary weaver with sleep o'ercome,

The factory bell sounds like 'Fee Fo Fum'.

How many who swagger this wide world through

Might just as well be called Ogres too!

Yes, I maintain, Ogres are less to blame

Than many persons I decline to name.

To eat up man and wife is far less cruel

Than to let 'em starve apart on water gruel!

And better swallow infants, fast as pills,

Then grind their bones to dust in cotton mills

And when we think of surplus population,

An Ogre's quite a blessing to the nation!

This contains tilts at conditions in the work house, ruthless factory owners, the exploitation of seamstresses as sensationally highlighted in Thomas Hood's 1843 poem 'The Song of the Shirt' and at the Malthusian interpretation of population growth.

When hero and heroine are turned into a bee and an orange tree, they are restored to normal by the Fairy Trufio, now a director of the New Grand Atmospheric Fairy Land Direct Railway, who arrives by the down line to open the new Bee and Orange Station. The story ends with the Ogre finding that the train can outstrip his seven league boots, and so he becomes chairman of the Grand Bubble and Squeak Amalgamated Railway and is drumming up support in parliament for its construction. It is the antithesis of Ruskin's celebration of Fairyland as the pastoral alternative to the industrial age. But it suggests that the progress linked to modernity might eliminate some of the social evils listed in Ravagio's song.

The level of cultural reference required to make sense of the extravaganzas was quite significant. *Telemachus* opened with a parody of the scene in Lord Byron's metaphysical drama *Manfred* in which he invokes the spirits of the universe – Calypso summons the spirits of brandy, rum, gin and whisky to give her consolation. The hit of *Theseus and Ariadne* (1848) was a Gilbertian patter song in which Charles

Mathews as Daedalus gave an account of a dream in which classical and modern figures were mixed up together. So Hannibal, Cato, Plato, Dido and Julius Caesar rubbed shoulders with Prime Minister Lord John Russell, the international adventuress Lola Montes, Lord Chancellor Lord Brougham, Prince Poniatowski, the Egyptologist Giovanni Battista Belzoni, the theatrical impresario Alfred Bunn and the Moroccan bandit Abd-el-Kader.

The Golden Fleece (1845) was inspired by the 'sensational success' of the performance of Euripides' Antigone in the Greek manner at Covent Garden. Planché said that he could not resist the temptation to burlesque 'not the sublime poetry of the Greek dramatist, I should have deemed it profanation – but the modus operandi of that classical period, which really illustrates the old proverbial observation that there is but one step from the sublime to the ridiculous.'[19] But since the humour depended in part on knowledge of ancient Greek theatrical conventions, The Times (25 March 1845), declaring The Golden Fleece 'one of Mr Planché's best pieces', warned 'If it does not prove so popular as some of his others, it will simply be because it requires more cultivation and knowledge on the part of the audience.' The Standard (25 March 1845) thought it 'scarcely one of the author's happiest efforts' but noted 'Nevertheless it was well-received and kept the audience in good humour.' However, the critic reported that while boxes and pit were crowded, the galleries had but comparatively few occupants.

References to contemporary musicians then in vogue in London, in Olympic Devils (1831) suggests a musically well-informed audience, as Orpheus sings in Hades:

> Oh! I on earth am famed for fiddling,
> I play concertos on a single string!
> Than Paganini, ah,
> Or Ole Bull far better,
> Mori, Cramer, Kiesewetter,
> Seem to me – La, la!
> But not alone upon the violin,
> I know the way to take the people in,
> On piano, harp, guitar,
> Than Hummel, Bochsa, Juli –
> O Regondi – I am truly
> Far more popular.

Niccolo Paganini (1782–1840), the only one of those names likely to strike a chord with present-day audiences, was one of the great iconic figures of the Romantic movement, a violin virtuoso with a scandalous private life. He had made his London debut in 1831. Ole Bull (1810–80), a Norwegian, was one of the most famous violinists of the nineteenth century. Nicolas Mori (1796–1839), the English-born son of an Italian wig maker, had been a child prodigy on the violin and later leader of the King's Theatre Orchestra. Johann Baptist Cramer (1771–1838), German-born pianist, composer and music publisher, had pursued his career entirely in England since 1800. Raphael Georg Kiesewetter (1773–1850) was a celebrated Austrian musicologist who organized an annual concert of vocal music from the sixteenth to the eighteenth centuries. Johann Nepomuk Hummel (1798–1837), the Austrian composer and most celebrated pianist of his day, was appearing in London in 1831. Nicholas Bochsa (1789–1856), the French harpist and composer, was musical director of the King's Theatre in London from 1826 to 1830. His annual solo concertos in London and the provinces in 1830s were hugely popular. Giulio Regondi (1822–72), guitar and concertina virtuoso and infant prodigy, was also performing in London in 1831.

Shakespearean parody and allusion were integral parts of Planché's humour, so much so that, reviewing *The Yellow Dwarf* at the Olympic, which was replete with them, *The Era* (31 December 1854) declared:

> To thoroughly enjoy the polish and piquancy of much of the dialogue, an intimate acquaintance with Shakespearean drama would be requisite, but the frequent recognition of the points of laughter and applause showed that the author had nothing to fear at this theatre from not gathering an intelligent audience within it walls.

This confirms Stanley Wells' suggestion, 'There seems no need to question the assumption that his public would recognize the allusions to Shakespeare.' He adds that:

> The reason for this familiarity is a matter of theatrical rather than educational history. Familiarity with Shakespeare was bred in the theatre, not in the classroom. This was the age of the Great Actor; and the prevailing repertory system made it possible for the regular theatregoer to become a connoisseur of performances in a way that is scarcely possible today ... Shakespeare's plays – in however debased versions – were more truly part of the living theatre a century ago than they are today.[20]

Indeed the parodies and allusions reflect the existing theatrical repertoire rather than the complete published corpus of Shakespeare, with *Hamlet* and *Macbeth* receiving the greatest number of references. The ghost scene from *Hamlet* was parodied in *The Discreet Princess* and the closet scene in *Graciosa and Percinet*. The 'is this a dagger which I see before me?' scene in *Macbeth* is parodied in *The Fair One With the Golden Locks* and the witches' invocation is sent up in *King Christmas* when the spirits decide to mix a Christmas pudding. The love scenes in *Romeo and Juliet* are parodied in *Graciosa and Percinet*. In *Once Upon a Time There Were Two Kings*, Corin emulates Orlando in *As You Like It* in pinning up poems about his beloved in the forest and carving her initials on trees. In *The Yellow Dwarf*, the dwarf's courtship of Princess Allfair is derived from Gloucester's wooing of the Lady Anne in *Richard III*. *The White Cat* opens with a parody of the opening of *King Lear* as King Wunsuponatyme at 80 tries to decide which of his three sons should be his heir. Many of the famous speeches are drawn on for humorous purposes. 'To Bee or not to Bee' in *The Bee and the Orange Tree* derives from *Hamlet*. In *The Queen of the Frogs* King Fulminoso parodies speeches from *Richard III* ('Now is the winter of our discontent') and *Richard II* ('Let us sit upon the ground and tell sad stories'). King Lear's invocation to the storm ('Blow winds and crack your cheeks, aye blow, ye cataracts and hurricanoes spout') features in both *The Deep, Deep Sea* and *The Island of Jewels*. Elsewhere there are allusions to *Hamlet* in *Beauty and the Beast*, *The Prince of Happy Land* and *Fortunio and His Seven Gifted Servants*; to *Macbeth* in *Beauty and the Beast*, *The Yellow Dwarf*, *The Island of Jewels* and *Fortunio*; to *The Merchant of Venice* in *King of Peacocks* and *The Yellow Dwarf*; to *Romeo and Juliet* in *King Charming*, *Once Upon a Time There Were Two Kings* and *The Yellow Dwarf*, to *Henry IV Part I* and *Twelfth Night* in *King Charming*; and to *A Midsummer Night's Dream* and *Othello* in *The Yellow Dwarf*.

Planché firmly defended the presence of a moral in his extravaganzas:

> Regardless of the opinion of the few self-constituted judges who contended that a moral was out of place in an extravaganza, and had evidently overlooked the fact that there is no very popular fairy tale without one, I most contumaciously persisted in my error.[21]

So Planché presented audiences with an impeccable set of Victorian aphorisms. The moral of *Riquet with the Tuft* was 'Love has power to embellish the ugliness of mortals, but virtue and talent alone can render the most beautiful happy.' The moral of *Puss in Boots* was 'Be content with what you have and make the most of it.' The moral of *Fortunio and His Seven Gifted Servants* was 'Kindly actions ever meet rewards.' The moral of *King Charming* was 'Indestructible are truth and love.' The moral of *The Discreet Princess* was 'As idleness of evil is the root, So safety is, of prudence, the rich fruit.' The moral of *The Island of Jewels* was 'If mortals would be happy here, below, The surest way is making others so.'

The Golden Branch (1847) was given a temperance framework. It opens in the Spirit Vaults and Private Still of the Enchanter's Castle where the enchanter Humguffin and his sister Mandragora assisted by Blueruino and other illicit spirits brew up noxious distillations which they have used to enchant Queen Benignanta of Arcadia (put to sleep for 200 years) and her admirer Prince Trasimenus (turned into an eagle). The Fairy Pastorella with the help of the golden branch plucked from the magic tree of entertaining knowledge reverses the enchantments and destroys the illicit still of the enchanter:

The time has come to stop your private still,

With ignorance in darkness brewing ill!

To make of simple mortals beasts and brutes,

The spirit of the age no longer suits.

Her aim, she says, is to 'change men for the better', to make them merrier as she makes them wiser. *The Daily News* (28 December 1847) approved, noting that 'it merits the approbation and applause of a critic, if only on account of its pleasantness, but also because there is a certain vein of didactic morality running through it which will benefit the present time.'

Although changing tastes in extravaganza and burlesque decisively left Planché behind, he remained the grand old man of the theatre. In 1872 William Tinsley published Planchés two-volume autobiography *Recollections and Reflections* which enabled him finally to get off his chest his resentments at the acclaim accorded to Beverley and Dance, whose contribution he manifestly felt to be subordinate to his own. In 1879 a handsome five-volume edition of his extravaganzas was published by Samuel French. The list of subscribers was headed by the Royal Library at Windsor Castle and by the royal dukes of Connaught and Cambridge, and alongside a glittering array of peers, playwrights, critics and actor-managers could be found the names of most of the current leading comic writers, E.L. Blanchard, H.J. Byron, W.S. Gilbert, F.C. Burnand, Robert Reece and William Yardley, still eager to honour the master of their craft.

Planché died in 1880, genuinely and widely mourned, but having outlived his vogue. A newer, broader, coarser form of burlesque had supplanted his delicate fairy fantasies, and by the end of the century, beginning indeed in the 1870s, burlesque itself was to be superseded by comic opera and musical comedy. Everything about the extravaganza has consigned it irrevocably to the theatrical past. Rhymed doggerel verse is now archaic. The musical parodies are of long-forgotten popular songs and operatic arias. The topical allusions are no longer comprehensible and the pun is now a completely despised and groan-worthy type of humour. However, the extravaganza did have a lasting legacy, in its influence on the pantomime opening which it extended and transformed decisively.

6

William Roxby Beverley
and the Triumph of Scene-Painting

Just as slapstick remained an integral part of the continuing appeal of pantomime, so too did spectacle. The Victorian thirst for the visual was nowhere more obvious than on the stage. The pictorial stage became the distinctive feature of the Victorian theatre.[1] In the eighteenth century in Sybil Rosenfeld's words, 'the emphasis was on the play and the players rather than the décor.'[2] This changed after leading actor-manager David Garrick employed the services of Philip de Loutherbourg in 1773. De Loutherbourg developed scene-painting (often of recognizable locales), stage machinery and innovative lighting as an integral part of theatrical production. The great exceptions to the relative absence of spectacle from the eighteenth century stage had always been opera and pantomime. Scene-painting and special effects had been a feature of pantomime production from the 1720s onwards.[3] The panorama featured in pantomimes from 1800, when *Harlequin Amulet* at Drury Lane depicted 'the most magnificent buildings in London', and *Harlequin's Tour* at Covent Garden had a succession of topographical scenes including Margate, Scarborough, Bath, Weymouth and Tunbridge Wells.

From the 1820s onwards scene-painting developed in twin directions: antiquarian accuracy for historical dramas and productions of Shakespeare and the romantic picturesque for melodrama, pantomime and opera. The antiquarian tradition reached a peak of achievement in Charles Kean's Shakespeare productions at the Princess' Theatre between 1850 and 1859.[4] The romantic mode achieved its own apogée at Covent Garden where between 1794 and 1845 the scene-painting was largely in the hands of the Grieve family, John Henderson Grieve (1770–1845) and his sons Thomas (1799–1882) and William (1800–44). They applied their talents equally to Shakespeare, opera and pantomime. John Grieve developed a particular wash for finishing his scenery which, when combined with the effects of gaslight, produced a brilliant visual impression. Although the term was not actually used until

1823, it seems to have been Grieve too who introduced the diorama (a more elaborate form of the panorama with lighting changes to give the illusion of movement) as a feature in the Covent Garden Christmas pantomime. The first one appeared in *Harlequin and Friar Bacon or The Brazen Head* – a sea voyage from Holyhead to Dublin – in 1820, after which it became a regular element of the pantomime. According to Sybil Rosenfeld, in the theatre the terms panorama and diorama became more or less interchangeable.[5] In 1871 *The Era Almanack* summed up the Grieves' achievement:

> In the brilliancy of their style and the strong feeling of reality which they communicated to the spectator, and in the taste and artistic beauty of their landscape compositions, they have since had few rivals and have never been excelled.[6]

The Grieves were briefly challenged by Drury Lane where Clarkson Stanfield (1793–1867) and David Roberts (1796–1864) undertook the scene-painting for a short time. Stanfield was the artist Dutton Cook credited with introducing the diorama into pantomime. The term was first used at Drury Lane in connection with the moving sequences of the building of the Plymouth breakwater in the pantomime *Harlequin and the Flying Chest* in 1823. The critics thought it was the best thing about the pantomime.[7]

Stanfield was a former seaman who had painted scenery at the Royalty and Coburg Theatres in London before joining Drury Lane in 1822 where he painted scenery until 1834, working for a time with his great friend David Roberts. He painted 550 scenes in 170 shows between 1816 and 1843 and became famous for his dioramas, painting sixteen in all. They became a particular attraction in the Drury Lane Christmas pantomimes between 1828 and 1833, providing a twenty-minute journey of moving travel views, from England to Gibraltar and Constantinople (1828), around Windsor (1829), over the Alps (1830), to Venice (1831), to the Niagara Falls (1832) and to the Nile (1833). 'These paintings,' said *The Examiner* (30 December 1837), 'belong in one word to the highest order of art.'[8] Stanfield abandoned scene-painting for easel painting, specializing in maritime scenes. He became a Royal Academician in 1835 and John Ruskin described him as 'the leader of the British Realists' and after Turner, 'the noblest master of cloud forms of all our artists.'[9]

David Roberts, who began scene-painting in Scotland in 1816, linked up with Stanfield at Drury Lane in the years 1822–6. But when tensions arose between them, Roberts decamped to work with the Grieves at Covent Garden between 1827 and 1830. There he sought to challenge Stanfield's diorama supremacy in pantomime before he turned full time to easel painting, becoming celebrated for his pictures of Spain and the Near East. He was elected as a Royal Academician in 1841.[10]

William Roxby Beverley (c.1810–89) was even more closely associated with pantomime than Stanfield or Roberts.[11] He came from a theatrical family, his father and grandfather being actor-managers and theatre owners in the north of England. His father, William Roxby, had taken the stage name of Beverley in honour of the Yorkshire town. His brothers Henry Beverley and Robert Roxby were also actors. Initially William both acted in comedy and painted scenery for the family theatres. His first engagement in London was in 1839 when he painted the scenery for the pantomime *Baron Munchausen* at the Coburg Theatre, then being managed by his brother Henry. Between 1842 and 1846 he was principal scene-painter at the Theatre Royal, Manchester.

The critical celebration of such scenic artists as Stanfield, Roberts and the Grieves demonstrates the increasing acceptance of scene-painting as an art form in its own right. This idea received powerful support as the century wore on. In a famous pronouncement, the pre-eminent Victorian art critic John Ruskin wrote in 1884 to actor-manager Wilson Barrett praising his production of the toga play *Claudian* and declaring: 'With scene-painting like that at the Princess' Theatre, (you) might do more for art teaching than all the galleries and professors of Christendom.'[12] This statement was regularly quoted in support of scene-painting. Oscar Wilde came resoundingly to the defence of scenic artists when he called in 1885 for critics 'to exert whatever influence they possess towards restoring the scene-painter to his proper position as an artist' adding, 'I have never seen any reason why such artists as Mr Beverley, Mr Walter Hann and Mr Telbin should not be entitled to become Academicians. They have certainly as good a claim as have many of those R.A.'s whose total inability to paint we can see every May for a shilling.'[13]

Leading painters also came to the support of the scenic artists. In an 1892 lecture, Sir Hubert von Herkomer declared 'Scenic art should in no way be held an inferior art ... All art is a struggle with the inadequacy of our materials for expression but in stage work the artist has more materials at his command than in any other form of artistic expression' and in 1904 Sir Lawrence Alma-Tadema declared that 'The art of scene-painting was indeed a beautiful art' and that 'the scenic artist had long since deserved some recognition beyond the occasional off-hand mention of his endeavours in the papers.'[14]

From the 1880s onwards *The Magazine of Art* ran regular features under the title 'Art in the Theatre' and gave scenic artists the space to argue their case. Soon books with titles like *The Art of the Victorian Stage* were being published. Eventually in 1904 the Scenic Artists Association was formed and in 1905 a major exhibition of the work of the great scenic artists was staged at the Grafton Galleries. Ironically it was not long before the nature of theatre and of scene-painting changed forever and the Victorian pictorial stage passed into history.

Looking back at the progress of scenic artists, W.J. Lawrence, who sadly never wrote the history of English scene-painting for which he had compiled eleven volumes of research notes, set out his thoughts in occasional journal articles. He noted that William Grieve was the first scenic artist 'to whom the public paid tribute by a "call" before the curtain.' That was at the premiere of the opera *Robert Le Diable* at the Italian Opera in 1832.[15] This began a tradition which was certainly honoured when it came to scene-painting for pantomimes. Lawrence also identified William Beverley as having been 'awarded the honour of being the first great artist who knew how to uphold the dignity of his profession.'[16] This was because scene-painters such as Stanfield, Roberts and Joseph Allen acquired their enduring reputations after they had abandoned scene-painting for easel painting. But Beverley, although he showed twenty-nine pictures at the Royal Academy between 1865 and 1880, never abandoned scene-painting and was celebrated as 'The Watteau of scene-painters'.[17] Tragically, none of Beverley's scene-painting, in common with that of most of his contemporaries, has survived for later generations to judge. He remains the greatest scene-painter of his age and in particular one of the major creators of the image of fairyland by report only. But the unanimity of critical opinion is very telling.

It would be unjust to discount the regular comparisons made by the critics to Stanfield, Poussin, Turner and Lorrain which suggests notable and consistent visual achievements by Beverley. According to the *D.N.B.*, he was engaged in 1846 by J.M. Maddox as principal artist at the Princess' Theatre in London.[18] But in fact he was in London in 1845 painting the scenery for the Princess' pantomime, *The Key of the Kingdom or Harlequin and Fairy Bluebell. The Era* (4 January 1846) was definitely not impressed by the show as a whole:

The opening comprised the usual quota of fairies, imps and human monstrosities, all laudably intent on dancing, howling and endangering the limbs of their respective neighbours. The author's wit seeming to have exhausted itself in a merciless plenitude of nursery antics, and an utter disregard of the shins, noses, and optics of his ridiculous characters ... At length a general uproar introduced us to Harlequin ... Columbine ... Clown ... and Pantaloon. After a lesson in sack jumping which gave Flexmore an opportunity of showing his unrivalled powers of tumbling, we come to a stupid scene in a Boulogne steamer, which not even the Clown's mirth-provoking antics could save from being hissed, both on account of its dullness and indecency. And after several scenes, none above mediocrity, the pantomime concluded with the 'Fairy Home'.

Apart from the clowning of Richard Flexmore, one of the more notable of Grimaldi's successors, no-one else in the cast received praise. However, the scenery, and staging did:

The beautiful scenery, and admirable management of the complicated machinery, amply atoned for the author's paucity of invention; let any who doubt us see the enchanted grotto, and the fairy conveyance to the equally excellent view from the golden tower, when they will say, as we did, with the poet, 'The force of nature could no further go.'

The critic concluded 'the superior scenery and pantomimic powers of Flexmore, will doubtless sustain this piece throughout the Christmas season.' *The Times* (27 December 1845) was much less severe on both the opening and the harlequinade. But the reviewer also noted: 'The scenery was certainly very pretty, and in many instances magnificent, eliciting great applause' with the enchanted grotto of Fairy Bluebell described as 'splendid'.

The following year Beverley did the scenery for the Princess' again for *The Enchanted Beauties of the Golden Castle or Harlequin and the One-Eyed Genie. The Times* (28 December 1846) reported:

> The strength of *The Enchanted Beauties of the Golden Castle* lies in its merits as a spectacle, which are first-rate, and cannot fail to make the piece attractive. The new and extensive scenery by Mr W. L. Beveridge [sic] and his assistants would alone render it successful, and the dresses and decorations are on a corresponding scale of excellence. The introductory portion was well received and the exertions of Columbine, Harlequin, Clown and Pantaloon produced a fair share of applause and laughter.

The Examiner (2 January 1847) proclaimed it 'incomparably the nearest approach to a good pantomime we have seen this year.' The reasons – 'exquisite scenery, machinery that works well, jokes which though not new are not dull, several clever changes, a pleasing Columbine and an excellent Clown.' *Bell's Life in London* (27 December 1846) declared the scenery of Beverley 'superb'.

But the following year Beverley was missing from the Princess', poached by Vestris and Mathews for the Lyceum, where he became a vital member of the team transforming the extravaganza into an all-out spectacle. Planché recalled his arrival, to work on the Lyceum production of *The Golden Branch*:

> In the scenic department we had for the first time in London an artist whose name was shortly to be one of the most celebrated in that peculiar (golden) branch of the profession – Mr William Beverley, with whom I had the pleasure of working for upward of six years. An ingenious machinist, as well as an admirable painter, he was of the greatest importance to me in carrying out effectively the many complicated changes which were necessary for the comprehension of the rather intricate plot of the piece, and which in less skilful hands might have endangered its success. Every point was so carefully arranged and so perfectly executed that, although we were so sorely pressed for time that the hour for opening the doors had arrived before we had finished the rehearsal, and consequently the last scene was never rehearsed at all, not a hitch nor a blunder of the

slightest description occurred to mar the intended effects, which were novel and beautiful enough to have saved a very inferior drama. The scenes in Arcadia, designed from the *chef d'oeuvres* of Watteau, presented a succession of *tableaux* certainly never previously equalled on the English stage, and obtained for Madame Vestris the most gratifying commendations from Edwin Landseer and other eminent artists, and gave a *cachet* to the reputation of the new management of the Lyceum for production of spectacular drama.[19]

The Times (28 December 1847) said:

The grand scene in Arcadia, with vistas of flowers and tall crystal columns ranged in avenues and the golden wood produced by the fertility of the branch, and afterwards opening into a novel fairy *tableau*, belong to the very first order of fanciful scenery and do the greatest credit to that rising painter Mr Beverley.

The Era (2 January 1848) praised the scenery as 'chaste, elegant and highly finished, elaborate in execution and splendid in effect.' It singled out the scene which ended act one, 'the most gorgeous exhibition imaginable, a very temple of flowers, designed, one would think, by an architectural Flora, and executed by magic hands; and this is so delicate withal, that its brilliancy is like moon rays, and its tints resemble those of the rainbow; there is nothing gaudy in the whole production, though everything belonging to it is rich.' *The Examiner* (1 January 1848) thought it 'quite remarkable for the care and beauty lavished on it.' *The Satirist* (2 January 1848) said 'the scenery is beyond all praise.' *The Standard* (28 December 1847) spoke for virtually all the newspapers when it declared 'As a spectacle there have been few pieces brought upon the stage comparable with *The Golden Branch* and its magnificence in this respect will be the talk of the town for many a day to come.'

There was a secret to achieving the successful evocation of fairyland. This was explained by scene-painter Frederick Lloyds in his *Practical Guide to Scene Painting and Painting in Distemper* (1875):

The great thing in painting fairy scenes is ... to use as pure colours and tints as possible, because, when you come to put brilliant coloured foils on the scene, in front of which there are already the brightest and most brilliant coloured dresses, it will be sure to look dirty, if the colours employed are not the purest. Pure grey, and plenty of it, would serve well, for instance, to set off your rich colours. Fairy scenes ... should be painted in the lightest possible manner, so as to have, especially in the middle and extreme distances, that airy, dreamy, indefinite look about them, so well exemplified by the beautiful pictures of Turner. Study closely those wonderful creations of his, trying to catch the spirit of them, and you can scarcely go wrong.[20]

Beverley's artistry was enhanced by the discovery and marketing by Winsor and Newton from 1832 onwards of white tempera paint powder. White tempera could outline painted objects on a flat or drop and could be blended with the new aniline pigments which were starting to come in from Germany. Suddenly scenery started to look brilliant because white, rather than the muddy grey previously in use, allowed gas lighting to be bounced back to the audience rather than absorbed. For maximum effect the painted canvas needed to be illuminated by gas and later limelight. In his account of stage effects, *The World Behind the Scenes*, Percy Fitzgerald noted:

> All the great triumphs of modern stage effect date from the introduction of a strong light. When gas was introduced, it was found that a more gaudy display of colours could be effected; but it was the application of the limelight that really threw open the realms of glittering fairyland to the scenic artist.[21]

W.J. Lawrence concurred, writing:

> To excel nowadays, the devotee of the double-tie brush needs to unite pictorial and constructive talents with mechanical ingenuity, and to possess a perfect knowledge of the possibilities of lighting. It was the skilful combination of these faculties at the outset of his career that gave William Beverley the fame and position he now enjoys.[22]

The 1848 Christmas show was *The King of Peacocks*, for which the *I.L.N.* (30 December 1848) reported that in the scenery, Mr Beverley had 'excelled himself', particularly in painting the deck of the Chinese junk ('very clever') and in the concluding scenic effect – a giant peacock feather fan opening up – 'one of the most elaborate and gorgeous (effects) ever seen.'

It was the scenery in *Theseus and Ariadne* which prompted the superlatives. *The Times* (25 April, 1848) said:

> The scenery, by Mr W. Beverley and Mr J. Meadows, surpasses, if possible, anything hitherto done for the decoration of burlesque. Mere magnificence is common enough, but here magnificence is combined with the best taste, and with truly classical feeling. The Cretan port, the bird's-eye view of the labyrinth and the departure of the galley are specimens of high scenic art.

The critics were now regularly drawing comparisons with Stanfield. *The Era* (30 April 1848) reported:

> The getting-up is extraordinarily beautiful. Such scenery as is here exhibited is quite equal to anything Stanfield ever produced upon the stage; words can scarcely do justice to the labours of Mr W. Beverley and Mr J. Meadows, who have thus outdone all their previous creations in the way of scene painting.

The Examiner (29 April 1848) said:

> There is a scene of the vines before the temple of Bacchus which recalls wonders of the
> painters as well as poets; there is a view of the Cretan labyrinth which Daedalus himself
> might have planned, so dizzy and bewildering it is, yet green and glorious withal; and
> there are some views of the ocean on which … Stanfield himself might deign to smile
> benignantly.

The one criticism was of the fight between Theseus and the Minotaur. *The Morning
Chronicle* (27 April 1843) said it was 'one of the least effective scenes in the piece,
and was by no means of a kind to satisfy the combative feelings of the audience; as
after a few blows on the horns the *Minotaur* trotted off without having made even a
feint at resistance, to be quietly slaughtered off stage.'

The Standard (25 April 1848), praising the way in which the Cretan city glided
onto the stage ('a luminous, novel and well-managed effect') and the labyrinth, the
departure of the galley and the vines outside Bacchus' temple, noted:

> The scenery of Mr Beverley is at all times a source of genuine gratification. Not only does
> it betray great variety and inventiveness, but a degree of artistic feeling which gives it a
> higher rank in the annals of stage painting than anything that has been produced since
> the days of Stanfield. Nothing more complete, picturesque and Poussin-like in design
> can be imagined than the *ensemble* which the last scene presents, with its tipsy revelries
> of fauns and bacchanals.

In the Easter 1849 extravaganza *The Seven Champions of Christendom*, *The
Standard* (10 April 1845), describing Beverley's scenery as 'superb', went on:

> This gentleman is fast achieving the fame to which his great talents so well entitle him.
> He has completely restored the character of scenic decoration, which since the
> retirement of Stanfield and Roberts, had obviously retrograded, and has revived the
> standard which those great artists had laboured to establish. His present efforts display
> his usually pure artistic feeling … The scene which closes the first act is unrivalled in its
> effect as a piece of fairy invention: the stage is spanned with delicate rocky arches
> entwined with coral branches and seaweed, canopying an azure lake, the eye running up
> a series of vistas, terminating with one of those aerial distances so grateful to the
> educated eye; while the swans on the water, the naiad shells, and the groups of sportive
> nymphs in the foreground complete a *coup d'oeil* exquisitely luminous and poetical.
> There is a desert landscape in the first act, a perfect study for harmony and grace of
> colouring; qualities also exemplified in the 'Enchanted Garden', notwithstanding the
> golden artificiality of the tone, and the florid lustre of the accessories. A composition of
> Egyptian architecture displays great breadth of drawing as well as depth and massiveness
> in the execution; and the perspective of the tapestried tents which form the last scene,

glowing with the armorial trophies of the seven champions, and animated with the crowd of burnished warriors, mingled with the white draperied princesses and their attendants is a tableau of diversified and matchless gorgeousness.

The Era (15 April 1849) concurred, saying:

It is hardly possible to do justice to the efforts of Mr Beverly, whose artistic paintings are beautiful in the extreme. This gentleman is essentially a poet. There is highest art in his creation ... it is but fair to remark that these extravaganzas would be nothing without his aid. He throws a charm over all that is said and done. He produces half the effect and more than half the attraction.

The critic adds that without seeking to depreciate the writer Planché, the musician Tully, the ballet master Oscar Byrne, the costume designer Bailey and the machinist Sloman, the highest achievement is that of Beverley and the other painter Gray. It is this kind of comment which clearly rankled with Planché.

It was *The Island of Jewels* which finally confirmed Beverley as the leading scene-painter of his day. *The Times* (27 December 1849) reported:

The piece throughout is one blaze of the most splendid dresses imaginable. In fact the dresses and the pictorial portion of the extravaganza could only have been conceived after a long course of Arabian Nights opium and pork suppers. Not to speak of the ball dance – the fresh green sea – doing one's heart good in the crowded hot theatre; the lively foliage of the island; the glowing faces and dazzling raiment of the 'precious stones' in waiting on King Emerald; the rare combination of scenic colouring and dress – a stupendous aquamarine gate, dreary basalt caverns, and the steel mountain in the Valley of Vapours – there was Madame Vestris in saffron satin, and Miss St. George in white ditto, and fairies in gauze; a whole *corps de ballet* in silk and gold, and every other attraction that could be devised.

All this was surpassed by the finale:

When wickedness has been duly punished and virtue rewarded, a vast column of palm leaves at the back of the stage slowly opens, each leaf bending towards the stage, and discovers a group of nymphs on a cushion, bearing aloft 'the Crown jewels' ... It seemed a web of silvery light. The jewels sparkled with more than the lustre of diamonds. All was a blaze of the most dazzling colour, and the curtain fell on the most exquisite *morceaux* of spectacle ever witnessed.

The Era (30 December 1849) proclaimed the scenery 'exquisite', compared it to the engravings of Turner's work, and said the show was worth seeing for Beverley's scenery alone. The *I.L.N.* (29 December 1849) said:

Of all Mr Planché's burlesques, the present, is, perhaps, the most elegant ever witnessed, and the way in which it has been produced the most gorgeous imaginable. The concluding scene ... is indescribably magnificent. The whole, also, was in perfect taste; and the piece must be pronounced a crowning triumph in the art of burlesque.

It was the finale in particular which caused a sensation. Planché described it in his *Recollections*: 'The novel and yet exceedingly simple falling of the leaves of a palm tree which discovered six fairies supporting a coronet of jewels, produced such an effect as I scarcely remember having witnessed on any similar occasion up to that period.'[23]

On *King Charming* as usual the scenery came in for superlatives. The *I.L.N.* (28 December 1850) summed up the general reception: 'It is impossible to bestow too much praise upon the scenery, painted by Mr Beverly and Mr Meadows: all was perfect.' *The Era* (20 December 1850) agreed, declaring that the final scene 'must be seen to be believed ... it is so splendid and bewildering.'

The pearls of Ormus are added to the rubies of Trebizond, and the emeralds of Viscapour glitter beside the diamonds of Golconda, thrown together with profusion, and yet with order. Then Mahomet's paradise has been deprived of a score of Houries who sit in a semi-circle on thrones of beaten gold backed by fans of waving silver, and graceful tissue. In fact Peru and California have yielded up their rubiest treasures to illustrate 'The Glorious Restoration of King Charming to the Throne of Fan-sea'.

The Standard (27 December 1850) said:

To describe the lustrous beauty of Mr Beverly's scenery would require a more glowing pen than ours. The pictures which are required to illustrate works of this ultra-imaginative school, where there is nothing real, tangible or natural, have prior to this time, exhibited but a small measure of invention, and, with this, more or less dryness and solidity of execution, Mr Beverly has undoubtedly created an epoch in the arts of stage embellishment, for to extreme grace and freedom of manipulation, he adds the much higher virtue of idea, and many of his efforts evince a power and variety of conception which we can but regret is developed in such an evanescent form ... In the composition of the fantastic allegories which identify the elfin kingdoms of romance, Mr Beverly displays a rare fecundity of device, and he has given the bizarre conceits of this class of scenic illustrations novelty of aspect as welcome as it is unexpected – investing it with an artistic and poetical interest which has never before been disclosed by the painter of 'flats and wings'. The same sensitiveness pervades his labours in the more legitimate domain of landscape, and none of his contemporaries have achieved pictures more remarkable for sweetness and harmony of effect ... than himself.

The Times (22 April 1851) on *The Queen of the Frogs*, the Easter offering of 1851, while praising the script, went on:

No one however, who witnessed the *Queen of Frogs* could conceal from himself the fact that the main success of the piece depended upon the scenery and decorations. Mr W. Beverley's help in the former department was of priceless value. To the excellence of this artist's talents we have often done justice, and the scenes in the present piece which emanate more immediately from his pencil are but justifications of what we have already said. He is the only veritable painter of these fairy legends – the only proper associate of Mr Planché in these pleasant passages of inconsistency and absurdity. His efforts on the present occasion are similar in tone and purport to those which have gone before. The Hall of Diana, the Quicksilver Lake, the gardens of Prince Nonpareil, and the Nuptial Bower of the Queen of the Frogs, breathe the very spirit of the 'unreal', and afford a fascinating insight into the realms of poetry and romance. The scenery, generally speaking, is not upon so vast and showy a scale as *King Charming*, excepting the finale, which, constructed upon similar principles as the celebrated close to that piece, is equally rich and lustrous in effect. A ring of dainty maidens support a capital of gold, which rises amid a suffusion of coloured fires, and develops other figures bathed in light, forming altogether a tableau of matchless and dazzling brilliancy. The applause which awaited this superb display was universal.

This was the general critical opinion. *The Era* (27 April 1851) said:

The scenery is ... remarkably beautiful, and Mr Beverley has performed another triumph. In the work of this artist ... lies the principal merit of the piece, for admiration never flags while the curtain is raised. The painting is so perfect that you cannot but regret its ephemeral character. It is full of poetry from first to last, and realizes all your notions of fairyland and of nature in her richest attire.

The *Morning Chronicle* (22 April 1851) said:

Nothing could surpass the beauty of some of the scenery ... The 'Quicksilver Lake' is an exquisite embodiment of one of the happiest conceptions of a delicate fancy, and the last scene surpasses in splendour even the *Island of Jewels* and *King Charming*. A more gorgeous effect was never produced in any theatre.

The Prince of Happy Land (1851–2), the Christmas offering, elicited from *The Era* (27 December 1851) praise for the 'smart jokes and very pleasant puns' of Planché's script, for the songs, dances and costumes, but – the sting in the tail for Planché – the play was the 'medium for introducing some of the most finished and beautiful scenery that ever was exhibited upon any stage.' The scenery was said to 'truly beggar all description':

Trees and foliage appear with more than usual loveliness – structures are raised which take the imagination captive, and the land of fairies seems realised. The opening scene presents the chamber of a lady who has never seen the sun. An extraordinary candelabrum almost fills the apartment, and a sky of point lace hangs overhead. Then comes a pleasure garden, where golden palm-leaves are suspended from silver stems. This scene reminds one of Turner's choicest pictures, as, indeed, for light and air, for touch and delicacy, for invention and taste, are many of Mr Beverley's best pieces. The closing view is the Golden Pinery; and here one vast pine is made to open into many compartments, each disclosing a young lady attired in silver ... It is a rare sight, and one wonders that scenic effect can be carried so far ... Mr Beverley, Mr Meadows and their assistants ... have evidently endeavoured to produce something beyond ordinary scene painting – and succeeded.

The Standard (27 December 1851) reported:

The scenic accessories ... exceed in aesthetic beauty anything that has preceded it – bold as the asseveration would seem to be. Mr. W. Beverly has achieved great renown for the composition of fairy effects, and his title is here distinctly consummated. The several scenes which illustrate the present extravaganza abound in those exquisite traits of imagination which we look for at the hands of genius.

Particularly praised are the Pleasure Gardens of the Fairies, the Princess' chamber and the Golden Pinery.

Declaring 'I have not seen such a fairy piece as this. The triumvirate Vestris, Planché, Beverley ... have opened Fairyland ... who is there will not take a peep?' the eminent critic George Henry Lewes rhapsodized about *The Good Woman in the Wood* (1852):

I must borrow hyperboles to express something of the admiring delight with which we witnessed *The Good Woman in the Wood*, ordinary epithets have so lost their value by the prodigal use made of them in criticism, that to speak within bounds would be speaking coldly and inaccurately. The Greeks would have boldly spoken of the *flabbergastuality* of this piece, but our poorer language is denied those reaches of genius! The Lyceum itself affords no standard of comparison. Never on any stage was there a scene of such enchantment and artistic beauty as that which concludes the first act of this piece, the *Basaltic Terminus on the Borders of Lake Lucid*. To say that in the long summer afternoons of reverie-peopled boyhood one had dreamed of fairy-land like this, would be to say that the wide-wandering fancy of a boy was equal to that of a Beverley; but Beverley is the fairy's own child; he *must* be a changeling; his childhood was spent among those regions, and now, in his serious and laborious manhood, the dim remembrances of that far-off splendour haunt his soul ... The fairies have had millions of worshippers, hundreds of poets, and one supreme artist, and that artist is William Beverley! In this *Good Woman in the Wood* there are several beautiful scenes, and the last scene – always a Lyceum marvel – is as marvellous as anything which former years have shown us; but, to my mind, the highest reach of scenic art is that closing scene of the first act.[24]

The Era (2 January 1853) was entranced by the finale of *The Good Woman in the Wood*. The tableau is declared:

the wonder and delight of a gaping and a crowded audience, who despair of ever conveying to their most credulous friends anything like a notion of what they witness. It is, indeed, a most elaborate spectacle, and withal, so chaste, so delicate, so perfect. It took poetry to invent, and genius to perform all this.

The critic describes the Testimonial presented to the Good Woman:

We see a large group of gems and flowers, the former all glistening in brilliant hues, the latter budding and afterwards blooming in various tints. These are borne by and garnished with living female figures, whose dark hair, and dainty limbs, and flashing eyes, add to the general effect. There has been some care shown in selecting these ladies, and an uniformity as to countenance and superior personal proportions is conspicuous. The prevailing feature of the whole scene is delicacy. There is something supernatural in the fineness of everything, from the light dresses of the fairies to the leaves on the trees. Tulips open and expand in transparent colours; figures of reposing nymphs move without any perceptible effort; and the scene unfolds itself, as it were, and grows before your eyes into something more and more wondrous, until a blaze of light is thrown upon the whole, and the curtain falls amid a burst of applause. Mr Beverley and Mr Meadows, the artists, have undoubtedly achieved considerable addition to their fame.

Beverley was called for by the audience and 'appeared in all the deshabillé peculiar to his craft.'

The Standard (28 December 1852) reported:

The scenery of Mr William Beverley is once more remarkable for its superb and lustrous beauty. As the inventor of fairy haunts this gentleman has no competitor, for while his imagination teems with delicate conceits touching magic bowers and elfin lakes, his pictures are exquisite as compositions. While his designs breathe a purity and elegance palpable to every one, the execution is replete with masterly skill, and the effects of colour visible in all his paintings are those only of the true and accomplished artist. The qualities which have so pre-eminently distinguished his productions in the former holiday pieces brought out at this theatre are equally manifested in *The Good Woman in the Wood* and the scenery is one entire succession of lovely effects – now dealing with the natural and picturesque, and now with those graceful elaborations of fancy which suggest the homes of the supernatural beings with whose vague and indefinite spirit he holds such intimate communion. Let the scene which terminates the first act, 'The Basaltic Terminus on the Borders of Lake Lucid', be cited as a most alluring example of those ingenious pictorial metaphors, which it is so exclusively his gift to create. Through a series of basalt arches, ribbed and glistening with burnished gold, a cerulean lake appears, confined in walls of fairy rock-work, the pinnacles of which rise in lofty towers on either side and seem bathed in golden refulgent light. The atmospheric effect of this scene is admirably managed, and the melting distances are executed with the ablest and most fascinating dexterity.

In *Once Upon a Time There Were Two Kings* (1853–4), it was the 'magnificent efforts' of Beverley that gained the accolade for his depiction of Sea-Weed Hall and his finale. *The Times* (27 December 1853) thought 'the merits of the piece lie chiefly in the scenic effects, the excellence of the costumes ... and the music' but 'the dialogue ... is greatly wanting in that point and piquancy which are so highly relished in this class of performance.' *John Bull* (2 January 1854) thought the show worth visiting for the scenery alone which was 'exquisitely beautiful'. *The Era* (11 January 1854) reported:

> Philosophers have told us that the bottom of the ocean is a vast forest resplendent with trees of a stature so gigantic and a form so varied that they find no type or equal upon earth. This then, Mr Beverley presents to us; all the various species of sponges, corals, and the rest with which we are familiar, interlacing a tangled forest of sub-marine plants, and the whole rendered sparkling bright and translucent by the play of the blue water and the beams of the soft stars. It is a beautiful scene, and when its attractions are enhanced by the dancing and the graceful groupings of fifty ladies of the ballet, the effect is truly magical. Still more magnificent is the closing scene, truly styled in the bills 'a dazzling prospect'. Here we have a new idea carried out of 'floating ladies' suspended in the air in most bewitching attitudes, and arrayed with an elegance and taste which for grace and beauty must be pronounced perfection. The applause of the audience at this scene was startlingly unanimous.

Despite the praise for costumes by Mr Brown and Miss Burt, the machinery of Mr Sloman and the 'appointments' of Mr Bradwell, it was Beverley who was called to take a bow after Act I and called again before the curtain along with 'all the performers'. 'The tribute to his genius, warmly and heartily bestowed upon him, was gratefully acknowledged.'

The Standard (27 December 1853) likewise praised Beverley's work in the finales of Act I and Act 2. Act I ended with the seaweed cavern:

> It is a study solely of seaweeds, the spreading and delicate tendrils of which span the stage in every direction, forming long vistas, and shading pools of azure water, which melt imperceptibly in the distance. The entire area of the stage has been pressed into the service of this striking scene. Sea-weeds of every variety are grouped and inter-laced, and we are well aware what rare diversities of colour nature has lavished upon these fruitful growths of the deep. The contrasts resident in the several tints present a polychromic tableau graceful and elegant beyond measure; while the slender shoots which web every

spot and corner upon which the eye rests make up one huge and boundless surface of delicate and impalpable tracery.

The finale of Act 2 was compared favourably to the finales of *The Island of Jewels* and *The Good Woman in the Wood*:

A gloomy, massive wall, bristling with turrets, bends over towards the spectators. All now is light and brilliancy, for upon the shelving surface are lines of golden leaves, tipped with violet and scarlet, while in the middle distance female figures are recumbent. An arch composed of silver ribs opens majestically behind, and from the top descends a pair of females, swathed in long, sweeping draperies, forming a sculpturesque group, singularly happy and poetical in design. The tastefulness of the tableau and its lustrous gorgeousness ravished the audience to the utmost degree.

The final extravaganza of the Mathews regime was *Prince Pretty-Pet and the Butterfly*. It was written by William Brough and was an original creation and not an adaptation of a pre-existing story. The *I.L.N.* (30 December 1854) recorded:

Mr Brough's Burlesque is always richly appointed; superabounds, indeed, with wit, jest and humour, and overflows with allusion, parody, and fun. His merits are in excess. Though he lacks, therefore, the point and finish which Mr Planché gives to his productions, there is a life-like exuberance in the joviality and bacchic sincerity of his mirth which is irresistible.

The Era (31 December 1854), however, did not share the *I.L.N.*'s enthusiasm, claiming that at two and a half hours it was much too long:

Strewed as it is with puns of a lively and telling character, it is too much to expect an audience to sit for two and a half mortal hours listening to an incessant play upon words which is just of sufficient interest to keep the mind on the rack lest any of the jokes should be lost. An extravaganza, unless full of startling incident, should never exceed an hour in representation; and clever and smart and witty, as we admit this production to be, we ask Mr Brough what demon it was that put it into his head to inflict upon poor mortals in search of Christmas cheer, well spiced but not too cloying, two hours and a half of incessant punning fired away at you without intermission and without remorse? The author really must bridle his exuberant humour.

But Beverley was on hand to supply relief in the form of his characteristic spectacle:

Especially we must notice the glorious effect of the Crystalline Haunt of the Butterflies, and the butterfly ball which therein takes place; and the concluding and most gorgeous tableau of all – the Throne of the Butterfly Queen. Every appliance of stage art is here brought into requisition – a gorgeous arched pedestal of liquid gold and precious gems in front – a raised canopied throne in the rear – floating fairies with their robes terminating

in vaporous clouds – beautiful coryphées at the wings, and a flood of light streaming on
the whole!

Despite the reviewers' strictures, something unique happened. Both Beverley and
Brough were called for and took bows – something that apparently never happened
to Planché.

Writing in 1883, journalist Michael Williams recalled 'Prince Pretty-Pet and the
Butterfly was extremely clever, but its wit proved too broad for an audience
habituated to the more delicate graces of the elder author [i.e., Planché], and so,
though the mounting was as perfect as ever, it is a fact that the piece did not draw,
was withdrawn long before the usual time.'[25] The Times (27 December 1854)
thought it lacked 'the elegance and neatness' of Planché but this was compensated
for by 'the amount of fun thrown into choreography and dialogue'.

John Bull (30 December 1854) thought it 'clever, but too laboured and too long'
but added 'In respect to the spectacle, this theatre has maintained its superiority. Mr
Beverley has almost excelled himself in the magical beauty of the scenery; and the
groupings and tableaux on the stage are brilliant and picturesque in the highest
degree.' The Daily News (27 December 1854) agreed that it was clever but suffered
from 'over-elaboration' with dialogues 'too protracted' which would benefit from
being condensed. 'The spectacle – the main feature, after all, of things of this kind –
was most beautiful, and several of the scenes called forth shouts and acclamations
from all parts of the house.' In the end, it ran for fifty-seven performances, compared
to the eighty-three chalked up by Once Upon A Time There Were Two Kings.

Charles Mathews, bankrupt again, relinquished the lease of the Lyceum in March
1855 and E.T. Smith immediately acquired the services of Beverley, his brother stage
manager Robert Roxby and premiere dancer Rosina Wright for Drury Lane. The Era
(23 December 1855) noted with approval:

> From the care and expenditure bestowed upon every department it would seem this year
> that the lessee Mr E.T. Smith, has determined to excel his previous achievements, and
> with the valuable aid of Mr William Beverley, to link the brilliant graces of a Lyceum
> burlesque with the humourous extravagances of what is traditionally recognised as a
> good old English comic Pantomime.

Hey Diddle Diddle or Harlequin King Nonsense and the Seven Ages of Man was the
first Drury Lane pantomime to employ Beverley's talents. The Era (30 December
1855) opened its review with an encomium on the new arrival:

> Time was when the principal pictorial effects were reserved for a diorama,
> unceremoniously thrust in immediately prior to the catastrophe; but this fashion is
> now exploded, and the scenic artist devotes himself to the absolute embellishment of the
> piece itself. Mr Beverley has hitherto had no opportunity of producing upon a stage of

large proportions one of those superb tableaux which for several seasons past he has been in the habit of creating at the Lyceum. To engage him, therefore, for Drury-lane Theatre was a wise step on the part of the management, for in the comparatively exhausted state of pantomimic invention, a special prestige is hard to be obtained by recurrence to what may be termed purely legitimate means. In the opening of HARLEQUIN KING NONSENSE AND THE SEVEN AGES OF MAN, the genius of this able and poetical artist displays itself with paramount conspicuousness, and twice during the first representation was the delight of the audience so keenly stimulated that cries for 'Beverley' echoed instinctively throughout the house. The occasions of these particular demonstrations were the scenes described as 'the Abode of Love' and 'the Realms of Perpetual Summer'. It is such fanciful localities as these that Mr Beverley loves to depict, and the town well knows that in the conception of such ideal spots – so delicate, so ethereal, so intangible – his imagination is boundless. Often as he has daguerrotyped the domains of fairydom, his power of producing these fictions faints and wearies not. Witness the 'Abode of Love' – with its azure lakes, its hues of golden vapour, its rich exuberance of flowers, its melting vistas – breathing, let the eye turn where it will, a chaste but voluptuous beauty, a tranquillity pre-eminently divine! To what standard can we compare these delicious embodiments of dream land but to his own? No one has ever been so daintily influenced by Queen Mab as himself; and scenic idealities like his, so exquisite in composition, so harmonious in colouring, and so pure, elegant and graceful in effect, surely mark an epoch in stage decoration. The transition from a gloomy winter landscape to the 'Realms of Summer', the scene in which the pantomimic transformations take place, belongs to another class of design for which Mr Beverley has obtained prodigious popularity. It is he who has taught us what fascinating results may be obtained from combinations of the female figure, draped in silver and gold, increasing in lustre as fresh floods of light are poured upon them, a *tableau* meanwhile gradually and majestically forming itself, until a picture is completed of surpassing radiance and brilliancy. The present instance of this gorgeous species of scenic development is equal to anything which Mr Beverley has devised before; and can panegyric be more emphatic than to say as much?

The Standard (28 December 1855) pronounced the visual *tableaux* 'gorgeous' and called Beverley 'a genius'.

See Saw Margery Daw was the 1856–7 pantomime. *The Times* (27 December 1856) thought the introduction 'too long and contains too much dialogue'. But the reviewer praised the scenery. Particularly admirable were the scene of 'Holiday's Winter Garden' and that of the 'Fairy Factory of Fancy', the latter 'one of those magnificent and gradually unfolding *tableaux* in which Mr W. Beverley has no rival.' The audience were 'enchanted with both, and not only recalled the gifted painter, but Mr Smith, the manager.' The sudden metamorphosis of the gorgeous palace to the humble cottage was 'admirably contrived, and effected with great rapidity.' The transformation scene took place in the 'Fairy Factory of Fancy' where Necessity and Holiday produced two teams of harlequin players, whose 'tricks and transformations … went off with a precision really wonderful, considering that it was the first night.' *The Era* (28 December 1856) declared that Holiday's Home in the Garden of Mistletoe 'forcibly reminded us of the glories of the Lyceum in its brightest days, and this is awarding no mean or invidious praise. It must, however, be seen, otherwise its marvellous effulgence and beauty cannot be understood.'

Little Jack Horner was the pantomime of 1857–8 and inspired a rhapsodic account from *The Era* (27 December 1857).

The opening scenery by Mr William Beverly upholds the fame of that ablest of scenic artists. In depicting the regions of the enchanter and the fairy, it is no news to tell the world that he displays an invention which, for grace and variety coupled with a warm poetical feeling, no artist who has hitherto painted for the stage has ever yet equalled. His pictures, in fact, constitute an epoch in the history of theatrical embellishment, being as remarkable in the novelty of their conception as for the delicacy and beauty of their treatment. His peculiar genius is again made transcendently visible in the new Pantomime, witness the 'Retreat of the Imagination' – a genuine Castle in the Air – the Golden Gallery, the draperied foliage, and melting distance breathing nothing but metaphor and illusion! The great scene, however, is the Palace of Coral, in which the transformations take place. Here we have one of those alluring configurations which alike ravish, dazzle and amaze the eye. Like the former instances of the same bright and luminous family, the scene is one of mutation, the field of coral which appears in the first instance gradually becoming alive with ascending shafts, upon which groups of Naiads stand in perilous eminence; while others glide imperceptibly from the sides and centres, until a gigantic tableau is formed, the gorgeous and resplendent lustre of which it would be impossible to describe, but the effect of which is overwhelming.

Then it was the turn of *Robin Hood* (1858–9) to inspire the magazine's admiration. Once again the review in *The Era* (2 January 1859) was dominated by an account of Beverley's scenery, the critic declaring that 'his fancies in the realms of fairydom become, as it were, brighter and brighter with every fresh necessity':

To this sensitive and highly-imaginative artist the present brilliant state of the Christmas scenery of the present day may be ascribed. The magnificent *tableaux* which he produced at the Lyceum were as novel in design as they were alluring in effect, and little wonder was there that they should not only captivate the town, but introduce a host of imitators whose efforts in the same forms of device were the sincerest flattery they could receive. The earnestness of contemporary rivalry has, however, only strengthened and enlarged the facility of Mr Beverley in the composition of the fairy haunts and the spectacular

ensembles to which we have alluded. The examples with which he presents us this year
are emphatic proofs of this, as well as of the variety and originality of his genius. What,
for instance, can be more refined and elegant in its conception than the 'Abode of the
Arcadian Fairies'? – an ideal study of unsurpassable beauty – the trees of Porcelain
crested with golden branches, which constitute the foreground, opening in the centre
and unfolding a vista through which a torrent of living water is seen sporting and
tumbling over a precipitous incline of rockwork. The effect of this is most charming and
when the stage is filled … with a myriad of shepherdesses, costumed after Watteau, the
beauty of the picture, so happy in its composition, so dainty in its development, and so
exquisitely glowing in its execution, completely ravishes the spectator and transports him
into regions so conceived, and so peopled, only in his dreams! The transformation scene,
the 'Retreat of the Wood Nymphs', is one of those mechanical combinations of which Mr
Beverley … is the sole creator. It realises itself through *media* that gradually became less
and less dense, until a gigantic fern is discovered, which, in its turn, opens silently and
imperceptibly, and reveals, as the scene grows, and the light becomes more effulgent,
nymphs without number reposing upon the interlacing branches of a silver oak in the
background, in attitudes the most graceful, and with the most perfect concealment of
the means that are resorted to to produce a *denouement* at once delicate, ethereal, and
lustrously, bewilderingly, magnificent. This vast scenic effort will, no doubt, be the talk of
the metropolis for some time to come.

Blanchard acknowledged Beverley's contribution charmingly by having Sylvia,
Queen of the Forest Fairies, declare in the Retreat of the Fairies:

Here fairy Beverley spell-bound holds you fast
Who every year exceeds in skill the last.

The scene of the Fairies' Retreat was proclaimed by *The Times* (27 December
1858):

the pictorial triumph of the Pantomime – one of those gradually unfolded masterpieces
almost panoramic in effect, since movement is requisite to the fulfilment of the entire
design, for which Mr Beverley is justly celebrated, and by which he may be said to have
originated a new school of scenic decoration. The *coup d'oeil* was dazzling and splendid
beyond description, and, amid a tempest of plaudits, Mr Beverley, Mr Smith and even
Mr Roxby (stage-manager) were successively brought before the footlights.

Reviewing *Jack and the Beanstalk* (1859–60), *The Era* (1 January 1860) while
praising the big heads of Dykwynkyn and the 'versatility and fecundity of his
imagination', nevertheless opined:

The chief glory of the opening consists, as heretofore, in the scenery, painted by Mr
William Beverley. This accomplished artist has given a peculiar character and

significance to all the pieces produced at the holiday periods of the year and to his refined and elegant inspirations may be attributed the interest which is now felt in spectacular theatricals, and the various fancies to which they have given rise. The charming originality of his fairy scenes, and the beauty of the pictorial effects, generated by his glowing pencil, have suggested a species of decoration of which every theatre in the metropolis now feels the influence. He is indeed Titania's own artist – the privileged delineator of fairydom, and the cognate regions of the supernatural! In the present pantomime he contributes two of his choicest pictures – pictures that a few years ago would have surprised, no less than enraptured the town, and defined him at once as the creator of a new epoch in scenic embellishment.

Beverley was called twice, to take a bow for each of these scenes. First there was the Grotto of the Pixies, which *The Times* (27 December 1859) called 'one of the most picturesque and original emanations from his pencil'. *The Era* described it:

The Grotto of the Pixies is one of those pictorial fictions upon which the eye could not repose without an interest bordering upon ravishment. A long vista of arched rock work, terminating in a point of brilliant light, which diffuses the gentle effulgence upon the sea-green waters below, constitutes an *ensemble* of surpassing loveliness, the zest of which is increased as the elfin inhabitants of the locality float gently from side to side, and form groups of engaging grace and beauty. In this scene a *ballet fantastique* is introduced in which a myriad of *coryphées* (headed by Mdlles. Morlacchi and Balbo) take part, and whose motions are reflected by the natant fairies in the background. All this is most alluringly conceived and produces a series of shifting pictures, the poetical expression of which touches the imaginative sensibility at once, and challenges the warmest admiration.

His second appearance was occasioned by the transformation scene, the Floral Home of the Good Fairy, which *The Times* said was 'a combination of colour, light and mechanical contrivance calculated no less to dazzle than enchant.' *The Era* called it:

one of those lustrous spectacles which fill the spectator with wonder as each successive *tableau* is formed, until the whole area becomes one blaze of light and fairy animation. In the golden *facade* which serves as the foreground of the scene, female figures in glittering raiment appear, while others, upon flowered pedestals at the sides, gradually steal into shape and brightness, the scene becoming more and more peopled with aerial configurations, emerging from melting perspectives, until the entire picture is completed. To describe this matchless *ensemble* is impossible. It is a display of pure enchantment, a composition eminently ideal, luminously beautiful – an illusion, in short, exquisitely dainty and brilliant. The combination of colours has been suggested by the most refined feeling, and the general effect, when the whole development is consummated, is superb in the last degree.

For his work on *Peter Wilkins* (1860–1) *The Times* (27 December 1860) dubbed Beverley 'the Claude Lorrain of pantomime' and said he had 'dipped his pencil in sunbeams to produce a "marvellous *coup d'oeil*", the flight of the flying women to their aerial city.' *The Era* (30 December 1860) declared of the transformation scene:

> It would be utterly impossible by words to do justice to this wonder of the scenic art. Mr Beverley has gone beyond himself, and, consequently, quite beyond anything that has ever been attempted of the kind before. It is called in the bills 'The Flight of the Flying Islanders to their Aerial Home, and Great Gathering of the Winged Women at the Trysting place by the Spreading Banian Tree'. The flying women, with their glorious wings, are the most heaven-like things we have ever beheld on the stage. Their wings, as gauzy as those on the fire-fly, are of great magnitude, and they seem to float upon the air out of heaven itself. If ever Elysium was duly portrayed by the art of man, it has been done by Mr Beverley at Drury-lane Theatre in this one scene. We need scarcely add that it was applauded to the echo, and the artist summoned to receive the congratulations of the audience.

Beverley was called twice to take a bow, once for his painting of Elfinland and again for the flight of the flying women.

The 1861–2 pantomime was *Harlequin and the House that Jack Built*. Beverley was called twice, for his sunrise effect in scene four and his transformation scene. *The Times* (27 December 1861) said:

> One might have thought that, after so many masterpieces of the kind which Mr Beverley has produced, his invention must have been quite exhausted. Not so, however, as he convincingly declared in the present instance. The metamorphosis of a dismal bullrush swamp into the dazzling and brilliant *tableau* which unfolds itself to the delighted gaze of the audience, as the scene gradually changes to 'Elfin land' is one of the triumphs of his skill.

The 1862–3 pantomime at Drury Lane was *Little Goody Two-Shoes*. Edmund Falconer had replaced Smith as lessee, and he retained the services of Blanchard but not Beverley. The scene-painting was in the hands of William Telbin and Thomas Grieve. The scenery was praised by the critics, but there is no mention of the artists being called.

This year Beverley was scene-painting *Riquet with the Tuft or Harlequin and Mother Shipton* at the Princess', illustrating another script by Blanchard. The show, said *The Times* (27 December 1862), was enhanced by 'the grace of some tasteful scenery' by William Beverley, assisted by Mr F. Lloyds. Particularly good were the

15. The Prince of Happy Land *at the Lyceum in 1851*

16. The Island of Jewels *at the Lyceum in 1849*

17. The 'Valley of Diamonds' in Sindbad the Sailor at Drury Lane in 1863

18. The Pixies' Grotto in Jack and the Beanstalk at Drury Lane in 1859

Lake of Lillies, the Enchanted Wood 'more picturesque though less gorgeous' and the transformation scene 'which was sufficiently brilliant and pretty to procure for Mr Beverley the honour of a call before the curtain.'

The Era (28 December 1862) praised the scene in which Mother Bunch and Mother Shipton mounted their broomstick and flew to Mushroom Marsh on a Misty Morning. It resulted in 'one of the more novel scenes that was ever put on a stage':

> There are some seventy or eighty enormous mushrooms, the chief fungus being Miss Hart, which gradually expand, and opening, disclose reclining in each mushroom, a demon dressed in red, with silver helmet and battle-axe, the effect of which is considerably enhanced by a strong green light being thrown upon the figures. When the mushrooms fully expand, the demons simultaneously rise, and beginning to dance, are interrupted by the appearance of Mother Shipton, when they fall upon their knees in three circles, producing a novel and effective tableau, which drew forth a burst of applause.

This scene is dissolved by the magic influence of Mother Bunch into:

> one of Mr Beverley's exquisite realisations of a fairies' haunt in the Lake of Water Lillies, where a ballet takes place by the attendant Gossamers, the Water Lily and the Gossamer Genie being the principal *danseuses* who performed a series of *pas* in a manner that deservedly elicited the warm acknowledgement of the audience. The ballet is one of the prettiest we remember to have seen.

The final visual delight was provided by the Bright Home of the Gossamer Fairy, the grand transformation scene, and 'we think without exception, a more beautiful scene of fairyland could not be imagined ... The brilliancy and magnificence of its *tout ensemble* drew down a unanimous and enthusiastic call for Mr Beverley who came forward and bowed his acknowledgements.' Blanchard acknowledged Beverley's contribution in the script, as the Gossamer Fairy declares the bet between Mother Bunch and Mother Shipton drawn:

> It's a drawn bet, and so, to do it cleverly,
> Suppose the wager's drawn, and drawn by Beverley,
> Whate'er he touches, he with taste expresses;
> And this will suit the Prince and the Princess's.

Falconer's second pantomime at Drury Lane saw the return of William Beverley to join Blanchard in the production of *Harlequin Sindbad the Sailor or the Great Roc of the Diamond Valley.* The *I.L.N.* (2 January 1864) declared:

> the pantomime has been placed on the stage with a gorgeousness that far exceeded our previous experience. On every scene Mr Beverley has expended the prodigality of his art.

The opening scene, Memnon and the Pyramids, was remarkable enough; but the second, the source of the Nile, was magnificent beyond expression. A cataract of real water, with a moon that looked a live one, shedding poetic light on the gauzy clouds near her, presented a scene of enchantment that was rapturously applauded by an overflowing audience. But there was something more than the scene; there was Mr Cormack's troupe of dancers, the maidens of the Nile, who descended the rocks in countless numbers, and then figured in a grand ballet of exceedingly picturesque character. It was early in the evening for a demonstration; but the audience were imperative, and Mr Beverley was brought forward to acknowledge the compliment.

Mr Falconer led Beverley out to receive his applause. *The Times* (28 December 1863) declared the Valley of Diamonds 'a masterpiece of stage painting'. 'Dark brown rocks of huge dimensions are heaped upon each other in masses distinguished by breadth and power of colour, and at distant intervals from each other the diamonds sparkle like great stars.'

The 1864–5 pantomime was *Hop O' My Thumb and his Eleven Brothers or Harlequin and the Ogre of the Seven League Boots. The Era* (1 January 1865) thought that the 'inventive genius of Beverley' was particularly shown in two tableaux. The Valley of Mosses and Lichens at Daybreak featured a series of grottos reflected in a stream running through them, fairies reclining on rows of rocks, mosses hanging in clusters from overhead and sleeping sunbeams who when awakened danced in yellow light. The transformation scene was 'The Ascent of the Rays of the Golden Light', in which clouds dispersed to show the glories of the sun, and fairies floated up and down before the rays, the combination of mechanical effects and scene-painting achieving according to *The Era* 'grandeur of effect'. The transformation scene, said *The Times* (27 December 1864), by its combination of brilliant colours 'gives a clearer notion of faery life passed in the air than any exhibition hitherto seen upon the stage.' It thought Beverley had 'surpassed himself' in the transformation scene and the Valley of Mosses and Lichens.

The Times (27 December 1865) noted of *Little King Pippin* (1865–6) 'Altogether the Drury-lane pantomime of this year is one of the most gorgeous spectacles ever witnessed by this spectacle-fed generation.' The transformation scene, 'The Fairy Factory of the Wheels of Fortune' with its wheels of burnished gold and all the operatives, young women in shining raiment, was 'a dazzling combination of brilliant colours and revolving figures … that surpasses even Mr William Beverley's previous achievements', and led to Beverley being called forward in what *The Era* (31 December 1865) called 'a tempest of applause'. *The Era* continued:

No-one is at work in the Beverleian Factory, which, when the floating clouds gradually disperse, is seen in a blaze of light, and full of Fairies, revolving, reclining, and apparently floating in the air as only Pantomime spirits can. While one wheel of fortune revolves before the audience, two more, at the back of the stage, carry very interesting loads of young ladies, as terrestrial 'merry-go-rounds' do at country fairs. From the higher regions strings of different coloured globes are let down, forming the prettiest kind of roof imaginable, and upon the 'revolvers' a silvery light is thrown with an extraordinarily brilliant effect. The dresses of those fairies nearer the front, and in a group by themselves, are of stronger colours, and the magnificence of the spectacle when the 'coloured fire' is turned on has never been surpassed.

Regarding *Number Nip* (1866–7) the critics heaped their customary praise on Beverley. *The Era* (30 December 1866) recorded of the Willow Island scene with its ballet:

> This ballet scene is charming both in idea and treatment, and is, at once, worthy of the Theatre and the artist. The water is supposed to flow into a grotto, arched over with towering rocks, and canopied with masses of trailing foliage and branches, which dip into the clear stream. The entrances to various caverns are seen, and from the banks of this secluded bay, in the very 'beautiful Rhine', the huge leaves of water plants rise in clusters. The Nixies, in delicately-tinted and filmy dresses, are discovered reclining by the river bank, and on a golden pavilion, buoyed up by lotus leaves, Nymphalin ... and Pipalee, her attendant ... float quietly into the secluded pool. A strong light is thrown from above on to the stage while the water nymphs go through an uncommonly pretty ballet ...The *coryphées* are each provided with a spear, and a shield shaped like a lotus leaf. They form all kinds of effective combinations, and spread themselves out, fan-like, after forming a close phalanx, hidden for a time under the broad and glittering shields. An exceedingly pretty effect is here produced by every lady of the *corps de ballet* having a row of deep silver fringe from the shoulder to the wrist. As the arms are extended these threads resemble sparkling drops of water.

The final transformation takes place after the marriage of Number Nip and Princess Carynthia, when the giant mountain disappears.

> The design develops itself quickly into a Fairy Lake, bordered by rocks, on which are seen sprays of coral. These 'stony limits' open, and make way for Fairies to glide out and take the places as if floating on the still water. At the back rises a light pavilion with a sapphire and amethyst canopy, and near the front of the scene are Nixies, which seem to rise and fall over the surface of the lake.

Beverley was called for by the audience after both these scenes and enthusiastically applauded. The manager Chatterton also appeared with him to take a bow.

Of *Faw, Fee, Fo, Fum* (1867–8) *The Era* (29 December 1867) reported:

> The Fairy Boudoir ... surpasses all Mr Beverley's previous efforts at this house. It recalled to the recollection of many of the audience the brightest days of the Lyceum

under Madame Vestris. The whole stage is draped in lace, with pendants of pearls, a golden temple rising at the back, supporting, or being supported, by living female caryatides, in garments of gold, glittering all over with diamonds. The effect of this was really charming – a scene of bewildering beauty, which fairly drove the audience wild with delight. There were calls for 'Beverley' before the scene was half developed, and they never ceased until the gifted artist appeared upon the stage to bow again and again his acknowledgements.

In *Grimalkin the Great* (1869–70), there were, thought *The Era* (3 January 1869), 'three splendid scenes' in the Opening, a Flowery Dell on a Summer's Morning, cornfields and the banks of a river, and the 'brilliant transformation in the Web of the Golden Gossamer':

The first is a Fairy dell, overhung with trees, luxuriant with thick foliage, fresh with the verdure of virgin spring. From the mountains in the distance, down a facile descent of moss-covered rocks, there pours a cataract of real water, divided into two streams. In the centre of this, on dry stones, are seated a myriad of Nymphs and Swains, dressed *a la* Watteau, while groups of Fairies nestle among the wild roses that bloom round the pool, which the accumulated waters form at its base. A more charming scene than this could not well be conceived. The splash and foam of the falling waters are so real, the verdure of the trees is so true to Nature in her best humour, the groupings are so easy and graceful, that the spectator feels himself to be in the presence of a highly idealised reality. The distinguished merit of this scene is that it is not simply effective from the theatrical point of view, but that it is also in the highest degree artistic. Painted in oil or water colours, on a canvas four feet by three, it would find a place on the line in the best rooms of the Royal Academy. This is Mr Beverley's great distinction – that he is above all an artist, and, in his conception, a poet.

The Times (28 December 1868), calling it 'certainly one of the most beautiful scenes ever produced by the genius of Beverley' noted that he had 'not only devised a picture striking in all its points, but he ha[d] infused the tone of Watteau into his colour, and the foliage of the background belong[ed] to the period of courtly pastoral as the costume of the figures.'

The transformation scene, The Web of Golden Gossamers, was pronounced by *The Era*:

another example of Mr Beverley's taste and artistic skill. The grouping is distinguished by harmony of form and the painting by a simple blending of colour, which is in the highest degree pleasing. There is nothing gaudy, nothing meretricious about the fairy picture, and the delight of the audience when it was fully unfolded before them, proves that the public are quite capable of appreciating good things in art when they can get them.

As *Beauty and the Beast* (1869–70) began, the stage was darkened and through the gloom two gigantic figures of Evil Genii were seen among the clouds to the left and the right. To the accompaniment of muted violins ('always so effective in these situations' thought *The Era*) the clouds partly opened at the back and through the haze a group of female figures were discovered floating in the air and gradually sinking towards the level of the stage. The mist rose and the sun began to glisten on the water in the extreme distance – an image *The Era* (2 January 1870) found 'Turnerian'. In the centre of the stage was a group of Peris. Others reclined under awnings of palm-fringed cloth, and on either side of the stage palm trees, long-leaved plants and all kinds of luxuriant growth hemmed in the 'Vale of Cashmere', as 'this exquisite scene by Mr Beverly is called.' Across the back of the stage was a huge archway of rock and through this the distant view was seen. 'The Vale of Cashmere is a specimen of painting in the literal acceptation of the term, and is worthy of Mr Beverly and the Theatre.'

On *The Dragon of Wantley* (1870–1) Beverley painted the 'Haunt of the Water Nymphs' where the personified rivers of England gather to celebrate the marriage of the Thames and the Medway. It was, said *The Times* (27 December 1870), 'one of those delicious, dreamy combinations of sparkling lake and light foliage, whereby Mr W. Beverley has gained his high reputation.' The *I.L.N.* (31 December 1870) said of this scene that Beverley 'displayed that marvellous power of landscape-painting in which he scarcely has any rival.' The transformation scene, the World of Waters, was declared by *The Era* (1 January 1871) to be 'a gorgeous spectacle in Mr Beverley's very best style. Britannia on a golden throne, surrounded by golden and silver attendants. The whole stage is one blaze of dazzling light.' *The Era* reported: 'Mr Beverly is, of course, summoned on to the stage, and cheered enthusiastically.'

On *Tom Thumb the Great* (1871–2) there were a succession of stunningly visual sequences, starting with the Doll's House opening. *The Era* (31 December 1871) reported:

> The prologue is in the highest degree fanciful and ingenious. ... This scene is enacted entirely by children, and extremely clever children they are, dressed up in pretty imitation of every imaginable style of doll ... The interior of the dolls' house is capitally managed. The front of the house removes in orthodox fashion, and then the three floors of a dolls' house are discovered with living dolls. In the bed-room the children are making beds and tidying up. In the parlour the dolls are receiving company. In the kitchen the cooks are at work with the dinner. The realism of this picture made the children shriek with delight.

The Garden of Dainty Delights followed in which the Enchantress La Faye summoned the spirits of music, poetry, painting and dancing to choose the subject of the pantomime. *The Era* said it was 'a celebrated Dresden China scene which will soon be the talk of all London. A picture so elegant and refined as this has seldom been seen or attempted':

> The whole stage represents a drawing-room ornament of Dresden China, and the blues, yellows, purples, violets, greens and ambers of the shepherds and shepherdesses, the golden cages, the baskets of flowers, when heightened by the limelight, form a picture of surpassing beauty. A little maiden in our immediate vicinity covered her face with her hands and whispered to her papa that it was all too beautiful to look at.

The scene ended with 'a superb Watteau ballet, the very perfection of taste, led by Mdlle Marie Gillet, a most graceful *danseuse*.' The transformation scene was 'one of singular beauty':

> Picture a bouquet of revolving flowers, each cup filled with gold and silver Fairies, tinted now with the golden glare of the sun, now with the silver rays of the moon, now with the ruby glory of the sunset, now with the pale greenish tint of a midnight landscape, and you may have some ideas of the beauty of Mr Beverley's Transformation Scene. How the veteran artist was called, and how the whole house shouted, need not be described.

In *The Children in the Wood* (1872–3), usually better known as *Babes in the Wood*, there was a succession of visual delights. The first spectacular scene was 'The Ivory Gate of Dreams', created by Beverley to give the impression of children entering the realm of dreams. In it, the distant objects were seen through a light film of gauze, supposed to represent a screen of gossamer web. The dream of the children was illustrated by groups representing fairy stories, which appeared to float through the air. The sequence ended with a ballet, 'A Gossamer Dream'.

'The Depths of the Forest' was 'one of the most elaborate scenes in the Opening of the Pantomime'. Huge trunks of trees lined the back of the stage and 'the gloom of the forest [wa]s suggested with the force to be expected from an artist of Mr Beverley's skill.' The final transformation scene, Queen Mab's Car, began at the back of the stage, supposed to represent a lake, from which the fairy car of Queen Mab advanced towards the footlights, led by milk-white doves and guided by Fairies. The birds were held by blue streamers and from the topmost heights of the stage hung long fibres of gold and silver. 'The central group of Fairies and the surrounding figures brought into the design have a very rich and brilliant, but singularly refined effect, and the whole Transformation may be described as a pretty idea, worked out in the best possible taste.' Beverley was called forward to acknowledge the applause.

The transformation scene in *Jack in the Box* (1873–4) was declared by *The Times* (27 December 1873), 'one of the most felicitous products of Mr Beverley's fancy, being not only beautiful but original.' Of the scene 'The Golden Land of Plenty; or, the Harvest Home of the Fairies', *The Era* (29 December 1873), declared 'Its name will suggest its nature, but not one half of its transcendent beauties. These we must leave the reader to see for himself, and can promise him something literally dazzling.'

On *Aladdin* (1874–5), everyone praised Beverley's scenery but actually wrote little about it. *The Times* (28 December 1874) reported that Beverley 'painted in his best style the interior of the cavern, the garden of jewels, the exterior of Aladdin's palace and above all, "the bright region of Fan-ta-See", the transformation scene.' The *I.S.D.N.* (2 January 1875) called the transformation 'an art-triumph' and reported 'a well merited call for the veteran artist'.

On *Whittington and His Cat* (1875–6), there were two major transformation scenes. One was on the voyage to Zanzibar. As *The Era* (2 January 1876) put it, the ship suddenly disappeared:

> leaving behind the rigging, which is covered with sea-weed, and up which swarm dusky urchins, whose head adornments send forth a dazzling light. Obedient to (the Fairy Bluebell's) summons nymphs and mermaids rise from their emerald beds and coral banks, and there takes place a 'grand Ballet of Marine Wonders', reflecting credit on the taste and ingenuity of Mr John Cormack.

It was one of the prettiest and best-managed transformation scenes that even the management of Drury Lane had ever produced.

The final transformation was pronounced 'remarkably pretty'. 'We see Water Nymphs rising from a lake supported on crystal columns; more nymphs gliding gracefully down the streams; more hovering in air on either side; and more emerging from water lilies. Coloured fires add to the brilliancy of the picture.' Beverley was called for by the audience.

Harlequin and the Forty Thieves was the 1876–7 pantomime. Beverley was now under exclusive contract to Drury Lane. *The Times* (27 December 1876) said he:

> rarely produces anything which does not leave an agreeable impression on the mind. On this occasion he has painted in his best style the Market-place of Bagdad and the Divan of the Genii, while the transformation scene lays claim to the merit of uniting taste and splendour.

Beverley was twice called during the transformation scene, transporting the characters to the Peri's Palace where a series of jars was transformed into living palm trees. *The Era* (31 December 1876) called it 'glorious'.

The visual highlights of *Harlequin and The White Cat* (1877–8) included, according to *The Era* (30 December 1877) 'a remarkably attractive scene', the Lake of Water Lilies and Fairy Grove by Midnight, 'which must be pronounced one of Mr William Beverly's best efforts' and the transformation scene in which a tangled brake opened up to reveal the distribution of the wedding cake and the bridal gifts of the fairies. *The Times* (27 December 1877) pronounced this 'a most gorgeous and dazzling scene, in which Mr William Beverley certainly equals, if he does not indeed surpass his previous triumphs.'

On *Cinderella* (1878–9), *The Times* (27 December 1878) said:

The scenery, throughout appropriate, occasionally, as in the representation of 'the illuminated ball-room' in Prince Amabel's Palace, splendid, had its gorgeous culmination, as was to be expected in the transformation scene, 'The Assembly of the Hours', a brilliant combination of many colours, irradiating numberless fairy forms.

The Era (29 December 1878) said the transformation was 'So beautiful and so bewildering in its loveliness' that Beverley and Chatterton were called to take a bow. It was the last of Chatterton's Drury Lane productions.

For Augustus Harris' first pantomime, *Bluebeard* (1879–80), Beverley was missing, replaced by three artists, Henry Emden, William Telbin and Frederick Fenton. This artistic team effort marked a distinct departure from the previous arrangement whereby the whole visual conception was in the hands of a single artist – Beverley. The presiding genius was now Harris who assigned painters to scenes after he had approved the overall conception.

On *Mother Goose and the Enchanted Fountain* (1880–1), Harris again had three painters: Emden and Telbin now joined by Henry Cuthbert, a decision presumably vindicated by the verdict of *The Era* (1 January 1881) which said 'the scenery throughout is absolutely beyond reproach, and reflects immense credit on the artists.' On *Robinson Crusoe* (1881–2), Harris employed six artists, Henry Emden, J.W. Hall, Walter Hann, Julian Hicks, J. Ryan and Brioschi, to provide the scenery for the fourteen scenes of the opening. After the controversial and heavily criticized *Sindbad* of 1882–3, William Beverley was summoned back to Drury Lane for *Cinderella* (1883–4) but now to be part of a team including Henry Emden, William Telbin, William Perkins and Thomas Grieve. Beverley was responsible for the Illuminated Palace Gardens, pronounced 'gorgeous' by *The Times* (27 December 1883) and 'grand' by *The Era* (29 December 1883), and for the transformation scene, 'The Home of Light and Love' which *The Era* thought 'At first it is beautiful in its simplicity. Later it becomes dazzling in its brilliancy.' But *The Times* thought coming directly after one of Harris' spectacular processions – the heroes and heroines of all the great pantomimes – it 'has some difficulty in holding its own.' The dominance of the procession at the expense of the transformation scene is indicative of the way the pantomime was going under Harris.

On *Whittington and his Cat* (1884–5), Beverley was only one of a team of six scene-painters – along with Grieve, Ryan, Emden, Leolyn Hart and W.B. Spong. *The Times* review (27 December 1884) did not mention the painters. Increasingly the reviews concentrated on the spectacle, the processions, the ballets, the special effects, and the costumes and took the painting for granted. The fact that *The Times* also failed to mention the artists in 1885, 1886 and 1887 is indicative.

On *Aladdin* (1885–6), the painting team was Henry Emden, William Perkins, Julian Hicks and J. Johnstone, with Beverley contributing the background to the procession, 'A Dream of Fair Women' and the transformation scene, 'Aladdin's Golden Dream', of which *The Era* (2 January 1886) declared 'Mr William Beverley has supplied the Drury-lane stage with another gorgeous example of his unrivalled genius as a scenic artist.'

For *The Forty Thieves* (1886–7), Beverley joined Emden, Perkins, Ryan, Telbin, Grieve and Hart. He painted the interior of the robbers' cave. They all provided, said *The Era* (1 January 1887), 'splendid artistic assistance'.

Beverley's final Drury Lane pantomime was *Puss in Boots* (1887–8). Emden, Ryan and Perkins did the bulk of the scenes, with the two great painters Beverley and Telbin painting one scene each, Beverley the panorama taking in the park, the vineyard and the hayfield, and Telbin the transformation scene, 'The Golden Honeymoon'. Beverley, whose eyesight had been failing, died on 15 May 1889 aged seventy-eight.

From the 1860s onwards, the tradition of scenery consisting of 'either cloths [painted canvas on rollers] suspended from the flies, or flats [painted canvas stretched on wooden frames] ... originally supported in two sets of wooden grooves' was increasingly superseded by the box set with side walls at an angle and with three dimensional 'built-out' scenery to enhance the flats and cloths.[26]

The scenic artists working with the new system and their actor-manager employers found themselves regularly accused of overloading the stage and swamping the play with unnecessary furniture, distorting and slowing down the action as long waits became necessary to accommodate ever more elaborate and lavish three-dimensional sets, all in the name of greater realism. There were three main critical standpoints: the traditionalists who supported simple painted back-cloths and sets, the atavists who sought to return to plain Elizabethan staging techniques and the modernists who advocated abstract scenery and lighting effects in place of realistic scene-painting and properties. It was the realists who prevailed and built-out scenery became the norm. Interviewed in 1885, Beverley said:

> They overload plays nowadays with decoration to the detriment of the drama. A sufficiency of mounting is in favour of a play, but an incessant introduction of unnecessary realistic work is against it. If you have good actors and actresses you don't require all this extraneous aid. Have as much painting as you like; that is legitimate art. A well-painted scene assists the poetry of a drama, for it stimulates the imagination; but a 'built-up' scene, full of elaborate realistic detail, distracts the attention of the spectator from the essentials of the drama, namely the poetry, the character, the acting. I condemn

all this straining after realism entirely, because it serves no artistic purpose. The audience know the scene is a sham, and no tricks of the carpenter, the 'property' man or the florist can convince them of its reality.[27]

But Beverley was one of the last surviving masters of the old-style scene-painting. The future lay with the realists and built-out scenery. At Drury Lane, the unified artistic vision of the single painter, like Beverley, was replaced by an ensemble in which a team of painters divided the duties between them.

Beverley had similarly strong views about how the whole genre was developing. Asked in the same *Sunday Times* interview what were his views about the state of pantomime in 1885, he said:

Well on that subject I had better not speak. For sixteen years I had the entire management of the productions at Drury Lane, and then pantomime was quite a different thing to what it is now. They are certainly more gorgeous spectacles now, and perhaps that is what people want. Years ago we would never have dreamed of spending the enormous sums that Mr Augustus Harris spends on his pantomimes. We looked formerly upon pantomime as belonging in a way to the 'legitimate drama', but then we endeavoured to tell the simple fairy story in the simple yet adequate manner.

Taking the Lyceum and Drury Lane years together, Beverley had for over thirty years provided London audiences with a vision of fairyland that entranced successive generations of theatregoers, an enchanted world of lakes and forests, grottoes and caverns, meadows and villages, castles and towers and palaces, where fairies, elves, goblins, wizards, pixies, witches, nymphs and naiads disported themselves. But it was the scale, style and approach of Harris, massive, spectacular and imperial, that was to triumph over the poetic visions of Beverley and Blanchard.

7

The Drury Lane Pantomime: The Creators

For the remainder of this book, we will view the evolution of pantomime through the prism of the Theatre Royal, Drury Lane. As A.E. Wilson, the early authority on pantomime, wrote in 1934:

> the history of pantomime must inevitably resolve itself into a history of Drury Lane. It was on the boards of the 'national theatre' that some of the first pantomimes appeared and earned the support of the public, and it was there that pantomime assumed the character of a fixed institution.[1]

Stanley Lupino, who when he grew up starred in Drury Lane pantomimes under Arthur Collins, recalled the importance of Drury Lane pantomime to him as a boy:

> In my boyhood Christmas was not Christmas without the pantomime – and of all pantomimes that at Drury Lane. Any small boy could be kept good for a whole year with the threat of forfeiting that annual treat. I know I would have taken a thrashing once a week willingly in order to secure the privilege, and it would have been easier than saving up my pennies ... all England wanted to see it and all the nurseries of the Empire lived on its memory as retold by mothers, grandmothers, and great-grandmothers.[2]

It is only fair to acknowledge that pantomime flourished everywhere, not just in London and that often in the big provincial cities, they were every bit as good as their London counterparts. Leopold Wagner acknowledged this in his book *The Pantomimes and All About Them* in 1881:

> Of provincial pantomimes, those of Leeds, Manchester, Liverpool, Birmingham, Leicester, Sheffield, Bradford, Edinburgh, Glasgow and Dublin, are the most important, and create quite a *furore* among playgoers in their respective towns during the holiday season. Notably among these may be mentioned the Pantomimes annually produced at the Alexandra Theatre, Liverpool, which, under the able and experienced direction of Mr Edward Saker, have of late years achieved popularity sufficient to attract very numerous

audiences not from neighbouring towns alone, but from afar ... the same may be said also of the Christmas productions at the *Grand Theatre, Leeds* ... Naturally, one would expect that at the 'Grand' Mr Wilson Barrett would produce every species of performance upon a scale of grandeur, and in this neither ourselves nor the public have been suffered to be disappointed; since Mr Barrett's Pantomime at Leeds was admitted last year to be superior to any London production. Manchester owns no less than three theatres, annually vying with each other in the matter of Pantomime supremacy ... It is needless to add that all the above theatres go to a very considerable expense in these productions; while it is not too much to assert that Mrs Nye Chart's excellent theatre at Brighton annually presents to its fashionable patrons a Pantomime little, if at all, inferior to a similar production in the West End of London.[3]

The Theatre Royal, Drury Lane, was one of the two patent theatres which were expected to uphold the hallowed traditions of the legitimate drama. Its cavernous size and capacity of 3,000 were always difficult to fill but like many theatres it was the success of the annual Christmas pantomime which often kept it afloat financially, allowing it to mount the programme of Shakespeare and opera which was expected of it. The Drury Lane pantomime was to become the standard by which all other pantomimes were judged; so much so that it was regularly dubbed 'the national home of pantomime'.[4] George Lancaster wrote in *The Theatre*, 'a Drury Lane pantomime is an English institution. We can no more do without it than roast-beef, plum pudding, and mince-pies.'[5]

In the hands of a succession of buccaneering capitalist entrepreneurs, it acquired and maintained this reputation. After a series of short-lived lessees had failed to make a success of the theatre, the lease was acquired in 1852 by E.T. Smith who was to run Drury Lane for ten years. Edward Tyrrel Smith (1804–77) was apparently the eldest son of Admiral E.T. Smith, though the acerbic grande dame of the British theatre, Geneviève Ward, suggested that if there was an admiral among his antecedents, it was a Phoenician admiral and that 'his features were decidedly of Semitic cast.'[6] Theatre historian Errol Sherson called him the greatest impresario London had ever known.[7] Ward recalled him as 'an extraordinary person, a born gambler from the cradle' and Edward Stirling, who was his stage manager at Drury Lane, described him 'a Jack-of-all trades and master of none'.[8] The journalist Edmund Yates remembered him as a 'shrewd, uneducated, good-natured vulgarian of a dreadful backslapping, Christian-name-calling familiarity'.[9] A.E. Wilson called him 'an engaging blend of Barnum, Crummles and Horatio Bottomley'.[10] Starting out in life as a navy midshipman, he was subsequently a Metropolitan Police constable, an auctioneer, a wine-merchant, a picture-dealer, a land-agent, a bill-discounter and Dunmow flitch-of-bacon restorer. Having become landlord of a Holborn public house, he perceived that money was to be made from the burgeoning entertainment industry. He entered it and there was almost no form of the business he did not try. The first of his speculative ventures was turning Crockford's gambling house in St. James's into a fashionable restaurant, the Wellington. From 1850 to 1852 he was lessee of the Marylebone Theatre and from there he moved on to Drury Lane. With limited capital, he took it on, the rental having been reduced from £10,000 to £3,500 because no-one wanted to take a risk on it. Smith sought to maximize his audience by reducing ticket prices, providing refreshments at affordable prices, abolishing box-keeping fees and introducing regular matinee performances of the pantomime.[11] He announced his intention of making 'Old Drury' a theatre of the masses, 'by bringing out spectacle, farce and thrilling melodrama', as well as pantomime.[12] In short, his production philosophy was one of commercial populism. The success of the pantomime and the spectacular stage adaptations of Uncle Tom's Cabin and Charles Reade's Gold meant 'the first season terminated with a handsome profit.'[13]

He dutifully staged Shakespeare and grand opera and engaged the great French actress Rachel and the flamboyant tragedian Gustavus V. Brooke but in the interests of the box office also staged a circus, and engaged 'the human fly', a man who walked on the ceiling of the theatre, to the dismay of upholders of the Lane's reputation. Later when he was running Her Majesty's Theatre, he was with difficulty restrained from introducing the prize-fighters Sayers and Heenan to the audience between the acts of the opera.[14]

It was not long before concern was being expressed about the nature of the fare on offer at Drury Lane. As The Times (27 December 1853) noted of Smith's regime:

> We are aware that there are critics who, not satisfied with looking at results, have an unseemly anxiety about the causes of things. These doubt whether the house has been kept open by strictly 'legitimate' means. A tragic season supported by a single 'star' (Gustavus V. Brooke) and followed by a period of horsemanship, topped with a bal masqué, does not seem to certain fastidious tastes the high road to that dramatic regeneration for which all England gasps, and is destined, we fear, to gasp for a long time

but it concluded:

> the sum total, that Drury-lane is a thriving concern, is a creditable finish to the items, however odd, various, and illegitimate they may look. Something like an instinctive power of hitting the taste of a large portion of the public must have more to do with the matter than many are willing to imagine.

The I.L.N. (31 December 1853) similarly highlighted the concerns about the standard of entertainment at the home of the 'national drama' and agreed with The Times that Smith had sought to cater to the tastes of his audience and in so doing had demonstrated the very English qualities of 'talent, instinct and perseverance'.

Not content with running Drury Lane, Smith continually embarked on new ventures, and as Stirling recorded his 'many ventures kept him poor', reporting 'A Jew friend observed to me: "Smith, sir, 's a wonderful man, keeps plenty of people in bread, earns lots of money, but can't keep it; none sticks to his fingers".'[15] He secured a renewal of his Drury Lane lease in 1862 on condition that he completely redecorated but he could not afford to. So he handed over the lease to Edmund Falconer for £5,000 on condition that he spend £7,000 on decoration. While running Drury Lane, he also leased Her Majesty's Theatre, Haymarket in 1861–2 and put on a season of opera. From 1861 to 1869 he was lessee and manager of the Cremorne Gardens, a pleasure ground which combined theatre, music hall, supper rooms, park, dancing and fireworks displays (it closed in 1877). He converted the Panopticon of Science and Art in Leicester Square into the Alhambra in 1858 for circus and music hall and ran it until 1861. Although by over-extending himself he had lost Drury Lane he had not lost his taste for management. He ran Astleys (where he presented 'Adah Isaacs Mencken in *Mazeppa*) from 1863 to 1866, the Lyceum from 1867 to 1869, where he introduced the Vokes Family, and the Surrey Theatre from 1870 to 1871. He opened the Cremorne Supper Rooms in Leicester Square, acquired the Radnor Tavern in Chancery Lane and took over a travelling circus. He leased the Highbury Barn in 1871 to create a theatre-cum-pleasure ground but it failed and he opened a dining room in the vaults of the Royal Exchange, which also failed. He acquired *The Sunday Times* for a short period in 1856, and stood for parliament in Bedford (setting up a newspaper, the *Bedfordshire Independent*, to promote his cause) but once again he failed, his campaign costing him £2,000. His final venture was the building of the Elephant and Castle Theatre in 1872, which he lost in 1873. It was an undertaking, according to Ward, 'which, he used to say, "broke his back"' – in other words, ruined him as an operator on a great scale. The net result, however, was retirement on a small competence to the neighbourhood of Kennington Park with another, and a more youthful, wife. 'I do not know her number, nor perhaps did he', said Ward.[16] According to Sherson, he died 'forgotten and almost in poverty' in 1877.[17]

The regime of E.T. Smith was followed by that of F.B. Chatterton. A rather different personality to the genial Smith, Chatterton was renowned for his fierce temper and chronic litigiousness. Geneviève Ward recalled that 'his outbursts of wrath behind the curtain were terrible. The humbler members of the company quailed before him' and that he had 'a passion for litigation, and he lived to see his folly.'[18] But to counterbalance this he was capable of immense generosity and was devoted to the drama. His friend, the actor-manager John Coleman wrote: 'Wilful, irascible, and wrong-headed as Frederick Balsir Chatterton often was in the days of his prosperity, he was always large-hearted and benevolent. Bad temper and false pride were his weak points; kindness and generosity were his strong ones.'[19] Coleman suggests that his temper may have been exacerbated by the pain he suffered from a spinal condition. But 'his dominant ideas ... were love of family, and .... an absolute reverence for the highest form of dramatic art. His first ambition was to restore the fallen fortunes of his family, his next, to make the National Theatre worthy of its great traditions.'[20] He supported his mother and family financially and conscious of his own lack of education, which had resulted from the straitened circumstances of the family in his youth, he ensured the best of educations for his brothers. Ward recalled that he kept old actors on his staff out of pure kindness, saying 'if I don't employ them, who will? What are they to do?'[21]

Frederick Balsir Chatterton (1834–86) was born in London, scion of a musical family: his grandfather had been a 'professor of music' at Portsmouth and two uncles, celebrated harpists. His father Edward, 'being rather a dare-devil and a ne'er-do-weel ... remained ... for many years a "Jack of all trades".'[22] He was sometimes a music publisher and musical instrument seller but spent many years as box office manager at a variety of theatres. Although he never wrote an autobiography, Chatterton gave a detailed account of his life to his friend John Coleman, who included it verbatim in his *Players and Playwrights I have Known* (1888). Frederick became stage-struck at a young age and thanks to Thomas Greenwood of Sadler's Wells, where his father worked at one time, he went on in the pantomime as a super and later pursued an undistinguished acting career at the Olympic and Soho Theatres. He decided on a career in management, spending a season with E.T. Smith at Drury Lane as box office manager before joining Charles Dillon as acting manager at the Lyceum in 1857. Dillon failed to make a success of management and in 1859 returned to his career as a provincial tragedian. Playwright Edmund Falconer took on the lease of the Lyceum in 1861 and Chatterton became his partner, having had a season as lessee of the St James' Theatre in 1859–60. Then in 1862, Falconer bought the lease of Drury Lane from Smith, investing the £13,000 he had made at the Lyceum, and he invited Chatterton to join him. Chatterton agreed, his ambition being to restore 'Old Drury to its position as the home of the poetic drama from which it has been deposed by E.T. Smith.'[23] Under Chatterton's influence, Drury Lane mounted productions of *King John, Henry IV, Faust, Comus* and *Manfred* but the productions masterminded by Falconer, notably the historical drama *Bonnie Dundee*, proved to be expensive failures. Falconer, according to Chatterton, 'got into a state verging upon imbecility, owing to his unfortunate infirmity' (which seems to have been alcoholism), and in 1865 was declared bankrupt.[24] The partnership owed £10,000. But Chatterton cleared the debts and in 1866 acquired the lease for himself, running the theatre until 1879. He initiated the policy that was to become associated with Drury Lane of alternating 'big, panoramic dramas and spectacular pantomimes'.[25] There was a successful series of Shakespeare revivals starring Samuel Phelps, an equally successful series of adaptations of Scott's Waverley novels and the annual Blanchard pantomimes. Chatterton was making £16–17,000 a year when he was fatally tempted to diversify. He was persuaded to join Benjamin Webster in his management of the debt-burdened Adelphi and Princess' Theatres and in 1874 took on the leases of both theatres alone. But as he ruefully recalled:

> I might as well have attempted to drive the horses of the sun. My poor old dad tried to dissuade me from this suicidal act, but it was in vain that he pointed out that three theatres were more than one man's work, however energetic he might be ... but I could not withstand the temptation.[26]

At first he sustained the other two theatres with the profits from Drury Lane but he then experienced a major downturn in his fortunes at the Lane. He quarrelled with the major star Samuel Phelps who departed, he engaged the Italian tragedian Enrico Rossi and his company, who failed, and his expensive productions of *Richard III*, *The Winter's Tale* and *Peveril of the Peak* also failed. He kept going by borrowing money 'at usurious interest'.[27] He was forced to dispose of the leases of the Adelphi in 1876 and the Princess' in 1878. He claimed that his losses up to Christmas 1879 were over £7,000 and he was banking on the pantomime to bail him out, but the pantomime was 'a miserable failure', he was unable to pay salaries, the Vokes Family (the stars of the pantomime) went on strike and Chatterton was forced to close the theatre. Edward Stirling says he was actually in debt to the tune of £36,000.[28] He lost the lease. His friends rallied round and several benefits were held for the Chatterton family which raised £800. The Gatti Brothers, who had taken Covent Garden for the Christmas season, engaged him as their manager for the 1880–1 pantomime. He produced *Valentine and Orson* but a quarrel with the Gattis about his benefit at the end of the season led to him severing his connection with the brothers. John Coleman takes up the story:

> The year after he left Covent Garden, yielding to bad advice, Chatterton was unfortunately induced to tempt fortune again by embarking on management at Sadler's Wells Theatre. The result was most disastrous. The receipts at no period of the season ever approached half the expenses. Nor was this the worst. As there was no capital to work upon, the productions were of such a character as to be absolutely ruinous to his reputation.

He opened on 29 September 1881 and the theatre closed abruptly on 4 February 1882 during the run of the pantomime *Ali Baba and the Forty Thieves*. John Coleman, who went to see it, recorded: 'It was, I think, the saddest sight I have ever witnessed. An empty house and a shabby, tawdry show which would have discredited a respectable barn ... It was evident he had reached the bottom of the bill.'[29] Chatterton never returned to management but sought to eke out a living as a reciter of passages from Dickens before dying of bronchitis and enlarged thyroid in 1886 virtually blind, penniless and aged only fifty-two.

After a hiatus of eight months, an ambitious, self-confident twenty-seven year old turned up with a bid for the lease. He managed to raise the required £3,000, won the lease and embarked in 1879 on the career that would make him, in Macqueen Pope's words, 'the most successful manager there since the time of David Garrick'.[30]

Augustus Harris (1852–96), popularly known as 'Gus', was actor, writer and above all, impresario and producer. The *D.N.B.* says he had 'a genius for stage management, in which in his time he had no English equal'.[31] His father Augustus Glossop Harris (1825–73), himself a former actor and then manager of the Princess' Theatre, was connected with Covent Garden for nearly twenty-seven years and also directed operas in St Petersburg, Paris, Berlin, Madrid and Barcelona. During the last four years of his life he produced the Christmas shows at Covent Garden. The younger Harris also started out as an actor in 1873, though Geneviève Ward recalled he had been 'very bad' as Malcolm in *Macbeth*.[32] He came to specialize in juvenile and light comedy parts. But his real talents lay elsewhere. He became assistant stage manager and then stage manager at Covent Garden and in 1876 produced Blanchard's Crystal Palace pantomime *Sindbad the Sailor*. After he took over Drury Lane, he established the regime that made his fortune and that of the theatre: the autumn melodrama, beginning with *The World* (1880), and the Christmas pantomime. He also produced highly praised seasons of opera at Covent Garden. On the melodrama and pantomimes, he was always co-writer and he sometimes acted too, though the *D.N.B.* reports 'he had few gifts as an actor.'[33] Like his predecessors he took on other theatres and in 1891 was managing Covent Garden, Her Majesty's and the Olympic along with Drury Lane. He also found time to serve on the London County Council and was Sheriff of London in 1890–9. It was in this capacity that he was knighted on the occasion of the visit of the German Emperor. He died in Folkestone on 22 June 1896 of exhaustion, diabetes and cancer, worn out by his exertions and aged only forty-three. Contemporaries left a vivid picture of his life as the great impresario. Journalist Richard Whiteing wrote:

> He began work long before he began breakfast ... The first person to arrive in the morning at 'The Elms' was his secretary Mr. Arthur Yates ... He brought with him all the latest letters and telegrams from Drury Lane Theatre, and took instructions on them while the chief was gently soaking in his bath. Then came the morning meal, not less important than the correspondence, for Sir Augustus was a mighty trencherman.[34]

His breakfasts were occasions, recorded Macqueen Pope, with secretaries in attendance, auditions going on and authors and scenic artists milling around.[35] The great costumer Charlie Alias was often in attendance, with Harris sketching on the tablecloth what he wanted in the way of costumes, 'Then he glanced at the newspapers, and rarely failed to find some flattering article about himself, for his great theatrical and operatic projects kept him constantly in the public mind.'[36]

He was the first producer to engage a permanent press agent. Initially it was Augustus Moore, the raffish journalist brother of novelist George Moore.

> He now turned his thoughts to the work of the day. Perhaps he had some dramatic author staying at the house who was collaborating with him in one of those mechanical and elaborate – yet in many respects happy-go-lucky – productions called 'Drury Lane Dramas'. If so, there would naturally be important conversations with him. After his patron had left for town, the collaborator, still remaining at the house, would go to his desk and do his best to combine instructions with original ideas. The work turned out on this curious system was naturally wanting in almost every quality of dramatic art, but it usually pleased the public, and that was enough for the authors ... It was now time, perhaps, for the great man's audiences with the managers of his provincial touring business, who came to discuss some grand project for the control of all the great provincial theatres.[37]

Macqueen Pope recalled:

> As a producer, he was a great stickler for accuracy. Everything must be dead right, down to the tiniest detail. He missed nothing. He was a fair and just man, everyone, including the stage hands, adored him. But if there was slackness, carelessness, inefficiency, then his wrath was terrible. His insistence on accuracy made the deepest impression on his staff.[38]

Gus would eat a gargantuan lunch 'And this gave him great vigour for the time being, and he arrived at the theatre with an energy that was simply appalling. His presence there was immediately felt in every department.'

> At the theatre he would remain all day, directing operations, receiving people with whom he had appointments, and with a strong guard between him and the bores. Then perhaps he would have to dash off to a committee meeting at a theatre, other than Drury Lane, in which he had an interest. This done, he returned to resume work in his private room, dictating, scheming, overlooking accounts, yet leaving it all suddenly from time to time to dart on to the stage and give an eye to a rehearsal. Back again in his room, perhaps he found another privileged visitor, and in the midst of their conversations he might pause to send an order to the City for shares in a financial undertaking. ... With his intense restlessness, he occasionally drove some of those in his employment half-crazy ... In conducting rehearsals, especially towards the last, he showed immense energy for a short time, and then tired and left someone else to take his place. As the day wore on he had another hearty meal, and then, the office work over, snatched a doze in his room, or sometimes slept for hours. On awaking, he dressed for the evening, and remained at the theatre until the performance came to a close. After that he supped at the Albion, or at a restaurant in Regent Street in which he had a pecuniary interest, and finally went home.

At home it is no exaggeration to say he was always absorbed in work. He would sit up for what was left of the night, planning out some great pantomime, conjuring up all sorts of scenes and situations, and thinking how he could surpass himself and best his last year's record. When the pantomime was written he went over it most laboriously with a view to its improvement and passed it on to one of his principal managers for further revision. This done, he took another turn at it, until what with his cuts, additions and interlineations, in all sort of coloured inks, the manuscript was a mystery to all but the learned in the craft. Dramas were also treated in the same way. ... He was so preoccupied with work that he often forgot important social engagements through sheer weariness of brain.[39]

In its obituary *The Theatre* suggested:

Perhaps if he had entrusted more work to his capable lieutenants his life might have been prolonged; but he had a distrust of the abilities of other people as compared to his own. He preferred to see his own work through, and no one could have been more entitled to the full credit of everything that was done in his name.[40]

In an article defiantly entitled 'The National Theatre' written for *The Fortnightly Review* in 1885, Harris set out his theatrical agenda:

The fact that 'Drury Lane' has been known from time immemorial as the National Theatre seems to have given a section of the public the prescriptive right to interfere in its management, and even to dictate to its proprietors and lessees the bill of fare which they should provide for its gratification. This benevolent intervention has usually taken the form of a more or less imperious demand for the exclusive performance at all risks of what its patrons are pleased to designate the legitimate drama, and a vigorous attempt to declare the intrusion of all other classes of entertainment little less than the wanton desecration of a time-honoured shrine. It is difficult to define what is meant by this cry for the 'legitimate'. Some would limit the application of the term strictly to Shakespeare; others, more liberally inclined, would extend it to any of the standard works of the old masters of the stage. The history of Drury Lane for the past century and a half is not altogether uninstructive. It may be briefly described as a perpetual struggle between the advocates of the legitimate and successive generations of managers who have always come sooner or later (often, alas! To their cost) to realise the truism which Mr Irving aptly expressed when he said that the drama 'must thrive as a business before it can flourish as an art'. In a word, the standing conflict at Drury Lane has been between theatrical theory on the one hand, and theatrical practice on the other.

He went on to rehearse the managerial dilemmas of previous lessees Garrick, Sheridan, Bunn and Macready as they sought to balance the demands of the public and the expectations of the elite. Turning to his own immediate predecessors, he noted that after E.T. Smith secured the theatre at a low rental, 'Mr William Beverly about this time invented transformation scenes, and his beautiful effects made the annual pantomime the sheet anchor of the new manager.' When Chatterton took over, spectacular productions such as *The Great City*, *Formosa*, *Amy Robsart* and *Ivanhoe* filled the theatre. When Her Majesty's Theatre burned down he brought in the Italian Opera 'on remunerative terms' and the popularity of the Vokes Family made the annual pantomime a success. But in due course the Italian Opera returned to the Haymarket, the public tired of the Vokes Family and lavish productions of *The Winter's Tale* and *Antony and Cleopatra* were shunned, leading to the closure of the theatre and rumours of its imminent demolition.

When Harris acquired the lease, he implemented at once the policy to which he had adhered since: 'My constant aim has been to gauge the taste of the theatre-going public with the greatest possible accuracy, and to follow intelligently in the matter of dramatic entertainment the unerring law of supply and demand.' The fate of his periodic experiments with Shakespeare confirmed the rightness of his judgement. *Henry V* with George Rignold, *As You Like It* with Marie Litton, *Othello* with John McCullough and *Julius Caesar* with the Saxe-Meiningen Company were all critical successes but box office failures.

> By this time I had become more and more convinced that popular drama was best suited to the public taste, and the triumph of *The World* proved my surmise to be correct. No such success had been scored at Drury Lane for many years; the play was eagerly sought for in every country where the English language is spoken and is even now making money for the fortunate purchasers of the acting rights.

He followed *The World* with *Youth* which 'crowded the house and gave a large profit.' Since then his only contribution to 'high art' had been the annual visit of the Carl Rosa Opera Company, which he hoped 'contributed to the increased appreciation of English opera in London.' His policy was confirmed:

> For the financial success of Drury Lane I am more than ever convinced that my guiding-star must be wholly and solely the taste of those I endeavour to please. If the public at large really wanted to see Drury Lane the home *par excellence* of the 'legitimate' they would have given a far more constant support to the various efforts of my predecessors and myself in this direction. They have failed to do so, and the only inference to be drawn from past events is that the demand in question comes rather from the dissatisfied minority than from the great mass of British playgoers. Experience is an unerring master and experience teaches precisely what the public ask for at Drury Lane. Leaving the ever-popular yearly pantomime out of the question, the requirements of an average Drury Lane audience are sufficiently clear. They demand a performance which must be, above all things, dramatic, full of life, novelty and movement; treating, as a rule, of the age in

which we live, dealing with characters they can sympathise with, and written in a language they can easily understand. It must be well mounted, well acted, and should appeal rather to the feelings of the public at large than to the prejudice of a class.

For those who wanted legitimate drama, he recommended the regime of Henry Irving at the Lyceum: 'He is the tragedian who seriously commands the attention of London audiences, and the dimensions of the theatre are exactly suited to his requirements.' As far as Harris was concerned, 'the limited extent of the demand, the success of Mr Irving, and the annual production of the pantomime, are sufficient to make any further experiment of the kind [i.e. 'legitimate drama'] under existing circumstance, almost out of the question.'[41] The extent of his wealth at death (£23,677.2s.9d., over a million pounds in today's money) demonstrated the rightness of his judgement and contrasted markedly with the poverty-stricken endings of his two predecessors. However, all three of these had devoted all their energies to ensuring that Drury Lane maintained its reputation as the 'national home of pantomime'.

For some years Gus' stage manager at Drury Lane for pantomimes and melodramas was his younger brother Charles (1854–97). He survived Gus only by a matter of months, dying of pneumonia aged forty-two in 1897, having been suffering from Bright's Disease and diabetes. He had enjoyed a long career as a major London stage manager after managing his first pantomime, *Little Red Riding Hood*, at Covent Garden when he was only eighteen. He had later stage managed at the Adelphi for the Gattis, at the Lyric for his brother-in-law Horace Sedger and most recently for D'Oyly Carte at the Savoy, where he had stage managed a succession of shows following the split between Gilbert and Sullivan: *The Nautch Girl* (1891), *Haddon Hall* (1892), *Jane Annie* (1893), *Minette* (1894) and *His Majesty* (1897). *The Era* (6 February 1897) said of him that he was 'a thorough master of his art and although occasionally a rough diamond, he was a good-hearted man and was much liked by his associates and subordinates.' The 'rough diamond' allusion may have been a discreet reference to Harris' well-known mastery of invective. The journalist J. B. Booth recalled that he 'acquired fame for his ability and his strong language, and was nicknamed "The Stage Damager".'[42] Macqueen Pope said, 'his language would paralyse a crowd of rough supers ... into awed silence and then lash them into hasty and accurate action when some absolutely new and original cursing followed.'[43]

Despite his own achievements, he was inevitably linked in the public mind with Gus and at Charles' funeral as reported in *The Era* (13 February 1897), the Reverend Alfred Poynder, rector of St Michael's in the Strand, stressed this, saying:

He and his brother Augustus were both hard workers, they commanded success where others had failed; great things were asked of them, and they rose to emergencies. They spent their short lives trying to make merriment and recreation for their day and generation. Night and day they toiled, and planned, and created success after success. Dauntless pluck and conscientious perseverance were the secrets of their short, busy, hardworked lives.

But Charles' widow was left in straitened circumstances, which Mrs D'Oyly Carte sought to relieve by staging a benefit performance for her.[44]

It was Harris' loyal henchman, Arthur Collins (1863–1932) who took over at Drury Lane in 1897. He had joined the staff of Drury Lane as a scene-painter, apprenticed to scenic artist Henry Emden, in 1881. When Collins expressed a desire to act, Harris sent him out on the road as an actor in a touring production of *A Run of Luck* and later as stage manager of a pantomime Harris was producing at the Grand Theatre, Glasgow. He graduated eventually to become stage manager at Drury Lane and Harris' right-hand man. When Harris died, he managed to raise the £1,000 necessary for an option on the lease, demanded by Lady Harris and her brother, Frank Rendle, the executors of Druriolanus. Drury Lane became for the first time in its history a limited liability company with Collins as managing director. He remained in charge until 1924, carrying on the Harris formula of spectacular melodrama and spectacular pantomime with success. Like Harris, Collins collaborated on the pantomime scripts. He was responsible for three major developments: he dropped the processions so beloved of Harris; he eliminated the remnants of the harlequinade; and he dispensed with the transformation, introducing instead an interval, playing the pantomime in two parts. This intermission was greeted with something like relief by the critics, given the fact that the shows regularly lasted for five hours. Macqueen Pope penned an appreciative portrait of Collins in his history of Drury Lane, writing of his retirement:

> He had loved The Lane and served it well. He was a charming man, this dark, keen-eyed companionable genius of the theatre, a man who hated to be alone, who loved the company of his fellow-men and colleagues. He talked almost unceasingly and he talked well. It was his joy to tell long stories, carrying on far into the night, and often he was to be found still talking at three in the morning, either in a dressing room or in his suite at the Savoy. He would go to Romano's to lunch, if there were no rehearsals on, and all well at the Lane, and when dinner time came around, it was not out of the way for him still to be there, conversing with his luncheon guests. He respected and loved his old chief and master, Sir Augustus Harris. He was a most loyal friend, and found jobs for his cronies, often creating them specially; and he would keep deserving cases in work so that they could qualify to join the Drury Lane Fund and make their old age safe. Yet he could be, and was, very scathing to those whom he considered at fault ... But he was just and fair to a degree. He closed an epoch and left with it. Unlike Gus Harris, he never fell foul of a critic ... Arthur Collins took into retirement with him a name which was respected and loved, and a brilliant record of success and achievement.[45]

Although Drury Lane was in the West End, its audience was far from exclusive. The received view of theatre audiences in London is that East End and West End theatres were different, distinct and separate both in audience and repertoire. This view has been superseded by the recent research of Jim Davis and Victor Emeljanow which suggests that the picture was far more varied and diverse. Investigating the audiences for theatres in the East End and West End, north London and south of the river Thames, with the aid of census returns, maps, playbills, transport timetables, local and national newspapers, they have shown that 'London theatre audiences in the mid-nineteenth century were so diverse that generic definitions are clearly inappropriate.'[46] London theatre audiences were much more mixed, cross-class, socially and physically mobile than has previously been allowed.

The Times (28 December 1852) described the Boxing Night audience for the first Christmas productions of the new management regime of E.T. Smith, Uncle Tom's Cabin and the pantomime Harlequin Hudibras:

> The house was full from the pit to the very highest gallery. The pit was crammed to suffocation; those who abode in the boxes were evidently distressed with the heat, and how those fared who occupied the topmost seats is very difficult to understand and very unpleasant to imagine. Men in shirt-sleeves, women with their bonnets half off, faces ripe for mischief, and the usual complement of those unearthly tones which a Christmas audience seems bound to utter, occupied the interval between the filling of the house and the rising of the curtain. Oranges, too, were eaten with customary eagerness, and the skins flung upon the heads of the persons in the pit, who sought to return the courtesy, but their performance falling short of their intentions, the occupants of the boxes came in for a share of wet orange peel. Standing-up fights there were, too, among the occupants of the upper regions, to the signal interest of all those who were lucky enough to get a sight of the combatants. But, on the whole, the audience behaved very decently for a Christmas audience. Never in one instance did a fight lead to a general engagement; and even the conversations across the theatre, or between gallery and pit, were full of politeness and good humour.

Similar descriptions appeared regularly in the annual Boxing Night review.

From the 1860s onwards more and more of the middle and respectable working classes patronized the theatre. This theatre-going was facilitated by the completion of the suburban railway system which made it convenient, improved street-lighting and policing which made it safe and the appearance of extended theatre coverage in the expanding popular press which made it fashionable. West End theatre audiences were not based on the local neighbourhood but became epitomes of the nation. Davis and Emeljanow conclude that by the 1880s:

the West End, in the upholstered ceremonial occasions at Irving's Lyceum or in the jingoistic autumn melodramas and Christmas pantomimes at Drury Lane did succeed in creating a surrogate or symbolic community, comprised of people with few geographical or spatial ties, but linked by a sense of belonging and common values. In this respect the West End and the values that it promulgated helped to create 'an imagined community'. It became the locus for the dissemination of nationalism and embodied the imperial values of the British nation-state.[47]

The change in the pantomime audience at Drury Lane was noted by a contemporary observer, Jimmy Glover, the musical director under Harris and Collins. Writing in 1911, Glover said:

The Drury Lane pantomime has wonderfully metamorphosed in the last three decades … It is ridiculous for people to state that pantomime has declined. It has not declined; it has, however, changed and increased its public … Chatterton's public was a few rows of five-shilling or seven-shilling stalls, a huge eightpenny pit, and a seething mass of sixpenny and fourpenny galleryites, who cat-called the 'opening' on Boxing Night till not a word on the stage was heard. The shilling pit and the sixpenny gallery boy shouted the latest music-hall songs. The better educated audience of to-day is not the chorus-singing urchin or patron of the seventies. The top gallery disappeared under the London County Council during the end of the Harris management and the stalls on Boxing Night have developed into a kid-gloved army of *dilettante* patrons, across whose apathetic well-dined and gloriously-gloved personalities it is a far run to get to the pit for a good honest round of applause.[48]

Glover highlights something that became a regular feature of Boxing Night pantomime performances until the 1890s – the boisterousness, noisiness and drunkenness of the audience that became a staple of Victorian reporting.

In a thoughtful essay on Boxing Day audiences, Jim Davis denounces much of the press reporting of audience behaviour as 'patronizing, condescending, implicitly containing and highly class-conscious' and reminds us that Boxing Day audiences were exceptional rather than typical, as the Boxing Day pantomime was a special occasion. He interprets their behaviour as 'a celebration of disorder, self-regulation and power by a crowd which, however out of control it might seem, was far more in control than the press accounts imply.'[49]

The Times' (28 December 1868) review of *Grimalkin the Great* at Drury Lane lends support to this view. The review opened with a description of the audience:

The scene exhibited before the curtain on Saturday marked no departure from the usage of late years, the house being crammed with a noisy and excitable multitude who went through their routine of sound and silence with a precision which might suggest the notion that holyday playgoers are subjected to as many rehearsals as the players whom they go to see. During the farce, which is merely intended to preface the treat of the evening, the occupants of the gallery, not without sympathisers in the pit, amused themselves with loud demonstrations of reciprocated friendship or hostility, of impatience or satisfaction, which rendered inaudible every word spoken on the stage. A new turn to the popular behaviour was given by the commencement of the overture to the pantomime, very cleverly constructed out of popular melodies by Mr Levey, the plebeians of the public having of late cultivated the art of accompanying the more favourite tunes played by the orchestra with the music of their own sweet voices. Their proficiency in this art, which really they have brought to a high degree of perfection, they make a point of displaying with great vigour whenever they have an opportunity of joining in the theatrical celebrations of St Stephen's Day ... When the curtain rose a buzz of satisfaction had succeeded the outcries of half an hour before, and all noise soon subsided into attentive silence, to be broken only when some special sign of admiration or mirth was required.

This was the pattern of audience reaction year after year. The first piece of the evening, whether farce or melodrama, would be totally inaudible due to audience noise, clearly indicating that they had only come for the pantomime. They fell silent as soon as the pantomime started but then participated by demanding encores of songs and dances, calling for the artist or the manager to come and take a bow and aiming quips and comments at the performers.

Typically at Christmas 1853–4 the Drury Lane programme began with Mark Lemon's sentimental drama *Gwyneth Vaughan* which just about survived, despite the crowd's shout of 'hornpipe' every time a character in sailor's uniform appeared. But the vaudeville *Delicate Grounds*, according to *The Era* (1 January 1854) 'a piece depending entirely on the audible utterance of those sentimental gallicisms which so clearly indicate its Parisian origin', was booed off the stage, not because of its perceived inferiority but because the audience had come for the pantomime and resented the delay in presenting it. When the pantomime arrived, it was greeted by an appreciative shower of orange peel and torn up bits of paper, and then watched with 'earnest attention'.

For the pantomime is and always has been the supreme example of the audience participation show. Relics of it persist to this day with the ritual cries of 'Oh no, it isn't' – 'Oh, yes, it is' and 'Look out behind you' from the spectators punctuating the action. As Dawn Lewcock comments in her essay on the subject:

This has no rational meaning, it adds nothing to the plot, but it allows the audience to interact with the comedians ... This encouragement of interjections from the audience in response to certain actions or behaviors on stage is deliberate and helps to bring out the conflict between good and evil, or wickedness and innocence, in which the audience is implicitly invited to take sides. This was seen particularly in the behaviour in the Penny

Gaffs, the rough popular entertainments enjoyed by the poorest audiences in London slums in the nineteenth century. In 1881 a *Sunday Times* correspondent decided to report on the pantomime in one and described how much the young audience encouraged the crude humor, the chases, and the slapstick, shouting at each other as well as the actors and particularly enjoying the clown battering at the actor dressed as a police constable. They were experiencing a kind of catharsis in seeing the characters behave as they might wish to themselves against the forces of law and order, whom they saw as their enemies.[50]

The acknowledged master of the pantomime genre from the 1850s to the 1880s was Edward Leman Blanchard. The *I.L.N.* (1 January 1876) called him 'the prince of modern pantomime inventors'. *The World* called him 'the genius of pantomime'. The comic magazine *Judy* presented him with the Ally Sloper Award of Merit as 'The King of Pantomime Writers'.[51]

Blanchard was born in London on 11 December 1820, the youngest of the six children of William Blanchard (1769–1835) and his second son by his second wife, Sarah Harrold (1784–1875). William Blanchard, a renowned comic actor, earned an entry in the *D.N.B.* and was a master of the comic drunk act. Edward imbibed his love of pantomime at his mother's knee. E.L. Blanchard's widow recalled:

> E.L.B. derived much of his inventive talent from his clever mother, who used to illustrate by *doll models* all the nursery stories on which he afterwards founded his pantomimes; and, at a very early age, he used to invent words for Little Boy Blue to speak, for the Old Woman who lived in the Shoe, Bluebeard's family etc., etc., which year by year he enlarged and improved until his true talent developed itself for stage purposes.

He was only five when his mother took him to see what was probably his first pantomime in 1825.[52]

After a brief period of schooling in Brixton, 1827–9, he was sent to Lichfield to be educated and remained there from 1829 to 1831, after which he accompanied his parents to America where his father acted on the New York stage. Back in England he resumed his education in Ealing. But his father's death in 1835 necessitated his taking on a job and he began what became a varied and prolific career as a jobbing writer. He was barely sixteen when in 1836 he became sub-editor of *Pinnock's Guide to Knowledge*. In 1841–2 he was editor of the weekly miscellany *Chambers' London Journal*, and in 1845–6 editor of *The New London Magazine*, but these jobs were poorly paid and short-lived. In 1844 he founded *The Astrologer and Oracle of Destiny* magazine, catering to his life-long interest in the occult and the spirit world. But the journal rapidly failed due to unforeseen circumstances when its financial backer disappeared.

Blanchard was a much-loved figure. Clement Scott, a lifelong friend and the co-editor of his diaries, wrote of his 'gentle, considerate and kindly nature', that he 'never lost the heartiness, the impulse, and the energy of a boy', that he was a 'sunny, light-hearted, affectionate companion', that he 'could not bear giving pain to any one', that he loved children and animals, that 'his tastes were simple and his habits healthy' and that 'friendship, nature and tobacco were the solace ... of his life.'[53] The *D.N.B.* called him 'one of the kindest, most genial and lovable of Bohemians'.[54] All of these qualities can be seen reflected in his pantomime scripts.

Scott's verdict on Blanchard was shared by fellow writer and critic Sir Frank Burnand who called Blanchard 'one of the gentlest of clever writers ... the kindest mannered man who ever murdered his aspirates. What Blanchard did not know in theatrical life, and journalism generally, was not worth picking up.'[55] Blanchard was at one time a keen spiritualist and took Burnand to a séance.[56] But his faith in spiritualism was severely dented though not entirely extinguished by the exposure of the Davenport Brothers as frauds and the downfall of Daniel Dunglas Home, parodied by Browning as Mr Sludge the Medium. His spiritualism was of the Christian variety as he invariably thanked God in his diaries for blessings bestowed.

At his funeral, the Reverend F.D. Perrot declared that his 'simple, childlike character may well be an example to all of us.' He described him as follows:

United with a geniality of manner and unalloyed kindness of soul, there was in him a deep spirit of humble religious feeling; and all who knew him can testify to his simple open-heartedness and frank honesty of purpose. The gift of giving pleasure to others was his in a peculiar degree, and in the use which he made of this gift is his best claim on our gratitude and memory. Most truly was he the friend of children – not alone of those who came into personal relationship with him – but of those of a wider sphere, of the people's children, to whose pure, innocent enjoyment he devoted no small measure of his great talents.[57]

Blanchard was an enthusiastic clubman, a member of the Wrekin Club, the Re-Union, the Friday Knights, the Urban Club and the Arundel Club, those Bohemian haunts of dramatists, journalists and artists, where they would stay up long into the night drinking, smoking, gossiping, joking and story-telling.[58]

He also became a mason. He evidently found comfort in these all-male environments away from the dramatic rows and money worries charted in his diaries. It was also a relief from the unrelenting pressure of work, which did not let up even at Christmas. His diary entry for Christmas Day, 1866, reads:

I spent my Christmas Day, as usual, *solus* in my chambers, working for *Daily Telegraph*. The housekeeper sends me up a slice of duck for my dinner, and I work on until three next morning to get ready with the heavy pressure of 'light' articles wanted; awfully tired.[59]

Similarly, his diary entry for Christmas Day 1871 records:

Christmas Day. A very hard working day in town. Kindly present from Murray of cigars with Christmas greeting. All day till midnight writing three or four columns for *Daily Telegraph*. Twice to office; my landlady sends me up a slice of her beef, and I give her £1.5s. for a Christmas-box. Weary at night, I go for supper at Arundel.

Things were little easier on Boxing Day:

Hard working all morning on *Daily Telegraph* work. Steak at Edinbro' with Scott and Sterry; then to Princesses's [where his pantomime *Harlequin Little Dicky Dilver* was being performed], looking in at Drury on my way [for his pantomime *Tom Thumb the Great*]; and down at office at 2 a.m. with Princess' notice [he was reviewing his own pantomime for the *Telegraph*], through drenching rain; called back at Arundel; commemoration of Belford's birthday; to bed at 4.30.[60]

He was willing to turn his hand to anything to earn a crust in the precarious world of Victorian journalism. He wrote illustrated guide books, comic songs and monologues, journal articles on anything and everything. He edited Willoughby's *Shakespeare* and wrote largely unmemorable novels (*Temple Bar, Confessions of a Page, Brave Without a Destiny*). He contributed to most of the short-lived comic rivals to *Punch* (*Mephistopheles, Fun, Puck*).

But his greatest love was the theatre. He wrote dramatic criticism for *The Era, The Sunday Times, Weekly Despatch, Illustrated Times* and *The Observer*. From 1863 to 1887 he was the chief drama critic of the *Daily Telegraph*. According to his *Era* obituary (7 September 1889) in the four years following his father's death he wrote thirty dramas, farces and burlesques and a number of pantomimes under the pen-name Francisco Frost. But at least three of the pantomimes were for amateur performance. Blanchard wrote the scripts, devised the tricks and played Harlequin in *The Three Men of Thessaly* (1838), *The Old Woman and Her Three Sons or Harlequin and the Wizard of Wookey Hole* (1839) and *Pat-a-Cake, Pat-a-Cake or Harlequin and the Baker's Man* (1840). They were performed in a school on the Old Kent Road for a week or so and admission was free. So these were hardly a source of income but in writing and staging them he was learning his craft. During these years he was also briefly manager of the short-lived Royal Manor House Theatre, in the King's Road, Chelsea, penning farces to keep the building open.

His farce *Angels and Lucifers* was performed at the Olympic Theatre to great acclaim in 1841 and he was retained by that theatre as its stock dramatist until 1846, turning out a stream of farces, dramas, comedies and travesties. His one-act farce

The Artful Dodge was first performed there in 1842 and, according to *The Era*, 'caught the fancy of playgoers and was for a long time received by them nightly with shouts of laughter.' It was 'wonderfully humorous and in parts screamingly comic'. Twelve months later he produced a 'capital and ... thoroughly good-humoured' parody of transpontine melodrama, *Pork Chops*. He 'ruthlessly burlesqued' *Antigone*, *Cinderella*, *Robinson Crusoe*, *Jack and the Beanstalk* and *The Merchant of Venice* in the period 1843–5. In 1845 he wrote the Olympic pantomime *Fortunatus or the Magic Cap and the Three Lucky Wishes*.

The Era noted approvingly that prolific as he had been he had never dramatized a novel or adapted anything from the French, 'a surprising circumstance, to say the least of it, and one that certainly redounds to his honour as a dramatic author.' This fact 'furnishes proof and confirmation strong of his originality.'

From 1846, he freelanced, working for various East End and South London theatres and embarking on the prolific pantomime career that would make his name. He wrote *The Birth of the Steam Engine* for the Victoria Theatre (26 December 1846) and *King Alfred the Great or Harlequin and the Enchanted Raven* for the Olympic (26 December 1846), recording in his diary for 26 December: 'Pantomimes produced: both hits and houses crowded'.[61]

What Clement Scott and his other friends did not know until his diaries came to light is that he was burdened by perpetual money worries as he sought to support 'innumerable relatives' and continual grief due to his separation from the woman he loved, who was for much of the time on the other side of the world. The diaries published after his death by Clement Scott and Cecil Howard give a remarkable, detailed picture of the career of a Victorian playwright/critic/journalist, the astonishing work-rate, the prodigious output and the unending demands from relatives for money.

As John Russell Stephens has shown, while it was possible for a playwright to earn a living from the theatre in the 1830s, this ceased to be true in the 1840s and 1850s when conditions in the theatre reflected the depressed economic state of the nation. For a writer, the money was to be made writing novels not plays. So Bulwer Lytton, who had been a highly successful playwright in the 1830s, gave up the stage and turned to novels in the 1840. Dickens, despite a life-long love of the theatre, did not seek a life in playwriting but made his fortune in writing novels. The situation changed in the 1870s and 1880s with the rise in status of the theatre and a change in the system of remuneration, pioneered by Dion Boucicault. Until Boucicault, playwrights were paid a flat fee. He developed a system of profit-sharing, with the writer getting a percentage of the box office take. This meant that long runs of plays and repeated touring of successes could provide a living wage. By the 1890s, playwrights like Oscar Wilde, Arthur Wing Pinero and Henry Arthur Jones could make a good living from playwriting. It was a far cry from the mid-century when several playwrights ended their lives destitute (Richard Brinsley Peake, George Dibdin Pitt, Westland Marston, C.L. Barnett) and there were stories of playwrights actually dying from starvation.[62]

Much of Blanchard's life was darkened by money worries, largely occasioned by the fact that he was not only supporting himself and his elderly mother, who lived to be ninety-one, but his improvident brother William and William's family. On 12 January 1867, he records sadly: 'Now 9 in family to support – belonging to other people.' Five of these were William and his wife and three sons. Blanchard seems to have taken personal responsibility for raising his nephew Walter, referred to regularly in the diaries as 'the dear boy', as he is taken to the zoo, the circus and the pantomime. In 1867 Walter departed to take up a post as a tutor at a private school in Brixton ('I shall miss him very much here'). On 7 February 1872, Blanchard was literally 'stunned' to receive a letter from Walter to tell him that he had married Blanchard's former housekeeper Mary. But he subsequently went to visit them in Bishops Stortford and, finding them 'well and happy', seems to have accepted the situation.[63]

From the outset the diaries are littered with laments about his poverty. On 4 October 1844, he writes: 'Domestic matters; all money again; heart-sickening, very'. The diary editors include a page from his September 1850 diary to show 'the straits he was put to through his excessive goodness of heart.' The bailiffs were occupying his lodgings because he owed three quarters rent and the poor rate. From 18 to 24 September he raced round borrowing money from friends and securing advances for songs not yet written and for his Bradshaw's Railway Guide authorship, in order to settle his debts, which he does by 24 September. On 16 February 1855, he writes: 'Pushed hard for cash and doubtful about the means for the forthcoming spring'; on 12 March 1855: 'scarcity of coin severely felt'; on 23 August 1855: 'quite upset this week entirely through money matters'. On 28 June 1855: 'Oppressed by the surplus population I have to provide for, and means getting apparently less every day.' On 12 May 1856, he records that he had worked till late but had been hindered by the arrival of his brother in the morning, 'pecuniary help asked and given. Heavy drains on purse from all quarters.' On 15 October 1855, 'W.B. [his brother] pressing very hard on spirits as well as on purse.' At the end of 1855 he records his total income for the year as £260, of which he has given over £60 to his brother.[64]

His financial trials continued. On 12 December 1857, he writes: 'Much indisposed and greatly upset mentally and domestically; paying a vast amount for no comfort, no happiness, or sympathy.' On 14 May 1858, 'Money pouring out like water for all sorts of expenses.' On 14 October 1858, W.B. turns up and Blanchard 'give[s] him [his] frock-coat as a protection against the cold weather.' He describes 1858 as 'a year in which I have been more heavily worked and more heavily drained financially than any yet experienced.' On 8 February 1859, he records: 'All day paying all sorts of bills, for which I find I am liable, and cruelly upset by fresh discoveries; have the greatest difficulty on meeting the expenditure so unexpectedly evolved'. On 16 June 1859, 'W.B. in afternoon, and – usual money pressure: very heavy and anxious about the future.' On 19 October 1865, he writes: 'The great domestic difficulty pressing heavily at the present; three nephews more to keep.' At the end of 1866 he records 'have ... been heavily drained by domestic troubles and ceaseless claims of my brother and his family.' In 1870, he still had six family members to support. On 21 January 1871, his brother William dies and 'closes his unfortunate career', removing at least one financial drain on him. As the nephews grew up and embarked on their own careers his financial burden also eased. In 1871, for instance, he arranged for his nephew Joey to go to sea, giving him a £10 outfit and all necessary expenses.[65]

Blanchard meticulously recorded his annual income in his diaries and we can trace its steady growth from 1849 when his annual income was £152.18s., peaking in 1877 with £708.17s. It fell back a little in the 1880s but remained reasonably consistent until 1887 when his health began seriously to fail and there was a marked decline to the final total in his last year of life, 1889, of £200.[66]

The steady increase was partly due to his prodigious workrate but also it reflected a change in his remuneration from a flat fee for his scripts to a royalty, on the lines that Dion Boucicault was promoting and at exactly the same time. For ten years, 1851–61, he provided the annual pantomime for Sadler's Wells. The contemporary press and later Allardyce Nicoll attributed most of these pantomimes to Thomas Longden Greenwood, co-lessee of the theatre, but it is clear from Blanchard's diaries that he wrote them, though he later formed a writing partnership with Greenwood, calling themselves the Brothers Grinn. But for most of these ten years, Blanchard received a flat fee of £10 for his scripts. In 1858 he calls £10 his 'usual payment', made by cheque from Greenwood, in this case on 25 January 1858. However, in 1860 Blanchard received £20 for the pantomime script *Harlequin Hans and the Golden Goose*. In 1861 Greenwood ended his lesseeship but his partner Samuel Phelps carried on alone and Blanchard seems to have negotiated a new deal, a royalty of £1 per night for the duration of the run. This netted him £45 for *Harlequin Sindbad the Sailor* in 1861–2 and £49 for *Cherry and Fair Star*, his last for Sadler's Wells, in 1862–3.[67]

From E.T. Smith at Drury Lane he received a flat fee. For his first pantomime *Harlequin Hudibras* he records on 14 January 1853 receiving 'the balance of £10' from Smith. This suggests that there had been an earlier payment but it is not recorded. By 1859–60 he was earning £35 (paid in two instalments) for his pantomime *Jack and the Beanstalk*. When Edmund Falconer took over the lease in 1862, Blanchard again seems to have negotiated a royalty rate for £1 per performance. *Little Goody Two-Shoes* brought him £76, directly reflecting the number of performances. Falconer's second pantomime, *Harlequin Sindbad the*

Sailor brought him £50. When Chatterton took over, Blanchard received £95 in four instalments for *Little King Pippin*. Subsequent pantomimes brought in much less: £50 for *Faw, Fee, Fo, Fum* (1867–8) which ran until 29 February, £54.10s. for *Grimalkin the Great* (1868–9) and for *Beauty and the Beast* (1869–70), £55 in three instalments, the last on 1 March. *The Dragon of Wantley* (1870–1) brought him £100 and *Tom Thumb the Great* (1871–2) £50. Thereafter the diaries do not record individual payments.[68]

There was one disaster. In 1864 Blanchard agreed to provide a pantomime for the English Opera House, Covent Garden for a flat fee of £100. Blanchard noted that Augustus Harris was to have £20 as commission. The script, *Cinderella*, was by the Brothers Grinn. On 18 January 1865 Blanchard received a cheque from Covent Garden, noting his share as £65, paying Harris his £20, suggesting Greenwood received only £15. In 1865 Blanchard provided Covent Garden with a new script, *Aladdin and His Wonderful Lamp*. It was a success but the English Opera Company went out of business and defaulted on the promised £100 fee. This had a drastic effect on Blanchard's annual income, down from £441.18s. in 1865 to £289 in 1866.[69]

Blanchard was both willing and able to tailor his scripts for particular performers, and during his long writing career there were several changes of personnel on the stage at Drury Lane. For several years the pantomimes were built around the talents of a diminutive juvenile star, Master Percy Roselle. Roselle had stolen the show in *Harlequin Sindbad the Sailor* (1863–4), playing the Old Man of the Sea, the king of the pygmies. For the next four years he was the star of the pantomime. He appeared in the title role of *Hop O' My Thumb* (1864–5); the title role in *Little King Pippin* (1865–6); as the shape-changing gnome king in *Number Nip* (1866–7); and as the Cornish Puck, Pigwiggin in *Faw, Fee, Fo Fum* (1867–8). But the following year he was missing and was not seen again at Drury Lane. In his brief heyday he had 'delighted' Blanchard and enchanted Lewis Carroll who wanted to write a play as a vehicle for him.[70]

The Roselle era was succeeded by the age of the Vokes Family. The Vokeses were recalled as 'distinguished and unique' among theatrical families by critic H.G. Hibbert and Jimmy Glover described them as 'one of the cleverest and most talented troupes of the mid-Victorian era'.[71] Glover was their musical director and toured the country with them in the repertoire of 'very humorous one act plays', some of them written by Blanchard, in which they performed between pantomimes. The Vokeses were the children of theatrical costumier Frederick Vokes and one after another they went on the legitimate stage in child roles. Fred Vokes (1846–88) was the star of the family. Trained by his father as a tailor, he soon abandoned this for the stage, making his debut at the age of eight. For a time he was assistant to the magician Professor Anderson, 'The Wizard of the North' and a callboy to actor-manager Samuel Phelps at Sadler's Wells. He was taught dancing by Flexmore, the clown successor of Grimaldi, and became a leading eccentric dancer. Glover described him as 'a wonderful dancer, and also a very fine black and white artist' with a mania for yachting.[72] Fred was joined on the stage by his three sisters, Jessie (1851–84), who took care of the troupe's business affairs, Victoria (1853–94) and Rosina (1854–94). They first teamed up as the Vokes Family in 1861 in Edinburgh and made their pantomime debut in *Humpty Dumpty* at the Lyceum Theatre in 1868–9. But in 1869–70 they moved to Drury Lane for *Beauty and the Beast* and remained there for ten years, missing only the pantomime *Jack in the Box* (1873–4) when they were on tour in America.

Victoria and Jessie never married. But in 1877 Rosina married Cecil Clay, brother of the composer Frederick Clay and described by Glover as 'that dear old Bohemian and English gentleman'.[73] He had devised an entertainment called *A Pantomime Rehearsal*. Rosina retired from the troupe, formed her own company and successfully toured America in a programme of comedies, including *A Pantomime Rehearsal*. She was replaced in the troupe by Fred's wife, née Bella Moore. The troupe had been joined by a non-family member Walter Fawdon who performed under the name Fawdon Vokes and outlived them all, dying in 1904. J.B. Booth recalled that the Vokeses lived opposite Drury Lane stage door and worshipped at St Paul's Church, Covent Garden, where they were so celebrated that people turned up to stare at them.[74] Under the influences of the Vokeses, dance became a predominant element in the pantomime and the fairy element took precedence over the comedy.

Although the *D.N.B.* says that Blanchard married twice, there is no mention of a first wife or marriage in the diaries and for many years he yearned for the great love of his life, Caroline Cadette Bollin, whom he called Carina and who figured in the diaries as C.C.B. She (1821–c.1909) was a remarkable figure in her own right and earned her own entry in the *D.N.B.* She and Blanchard first met in 1839 and a romance seems to have developed but it ended in 1842 – 'the fatal year of separation' he called it. Carina married artist William Morris Alpenny in 1843 and bore him a daughter. But the marriage was an unhappy one and she fled to Ireland where in the 1850s she ran a flax farm. (She is first mentioned in the diaries on 12 March 1852 engaged in this capacity.) It is not known what became of Alpenny or what caused the breach with Blanchard. A likely explanation would be the impossibility of marriage, given the large number of relatives he was supporting. But she was back in London in 1855 and resuming a relationship with Blanchard, who was in a state of permanent ecstasy. On 1 May 1855, he sees her for the first time since 1844 ('magical memories of the bygone. Lovely moonlight night and long walk home'). They meet again on 3 May ('tales of the past and confessions of the heart') and on 8 June he notes 'dreamy and speculative, heart and head enthralled'. Then on 2 July

Carina writes to say she wishes the relationship to be 'fraternal for the future, but nothing more'. Then from 12 to 25 September they spend a week together in Hastings:

> happiness and home beyond my hopes. Thrilling meeting; stroll by starlight by the beach. Old times and old loves recalled; the attachment of sixteen years found not to have abated one jot of warmth; fidelity yet in the world ... Little sleep in consequence of the delicious reveries indulged in.

He describes 15 September as:

> the most enjoyable day I ever had in my life; the realization of all that my early youth dreamed of, and time makes at last a recompense for the sorrows and sufferings of the past; regrets repaid by atonement, but the separation already dreaded more and more.

Evidently he wants to marry her but he notes sadly on 11 October 1855 'Struggles between love and duty, and latter victorious after severe contest.' The duty is evidently to the family he is supporting and the consciousness of the money worries peppering the diary. On 30 October 1858 he records despairingly 'C.C.B. is lost to me for ever!' which must mean that marriage had been ruled out, as they continued to meet periodically for theatre visits, walks, dinners and even a séance until she dropped a bombshell in 1862. She had become a leading proponent of emigration for middle-class women, a cause to which she was to devote her career. On 13 September 1862 Blanchard received a letter from Carina announcing that she intended leaving for Otago, New Zealand, accompanying a shipload of female emigrants. He saw her off on 26 September, describing the event as 'severely felt, and terribly depressing my spirits.' She stayed in New Zealand for ten years and although she wrote regularly to Blanchard, she married a chemist, George Richard Howard, in 1867 and it was only at his death in 1872 that she returned to England.[75]

In the meantime he records his loneliness and unhappiness in his diaries. On 31 December 1866, he writes:

> thus goes out a year of (to me) almost unprecedented hard work and domestic worry God be thanked! – though I had few happy hours in it, I have done much, I believe, to make others happy; and again I hope the severe trials, to which my life has been subjected will soon end, and that at last the peace I have so long prayed for will be mine.

On 31 December 1868, he records:

> Utterly overwhelmed with domestic misery. Walter [his nephew] and I take a stroll through the town, and wish a Happy New Year to unsympathising people. See the Old Year out at home with only the boy to give me a word of greeting. God bless him! And so exit 1868, a year of singular unhappiness.[76]

But when Carina returned they agreed to marry, and on 11 June 1874 Blanchard wedded the woman he called 'the heroine of the story of my life' and achieved 'the realization of hopes hardly dared to believe would ever be fulfilled.' There was a brief honeymoon in Margate. Scott notes that 'Carina gave to this lonely, dispirited and forlorn man the happiest hours of ... his life.' On 1 January, 1882 he included in his diary a quotation from Wordsworth which he thought perfectly described his wife:

The reason firm, the temperate will,
Endurance, foresight, strength and skill,
A perfect woman, nobly planned
To warn, to comfort, and command;
And yet a spirit, still and bright
With something of an angel light.

She continued her work for female emigration with a succession of voluntary societies during the 1870s and 1880s, writing regularly on the subject, under the pen-name Carina, for women's magazines.[77]

In 1888 a light opera called *Carina* was given at Opera Comique. It was virtually Blanchard's last stage composition. Errol Sherson in *London's Lost Theatres* recalled that he had named it after the woman he had loved and (temporarily) lost, noting the happy ending when they were reunited 'in the autumn of his life, to be a comfort to him in his last days.' Sherson called this true-life story 'one of the most romantic I have ever known' and added that it 'has the distinct advantage of being absolutely true and ending as all tales should with "they lived happily to the end".'[78]

Carina had actually been written in 1885 with a score, unusually, by a woman composer, Julia Woolf. But before it was staged in 1888 the libretto was substantially rewritten by Cunningham V. Bridgman and during the run Charles Collette made such a success of the role of a comic Irish servant that the part was built up and given two new songs. It ran for more than 100 performances in this form and then toured for four months, during which time Blanchard died.

The opera was based on an eighteenth-century French play *La Guerre Ouverte* (1786). The plot hinged on the outwitting of a general who wants his daughter to marry a wealthy merchant. Her true lover manages to rescue her from this fate. One can understand the resonance of the story for Blanchard. Kurt Gänzl says the plot and book were 'unextraordinary', the lyrics and dialogue 'workmanlike but lacking in genuine interest and humour' and the music 'more academic than lyrical'. But its successful run must have gratified Blanchard.[79]

Eventually the punishing schedule of work he undertook exacted its toll. During the 1880s his diary increasingly records the breakdown in his health: 2 May 1882, 'unable to do much work, as feel I am getting "stricken in years"'; 10 December 1883, 'quite the invalid'; 16 January 1884, 'too ill to go out – hardly able to write a line.' On 31 December 1884 he is too ill to go to the midnight service and describes himself as having been all year 'a confirmed invalid from a chronic complaint, which weakens me greatly.' On 22 May 1885 he fell down the stairs and was unconscious for two hours. On 31 December 1885 he records: 'Self very weak and shaky; do not rise till past noon; still no appetite; and I here record with gratitude the close of a year that has brought with it an increase of my domestic happiness and no serious financial loss.' But this situation was soon to change as he records on 31 December 1887 'impaired health and a greatly diminished income'. On 12 June 1889 'so weak; can only take a cup of tea and bread-and-butter in place of dinner. Cannot get on with my work.' His last diary entry was made on 3 July and on 4 September 1889 he died, aged sixty-nine. The doctor said: 'It was a case of gradual decay. He was "worn out".'[80]

But Blanchard was only one of the team at Drury Lane whose combined efforts produced the annual spectacle to entrance both old and young. If Blanchard provided the script, words, lyrics and imaginative concept, others were on hand to give visual and aural life to his fancies. For much of his time at Drury Lane the scenic designer was William Beverley, the master of his craft (see Chapter 6). But a further visual dimension was provided by Richard Wynn Keene (1809–87) who went by the pseudonym Dykwynkyn in his pantomime work. Richard Wynn Keene was born in Birmingham, moving to London with his parents around 1830. He married in 1834 but his wife left him ten years later. He is first encountered as a manufacturer of cement and terracotta. In 1838 he obtained a patent for a process to improve the manufacture of cement. He exhibited at the 1851 Great Exhibition, showing samples of mosaic created in terracotta. But alongside this he was developing a second career as a creator of masks, properties and dresses for the stage. It seems likely that his first professional involvement in the stage came in 1851 at the Marylebone Theatre, managed by E.T. Smith (for whom Blanchard was providing pantomime scripts). What more natural then that when Smith took over the lease of Drury Lane and brought in Blanchard to write his pantomime scripts that Dykwynkyn should join them. He was involved in 1852 in the very first Blanchard Drury Lane show, *Harlequin Hudibras*, billed as the designer of the 'Hudibrastic characters' and modeller of the masks. Thereafter he provided the grotesque masks or 'big heads' as they were known, traditionally worn by the performers in the opening, for every pantomime at Drury Lane from 1852 to 1867–8. In 1868–9, William Brunton provided the masks for *Grimalkin the Great* at Drury Lane, as Dykwynkyn was at the Amphitheatre Liverpool providing masks for the pantomime *Harlequin Jack Sprat*. He was back at Drury Lane for *Beauty and the Beast* in 1869–70. But thereafter he is mysteriously missing.

During his time at Drury Lane, however, he was a vital part of the artistic team. Blanchard notes in his diaries having consultations with Dykwynkyn and Beverley about the realization of his scripts (9 October 1857, 25 November 1865) and recording his death on 28 November 1887 calls Dykwynkyn 'my old artistic friend'.[81] His contributions to the pantomimes led to encomia. T.W. Robertson called him 'the presiding genius of all theatrical Christmas revels' in an article, 'Dykwynkyn at Work' in *Belgravia*, and *The Era* (29 December 1867) called him 'the Tycoon of the Theatrical world, who is heard of and known by his work, but never seen.'[82]

His reticence may have been due to the fact that from 1846 he was profoundly deaf. This was only one of many misfortunes to befall him. There were, as with Blanchard, money worries. In 1864 he was declared bankrupt with debts of £520 but he was discharged in 1865. In 1880 he was paralysed either by a stroke or an accident and thereafter unable to work. Reduced to poverty, he was sustained by periodic charitable collections and small weekly sums from the Dramatic and Musical Sick Fund. After several years of physical and mental decline he died aged seventy-seven in 1887.

Alongside his work on the pantomimes, he also designed carefully researched costumes, armour and properties, under his proper name Richard Wynn Keene, for productions of Shakespeare and Byron at Drury Lane. After he left Drury Lane, he provided masks for the pantomimes at the Surrey Theatre, in 1873 (*Jack and the Beanstalk*) and 1874 (*Cherry and Fair Star*) and linked up again with Blanchard in his productions at the Crystal Palace, *Jack and Jill* (1872) and *Cinderella* (1874). In 1876 he was called upon to design the animal and bird masks and the dragon for Wagner's Ring Cycle at Bayreuth. In 1877 he was head of the decorative department at Her Majesty's Theatre, presiding over the realization of a programme of operas. In 1879 Augustus Harris recalled him to Drury Lane to collaborate on the provision of properties. But any permanent comeback was halted by his paralysis in 1880.[83]

His work regularly earned critical praise. Of *Hey Diddle Diddle*, *The Times* (27 December 1855) noted, 'a praiseworthy feature of the pantomime which immediately forced itself upon the attention was the artistic spirit and comic expression of the masks, designed by "Dykwynkyn"', and of *Little Jack Horner*, the *I.L.N.* (2 January 1858) declared, 'the masks are singularly expressive and do credit to the remarkable artist by whom they have been invented.'

Music and dance were vital ingredients in the pantomime and a succession of talented musical directors composed and conducted the scores for Drury Lane. The score for *Harlequin Hudibras* was by John Blewitt, who had been conducting at Drury Lane for twenty years. *The Era* (2 January 1853) complained that it was 'so slovenly performed that we frankly confess there was much to us but ill-understood.' It was Blewett's last score for Drury Lane for he died in 1853 aged seventy-three. Between 1853 and 1857 several different composers were used. A Mr Hayward provided the music for *Harlequin King Humming Top* in 1854–5. But for 1855–6 the experienced J.H. Tully took the baton. For *See Saw Margery Daw* in 1856 the composer-conductor was Herr Anschutz, whose score, said *The Era* (28 December 1856), was 'from the overture to the end full of sparkling vivacity, and is genuinely characteristic.' From 1857 to 1861 Tully held the baton, earning praise. Of *Robin Hood, The Times* (28 December 1858) noted:

> the music, which, though always well selected and well arranged, as full of character as of life and bustle (Mr J.H. Tully, the most practised and fluent of pantomimic musicians, being the composer), is seldom 'in order' at the outset, was played by the members of the orchestra under Mr Tully's direction with such spirit and precision throughout that one might have fancied it the last instead of the first performance of the season was under consideration.

When Edmund Falconer took over the lease, he brought in a new musical director, John Barnard, who conducted until 1867. After Chatterton acquired the lease he recalled Tully, who provided the music for *Faw, Fee, Fo, Fum* in 1867–8. But on 28 January 1868 he died. He had been a child actor and singer, making his debut at thirteen. He became in adult life a composer-conductor-chorus master at Covent Garden (under Madame Vestris) and Drury Lane (under Alfred Bunn and later E.T. Smith), composing operettas and burlesques. Blanchard called him 'my old friend' when reporting his death. Tully was succeeded in 1868–9 by W.C. Levey, whom *The Era* (31 December 1871) said 'has one of the best orchestras in London under his command and not only arranges but composes the best music.' He composed and conducted until 1873–4. Then from 1874 until 1878 Karl Meyder composed and conducted the music. When Harris took over in 1879 Ferdinand Wallerstein assumed the conducting and composing duties. From 1881–2 to 1885–6 it was Oscar Barrett, later to challenge Harris' pre-eminence as a pantomime producer.

Whereas ballet in Britain in the twentieth and twenty-first centuries is regarded as part of high culture, in the second half of the nineteenth century it was integral to popular culture. Unlike the continent where the opera houses at which ballet was performed were supported by government subsidy and aristocratic patronage, in Britain ballet was part of popular theatre and depended on commercial success to survive. There had been a vogue for romantic ballet in the first half of the nineteenth century, produced in particular at Her Majesty's Theatre in the Haymarket, performed by foreign dance stars and supported by upper-class audiences. But this vogue had given way to a fashion for opera in the 1850s. Thereafter ballet in Britain survived as a feature of music hall and pantomime, where the appeal to the mass audience was visual spectacle, exoticism and scantily clad females. At the Alhambra and Empire music halls in Leicester Square from the 1860s to World War I, full length, large scale ballets, often running for six months at a time, attracted large audiences. Meanwhile at Drury Lane, Covent Garden, the Lyceum and other popular theatres, ballet was one of the regular features of pantomime and extravaganza.

At Drury Lane, the ballets were choreographed initially by specialist ballet choreographers: Madame Louise, who ran her own dance school, choreographed *Harlequin Hudibras* (1852), *King Humming Top* (1853) and *Jack and Jill* (1854). Emile Petit choreographed *See Saw Margery Daw* (1856) and *Little Jack Horner* (1857). In 1860 John Cormack (1827–90) joined the Drury Lane company as Harlequin and also assumed choreography duties, undertaking both every year until the end of Chatterton's regime in 1878–9. When Edmund Falconer took over as lessee he brought in Oscar Byrne to choreograph the Ballet of Bouquets, featuring ballerina Lydia Thompson as a special feature. But thereafter it was Cormack who choreographed the ballets as well as devising the harlequinade 'business'. *The Era* called Cormack a 'Ballet Master with few equals' (2 January 1870) and 'the most ingenious and indefatigable of ballet masters' (1 January 1871).

Like John Cormack, John D'Auban was a performer as well as a choreographer. He became one of the leading choreographers of his age. Credited with developing skirt dancing (a more decorous version of the uninhibited French can-can) and hailed as the champion star-trap jumper, he became associated closely with both the Savoy and Drury Lane. He was born in Dublin into a theatrical family called Dobbin, who changed their name to the more aristocratic sounding D'Auban in 1848. He made his stage debut dancing an Irish jig when only five and thereafter toured the British Isles as part of the family dance troupe. Teaming up with his sister Mariette as Harlequin and Columbine, he made his London pantomime debut at the Marylebone Theatre in 1862–3 in *King Hal ye Bluff, Anne Boleyne ye fayre, or Harlequin Herne ye Hunter and the Good Little Fairies of the Silver Ferns*. He danced in many of the pantomimes and burlesques at the Alhambra produced by John Hollingshead between 1865 and 1868 and then joined Hollingshead at the Gaiety, where between 1868 and 1880 he developed a career as choreographer and earned not just a national but an international reputation. Beginning with *The Sorcerer* in 1877 he choreographed all the Gilbert and Sullivan operas apart from *The Gondoliers*, whose opening clashed with the Drury Lane pantomime. In 1880 D'Auban choreographed and appeared in *Mother Goose* at Drury Lane. He remained there as choreographer and ballet master until 1909, regularly performing in the Christmas pantomime.[84] This then was the team that set the standard for pantomime which other managements sought to emulate or even to top.

8

E.L. Blanchard and the Drury Lane Pantomimes: The Smith Management

Blanchard cut his dramatic teeth on extravaganzas and burlesques performed not at Christmas but in spring and autumn. There was *Cinderella* at the Olympic (8 April 1844), *Jack and the Beanstalk* at the Victoria (2 September 1844) and *Robinson Crusoe* at the Strand (12 May 1845). His first Christmas pantomimes appeared in 1845–6 as he provided scripts for the minor theatres: *Fortunatus or the Magic Cap and the Three Lucky Wishes* at the Olympic (26 December 1845), *The Birth of the Steam Engine or Harlequin Go-Ahead and Joe Miller and His Men* for the Victoria (26 December 1846) and *King Alfred the Great or Harlequin and the Enchanted Raven* (26 December 1846) at the Olympic.

In 1847 he wrote *The World of Wonders or Harlequin Caxton and the Origins of Printing* (under the pseudonym Francisco Frost) for the Victoria (26 December 1847) and *Eyes, Nose and Mouth or Harlequin Prince Perfect and the Birth of Beauty* for the Marylebone Theatre (26 December 1847). In 1848 came *Harlequin Lord Lovel or the Mistletoe Bough or Lady Nancy Bell and the Fairies of the Oak* for the Surrey (26 December 1848), *William the Conqueror or Harlequin Harold and the Sack of the Saxons* (26 December 1848) for the Olympic and *The Land of Light or Harlequin Gas and the Four Elements, Earth, Air, Fire and Water* (26 December 1848) for the Victoria.

Curiously, there were no pantomimes in 1849 or 1850. The explanation may be that Blanchard was travelling a good deal to revise guide books and was busy with journalism. He was also writing, in 416 double-columned pages, the third series of *The Mysteries of London* after its originator, G.W.M. Reynolds, fell out with the publisher.[1]

Pantomime-writing resumed for the 1851–2 season and he wrote three: *Harlequin Blue Cap and the King of the Golden Waters* (26 December 1851) for the Surrey, *Sir John Barleycorn or Harlequin Champagne and the Fairies of the Hop and Vine*

(26 December 1851) for the Marylebone and *Harlequin and the Yellow Dwarf* (26 December 1851) for Sadler's Wells.

The first thing that strikes one about these pantomimes is the extraordinary eclecticism of the subject matter, ranging from scientific developments and allegories to folklore, fairy tales and balladry. The pantomimes which celebrate the great scientific advances of the age were all produced at the Victoria. *The Birth of the Steam Engine* (1846) opened with the entrance of the Emperor of Topsy Turvey, 'whose old-fashioned ideas are quite opposed to the new order of things introduced by the "Birth of Steam".' The railways have turned everything upside down. *The Daily News* (28 December 1846) reported:

> The entertainment is carried on through eight stations and stops at last at 'the grand terminus of pantomime in the realms of laughter'. While passing through these several stations, the principal topics of the day, social and political are introduced in a grotesque and laughable form, by means of the mechanical contrivances usual, from time immemorial, on these occasions. There was, now and again, a little awkwardness in shifting the machinery, but, on the other hand, the scenery was excellent, and, on the whole, the piece received a boisterous reception from an audience crowded to inconvenience.

This celebration of the railways was entirely in line with the enthusiasm generated by their development. The railways epitomized technological advance – a new method of transporting people and goods speedily and in bulk, of unifying nations and, in the words of the celebrated epigrammatist Sydney Smith, 'abolishing time, distance and delay.' Their coming in art and literature was hymned on a remarkable scale of imagination and power and great were the claims made by contemporary enthusiasts such as E. Foxwell and T.C. Farrer, who in 1889 wrote that 'Many, if not most, of the distinctive phenomena that constitute the "nineteenth century" are directly due to railway speed.' They listed these phenomena as the diffusion of wealth, the universal spirit of competition, independence of manners, realism in art, the unprecedented growth in population, the cheapness of most necessaries, the ending of feudalism and the beginning of freedom.[2]

The 1847–8 Victoria pantomime was *The World of Wonders*, whose theme was the triumph of Intelligence and Learning 'by the gigantic agency of the Press' over Ignorance and Superstition. This led *The Era* (2 January 1848) to describe it as an 'intellectual pantomime'. The first scene is set in the Abode of Stupidity in the dark depths of Ignorance where slaves are forging the fetters of Ignorance and Superstition, watched over by the giant fiends of Crime and Poverty. But gradually this location is superseded by the Temple of Intelligence. Intelligence waves his wand (a giant quill pen) to disperse the clouds of ignorance and his fairy attendants appear, including Typographica, the genius of the printing press. Intelligence

promises to free the people and decrees a pantomime on the history of printing,
summoning up personifications of all the contemporary newspapers. The schemes of
Stupidity and his associate Prejudice are defeated as poetry, painting, music,
sculpture and navigation are sent through the land to diffuse their humanizing
influence. There is an allegorical tableau of the progress of printing from the days of
William Caxton to the present. The subplot has Caxton's apprentice Wynkyn de
Worde and the villainous Sir Geoffrey Crinkumcrankum in competition for the hand
of the fair Rosabella. With the help of the fairies, Wynkyn triumphs. The last scene
of the opening takes place in the temple of Typographica with all the different styles
of lettering personified. The characters of the opening are then transformed into the
personalities of the harlequinade and Ignorance and Superstition are kicked and
beaten by Clown and Pantaloon. The final scene of the whole show takes place in the
Fairy Palace of Printing in the Dominions of the Press, the whole of the Alphabet
being present in double columns. *The Era* concluded: 'The Pantomime is a good one,
and will attract very many full houses.' Blanchard celebrated the progress of printing
and the development of the press as the key to the spread of intelligence and the
banishing of ignorance and prejudice, crime and want. He included all classes in its
benefits, for when Stupidity asks to be allowed to keep the lower orders in thrall,
Intelligence replies:

> Inspired by me all men have equal claim
> I make the peasant and the peer the same

Truth encourages Intelligence in his campaign, promising that if he perseveres an
ideal state of affairs will prevail:

> When statesmen shunning parties' claim
> Shall make their country's good their aim,
> And earth receives, what earth intends,
> The bounteous food that nature sends;
> When men shall feel, as I'll explain it,
> That giving happiness, they gain it,
> And wages fair shall be paid each one,
> By whom a fair day's work is done.
> Then England shall indeed be blessed,
> And want shall ne'er oppress her.
> For Truth will dwell an honoured guest,
> And all mankind shall bless her.

This was a potent message for the 'Hungry Forties' and one likely to provoke cheers
in the working-class audience of the Vic.

As if to underline the theme of education, the action of the pantomime took place against scenes reproduced from old engravings of Caxton's house with its view of Charing Cross; Lambeth Marsh and the Ferry of Old Thames; and a 'well-executed' painting of Shakespeare's House.

This highly didactic pantomime was revived at the Marylebone Theatre on 26 December 1856, attributed to Francisco Frost, but re-titled *Tit, Tat, Toe, – My First Go or Harlequin N.E.W.S. and the Fairy Elves of the Fourth Estate*. Its appearance was welcomed by *The Era* (28 December 1856) which praised the new manager Sam Emery: 'Mr Emery has aimed well as to an inspiring intellectual subject, the germ of which begat present civilization; and we gladly, therefore, hope that the results of his teaching may be most beneficial.'

The theme of the 1848 Victoria pantomime, *The Land of Light or Harlequin Gas and the Four Elements, Earth, Air, Fire and Water* was the triumph of gaslight. Gas lighting had been introduced into London in the first decades of the nineteenth century. The first parliamentary act to incorporate a gas company was passed in 1810. By 1823 40,000 gas lamps were lighting 215 miles of London streets and from 1840 gas lighting was increasingly used in private houses.[3]

Blanchard's pantomime, submitted to the Lord Chamberlain under the title *Earth-Air-Fire-Water or Harlequin Gas and the Flight of the Fairies*, was based on the battle between Science and the Fairies. But the first night of the pantomime was overshadowed by tragedy. When the theatre opened for the evening on Tuesday, so many people crowded in seeking places in the gallery that the handrail of the stairs collapsed and two lads, William Phillips (aged eleven) and John Castillo (aged fifteen), were killed and several others injured. This is grim evidence of the popularity of the shows.[4]

The story begins in the Shadow Swamp in the dominion of darkness where the fairies (Oberon, Titania, Puck, Robin Goodfellow, Queen Mab and Friar Rush) have retreated to the Goblin Coal Mine 5,000 miles below the earth to escape the advance of Science. There is a crash and Science appears attended by four navvies, explaining that she has been teaching Brunel to form a tunnel 'through the earth to save all time and bother', a reference to the recent completion and formal opening in 1843 of the Thames Tunnel, constructed by the Brunels father and son. Summoning her Sprite Gas, Science with a wave of the wand conjures up 'the Lustrous Land of Light', 'designed', said *The Era* (31 December 1848), 'to include every description of artificial light with which we are acquainted.' A wager is made between Science and Oberon that the powers of the former will outdo those of Fiction as represented by the Fairies. The objects of the trial are two rivals for the hand of the heroine. Interestingly in class terms, the rivals are a humble woodsman, Walter, and an aristocrat Lord Tomnoddy (generic term for a fool), both in love with Lady Emmeline. Science and the Gas Sprite support Walter and the Fairy King Oberon,

Lord Tomnoddy. The Gas Sprite helps Walter elope with Emmeline by use of a balloon and a steamboat. The victory is awarded to Science who decrees a harlequinade to entertain everyone, and Oberon helps convert the characters of the opening to those of the harlequinade. Science declares:

My flickering Sprite shall join you on your rambles
And Gas shall light your merry Christmas gambols,
With Earth-Air-Fire and Water, you'll confess
That we have got the *Elements* of success.

The Era reported: 'The tricks and transformations are executed with much vivacity, humour and dexterity, and are, moreover, well chosen, and some of them are novel.' The conclusion in the Hall of Magic Science was declared 'exceedingly brilliant and attractive and puts a fitting termination to the whole affair.' For Blanchard, the scientific and technological changes of the age (the railways, the popular press, gaslight) were a positive good, not only representing progress but advancing education and democracy. The pantomime was being actively used to vindicate them.

History, or rather historical folklore was the order of the day at the Olympic. *King Alfred the Great or Harlequin History and the Enchanted Raven* begins in 'The British Walhalla or Hall of Heroes', which the *I.L.N.* (26 December 1846) thought was 'a good notion ... where the most important characters in history are grouped after the style of Madame Tussaud's exhibition, and deliver various opinions.' On pillars are seen medallions of the Kings and Queens of England and in niches busts of particular historical figures, Fair Rosamond, Wat Tyler, Jack Cade and Sir Walter Raleigh, who speak at various points. It is an interesting choice of characters: two rebel leaders, a murdered king's mistress and an executed adventurer, figures as much of folklore as of history. The presence among the historical figures of two rebels, Jack Cade and Wat Tyler, can only reflect the anxiety about the rise of Chartism, in whose rhetoric such populist rebel leaders figured. Equally significant is their rejection in favour of a celebrated monarch who led the English to victory against the Danes to assert English nationhood. History's attendants, Doubt, Prejudice, Research and Reflection appear, and then a large volume inscribed 'History of England by Hume and Smollett' rises through a trap door and History steps out. She examines the past year for themes for pantomime:

Two ministries [Sir Robert Peel and Lord John Russell] – Free
Trade – the League victorious [The Anti-Corn Law League] –
the health of towns considered – the Pacha's Visit [The visit
to London of Ibrahim Pasha, the ruler of Egypt] ... The statue
[the controversy about where to site the statue of the Duke of

Wellington] ... I must admit, the year does England credit.

But in this age of peace my strength relaxes

Give me the good old times of wars and taxes.

Two old friends of History appear, Fable, seen as an old man dressed as Aesop, and Travestie, dressed in a caricatured form of modern costume. They consider and reject Rosamond, Tyler, Cade and Raleigh and Travestie suggests King Alfred. Since nothing much is known about him, History leaves it to Fable and Travestie and retires.

King Alfred opens as the Danes under their King Guthrum return to Uffington Castle, having defeated the Saxons. The enchanted raven banner of the Danes warns of danger but Guthrum defies it and insists on marching to Stonehenge. Alfred, a fugitive from the Danes, takes refuge at the Druid's Cave and Blowing Stone of Kingston Lisle, where the Druids, also in hiding, give him a magic harp to charm the Danes. Taking refuge in the cottage of Dame Winifred, he is set to watch the cakes and allows them to burn while plotting his strategy. He is joined there by the Saxon lovers, Edwin and Elfrida, who have escaped from captivity at Uffington. Alfred rallies his troops and after distracting the Danes with his harp, and identifying their weak points, leads an attack and defeats Guthrum in combat, at which point Fable appears, transports them to the Fairy Land of Fable where the characters are transformed into those of the harlequinade and at the end, Saxons and Danes make peace.

The Times (28 December 1846) noted that the performance of the tragedy of *Jane Shore*, which came first, was reduced to a dumb-show spectacle by the 'time-honoured' custom of Boxing Night by which the actors were drowned out by 'an incessant fire of comic commentaries from the sprightly occupants of the pit and the gallery' but that quiet prevailed as soon as the pantomime started and that at the end it was 'announced for repetition with universal approval.'

It looks to have been intended as a parody of Sheridan Knowles' 1831 drama *Alfred the Great*, which contained the burning of the cakes, the impersonation of the harpist and the enchanted raven banner and in which the great William Macready had starred, though the script instructs the actor playing Guthrum to do so in the manner of current theatrical superstar Charles Kean. Guthrum's first line upon entering is 'Now is the winter of discontent' and Richard III was a role that Kean played regularly in his career.

In the context of the consideration of Wat Tyler as a pantomime theme it should be noted that the 1849–50 pantomime at the Victoria, not by Blanchard, was *Harlequin Wat Tyler or Jack Straw's Rebellion and the Fairies of the Land of Flowers*. The Tory journal *John Bull* (29 December 1849) disapprovingly noted 'the Victoria pantomime assumes a political tone', and that the harlequinade had political allusions 'betraying a leaning to the liberal school.' In the pantomime opening,

Richard II hunting with his uncles in Greenwich Park is told that the poll tax is to be imposed on the people. 'Levy a tax? What do my people say?' he asks. He is told 'they grumble, sire, but they pay.' However, when the tax collector tries to levy the tax, he is murdered. Wat Tyler, described as 'The Chartist of 1381', rebels and is later killed by the Lord Mayor of London, Sir William Walworth, described as 'Defender of the Filth'. In the harlequinade, a box labelled 'Manchester Goods' is opened to reveal a portrait of Anti-Corn Law campaigner Richard Cobden with the words 'Cheap Bread' written beneath it. There seems to have been nothing similar in any of the other London theatres.

The 1848 Olympic pantomime was *William the Conqueror or Harlequin Harold and the Sack of the Saxons*. *The Era* (31 December 1848) reported that the manager William Davidson had got the show up at short notice, the theatre having been closed for repainting and refurbishment. Nevertheless 'the house was crowded in every part' for the programme of *She Stoops to Conquer* followed by the pantomime, and:

> as is usually the case on 'Boxing Night', the gods, though less uproarious than in some other of the minor theatres, were too impatient for the pantomime to allow much of the dialogue to be heard. Indeed, all the 'heavy' parts of the play passed in dumb-show, and it was only during the more comic scenes that the clever acting ... induced a temporary cessation of the clamour.

Eventually quiet descended when the pantomime began and it opened in the Factory of Fun, in the World of Waggery, where jokes and puns are manufactured to order. The Genius of Fun, lamenting that from continuous demands made on her, she has been reduced to her last pun, is astounded to receive a cheque for a new pantomime and draws a bill for fifty puns at sight upon history. The bill being discounted, the Norman invasion is chosen as the subject for the pantomime. This was probably because of the publication in 1848 of Bulwer-Lytton's novel, *Harold, the Last of the Saxon Kings*, which dealt with precisely this subject.

The story itself, summarized in *The Era* (24 December 1848), begins at Hastings Castle with a distant view of the English Channel by daybreak, where Grimmug, a venerable Saxon sentinel, is keeping watch on the battlements. Edwin, a young fisherman in love with Edith, daughter of the governor of the castle, climbs in to meet her. Earl Wottagoth, Edith's father and the governor of the castle, returns from fighting the Norwegians and orders breakfast al fresco. The guards discover Edwin and denounce him as a spy. He is imprisoned in the dungeons but helped to escape by the spells of a fellow prisoner, the Scandinavian sorceress Norna (the equivalent of the sorceress Hilda in Lytton's novel). William of Normandy and his army land at Pevensey Bay, bearing banners inscribed 'First Come, First Served' and 'Everything or Nothing'. Harold challenges William to single combat to settle the dispute but this being refused, the two sides engage in battle until Fun intervenes to change them into the characters of the harlequinade.

The *I.L.N.* (31 December 1848) reported that the pantomime was produced with 'entire success'. The opening was:

> very cleverly written, far more so than we usually look for in the pieces of this kind, and every well-known incident is turned to humorous account, even to the battle of Hastings, in which there is a terrible combat between *Harold* and *William the Conqueror*. The change from this scene to the fairy temple, in which the transformations for the harlequinade, take place, was most elaborate and beautiful, and rewarded with long-continued rounds of applause.

The Era (31 December 1848) reported that in Blanchard's script 'There are many and appropriate hits ... some so fine and delicately sharp' that they were missed by the vulgar. *The Times* (27 December 1848) thought that the hits in the harlequinade at the events of the day were 'none of them ... so striking as to demand special notice.' They included references to the sighting of a sea serpent, the overthrow of King Louis Philippe of France, emigration, gutta percha, the chef Alexis Soyer, the state of the drama, the condition of the national defences and the baby jumpers. But 'the action of the pantomime was kept up with great life and spirit ... The scenery, most of which is entirely new, does much credit to the painters, and the concluding scene is one of great brilliancy, and displays considerable mechanical ingenuity.'

For the 1848–9 Surrey pantomime *Harlequin Lord Lovel or the Mistletoe Bough or Lady Nancy Bell and the Fairies of the Silver Oak* Blanchard turned to old English balladry, contriving a plot which merged *The Mistletoe Bough* and *Lord Lovel*. So Druids and the mistletoe kiss intertwine with the story of Lord Lovel who goes travelling 'strange countries for to see', leaving behind him his beloved Lady Nancy Bell. He returns after a year and a day to find that she has just died. He dies of grief and from their respective graves grow a rose and a briar.

Blanchard's version begins in the Druids' haunt by moonlight where the Druids recount their quarrel with Baron Allaflam, who has given them notice to quit Stonehenge, which is on his land. They deliver a warcry 'Freedom and Stonehenge' and resolve to be avenged by setting fire to the forest and causing the death of the Baron's daughter Lady Nancy Bell, who is due to marry Lord Lovel. The Fairy of the Oak intervenes to save the forest from destruction. Instead the Druids cast a spell on the mistletoe bough so that when she and Lord Lovel kiss under it on their wedding day, she will die. After a grand wedding banquet with an immense variety of dishes from turkey to boar's head carried in to the theme of 'There's a good time coming, boys' (in which the audience in pit and gallery joined 'heartily and loudly' reported *The Standard*), Lady Nancy proposes a game of hide and seek during which she is supposed to die, but again she is rescued by the fairies.

The Times (27 December 1848) reported that 'The Theatre was crowded in every part to inconvenience, and hundreds were compelled to go away for want of accommodation.' The critic of the *I.L.N.* (3 December 1848) was unable to give a full account of the pantomime as the crowd was so dense that he could only see by jumping up to get a glimpse of scenes above the heads of standing spectators. But he reported that the regular bursts of laughter suggested a hit. The pantomime was preceded by a three-act drama, *The Secretary*, 'very tragic, very dull', of which *The Daily News* critic (27 December 1848) reported that he could not hear a word.

The Times said that the combination of the two ballads produced alternately:

> scenes of a beautiful woodland character, of which groves of oak, peopled by Druids and fairies, were the chief characteristics and ludicrous and grotesque representations of Lord Lovel's courtship of the fair Nancy Bell, and the preparation made by him 'strange countries for to see'. Of these it is enough to say that the scenes, in point of artistic excellence and stage effect, were truly admirable, and that the latter were grotesque and amusing enough to keep the house in a roar of laughter.

The Era (31 December 1848) thought the pantomime 'perfectly successful' and pronounced:

> 'The opening' by the talented Mr Blanchard is smart and clever; the 'comic scenes' really *comic*; the scenery, dresses and properties, gorgeous in the extreme; the music, light and pretty; the tricks and mechanical transformations obedient to the magic bat of the motley hero; and the Pantomimist the best in London.

The Standard (27 December 1848) thought the scenery 'highly creditable' and particularly praised 'the magical metamorphosis and sudden appearance of the fairies of the Silver Oak in the sylvan temple of the enchanted forest of golden leaves, with the apotheosis of the oak' which signalled the transformation of the characters of the opening to those of the harlequinade.

Then there was a series of allegorical narratives. One of the most extraordinary and surrealistic was *Eyes, Nose and Mouth or Harlequin Prince Perfect and the Birth of Beauty*, Blanchard's 1847–8 offering at the Marylebone Theatre. It followed a performance of the heavy eighteenth-century tragedy *Jane Shore* by Nicholas Rowe. According to *The Times* (28 December 1847): 'The uproar throughout the tragedy was so great that it was utterly impossible to catch more than an occasional sentence and all that we can say about the performance is that the piece, as usual at this theatre, was extremely well put upon the stage.' But as soon as the pantomime started, 'the storm in a great measure abated, and all was hushed in comparative repose.'

The pantomime begins in the Abode of Ugliness where the Demon King of Ugliness informs his attendant sprites that he is engaged in a life and death struggle with the Queen of Beauty and about to be attacked by the combined forces of Beauty, Verri Pretti and Sunbeam. If defeated, he would see his empire dissolved. The conflict focuses on Prince Perfect and his search for a wife. So the King of Ugliness sends for the abominable Fright and orders him to ensure that Prince Perfect chooses a 'perfect fright' as his consort. But in the next scene, the Isle of Beauty by the Lake of Loveliness at sunrise, the Queen of Beauty causes Prince Perfect to behold a vision of Princess Paragon. He returns to his castle and inserts an advertisement in the *Morning Post* headed 'Matrimony – a wife wanted.' Ambassadors come from the North American Indians, from China and from 'the Ethiopian Court of the Congo' with portraits of eligible princesses but Perfect fails to find Princess Paragon. At the suggestion of Fright, who has insinuated himself into his court, Prince Perfect sets out to find a wife. Accompanied by his valet Scrimble-Scramble, he travels through the Empire of Eyes to find nothing but Amazonian damsels with huge eyes. He flies to the Nation of Noses, to find female divinities with huge noses. Finally seeking 'The Great Mouth' he ends up in the Abode of Ugliness where Ugliness and Beauty confront each other and the fairy Sunbeam intervenes to transform the scene to the Bower of Beauty and the Prince and Princess, the object of his search, are transformed into Harlequin and Columbine for the harlequinade. At the end, they are united in the Fairy Court of the Realms of Beauty, 'a superb tableau' according to *The Daily News* (28 December 1847).

The Times thought the show 'a triumph' and *The Era* (2 January 1848) thought it 'entirely successful', particularly praising the masks ('very funny') and the scenery ('exceedingly good'). *The Standard* (28 December 1847) noted:

> The success of the pantomime, of course, mainly depended upon the extravagance of the scenes, and perhaps there never was a happier accumulation of frightful monstrosities than is to be found in the Nation of Noses and Empire of Eyes, over which the demon of ugliness has dominion. The tricks and transformations, the sudden transitions and scenic effects, elicited the warmest applause; and on the conclusion of the performance, the unanimous approval of the audience established the success of the pantomime.

For the Marylebone Theatre in 1851 Blanchard (under the pseudonym Francisco Frost) wrote *Sir John Barleycorn or Harlequin Champagne and the Fairies of the Hop and Vine*, a celebration of drink. The opening scene takes place in the Great Brewery of pantomime where in a great vat a pantomime is being concocted by elves from jokes, hits and skits, under the superintendence of the Genius of Fun. The centre of the Vat opens to reveal the well-known image of Sir John Barleycorn, the personification of malt liquor, with a foaming tankard of ale in his hand. Fun exclaims:

Hail, glorious John, old England's fame and boast;
This is the stuff that Britons prize most;
Be this our subject – real old English ale;
Who sees that head will never find it's stale

The sprite Corkscrew is summoned and instructed to aid Sir John who is seeking a wife. From his cottage in the village of Richingrain, Sir John inspects and rejects several village lasses and sets his heart on the fair Light-Heart, who is already being courted by Champagne. So, with his attendants Pale Ale and Extra Stout, Sir John proceeds to the Abode of Old Port in the Wood, the guardian of the fair Light-Heart. Here a contest takes place between the Knight of the Vine and the Knight of the Hop, ending with the escape of Champagne with Light-Heart, who is conveyed to his castle on the banks of the Rhine. But Light-Heart rejects Champagne's advances. Sir John and his followers attack the castle with a battery of soda-water bottles and Corkscrew, insinuating his body through the wall, opens the gates of the castle to the Barleycorn Barrel Army. Champagne, Light-Heart and their followers take refuge in the wine vaults of the castle. But finally in the Bower of Beauty in the regions of enchantment the characters are transformed into the figures of harlequinade, with Champagne as Harlequin, Barleycorn as Clown and Light-Heart as Columbine. The pantomime ends with a truce granted on condition that the Hop and Vine join forces to cheer the hearts of mankind at Christmas. So while it celebrates the Britons' love of beer and ale, it is happy to compromise with continental wine in the interests of general good cheer.

The Era (4 January 1852) reported of the pantomime:

It is probably one of the most original in subject, and most effective in treatment that has ever been offered to the public at this or any other theatre. There is a remarkable freshness in the notion of embodying the various beverages, and exhibiting, through this medium, the contest between the rival powers of the Hop and the Vine for the possession of Lightheart, and the allegory is admirably sustained by the succession of scenery through which the idea is carried to its culminating point in the transformation of the characters ... the tricks and changes of the harlequinade are both numerous and novel ... the scenery of Mr Mildenhall, shows a fertile design and a skilful artistic pencil; and the last scene representing what the bills call the 'Glittering Regions of Enchantment' is truly a dazzling display of splendour, involving an expenditure which must have been considerable ... No expense has been spared in its production, and the style in which it has been placed upon the stage is only a satisfactory proof that the lessee, Mr E.T. Smith, is not only indefatigable in his exertions to raise the reputation of the establishment under his direction, but regardless of outlay when he has an entertainment that seems likely to please the public.

You could not have asked for a better review. The only problem for the scholar analysing the reviews is that Blanchard wrote it himself, as he revealed in his diaries. On 29 December, he went to the Marylebone to see the pantomime from a private box. 'Much pleased with pantomime' he wrote. On 31 December, he noted: 'Write notice of Marylebone for *Era*' and on 4 January 1852 the review was published.[5] To be fair, there seems to have been some striking imagery in the show, for example the attack on Champagne Castle by a battery of soda bottles which peppered the castle with corks. The Champagne army consisted of inverted wine glasses and foil-tipped bottles with cigars for spears.

The fourth source of pantomime stories for Blanchard was fairy tales. For the Olympic in 1845–6, Blanchard supplied *Harlequin Fortunatus or the Magic Cap and the Three Lucky Wishes* which took its basic idea from an old German folk tale, first printed in 1509 and later published in a variety of forms and languages, including a play by Elizabethan playwright Thomas Dekker in 1600.

Blanchard's pantomime opens in the Hall of Hypochondria in the dominion of Dreams. It is painted blue (for 'the blues') and features winding corridors stretching into the distance 'à la Martin' (recalling John Martin, the celebrated painter of heaven, hell and apocalypses). There are pestles and mortars labelled 'Woes for the Wretched', 'Grist for Grumblers', 'Meals for the Miserable' and 'Dumps for the Desponding'. The Demon Dismalgrowl appears, his attendants singing:

Sow the seeds of sadness! Pluck the weeds of gladness!
Make the world as sad as the world can be.

The Demon complains that the world is getting happier, what with the abundance of funny publications and the popularity of burlesque on the stage. Nightmare arrives and reports that the Fairy Lightheart has vowed to destroy Dismalgrowl's kingdom and banish the blues and even to make Prince Megrim, who never smiles, laugh. The Demon says that this means war.

Then in the Wondrous World of Wideawake, at sunrise, Fairy Lightheart finds her agent, the peasant Fortunatus, asleep, put under a spell by Nightmare. She promises to unite him with Princess Floribella, whom he loves, and who loves him. She wakes him and gives him a magic cap that will grant three wishes and an ever-filling purse of gold. Fortunatus proceeds to the royal palace, and seems to gain the favour of Emperor Glumpyglump by filling the treasury from his purse. But when the Emperor tries to arrest him, he puts on the magic cap, wishes for invisibility and vanishes. A herald announces that by order of the Emperor anyone who can make his son, Prince Megrim, laugh can have anything he wants. Floribella has turned down the advances of Megrim on the grounds that he never laughs. Fortunatus turns up and suggests a pantomime at which Megrim roars with laughter. The hand of Floribella is his reward. When the Emperor asks where the pantomime is, Lightheart appears and turns them all into the characters of the harlequinade ready for the comic business of the show, at the end of which Fortunatus and Floribella marry in the 'refulgent' Hall of Brilliants.

The Era (4 January 1846) noted that the show was 'received with much applause by a house crowded in every part' and pronounced the opening 'cleverly written'. The Times (27 December 1845) thought the scenery 'very excellent' and the dresses and properties done 'in the very best style'. The Standard (27 December 1845) praised the scene of the lake at sunrise as 'exceedingly beautiful' but noted with a hint of disapproval that the harlequinade was particularly boisterous ('A more than usual number of slaps in the face, pilfering from tradesmen and from unprotected females fill up the business').

Blanchard turned to an old Persian fairy tale for his Surrey pantomime of 1851–2, *Harlequin Blue Cap and the King of the Golden Waters or the Three Kingdoms, Animal, Vegetable and Mineral* which he wrote under the pseudonym Hafizd Fun, acknowledging the origin of the story. The pantomime opens in the Abode of the Fairy Trifla, Queen of the Realm of Sweets, in the island of Shooga Candi amidst the Golden Seas. The fairies, Sweet Cake, Bonbon, Liquorice, Peppermint, Cloves, Hardbake and 'a host of luscious names familiar to the infantine ear', appear followed by Queen Trifla who rises in her temple of Barleysugar. She explains that Emperor Alicampane, ruler of the Golden Seas, plans to marry his daughter, Princess Saccharina, to Grimguffin, King of the Ugli Isles. She loves Prince Bluecap of the Knursawry Isles and Trifla tells the fairies that they will aid the Prince to win the Princess. There is a fairy ballet to end the scene.

In the Golden City, the Emperor announces the forthcoming marriage of Saccharina and Grimguffin and promises to distribute 10,000 crowns to the people to mark the occasion – but he will keep it in the royal chest in case they are tempted to spend it. Prince Bluecap appears to claim the Princess. The Emperor agrees to approve the match if Bluecap brings him a treasure from each of the Animal, Vegetable and Mineral Kingdoms, an idea inspired by the exhibit classifications at the Crystal Palace.

In the Animal Kingdom, a panorama peopled by a variety of animals, 'a Pictorial Zoological Garden' says the script, the fairies produce for Bluecap a sagacious dog who helps drive off Grimguffin and his men who have followed Bluecap. He moves on to the Vegetable Kingdom, where the castle (modelled on the Crystal Palace) and kitchen garden of King Cauliflower are protected by a Turnip Guard. King Cauliflower appears, attended by Brussel Sprout pages, and the vegetable army of salad, potatoes, beans, peas, scarlet runners, onions, spinach and so on pass in review before the King and the Prince. The dog locates a magic spade which can identify gold in the ground and cause new crops to spring up. This is presented to Bluecap after the dog restores the head of an accidentally decapitated turnip guard. Then in the mines of darkness in the Mineral Kingdom, Bluecap uses the magic spade to uncover a store of solid gold. He returns to Alicampane with the dog, the spade and the gold, but the Emperor reneges on his promise and the Prince uses the spade to transform the scene to the 'Hive of a Thousand Sweets in the Palace of a Million Pleasures' where the fairy Trifla converts the characters into the traditional figures of the harlequinade, at the end of which Bluecap and Saccharina are united, in the Pavilion of Shooga Candi.

The Era (28 December 1851) noted that 'The opening displays a magnificent series of fairy scenery; and is plentifully interspersed with witticisms in verse ... The whole plot is effectively worked out in all its quaintness and drollery through a mass of gorgeous and romantic scenery.' The I.L.N. (27 December 1851) thought William Calcott's scenery 'exceedingly beautiful', the temple of sweets 'a most remarkable and effective scene' and praised the manager Richard Shepherd for showing 'great taste and liberality in getting up' the show.

The Daily News (27 December 1851) reported that the play preceding the pantomime, Richard Lalor Sheil's Evadne, was listened to with more attention than usual on these occasions, but The Standard critic and The Times (27 December 1851) said it was performed in dumb show due to the 'unflinching determination of a large portion [of the audience] to maintain the right to drown the first piece on Boxing Night.' But, said The Daily News, the start of the pantomime was greeted with great excitement. 'There was abundant evidence in the first scene that the manager was determined not to be surpassed by any of his rivals on the more aristocratic side of the water ... the pictorial effects are of the most striking description.' Interestingly, The Daily News noted 'the pantomime ... partakes in the opening more of the character of a burlesque than of an ordinary harlequinade, and is overflowing with parodies and satirical hits at the topics of the day', evidence of the merger of genres. The critic reported: 'The fun was well kept up to the end, and the scenery was of a more meritorious character than we have been accustomed to find at this transpontine establishment ... the pantomime was pronounced a decided hit.'

The Standard (27 December 1851) found 'the whole of the opening was utterly deficient in plot and the dialogue rather slow' but 'for magnificence of scenery, dresses, etc., and efficiency in company, we think it will more than bear comparison with any in the metropolis.' It cited in particular the Golden City, 'the colours in which were really so beautifully blended, and with such taste and view to dramatic effect, as completely to stop the progress of the piece' until the manager, Richard Shepherd came forward to take a bow in answer to repeated calls. The same thing happened at 'the Hive of a Thousand Sweets': 'It is almost impossible by mere description to do justice to this really splendid scene, which we have never seen anything of the kind to surpass.' So the final verdict was that the show may be regarded as a 'decided and most successful hit'. Blanchard saw the show from a private box on Boxing Day and recorded 'all goes off gloriously.'[6]

Harlequin and the Yellow Dwarf or the Enchanted Orange Tree and the King of the Golden Mines, the 1851–2 pantomime at Sadler's Wells, was attributed by the contemporary reviewers and subsequently by Allardyce Nicoll to T.L. Greenwood.[7] But Blanchard records in his diary on 31 October 1851, 'write first scene of Sadler's Wells pantomime' and he was in a private box to watch it on 27 December, his customary procedure on pantomimes he had authored.[8] *The Era* (28 December 1851) reported that the play preceding the pantomime, *The Lady of Lyons* 'was listened to with very marked attention and the actors repeatedly received the applause of the audience.' *The Times* (27 December 1851) reported, on the contrary, that the denizens of pit and gallery paid scarcely any attention to it, preferring to amuse themselves by whistling, shrieking, laughing, drinking gin and gingerbeer, sucking oranges and pelting each other with the peel, and, 'in not a few instances, we are sorry to say, with regular fighting.' The pantomime, however, 'received a fairer hearing and elicited an ample share of applause; as, indeed it well merited.' *The Standard* and *The Daily News* (both 27 December 1851) also reported that the play could not be heard because of the noise and that orange peel duels filled the half hour between the end of the play and the start of the pantomime. Given the dates of the reviews, it is possible that *The Era* critic saw the play on a different day to the others.

The pantomime was based on a story in *Mother Bunch's Fairy Tales*. Mother Bunch, like Mother Goose, was an Old English folkloric figure to whose authorship eighteenth-century English translations of French fairy tales – in her case by Madame d'Aulnoy – were attributed. The show opens with a typical debate between Tradition and Progress. In the ancient court of revels in Old Style's Christmas hall the Abbot of Misrule superintends the 'ancient sports and fooleries', attended by a group of historical celebrities, King Arthur, Henry VIII, Anne Boleyn (carrying her head in her hand), Queen Elizabeth I, Sir Walter Raleigh, Sir John Falstaff and Dame Quickly among them. The principal feature of the scene is a lively performance of the Sir Roger de Coverley dance. In the midst of the fun, the host Old Style enters and, addressing the revellers, expresses his regret at the innovating spirit of modern days and urges that the rage for improvement be resisted, so far, at least as time-honoured sports are concerned. At this point, New Style, in the person of a Bloomer, appears, declares the festivities out of date and refers to the 'goahead' spirit in America which has lately produced unequalled reaping machines, impregnable locks and unapproachable yachts. To show what she can do, she changes the scene to the Temple of New Style in the Region of Design where a dance is performed by a troop of Little Bloomers, Misses Tightwaist, Bluestockings, Shortskirt and Trimtrowsed. After further discussion on the spirit of Progress, New Style agrees to Old Style's plea to spare the good old pantomime from the threatened destruction of ancient pastimes and the Yellow Dwarf is summoned to assist in carrying this out. The use of Bloomers to embody progress and the counterpointing of American inventions and British tradition was highly topical as it was in the summer of 1851 that Mrs Amelia Bloomer arrived from America with her disciples to crusade for healthy and rational dress, including trousers for women. They were subjected to immediate and sustained ridicule in a stream of cartoons, jokes and satires. The opening traces the rivalry of the Yellow Dwarf and California, King of the Golden Mines for the hand of Princess Allfair, before the transformation into the characters of the harlequinade and the finale in the Palace of Rainbows. Again events in America had inspired the character of the King as in 1847 gold was discovered in California, the gold rush ensued and 1849 had seen the arrival of the first consignment of Californian gold in Britain.

Topicality too featured in the harlequinade with its opening scene in the new terminus of the Great Northern Railway at King's Cross and allusions to Bloomerism, vegetarianism, city improvements, the great submarine telegraph opened to the public in November 1851, Bramah's patent lock, cheap omnibuses, and the French coup d'état of Louis Napoleon in which English and French Assurance Offices saw French liberty assured by the sword and English life, by the law.

The reviews all praised the scenery of Frederick Fenton: 'excellent' (*The Times*, 27 December 1851), 'most beautiful' (*The Era*, 28 December 1851), 'of rare excellence' (*I.L.N.*, 27 December 1851). All three praised Greenwood as the writer of the pantomime, making no mention of Blanchard. *The Standard* (27 December 1851) thought the piece 'chiefly remarkable for the scenery and stage tricks ... the piece can never, perhaps, become an effective one, in consequence of its want of humorous dialogue and pointed satire', but thought it would amuse a holiday audience with its tricks.

Thomas Longden Greenwood (1806–79) was the fourth-generation member of a scene-painting family who had worked chiefly at Sadler's Wells. Greenwood joined the staff of the theatre, rising under actor-manager Robert Honner in 1839 to become business manager and resident writer. In 1843 he became manager himself, joining forces with the actor Samuel Phelps in 1844. Together they ran Sadler's Wells from 1844 to 1860 when Greenwood retired from management, followed in 1862 by Phelps. During their long and celebrated period of management, Phelps produced the Shakespeare and other classic plays and Greenwood was responsible for the pantomime. Interestingly Greenwood is not credited with pantomime scripting before 1850, his earlier work being melodrama, notably dramatizations of *Oliver Twist* and *Jack Sheppard*. Allardyce Nicoll credits Greenwood with the Wells pantomimes for 1850, 1851, 1852, 1853 and 1857.[9] However, it is clear from Blanchard's diaries that he wrote the pantomimes of 1851, 1852, 1853 and 1857 as well as those for 1856, 1860 and 1861, which are credited to him by Nicoll, and the pantomimes for 1854, 1855, 1858 and 1859 which are not listed in Nicoll.[10] So in effect he was the real author of the annual Wells pantomime every year from 1851 until the end of the Phelps–Greenwood management.

It is clear that Blanchard played an important part in the Wells set-up. In his biography of Phelps, published in 1886 and based on personal knowledge, the actor-manager John Coleman recorded that Phelps was considerably aided by his partner Greenwood who:

> not only attended to the financial department, and took the weight of the production of the pantomime off his hands, but he also watched the waves of public opinion, and steered the ship in accordance therewith. Then he had the advantage of the sagacious advice of his friend Edward Leman Blanchard, who, it is now known, was the editor of 'Phelps' Shakespeare.[11]

The first mention of Greenwood in Blanchard's diaries comes in 1846 when Blanchard delivered a piece called *Bear and Forbear* to him at Sadler's Wells.[12] There is no evidence that Blanchard wrote the 1850 pantomime, *Harlequin and the House that Jack Built for 1851 or the Genie of the Ring and Aladdin's Wonderful Lamp*. It was what the *I.L.N.* (28 December 1850) called 'a sort of *pièce de circonstance*', opening in the enchanted workshop of Jack-of-all-trades who announces to his work people that he intends building a house of industrial exhibition. He creates the Crystal Palace, introducing to his workmen some of the celebrities expected to visit it, among them Jenny Lind and the Prince of Nepal. But Invention turns up and points out that the Great Exhibition is not due to open until May and they have to put on a show on Boxing Day and with the aid of the fairies, she selects the story of Aladdin which is then told in the form of a pantomime. According to *The Times* (27 December 1850), it was 'composed and arranged by Mr Greenwood.' Although Greenwood did not return to management apart from brief spells at Astley's and the Princess' Theatre after he left the Wells, he continued to write, specializing in pantomimes. In fact he formed a partnership with Blanchard, collaborating with him as the Brothers Grinn, and they remained friends until Greenwood died. Blanchard records his death on 10 May 1879 and the fact that he and his wife attended the funeral on 15 May, describing him as 'our dear old friend'.[13]

By 1852–3 Blanchard was in demand. He was asked by theatre managers in Liverpool and Edinburgh for new pantomimes but apparently refused. He rejected a request from Eliza Vincent, the actor-manager of the Victoria, even though he had furnished pantomimes for the Vic in 1846, 1847 and 1848.[14] It may have been that he now considered this venue too downmarket, for he had secured in 1852 the prized assignment of furnishing the pantomime for the Theatre Royal, Drury Lane. E.T. Smith, who also ran the Marylebone Theatre (1851–3) for which theatre Blanchard had provided the pantomime in 1851, was the new proprietor at Drury Lane. Blanchard also agreed, as in 1851–2, to provide the pantomimes for the Surrey and Sadler's Wells.

The press attributed the Wells pantomime to Greenwood. For example, the *I.L.N.* (1 January 1853) said:

> The pantomime at this house is always good; and on the present occasion is excellent. 'Whittington and His Cat' may be an old subject, but it is one that can never be outworn; and Mr Greenwood has elaborated it with the skill which only time and practice can bestow.

But Blanchard's diary reveals that he wrote it, received ten pounds in payment and attended the production ('the best pantomime (thought to be) of the season').[15]

Whittington and His Cat or Old Dame Fortune and Harlequin Lord Mayor of London was an optimistic tale for hard times. It opened with a moonlit view of the mismanaged Abode of Miss Fortune who with Miss Hap, Miss Anthrope, Miss Chance, Miss Chief and other evil spirits laments the supposed arrival of 'the good time' which has been so long coming and the fatal absence of all future cause for grumbling. The scene is transformed to the Wheel of Fortune in the Palace of Rubies, the residence of Old Dame Fortune who is prescribing a cure for her daughter Miss Fortune's *ennui* and is demonstrating her willingness to aid those who practice industriousness and hard work. She suggests a grand pantomime to illustrate the story of Dick Whittington.

Dick, a penniless youth in search of a fortune, is taken on as a kitchen boy by merchant Hugh Fitzwarren. Although he works hard, he is ill-treated by the cook and the clerk and befriends the equally ill-treated Cat. He sends the Cat on a trading venture to the Barbary Coast where he earns renown by disposing of the rats. Dick runs away but is urged by the bells 'Turn again, Whittington', returns to Fitzwarren's warehouse for the transformation at the end of which he marries Alice Fitzwarren and becomes Lord Mayor. The harlequinade satirized dishonest politicians, cheating tradesmen, humbugging moralists and competing theatrical managers. The scenery of Frederick Fenton and Meadows was praised by *The Era* (2 January 1853) and *The Morning Chronicle* (28 December 1852), particularly the Abode of Misfortune, the Revolving Wheel of Fortune, the Banqueting Hall of King Flipidee Flobbidee, Fitzwarren's House and the Road to Highgate.

Blanchard was now moving increasingly into fairyland for his subjects. For the Surrey in 1852–3, his pantomime was *Harlequin and the World of Flowers or the Fairy of the Rose and the Sprite of the Silver Star*, allegedly based on an untranslated German tale by Herr Krackjaw Hawhawhausen, but in fact a Blanchard original. The evening began with *Uncle Tom's Cabin* which, according to *The Times* (28 December 1852) was:

got through rather dully, and we should think little to the edification of anybody, for a large portion of the audience were evidently little interested either in the horrors of slavery or the particular fate of Uncle Tom, and kept up a succession of noisy demonstrations from beginning to end.

An hour's wait for the pantomime made the audience restless but the lessee Richard Shepherd appeared to apologize for the delay and once the pantomime began 'everybody was again in a good humour.'

The show began in 'the glittering regions of the silver star' where No-Wun-No-Zoo, the Sprite of the Silver Star reigns. He has fallen in love with Rosabelle, the beautiful daughter of Baron Zourkroutz, burgomaster of Dondemendblitzen, a town on the banks of the Rhine. The Sprite descends to earth with his attendants to woo her. But the fairy queen of the roses, Rosalia, first seen in 'the Abode of Fairies in the World of Flowers', takes Rosabelle under her protection, and encourages the suit of a humble lover, Rodolph, the burgomaster's head gardener who also loves her. No-Wun-No-Zoo makes repeated attempts to carry off Rosabelle. His first attempt is foiled when Rosabelle plucks a magic rose which causes a bower of roses to surround and defend her and Rodolph. Later as Rosabelle and her lover are sailing on the Lake of Waterlilies at sunset in a fairy galley drawn by swans, No-Wun-No-Zoo raises a storm and in the midst of the tempest he conveys both to the 'cloudy realms of gloom'. But once again Rosabelle has recourse to magic, kissing a bouquet of roses which breaks the sprite's spell and results in Rosabelle and Rodolph being conveyed to the Valley of Bluebells, where the transformation to the harlequinade takes place.

The Times reported that:

In this, the first part of the performance, there are a variety of very tasteful and brilliant spectacles. Some of the scenes are indeed of singular beauty and excellence, especially the Lake of Water Lilies and the Valley of Bluebells. In point of colouring and general effect they surpass anything that has yet appeared in the Transpontine theatres, and the delight of the audience knew no bounds.

There was general praise for W.J. Calcott's scenery, pronounced 'gorgeous' by *The Era* (26 December 1852) and 'magnificent' by *Bell's Life in London* (2 January 1853). *The Morning Chronicle* (28 December 1852) said:

the favourable reception which the pantomime certainly obtained must be attributed rather to the great beauty of the scenery than to the humour of the dialogue or the novelty of the pantomimic incidents. Some of the strange effects are really magnificent, and well deserved the applause of a house which was crammed from the floor to the ceiling.

The Times also noted of the harlequinade that it contained 'a great many of the old stale tricks and jokes intermingled with allusions to passing events.'

For the Marylebone pantomime *Undine, the Spirit of Water or Harlequin Teetotum and the Chinese Cup and Sorcerer* Blanchard employed his nom-de-plume, Francisco Frost, and took as the central figure the water nymph Undine who featured in the 1811 fairy romance of the same name by Friedrich, Baron de la Motte Fouqué. He then involved her in a fanciful battle of beverages with characters named after brands of Chinese tea. Emperor Congou, named after the Chinese black tea, is at war with King Coffee. His daughter, Sue-Chong, is loved by young Hyson of the Green Tea faction, who is disapproved of by the Emperor. They elope to the Land of Lump Sugar where the fairies of the Sugar Loaf aid them. Learning of a magic cup, belonging to the Chinese sorcerer Hanki Panki which will grant its possessor every wish, they hasten to obtain it. But they are pursued by the Emperor's regiment of spoons until Undine intervenes, changes the scene to the wondrous world of waters complete with water-wheels, fairy fountains and waterfalls and there effects the transformation. *The Era* (2 January 1853) declared the pantomime 'remarkably full of business and much above the average'. E.T. Smith gave up the lease of the Marylebone in 1853 to concentrate on Drury Lane and Blanchard would thereafter no longer supply the minor theatres.

Latterly Drury Lane pantomimes had been getting a bad press. The 1846–7 pantomime, *Harlequin and St. George and the Dragon* by Maddison Morton was proclaimed by *The Examiner* (2 January 1847):

> the worst pantomime we ever saw. The solitary piece of fun in it is Mr Payne's equestrian feats in the character of *St. George*. He rides a hobby-horse and reviews his fellow champions as a veteran would a parcel of raw recruits, before they set forth on their adventures ... We may also mention with some praise the impossibly preposterous Black Masks of the Court of King Ptolemy. The rest is rubbish ... We left the theatre with no livelier sensation than of dust, brimstone, fatigue, and a horribly dull exaggeration of the dullest of all possible jokes.

The Daily News (28 December 1846) called it:

> tedious enough and wanting in what should be the pantomime's essence – viz., fun. But the fun of a pantomime has of late years been confined to a burlesque introduction, the remainder being only noticeable for a few novel transformations, having now and then, some point, popular or political. On the present occasion, the introductory part was burdened by a very short dialogue of no merit, and, notwithstanding the bustle and rapidity of the action, was so confused and wanting in drollery as to draw down frequent bursts of hissing ... the real business of the pantomime was equally unfortunate. No topic of the day was successfully touched on; ... the tricks and changes were as

commonplace as if neither chemistry nor the science of machinery had made any progress in the last ten years; and the mythic personages ... seemed to be under the influence of the general drowsiness.

The Satirist (3 January 1847) thought some of the actors were drunk on the opening night and complained about the 'lamentably slow' pace of the performance.

In 1847–8 the pantomime was *Friar Rush or Harlequin King Gold* by Alfred Crowquill and Albert Smith. *The Daily News* (28 December 1847) said that the pantomime was:

> enormously long, and before the close the audience exhibited signs of something more than weariness. Of the introductory part, from which the piece derives its title, we confess ourselves unable to give any account, for though we studied the wordy programme painfully and laboriously, we could not make ourselves understand either what we saw or what we read.

When it came to the harlequinade:

> Most of the tricks were practical jokes, of a threadbare kind – cuffs, kicks, and other manual witticisms, leaps through windows etc. Many of the transformations failed, owing to the defective working of the machinery; and scenes, evidently meant to be funny, were suddenly brought to a lame and impotent conclusion ... It went off with extreme coldness; the audience for the most part preserved a profound silence till the fall of the curtain, when expressions of disapprobation had a decided preponderance.

It was reported in *The Satirist* (2 January 1848) that the disasters of the first night were later eliminated and the pantomime shortened, and the tricks and scenery worked well subsequently. For Christmas 1848 the Cirque National de Paris was engaged for the season by lessee Alfred Bunn and there was no pantomime.

Blanchard's arrival at Drury Lane was to prove epoch-making but it did not begin particularly auspiciously. Both press and public evidently saw the arrival of E.T. Smith as manager as an event of significance. *The Times* (28 December 1852) reported, 'never was a house better filled than Drury-lane last night. The combined attractions of a new manager, new decorations, a troupe partly new, and two new pieces, have done wonders for this the disowned among the metropolitan theatres.'

The performance began with Edward Fitzball's adaptation of *Uncle Tom's Cabin* which *The Times* critic thought crude, lachrymose and badly acted and which was 'listened to with far greater patience than it deserved.' It was followed by the pantomime, Blanchard's *Harlequin Hudibras or Old Dame Durden and the Droll Days of the Merry Monarch*. Blanchard, perhaps inspired by his move from East End theatres to the grandest home of the national drama, chose to base his pantomime on a seventeenth-century satirical poem by Samuel Butler, thus proving that you could make a pantomime out of absolutely anything. But he mixed it up with a nursery rhyme and ensured a setting with distinct scenic and costume possibilities.

The Times noted that the author had mixed up Charles II, Hudibras and Dame Durden 'for no imaginable purpose but to make fun of them, and in this he succeeds.' The critic's bemusement is understandable. Samuel Butler's *Hudibras* mocked the hypocrisy and self-seeking of the Puritans. It was published in three parts between 1663 and 1678, thus indicating the reign of Charles II, 'the Merry Monarch'. Dame Durden was the central figure in a popular song who kept five men-servants 'to use the spade and flail' and five women servants 'to carry the milken pail.'

The pantomime expresses fully formed Blanchard's philosophy. It is one of celebration of the age of equipoise and enthusiasm for monarchy and 'Merrie England'. *Harlequin Hudibras* opens with a dispute between Antiquity and the Genius of Improvement. Antiquity is a gray-haired old man in a purple robe who lives in a grotesque 'Old Curiosity Shop' wherein he has stowed away 'specimens of exploded usages, obsolete notions, customs of days gone by, and worn out things of the past'. These include an old mail coach, Joe Miller's Joke Book, a horoscope cast by Dr Dee, the first issue of *The Gentleman's Magazine*, old street lamps, suits of armour and pairs of knee-britches. These will soon be joined, he says, by Blackfriars Bridge and Smithfield Market, both scheduled for demolition and replacement. He is attended by his faithful elves Moth, Mildew, Rust and Cobweb. The Genius of Improvement is a pretty girl in a yellow-spangled dress who appears from the dial of the electric telegraph and with her fairy wand summons up an image of the Crystal Palace at Sydenham by moonlight with fountains playing. It was to be officially opened by the Queen in 1854. There the *corps de ballet* dance to represent the union of the arts and sciences. Antiquity is persuaded by this to enter into alliance with Improvement to present the pantomime ('that is a good old custom every year/with which I never want to interfere/one for our children's sake we could not spare'). The Genius of Improvement proclaims her message:

I'm full of glorious projects for the people,
The working man shall find me raise his station,
I'll give him health – his children education,
Link the whole world in one vast railway chain,
'Till wiser grown, men never war again.

But peace and progress go hand-in-hand with respect for the past and tradition.

However, it is a past which rejects Puritanism and endorses monarchy. The scene changes to the Valley of Mountain Mist and the village of Sumware near Worcester and Dame Durden's farm 'with the serving maids and men busily occupied at their several employments as transmitted to us by the well-known glee.' Their labours are interrupted by the arrival in disguise of Charles II, fleeing from his defeat at the

Battle of Worcester. Charles makes love to Dame Durden's beautiful niece Alice until compelled to flee by the arrival of Sir Hudibras and his squire Ralpho seeking to recruit soldiers for the Roundhead Army. Hudibras courts Dame Durden, anxious to lay hands on her 'jointure land'. A bear-baiting follows and since it is condemned by the Puritans, Hudibras tries to stop it and ends up in the stocks. On his release, he recruits a force of local rascals and sets out to find the fugitive Charles. Charles meanwhile hides in the Royal Oak and then the kitchens of Boscobel Manor where he knights the roasting loin of beef, to create 'sirloin of beef', an act that folklore generally assigned to his grandfather James I. Charles poses as a cook when Hudibras arrives. 'A dance of a lively old English character' ensues, during which Charles escapes. Hudibras repairs to the Dark Dwelling of Sydrophel the Astrologer to learn something of his suit with the widow, only to be shown the restoration of Charles II on 29 May 1660, at Cheapside. Hudibras, Alice and Dame Durden are in the crowd. Hudibras says he has given Alice to Ralpho as wife. Charles says that a gift like that is now in his power and has Hudibras committed to the tower. Antiquity and Improvement return and summon up the Palace of Progress in the Region of Art where Art and Science are linked with Peace, Progress and Improvement. The transformation to the harlequinade takes place and the final scene is set in the Palace of Poetic Invention on the Borders of Burlesque.

Some of the critics had problems with Blanchard's opening. 'The opening was somewhat too long ... and it was not, perhaps, strictly intelligible' thought *The Morning Chronicle* (28 December 1852), and *The Daily News* (28 December 1852) said: 'For the spoken fun of the pantomime we cannot say much, as it was often rather obscure, and the actors seemed sadly deficient in their parts.' *The Era* (2 January 1853) disparaged the music, which it said 'was arranged by the veteran Blewitt, but so slovenly performed that we frankly confess there was much to us but ill understood', though *The Times* thought the score 'excellent'. However, there was general praise for the harlequinade, the dancing and the scenery, which was by Messrs Mildenhall, Nicolls and Cooper. *The Daily News*, for example, reported that the 'beautifully painted' depiction of the Crystal Palace at Sydenham provoked prolonged applause, and pronounced the rest of the scenery 'splendid', notably the village of Sumware in 'a fine sunny landscape', a view of Cheapside in 1660 and 'the grand fairy tableaux, both of which were as gorgeous as anything ever produced at the Lyceum, and elicited the warmest and most universal approbation.' There was a mishap when Dame Durden accidentally fell into the orchestra but the actor seems to have been uninjured. Edward Stirling, who stage managed the production, confirmed that it had been 'fairly mounted, considering the scanty resources at [Smith's] disposal.' Officially then it was deemed a successful launch for the Smith regime.

For 1853 Blanchard wrote the Drury Lane pantomime, *Harlequin and King Humming Top or the Land of Toys*, the Sadler's Wells pantomime, *Harlequin Tom*

Thumb or *Gog and Magog* and *Mother Goose's Golden Goslings* and *Jack the Giant Killer* for Birmingham. He travelled to Birmingham to see the production on 4 February 1854 and recorded in his diary, 'much pleased'.[16]

King Humming Top was the first of a series of highly imaginative and fanciful pantomimes based on nursery rhymes or nursery toys. As with *Harlequin Hudibras* Blanchard was aiming high but, as it seemed, too high for some of the critics. For he received similar comments to the previous year. *The Times* (27 December 1853) noted that it required 'a good deal of close attention clearly to understand the development of the fable.' *The Daily News* (27 December 1853) thought the opening neither intelligible nor coherent and *The Morning Chronicle* thought the opening 'rather an intricate one' and too long. The *I.L.N.* (31 December 1853) also thought it too long but believed that after judicious cutting it would succeed as a holiday amusement.

The pantomime opened in the Realms of Novelty where Success, Capital, Enterprise, Fashion, Invention and Design are discovered awaiting the arrival of Novelty on whom they are attendant. Novelty presently arrives in her emerald car, having just left Ireland where 'like many more' she has been on an Irish tour and attending the Irish Industrial Exhibition which signalled a change in Ireland's economic fortunes and where the great novelty was that 'Hibernia ceased to grumble.' Queen Victoria had visited Ireland in 1853 and the Irish Exhibition had run in Dublin from 12 May to 31 October. Novelty claims to have had her hands full this year, what with submarine electric telegraph cables, one laid between Downpatrick and Donaghadee and one projected between France and Algeria, mysterious table rappings attending the arrival of Spiritualism in Britain, a new sewing machine and the novelty of a Shakespearean actor (Gustavus V. Brooke) filling Drury Lane. Novelty's final contribution to the year is an entirely new Christmas pantomime, *Harlequin and King Humming Top*.

The story begins in the Prismatic Pavilion of Prince Chameleon on the banks of the Enchanted Stream. Prince Chameleon, though possessed of everything that can contribute to enjoyment, disbelieves in the existence of happiness and, disgusted with life, is about to terminate it by throwing himself in the stream. At this point the Spirit of Happiness emerges from the rainbow that spans the stream and promises to convince him of the error of his view by showing him that happiness can be derived from the simplest of pleasures and from the earliest age. After a grand ballet, the Prince is led to the Magic Mulberry Tree in the Garden of Childhood where the earliest indication of happiness can be heard in a childish chorus of 'Here we go round the mulberry tree.' The Prince here encounters Marbles, Hopscotch and other childhood games and is conducted to the Territory of Toys in the Island of Youthful Delights. Here all the inhabitants of the world of toys are personified and the Prince meets King Humming Top and his army of tops and Princess Skipping Rope and her retinue of kites and the Herald Jack in the Box. He falls for Princess Skipping Rope.

Word comes that the Queen of Beauty is threatening to invade Toy Territory and after some warlike preparations, refuge is taken in the Hall of Sports and Pastimes where cricket, archery, rowing, fencing, angling and other athletic sports are called to repel the invasion. The Queen of Beauty is too potent to resist. The toys symbolic of boyhood are compelled to retreat and the Prince enters the Labyrinth of Love, passes through the Bower of Beauty to reach the Haven of Happiness and become possessed of True Love, and finds real happiness at last. In the Palace of Pleasure, the home of youth, the transformation takes place and the harlequinade follows. The pantomime was supposed to end in the Hall of Christmas Revels with the 'extraordinary' novelty of 'Les Femmes Volantes; or Flying Women from the Theatre de l'Ambigu, Paris, who, suspended in the air, without any visible framework, . . . form aerial groups of the most surprising character.' Unfortunately they could not appear on the opening night as their apparatus had been detained in customs. But eventually they made it onto the bill.

The story was evidently intended as an allegory with a human being achieving happiness in childhood and growing up to find love in adulthood. But *The Times* critic missed the point, complaining:

> It is with the politics of this strange country that we are sore perplexed. We find that it is invaded, but cannot conceive why or by whom. We see two regiments of kites and pegtops, who seemed to be loving subjects under one monarch, arrayed in order of battle against each other, without being acquainted with the cause of discord.

Nevertheless, the critic conceded:

> spectacles of this sort are usually deemed satisfactory if the eye is gratified and the fancy a little enlivened, and on this account the Drury-lane introduction is entitled to much commendation. The costumes of the personified toys are comic and ingenious, a consistent picture being produced by the scene in which they move, being a representation of a town composed of toy houses with rows of toy trees.

The Morning Chronicle (27 December 1853) declared: 'The Spectacles that occur in the course of the piece were got up with great splendour. Each one seemed more gorgeous than its predecessor, and the finale was a blaze of brilliancy.' *The Era* (1 January 1854) concluded, 'all the departments have been efficiently filled, and the result is one of the most perfect and entertaining Pantomimes which this season has brought forth.' This suggests that the combined efforts of scene-painters Nichols and Cooper, mask-maker Dykwynkyn, composer Mr Hayward and director Edward Stirling had succeeded in providing sufficient spectacle to compensate for the problems posed by Blanchard's script.

For the Wells Blanchard scripted *Harlequin and Tom Thumb or Gog and Magog and Mother Goose's Golden Goslings*. He was paid £14 for it by Greenwood and saw it on 29 December 1853, recording 'very good for changes and capital clown, Nicolo Deulin'.[17] The pantomime began in the Guildhall where the statues of Gog and Magog, the giants of Albion slain by Brute, the legendary founder of the British race and here representing the past, come to life. They lament the endless progress of modern improvements. But in one of his celebrations of progress, Blanchard introduces the Spirit of Improvement in the Palace of Progress, a representation of the Crystal Palace, and outlines the various improvements she plans: the closure of Smithfield Market, the suppression of Bartholomew or Bartlemy Fair ('That you're a nuisance needs no ghost to tell/your air is foul – fare better and farewell'), the removal of duties on coal and the cleaning up of the polluted Thames. But Mother Goose appears to plead for one tradition from the past – the pantomime. Improvement agrees and the golden goslings appear, each carrying a letter which makes up the name of the proposed pantomime: *Tom Thumb*. There is a dance of children to celebrate the choice and clouds clear away to reveal the interior of the cottage of Gaffer Thumb. Tom falls out of his cradle into the pudding. A tinker carries the pudding away. A cow devours the pudding and disgorges Tom, who is carried by a raven to the castle of the Giant Grumbo where he rescues Princess Poppet, King Arthur's daughter, from the giant. The giant swallows him but then disgorges him. Tom seeks to escape by swimming the moat but is swallowed by a salmon which is then caught and served up at King Arthur's table. Tom emerges from the salmon and claims the hand of the Princess whom he has saved. When Arthur proves reluctant, Mother Goose transfers the characters to the Pavilion in the brilliant Butterfly Palace in Fairyland where they are transformed into the characters of the harlequinade. At the end of the show in the Glittering Palace of Progress, Tom Thumb and Princess Poppet are united.

The theatre was so crowded that when *The Morning Chronicle* (27 December 1853) critic arrived late, he was crammed into a crowd and claimed not to have been able to see or hear the show. The *I.L.N.* (31 December 1853) critic similarly reported 'The house was excessively crowded, and so impatient that it was exceedingly difficult to catch the plot of the performance.' *John Bull* (2 January 1854) thought the pantomime 'a more elaborate affair than has been seen on this stage for some years' but added 'As for the plot, we give it up, as the very best riddle we have had propounded to us this season.' The evening had begun with *The Lady of Lyons* but it was totally inaudible because of the audience noise.

The Era (1 January 1854) reported:

The opening is remarkable for a series of scenic and mechanical changes which, we presume, are due to the constructive design, as well as the artistic execution, of Mr F. Fenton. The change from Guildhall, with its illuminated western window, to the glittering regions of Progress, with steam-engines and huge propellers in action, is extremely effective; nor less so is the sudden transformation of a bright sunlit landscape, representing the granary and homestead of Gaffer Thumb, to a moonlight view of the Giant's Castle. The rapidity with which the change is made, and the startling contrast of the scenes themselves fairly take the audience by surprise.

This was the general view of the critics.

It was nursery rhymes again that provided the framework for the 1854–5 Drury Lane pantomime, *Jack and Jill, Harlequin King Mustard and the Four and Twenty Blackbirds Baked in a Pie*. The narrative was topical in that it was inspired by celebrity chef Alexis Soyer, his cook book and his cookery maxims, currently much in the news as he was providing kitchens to feed the troops in the Crimea.

The Crimean War was, as *The Times* (27 December 1854) critic observed, preoccupying the minds of the audience: 'Can an Englishman – a true Englishman – take a cup of tea or coffee without thinking of Sebastopol or swallow a glass of grog, without an inward vow for the speedy annihilation of the Czar and his legion of serfs?' However, the pantomime provided an opportunity for escape:

> whatever the condition of things, there must be element for laughter in the deeds and appearance both of ourselves and our neighbours … And thus, we gentlemen and plebeians of united Britain, although the actual moment is possibly one upon which hangs our future destiny as a political Power … can afford to laugh when seemingly it would far better befit us to weep.

There was no doubting the patriotic feeling of the audience. The pantomime opened with a medley overture by J.H. Tully which culminated in 'God Save the Queen' and the French anthem 'Partant pour la Syrie' which provoked great enthusiasm in the audience, every stanza greeted with waving of hats and handkerchiefs and applause. It was 'encored with acclamations', not, as *The Times* pointed out, because of the beauty of the music but the patriotic sentiment associated with the Crimean War. *The Morning Chronicle* (27 December 1854) reported 'We have seldom seen a finer burst of national feeling than on this occasion.' Similarly the harlequinade culminated in a grand military and patriotic extravaganza with an Allied Army quadrille, allusions to the Crimean victories, the distribution of military honours and the playing of 'God Save the Queen', 'Partant pour la Syrie' and 'Rule Britannia' with panoramic effects. It was all vociferously cheered by the audience.

The message of the pantomime was the necessity for young women to learn how to cook, one of the regular affirmations of traditional gender roles that featured in Blanchard's scripts. The pantomime opens in the Hall of Hypochondria in the Dark Domain of Dullness where the 'blue devils', Fog, Drizzle, Spleen, Indigestion, Quarter-Day and Taxation are concocting an extra dose of melancholy for the millions, to the delight of their chief Miss Ann Thropy who enters riding on her favourite nightmare. They are all put to flight by the arrival of Good Humour in her Christmas car – the car formed of a punchbowl and riding on pudding wheels, attended by Lightheart and Sunshine – and she invokes the shades of Mrs Glasse, Dr Kitchener, Mrs Rundell and 'the rest of our peptic preceptors' (i.e., cookbook writers) to furnish a good recipe for a Christmas dish. Hannah Glasse, celebrated eighteenth-century cookery writer, emerges from the pages of 'Soyer's Shilling Cook Book' and adapts one of her ancient recipes to the making of a Christmas tale. The story of Jack and Jill is chosen. The scene shifts to Jill's cottage and enchanted kitchen garden on the borders of Fairyland. Jack and Jill are in love and as Jack helps Jill to fill her bucket at the well, the brickwork of the well is disturbed and discloses the will of Jill's father, saying she may not marry until she bakes a cake. Jack catches twenty-four blackbirds and 'a pocketful of rye' for Jill to bake a pie, but she confesses she is ignorant of the culinary arts. Jack rubs two lucky sixpences together, creates a magic shilling and summons Mrs Glasse. Mrs Glasse comes to her aid and animating the fruit trees makes her acquainted with the mystery of preserves. Forty dancers now perform a ballet of preserves, cherry, damson, strawberry and so on, led by Queen Golden Marmalade. Returning home, Jill finds that her kitchen utensils, kettle, saucepan, frying pan and so on have been brought to life by Mrs Glasse. They teach her about their various uses. With this 'remarkable retinue', Jill now goes to the court of King Mustard at Cruet Castle in Tablecloth Territory. The King introduces her to the royal family of the Peppers, Queen Vinegar, Princess Sweet Oil 'and the other inhabitants of this continent of condiments'. The Army of Zests, 'composed of grotesque embodiments of the most esteemed relishes in vogue' is next passed under inspection. But the jealous Queen Vinegar lures Jill to the abode of Chutnee, Sultan of all the pickles, whose subjects are natural enemies of the 'sweets' and causes her to lose her way in the Labyrinth of Salt. The Preserves persuade Jack to upset his pail on the hill above and the water, penetrating the salt mine, causes the stalactite saline columns to melt and reveal the Blackbird pie, duly completed in the Emerald Temple of Salad where the sweets and sours mingle happily. The transformation and the harlequinade follow.

Evidently the critics had at last realized the nature of Blanchard's inventive imagination. *The Times* declared that 'the infinite promise of the title' was 'more than infinitely performed' and hailed Blanchard as 'the imaginative and bay-crowned inventor of the present harlequinade.' The critic thought it all 'cleverly done. The caricatures are grotesque and droll, especially those of the kitchen utensils and the pickles; the ballet of the fairies ... is extremely pretty and well-arranged; the scenery is good; and the principal active personages are portrayed with great spirit.' The Temple of Salad 'pleased the spectators so much that they called uproariously for Mr Smith, and the worthy manager stepped forward to the summons.' The *I.L.N.*

(30 December 1854) called it 'a remarkable success' and Blanchard's script 'highly meritorious', the pantomime cast 'very strong', the models by 'the great Dykwynkyn' 'amazingly funny', the scenery by Cuthbert and Nichols 'unusually splendid' and it said the final tableau closed the pantomime 'with a series of triumphs'. *The Era* (31 December 1854) said: 'Altogether, the Pantomime reflects credit upon everybody concerned, especially Edward Stirling, the stage manager, under whose judicious care it has been produced.' *The Daily News* (27 December 1854) called it 'a very brilliant and effective spectacle'; *John Bull* (30 December 1854) called it 'clever and effective'. *The Standard* (27 December 1854) said 'the scenery is dazzlingly beautiful and would alone be worth a visit.' *The Morning Chronicle* (29 December 1854) concluded that it was 'to the full as diverting, funny and extravagant as one would wish to see' and since the young were the best critics of a pantomime, judged by 'the merry laughter of the children, alternating with their shouts of delighted wonder', it should be pronounced 'Triumphant'. The *Chronicle* also thought that 'It surpassed in grotesque absurdity' Blanchard's previous burlesques.

Stirling recalled that *Jack and Jill* was produced 'with increased expenditure. Smith always paid great attention to his Christmas work, knowing its consequence to his treasury.'[18] Blanchard went to see it on Boxing Day and recorded, 'crowded house and all goes off admirably.'[19] It ran until 24 February.

The 1854–5 Sadler's Wells pantomime was *Harlequin Ali Baba and the Forty Thieves or Morgiana and the Arabian Nights*. There is apparently no copy in the Lord Chamberlain's collection either attributed to Blanchard or Greenwood or Anonymous. But in his diary Blanchard records that he had written an altered opening scene for Sadler's Wells on 27 November and delivered it to the theatre, though he does not name the play. He reviews it on 28 December for *The Era* but looks in again on the show on 29 December, noting 'by no means realizing the expectations I had formed of it.' He takes his nephew Walter to see it on 6 January ('A very pleasant night; the boy delighted'). On 4 January 1855 he records receiving £10 from Greenwood for the pantomime script. The press as usual attributed it to Greenwood.[20]

The first scene represents the exhausted fountain of Amusement, where the Spirit of Amusement, 'intended' thought *The Times* (27 December 1854) 'to typify the distressed manager or author on the look out for novelty', deplores pathetically the gradual drying up of her springs, and passing in review the various theatrical experiments of the past season (*The Corsican Brothers* at the Princess', *The Spanish Dancers* at the Haymarket and farewell performances of G.V. Brooke). At last she calls her old friend Imagination to her aid, and Imagination suggests the East as a setting, since everyone's attention is currently directed there (because of the Crimea War) and the scene changes to the Enchanted Forest where Ali Baba is cutting wood. *The Times* reported:

the story is followed in most of its details, but the leading parts are so well sustained by Mr W.H. Payne, the veteran pantomimist [as the robber chief Abdallah] and his sons [playing Mustapha and Morgiana] that the opening is rendered unusually brisk and effective. The dismemberment of Cassim and the subsequent stitching up by the cobbler of his scattered anatomy are shown after a very humorous fashion. And the scenery of the whole of the introduction, painted by Mr [Frederick] Fenton, is extremely good – the hall of 1,000 Arabian Nights and the Palace of Imagination, in the realms of Fancy, equalling anything of the kind which has ever been attempted at this establishment. Some grotesque dancing here introduced by Morgiana (Mr Henry Payne), and some figure dancing by Mr Frampton's pupils add considerably to the effect of this portion of the entertainment. The transformation takes place in the courtyard where the famous forty are concealed in oil jars.

The *I.L.N.* (30 December 1854) fascinatingly interpreted the show as 'aesthetic':

The subject of this piece may be said, by way of distinction, to be even aesthetic – hard and inappropriate as the term may seem to the treatment of something supposed to be so unphilosophic as this sort of drama. The aim is a serious one – to point a moral *apropos* of the stage. The imaginative is here successfully opposed to the melodramatic and terpsichorean and the triumph of the spectacle is awarded to legitimate drama. Mr Greenwood treats all other forms of stage-art as 'exhausted fountains of amusement' and leads his characters through various changes to the inexhaustible in the poetic play.

The harlequinade was, said *The Times*, 'rife with strong satirical hits, and is not devoid of political allusions, which are smartly yet delicately handled.'

The evening opened with Home's gloomy tragedy *Douglas*, which could not be heard, but *Ali Baba* was expertly produced by Greenwood and W.H. Payne, previously at Covent Garden. *The Times* said the show 'is in every respect calculated to maintain the reputation of this house for its pantomimic productions; and that such was the unanimous verdict of the large and enthusiastic audience which last night thronged within its walls, is a fact which admits of no disputation.'

Blanchard, reviewing his own show in *The Era* (31 December 1854) pronounced the pantomime 'one of the best and busiest of the season. It has all the essentials of pantomimic vitality: unflagging fun, smart satirical hits at the vulnerable points of social life, quick action and an admirable corps of pantomimists.' He described in appreciative detail the pantomimic acting of W.H. Payne, and praised the harlequinade and the scenery of Frederick Fenton:

The scenery … exhibits remarkable powers of imagination as well as great pictorial skill. The illustrative panorama displaying the most popular stories in the 'Arabian Nights' is an exquisite series of paintings, and the transformation scene is conceived in great taste and executed with great ability.

He concluded: 'Never has the tact and talent of Mr Greenwood been more strongly manifested than on the present occasion.'

Blanchard tried something even more ambitious in the 1855–6 Drury Lane pantomime, *Hey Diddle Diddle or Harlequin King Nonsense and the Seven Ages of Man*, nothing less than a show based on the celebrated 'Seven Ages of Man' speech in Shakespeare's *As You Like It*, with a plea for more intellectual fare for children. The pantomime opened in the Hall of Nursery Rhymes in the dominions of King Nonsense. This is the first of the seven ages and the monarch is surrounded by the heroes of nursery literature, among them Little Jack Horner, Little Red Riding Hood, Simple Simon, Humpty Dumpty, Little Tom Tucker, Old Mother Hubbard and her Dog, and Little Boy Blue. On the wings were medallions illustrating all the familiar nursery rhymes, such as 'Hey Diddle Diddle', 'Ding Dong Bell' and 'Ride a Cock Horse'. The Spirit of Common Sense arrives and the King remarks that Common Sense has had little influence thus far on Kings, the Law or the City. Routine and Redtape enter but in conflict with Common Sense are banished to Noodledom, 'amid the execrations of the audience'. Routine had an office inkstand for a cap, carried despatches from the Baltic and the Crimea, and bore a legend announcing that his office hours were from ten to four. Redtape 'elicited shouts of laughter', reported *The Times* (27 December 1855), 'seeing that he looked like nothing but a gigantic bundle of that article taken from a stationer's window.' In a classic demonstration of compromise, Common Sense proposes an alliance with Nonsense to improve the intellectual quality of infant literature. The proposal to dramatize the 'Seven Ages of Man' speech in a pantomime is agreed.

The second age – that of the schoolboy – introduces the village of Prettywell-cum-Thankye, with a distant view of the church and surrounding country. Here there is a village school where Hobbledehoy the dunce leads Young Hopeful into various adventures and misadventures. They play truant to go fishing, but Hobbledehoy falls in the water. He climbs an apple tree to pilfer apples but the branch breaks under his weight and he falls to the ground. Hopeful is attracted to the pretty Rosa, a pupil at Miss Starch's Girls' School opposite the Boys' School. There is a severe schoolmaster Dr Birch who canes the pupils for misdemeanours such as copying from each other. Eventually, playing at cricket with the boys on the border of the river, a well-aimed ball knocks him into the water, 'to the intense delight of the juvenile portion of the audience', reported *The Times*.

The third age – that of the lover – takes place at a blacksmith's forge and neighbouring inn as Young Hopeful courts Rosa, the ward of the local Justice of the Peace and writes her a sonnet. But the Justice separates the lovers and encountering Sergeant Kite recruiting young men for the army, Hopeful enlists as a soldier – the fourth age – in order to become more worthy of Rosa's love.

Hopeful and Rosa meet secretly in the old abbey ruins and there encounter the Spirit of Love who transports them to the Bower of Bliss where a grand ballet takes place featuring the Spirit of Love and her attendants Hope, Desire, Happiness, Joy and Delight, and signifying the falling in love of Hopeful and Rosa.

The fifth age – Justice – takes place in the Justice Hall where the Justice begins by sentencing two farm labourers to a fortnight in jail with hard labour for leaving their work to attend a military review. This was an allusion to an actual case which took place in Essex and was greeted by the audience with boos, presumably directed against the harshness of the penalty. The Justice wants Rosa to marry Hobbledehoy, now a wealthy country squire. Instead Rosa elopes with Hopeful. In the ruined Cottage of Old Age – the sixth age – Hopeful and Rosa are pursued by the Justice, Hobbledehoy, Dr Birch and Sergeant Kite. Old Age disappears through the hearth. The Spirit of Love appears and a wintry scene of snow is changed to 'the bright realms of perpetual summer'. The characters of the opening are transformed into those of the harlequinade and the show ends at a late hour with 'a most brilliant scene of fairyland' which 'sent every one home in good humour.'

The Times thought that the introduction based on 'The Seven Ages of Man' was 'novel in conception and ingenious in execution, and this part of the pantomime gave unqualified satisfaction.' But the critic felt that the harlequinade fell flat. 'The fun frequently halted and went lame, and even the tricks and transformations refused to run smoothly. The audience were now and then impatient.' *The Era* (30 December 1855) praised the school and village scenes: 'The pranks of the boys in the scene of the Village School, and the eccentricities of the recruiting party in front of the Blacksmith's forge are capital, and we remember nothing more genially droll in the shape of introductory matter.'

A major talking point was the arrival at Drury Lane of William Beverley as scene-painter. His debut was a triumph. His name was called as soon as the curtain went up on the 'charmingly painted' scene of the village of Prettywell. The manager E.T. Smith was called to take a bow when 'The Abode of Love' and the 'Realms of Perpetual Summer' were revealed. Beverley's brother Robert Roxby had taken over as stage manager and *The Era* reported that the staging had been speeded up, the stage machinery perfected and the show judiciously cut after the opening night, thanks to Roxby.

The Morning Chronicle (27 December 1855) pronounced the pantomime 'unusually brilliant ... it was produced with a wealth and magnificence of appointment that enabled it to compete with any of its rivals, and it obtained, throughout, the continuous applause of a crowded house.' It declared the masks and properties of Dykwynkyn 'exceedingly clever and characteristic', the music by J.H. Tully 'most happily arranged' and William Beverley's scenery 'exquisite'.

John Bull (29 December 1855) reported:

A few years ago Pantomime appeared to be in danger of extinction. The witty parodies, by Mr Planché, of the most fanciful and elegant fairy-tales, especially those written by the Countess D'Aulnoy, had set the public 'all agog' for Burlesque. Somehow the old Grimaldi style of entertainment seems to have taken deeper root in the national heart than we had imagined. There was only one exception to the dominance of pantomime this year, the burlesque at the Olympic.

Hey Diddle Diddle, it thought, 'excels any which Mr Smith has yet produced at Drury Lane.'

The Standard (28 December) rather dismissively thought 'The Seven Ages of Man' 'not a bad idea for the preliminary scenes of a harlequinade, and Mr E.L. Blanchard has dealt with this grave Shakespearean text with tolerable ingenuity.' But it pronounced the visual tableau 'gorgeous' and called Beverley a genius. 'The scenery of the opening is, in a word, replete with glowing beauty and rich in those effulgent devices which allure and enrapture the eye.' Blanchard went to see the show on 26 December and recorded: 'Everything in the opening goes off wonderfully well; house crammed.'[21]

The Sadler's Wells pantomime for 1855–6 was *Harlequin and Puss in Boots or All the World and His Wife and the Ogre of Rats Castle*. It opened in the Retreat of All the World and His Wife where All the World and His Wife review the events of the passing year and bewail, with the smaller circles of the great world, the embarrassment that attends their respective spheres. Novelty and Mirth are found to be still in existence and by their agency the audience is transported to the Land of Fable, where the subject of Puss in Boots is chosen for pantomimical elaboration. The original story was closely followed, with the miller's legacy leaving Jocelyn, the hero, with the cat Grimalkin. King Log, Emperor of the Woodenheads, not having any appetite, his daughter Princess Gloriana goes in search of game to provide her father with a tasty morsel. Puss comes to her aid with a plentiful supply of hares, rabbits, pheasants and partridges, with which he arrives at the Palace of King Log, claiming they are gifts from his master, the Marquis of Carabas. Puss leads the King on a trip to see the Marquis' lands, displaying his physical prowess by seeing off an invasion of long-tailed Muscovite rats among the corn. The ogre of Rats Castle appears to take revenge for the defeat of the rats and carries off a couple of reapers to provide his supper. Puss pursues, fights off the Rat guards and persuades the Ogre to turn himself into a mouse, which Puss then devours, receiving the King and his train at the castle which he declares to be that of the Marquis of Carabas.

The Times (27 December 1855), noting that unusually the first piece, *The Lady of Lyons* was listened to with 'a considerable degree of attention and favour', apart from a few comical criticisms, 'which set the whole house a-laughing' and every so often 'an amateur pugilistic "set-to" among the juvenile occupants of the pit', but 'upon the whole the holyday folks were extremely decorous, all things considered.' *Puss in Boots* was declared 'A very good pantomime' on the whole.

> The grotesque masks of some of the figures and the awkward scrapes into which it was their doom constantly to fall kept the good-humoured audience in a continual roar of laughter, which proved how successfully the getter-up of this part of the entertainment [unnamed] had hit the fancy of the public.

The scenery was 'very splendid' and the topical allusions were relished, particularly the repeal of newspaper stamp duty which caused a host of penny papers to spring into existence with titles like the Whitechapel Gazette and the Pimlico Courier. *The Era* (30 December 1855) said the show:

> has the peculiar pantomimic merit of dealing with a good story, told in rapid action, as arranged by Mr Greenwood, and giving a plot that furnishes unflagging fun throughout its development. ... The incident of the capture of the game, with really life-like hares, rabbits and partridges ... is very funnily contrived in the true spirit of burlesque.

It went on: 'The Harlequinade has, however, even superior merits, for the practised hand of the lessee, Mr Greenwood, has dealt so effectively with every available topic that each scene is a smart satire on the vulnerable follies.' Its only drawback from an audience point of view was the omission of the song 'Hot Codlins' which was vociferously but in vain demanded. *The Standard* (28 December 1855) said *Puss in Boots* was 'as lively, bustling, absurd and extravagant an affair as it would be well possible to imagine.' *The Examiner* (29 December) said: 'At SADLER'S WELLS the pantomime is always of the old school, which we take to be perhaps the best, well enough written for its purpose and successfully produced.' It kept 'a good natured audience in incessant laughter'. Blanchard's diary records his writing the introduction and comic scenes for Sadler's Wells on 24, 26 and 27 November and consulting with Greenwood. He saw the pantomime on 29 December 1855 and pronounced it 'very good'.[22]

The 1856–7 Drury Lane pantomime was *See Saw Margery Daw or Harlequin Holiday and the Island of Ups and Downs*, which *The Times* (27 December 1856) thought with a few judicious cuts was 'destined to enjoy as long a lease of existence and as widespread a popularity as any of its immediate predecessors.' It was preceded only by a light *comedietta*, *Simpson and Co.*, evidence that the management had at last recognized that the audience came for the pantomime and tended to be annoyed if it was too long delayed. Even so it was greeted, said *The Era* (28 December 1856), with 'the usual display of impatience by the audience who wanted the pantomime.'

The plot of the pantomime proceeded:

from the fertile imagination of Mr E.L. Blanchard, to whom the regions of metaphorical burlesque are a natural element and monstrous pasteboard heads as much 'a feeling' as 'high mountains' to the poet. The time-honoured nursery rhymes upon which it is founded are put to symbolical uses, and a moral lesson is endeavoured to be imparted.

It opens in the Region of Reverses in the World of Ups and Downs with a globe upon which rests an enormous see-saw at each end of which is a group representing on the one hand wealth and abundance and on the other poverty and rags, with three figures in the foreground representing the three classes of society. 'A clever device of mechanism metamorphoses Wealth into Poverty, and *vice versa*, according to whichever end of the see-saw happens to be uppermost; and thus are shadowed forth "The Ups and Downs of Life", to reconcile which constitutes the quasi-philosophic purport of the *masque*.' The appearance of Holiday, the Genius of the Season with her attendants Sport and Pastime cuts short the 'somewhat prolix dialogue' between 'Up' and 'Down'.

> Snubbed, of course, by 'Up', who is a snob, and approached by 'Down' with befitting humility, Holiday proffers some excellent counsel to the opposing parties – a 'coalition', in short, for the attainment of the largest possible amount of festive and seasonable recreation. This good advice is accepted; a reconciliation is agreed on; the social poles, like 'extremes', meet for the accomplishment of a common object.

There could be no better or more emblematic allegory of the Age of Equipoise than this opening.

Just as everything is settled to 'universal satisfaction' Dame Necessity arrives to claim from Holiday her annual tribute in the shape of a Christmas pantomime. There being a shortage of subjects, Necessity's favourite child, Invention, is called upon to name a topic. Necessity will point the moral and Holiday will adorn the tale. Holiday invites all the personages to her abode in the Green Bower of Mistletoe and Winter Garden of the Fairies and there, after a grand ballet, the subject of the pantomime is agreed – the nursery rhyme *See-Saw, Margery Daw*. The moral is that 'those who labour alone are entitled to a holiday.' But the lesson is, as in *Jack and Jill*, the necessity for women to learn the required domestic skills.

At the Golden Gates leading to the Palace Gardens of King Huggamugga, various tradesmen gather to complain of the temper, idleness and contempt for work of the King's daughter, Princess Margery Daw. Suddenly the Princess herself enters and threatens imprisonment and the imposition of double taxes on all those who venture to speak of work in her presence. Artisans who have already spoken are made to form footstools for the Princess to step on and then taken away under guard. Dame Necessity enters in a cloak asking for alms, which she is refused. She resolves to make Margery Daw change her tone. In the interior of the Palace King Huggamugga is seated on his throne, receiving in turn the attendants on his daughter to complain of her conduct. She enters followed by her suitor Prince Popinjay whom she boxes on the ears and dismisses. Necessity now appears to teach Margery Daw 'a wholesome lesson' and with her crutch changes the Palace into the cottage of Necessity where Margery Daw is set to work a sampler of needlework within a specified time. She is given an enchanted work box for this purpose. Its contents, needles, pins, buttons, bodkins and so on, are magically animated and assist her in completing the task. She is converted to the view that 'the dignity of labour and toil is intimately associated with, and contributes to the true nobility of nature.' Necessity hastens to reward her, conveying her in a silkworm car to the Iron Mine of Labour. There they encounter miners with their pickaxes at work. Necessity declares:

Far from the light of day even underground
You see that hardy workmen yet are found
Who labour hard to furnish what no doubt
The world would puzzled be to do without
Even Kings and Queens would never live with ease
Until they had the toil of men like these.

The Princess concedes her conversion to the principles of Labour. The Spirit of Labour appears and decrees the reward 'for all good children who work hard' – holiday. Holiday appears to convey them to their promised treat in the glittering Fairy Factory of Fancy where the transformation takes place.

The Times critic thought the introduction too long, too slow, and 'contains too much dialogue', though *The Daily News* thought it not too long and *The Morning Chronicle* said 'The opening is satirical, without being gross, witty without being personal, and clever without being offensive.' *The Times* in common with *John Bull* (29 December 1856), *The Daily News* (27 December 1856) and *The Morning Chronicle* (27 December 1856) praised the scenery.

The Era (28 December 1856) praised the *corps de ballet* of 100 representing the spirits of Fairy Kisses under the Mistletoe for its 'grace and *esprit*'. The music, composed and conducted by Herr Anschutz was 'full of sparkling vivacity'; the dresses and appointments were 'elegant, fairy-like and unique'. *The Era* added: 'No small share of praise is due to Mr Robert Roxby, who has superintended the whole production.' The review concluded:

We predict a long run of success to the Pantomime at Drury-Lane. It merits it in every respect, for it has been produced by the spirited lessee with a liberality and a total disregard for expenditure in catering for the public, which we are certain the public in return will duly appreciate.

The 1856–7 Sadler's Wells pantomime was *The Fisherman and the Genie or Harlequin Padmanaba and the Enchanted Fishes of the Silver Lake*. It was based on the Arabian Nights tale and is attributed to Greenwood by *The Era* (28 December 1856) but was in fact by Blanchard. Blanchard records in his diary that he went to Sadler's Wells on 29 December to see *The Fisherman and the Genie*, recording 'slow, my ideas not carried out – but it goes off well.'[23]

It was preceded by *Venice Preserved*, 'without exception the most lugubrious of legitimate dramas', according to *The Times* (27 December 1856), but 'The solemnity of the tragedy . . . seemed only to dispose the gods all the more for the hilarity of the pantomime, which passed off with such riotous applause and such exuberant merriment as one does not often now-a-days meet with in our popular assemblies.' But *The Era* (28 December 1856) claimed that most of the language of the play could not be heard over the din from the 'gods'. *The Daily News* (27 December 1856) noted:

> The plot of the pantomime closely follows that of the well-known Eastern tale which gives it the title, which enabled the audience to follow its development with greater ease and satisfaction than is generally the case with the elaborate intricacies of Christmas pieces.

The pantomime opens on a huge chessboard with the Black King and the White King contending for mastery until the Spirit of the Rainbow, attended by fairies dressed in the seven prismatic colours, appears and promises to produce a colourful spectacle as a contribution to Christmas. The next scene reveals 'the glowing prospect of an Oriental sea' with Padmanaba fishing. He saves the Princess Tootsi Pootsi, daughter of the Sultan of the Kingdom of Pearls, from drowning. Then he finds a sealed bottle from which he frees the Genie, from whom he receives four coloured fish which he takes to the Sultan, who has offered a reward to whoever brings him fish. Padmanaba claims the Princess as his reward. But the Black Enchanter abducts the Princess and the scene changes to the City of Colours, 'a fine tableau which brought down the applause of the house', where the transformation takes place. *The Daily News* thought:

> The practical joking and tricks were extremely well performed. They were so rapid in succession and sharp in execution that the audience had not time to allow one burst of laughter to subside ere it was followed by another. The hits at the social, political, and fashionable follies of the day were nothing near so palpable, and they generally fell flat on the ear and eye.

The show finished with a 'brilliant scene representing the "jewelled Temple of Aluminium" in the regions of Fairy Land.' The critic concluded that 'the scenery throughout is more chaste and elegant than gorgeous, and does credit to the taste of Mr Fenton.'

The Times declared the harlequinade 'the real business of the evening ... that exhaustless succession of practical jokes of which an English audience never tires ... at all events, the laughter is uproarious, the audience delighted and the piece successful.' *The Era* was full of praise for the scenery, several of the scenes which included the Palace of Rainbow, Fisherman's Cottage on Enchanted Lake, the Magic Grove, the City of Colours and the Fairy Temple eliciting applause. Particularly impressive was a diorama of an African scene, 'beautifully painted by Mr Fenton on a gigantic scale' which led to calls for the artist, who, however, did not appear. 'Beyond the scenery, in the opening, there is really nothing to call for a remark. The legend is badly rendered, and leaves the audience to put its own construction upon it, and who soon began to show equivocal marks of tediousness.' In general, it seems the critics did not rate the opening very highly but thought the show redeemed by the harlequinade and the scenery.

The Drury Lane pantomime for 1857–8 was *Little Jack Horner or Harlequin ABC*, for which, recorded *The Times* (28 December 1857), 'a larger concourse of people probably never assembled within the walls of Drury-lane Theatre.' The critic now seriously suggested that they drop any accompanying piece to the pantomime, as the farce *Too Much of a Good Thing* was effectively played in mime for not a word of the dialogue could be heard in the stalls:

> as the inhabitants of the 'upper regions' were more unruly, uproarious and obstinately overbearing than in any previous instance we can remember ... How easily these excesses might be averted by limiting the spectacle on Boxing Night to the pantomime ... will be evident to the plainest understanding.

Blanchard was this year trying something even more ambitious than usual in his opening and more demanding on his audience, nothing less than a plea for literacy, knowledge, intelligence and imagination. He took up ideas he first explored in *The World of Wonders*. His approach divided the critics. The *I.L.N.* (2 January 1858) thoroughly approved:

> The pantomime was ... by Mr E.L. Blanchard and, like all that gentleman's productions, designed for the edification of the rising generation, as well as for the amusement of 'children of larger growth' ... Some are for the unbending of the mind altogether, and demand from the Christmas pantomime only extravagance and caricature, and absurd masks and impossible accidents – signs that signify nothing, 'sound and fury', and Folly with her cap and bells provoking laughter without reason. Such critics would reverse the prudent adage of our forefathers, which recommended us 'to be prudent and wise' – an adage, too, generally applicable to Christmas festivities. Mr

Blanchard has been mindful of the maxim on all occasions; and, on the present, has been laudably careful that his mirth should have a meaning. The pleasure derivable from his composition is enhanced by its merit. The *utile in dulce* is his motto. His pantomime is a symbolical poem, or allegorical burlesque, in which certain attributes of mind and adjuncts of the schoolroom are personified. Nor does he fear that the nursery denizens will fail to apprehend and identify notions and presentments as embodied on the stage. The 'Grand Ballet of the Belles Lettres', as danced by Rosina Wright and her century of fair companions, was immediately intelligible to the audience, senile or infantile.

The Times disagreed, pronouncing the opening 'a mistake':

People do not expect to be edified or instructed at a pantomime, but to laugh 'quand-même' [any-how]. 'Ignorance', 'Intelligence', 'Imagination', 'Perseverance', 'Anagram', 'Proverb' etc. may do famously as symbolical personages in a poem; but in a pantomime they are rather bores than otherwise. Thus the commencement of the burlesque, where 'Intelligence' is engaged in strife against 'Ignorance', only becomes interesting when 'Imagination', enlisted on the side of the former, conveys us to one of her own airy castles, in the precincts of which we are treated to a splendid choreographic display. Here 'nearly 100' fair daughters of Terpsichore, with that clever and vivacious 'scorner of the ground', Miss Rosina Wright ... arrayed in ethereal and sparkling costumes, executed a series of evolutions, under the name of 'Grand Ballet of the Belles Lettres' which, allegorical or literal, mattered little to the audience, since it was the first thing to rouse their enthusiasm. Miss Rosina Wright danced in her most animated style and ... put the house in good humour with the pantomime, which from that moment never once 'flagged'.

The Standard (28 December 1857) approved of the moral but felt it had been achieved at the cost of humour:

However great the ingenuity may be which is displayed in the opening ... the wit is of the very smallest; we do not remember one attempt at smartness, much less brilliancy from first to last. Indeed the author appears to have purposely eschewed fun and humour in the dialogue, and to have laid great emphasis on the morality of the piece, and its fitness for scenic displays. In both he has greatly succeeded. To the younger branches of his visitors he reads a lesson which cannot fail to last them during the holidays, while the opportunities presented to the scene-painter and decorator are singularly opportune and happy.

There was general agreement that the scenery was the outstanding feature of the pantomime, *The Times* reporting that the Fairy Aquarium was:

one of the most gorgeous, ingenious and magnificent of all those elaborate scenic combinations for which Mr W. Beverley is specially celebrated ... As its wonders gradually revealed themselves, and the circumambient air, no less than *terra firma*, became densely peopled with floating nymphs and soaring fairies, the applause was vociferous and continuous, and a summons first for Mr E.T. Smith, the manager, and next for Mr Beverley, the artist represented the climax of excitement.[24]

Little Jack Horner opens with Doctor Syntax, the parodied clergyman/schoolmaster whose exploits were recounted in verse by William Combe (1741–1823) and drawn by Thomas Rowlandson (1756–1827). He is surrounded by the real-life authors of improving works, Mrs Sarah Trimmer (1741–1810), and 'Peter Parley' (1793–1860), who wrote didactic stories for children; the grammarian Lindley Murray (1745–1826), 'the father of English grammar'; and Edward Cocker ('Old Cocker'), the seventeenth-century author of a treatise on mathematics. With heads provided by Dykwynkyn, they are all found stirring up a giant inkpot with their pens. They are watched by a group of wretchedly clad children under Tag-Rag and Bobtail. The souls of the children are competed for by Ignorance, attended by Prejudice and Superstition ('As soon as man is born, I hold him mine, and mine he shall remain … Ignorance is bliss'), and Intelligence, attended by the Fairies Discovery and Invention. Intelligence announces that she has just arrived from India and will cross the Atlantic by electric cable next summer. This shows the pantomime linking itself directly with modernity, and celebrating something seen as 'an essential part of the new imperialism'.[25] In 1856 the Red Sea and India Telegraph Company was founded to link Constantinople with Alexandria, and Suez with Aden and Karachi. The Red Sea cable was laid in 1859 but broke and after costing £800,000, never transmitted a single message. A transatlantic cable had been laid in 1857 and 1858 but after transmitting a few messages it died. The first workable submarine cable from Britain to India was not actually inaugurated until 1865 and the transatlantic cable in 1866.[26] Intelligence enlists Imagination, who has a castle in the air, and fairy attendants, the children of the Air. Intelligence believes that Imagination is vital: 'Whilst I instruct, her aim is to amuse, to gild my facts with Fancy's brightest hue, her aid I'll seek.'

In his country cottage, Jack Horner is trying and failing to learn his letters. He wants to kiss the fair Rosetta but she won't let him until he has learned them. The Grenadier, the five little pigs and the mouse running up the clock all appear from the familiar nursery rhymes. Jack, given a Christmas pie by his parents, puts in his thumb and pulls out a plum.

Ignorance and Intelligence fight for the soul of Jack Horner. Intelligence sends him a mentor in the form of Proverb, who speaks entirely in proverbs, and who seeks to get him to pay heed to Intelligence. Having succeeded, he grants Jack the sword of Perseverance with which to attack the parts of speech. Ignorance sends an army against him, personified embodiments of Two Syllables, Three Syllables, the

Multiplication Table, the Wine and Spirit Measure, Coal Measure, Apothecaries' Weight, Troy Weight, Avoirdupois Weight, Dry Measure, Long Measure, Solid or Cubic Measure and a small force of pot-hooks and hangers under Sergeant Penknife. Jack defeats them and enrols them as his allies. Ignorance now sends against him personal pronouns, auxiliary verbs, arithmetic, geography and algebra, all of whom he defeats and enlists on his side. Finally Ignorance despatches him on a bogus mission to the depths of the sea, where nothing can be known. But Ignorance is fooled as Proverb appears to Jack and tells him the electric telegraph runs through the sea: 'And where that goes Intelligence must be/so Jack finds knowledge even in the sea.' Intelligence appears and takes Jack to the Grand Fairy Aquarium, a palace of coral, 'raised by Imagination in honour of her visitor, Intelligence', where the characters are transformed into those of the harlequinade whose comic business ends in 'The Happy Home of Intelligence – the Circle of the Sciences – Art and Science Bearing Commerce Over the Globe.'

Blanchard's 1857–8 Sadler's Wells pantomime, *Harlequin Beauty and the Beast or Little Goody Two-Shoes and Mother Bunch's Bookcase in Babyland*, caused him problems as he attempted to write it while distracted by severe domestic difficulties. He records in his diary on 8 December 1857: 'All day at work writing second scene of Sadler's Wells opening, which take, and after sit up till 3, cogitating over remainder.' He received from Greenwood on 25 January 1850 'the usual payment of £10 per cheque for Wells pantomime'. But having seen the show on 29 December, he noted: 'Scenery good, but wasted thought and energy as usual.'[27]

The evening began with Kotzebue's gloomy melodrama *The Stranger* which was listened to with uncharacteristic attention, noted *The Times* (28 December 1857), though *The Era* (27 December 1857) reported the usual barrage of noise during the performance. The pantomime opens with Mother Bunch's Book-case in Baby-land and the curtain rose to disclose Mother Bunch, Mother Glass, Mother Shipton, Mother Goose, Mother Redcap and Mother Hubbard with their brooms stirring up the contents of a huge cauldron, inscribed 'Mother Bunch's Infant Food'. A wrangle between the ancient females is interrupted by the appearance of Goody Two-Shoes who allays the strife and says her pupils have been so good that she has promised them a pantomime. Mother Bunch replies 'I've none but the old ones' and Goody Two-Shoes replies:

> None are like the old. There's even some who never heard them told.
> As long as children in the world exist,
> So long to those old stories will they list.

Mother Bunch waves her wand and the scene changes to 'a charming view' of the 'many-storied tower of fairy tales in the land of legendary lore'. Thereupon severally appear Jack the Giant Killer and the two-headed giant Grumbo, Valentine and

Orson, Puss in Boots, the Ogre, the White Cat and the Yellow Dwarf. Goody Two-Shoes rejects them all in favour of Beauty and the Beast. The scene changes to the courtyard of a merchant's dwelling where Beauty, the merchant's youngest daughter, is seen tending her favourite rose-tree. Her cruel sisters, Fatima and Lankinella, respectively short and obese and thin and tall, pass the time demonstrating their contempt for Beauty and ill-treating two black slaves, who retaliate, one by dropping an open razor on Fatima's toe and the other by pouring hot water down Lankinella's back. Scanderino the merchant is summoned away to deal with a panic in the city and asks what presents they would like: Fatima chooses a turban and Lankinella a dress. Beauty asks for a rose. In a picturesque snow forest the merchant is menaced by an elephant and a rhinoceros and swoons. He awakens in the Beast's palace where a 'capital' procession of beast-courtiers pay him homage – monkey-pages, lion-lords, tiger-grooms, cat-headed maids of honour, a goose-headed doctor, an owl-headed chancellor and so on. They feed him food and drink but are horrified when he plucks a rose. The Beast appears with his griffin-guards and only releases the merchant on his promise to send Beauty in the palace. Beauty goes to save her father's life but falls in love with the Beast, who is transformed by her love into a prince before the harlequinade commences. *The Times* declared:

> Every lover of pantomimes will know that when the scene changes to 'Beauty's Nuptial Bower in the Region of Roses', the scene-painter presents you with his choicest *tableau*. But the extreme beauty of the scene and the brilliancy of the costumes took the audience by surprise, for Sadler's Wells seemed about to realize the glories of the Lyceum spectacle under Madame Vestris' management. The applause was enthusiastic, and loud calls for Mr James bore tribute to the ability and promise of the young scene-painter.

The *I.L.N.* (2 January 1858) thought James' nuptial bower 'goes far to rival the elaborate specimens of the west-end.' *The Era* (27 December 1857) agreed, saying the scene 'reflects the greater credit upon the talent and ingenuity of Mr Charles Stanfield James.' *The Era* also thought the opening boasted 'a great deal of grotesque Pantomime fun and sparkling burlesque dialogue'.

The hit of the harlequinade was a baby-Clown, proclaimed by *The Times* 'the smallest and fattest performer surely that ever trod, or toddled, or waddled, upon the stage.' He was the youngest son of Nicolo Deulin, the adult Clown. The child's tricks and tumbling had the audience roaring with laughter. There were also the usual hits at the events and follies of the day. *The Era* reported that:

> One of the great hits of this portion of the Pantomime was the introduction of a figure of justice in a sign-painter's establishment where justice blinded gives a thousand a year to the retiring Proctor of Doctor's Commons, and twopence a day to the discharged soldier; refuses a license to the Argyll Rooms; and grants one to the Holborn Casino; and so

forth, ending by justice becoming 'wide-awake', and honouring [Indian Mutiny heroes Sir Henry] Havelock and Sir Colin Campbell with a peerage and a pension.

The Era concluded that 'the beauty of the scenery in the opening, and the sharp points and broad practical fun of the comic business, capitally sustained by a blithe band of pantomimists', guaranteed success.[28]

Perhaps in reaction to the mixed reception of his educational allegory, Blanchard turned to more traditional fare for the 1858–9 pantomime, the legends of Robin Hood. This met with the whole-hearted approval of *The Times* (28 December 1858) who declared *Robin Hood or Harlequin Friar Tuck and the Merry Men of Sherwood Forest*:

> beyond comparison the most attractive that has been witnessed for many years. In magnificence of scenery, costumes, and decorations it has rarely, if ever, been surpassed, while the materials presented by the legends appertaining to Robin Hood have enabled Mr E.L. Blanchard (since nearly a quarter of a century one of the chief high priests of pantomime) an opportunity of investing his introductory burlesque with a degree of histrionic interest which was almost wholly absent from its immediate predecessors of 1856 and 1857.

The *I.L.N.* (1 January 1859) began its review with an encomium on Blanchard:

> Foremost of those writers who have added literary value to the *libretto* of pantomime is Mr E.L. Blanchard, who has now for some years enjoyed the monopoly of supplying the seasonable article to Old Drury. Like Pope, Mr Blanchard is the poet of common sense, and frequently burdens his verses with sober truths, feeling, probably, that at Christmas time, as at all other times, people should be both 'merry and wise'. His greatest successes have arisen out of palpable hits of this sort, preferred by him to the subtlest pun or the funniest parody.

The Times noted that everything went smoothly on the opening night from the stage machinery, which worked without a hitch, to the music of J.H. Tully, 'the most practised and fluent of pantomimic musicians', which was 'as full of character as of life and bustle' and played under Tully's direction with 'spirit and precision'. The shortness of the first piece, the farce *Latest from New York* was 'not the least agreeable incident of the evening'. It enabled the pantomime to begin before 8.30. The orchestra striking up the overture ('a capital medley, constructed on favourite airs, chiefly old English, appropriate to the scenes about to be revealed') attracted the attention and eventually the silence of the audience, who had received the farce with their customary mixture of noisy turbulence and uproariousness. Then, said *The Times*, the introductory burlesque 'though long, is so good, and offers so many excellent opportunities for scenic and decorative display, that it never for an instant flags.' Blanchard began with a tilt at the dominance of Italian opera in the capital. In the Hall of Harmony, filled with musical instruments suitably embodied, the Genius of Music appears, with her attendants Do, Re, Mi, Fa, Sol, and La. Music summons her fashionable child, Italian Opera, who appears with three heads (to represent Covent Garden, Drury Lane and Her Majesty's, the homes of Italian opera) and boasts of her success: 'I'm the rage – my fame goes on crescendo.' But then enters English Opera, 'your neglected child', prompting Music to say: 'I almost had forgotten your existence' but predicting bright days in store, and Canterbury Hall, 'not least, though last', the home of 'nigger minstrel' troupes. They are followed by English, Irish, Scottish and Comic Songs, 'songs to all endeared/Over the world how many hearts you've cheered.' It is from the old English ballads that the Year 1858 appears to choose the subject of the pantomime and settles on Robin Hood.

In the Arcadian Haunt of the Forest Fairies, the fairies decide to support Robin Hood against the Sheriff of Nottingham. Robin meets Maid Marian in a forest glade and they are joined by the merry men. Robin, who had robbed a pedlar, complains that his food for sale was adulterated, a reference to a much publicized contemporary problem. The outlaws waylay a butcher, Robin buys his clothes and wares and they proceed to Nottingham Fair where they excite the suspicion of the sheriff by carrying off all the prizes for the traditional English pastimes. These include sack-racing, climbing the maypole and archery. 'All this is represented,' said *The Times*, 'with graphic minuteness and wonderful animation, into which the members of the ballet entered with just as much spirit and vigour as they had already displayed in the foregoing scene, where the quaint French pastoral imparted such a widely different physiognomy to their evolutions.' The outlaws are arrested by the sheriff but escape and are pursued to Sherwood Forest where they are on the point of surrendering when they are rescued by the Fairy Queen, who transports them to the Retreat of the Fairies in the Region of Bluebells and Wild Flowers for the transformation. *The Times* proclaimed the scene of the Fairies' Retreat 'the pictorial triumph of the Pantomime'. Smith and Beverley were duly called forth to take a bow, as they had after the scene of the Arcadian Haunt of the Forest Fairies.

The Era (26 December 1858) saw this as part of a trend, noting:

> With this attention to lavish scenic display, much of the original humour of Pantomime has departed, but that the taste for it on the part of the public has not gone too, may be judged from the fact that out of two dozen pieces producing Christmas novelties, only three have adopted the more refined form of extravaganza.

The scene-painting and the ballets attracted the now-customary superlatives, with the sequence of Old English games and pastimes particularly appreciated.[29]

The 1858–9 Sadler's Wells pantomime was *Harlequin and Old Izaak Walton or Tom Moore of Fleet-street, the Silver Trout, and the Seven Sisters of Tottenham. The*

Times (28 December 1858) attributed the script to Greenwood but it was definitely by Blanchard. He records in his diary a visit on 22 September to discuss the subject of *Izaak Walton* with Greenwood and on 27 November that he was busy all day making a fair copy of the Wells pantomime. Blanchard sees it together with *Macbeth* on 22 January and notes that the pantomime was performed in an hour and a quarter.[30] On Boxing Day it had been paired with *The Lady of Lyons*.

The *Times* noted that 'The Thames, its impurities, and the many schemes for its purification, are subjects obvious to the satirist.' The pantomime opens at the Muddy Mountains of Old Father Thames, where the god of that once pure river is bewailing his unfortunate condition. Town Talk, the Press, Public Opinion and General Indignation are pressing for a cure. The great physician, Dr Board of Works, is sent for, and drives in a car drawn by snails, an allusion to its slowness to act. He prescribes physic – a heavy drain – but Father Thames resolves to throw all physic to the (Isle of) Dogs and take his own course. So he pays a visit to the River Lea in a beautiful region indicated to be the Peerless Pool of the Water Nymphs. He finds her complaining of the gradual disappearance of the fish, in particular a favourite pike, due to the famous angler, Izaak Walton. The fresh water fish call for revenge. Marriage is suggested as a cure for the angler and the 'Fair Maid of Tottenham' Maude, the milkmaid, is to be used as bait to tempt the angler. Old Izaak Walton's abode in Fleet Street, accurately depicting the original dwelling, next introduces the real life angler Izaak Walton (1593–1683), his fictional apprentice Tom Moore and Tom's famous jackdaw. They go off to fish the River Lea. A diorama illustrates their progress from Fleet Street to Tottenham Fields. They at last arrive at the Farm of the Seven Sisters, who each try to captivate the heart of Izaak. He shows a preference for Maude but she loves Tom Moore. The sisters only agree to Tom's proposal on condition that he performs two impossible tasks: recovering a bracelet from the bottom of the river and obtaining a rook's nest from the top of a poplar tree. He does so, helped by a trout he has rescued from Izaak and the jackdaw he has befriended. But the six sisters repudiate their bargain, so the Fairy of the Lea turns them into trees and unites the lovers. Rewards and punishments are meted out in 'a magnificent scene – the Palace of Pearl in the Realms of Crystal'. The *Times* said:

> We cannot speak too highly of the scenery, much of which is by Mr C.S. James, a young artist of great promise. The Palace of Pearls would, for gorgeousness and taste, bear comparison with some of the best displays of Madame Vestris herself.

The *Era* (2 January 1859) called it 'a capital pantomime, full of wit, whim, fun, and genial satire … It is long since so good an opening has been devised, and its local interest … renders it all the more acceptable to the resident population of this district.' It said: 'The scenery … will for its truly artistic qualities delight the fastidious eye of the connoisseur as well as thoroughly fascinate the more impressionable public.' The audience called for James who came forward and took a bow.

The subject of the polluted Thames was immensely topical, for 1858 was the year of 'The Great Stink'. For years the Thames had been polluted, and polluted water was a major cause of cholera outbreaks. By the 1850s there were sixty sewer outlets into the river and in the hot summer of 1858 the stench was so great that MPs were unable to conduct their business in the Houses of Parliament. The *I.L.N.* (30 September 1854) called the Thames 'a stream of death, instead of a river of life and beauty'. In 1855 a London-wide Metropolitan Board of Works had been established which took responsibility for dealing with London's sewage. Joseph Bazalgette was appointed its engineer but because of 'professional jealousy, idiotic power games and bureaucratic obstruction' work did not begin until 1858 when, under the stimulus of the Great Stink, Chancellor of the Exchequer Benjamin Disraeli pushed through a change in the law and found the £3 million necessary to begin creating a modern sewerage system for London. Its highlight was the Victoria Embankment containing the sewers. Work began on it in 1864 and took six years to complete. It was opened in 1870.[31]

The subject was so topical in 1858 that the Surrey Theatre also featured it in its Christmas pantomime. Where Blanchard's pantomime merely began with the polluted Thames and later wove in the historical figure of Izaak Walton and the folkloric figures of Tom Moore and the seven sisters of Tottenham, C.J. Collins' *Harlequin Father Thames and the River Queen or Ye Lorde Mayor of London* was a much more systematic and hard-hitting satire, with 'strictures on city and Corporation abuse; the Board of Works and its half-measures; Commissioners of Sewers' and so on.

The Era (2 January 1859), calling Collins' show 'as near the perfection of what a Christmas entertainment should be as it is well possible for so heterogeneous a species of amusement to be made', described it as 'a sanitary epic, based on the abominable and abnormal condition of the Thames.' It went on to characterize the plot:

> The River – feeling itself an institution of the country, and, like other corporate bodies endowed with mortal antipathy to change, resists, in the person of its presiding deity, Father Thames, every attempt on the part of Purity, Queen of the River and the Spirit of Health, Sanita, to purify or reform his muddy course. In this struggle all the opposing and concurrent elements pertinent to the subject, such as the Board of Works, the bridges, sewers, and parks are personified and ingeniously brought in as the *dramatis personae*, to carry out, with significant effect the plot and scenes of this admirable Burlesque, Father Thames being, however, finally worsted and compelled to yield to the march of progress.

It concludes with a parody of the last act of *Richard III* as Father Thames is beaten in mortal combat with Sanita at Richmond. Her victory is celebrated with a Grand

Horticultural Show in the Floral Pavilion of the River Queen. *The Era* noted that the show had elicited 'unbounded laughter and enjoyment from the audience, who relish, with unmistakable delight, every blow aimed at public and familiar abuse.'

The 1859–60 pantomime for Drury Lane was *Jack and the Beanstalk or Harlequin Leap Year and the Merry Pranks of the 'Good Little People'*. Blanchard took his topical cue from the fact that 1860 was a leap year and the pantomime followed the structure of the year, which meant uniquely that the harlequinade was completely integrated with the opening.

The show opened in the Atmosphere forty-five miles above the earth where Old Moore and five other almanacs, Zadkiel, Hannay, the Illustrated, Pocket and Nautical Almanacs, gather to predict the future. Almanacs, handbooks of astrological projection, were very popular in the nineteenth century. Prominent among them were Old Moore's, named after the astrologer and schoolmaster Francis Moore and first published in 1699, and Zadkiel's. Zadkiel was the pseudonym of Richard James Morrison (1795–1874) and was taken from an angel in Rabbinical lore. He accurately predicted the death of Prince Albert in 1861. The one thing the Almanacs find that they cannot predict is the Weather. Weather appears in her Aurora Borealis car with her attendants Heat and Cold and confirms that she is completely unpredictable, particularly with 1860 being a leap year. Weather summons Snow, Hail, Sleet, Mist, Rain and Dew and then recites the rhyme 'Thirty Days hath September', and as they are mentioned personifications of the twelve months enter. The astrologers call for a pantomime to cheer up the people, whatever the weather. Weather unlocks the Don-Jon in Jackland, revealing all the heroic Jacks, Jack Frost, Jack Cade, Jack Straw, Jack the Giant killer, Jack and Jill, Jack in the Box, Jack Horner, Jack Sprat and Jack and the Beanstalk. Zadkiel chooses Jack and the Beanstalk and Weather says each month will represent a different scene. The story of Jack and the Beanstalk begins in his cottage in wintry Devonshire in January, where Jack and other boys are snowballing. Goody Greyshoes reveals that he is not her son, as he supposed, but was found abandoned on her doorstep. A lawyer and bailiff turn up to reclaim the cottage for unpaid rent; they are driven off and thrown into the horsepond. Scene Three, the Grotto of the Pixies, takes place in February, with Queen Prism summoning the Pixies, 'The Good Little People' and her attendant Crystalline identifying Jack as the son and heir of Prince Caradoc, dropped by the giant when he was carrying off his father. She will help him avenge his father and defeat the Giant. The scene ends with a grand ballet. Scene Four takes place in March on a breezy heath with Goody Greyshoes giving Jack a calf to sell, Jack selling it to Crystalline (disguised as a farmer) for five beans and Goody throwing the beans disgustedly away. In scene Five, April, the Pixies appear with sacks of guano and lime phosphate and watering cans and cause the beanstalk to grow up into the sky. Jack decides to ascend it. In scene Six, May, Jack climbs to the giant's castle, and receives his father's sword from the fairy of the harp and the promise of reward from the fairy with the magic hen which lays the golden eggs, if he frees them from their captivity. He uses the sword to kill the Giant's baby and behead the Giant. In scene Seven, June – the Festival of the Flowers – Queen Prism assembles all the characters in her floral home for the transformation, welcoming the leap year of 1860.

The harlequinade continues the succession of months. July has a seaside scene and a marine parade, with riflemen formed to repel a French invasion. August, set in the village and mansion of the Marquis of Flowerdale, has a sequence of high days and holydays. September has a street in London in 1759 transforming to the same street in 1859, where everything is new and fast. October is set in a Kentish Hop Garden and a well-known brewery, November sees Bonfire Night and fog, and December 'the merry halls of happy old Christmas', and the finale.

The Times (27 December 1859) thought *Jack and the Beanstalk*:

> surpasses any of its predecessors since Mr E.T. Smith was lessee, Mr W. Beverley 'scenic artist', Mr Robert Roxby stage manager, and Mr E.L. Blanchard, inventor of the introductory burlesque. Complex as are the mechanical contrivances, gorgeous the pictorial displays, and almost countless the incidents, the pantomime had apparently been rehearsed with such care and efficiency that scarcely a single 'hitch' or failure marked the progress of the evening. Thus the delight of the holyday audience ... was unchecked, and a success achieved as complete and triumphant as it was richly merited.

This was the general verdict of the press. The opening production, *King René's Daughter* was, said *The Times*, 'listened to with tolerable complacency, but long before the conclusion little better than an exhibition of dumb-show.' *The Era* (1 January 1860) recorded hooting and jeering during the play and the 'gods' pelting the pittites with orange peel. But they fell silent for the pantomime. *The Times*, which was sometimes impatient with Blanchard's elaborate allegorical openings, thought the first scene, with the weather, the months and the Jacks, might have been cut, despite the loss of 'some good singing, grotesque masques, strange combinations and striking scenery, together with the evolutions of a brilliant *corps de ballet*', because it was a 'not very intelligible allegory' and delayed the start of the story proper, which was 'all ... excellent and all diverting'.

But other critics hailed the improved literary quality of the pantomimes. The *I.L.N.* (31 December 1859) reported:

> The composition of pantomimes, notwithstanding a vulgar notion to the contrary, has of late days greatly improved. In the days of 'Mother Goose' they made no claim to literary status. But nowadays they are carefully written by literary men, and aspire to literary merit ... The burlesque openings to pantomime are innovations which might have been resented, but that the dialogue openings had preceded, and already violated the rule

which required that the only media should be signs and gestures, exclusive of words. The union of Burlesque and Pantomime is, however, now an ordinary occurrence, and certainly gives great piquancy to the entertainment.

Turning to the productions, the *I.L.N.* declared Drury Lane to be:

first in dramatic and national rank, and as a pantomime theatre ... decidedly of the first class. The energetic manager selects every year the best author, the best scene-painter, the best mask inventor, the best musical composer and the best machinists that can be had for love or money ... First in degree stands Mr E.L. Blanchard, whose choice of subject testifies to his usual judgement ... Our author, too, has availed himself of the privilege of burlesque, and 'embellished' his dialogue opening with puns and parodies, contrary to his usual practice, which was content with an imitation of Pope's elegant versification ... In the present he deals with an oft-used story, but the mode in which he treats it is new.

The Era (25 December 1859) almost certainly had Blanchard in mind in its annual meditation on the forthcoming Christmas entertainment. Recognizing the powerful impression pantomimes made on children, *The Era* welcomed a perceived improvement in their literary quality:

Regarding the vividness of the impression left upon the youthful mind, and the permanence of the words and images at this season retained, it is with no little satisfaction that we have recognised lately the better style of Christmas entertainments provided. A higher standard of intellectual enjoyment has been taken, and though of necessity the subjects dealt with must be apparently puerile in their nature, they are treated with a greater flow of fancy, and written with more literary care and taste than they were within the days of our early remembrance. The mere utterance of nonsense, or, what was infinitely more reprehensible, the coarse expletives of slang, do not disgrace the dialogues of the openings as they did formerly, and the union of fairy extravaganza with the old style of grotesque action has at least had the advantage, that a superior class of writers is employed upon the authorship, and a higher range of dramatic talent brought to bear upon the adequate illustration of the characters to be embodied. Scenic aid of the greatest order of art is freely imparted, and the finest specimens of pictorial design will be found in the stage pictures which our theatrical artists have produced for the embellishment of the Pantomime.

For Sadler's Wells, the pantomime for 1859–60 was *Harlequin Hans and the Golden Goose or Old Mother Earth, the Little Red Man and the Princess Whom Nobody Could Make Laugh*, based on the Brothers Grimm stories. His diary reveals Blanchard making a fair copy of the opening and posting it to the Wells on

5 December, and receiving from Greenwood a fee of £20 for it on 19 January 1860. Blanchard saw the pantomime from a private box on 27 December 1859.[32]

The evening opened with *The Lady of Lyons* which, said *The Times* (27 December 1859), 'was got through with as much success as could have been expected on such an occasion; the audience, notwithstanding their impatience for the pantomime, conducting themselves on the whole with quietness and decorum.' The pantomime, attributed by *The Times* to Blanchard and Greenwood, began with an interesting political allegory which was anti-war in sentiment, for though in 1859 the wars currently raging were the Second Chinese War and the War of Italian Liberation, and it was not long since the campaigns of the Indian Mutiny and the Crimean War had preoccupied the public, there was the threat of war with France after an assassination attempt on Napoleon III with a bomb made in Birmingham.

Old Mother Earth is much disturbed by the contests and commotions that prevail among the nations, and is found in her abode, about to be attacked by a 'Chinaman, Nigger, Yankee, and European' all armed and asking:

Now, what's the matter? Why this dreadful riot?
Can't you let Mother Earth grow old in quiet?
What does it mean?

Peace and Plenty make their appearance, and declare that war is the cause of all the uproar, on which Mother Earth gives her opinion that 'it is all a pack of nonsense' and ought to be ended. In this opinion John Bull, who enters, heartily concurs, observing:

I'm sure you're right; these poppings, spears and axes
Impose on me most inconvenient taxes

The Little Red Man, whose province it is to 'create fun', introduces himself, and after a long colloquy, in which Peace, Plenty and Old Mother Earth take part, deploring the evils of war, we are taken to the realms of Plenty. A pantomime is decided on to cheer up Mother Earth and the story begins in the interior of the Charcoal Burner's hut. Here Karl Koken and his ill-treated son Hans reside. They are informed by a courier pursued by wolves, who takes refuge in the hut, that there is a melancholy princess whose father will give her hand and half his kingdom to the man who makes her laugh. Father and son resolve to do so and quarrel over who will win the Princess. The Little Red Man, after he appears as an old woman and is ill-treated by the father, favours Hans, who is kind to him, and acquires for him a supernatural golden goose, found in an enchanted oak on the borders of the Black Forest. One of its qualities is that it causes all who touch it to adhere to it. On his pilgrimage to the palace of the melancholy Princess, Hans encounters many opponents but as each touches the goose they stick to the creature. By the time Hans reaches the Palace, he has so many people attached to the goose that the Princess bursts out laughing and Hans wins the prize. Peace and Plenty return and in the midst of a 'brilliant scene' called the 'Arcadian Home of Peace', the transformation takes place and the usual tricks and fun of the harlequinade follow, until the show ends in 'The Palace of Peace in the Realms of Common Sense'.

The Times noted: 'There are some very fine scenes and spectacles brought out in the course of the piece.' *The Era* (1 January 1860) said:

> The scenery by Mr Charles Stanfield James, shows this young artist to be rapidly advancing in his profession to the foremost rank. The Golden Gardens in the Plains of Plenty, and the necessary climax now of all Pantomime openings, a glittering Transformation Scene, where golden palm trees spread out and droop their branches to admit the revelation of fairies in gorgeous dresses of gold and silver tissue, may vie with the scenic wonders of any theatre.

Of the show, the critic wrote:

> The fun of the opening … is prolonged throughout the harlequinade which is of a rapid and bustling character that allows no interval for a moment's weariness. It is rife with smart sallies and ingenious references to current events and the changes are dextrously contrived.

The *I.L.N.* (31 December 1859) said, 'the episodes … abound with original and mirth-exciting situations … A great feature … new and elaborate scenery by Mr C.S. James, which, with the piece itself, was received with approbation.' *The Era* (1 January 1860) noted that:

> the great feature of the opening, apart from the scenery, is … the Little Red Man, very cleverly represented by a child, Miss Eliza Collier, whose odd appearance in a quaint elfin dress of a colour suggested by the name, and whose droll action rendered all the more funny by the apparent solemnity with which it is gone through, form a highly-diverting addition to the broader pantomimic humour of the opening.

The Drury Lane pantomime subject for 1860–1 was derived from Robert Paltock's novel, *The Life and Adventures of Peter Wilkins* (1751), which was similar to and in its day as popular as *Robinson Crusoe*, though now completely forgotten. Blanchard called his version *Peter Wilkins or Harlequin and the Flying Women of the Loadstone Rock*. It opens in a tin mine in Cornwall where Peter Wilkins is one of the miners. He seeks to fill his mind with book knowledge and is cruelly oppressed by the mining captain Black Ralph, who wishes to knock the knowledge out of him. Peter's ill-treatment is interrupted by the annual visit of the mine's owner Earl Polwholfoltolderyddol FitzArthur Trevanion and his beautiful daughter Constantia. Peter is smitten by Constantia and he shows her round the mine, and in parody of the garden scene from *The Lady of Lyons* 'they walk up and down like Claude Melnotte and Pauline.' When they leave, Ralph punishes Peter for his presumption by leaving him alone in the mine, imprisoned. He hears mysterious rappings, a reference to the then current craze for spiritualism. Feldspar, the chief Kobold or Goblin of the Mine, rises up on a trap on a fossil Labyrinthodon, which it is predicted will one day be seen at the Crystal Palace. He summons all the other little kobolds and tells Peter there is a land of elves at the centre of the earth. He can see it through a magic crystal. The crystal is handed to Peter and the scene changes to the elfin land in the crystal sphere. Feldspar makes Peter invisible but he gives himself away when applauding the singing of Nymphidia, Queen of the Elves and her attendants. As punishment for entering their realm, the Queen predicts that he will forget his sweetheart and fall for another. Peter drinks fairy wine and disappears. He wakes up at Trevanion Castle on the Cornish Coast near Lands' End. He encounters Constantia again. The Earl, her father, who is in need of money, arranges to wreck the good ship *Adventurer*. But Jack Robinson, first mate of the ship, and the pilot and crew disperse the wreckers. Peter, who has been reading *Robinson Crusoe*, is recruited as cabin boy and the Earl exits pursued by his creditors.

On board the *Adventurer*, the sailors, all talking in nautical terms ('splice the mainbrace', 'belay the binnacle', etc.) reel in various marine oddities, a Large Sole, John Dory, Ann Chovy, Dog Fish and a Whistling Oyster, and finally a mermaid. They all dance to J.L. Toole's 'Whistling Oyster' song. The ship is then drawn by the magnetic force of the Loadstone Rock and wrecked. Peter lands on the rock and goes through an aperture to find himself not in the Antarctic, as in the novel, but on the island of Flying Women in the Indian Ocean at sunrise. He encounters the strange race of flying women, the Glumms and the Gawries. Peter falls for a winged woman, Yourawkee. Her sister Hallycarnie rescues Jack Robinson. The captain and crew turn up and they are all taken by the flying women to the aerial city of the Glumms and Gawries where Peter plans to wed Yourawkee. But Nymphidia appears and tells him he is now being untrue to his original sweetheart and must roam through the world in motley guise to make amends until she receives him in her Fairy Home. This signals the transformation to the harlequinade. *The Times* (27 December 1860) declared that the success of its predecessor meant that *Peter Wilkins* had much to live up to. But it succeeded and 'was an unequivocal success from first to last.' The opening was said to be:

> if anything, longer and more elaborate than usual; but the familiar story (which Mr E.L. Blanchard has handled with his accustomed cleverness) includes a more than ordinary choice of incidents, the interest is well kept up, and a variety obtained, the want of which is often fatal.

But he had taken fewer liberties with the story than the Keeleys in their Covent Garden version thirty years before. The critic praised the contrast between the dance of the goblins ('as grim and fantastic a display of choreographic art as was ever witnessed') and the 'picturesque and graceful' ballet of the elves in Elfinland. When Elfinland appeared in the Crystal Sphere 'the magic paraphernalia and glittering beauty' of the scene elicited a spontaneous call for Mr Beverley, who appeared from the wings to acknowledge the honour. 'The metamorphosis from subterranean gloom to superaqueous light is extremely felicitous; and equally welcome is the change from the distorted physiognomies of the mine-goblins to the unmasked and smiling faces of the elves.' J.H. Tully's music was 'full of life and vivacity', Mr Robert Roxby had zealously supervised 'the very complicated scenery and stage accessories' and E.T. Smith had another hit. 'Nothing is wanted, in short', said *The Times* in its customary reservation, 'but a little judicious curtailment (especially in the opening scenes)' to render *Peter Wilkins* a model 'Christmas Pantomime'. *The Era* (30 December 1860), on the other hand, declared:

> Mr E.L. Blanchard is the Prince of Pantomime Writers. He must be a lineal descendant of some high and puissant Fairy Queen – Queen Mab, in all probability – or else he would never have been gifted with the faculty and power which he exhibits of dealing with mythical lore.

The Era suggested that Blanchard had now introduced an extravaganza element into the Drury Lane pantomime in that 'He has been more studied in his dialogue – studied, we mean, with regard to the points thereof. Almost every line sparkles with them, and they are all exceedingly telling.' Blanchard saw the pantomime on Boxing Day and recorded that he was 'very much pleased with the way in which it is acted.'[33]

In 1860 E.T. Smith took over Her Majesty's Theatre for one season and Blanchard was invited to provide the first ever pantomime to be staged at that august operatic establishment. The main attraction was an English version of the French comic opera, *Queen Topaze*, by Victor Massé and Smith engaged his regular Drury Lane team to provide a pantomime. The result was *Harlequin and Tom Thumb or Merlin the Magician and the Good Fairies of the Court of King Arthur*. Reviewing this first pantomime at that theatre and one which Smith declared to be aimed directly at children, *The Times* (27 December 1860) noted:

> On seeing the piece ... we understand more clearly what the lessee means in saying that 'the greatest care has been taken to make it suitable to the tastes of children'. The harlequinade is reduced in length, and the introductory extravaganza, also short enough, is not deformed with too much of the verbal torture which is considered appropriate to this species of entertainment ... there is less of talk, and more of action, and a great deal more of real fun. The action is broad and intelligible, and the whole attention is concentrated on points easily caught. The story of Tom Thumb is well adapted for such an experiment.

Miss Lilia Ross was a great hit in the title role.

> Surely, never before has such a mite of humanity been seen on so huge a stage as this little creature … who did her part wonderfully; speaking out what she had to say with the most perfect self-possession, and loud enough to be heard to the extreme corner of that immense building. Apart from the amusing things she said and did, the fact that they were said and done by so small an atomy … was laughable enough.

Tom Thumb is lost in a honey pot, carried away in a bag of cherry stones, devoured and disgorged by a red cow, then carried away through the air by a crow, goes down the giant's throat, is found in a salmon, drowned in a punchbowl and comes forth at King Arthur's court riding on a mouse and equipped as a knight. He is killed by a cat but revived by the fairies and borne away to fairy land, which was displayed in the final transformation scene, 'a triumph of scenic art which created vast enthusiasm.' *The Times* critic noted that the harlequinade was:

> much as usual … It is the introduction which will always prove the prime attraction. The red cow and other beasts were set forth upon the stage with great skill that created no small mirth. Seldom has a pantomime been known to run better on a first night, and we anticipate for it a great success.

The *I.L.N.* (5 January 1861) declared:

> Mr Blanchard has been very careful in the opening libretto; the writing is very even and good; the verses deserve a better fate than to be spoken behind the pasteboard curtain of masks, even when those masks have been designed by that astounding artist, Dykwynkyn.

But even better was the scenery, which, 'painted by Messrs Charles Drew, Sanders etc., under the direction and superintendence of Mr Beverley, is far superior to anything ever seen on that vast stage.' The scenes included the interior of Gaffer Thumb's Cottage, Rosewater Lake and the Romantic Haunt of the Fairies ('a very chaste and beautiful scene'), 'the vast and magnificent Turrets and Terrace of Giant's Castle' and The Banqueting Hall of King Arthur which Merlin changes to The Grand Chameleon Temple of the Fairies, with its triple changes of colour and 'resplendent effects of light'. *The Era* (30 December 1860) similarly praised 'this unparalleled combination of scenic marvels' and 'some of the most marvellous effects of light and colour which the stage ever witnessed.' It praised Blanchard's 'ingenious libretto', Robert Roxby's stage management, the 'admirable' models, including the Cow 'executed solely by the hands of a rising young artist, Mr H. Adams', and Tully's 'brilliant and appropriate music'. *The Standard* (27 December 1860) observed that two of the faults of the metropolitan pantomimes were 'a certain looseness of dialogue' and 'a tediousness', and that *Tom Thumb* was entirely free of these faults, the dialogue being 'good, crisp and witty'. Scenery and costumes inspired the usual superlatives. But E.T. Smith relinquished his lease after one season, confiding to Blanchard that he had lost £21,000 on the season. On 4 January 1861 Blanchard visited the shows, proclaiming *Queen Topaze* 'very bad' and *Tom Thumb* 'good'. He had been there on 29 December for the first morning performance, which, he wrote 'goes off very well, but a very indifferent house. Little Lilia Ross very good'.[34]

Blanchard displayed his loyalty to E.T. Smith when Smith took over Astley's in 1863 and turned at once to Blanchard for a pantomime. Astley's had stood empty and unlet for several months and Smith secured it only on 23 November 1863. He had, recalled *The Era* (27 December 1863), only three weeks and four days to get everything in place. Smith had announced that he intended conducting the theatre 'upon those principles by which he had raised Drury-lane from a state something like disaster to one of great prosperity.' Blanchard, assuming his old pseudonym Francisco Frost, provided a script called *Harlequin and Friar Bacon or Great Grim John of Gaunt and the Enchanted Lance of Robin Goodfellow.* But his diary recalls that on 16 July 1860, he had prepared a copy of a pantomime, *Harlequin Chaucer and Grim John of Gaunt* for Astley's.[35] So this may well be a recycled version of that script.

The Era (27 December 1863) proclaimed the pantomime:

> especially suited to the younger members of the community, for it combines good historical knowledge with unmistakable fun, and so well are the two blended, that one is as attractive as the other. Through the instrumentality of the broadest scenic arrangements, certain lessons are inculcated which will never be forgotten, for the father of English poetry, Geoffrey Chaucer, is presented to the young mind in his habit as he lived, and Grim John of Gaunt has a portion of his history told through the agency of the eye. This we hold to be a novel and most salutary element that Mr Francesco [sic] Frost has introduced into Pantomime writing.

It opens in a fairy encampment by moonlight with mushrooms for tents – a scene that provoked spontaneous applause. Oberon, the King of the Fairies, enters, accompanied by Robin Goodfellow and Imagination. Old Pantomime arrives, complaining of the dearth of good plots for pantomimes. Imagination offers Chaucer's Canterbury Tales and a 'splendid' ballet closes the scene. The scene shifts to the Tabard Inn at Southwark, which is recreated from an old print on the stage. Here we are introduced to Chaucer the poet as a young man, mine host of the Tabard and Rose the barmaid, as well as the Canterbury Pilgrims. Grim John of Gaunt arrives and gets involved in a set-to with Chaucer as they vie for the attentions of Rose. The Pilgrims set out after a lively morris dance by the *corps de ballet*. This is followed by a 'pretty representation of the country near Canterbury' as pilgrims travel and then John of Gaunt consults Friar Bacon in his laboratory at Oxford and he obtains a love philtre to conquer Rose. But he is foiled by Chaucer with the aid of Robin Goodfellow and his magic lance. Chaucer beats Gaunt in a comic tournament. The transformation then takes place. *The Times* (28 December 1863) described it:

> a grand affair – dazzling scenery, glittering stars, cascades of sparkling water, in the midst of which fountain nymphs of the loveliest forms, and all the most bewitching spirits of air and earth are seen floating, flying, and reclining, illumined by an intensely bright light, render this scene a perfect triumph, and it drew forth thundering applause from the beholders.

The Era called it 'one of the pantomime wonders of the season'. The harlequinade followed 'with the requisite amount of funny tricks and burlesque allusions to current events'. The pantomime concluded with the 'Grand Finale of the Salamandrine Temple'. The scenes were painted by Albert Callcott, C.S. James, W. Bradfoot and James Gates, the latter being responsible for the transformation scene. He and Smith were called for and took a bow. The music was by J.H. Tully. 'He was most warmly received on his entrance and his overture received the honour of an encore.' The comic business elicited roars of laughter, the house was crammed and *The Era* thought Astley's had not had such a house for many a year.

The *I.L.N.* (2 January 1864) said, presumably in view of Smith's record at Drury Lane, 'it was generally expected that a great hit would be made here and the expectation has been realised.' The reviewer pronounced the ballet at the end of the first scene 'excellent' and the fairy camp set 'gorgeous', the scene of the Tabard Inn 'splendidly executed', the transformation scene with its use of real water produced 'a remarkably brilliant effect' and the musical adaptations were 'particularly sparkling ... owing to the taste, judgement and skill of Mr Tully'. Blanchard records receiving £20 from Smith on account for the pantomime on 15 December 1863. On 18 May he received from Smith £10 which he accepted as 'payment in full for Astley's pantomime, as he has had severe losses this year.' The total of £30 was much less than his customary royalty fee, and bespeaks his generosity towards his former patron, a generosity particularly marked as when he saw the show on 1 January, he recorded: 'Opening fair but not carried out.'[36]

Amazingly, in view of his payment experience in 1863–4, Blanchard once again contributed the pantomime for Astley's in 1864–5, this time in partnership with T.L. Greenwood in their guise as the Brothers Grinn. The show bore the extraordinary title of *Harlequin Jack Sprat or The Three Blind Mice; Great A! Little A! Bounding B! The Cat's in the Cupboard and She Can't See*. It was aimed directly at the children and merged a record number of nursery rhymes: 'Robin the Bobbin', 'Sing a Song of Sixpence', 'There was a Jolly Miller', 'AaB', 'Three Blind Mice' and 'Jack Sprat'.

It opens in Tom Tiddler's Ground in the centre of the earth. This was the name of a children's game rather like tag in which the children chant 'Here we're in Tom Tiddler's Ground, picking up gold and silver' and are chased by Tom Tiddler until someone is caught and takes over as Tom. The labours of Tom and his followers picking up gold and silver are interrupted by the arrival of Merry Christmas Time and the five leisure hours, Seven, Eight, Nine, Ten and Eleven, who demand amusement. The fairies Amusement and Happy New Year decide on a pantomime and select the story of Jack Sprat. In the Abode of Amusement there is a parade of mythological figures – Jupiter, Minerva, Saturn, Ceres and Diana – followed by the signs of the Zodiac. They are all on horseback, utilizing the horses which were the distinctive characteristic of shows at Astley's. This is followed by a ballet of the Four Seasons, the dancers clad in emerald green for spring, amber for summer, crimson for autumn and pure white for winter. *The Era* (1 January 1865) pronounced it 'something more than ordinarily magnificent'.

The story proper begins in Mother Shipton's hovel on Toadstool Heath where the old witch is being harassed due to the mischief-making of Tell-Tale-Tit, laundry maid of King Robin de Bobbin. Mother Shipton is rescued by Jack Sprat and she rewards him by finding him a potential wife, Joan the daughter of the Jolly Miller, for whom Jack goes to work. But Tell-Tale-Tit, seeking revenge on Jack, launches an attack on the miller's flour with the three blind mice to prevent the Miller fulfilling an order from King Robin de Bobbin. Mother Shipton, using the letters AaB as a spell, releases the cat from the cupboard and he sees off the three blind mice, cutting off their tails with a carving knife. The Jolly Miller refuses to give his consent to his daughter's marriage to Jack unless Jack provides him with the laundry maid's nose. Mother Shipton and her fellow witches bake twenty-four blackbirds in a pie, and with it Jack gains admittance to the palace of the notoriously greedy Robin de Bobbin, while the king is in the counting house and the queen is in the parlour eating bread and honey. But Ralph the Raven escapes from the pie, pecks off the maid's nose and flies away with it. Jack is forced to pursue to retrieve it and gain the hand of the Miller's daughter.

But all was not well on Boxing Night. The scene in which Jack pursued the Raven to his Nest was not ready and the action moved from the pecking off of Tell-Tale-Tit's nose directly to Charles Brew's transformation scene in the subterranean Dwelling of the Gnomes, which *The Times* (27 December 1864) pronounced 'really striking and brilliant'. But the review concluded by saying: 'An exceptional number of "hitches", even for a first night, severely tried the patience of the audience, and the green curtain fell prematurely on the final scene, "The Palace of the New Year"'. The reviewer added: 'No doubt these shortcomings will be speedily remedied, and then the dances, dresses, horses, processions, and fairy scenes will enable the pantomime at Astley's to take rank with any of those at the larger theatres.'

A year later Greenwood alone took on the writing duties for the Astley's pantomime. Once again nursery-rhymes inspired: it was *Harlequin Tom Tom the Piper's Son, Pope Joan and Little Bo-Peep or Old Daddy Long Legs and the Pig that went to market and the Pig that stayed home*. *The Era* (31 December 1865) pronounced it 'a marvel of dramatic construction out of what would appear to be highly impracticable materials. It is smartly written, fully of telling parodies, and is excellently supported by the performers.' The music of J.H. Tully and the scene-painting, particularly the transformation scene of Charles Brew earned plaudits. But Smith was unable to make a go of Astley's and surrendered the lease, in October 1866, moving on to his next ill-fated venture.

Blanchard's 1860 Sadler's Wells pantomime was *Harlequin Sindbad the Sailor or The Fairy of the Diamond Valley and the Little Old Man of the Sea*, its narrative derived from the Arabian Nights. The first piece played was the 'doleful' tragedy of *Jane Shore*, which, according to *The Times* (27 December 1860), confirmed by *The Era* (30 December 1860), 'was listened to with singular quietness, even by the gentlemen seated in their shirt sleeves in the gallery, though there might be heard occasional manifestations of impatience for the promised pantomime.' The writer, says *The Times*, was E.L. Blanchard, whose aim seems to have been 'a combination of the humour and spectacular brilliance of the extravaganza with the fun and frolic of the pantomime.'

The show opens in the Fungus Crypt of the great Wine and Spirit Vaults where representatives of all the old liquor compounds are met in council and are concerting measures to resist the invasion of the French light wines. They are presided over by King Jollity and each in turn seizes the opportunity to set forth his peculiar qualities, beginning with Irish Whisky and including Scotch Whisky, Rum, Gin, Brandy, Porter, Stout, Pale Ale and Sherry. Having heard them, King Jollity comes to the conclusion that 'prudence with jollity is best allied' and when Undine, the water spirit, canvasses the merits of water, he orders Stout and Porter about their business, wishes French and English wines to 'pour themselves all out' and spirits to evaporate, and then calls for water. The idea of resisting the French invasion of wines being abandoned, the scene changes to an 'Aquatic Palace' where Undine condescends to amuse the party with an aquatic excursion in which they can trace the adventures of Sindbad.

In the port of Balsora a ship is being prepared to trade in foreign parts, and here is found Sindbad in reduced circumstances, but longing to retrieve his fortune. Through the agency of Undine, Sindbad is supplied with a store of merchandise and a pocket full of money. He embarks on the ship to dispose of his goods. The Captain, Ali, abandons him on a desert island and appropriates his merchandise with which, in due course, he arrives at the Golden Gates of the palace of King Mirage to whom he offers the goods for sale. The theft of the goods is suspected and he is thrown into prison. Sindbad meanwhile is carried by the Roc to the palace of King Mirage and the King offers his daughter Gulbeyaz to the man who will procure for him the largest diamonds. Under the care of Undine, and carried by the Roc, Sindbad reaches the Valley of Diamonds where he collects diamonds, encounters the Old Man of the Sea and returns to claim the princess. King Mirage seeks to renege and the fairies intervene to settle the dispute while the transformation to the harlequinade takes place, where the scenery includes a view of Sadler's Wells in the olden days, Islington a hundred years ago and a number of familiar local scenes. The show ended with 'a magnificent representation' of the Golden Hall of Gems.

The Times felt:

> Throughout the piece the dialogue is well sustained, and occasionally humorous, but there are not many pointed allusions to passing events. The spectacles were striking – one or two of them even splendid – and the ballet dances ... were witnessed with immense favour by the audience ... the new pantomime received unequivocally the stamp of universal approbation.

There were various references to Garibaldi (all cheered) and King Mirage was modelled on King Ferdinand II of Naples and Sicily (nicknamed King Bomba), the villain of the Italian liberation struggle. 'Put on more taxes, grind the people down, and should the rogues object, bombard the town' says King Mirage.

The Era (30 December 1860), noting that the 'enchanting story' was 'pleasantly treated by Mr E.L. Blanchard', lavished its praise on Charles S. James' scenery ('the splendid scenery and effects ... are in every way calculated to render the illusion complete'). The scenes included the Fungus Crypt in the Great Spirit Vaults, the Aquatic Temple of Undine, a panoramic view of the port of Balsora and The Valley of Diamonds, which was greeted by 'a perfect storm of applause' which brought Mr James onto the stage. 'He was again enthusiastically summoned' in the 'unrivalled Transformation Scene' which involved real water.

The *I.L.N.* (5 January 1861) noted: 'There is a certain amount of good writing and of the usual fun in this piece; and the scenery is very good, specially the grand transformation scene, as also the ... scene called the Diamond Valley.' *The Standard* (27 December 1860) thought the pantomime 'perhaps the best that has been put upon these boards, even during the present management' and said the name of the author, E.L. Blanchard alone guaranteed excellence. But there was praise too for the good artistic skill of the scene-painter C.S. James, especially his 'splendid' transformation scene.

Greenwood had ended his lesseeship and Phelps carried on alone for two more years. Blanchard watched the show with Phelps on 27 December. Blanchard negotiated with him not a flat fee but a royalty of £1 per night. This resulted in his getting £15 from Phelps on 11 January and £30 on 1 March, £45 in all for the run of *Sindbad*.[37]

Blanchard's 1861–2 Sadler's Wells pantomime was *Cherry and Fair Star or Harlequin and the Singing Apple, the Talking Bird and the Dancing Waters*, based on one of Madame d'Aulnoy's fairy tales. It was his last for the Wells as Phelps relinquished his management in 1862. Blanchard received £49 for the script, indicating forty-nine performances. He saw the show on 27 December, recording 'See Fenton – funny and transformation scene good'. Charles Fenton was playing Prince Cherry.[38]

The pantomime opens in the court of Queen Mab where the unruly elf Hobgoblin arrives after a period of exile in London. He confirms Queen Mab's complaint that all the wonders once accomplished by the fairies are now achieved by modern science. He cites the underground railway, iron-plated ships, the telegraph system and the Thames Embankment with its sewerage system. Mab summons the spirit of the age, the Great Excitement, who explains that society is in the grip of novelty and great excitement is caused by the latest popular song, sensation dramas like *The Colleen Bawn*, a new speculation on the stock market, a striking sermon or a daring trapeze artist. Mab asks if anything lasts these days and is told that the Christmas pantomime does and the spirit urges them all to meet him at Sadler's Wells for *Cherry and Fair Star*.

On a lonely island, Cherry and Fair Star, two young people rescued from the sea as babies and raised by the pirate Captain Kyd, are bored with their life and wish to leave but as Fair Star's hair yields jewels when combed, Kyd wants to prevent this. Cherry has a broadsword duel with Kyd and is beaten but the Spirit of the Shell appears to rescue them and transport them away on the Golden Galley. They arrive at the court of King Whiteheart, Emperor of Bigaroonia, who is under the thumb of his dictatorial mother-in-law, Queen Blackheart. It is she who eighteen years earlier had caused the two children to be set adrift at sea. Blackheart's waiting-woman Feintise now seeks to dispose of Cherry by persuading him to go after three treasures to delight his beloved Fair Star: the Dancing Waters which preserve beauty, the Singing Apple which improves wit and the Talking Bird that will tell them all they want to know. Accompanied by Kyd, who he has taken on as his valet, Cherry passes through the Valley of Granite Rocks to the Luminous Forest where he obtains the Dancing Waters; the Great Libyan Desert where he gets the Singing Apple; and the Snow Mountain, where he meets the Talking Bird but is turned to stone when he touches it. Fair Star, guided by love, has followed them, charms the bird with a song, frees Cherry from the spell and returns with the three trophies. The Bird reveals that Fair Star is the King's daughter and Prince Cherry her cousin, and they were cast adrift by Blackheart to enable her to secure the throne. She now closes in with her guards but Queen Mab intervenes to transport them all to her sunlit Floral Home for the transformation, at the end of which the lovers are united.

The Era (29 December 1861) recorded that the serious play was Henry Hart Milman's *Fazio*, in which a 'densely-packed audience' were kept somewhat in check by the good acting displayed by the leading *artistes*.

> No sooner, however, had the curtain descended on the *finale* than the fun began, and the proverbially quiet audience of Sadler's Wells became transformed into a laughing, noisy, hilarious, and unruly one. In the pit orange peel, and even the juice fruit itself, was scattered far and wide, and as the gallery folks are not generally slow to take up a *cue* of this description, the missiles soon came down so fast and thick that one might almost have imagined that the roof was off the house, and that the elements were pouring down their wrath in orange peel.

Bags of flour were also emptied on the pittites from the gallery and several fights broke out. Even when the musicians entered and the orchestra struck up, the most popular airs were accompanied by screeching and whistling. Eventually the audience settled down.

The Era noted that the script was by Blanchard and:

> it was treated by the author from a novel point of view, being written in that now popular punning style that takes so well in the West End Burlesques; and innumerable as are the Christmas pieces that have emanated from the pen of Mr Blanchard, he has never bettered the one under notice.

The Examiner (11 January 1862) recorded: 'The great and rare merit of the pantomime is that it keeps the house alive with constant laughter.' *The Era* praised the scenery:

> The subject is one that gives plenty of scope for scenic effect; and the Basaltic Cavern, with the Sea Shore and Corsair's abode, the Granite Rocks by Sunset, and the Luminous Forest, were all triumphs of Mr C.S. James's skill, which were eclipsed by the Transformation Scene, the Amber Groves of Queen Mab's Floral Home by the Waters of Perpetual Youth and Beauty. It opened from the previous scene, representing the Snow Mountains in the Frozen Regions, and displayed a magnificent globe, the upper half of which was gradually raised until it formed a canopy for the whole, the lower part at the same time unfolding, and hanging as a drapery all round, disclosing a group of Fairies in silver and lace, who held festoons of the same material. In the front of this was a series of alcoves, filled with Fairies similarly attired, while the background was composed of crystal fluting, interspersed with silver and gold, and the sides were ornamented with flowers.

The Examiner thought 'the scenic effects vie in brilliance with those of the West-end theatres', a view shared by most of the critics. The opening, said *The Era*, was 'full of broad and witty sayings of the leading topics of the day', and Charles Fenton as Prince Cherry kept the audience laughing whenever he appeared, though the most humorous performance came from Mr C. Seyton as the corsair Captain Kyd, a strongly caricatured melodrama stage villain.

The harlequinade was not a long one but:

> what was done was to the point, and the hits at the Yankees, the new Census Return, Mr [Charles] Spurgeon [the popular preacher] and the Gorilla [a reference to the Wilberforce-Huxley evolution debate] were all happily done, while the tricks ... worked without hitch or hindrance. The change of a Railway Terminus to the Sea-Beach at Ramsgate, was one of the best in the harlequinade.

Clown and Pantaloon did a seasickness act that convulsed the gallery and Clown performed some solos on a diminutive banjo and played a tune on a row of flower-pots.

The 1861–2 Drury Lane pantomime, *Harlequin and the House that Jack Built or Old Mother Hubbard and her Wonderful Dog*, was destined to be Blanchard's last for the E.T. Smith management at that theatre. It was deemed by critics to be one of his best. *The Era* (29 December 1861) began its review with the resounding statement: 'The Theatre Royal, Drury-lane is the temple of Pantomime, and Mr E.L. Blanchard is its High Priest.' It declared that in the present pantomime Blanchard had 'excelled' himself:

> In construction it is the most artistic Pantomime we have ever witnessed ... The manner in which the dual stories involved in the title of the Pantomime have been amalgamated is in our opinion a triumph of dramatic skill, and exhibits Mr Blanchard's genius most conspicuously.

The Times (27 December 1861) declared with approval, 'the pantomime has the merit of being a thoroughly English pantomime in every particular. The characters are English, the scenery is English, and the incidents, ludicrously as they are exhibited, are English too.'

Blanchard cleverly merged the two nursery rhymes, *The House that Jack Built* and *Old Mother Hubbard*, and attached them to a plot which travestied the familiar elements of melodrama, the wicked squire, the poor but honest country boy and the innocent milkmaid. The pantomime opens in Mother Hubbard's cottage where folklore figures Mother Hubbard with her dog, Dame Trot with her cat and Dame Wiggins of Lea with her goose meet in conclave to discuss their plans to thwart their common enemy, the young squire of Rookwood, who has decreed that in his domain all witches shall be burned alive – and the three dames are practitioners of witchcraft.

'No little amusement' is provided by the rivalry between Mother Hubbard's dog and Dame Trot's cat 'for supremacy at the domestic hearth'. *The Times* noted that Blanchard had raised Mother Hubbard's dog 'to the dignity of that far more important personage, "Puss in Boots", the Talleyrand of fabled quadrupeds'. The Squire arrives seeking to arrest honest Jack as a vagrant and snatch a kiss from unwilling village maid, Rosetta. When Mother Hubbard tries to intervene, the Squire orders her arrested as a witch and the three old women disappear on their broomsticks.

In scene two, the witches' glen by moonlight, the three old women perform an incantation, directly parodying the witches' incantation in *Macbeth*, to summon up supernatural aid. One of the heads to peep out of their cauldron is that of an attorney, who states with legal precision that by force of an ancient forest law, whoever can build a house on common ground between sunset and sunrise, the house and the ground on which it stands becomes his property and that of his heirs in perpetuity.

In scene three, on the village green with a roadside ale house in the background, the new and grasping young squire arrives and is installed in possession of his lands and tenements after a village festival. He tries again to steal a kiss from Rosetta, is prevented by Jack and has Jack arrested. Mother Hubbard's dog gets the key to Jack's chains from the Squire and frees him and he is pressed into service by the witches. In scene four, the house is built for Jack by supernatural means and he becomes as great a man as the squire. In scene five, the Squire, who has lost his way while out hunting, inveigled by the 'Will of the Wisp', Mother Hubbard's agent, is attacked by a swarm of frogs and on the point of being submerged in the fens, is rescued by the dog. As the price of his rescue and in atonement for his past misdeeds, he signs away his estates to Jack, who is with the Squire and the rest of the characters transported to the region of Elfinland, where the transformation takes place, with Jack urged to 'get good houses night and day. And give a hint of British Expedition to our Great International Exhibition', a reference to the planned 1862 International Exhibition in South Kensington.

On the basis of this plot there was plenty of burlesque fun and scenic splendours. Among the ingredients thrown into the magic cauldron were 'three hairs from a gorilla riven' and 'a lecture that was on him given', presumably a reference to the famous confrontation between T.H. Huxley and Bishop Samuel Wilberforce in late 1860 when the latter enquired if the former was descended from an ape on his mother's or his father's side. This reference elicited 'a roar' from the boxes, pit and gallery. The witches were all appropriately grotesque. 'The Witches Glen' scene was 'one of Mr W. Beverley's most graceful and well-executed performances'. At the end of it there came a fairy ballet, pronounced by *The Times*: 'new in design and brilliant in effect, the effect of numbers being admirably combined with that of picturesque and tasteful grouping. This created a "furore".' Scene three, the young Squire's installation, involved a realization of W.P. Frith's painting *Coming of Age in the Olden*

Times, and a complete demonstration of Old English sports, masques and processions. The 'Sir Roger de Coverley' was danced and there was a procession of mummers, including Robin Hood, Little John, Valentine and Orson, St George and the Dragon, Mother Goose, Stiltwalkers, Morris Dancers and a Bear and his Keeper. In scene four, Beverley's sunrise effect caused him to be called forward for a bow. The building of the house by more than 100 tiny labourers was, said *The Times*, 'one of the most happily conceived and thoroughly effective scenic contrivances that ever enlivened the introductory burlesque which of recent years has played so conspicuous a part in our Christmas pantomimes.' In the house, once erected, the audience were shown the malt that lay in the house, the rat that ate the malt, the cat that killed the rat, the dog that worried the cat, the cow that tossed the dog, the maiden who milked the cow, the man (Jack) who kissed the maiden, and the priest and the cock that crowed in the morn, 'the whole routine, indeed, of the nursery tale, vividly and humorously represented.' The transformation scene by Beverley was declared by *The Times* to be 'unique'. Beverley, Smith and stage manager Robert Roxby ('zealous and indefatigable') were all called forth to take a bow.

The Era reported that the theatre was packed, that the audience was 'not so obstreperous as heretofore' and only one fight in the topmost gallery took place. It was, however, 'very determined in character' and required three policemen to halt it. But when the orchestra struck up the overture, a medley of popular tunes composed by J.H. Tully with his 'accustomed ability and success', the pit and galleries joined in 'with a unanimity and harmony that would have done honour to the training and rehearsal of a Hullah', that is John Hullah, the pioneer of singing teaching and musical sight-reading. The overture ended with 'God Save the Queen', which, said *The Era*, 'was taken up with one voice by the audience, and then unanimously redemanded, Boxes, Pit and Galleries joining in the choral prayer which constitutes England's National Anthem. This was the most touching incident of this exciting evening.' The fervour of the singing was doubtless a response to the death on 14 December of Prince Albert, whose funeral had taken place on 23 December. Thereafter Blanchard's fortunes would be tied to first the Falconer and then the Chatterton managements.

9

E.L. Blanchard and the Drury Lane
Pantomime: The Chatterton Management

By the time of the 1862–3 Drury Lane pantomime, *Little Goody Two-Shoes or Harlequin Cock Robin*, the lease of Drury Lane had passed from E.T. Smith to the playwright Edmund Falconer. *The Times* (27 December 1862) noted that it was E.T. Smith who, having resolved that 'his house should be the pantomime house *par excellence*', realised what his predecessors had failed to appreciate 'namely that it was more than useless to present *George Barnwell* or *Jane Shore* to an audience who regard them as an infliction, on which not even the semblance of attention was to be bestowed.' So he had put on the shortest pieces possible before the pantomime. Falconer did the same but even the short curtain-raiser, Falconer's own 'comedietta' *Next of Kin* was completely inaudible due to audience noise. They only subsided into 'respectful silence' when the pantomime commenced.

The Times underlined the mixed composition of the audience:

> the stalls and boxes presented an appearance more than ordinarily brilliant for a holyday that is mainly plebian [sic], while the gallery was crammed with occupants of the good old British school, rough seekers of enjoyment, who during the progress of the short drama that prefaced the pantomime, indulged in recreations of their own.

Falconer had 'wisely', said *The Times*, retained the services of Blanchard but not Beverley and the scenery was now in the hands of William Telbin and Thomas Grieve. The subject of the new pantomime was the story of *Little Goody Two-Shoes*, first published in 1765 and generally attributed to Oliver Goldsmith. It had been utilized as a pantomime subject since at least 1803. Blanchard took the essential ingredients and combined them with several nursery rhymes: 'Little Boy Blue', 'Ding, dong, bell, pussy's in the well' and 'Who killed Cock Robin?'. Dykwynkyn did the masks, 'exhibiting', said *The Era* (4 January 1863), 'physiognomical traces of every variety of human passion'. John Barnard provided the music and Oscar Byrne, the choreography.

It opens with Little Goody Two-Shoes running a village school and seeking to make money so that she may marry her penniless admirer, the shepherd Little Boy Blue. When the school assembles, there is a scuffle between good and bad boys and Tommy Green, the bad boy, takes Goody's cat and puts him in the well, whence he is rescued by Tommy Stout. The squire Sir Timothy Gripe comes to collect the back rent owed him for the school, offers to remit it in return for Goody's love but when she rejects him, forecloses on her. At a hunting lodge on the borders of the forest, Little Boy Blue receives a message by pigeon telling him of Goody's financial problems. The fairy Good Nature appears, disguised as Goody Peabody, and gives him a basket of goodies, eggs, butter and so forth, which never runs out and allows him to raise money to help Goody Two-Shoes.

Goody now convenes her school at the Bramble Brake in the depths of the forest and the children play happily. Tommy Green, who hates the happiness of the others succeeds in summoning up the Demon Envy, and at Tommy's request the Demon promises to kill Goody's favourite bird, Cock Robin. Good Nature transports Goody Two-Shoes to the Haunt of the Wood Nymphs in the fairy dell. *The Era* reported that 'the scene met with round after round of applause' for the 'magnificent' scene-painting. There she is transformed into a forget-me-not in a dream and joins the other personified flower fairies, 100 of them – primrose, cowslip, violet, honeysuckle, bluebell, daisy, foxglove and so on – in the 'ballet of the bouquets', one of Byrne's 'best ballets' thought the *I.L.N.* (27 December 1862).

After the ballet, we are in Woodland avenue, leading to Buttercup mead, where Boy Blue reveals he has paid the rent and Goody Two-Shoes is elected Queen of the May and they go off to join in Mayday Sports. In the next scene, the exterior of Goody Two-Shoes' cottage with a view of the village, Envy gets the Sparrow to kill Cock Robin and successively the fly, the fish, the beetle, linnet, owl, lark, rook and bull are all brought on stage. Goody is heartbroken, Tommy Green penitent and Fairy Good Nature appears to preach forgiveness and good will:

I am Good Nature, stranger not to you;
You have preserved me constantly in view.
Often has England felt my power in it,
And never more than at the present minute.
Whilst silent mills and smokeless chimneys stand,
And dire Distress stalks grimly through the land,
My impulse warm pervades each generous heart,
And all in aid have nobly done their part.

This is a reference to the distress caused by the 'cotton famine' of 1862 – due to the American Civil War.

She unites Goody and Boy Blue and to provide all plentiful employment, commands the clowns 'Make a Great Exhibition of enjoyment'. In place of the ordinary transformation scene, there was a 'beautiful view' of the interior of the 1862 International Exhibition at South Kensington. After this first scene, the clowns performed in the interior and exterior of the international lodging house, the shellfish shop, cobbler's stall and music warehouse, the Islington Agricultural and Great Dog Show, Cat Show and Flower Show, and the exterior of Marine Stores, Public House and Sailor's Home. Much of the humour was inspired by the overcrowding of London during the summer. It concluded with a tableau representing 'England's glory and riches brought by her ocean waves.'

There was praise from the critics for the scenery, particularly 'the Bramble Brake in the Depths of the Forest' and 'the Haunt of the Wood Nymphs' ('Magnificently painted', said the *I.L.N.* (3 January 1863)), the dancing of Lydia Thompson as Goody Two-Shoes, the ballets of Oscar Byrne and the comic business of the harlequinade. The *I.L.N.* (3 January 1863) concluded: 'Altogether this pantomime is a superior production, and equal to the best ever produced at the national theatre … the whole, indeed, was a brilliant triumph'. Blanchard netted £76 on the basis of a one pound royalty per night for the seventy-six nights of the run.[1]

As the connection with Sadler's Wells ended, Blanchard was engaged by Henry William Lindus, manager of the Princess' Theatre in Oxford Street, to provide the pantomime. Blanchard chose as his subject *Riquet with the Tuft or Harlequin and Mother Shipton*, the Perrault fairy tale as anglicized in *Mother Bunch's Fairy Tales*, and further anglicized it, with a dose of English folklore. So it opens with Mother Bunch visiting Mother Shipton at the Dropping Well of Knaresborough where two dozen birch brooms dance. The result of the meeting is a wager with Mother Bunch betting that Prince Riquet, who is extremely ugly but good and sensible, will secure an admirer before the beautiful but silly Princess Amouretta. Mother Shipton had presided at Amouretta's birth and Mother Bunch at Riquet's. Villagers seek to attack Mother Shipton; she petrifies them with water from the Dropping Well and the two old women escape on the same broomstick. They fly to the Mushroom Marsh on a misty morning where Mother Shipton animates the mushrooms and invokes the mushroom elves as her helpers. They move on to the Lake of Lilies where Mother Bunch enlists the fairies to assist her. King Rumbustical the Rampageous of Little Brittany, father of Amouretta, indicates that he will bestow her hand on the first worthy suitor to present himself. Three princes appear: the short and stout German Prince Mannikin of the Principality of High-Ho-Slackenbach, the tall and thin Oriental Prince Gogmagog, chief of Petty Tartary and Prince Riquet with the Tuft. The King is anxious to marry his daughter off 'Ere, by some revolution, off I'm carried. I have heard sometimes such things people do, Forswearing royalty in an Otho too; And ere this crisis comes, I wish my daughter to wed.' This is a reference to the forced abdication of the unpopular Bavarian King Otto of Greece in 1862. Although Riquet is ugly, Amouretta recognizes his voice as one she has heard in the enchanted wood promising her wisdom. Despite his looks, the Princess falls in love with him and gains wisdom. He gains beauty and they will be married. The wager between Mother Bunch and Mother Shipton is declared a draw. The characters are transported to the Bright Home of the Gossamer Fairy for the transformation to the harlequinade. The four scenes of the harlequinade take place in Green Park, Mr and Mrs Ticklebirch's Academy and the exterior and interior of an underground station, facilitating comic knockabout involving schoolboys, soldiers and railway staff and passengers.

The Times (27 December 1862) said: 'Around a plot so slender Mr Blanchard has contrived to twine some smart dialogue, unusually devoid though it is of those puns and that far-fetched play upon words with which modern burlesque bristles.' The show was enhanced by 'the grace of some tasteful scenery' by William Beverley and Frederick Lloyds. The *I.L.N.* (3 January 1863) called the pantomime 'one of the most elegant of the season, and an indubitably great success ... the scenery is charming ... the Burlesque scenes are cleverly acted ... the comic business is also good ... perfect in all its departments.' *The Era* (28 December 1862) praised the show in similar terms, singling out the scenery of Beverley, 'the illustrator *par excellence* of fairy scenery and humour', the ballet of the gossamer fairies, 'one of the prettiest we remember to have seen ... the simultaneous and graceful movements of the *corps* reflected the highest credit upon them' and the stage management 'so excellently arranged by Mr Robert Roxby: the machinery ... worked admirably, there not being a single delay or impediment in the scenery during the whole evening.' Blanchard noted in his diary: 'Kindly notices in all the papers of my pantomimes'.[2]

Blanchard went to see the Princess' pantomime on 2 January 1863 and recorded: 'Well pleased with pantomime; well played and beautifully put on the stage' and he noted there was 'very bad business going at all theatres except Drury.' But tragedy marked the pantomime. Blanchard recorded on 23 January that there had been a fire at the theatre and two ballet girls had been burned to death and Robert Roxby badly injured trying to douse the flames. He was never fully to recover and died on 25 July 1866 aged only fifty-seven as a result of the injuries he had sustained. On 5 February 1863 Blanchard recorded that he had written an account of the funeral of the 'poor little ballet girls' and had contributed to a subscription for their families.[3]

Falconer's second pantomime for Drury Lane saw the return of William Beverley to scene-painting duties, a return widely welcomed by the critics. Blanchard returned to the subject of his 1860 Sadler's Wells pantomime, Sindbad the Sailor, for

Harlequin Sindbad the Sailor or the Great Roc of the Diamond Valley but with an entirely new framing story.

The Times (28 December 1863) noted 'the good humour and the good manners of the vast multitude' which allowed the opening farce, *A Roland for an Oliver*, actually to be 'heard and understood without the slightest difficulty.' The only example of conflict was in the long interval between the farce and the pantomime when the 'gods' pelted the pit with orange peel. When the overture began, the 'gods' joined in the popular airs it comprised. 'But all the noise, musical or otherwise', ceased when the curtain slowly rose and revealed the Great Pyramid of Egypt.

The introductory scene was inspired by the recent discovery of the source of the Nile by Captain John Hanning Speke and Captain James Grant, an event which had caused great excitement in the press. Cheops, the founder of the Pyramids and representative of the glories of the Ancient world, wakes from a sleep of three thousand years and is shocked to learn from the Spirit of the Nile that the source of the river is about to be discovered by a stranger. Cheops resolves to arrest the progress of Young England, who appears in the costume of a rifleman. But this youth overcomes all obstacles, talking down the Spirit of the Past, a gentleman dressed in the costume of the Regency, solves the Riddle of the Sphinx and drives from the field wicked figures representing the Seven Wonders of the Ancient World. He duly discovers the source of the Nile, a victory for progress and discovery. From a mass of mountainous rocks with a cascade of real water, a troop of peris, 100 in all, descend. Some covered in giant palm leaves and others carrying blossoms, they form themselves up into one enormous flower, producing, according to *The Times*, 'a singularly beautiful effect, highly creditable to Mr [John] Cormack, the inventor of the ballet'. To amuse Young England, the Spirit of the Nile, who has fallen in love with him, tells him the story of Sindbad the Sailor.

Similar to the Sadler's Wells narrative, this version shows Sindbad, reduced by extravagance to hawking melons, at the seaport of Bassora. A fraudulent old merchant, Ali Ben Rumpling, who is shipping a cargo, refuses to help him. But the Spirit of Enterprise provides Sindbad with a rich cargo, which he ships on Ali's vessel. However, Ali steals the goods and Sindbad pursues him to the court of the Indian King El Elnee. He falls in love with Princess Ivora and is promised her hand if he will secure for the King the largest gem in the Valley of Diamonds.

Having entered the Valley of Diamonds and found himself unable to escape, Sindbad is helped by the fabled bird, the Roc. *The Times* reported: 'The huge creature with outspread wings descends from the top of the stage, takes the slim little mariner in its claws, and re-ascends triumphant. This feat is capitally managed.' The next scene is on the Isle of Pigmies where Sindbad becomes the prey of the Old Man of the Sea. Although he escapes from him, he is overpowered by pigmies and taken, with Ali, who has also been captured, to the Basaltic City of the Dwarf

Kingdom where a fire is kindled to cook Ali and Sindbad. But they are rescued by the Fairy of the Diamond in time for the transformation.

As usual Beverley received considerable praise. The *I.L.N.* (2 January 1864) declared 'the pantomime has been placed on the stage with a gorgeousness that far exceeded our previous experience. On every scene Mr Beverley has expended the prodigality of his art.' It was also recorded that the audience demanded Beverley's appearance to take a bow after the opening scene. *The Era* (27 December 1863) praised all aspects of the production, but went out of its way to compliment Blanchard: 'The author has done his work capitally ... and has handled the incidents dexterously and boldly, and has written the dialogue in a style that might not please Constantinople and Cairo, but which delights London, for which it is composed.'

But the surprise hit of the show was juvenile performer Percy Roselle, playing the Old Man of the Sea. *The Times* reported:

> Dramatically considered the incident of the little old man, who has almost acquired a proverbial celebrity as the symbol of an encumbrance, may be regarded as the best in the piece. Master Percy Roselle, who seems not to be above seven years of age, is a most extraordinary specimen of precocity, speaking with the utmost distinctness, and representing with terrible truth the inebriety which causes him to fall from the shoulders of his victims.

The *I.L.N.* endorsed this judgement, declaring: 'This lad's performance was a perfect gem, and will add greatly to the reputation of the pantomime. He was deservedly recalled to receive the congratulations of the audience, who were evidently astonished at so much histrionic skill in one so young.' So great was Roselle's impact that for the next four years the pantomimes would be scripted specifically to create star roles for him. Blanchard records a second cheque of £25 from Drury Lane on 15 February, suggesting a run of fifty nights for the pantomime.[4]

There was a second pantomime for the Princess' Theatre, now under the management of George Vining. This one was *Harlequin and Little Tom Tucker or The Fine Lady of Banbury-Cross and the Old Woman who lived in a Shoe and had so many children she did not know what to do*. It was attributed to the Brothers Grinn, the name concealing a collaboration between Blanchard and Greenwood. *The Times* (28 December 1863) called it 'one of the best pantomimes which has been placed on the London stage for years.'

> Its compiler seems to have laboured to undo much of what in late years has been accepted as essential to the fitting production of Christmas extravaganzas, and to revive pantomime as it existed, or is supposed to have existed, in the good old times when the heroes of the nursery were brought out on the stage, and the success of the piece depended much on the fidelity with which they realized the anticipations formed

concerning them ... To enlist as widely as possible the sympathies of children, for whom this pantomime was written, the authors calling themselves the Brothers Grimm [actually Grinn], have selected not one or two, but a whole dictionary of nursery rhymes and stories, and connected all the principal personages whose lives and actions they concern by an elaborate and fanciful pedigree.

This involved Little Tom Tucker becoming the eldest and favourite son of the Old Woman who Lived in a Shoe, and Mary, Mary, Quite Contrary, becoming the daughter of Old King Cole and identical with the Fine Lady riding a horse to Banbury Cross. The pantomime opens in Old Cocker's Cabinet of Calculation, where the audience is introduced to numbers, the value of holydays and favours bestowed by fairies on good boys and girls.

The story proper begins in the Shoe with Dame Tucker besieged by a regiment of ragged and hungry children who are fed on thin soup and beaten with a birch broom before being sent to bed. Tom, the eldest son, artist and musician, helps support the family and is allowed a later bedtime. He learns that Princess Mary, daughter of Old King Cole, has been carried off and imprisoned by Taffy, Welshman and Thief, who is depicted as a wild man of the woods with a mass of red hair. Tom resolves to rescue her. Tom makes his way to Taffy's retreat in the Land of Leeks and gains admittance by singing for his supper, finding the Princess held prisoner in an enchanted garden. A beautiful white charger has been provided by Tom's fairy friends to aid her escape but at the last moment, her contrary disposition asserts itself, she refuses to leave and Taffy rushes in to turn her to stone. Old King Cole mourns the loss of his daughter and is further afflicted by gout. Neither Zadkiellissimus or the fiddlers three can comfort him. News arrives that a statue resembling Mary on a fine horse has arrived at Banbury Cross and the King sets out to see it, recognizes it but cannot reanimate it. Tom succeeds in bringing her to life, Taffy is confounded and the transformation follows.

The enchanted garden was a particular success. *The Times* described it as 'a terrestrial Paradise' as 'one by one the "Silver bells of cockleshells and cowslips all of a row" gently raise their heads, and opening their foliage, disclose within the fairy guardians of the place.' But even this was eclipsed by the transformation scene.

It is a success which has not been hitherto achieved upon the stage, and as its full beauty grew upon the audience ... it awakened their enthusiasm to such a pitch that the artist Mr F. Lloyds was three times re-called, and in the last instance, in compliance with urgent demands, he appeared upon the stage hand in hand with the lessee, Mr George Vining. The scene may be said to consist of several parts. In the first, as the clouds slowly disperse, a lake illumined by moonlight is seen, to all appearance covering the stage. The water is real, flows in freely at the back and ripples gradually towards the front of the stage. All this is perfectly easy to see and to understand; but the astounding part is that the surface of the lake affords as brilliant a reflection as could be gained from a mirror. Nautilus shells float gracefully from side to side, and fairies reclining in them toy with the wave as it passes and throw up jets of water with their shells. Then the moonlight fades, and glow-worms and fairy lamps at the edge of the lake find their sparkle reflected in its surface. Finally, the whole character of the scene changes. The water remains, but groves of tropical verdure spring up on all sides, flowers and silver bells glitter on every branch, and shells, with what seems to be a fringe of diamonds drooping gradually forward, reveal the hiding place of the fairies. These mount and mount till in the background towers a monument of living figures, reflected like the rest in the lake below.

The Era (27 December 1863) called it 'as poetic and lovely a scene as we ever saw' and praised 'several beautiful pieces of scenery throughout the Pantomime', which were the work of Messrs Walter Hann, John Gray and A. Lloyds as well as Frederick Lloyds.

The Era said that the various nursery rhymes had been 'cleverly blended' in the opening and 'as a whole, nothing could be more successful than the entire prologue to the Pantomime'. The harlequinade was 'full of wit and rough humour', 'all the most important events of the year were happily ridiculed ... the tricks, though not particularly new, were effective and worked well.' *The Times* thought the harlequinade 'in every respect worthy of such an introduction.' For the Princess' Blanchard records a £10 advance from Lindus on 26 June on account for the pantomime and £16 'balance of pantomime' on 8 January 1864, £26 in all, suggesting a flat fee rather than a royalty. One puzzle is that he records that it is Lindus who is paying him even though he had been replaced in May 1863 by George Vining as lessee and manager.[5]

There was also a pantomime for Drury Lane's great rival, Covent Garden. On 13 August 1864 Blanchard met with the committee of the Royal English Opera House, Covent Garden, and agreed to provide the 1864 Christmas pantomime for a flat fee of £100, as the Brothers Grinn. This meant collaboration with Greenwood and they met by appointment at Covent Garden on 27 August and arranged with the manager Augustus Harris the subject of the show. Interestingly Blanchard notes that Harris is to have £20, presumably commission. He saw the show on 27 December and records 'transformation scene capital'. On 18 January 1865 he received a cheque from Covent Garden, noting his share as £65 and on 19 January he paid Harris his £20. This suggests that Greenwood only got £15, indicating perhaps a minor share of the writing.[6] The show was *Cinderella or Harlequin and the Magic Pumpkin and the Great Fairy of the Little Glass Slipper*. It opens with an argument in the Hobgoblin's Hermitage on the mountain top between two characters new to the story, the grumbling Hobgoblin and the good fairy Papillon who argue over the fate of Princes Ugolino, who is rich, fat, selfish, indifferent and lazy. Hobgoblin, himself a misanthrope and recluse, is determined that the Prince will never change. Fairy Papillon is determined that he will fall in love and be transformed by marriage. So a contest begins. The Prince, attended by his private tutor, Grimguffin, and a hawking party, loses his way in the wood, and conveniently strays into the Butterfly Haunt in the Dell of Delight where the fairy Papillon shows him, through a vision, the face and form of Cinderella reflected in a fountain. Instantly enamoured, the Prince orders a grand ball to take place at the palace, to which 'every woman in the world' is to be invited, in the hope of finding the vision. The invitation arrives at the home of Baron Pumpolino, who accepts on behalf of himself and his two eldest daughters Thisbe and Clorinda. Father and daughters ill-treat Cinderella. But the fairy Papillon arrives, and provides dress, coach, horses and attendants with the warning that they will all vanish at midnight. In the palace ballroom, the Prince recognizes Cinderella and pays her court. But Hobgoblin alters the clock, causing her to overstay her time and she flees in rags after her coach, horses and so on are turned back into pumpkin, lizards, rats and mice. But the Prince finds her slipper and uses it to track her down. Papillon is victorious. The two supernaturals then effect the transformation of the characters for the harlequinade, at the end of which Cinderella and a transformed Prince are united.

The Times (27 December 1864) recorded that the pantomime was a visual treat:

> Seldom has such splendour of scenery, costume and ballet, such elaboration of mechanical contrivance, been lavished upon a pantomimic burlesque. Mr Grieve, in the 'Butterfly haunt', as in the 'Fairy's Chronometer and Flight of the Hours' [the scenic prelude to the transformation], fairly surpasses himself; the first is as genuine a bit of scenic painting as the last is a marvel of ingenious construction and development.

Scene-painter Thomas Grieve was called after both scenes and took two bows, joined on the second occasion by Augustus Harris. *The Era* (1 January 1865) said:

> The crowning glories are, as usual, achieved by the union of scenic and ballet attractions. To begin with the ballet scene *par excellence*, nothing more exquisitely delicate and beautiful has ever been imagined than the Butterfly Haunt, painted by Mr T. Grieve. A calm and unruffled lake, finishing in flowery banks, occupies the breadth of the stage. From the surface rises an island, covered with delicate foliage, and showing the cliffs at the back. The enormous rock is pierced by two arched caverns, while to the left a distant and higher lake is seen, partly surrounded by mountains, and having a waterfall leaping down to the plain beneath. The wings of this lovely scene are formed by flowers and overhanging trees. A burst of long sustained applause greeted this specimen of Mr Grieve's imagination and skill ... As a Transformation Scene, the Flight of the Hours will bear comparison with all those gone before, at this or any other theatre. The stage has been, perhaps, seen more crowded with figures on former occasions, but as an

exquisitely designed final *tableau*, in which the necessary glitter is regulated by absolute purity of taste, this Flight of the Hours has probably never been excelled. The cover for the scene is a clock-face, taking up its whole width and height. The figures marking the hours disappear and in their place fairies are seen. After the total expanse of screen has sunk down, the stage is flooded with light, which falls upon large radiating fern leaves. On the tip of each leaf a fairy is placed in a reclining position, while others are grouped in the front, under golden palms.

The ballet scenes were praised unreservedly by *The Era*, though *The Times* thought they went on too long. However, the critic conceded that the ballet corps of the English Opera was 'used to excellent advantage', that the *Pas de Papillons* 'in which Mdlles Duchateau, Montero, and Bonifanti are conspicuous as principals ... is very pretty, and like its still more attractive successor, the *Pas Mythologique* (costumes à la Louis XIV), highly creditable to the taste and invention of M. Desplaces.' Also praised was the quick-fire change transforming Cinderella, pumpkin and animals.

The experienced pantomimists W.H. Payne and his son Fred Payne were singled out for praise by both *The Times* and *The Era*. *The Times* thought the comic business 'admirable', and the humour of W.H. Payne as Baron Pumpolino and Fred Payne as his head footman Pedro 'inimitable'. The comic scene of the Baron getting ready for the ball and the grotesque dance of Pedro the footman, which had to be encored, were both praised.

The harlequinade was, said *The Times*, 'short and excellent, the "business" being kept alive from first to last with unflagging spirit by, perhaps, as thoroughly efficient a pantomime quartet ... as could now be anywhere obtained.' The quartet were the brother Harry and Fred Payne, Mddle Esther and Paul Herring, who having played the Prince's Chamberlain, Squaretoso, assumed the role of Pantaloon in the harlequinade. The brothers Payne performed a séance after the manner of the spiritualist Davenport; and a juvenile imitator of popular tenor Sims Reeves, Master Edward Sanders, contributed a song. But the hit of the harlequinade was Senor Donato, a one-legged Spanish dancer, 'a real phenomenon in the fullest acceptation of the term'. Young, good looking and graceful, manipulating a shawl and castanets, he performed ten minutes of dazzling evolutions, returning to take his bow with his crutch. He was twice called back and vociferously cheered. *The Times* concluded:

There is a profuseness of splendour about the whole show which shows that no expense has been stopped at, and that the directors of the English Opera (limited) were fully bent upon giving their patrons a Christmas pantomime brilliant in all respects.

The Era agreed: 'Every accessory of the superb spectacle here is in the most perfect taste, and speaking generally of this splendid Christmas entertainment, it shows a lavish profusion which has not of later years been excelled.' It praised the script:

> The hilarious Brothers Grinn ... have supplied a burlesque opening written with the usual neatness and free from those parodies which are not always in the most irreproachable taste. The popular questions of the past year are pointedly alluded to; and without the slightest approach to vulgarity a few gentle reproaches are uttered to those who delay the coming of certain things which are to beautify London.

The reference here is to Landseer's four bronze lions for Trafalgar Square, not completed until 1867.

The 1864–5 pantomime for Drury Lane was devised specifically with Percy Roselle in mind. It was Hop O' My Thumb and His Eleven Brothers or Harlequin and the Ogre of the Seven League Boots. The story was one of Perrault's fairy tales, dating from 1687 and first translated into English in 1729. The pantomime opens in Cloudland where the witch Okriki supervises the making of the Seven League Boots for the Ogre Fee-Fo-Fum. They are tested by exposure to Hail, Frost, Rain and Snow and then delivered to the Ogre. The four winds raise a storm so that the Ogre, who is also a wrecker, may acquire treasure from wrecked ships. The Man in the Moon halts the storm and calls in the twelve signs of the Zodiac and several famous constellations to find a youth to punish the Ogre. Orion (pronounced O'Ryan and speaking with an Irish accent) recommends Hop O' My Thumb. The Man in the Moon descends to the Valley of Mosses and Lichens and enlists the help of the Sunbeams, one of whom enters the Ogre's castle to assume the form of one of his daughters. The Thumbs, father and mother, are so poor that they abandon their twelve children in the northern Pine Forest. The children find their way to the Ogre's castle where they are welcomed by the Ogre's twelve daughters, who hide them. While the Ogre is drunk, the brothers and sisters flee from the castle, going to the Snow Mountains and Icy Plains of the North; one of the Ogre's boots is stolen by Hop O' My Thumb and the Ogre chases him until he is rescued by the Sunbeams and this leads to the transformation scene.

The Times (27 December 1864) described Blanchard as 'a comic lyric poet of no small pretentions'. Again 'the inventive genius of Beverley' was praised, especially for his tableaux, the Valley of Mosses and Lichens at Daybreak and the transformation, 'The Ascent of the Rays of the Golden Light'. The ballets, choreographed by John Cormack, were admired, in particular an alphabetical ballet in which twenty-six young ladies stepped out of a Christmas book and formed themselves into different words. But again it was Percy Roselle who astonished the critics. The Era said that Hop O' My Thumb was played 'with infinite spirit by the clever Master Percy Roselle, who is an extraordinary actor for his size and age.' The I.L.N. (31 December

1864) called him 'a marvellous boy'. His performance evidently set the tone for the production, which, said *The Era*, included:

> a capitally designed juvenile scene ... in which the Pine Forest suddenly becomes peopled with kind and charitable little elves, who slide down to earth from the branches of trees, and after going through all kinds of quaint exercises, proclaim themselves friends of Hop O' My Thumb and his benighted brethren. The stage is full of these little figures, who turn head over heels all together, and lie flat on their faces with the oddest effect possible.

Blanchard saw a morning performance of *Hop O' My Thumb* at Drury Lane on 27 December 1864 and noted sourly 'As usual, not half the effects carried out.' He received £50 on account for the Perrault from Falconer and Chatterton on 14 January 1865. There is no further record of payment but he notes on 25 March, 'ninety-ninth and last night of Drury Lane pantomime', suggesting that on the royalty rate he was due £99.[7]

Blanchard alone supplied the pantomime for the Royal English Opera, Covent Garden, in 1865. It was *Aladdin and the Wonderful Lamp or Harlequin and the Flying Palace*. *The Times* (27 December 1865) pointed out that 'the brilliant success of the pantomime last Christmas raised expectations with regard to its actual successor not by any means easy to meet', particularly since the 'chief attraction' of *Cinderella*, the one-legged dancer Senor Donato, had died in the meantime. But the new pantomime was an 'unequivocal success', bringing together the talents of 'those incomparable pantomimists, the Messrs Payne, father and son'; Thomas Grieve and his 'clever son' Walford Grieve who designed and carried out the transformation; the 'gorgeous company of Terpsichoreans, whose evolutions, "poses" and glittering attire lent such *éclat* to the most conspicuous scenes of the pantomime last year'; W.H. Montgomery who composed and arranged the music; and 'the multifariously busy Mr E.L. Blanchard' who wrote the script. The critic concluded:

> On the whole the introductory burlesque, now invariably by far the most important part of our pantomimes, is in some respects even superior to that of last year – more marked in character, more varied in incident, more humorous in detail, and more splendid (though that was hardly possible) in *mise-en-scène*.

It opens in the abode of Abanazar, the African magician. Mr (Harry) Payne Sr played Abanazar as 'a semi-serious grotesque' and Mr (Fred) Payne Jr, his dumb slave Kazrac, as 'a hyper-comic grotesque individuality – both infinitely diverting.' Seeking an object which would make him all-powerful, Abanazar summons up an efreet, Bo Ghee, who tells him of a wonderful lamp in the mountains of Cathay which can only be secured by an innocent youth. In a street in Canton, Aladdin accidentally sees and falls in love with Princess Badroulbadour on her way to the Royal Baths. The princess' procession is accompanied by a grand ballet, with the three dancing stars of the Opera (Mdlles Duchateau, Montero and Pancaldi) with 100 ladies of the *corps de ballet*, all 'magnificently attired' in Chinese costume. They were grouped and placed 'with a skill and fancy to which M. Desplaces has long accustomed the frequenters of Covent Garden' in an elegant ballet that resembled a cross between Offenbach and Adolphe Adam. Abanazar and Kazrac turn up, the magician posing as Aladdin's long lost uncle, and Widow Ching-Ching allows her son Aladdin to accompany him. In the Cedar Valley of the Blue Mountain, the whereabouts of the Lamp is revealed by a magic ring. Aladdin enters through a cavern the garden of jewels and finds the lamp but drops it and Abanazar furiously pushes Kazrac in before the entrance closes. Kazrac joins forces with Aladdin. Aladdin rubs the ring and produces the Genius of the Ring who takes them to the garden of jewels where Aladdin collects a fortune in gems and thus arranges their escape. This scene also included a grand ballet of Jewels, by Mdlles Borelli and Carey with the ladies of the corps, 'quite as pretty and, with regard to costume, quite as characteristic, if not on so pretentious a scale, as the other'. The audience 'dazzled ... with the variegated and brilliant effect of the daintily personified precious stones' greeted the ballet with 'unanimous and hearty applause'.

In the next scene, Aladdin returns to his mother and gives her the lamp. Polishing it, she releases the Genius of the Lamp who asks for orders. Aladdin produces gifts for Badroulbadour's father and is accepted as son-in-law, and a palace for Aladdin is produced. Outside the new palace, the Princess trades the old lamp for a new one from a disguised Abanazar and the palace flies away with Abanazar and the Princess in it. Aladdin pursues and with the help of the Genius of the Ring, arrives in Africa in time to save the Princess from Abanazar, who is carried off by Bo Ghee. The Spirit of the Diamond appears to effect the transformation to the harlequinade, which consists only of three scenes, before the happy ending in Aladdin's home.

The Times was particularly impressed by the transformation scene, in which Mr Grieve 'by a most skilful combination of lights and colours, an artistic distribution of the various figures that give life and movement to his gradually unfolded picture, a mechanical contrivance as ingenious and an invention as ready as ever, has equalled any of his previous efforts in this way.' Grieve was called for by the house and emerged to receive 'the tribute of applause from all parts of the house'.

The Era (31 December 1865) declared the pantomime was put on the stage 'in a singularly perfect manner', thanks to stage manager W. West. It said Blanchard:

> treated the life of the Chinese *gamin* with such tact and good taste that the very old story of the very old lamp seems to possess quite a new interest. From Blanchard may be always expected polished versification, thoroughly adapted for the ears of children, and neither in the songs nor the dialogue of his Christmas productions is ever to be detected

the least deviation from the golden rule. In these days, when slang is frequently spoken, and coarse allusions often made in the ordinary course of burlesque, the utter discountenance of this literary vice certainly deserves the warmest acknowledgement.

The Era critic was dazzled by the sets, particularly the street in Canton, with its shops, archway, many-storied pagoda and enormous throng of extras in Chinese costume. Like *The Times*, *The Era* praised the series of 'intensely original dances and picturesque groupings' arranged by Desplaces, the theatre's ballet master, 'the most exquisite taste' in the choice of colours for the costumes and the costumes themselves: 'truly magnificent'. *The Era* described the transformation scene in the haunt of Bo Ghee:

> The 'Haunt' is represented by a thick screen of leaves, taking up the entire width and height of the stage … The leafy screen rises and discovers one brilliant figure standing on a golden ball in the centre of the stage. The strongest light is thrown upon this figure, which appears to float on the surface of a clear lake. The transparencies then sink from view, and discover what we must presume to be the bottom of the sea, but instead of finding it covered with 'dead men's bones', we see only every exquisite form of seaweed and coral. Long sprays then slowly rise from the bed of the sea, having nymphs of flesh and blood at the end of each. In the front of this beautiful scene enormous mussel shells open, and discover more living and breathing loveliness, while at the back rises Apollo in a car drawn by white horses. Phoebus continues his upward flight while the orchestra plays the time-honoured 'Glorious Apollo' and a flood of dazzling light is poured upon this splendid *tableau*.

The success of the show, however, turned to ashes as the English Opera Company went out of business and defaulted on the promised payment of £100 to Blanchard for his script. He had seen the show on 28 December 1865 and declared it 'splendidly got up'. But the loss of the £100 had a dramatic effect on his annual income. It had been £441.8s. in 1865 but at the end of 1866 he recorded his annual income as £289.[8]

The 1865–6 Drury Lane pantomime was *Little King Pippin or Harlequin Fortunatus and the Magic Purse and Wishing Cap*. The context of the production was one of improvement. *The Era* (31 December 1865) noted 'a marked advance has taken place of late years in the literary merit and artistic embellishment of these annuals, and this season it will be observed the characteristics to which we allude have been more than usually prominent' and it announced 'the complete success of all the novelties produced this Christmas'. It opined: 'In no other kingdom of the world is so much invention, thought, skill, talent and money expended in the entertainments for the people.' *The Times* (27 December 1865) noted:

19. *Blanchard began his pantomime career writing for the minor theatres – here the turnip army in* Harlequin Bluecap and the King of the Golden Waters *for the Surrey Theatre in 1851*

20. *For 11 years, Blanchard produced the pantomime for Sadler's Wells – here,* Harlequin and the Yellow Dwarf *in 1851*

21. *Blanchard pantomimes usually had a moral. In* Little King Pippin *(1865) it was an attack on the corrupting effect of avarice, highlighted in this scene in the Temple of Mammon*

22. *The pantomimes sometimes contained explicit political comment. In* Jack in the Box *(1873), the three ministers of King Cockalorum were made up to look like Gladstone, Disraeli and Home Secretary Robert Lowe*

23. *In his Drury Lane pantomimes Blanchard became one of the century's principal exponents of the classic fairy story – here, the giants in* Faw, Fee, Fo, Fum; or, Harlequin Jack the Giant Killer *(1867)*

24. *As the century wore on, and perhaps responding to British imperial expansion, orientalist settings and subjects became increasingly popular, as here in* Beauty and the Beast *(1869)*

It was as a pantomime house that Drury-lane recovered its ancient legitimacy – Mr E.T. Smith, when he became its manager, did not indeed effect much towards the revival of the poetical drama; but nevertheless by opening his theatre every Christmas for the production of the national entertainment on a large scale, he restored to it a character which it had lost, through all sorts of odd uses and abuses, and Messrs Falconer and Chatterton who have completed the rehabilitation of this old establishment, have not forgotten the basis on which they took their first footing. They spare no pains or cost to render their pantomime one of the grand sights of the season ... the state of the house last night, crowded by an audience assembled to witness the new pantomime ... bore ample testimony to the towering importance of Drury Lane as the seat of pantomime in Central London.

The critic also noted a new development:

Through the increased taste for music in modern times, the 'gods' have now a method of showing their sympathies, unknown not only to their fathers but even to their elder brothers. Every popular tune that occurred in the overture – and it was made up of little else – was accompanied by the galleries *en masse*, and while we record that the volume of sound was astounding, we are bound to add that the execution of the vocalists was precise.

Little King Pippin was based on a German folk tale of 1509, dramatized by Hans Sachs in 1553 and Thomas Dekker in 1600. It began, said *The Times*, 'as usual with Mr Blanchard ... with a moral allegory' which aimed to show 'that perfect happiness is by no means the necessary consequence of an ample fortune'. It opens in the temple of Mammon, where his votaries gather: a merchant with his ledger, a city speculator with his share list, a money-lender with his interest tables, a tradesman with a scroll inscribed with 'LARGE PROFITS AND QUICK RETURNS' and a contractor with a scroll inscribed 'WAGES GRIND, FORTUNE FIND'. They join in a chant:

Hear us! Mighty Mammon, pray,
Richer make us every day!
Every hour increase our store,
The more we have we want the more.

A loud clinking of money is heard, the votaries prostrate themselves before the shrine and Mammon rises and receives the petitions from his votaries:

Ha! Ha! they've offered up to me,
All that makes life agreeable, I see;
Love, Friendship, Truth, Hopes earthly and divine
All Sacrificed at Mammon's golden shrine

Fortune appears and denounces the power of money. But Mammon argues that money can bless as well as curse. Fortune asks for an inexhaustible magic purse, full of gold, to see what good money may do. Mammon grants Fortune's wish. The scene shifts to the Abode of Fancy on the Summit of Mount Olympus. Mammon and Fortune arrive and greet Agreeable Fancy. Mammon declares:

> Fancy doesn't pay –
> My speculations head another way.
> Whilst you are making jokes, I'm making p'unds
> Outbreaks of Fancy don't affect the Funds.
> Of your name in the Share List there no knowledge is.

Fancy replies:

> Yet I invented all the old mythologies,
> And I suspect your modern railway schemes,
> Are only formed of Fancy's wildest dreams.

Fancy is challenged with producing no results and claims substantial results:

> But for me all boys
> And girls would lose the greatest of their joys
> I tell them fairy legends – show each lad
> How the good prosper – how are served the bad.
> To me at Christmas time each heart rejoices,
> I hear it from a thousand silvery voices.
> Here are a few small children of my own
> That every schoolboy in his time hath known.

There then appears successively 'a series of personations ... as the Dykwynkian embodiments of Drury Lane Pantomimes', with masked figures as Masters Hudibras, Humming-top, Jack Horner, Robin Hood, Peter Wilkins, Sindbad, Hop O' My Thumb, Miss Margery-Daw and Little Goody Two-Shoes, a retrospective of the previous Blanchard pantomimes to date.

The purse is offered by Fortune to Fortunatus of Famagusta, a youth newly home from college, who finds his parents impoverished. He takes the purse to the court of King Pippin and uses the wealth to buy from the King a wishing-cap which will transport the wearer wherever he wants. The newly acquired wealth makes Pippin avaricious and tyrannical, and this provokes a revolution as the people seek to participate in the wealth. To escape Pippin and Fortunatus wish themselves a thousand miles away and end up in Flanders, where Fortunatus' parents have become servants of the Earl. The Earl of Flanders decrees a tournament to win the hand of his daughter Agrippina. Fortunatus wins but when the Earl discovers that his putative son-in-law is the child of servants, he forbids the marriage. Fortunatus wishes himself and Agrippina several miles above the earth where Fortune appears to pronounce the moral of the tale:

I've tried you with the purse; you've seen my lad,
Money is either a good thing, or bad,
According to the use that we apply it,
Whene'er again upon the earth you try it,
Remember this one line, to save verbosity,
Prudence should govern even generosity.
And now behold, whilst good advice bestowing,
How fancy sets the Wheel of Fortune going!
For this design we give to Beverly thanks,
Here you may draw all prizes and no blanks.

The Times reported: 'As in most modern pantomimes, the introduction is the most important part. It surpasses in magnificence every attempt made even at Drury Lane.' The transformation scene, The Fairy Factory of the Wheels of Fortune, was said to surpass all Beverley's previous achievements and provoked a storm of applause requiring Beverley to take a bow. *The Era* (31 December 1865) declared: 'Mr Blanchard's literary resources seem as inexhaustible as the purse of Fortunatus and if the prosaic times allowed rhymers to be crowned with bays by their admirers, he would be buried at once under a perfect forest of leaves.' Percy Roselle was the unquestioned star. *The Era* recorded: 'That extraordinary child-actor, Master Percy Roselle, gives a speech on covetousness with an earnestness and truth to nature nothing less than extraordinary.' Blanchard saw it on 27 December 1865 and records: 'Delighted with Percy Roselle; the other little things not done so well as they might have been.' He also records receiving three cheques for £25 each on 15 January, 6 February and 3 March and £20 on 7 April, settling the account for *King Pippin*: £95 in all.[9]

The 1866–7 Drury Lane pantomime was *Number Nip or Harlequin and the Gnome of the Giant Mountain*. It was the first pantomime produced under Chatterton's sole management. To create his plot Blanchard merged two German fairy tales, Johann Karl August Musäus' *Rübezahl*, the story of the 'Silesian Puck', and the Brothers Grimm's *The Cobbler and the Elves*.

Number Nip opens with some stringent comments on the state of theatrical taste. Scene One is the Retreat of Romance by sunset. Romance is discovered pensively reclining on a broken column in a statuesque attitude, attended by her favourite heroes and heroines of Romance: The Bleeding Nun, The Red Rover, Alonzo the Brave, The Mysterious Bandit, The Wood Demon, Sixteen-String Jack, the Red

Cross Knight, Lady Audley and their attendants. The chorus sing sadly that they are out of date and their stories excite jokes and jeers. Romance declares:

> My banished children – tho' I can't forget
> Romance is exiled – that her sun hath set –
> I love to think, when – like my Gallant Rover –
> You were all *hotly pressed* and 'Red' all over.
> Here let all mourn romance's lost domain

Burlesque arrives:

> 'Slap!' also 'Bang!' and likewise 'Here again!'
> I always use slang phrases of the day;
> Familiar I admit – but that's my way.
> I give myself – by way of notoriety –
> The easy airs of *Music Hall* society.
> 'I'm Costermonger Joe', the gallery's frantic,

There follows a lengthy exchange of puns between the two characters as Burlesque claims to be able to fill the theatres and to be over in an hour or so. Romance declares: 'Oh! Doctor Johnson, what wouldst *thou* have said?' *Johnson's Dictionary* is brought on and Mother Tongue emerges from it; she complains that Burlesque has tortured and distorted the English language shamefully. Burlesque replies:

> Well, I admit my faults; I know that yearly
> I have mocked at much men ought to value dearly,
> Nay, I have seemed to parody sometimes
> Life's purest poetry in doggerel rhymes.
> But this confessed, with promise to amend,
> I think your reprimand may fairly end.
> I've done the stage some service – and they know it –
> No more of that – but if, as says the poet,
> Unto my share some trivial errors fall,
> Seeing what supports me, you'll forgive them all.

Four ladies of the ballet come forward, each bearing a letter in front of her dress. The four form LEGE until the final letter is changed to S. The letters indicate the importance of the ballet to burlesque. The ballet ladies dance round to a familiar burlesque air, followed eagerly by the Heroes and Heroines of Romance. Romance laments this development but says, 'there's a day will come' and Mother Tongue proclaims the virtues of cheap editions of the classics.

It *has* come. See!
Dickens and Scott and Shakespeare! Glorious three!
The Poor Man's library, with treasures filling,
Sixpence for Scott! – all Shakespeare for a shilling,
With, just as cheap, the poets who have sung
The splendid triumphs of their Mother Tongue.

Romance and Burlesque agree to go into partnership as a Limited Liability Company. Mother Tongue summons the four quarters of the world to give their news. Europe talks of war between Austria and Italy, Asia says: 'India improves – no doubt you are well aware of it. A great possession! England should take care of it.' Africa says: 'Soon men like Burton, Barth and Baker, Won't leave me one uncultivated acre.' This refers to the activities of explorers Richard Burton, Samuel Baker and Heinrich Barth in mapping and claiming areas of 'darkest Africa'. America sings the praises of the Atlantic Cable. Then Young Australia intervenes:

I'm only in my infancy I know,
But Young Australia will a giant grow.
I speak your language. Englishman by Birth.

He promises to repay the instruction by the Mother Country with gold and corn, and Mother Tongue happily declares:

To make instruction pleasing to the ear
No tongue is like the mother one, my dear.

Europe, Asia, Africa, America and Young Australia each speak up in favour of themselves as the pantomime locale but Romance clings to the Rhine. So the story proper opens on the Willow Island of the Drachenfels in which the water fairies are assembled under their Queen Nymphalin. The Queen decides to intervene to quell the depredations of Number Nip, the shape-changing Gnome King, who vexes the Silesian peasantry. She will do this by ensuring his marriage. Her attendant Pipalee is sent to watch him and assumes the guise of a peasant girl working for Hans Hansel and Gammer Grethel. Prince Ratibon on his way to visit his fiancé is misdirected by Number Nip. Princess Carynthia of Silesia appears with six huntsmen. The huntsmen are frightened off by Number Nip, who woos the Princess in the guise of a ploughboy. Engaged by Hans, he terrifies the farm labourers, animates the turnips and carries off the Princess to his palace in the centre of the earth. Ratibon arrives and orders the labourers to attack the base of the mountains. In the Gnome King's palace Pipalee, now attending the Princess in the guise of Brinhilda, advises that the Gnome King is not a bad match and urges Number Nip to mend his ways, and in particular repair the damage done to Hansel who, ruined as a farmer, has become a cobbler. A troop of elves are sent to produce enough shoes to set Hans up successfully in this trade. Other acts of benevolence endear Number Nip to the peasants and he marries the Princess, who did not love Ratibon – the proposed marriage had been a state alliance. The grand transformation scene is 'Nuptials of Number Nip or wedding dowry for the Earth's Treasures'.

The critics heaped praise onto Beverley. For example, the *I.L.N.* (29 December 1866) found his 'Willow Island on the Drachenfels' 'remarkably beautiful' and the final transformation 'One of [his] most gorgeous efforts'.

Percy Roselle was once again the focus of attention. *The Era* reported, 'that clever little actor, Master Percy Roselle, is again the centre piece of the Christmas banquet, and as Number Nip performs with an ease, spirit, and a mock-regal dignity productive of infinite amusement. He sings, too, with perfect intonation, and once more takes the very juvenile lead in his own emphatic manner.' *The Times* (27 December 1866), paying tribute to the team which put the pantomime together (author Blanchard, artist Beverley, composer Tully, ballet-master Cormack, clown Boleno and mask-maker Dykwynkyn), declared: 'All the elements that make a Drury-lane pantomime, the great "fact" of the Christmas holydays are to be found in *Number Nip*' and the *I.L.N.* declared 'the success of the pantomime was throughout triumphant and for general harmony and effect the performance has never been equalled.' Blanchard, however, who saw *Number Nip* on 29 December 1866, confides to his diary 'I am disappointed as usual', but it came at the end of a 'year of unprecedented hard work and domestic worry' which may account for his mood.[10] Nothing is recorded about remuneration for the script.

The 1867–8 Drury Lane pantomime was *Faw, Fee, Fo, Fum; or, Harlequin Jack the Giant Killer*. *The Times* (27 December 1867) noted that although the two major theatres, Drury Lane and Covent Garden, were staging pantomimes, many West End theatres now ran straight plays at Christmas. But in the East End and the suburbs, pantomime reigned supreme, and 'a comparatively new feature in the history of English drama' was the spread of pantomime to the provinces.

Blanchard included in the story a role fashioned specifically for Percy Roselle, Pigwiggin, a character in Michael Drayton's 1627 fairy poem *Nymphidia*, a mischievous diminutive fairy who challenges King Oberon for the love of Queen Mab. The pantomime opens on the Giant's Causeway in Ireland by moonlight. Twelve leprechauns, armed with spades and glow-worm lamps, speaking in stage-Irish dialect, search for the magical four-leafed clover among the basaltic columns. They are interrupted by the arrival of giants of all nations, led by the Irish Giant, who agree that they will seize the land and cause evil to hold sway. At the Golden Garden of the Peerless Pool, the Fruit Fairies gather, headed by the chief Nectarine, are joined by the leprechauns and resolve to defeat the giants. The agents for this work will be Pigwiggin, a sort of Cornish Puck, and Ondine, the fairy of the Pool, who being governed by a law made on purpose for water nymphs, is found to become human whenever she touches land. She transforms herself into an English peasant boy. In a Cornish fishing village, Ondine finds Jack flying his kite. Jack, inspired by Ondine and falling in love with Adelgitha, daughter of the Duke of Cornwall, resolves to defeat the giants who now attack Cornwall. Aided by Pigwiggin, Jack acquires the sword of sharpness, the coat of darkness and the shoes of swiftness as magical aids. He catches the one-headed giant Cormorant by baiting a hook with a leg of mutton; encounters and slays the two-headed Blunderbore; and then seeks to tackle the three-headed Faw-Fee-Fo-Fum who has captured Adelgitha. He uses a series of stratagems to defeat the giant, tricking him into eviscerating himself. Jack finishes him off with his own club. The magic horn is blown, all other giants are destroyed, the castle walls shake, virtuous elves dance round the giant's body and Jack, revealed to be Prince Johannes, son of King Arthur, is united with the rescued Adelgitha. The ruins of the giant's castle, where the four-leaved clover has been found, dissolve into the Fairy Boudoir and all are made happy, the fairies rewarding Jack with a thousand costly jewels.

By 1867 *The Era* (27 December 1867) was according the Drury Lane pantomime classical status:

The name of 'Old Drury' has rendered the Pantomime classical. The glorious traditions of the Theatre have consecrated nonsense and given the stamp of legitimacy to a form of entertainment which, both in its parentage and nature, is decidedly illegitimate. If the Christmas pantomime, as it has been known for the last seventy years or so, had never been seen until Thursday night, we should have the critics exclaiming that pieces of this class are unworthy to be performed on the boards consecrated by the poetry of the divine Shakespeare. But see what time and custom can do in this conservative land of England. Time can pull down, but Time can also build up, and Time in his course has built up the Pantomime into an institution, as venerable as Magna Charta, as sacred as the 'Bill of Rights', as dearly cherished as Habeas Corpus. The Pantomime is considered as worthy of the boards of Old Drury as the works of Shakespeare himself. Indeed, Shakespeare, mighty magician as he is, could not make the theatrical ends meet without the Clown's string of sausages to eke them out. We have ventured to call the Pantomime 'nonsense'; let us hasten to add that it is the most innocent, the most amusing, the most enjoyable of nonsense. Old as well as young can enjoy it thoroughly, and the draughts of delight which we take in on Boxing Night leave neither headache nor heartache behind them.

The Era, noting that it was Blanchard's eighteenth pantomime for Drury Lane, marvelled:

After so many efforts we might expect him to flag a little, for writing a Pantomime is not so merry an employment as witnessing one; but, so far from this, Mr Blanchard has excelled many of his previous efforts. His work is, as usual, distinguished by much pleasant fancy, by pretty conceits, and by, occasionally, a vein of true poetic feeling. There is never anything coarse in Mr Blanchard's Pantomimes. He always writes for ladies and gentlemen, big and little, and he has the true man's faith, that these are to be found in the gallery, as well as in the boxes.

Blanchard records two payments of £25 for the pantomime (8 January and 13 February). But since it ran until 29 February (eighty-four nights in all) there will have been a third payment to complete the royalty.[11]

Faw, Fee, Fo, Fum marked the last Drury Lane pantomime appearance of Percy Roselle, who had been their undoubted star for the four years following his sensational debut as the Old Man of the Sea in *Harlequin Sindbad the Sailor* in 1863–4. His celebrity and the reaction to it is revealing about a key Victorian attitude. His career also throws up two mysteries: was he really a child or was he a dwarf/midget and what became of him?

There was a 'cult of the child' in the Victorian Age, or rather several cults. One was the idealized innocent, artless and spontaneous, as depicted in two of the dominant value systems of the nineteenth century, Romanticism and Evangelicalism. For Romantics, the child represented 'a pure point of origin deeply connected to the natural and primitive world and as yet unmired by the sullying forces of language, sexuality and society.' For Evangelicals children were not only to be instructed and disciplined but 'to be closely observed because they offered adults glimpses of an original heavenly purity.' Both value systems subscribed to a view of childhood as 'a paradise of innocence and purity'. Victorian books, poems and paintings are replete with such images and it is a view now conventionally associated with such writers as Charles Dickens, Lewis Carroll, J.M. Barrie and John Ruskin.[12]

But there was another form of appeal, particularly associated with stage children. This was precocity, the ability to successfully mimic adults, an appeal memorably satirized by Dickens in the character of 'the Infant Phenomenon' in *Nicholas Nickleby*. It was the dominant characteristic of child stars who flourished throughout the nineteenth century, the most celebrated being Master Betty (1791–1874), William Henry West Betty, dubbed 'the Infant Roscius' (after the celebrated Roman actor). He was a sensation in the early years of the century, playing such adult roles as Richard III and Shylock, and was the prototype of such performers. But quite apart from such stars, children were integral to the Victorian stage. There were all-child stage productions from the 1860s to the 1890s. There were plays with leading roles for children (twenty-two between 1887 and 1891 alone). Child sequences in pantomime were particularly prized. An estimated 10,000 children were employed during the pantomime season.[13] They were in demand to play small animals, flowers, elves and pixies as well as for dancing, marching and drilling sequences in which they were regularly described as 'Lilliputian' as they sought to mimic their elders. For some of the adult spectators in the audience there was also an undeniable erotic attraction to child performers both male and female.[14]

From the 1870s there was mounting concern about the health and safety of pantomime children and campaigns were mounted first by social reformer Ellen Barlee and later by Millicent Garrett Fawcett to secure legislative protection for stage children. The 1879 Children's Dangerous Performances Act banned the engagement of children under fourteen in stage business 'of a kind which would endanger life and limb'. The 1876 Education Act made attendance at elementary school compulsory between the ages of five and thirteen, though managements were rarely prosecuted before 1889, when the London School Board brought several prosecutions for the employment of school age children on the stage. One such led Oscar Barrett, manager of the Crystal Palace, to remove all children aged between five and thirteen from his pantomimes. In 1894 the Prevention of Cruelty to Children Act prohibited the employment of children under ten and regulated that of older children by licenses granted by police magistrates. The plight of child performers was addressed in detail by Ellen Barlee in her 1884 book *Pantomime Waifs*, for which the Evangelical reformer Lord Shaftesbury provided a thunderous preface declaring that the book highlighted the 'sources of mischief and suffering, affecting principally children, many of tender years, who, physically and morally, are in fact sacrificed for no purpose other than to administer to the pernicious amusements of the populace, high and low, in our great cities'.[15]

None of this legislation would have affected the career of Percy Roselle. It is possible to reconstruct part of it by reference to that of his sister Amy Roselle, who became a well-known actress and met a tragic end. Married to handsome leading man Arthur Dacre, she embarked with him on a tour of Australia which failed and left them in reduced circumstances. Depressed by the failure, Dacre shot his wife dead and cut his own throat on 16 November 1895. *The Theatre* magazine published an appreciative obituary.[16] It revealed that her real name was Hawkins and that she had been born in Glastonbury in 1854, had in childhood appeared on the stage with her brother Percy and was like him looked on as 'an infant prodigy'. Her father, a schoolmaster, was 'so far alive to the precocious intelligence of the two children that he gave up his profession and became a theatrical manager in their interests and his own – in the provinces, where they soon obtained a large following'. At sixteen, spotted acting in Exeter, she was recruited by E.H. Sothern to support him in the provinces and later at the Haymarket Theatre, making her West End debut in 1871. She later supported such leading actors as Samuel Phelps and William Creswick, becoming 'One of the most graceful and sympathetic actresses on the stage within the last quarter of a century'.

These details make sense of some of the references to Percy. The West Country connection would suggest the statement of *The Illustrated Sporting and Theatrical News* (21 November 1868) that Percy made his stage debut in Bristol in 1859 aged five has some validity. If the age is true, it would suggest a birth date of 1854, the same as Amy, but it is possible that several years were knocked off his age to emphasize his precocity – a common practice in the nineteenth century. *The Musical World* (2 January 1864) claims that he played the Old Man of the Sea 'very cleverly' as a child of five or six. That would give him a birth date of 1857 or 1858, again suggestive of tampering with the actual age. The father's role as manager makes sense of an entry in the diaries of Frederick Wilton, Stage Manager of the Britannia Theatre, Hoxton, which indicate that Percy was playing roles in straight plays and burlesques together with Amy in 1864 but that on 16 June 1864 Wilton told his father that his engagement would terminate next Saturday week.[17] Percy did not only play in pantomime. In 1865 and 1866 he was in the cast of *King John*, playing Prince Arthur to Samuel Phelps' King, and earning from playwright Andrew Halliday in *London Society* 9 (January 1866) the tribute that Percy was 'the only actor among them who touches nature.'

But rumours were beginning to circulate about his real age. Lewis Carroll went to see him in *Little King Pippin* and wrote in his diary on 17 January 1866 that it was 'the most beautiful spectacle I ever saw in Pantomime. Percy Roselle's acting is quite the gem of the whole thing', but adding 'Miss [Kate] Terry tells me he is 18 or 19; he looks about 8'. But Carroll was so enchanted by him that he wanted to write a play for him; it never eventuated.[18] Playwright George R. Sims in his 1917 autobiography stated flatly the Percy was 'a dwarf and played children's parts in the Drury Lane pantomimes as "Master Percy Roselle" after he had come to man's estate.'[19] However, a review in *The Athenaeum* (22 February 1868), of a book on dwarfs and giants, referred to the current pantomime *Jack the Giant Killer* at Drury Lane, in which Joseph Irving was playing Jack. The review said that the role had doubtless been intended for Percy Roselle but implied that his voice had broken, making him unsuitable for it. This suggests that he was in 1868 still in his teens. The *I.L.N.* (28 December 1872) reported that the Christmas Pantomime at the Pavilion Theatre, Mile End, was *Harlequin Hop O' My Thumb* by Frederick Marchant and was:

> produced on a scale of great splendour. One of the most important engagements made is that of Percy Roselle, for some years the hero of Drury-Lane pantomimes, who here makes his first appearance in England since his successful tour in the United States.

His sister Amy had been touring the USA in 1871–2 and Percy is recorded as making his New York debut on 30 October 1871 in the title role of *The Boy Detective* at

Wood's Museum and Menagerie. He was announced as being 'only fifteen years of age'.[20] *The Era* (29 December 1872) reported: 'Master Percy Roselle long since won his laurels at Drury-lane, and now at the East, as well as the West, he has been received with the enthusiasm to which he is undoubtedly entitled by his unmistakable merit.'

There is no further reference to him after 1872. No obituary has been found. But there is no denying his impact in his brief heyday. He was still remembered as a juvenile star in an *Era* article (5 January 1895) surveying 'Pantomimists of Other Days', and in his 1920 autobiography *A Playgoer's Memory*, the critic H.G. Hibbert called Percy 'The Master Betty of his Day'.[21] This all suggests that he had no adult career and, dwarf or not, never made the transition from juvenile roles.

The Drury Lane pantomime for 1868–9 was *Grimalkin the Great or Harlequin Puss in Boots and the Miller's Son* which *The Era* (3 January 1869) thought 'the best Pantomime that Old Drury has offered its patrons for many years past.' Its attractions were:

> a fanciful story fancifully treated by Mr E.L. Blanchard, Fairy scenery from the artistic and graceful pencil of Mr William Beverley, lively music from the score of Mr W.C. Levey, gorgeous, elegant and fantastic dresses from the designs of Mr William Brunton, artistic groups and characteristic dances arranged by Mr Cormack, and a variety of practical comicalities invented and carried into execution by Mr Harry Boleno and Mr C. Lauri.

The Times (28 December 1868) pointed out that 'it is the principle of the genial author always to point his tale with a moral, set forth in that prefatory allegory which in modern times has been regularly established as a new introduction ... to the pantomime'. But the critic worried that the moral to be taken away from the story might be a belief in fraud. *The Era* identified the moral as being the need to show kindness to animals. Many years later Bruno Bettelheim pointed out that the moral of *Puss in Boots* is 'even the meekest can succeed in life'.[22]

In fact, Blanchard began the pantomime with an allegorical encomium on industry. As *The Times* reported:

> When the curtain ascends, our eyes are at once feasted with the view of the interior of a beehive, the bee from time immemorial having been regarded as the type of industry, and a knowledge of this fact having been universally diffused even among the least cultivated of our countrymen by the muse of Dr Watts.

Isaac Watts (1674–1748) was remembered as the author of *Divine Songs for Children* (1715), containing many celebrated aphorisms, among them 'How doth the little busy bee/Improve each shining hour/And gather honey all the day/From every opening flower.'

The interior of the hive contained enormous honeycombs and the bees were played by children. A bluebottle fly, type of an idle vagrant, is captured by the bees and tells the Queen Bee, Hymenoptra, about the miller's sons. The eldest two plan to destroy the beehive to lay hands on the honey. But Jocelyn, the youngest, 'would not hurt a fly.' The Queen orders the wicked brothers punished and the good brother rewarded.

In the story proper, the miller of Normandy has died and in his will left the mill to his eldest son Richard 'the glumpy' and the donkey to his second son, Robin 'the greedy'. The cat Grimalkin is left to the youngest son, Jocelyn 'the kind'. Jocelyn saves the beehive from destruction by his brothers and is given by the bees a cake. He feeds it to the cat who acquires thereby the powers of speech and reason. The brothers try to kill Jocelyn but he is rescued by Puss and escapes. The bees sting the brothers.

The cat persuades Philip the Podgy, King of Little Bretagne, that Jocelyn is the Marquis of Carabas and lives in a castle actually occupied by the magician Hankipanki. Puss tricks the magician into a series of transformations (lion, girl of the period, fast young gentleman) culminating in a mouse, which the cat then eats. Jocelyn becomes master of the castle and husband of Princess Rose D'Amour. The transformation takes place in the Glittering Web of Golden Gossamers.

A novelty introduced by Blanchard was a satire on the sensation scene in Boucicault's 1868 hit play *After Dark*, in which the heroine was tied to the railway track and rescued by the hero in the nick of time. In the pantomime Jocelyn, drugged by his brothers with an opiate contained in a peppermint lozenge, is laid across the tramway used for conveying the miller's trucks laden with sacks of flour. He is rescued by Puss in the nick of time and, said *The Times*, 'the same applause is excited as when the existence of the lady or gentleman is menaced in more serious dramas.' Intriguingly there was no sign of Percy Roselle, whose era of dominance at Drury Lane was now at an end. Grimalkin was played by Joseph Irving, who had played Jack in *Jack the Giant Killer* and now, said *The Era*, 'imitates the actions of a cat with amusing felicity'. Blanchard received only £54.10s. apparently (£25 on 8 January, £20 on 25 February and £9.10 on 15 April), suggesting a shorter run for the pantomime than usual, unless he omitted details of a further payment from the diary.[23]

For the pantomime of 1869–70 Blanchard chose *Beauty and the Beast or Harlequin and Old Mother Bunch*. It was, said *The Times* (28 December 1869), 'tremendously wellknown … But it derives its novelty from Mr Blanchard's ingenious treatment'. Blanchard merged the familiar story with Thomas Moore's *Paradise and the Peri* to create his narrative. It was the first Drury Lane pantomime to feature the Vokes Family, who were to become a fixture at Drury Lane under the Chatterton management.

The Vokes Family was recalled as 'distinguished and unique' among theatrical families by critic H.G. Hibbert.[24] Fred Vokes (1846–88) was the star of the family. Making his debut at the age of eight, Fred was taught dancing by Flexmore, the clown successor of Grimaldi, and became a leading eccentric dancer. Fred was joined on the stage by his three sisters, Jessie (1851–84), who took care of the troupe's business affairs, Victoria (1853–94) and Rosina (1854–94). They first teamed up as the Vokes Family in 1861 in Edinburgh and made their pantomime debut in *Humpty Dumpty* at the Lyceum Theatre in 1868–9. But in 1869–70 they moved to Drury Lane and remained there for ten years, missing only the pantomime *Jack in the Box* (1873–4) when they were on tour in America. Under the influence of the Vokeses, dance became a predominant element in the pantomime and the fairy tale element took precedence over the comedy.

In *Beauty and the Beast*, the curtain rises on Mother Bunch's 'juvenile depository' for the sale of toys and story books where a small boy is telling his chums a fairy story. A dispute arises on the subject, Mother Bunch makes her appearance and, as a representative of the good old times, sings a song in honour of the good old nursery lore. To give her young friends a treat, Mother Bunch summons a flight of ladybirds. One of them, assuming a human form, promises to afford them ample amusement. The children gone, Old Custom rises in a Snapdragon Car, complaining that he is banished from his native land. He summons his henchmen, Twelfth Cake, Valentine, Shrove Tuesday, Oyster Grotto, Guy Fawkes and Dunmow Flitch. Old Custom complains that they are now outmoded and overlooked but Mother Bunch promises to take care of them, while hailing the embodiments of modern improvement who now appear; the Thames Embankment, Holborn Viaduct, Blackfriars Bridge, the Thames Tunnel, the Electric Telegraph ('now purchased by the nation') and the newly opened Suez Canal. This last gives them the location for the pantomime – the East.

The pantomime opens in the Vale of Cashmere where Azalea the peri is expelled for the sin of disobedience. She appeals in vain against her expulsion to the principal peri and the sisterhood but they lecture her on her sin. Hope, the Spirit of the Rainbow appears, and sings to her that she may find goodness on earth and that will alleviate her condition, and she sets off for earth in better spirits.

The story proper has the merchant Ali take his leave of his three daughters in a caravanserai on the borders of the Persian desert. He asks his three daughters, Lankinella, Fatima and Zemira, nicknamed Beauty, what presents they would like. The eldest two ask for exorbitant gifts: a handsome dress for Lankinella and jewels for Fatima; Zemira asks only for a rose. Ali and his servant Scanderino are set on by robbers in the Forest of Apes but the robbers are frightened off and the victims hospitably received by the monkeys. Ali plucks a rose from the garden of the palace of Prince Azor, the Beast, who is all black, with the legs and body of a man, the head of a gorilla and the mane of a lion. He threatens to kill Ali unless Beauty takes his place at Azor's Palace. She does, Azalea accompanying her as a servant. Instead of revulsion, she expresses love for Azor who is transformed into his own shape and united with Zemira. For having helped accomplish this, Azalea is pardoned and resumes her place among the sisterhood of peris in the Fortunate Islands for the final transformation.

The Era described the ballet of the peris with Jessie Vokes as the Principal Peri:

> The dresses are most elegant, and in the matter of colour are in perfect accord with their surroundings. A good effect is produced by light blue veils, which fall over the blue and gold skirts, ornamented with the roses of Cashmere. Every coryphée carries in her hand a small spray of gilded leaves, and those are made good use of in the groupings, which precede and follow Miss Jessie Vokes' solos. The Drury-lane corps is very numerous, and the dances throughout the Pantomime are the invention of Mr John Cormack, a ballet master with few equals. The *Pas Seul* of Miss Jessie Vokes is well received, as it unquestionably deserves to be, for the young lady has already won her way to the topmost height in her Profession. At the close of the scene the whole of the ballet ladies form a group at the back, and the climax of brilliancy is reached when the lime-light is thrown on the dresses and the glistening sprays.

Rosina Vokes played Fatima and Victoria Vokes, Zemira. *The Era* said:

> Anything more charming than Miss Victoria's appearance in her green satin dress, her white satin Turkish continuations, and her strings of pearl ornaments, it would be difficult to conceive. She not only looks uncommonly pretty, but dances with remarkable vivacity, and has an admirable idea of burlesque acting – not in coarse and sensuous form, but on its higher and worthier ground.

W. Fawdon Vokes played Scanderino the valet and Fred Vokes, Prince Azor.

> The Forest of Apes, in which Ali and Scanderino are set upon by thieves, is one of the great effects of the Opening. At first the stage is almost unoccupied, but gradually the trees with their branches growing into the earth literally swarm with monkies. The robbers are frightened away, and Ali and Scanderino are in an abject state of fear. The apes are led by a superior animal, a baboon, personated with great spirit by Mr Mitchenson. A more diverting scene than this we do not remember to have seen in any of the preceding Pantomimes at Drury-lane.

In Azor's Palace:

> a singularly original and pleasing ballet is performed. The Persians, richly dressed, enter, carrying fans of ostrich feathers and dance to a very melodious and graceful specimen of the 'Mazurka', composed by Mr W.C. Levey. The adult persons of the feminine gender

are followed by a number of juveniles. The second and third beat of every bar are struck on two bells fixed to the fans, and the effect is delicate and pretty beyond description.

Also showcased were the dancing talents of Fred Vokes. *The Era* said: 'In his own peculiar line he stands alone. His marvellously lithesome manner is something to notice, and Mr F. Vokes constantly gives the idea that he is about to kick his legs into the pit.' With Scanderino, he did a comic shadow dance, each of them doing precisely the same steps. After the uniting of the Prince and Beauty, he, Beauty and Fatima join in a Dance of Exultation. Blanchard received £55 from Chatterton for the pantomime, which closed on 26 February: £25 on 29 December, £25 on 29 January and £5 on 1 March.[25]

The Drury Lane pantomime for 1870–1 was *The Dragon of Wantley or Harlequin and Old Mother Shipton*. *The Era* (1 January 1871) began its review with an encomium on the production personnel:

Mr F.B. Chatterton still continues the 'monarch of all he surveys', the happy Proprietor of our finest London theatre. He is still assisted in his Christmas councils by Mr E.L. Blanchard, that popular king of Pantomime, who becomes younger as he grows older, who writes better the more he writes, and who is a happy example of refinement and simplicity of heart in these somewhat rowdy and certainly very *blasé* days. Mr Beverly remains faithful at his post inventing new harmonies of colour, rearranging and twisting as in a kaleidoscope old effects, and making the most of the fine stage which he has so often peopled with fairies, and on which he has placed so many brilliant spectacles. Mr Cormack, most ingenious and indefatigable of ballet masters, is ready still with his inventive genius, and shows how novelty in art is as inexhaustible as change of harmony. And Mr Edward Stirling passes his practised eye over the suggestions of all these artists, improving here and making additions there, devoting untiring energy and unflagging zeal to the extremely difficult task of superintending such a large establishment. The music is still safe in the hands of Mr W.C. Levey, most melodious of composers, under whose presidency a well-trained orchestra adds spirit and life to the holiday entertainment.

It was noticed that 'a certain melancholy and depressed feeling' prevailed in the house on Boxing Day and this resulted in a more subdued and decorous reaction than usual to the show. The implication is that this was a result of concern raised by the Franco-Prussian War, with the emperor Napoleon III defeated and captured and Paris awaiting attack. The British had contributed £300,000 towards the relief of the sick and wounded of the conflict. There was considerable sympathy with the plight of the besieged and starving Parisians. The programme opened with a farce 'Rule Britannia', and this was greeted with unwonted decorum and attention. 'It was not a Boxing Day as of old'; everyone seemed to be on their best behaviour.

The source of the pantomime was *The Dragon of Wantley*, a traditional ballad first printed in 1685 and collected in Percy's *Reliques*. It tells of the gallant knight, Moore of Moore Hall, who having acquired new armour in Sheffield, kills a dragon that has been terrorizing the area around Rotherham. There was a sixteenth-century More family at More Hall in Wortley (obviously corrupted into Wantley); Sheffield was known for making armour; and a cave near Wharncliffe was known from the early eighteenth century as the Dragon's Den. Henry Carey turned the story into a burlesque opera in 1737 at Covent Garden. There was a burletta of *The Dragon of Wantley* at the Royal Circus in 1807 and pantomime on the subject in 1824 at Covent Garden and in 1849 at Sadler's Wells. It was evidently the war which lay behind Blanchard's choice of subject.

The pantomime opens in the workshop of time where Old Father Time, standing in front of a huge clock and consulting the Day-Book for 1871, debates the nature of time with Love, who reprimands him for producing the current war. ('Love's much more nice and equally exciting'.) Britannia appears to support Love ('with Love to help us, we tried all we knew to heal the many wounds produced by you') and to report that five of her counties, Yorkshire, Lancashire, Hampshire, Rutland and Kent are struggling for precedence. Yorkshire is called upon to prove its claim.

The scene changes to the Haunt of the Water Nymphs where the personified rivers of England gather to celebrate the marriage of the Thames and the Medway. It was, says *The Times* (27 December 1870), 'one of those delicious, dreamy combinations of sparkling lake and light foliage, whereby Mr W. Beverley has gained his high reputation'. The nymph Crystilla sings 'a charming rippling song, a graceful specimen of Mr Blanchard's poetical powers, tenderly set to music by Mr Levey.' This is followed by the first of the ballets. *The Era* reported:

> Nothing could well be in better taste. The dresses of the young ladies are made to imitate river flowers, and they carry in their hands gold bulrushes with emerald green stems. The groupings, aided by a brilliant lime-light, are quite dazzling.

The scene changes to Mother Shipton's dwelling at the Dropping Well. Mother Shipton has been urged by the villages to prophesy but they dislike her predictions and prepare to attack her as a witch. But the gallant and impoverished knight, Moore of Moore Hall, arrives to prevent her being ill-treated and thus secures her friendship. He needs her help because he is in love with Lady Joan, daughter of the Baron of Wantley, as his squire Jingo is with her maid, Miss Madge. Sir Guy the Grim, Lady Joan's guardian, returns from hunting. He proposes marriage to Lady Joan, in order to get his hands on the estates, but she refuses him. Moore presses his suit but she remains undecided. Mother Shipton prophesies the appearance of a dragon. The scene ends with a 'spirited break-down, danced to perfection by the Vokeses and the rest of the company.'

Scene Four, which 'will be talked of ere long in a thousand nurseries', was the customary Drury Lane scene entirely performed by children. This time it was the farmyard and the village of Wantley at sunrise, where Dame Durden calls up her serving men. It is 'one of those grotesque exhibitions of rural life which are always popular in pantomime,' said *The Times*. *The Era* described it:

The whole of the daily work in a farmyard is shown with pantomime action by the children. The cock crows – the early village one; the dog barks at being disturbed in his slumbers. Soon all is activity. The maids pass along with their milking pails, the men reaping and shoe their horses, unload the wagons, blow the bellows, carry 'grist to the mill', and set to work at tailoring. The pedlar is pestered by the girls; a wedding party arrives, and the day ends up with a harvest-home jollification. A clog dance, invented by Mr Cormack, and danced to perfection by the youngsters, is interrupted by a frightful apparition. The Dragon of Wantley appears on the top of a hill snorting out fire and flapping his hideous wings. The villagers rush off paralysed with fright.

Outside Moore Hall, Sir Guy urges Mother Shipton to conjure the dragon away but she will not, predicting that the slayer of the monster is destined to marry Lady Joan. The cowardly Sir Guy leaves the task to Moore, to whom the people appeal for help and who is equipped by Mother Shipton with a suit of spiked armour, made of Sheffield blades.

In Scene Six, the Dragon's Glen, the Dragon sleeps protected by the witch Sybilla. Mother Shipton puts her to flight and Moore kills the dragon, presenting its head and tail to Lady Joan who accepts his hand in marriage. 'Thus from all dangers be our country freed, by England's heroes in our time of need,' says Mother Shipton. The nuptials are celebrated in the transformation scene, the World of Waters. 'This is a gorgeous spectacle in Mr Beverly's very best style. Britannia on a golden throne, surrounded by golden and silvern attendants. The whole stage is one blaze of dazzling light.' Britannia, noting that all rivers lead to the sea, our national destiny, declares:

Soon let us hope all wicked war will cease
I bind all over to preserve the Peace.

The Era reported: 'Mr Beverly is, of course, summoned on to the stage, and cheered enthusiastically.' It concluded: 'Mr Blanchard never did better work. It is really a treat to come across so much grace and sweetness. This seems to us a model of a Fairy Opening.'

The Vokes Family starred, Fred as Moore, Fawdon as Jingo, Victoria as Lady Joan, Rosina as Miss Madge. *The Era* reported:

We find the famous Vokes family brighter and more irresistible than ever. Mr Frederick is here as exhilarating as champagne, and as light as the cork. Mr Fawdon accompanies him as the Squire, and shows what a true Pantomimist he is; Miss Victoria, who has shown herself this season to be a high-class dramatic artist, plays burlesque as it ought to be played, Miss Rosina is the most fascinating of soubrettes, and Miss Jessie leads the dancing with delightful grace.

The Times declared:

> We have no hesitation in declaring that the *Dragon of Wantley* is one of the best and most amusing pantomimes that have been seen for many years. The story is told in a brisk, lively manner, without any of those drags that often so heavily retard the flight of fancy. And all praise should be given to the Vokes family, who, numerous as they are clever, fill nearly every part in the introduction.

Blanchard received from Chatterton two payments of £50, thus £100 in all (30 December and 2 March).[26]

The 1871–2 Drury Lane pantomime was *Tom Thumb the Great or Harlequin King Arthur and the Knights of the Round Table*. It was the year in which the Prince of Wales had nearly died from typhoid fever and had made a miraculous recovery. Both *The Era* (31 December 1871) and *The Times* (27 December 1871) noted that this provoked outbursts of patriotic sentiment. *The Era* reported:

> The enthusiasm with which the holiday people echoed back the orchestral strain of 'God Bless the Prince of Wales' was everywhere noticeable, and these fervent ebullitions of loyalty might be confidently referred to as a genuine assurance of attachment to the Throne, and as a proof of the deep sympathy felt among all classes for the illustrious patient whose illness caused such great anxiety to every member of the Royal family.

In its review of *Tom Thumb*, *The Times* noted that on Boxing Day it had been repeated three times by popular demand and *The Era* ended with 'At every performance this week the music of "God Bless the Prince of Wales", given by Mr W. C. Levey after the overture, has created a wonderful demonstration of loyalty.' *The Times* included a report headed 'East End audiences and the Prince of Wales' arguing that working-class East End audiences were a good test of loyalty to the throne and that it was frequently asserted that they had 'conceived a permanent dislike to the established order of things' and veered towards Republicanism. But at the Pavilion and the Standard when 'God Bless the Prince of Wales' was played: 'At the former, the audience rose up, comported itself respectfully, and, at the end, cheered heartily; at the latter, the sibillation of a few malcontents in the gallery was quickly drowned in a general shower of applause.'

The Era used the occasion for an encomium on Blanchard:

> Age does not stale nor custom wither the infinite variety of our Christmas poet. He puts in other hands the enchanter's wand, and out of his imagination pour Fairies, Will o'the

Wisps, Sprites, and all the Spirit-world of Christmas-time, but he is, indeed, the enchanter, for he possesses the singular art of never repeating himself, and, on the contrary, of making each year's Pantomime superior to the last. For twenty-two years this magician, this Father Christmas, has wreathed us in smiles and pelted us with the toys of his fancy, and looking back at this almost complete slice of a century, he would be a clever man who could wander through the long list and select one of the number which so admirably suits its purpose as the Christmas Annual for 1871, called TOM THUMB THE GREAT... This is emphatically a Pantomime for children – the children so loved by the author, who crowd about him at Christmas-time, and rifle his pockets of all the good things he has hoarded up for them. It flows over with loving-kindness and that particular delicate and pure fancy which suits the innocence of childhood, and is so esteemed by those of a larger growth who would imitate childhood's simplicity. ... Elsewhere the purely comic business may be sacrificed for the glitter of pure extravaganza, and the entertainment may be overladen with costly magnificence; but here, at old Drury, combined with most welcome glitter are found the very effects which children most love. How the little ones will chatter about the great Dolls' house in action! An original and charming effect; and then for months to come we shall hear nothing but descriptions of how the old cow swallowed the Boy – how he was tumbled into the gaping mouth of giant Blunderbore, returned into a convenient moat, and finally taken to King Arthur's court in a monstrous Salmon. Add to these effects the mischievous schoolboys who bully old Gaffer and Goody, the frequent dances and songs, and finally, the superb pantomimic art of the Vokes Family ... and we have at once a Pantomime which can have no rival.

The story of *Tom Thumb* is an old one, first printed in 1621 but believed to be much older. Despite the script's references to Alfred Tennyson's *Idylls of the King*, the principal inspiration for the pantomime was the old story itself with some assistance from Henry Fielding's satirical comedy *The Tragedy of Tragedies or The Life and Death of Tom Thumb the Great* (1731), from which Blanchard borrowed the character of Queen Dollallola.

In Blanchard's version Dollallola is not the queen of King Arthur but the Queen of Lowther Arcadia, a reference to the upmarket shopping venue in Victorian London. She presides over a doll's house which is inhabited by every kind of contemporary doll: tin soldier, wooden drummer, Chinese tumbler, rocking horse, characters from the toy theatre drama *The Miller and his Men*, Jack in the Box, Black Sal and speaking dolls, Light Hair, Dark Hair, Soft Hair, Blue Eyes, Hazel Eyes and Pretty Face. As the clock strikes midnight they come to life to complain about their maltreatment at the hands of the children. They resolve to divert their infant owners from their toys by summoning up for them the image of a pantomime to engage their attention. Then in the Garden of Dainty Devices, the Enchantress La Faye summons the spirits of music, poetry, painting and dancing to discuss the subject of the pantomime. They decide to do a story set in King Arthur's time because Poetry has covered it with Tennyson's *Idylls of the King*, Purcell has done it in music, Painting has 'illustrated everything he did' and Dancing is confident of creating an appropriate ballet. 'The design of this scene is exceedingly pretty,' said *The Daily News* (27 December 1871), 'it is the vivification of the daintiest china shepherdess that ever graced a drawing room side table.'

The pantomime proper begins in the cottage of Gaffer and Goody Thumb who, tormented by mischievous schoolboys, wish for a child no bigger than a thumb. The magician Merlin, passing by, grants their wish and Tom Thumb appears but soon disappears. He accidentally falls into a pudding being made by Goody Thumb, is tied up in a pudding bag and consigned to the saucepan. He performs such gyrations in the bag that a terrified Goody Thumb gives the pudding away to a tinker. King Arthur and his knights call at the cottage and Merlin tells of an ancient legend that the King of Britain must abandon his life of pleasure and search for a small child who will act as his friend and guide, lest he lose his kingdom. In a village near the giant's castle the tinker, alarmed by the animation of the pudding, drops his bag and flees. Tom emerges, to be successively swallowed and disgorged by cow, crow, giant and salmon, until he is knighted by King Arthur. But in an addition to the story, the King becomes jealous of the attachment of Princess Guinevere to Tom and sends him at the head of an army to fight the Anglo-Saxons, hoping he will be killed. In a topical reference to the 1871 Cardwell army reforms that abolished the purchase of rank, Tom announces that promotion in the army will be by merit. However, Tom and Arthur are reconciled when Tom claims not to be the marrying kind and unites Arthur and Guinevere. Finally in the Druid's Temple Merlin uses an elixir to reduce his age to twenty-one and win the love of the enchantress Vivien before transporting everyone to Fairyland for the transformation.

Central to the Opening was the Vokes Family. *The Era* declared:

> of one fault the Vokes can never be accused. Sameness and tameness are unknown to them. They are always original, always new and fresh. They are delightful companions. Mr Frederick is unequalled as a Pantomimist, Mr Fawdon is invariably funny, the art of Miss Victoria almost surpasses art, it borders on genius, Miss Jessie fills in the picture and makes it complete, while Miss Rosina possesses a fund of bright and delightful humour, such as is rarely found.

Fred played King Arthur and Fawdon, his jester Dagonet. The knights were all played by women, led by the Vokes sisters. Victoria was Sir Tristram, 'all purple and gold, a Knight so beautiful, that ladies would faint at the sight of him, with a springy step and a laughing air which make merry the atmosphere he breathes.' Jessie was Sir Lionel, 'a brave and active young knight, gorgeous in gold and scarlet'. Rosina was Sir

Caradoc, 'all silver armour and apple blossom, the liveliest, merriest knight of all the Round Table, whose every step is a suggestion of fun and whose smile is deadly in its effect.' There were regular dance scenes to highlight the terpsichorean talents of the Vokes, in particular a scene of King Arthur and his knights making a pie in the kitchen accompanied by much singing and dancing. *The Times*, which thought Blanchard had 'resolved to be amusing and is less formally ethical than on previous occasions' praised him for 'affording opportunity for the exhibition of a grotesque chivalry at once comical and brilliant, in which the talent of the inimitable Vokes family is displayed.' It also praised Master John Manley as Tom, 'a diminutive actor of wonderful precocity'. *The Era* thought that Manley 'deserves much credit for his sharpness and lively appreciation of fun.' As always Drury Lane pantomimes were characterized by the excellent ballet scenes, devised by John Cormack, and scenes involving children, not just the dolls' house but also the military manoeuvres performed by Tom Thumb's Lilliputian army on Little Cove Common. *The Daily News* praised Levey's music 'always scholarly and effective' and particularly 'the capital music of a very pretty ballet of Dresden china *figurantes*'.

The Era concluded 'we have seldom seen a Pantomime Opening more meritorious than that to *Tom Thumb*' and lavished praise on Beverley for the scenery, John Cormack for arranging the dances, Levey for composing the music, Mr Tucker and assistants for the elaborate machinery, Mrs Powell for the floral arrangements and F. B. Chatterton, the manager. Blanchard records only one payment of £50 from Chatterton.[27]

Blanchard produced a second pantomime in 1871, this time for the Princess' Theatre, *Little Dicky Dilver and His Stick of Silver or Harlequin Prince Pretty Boy and the Three Comical Kings*, written in collaboration with T.L. Greenwood as the Brothers Grinn. This was no doubt the result of the fact that F.B. Chatterton of Drury Lane had gone into partnership with Benjamin Webster at the Princess' and the Adelphi Theatres. In this pantomime Blanchard reworked ideas he first explored in the 1851 Surrey pantomime *Harlequin Prince Bluecap*. The show opens in the Temple of the Drama which is derelict, its columns tottering, its roof admitting the rain and dense fog enshrouding it. The Spirit of the Drama summons up a succession of Shakespearean characters but dismisses them as unsuitable, for in the modern burlesque spirit, Shylock is represented as a dealer in old clothes, Hamlet as a spirit medium, Macbeth as a tobacconist's figure, Othello as 'Bones' in the Christy Minstrels and Prospero as a street conjurer with Caliban as his dancing bear. Drama calls to her aid Success who summons Fashion and Novelty with their attendant Follies and Favourites who review the peculiarities of taste, fashion, dress and excitement which have preoccupied the public mind in the past year. 'Many of the caricatures, too evident to be mistaken and too substantial (as in the case of Sir Roger Tichbourne) to be overlooked, are greeted with enthusiasm by the gods' said

The Era (31 December 1871). There followed a ballet of the nymphs of Fashion, each with a scarf of mauve, amber, blue, crimson or green, who wove such dance patterns that 'the entire effect made the interwoven hues become absolutely dazzling.' *The Era* called the ballet 'magnificent'; *The Times* (27 December 1871) 'singularly picturesque and suggestive'.

The scene changes to the Barley Shooga Palace in the Isle of Kandy where King Ali Campagne is vexed because his daughter Princess Sugar Plum has rejected the wooing of the diminutive Prince Pretty Boy, an eight year old, who is attended by a retinue of baby soldiers, armed with guns and fixed bayonets. She prefers the attentions of Dicky Dilver, who has entranced her with his knowledge of the latest music hall songs and mastery of the breakdance. King Ali Campagne will only approve his suit if he travels to the kingdoms of animal, vegetable and mineral and brings back a treasure from each. Dicky Dilver sets forth to the primeval world 'where Darwinian philosophy reigns supreme' (both *The Era* and *The Times* recognized the reference) and where various animals typify the 'descent of man'. Leo the Lion is monarch and, said *The Era*:

> a very funny sparring match between the Lion and the Unicorn ends in the victory of the latter. The comparisons to official personages of the present day are well carried out. For instance, two yokels pull a wagon along, while the horse is the driver; a donkey rides upon a man's back; monkeys discuss Court scandal; and an owl and a jackdaw are learned in the law, coming to conclusions of some sort between themselves which cannot always be said of their degenerate descendants. A hare, instead of running away from the sportsman, actually fires at him, and shakes her head dolefully upon missing her aim. All this scene is far beyond the ordinary scope of pantomime, and we are glad to say was fully appreciated.

From the animal kingdom Dicky moves to the vegetable kingdom and the Castle of King Cauliflower 'on the Border of Botany' where a grove of columns, each in the form of a celery stick, is tenanted by beans, peas, potatoes, radishes, lettuces, carrots, turnips and so on, personified by an immense troupe of supernumeraries:

> each with a cleverly-modelled head, full of grotesque character. The various expressions are quite remarkable for quaintness and originality. So much care revealed in a comparatively secondary matter is a proof of the high merit of this Pantomime throughout. A series of evolutions, conducted with great skill, and arranged by Mr Cormack with his usual ability, furnishes plenty of amusement for the young folks.

Finally Dicky visits the mineral world ruled by King Gold, King Coal and Silver Stick, returning with his three treasures and winning the hand of Princess Sugar Plum. The final transformation scene, in which *The Times* thought Frederick Lloyds surpassed expectation and *The Era* called 'an exquisite scene', was 'the Wondrous World of Animated Nature'. *The Era* said:

Mr F. Lloyds has given the rein to his fancy and let it wander unchecked into a perfect dreamland of exotic vegetation and tropical flowers in which the gigantic animals of the earlier world gradually disappear and their places are filled by the more graceful forms of sylphs and fairies. Fold after fold of gorgeous blooms and foliage reveal themselves surrounding lovely figures clothed in costumes which harmonise with the rich hues of the floral accompaniments and form altogether a scene of almost unrivalled splendour, enchanting the audience, who called Mr Lloyds to the footlights and overwhelmed him with applause.

The harlequinade followed and the whole ended at the Glittering Palace of Prosperity, but not, the critic noted disapprovingly, until 12.45 a.m.

The Era (31 December 1871) declared:

No Pantomime of the present season is written with greater refinement and elegance. The dialogue is neat and pointed, the speeches not too long, the jokes sufficiently smart, and what is especially to be commended in an entertainment so largely patronised by ladies and children, entirely free from vulgarity

and concluded 'the entire pantomime went exceedingly well' apart from its length. In addition to praising the Brothers Grinn and Frederick Lloyds, the critic praised the 'inventiveness' of dance master Cormack, the 'gorgeous costumes' of Mr Vandyke Brown and Miss Gouthier and the 'clever' music of W.H. Montgomery. The overture had concluded with 'God Save the Queen' and 'God Bless the Prince of Wales', 'both airs being received with deafening cheers.' Also a song sung by Miss Parkes as Dicky Dilver referring to the Prince of Wales' recovery from his near fatal illness, 'produced a burst of loyal cheering from a very crowded house' reported *The Times*.

The 1872–3 Drury Lane pantomime was *The Children in the Wood or Harlequin Queen Mab and the World of Dreams*. The story, first recorded in 1595 and later better known under the title *Babes in the Wood*, originally ended tragically with the two children dying, but after it reached the stage (first in 1793) the tragic ending was increasingly replaced by a happy one. Blanchard's version went with the happy ending.

The Era (29 December 1872) began its review with an encomium on Blanchard:

A Drury Lane pantomime from any other writer than Mr E.L. Blanchard would be something in the nature of an anomaly ... to his infinite credit, Mr E.L. Blanchard never forgets that he is writing for children as well as adults, and no one can reproach him with producing a single line in which grossness of allusion or expression, or vulgarity of any kind, may be detected.

The pantomime opens in the study of the celebrated Elizabethan wizard Doctor Dee, who is consulted by Geoffrey Nimble Legs, the running footman of Sir Rowland, the wicked uncle, as to the future fortunes of his niece and nephew. Consulting the horoscope, Dee discovers that they will live for 300 years. For confirmation he summons a variety of liquors, 'fantastically personified', followed by twelve of the most celebrated inn signs, among them The Goat in Boots, The Green Dragon, The Cat and Bagpipes, The Cork and Bottle and The Spotted Dog, also personified, all disaffected by the passing of the 1872 Licensing Act which aimed to restrict the issuing of liquor licenses. The personified inn sign Old Mother Redcap disapprovingly lists the restrictions placed upon the public houses by the new law:

Some folks have lately come to think
That other folks ne'er want to eat or drink
That bread and cheese and beer must lead to crime
Should they be swallowed past a certain time.
Policemen pop and pounce most readily
On all who are seen to walk about unsteadily.
On slippery pavements if a slide there is on
And down you go, you're taken up – to prison!
The law is paternal, turn out, turn out,
At hours nocturnal turn out.
At club you may stay, till the dawn of day.
But with us you have to turn out.
We shall see how the law will turn out.

The Era noted: 'Mr Blanchard treats this new form of paltry tyranny playfully but incisively.' Criticism of any legislative restriction on drinking was a regular theme of pantomime scripts and invariably received audience applause.

The story moves on to Magpie Hall, the residence of Sir Rowland. He arrives and is served a sumptuous feast but seats the children, William and Mary, on low stools with bowls of gruel. Sent to bed, the children enter the world of dreams and realm of Queen Mab where they contemplate a series of *tableaux* representing favourite fairy tales: Jack the Giant Killer, Puss in Boots, Little Red Riding Hood, Aladdin, Blue Beard, Cinderella and Four and Twenty Blackbirds baked in a pie. Queen Mab is accompanied by her attendants Somnambula, Morphea, Somnola, Fantasy, Whimsy and Shadowina. Somnambula sings a gracefully written song, composed by W.C. Levey, and entitled 'Beautiful Dreams'. The sequence ends with a ballet: 'A Gossamer Dream', devised by John Cormack, which was 'pretty and fanciful, and the grouping of the ladies, as they form various combinations with their scarfs is exceedingly effective,' said *The Era*. It also noted approvingly 'the dresses are remarkably chaste'. The ballet ended with the appearance of a giant peacock, its tail made up by the dancers each holding a large feather.

Next morning Sir Rowland comes to breakfast in a bad humour, having been tormented by Queen Mab with hideous dreams. He hires Walter the Woodman and Rufus the Ruffian to dispose of William and Mary. They take the children to the woods where in the Foxglove Dell, there came what *The Era* called:

> one of the prettiest effects we have ever seen in a pantomime … When entering the forest the children are supposed to hear the melody 'the harp in the air' and to think of dreamland. The Fairies are watching over them, and each flower opens to show a girl's face, which disappears when the flowers close.

When Rufus tries to kill the children, soft-hearted Walter intervenes to stop him and the children escape. They cry themselves to sleep and a flock of forest birds cover them with leaves for warmth and squirrels bring nuts to save them from perishing of hunger. The birds and squirrels were played by children. *The Era* reported that Cormack's 'labours in drilling and training the juvenile super-numeraries must have been sufficiently arduous. The result is all that could be desired, and the scene goes capitally.'

Rufus returns to claim the reward for killing the children. But Sir Rowland, who has now repented of his evil intentions, refuses to pay him and defeats him in single combat. Walter brings back the children safe and sound and the Opening ends with a transformation scene, based on Queen Mab's Car, 'a pretty idea, worked out in the best possible taste', said *The Era*.

The Vokes Family once again starred: Fred as Sir Rowland, Fawdon as Geoffrey Nimble Legs, Victoria and Rosina as the children William and Mary and Jessie as their longsuffering governess, Mistress Winifred.

> The 'babes' object to studies of any kind, burst into tears and lamentations on the slightest provocation, and sedulously cultivate all the little airs and graces permitted to people of their tender years. Their disposition is sportive, swinging and skipping-rope exercises being the delight of charming Miss Mary and leap-frog being the favourite diversion of Master Willie.

Fred Vokes made a distinct impression as the wicked uncle:

> Mr Frederick Vokes personates the fiery nobleman with a quaintness and originality most amusing. He is capitally made up, with a bald head and a moustache that bristles up whenever his fits of rage are coming on, Sir Rowland's temper is sorely tried at Magpie Hall … when Sir Rowland sits down to dinner he finds a small pig in the soup, and various other things happen for which the servants are belaboured with ladles, knives, and forks … Sir Rowland takes the lead in a general dance, throws his long legs over the

heads of nephew and niece, and goes through a variety of contortions suggesting the absence of bones in his physical construction ... The eccentricity of this member of the gifted Vokes family of dancers and the grace and finish of the others are in pleasant contrast. The dance was encored and will, we imagine, be redemanded every night.

There was another dance before the final transformation, done in a 'spirit of grotesque humour'. *The Times* (27 December 1872) pronounced it 'one of the best successes of Mr Chatterton's successful management'. Blanchard notes in his diary: 'The Wood pantomime ... goes off well.'[28]

In 1872 Blanchard provided two other pantomimes. Besides his Drury Lane annual, he initiated a connection with the Crystal Palace, for which he was to provide the annual pantomime until 1876. He began with *Jack and Jill or Old Dame Nature and the Fairy Art*, which he described as 'a grand masque' and which, perhaps in deference to the educational mission of the Palace, he based on the operation of W.E. Forster's 1870 Education Act, which sought to extend the school system by creating elected school boards, empowered to levy an education rate.

Jack and Jill opened on 21 December 1872 and the *I.L.N.* (20 December 1872) said: 'Mr Blanchard has now quite a reputation for the production of poetic pantomime which in the present instance he has completely justified' and declared the show 'a great success'. The curtain rises on the Dense Mists of Ignorance, with Ignorance becoming a patron of Crime, Superstition, Stupidity, Poverty and Prejudice. Together they form chains to fetter the human mind. A tribe of street boys, called the Little Errors, and consisting of thieves, coiners, hawkers and garrotters, appear and announce with a groan that everyone is now to be educated – as a result of the Forster Act – and they discuss the propriety of smashing up every school board. Science arrives and calls in aid the magic of Art, whose temple ('a very tasteful set') receives Painting, Poetry, Music, Sculpture, Architecture, Medicine, Agriculture and Navigation who arrive in miniature gilded chariots, drawn by miniature ponies. Ignorance defies them and engages Art in competition for the souls of Jack and Jill. Art invokes the aid of Dame Nature.

First another discussion ensues as to the tricks which Art has played in trying to improve Nature, a 'girl of the period' being introduced as an illustration of this development. Art boasts of her last achievement – the Aquarium – and Nature unfolds the 'wonders of the deep' with a dance of sea creatures: soles, plaice, codfish, crabs, oysters and octopus. Next is presented the abode of Dame Nature in the Happy Valley where Art laments the absence of bridges, railways, steamboats and electric light. Here 'by the aid of a host of children in dresses of many colours, a remarkably pretty effect is produced' and there is a grand ballet of the fruits. 'The coryphées, headed by the clever Misses Elliott, execute a variety of graceful movements, and at the end, each bearing a basket of flowers, form themselves into a charming group.' Nature, Science and Art agree to co-operate to defeat Ignorance.

The next scene introduces Jack and Jill at the cottage of Diggory Dock, where we meet Diggory's domestic pets, Puggy Muggy the dog, Tootsy Pootsy the cat and the historical mouse that ran up the clock. Jill, the farmer's daughter, has many suitors – the Butcher, the Baker, the Candlestick-Maker, the Tinker, the Tailor, the Soldier, the Sailor, the Apothecary, the Ploughboy and the Thief – all of whom are individually introduced to be rejected by Jill, who remains faithful to Jack. Jack and Jill wish to marry but have no money, and having no education, lack the means to make any. They begin to make a pie and Fairy Art appears disguised as a beggar to offer them her Little Page of Useful Knowledge, an edition of Mrs Glass' Cookery Book, to instil culinary skills in Jill. To Jack she presents the Staff of Perseverance and they prepare to mount the hill to fetch a pail of water. In the picturesque village of Prettiwell, Jack and Jill follow the path of progress to the Fountain of Knowledge, but both Jack and Jill come tumbling down. Old Proverb appears and introduces Jack to the Ladder of Learning and he determines to climb by the aid of the Staff of Perseverance. His resolution is hailed with delight by the villagers and a 'charming rustic ballet' ensues.

The first stage of Jack's progress brings him to Old Cocker's State Cabinet. This is Edward Cocker (1631–75), whose treatise on arithmetic enjoyed great popularity and gave rise to the expression 'According to Cocker'. Old Cocker is attended by his numerals and casts up his accounts, initiating Jack into the mysteries of arithmetic. The teacher puts his pupils through their paces; Jack proves an apt scholar but makes fun of his tutor, turning Euclid's Elements to the purposes of caricature. ' "Running Hand" and "Square Foot", both personified, are the funniest practical jokes we have ever seen or heard of', said *The Era* (22 December 1872). Cocker takes Jack by rapid strides to the top of the hill and introduces him to the alphabet. Then the story of the House that Jack Built is exemplified. There come in quick succession the historical malt, the rat that ate the malt, the cat that killed the rat, the dog that worried the cat, the cow that tossed the dog, the maiden all forlorn, the priest all shaven and shorn, and the cock that crowed in the morn. Here too in alphabetical order come twenty-five representatives of different trades. They combine to construct the house and then join in an alphabetical chorus 'which was deservedly encored'. In the next scene we return to the Depths of Ignorance, the occupants dancing with desperation in view of Jack's success. Art, Science and Dame Nature reappear; the lovers are united, Ignorance is vanquished and the allegory concludes with a grand transformation scene – entitled 'Endymion – a dream'.

The Harlequinade opens with a scene in St James's Park in which Clown and Pantaloon play battledore and shuttlecock with a baby, play practical jokes on Her Majesty's forces, introduce a wooden-legged *première danseuse* and drill an army of old women. Next at Mrs Wringem's Laundry a policeman, 'an active and intelligent officer' is washed and hung out to dry. The whole laundry is then converted into a gigantic policeman, and he in turn gives way to a pair of rival pubs. This scene allowed for 'some amusing hits' at the new Licensing Act, a placard being exhibited to the effect that no person under seventy can be served. The closing scene, 'an International Tableau', was 'chiefly remarkable for the introduction of a series of cataracts of real water, which have an astonishing and pleasing effect'. It was the Niagara Falls and the groupings were emblematic of peace and goodwill between Britain and America. *The Era* concluded:

> Mr Blanchard's admirable lines – wonderfully superior to the ordinary run of Pantomime openings – the beautiful scenery, the tasteful groupings, and the excellent acting of all concerned, should secure for *Jack and Jill* an unprecedented amount of popularity. The transformation scene 'Endymion' reflects great credit on Mr Charles Brew, and it is only fair to say it was hailed with enthusiastic plaudits by the immense audience.

The Daily News (23 December 1872) declared *Jack and Jill* to be outstanding:

> in excellence of construction, in exuberance of fun, and in beauty and splendour of scenery and decoration. It has, what is not always considered indispensable in pantomime, a congruous and intelligible plot, and a mildly didactic, but what is sure to be popular purpose ... and its purpose is to show how knowledge can and ought to beat ignorance, and how useful is 'culture', even in carrying out the homely but indispensable object of keeping the cupboard warm and plentitudinous. Mr E.L. Blanchard has written his allegory in pleasant and popular language, and Messrs Brew and Fenton have furnished it with scenic illustrations of beauty and magnificence such as we have rarely seen equalled on the pantomime stage. Competition seems this year to have put each artist on his mettle, and the result is two scenes, one from each, either of which might alone be held responsible for success.

Frederick Fenton was responsible for the Abode of Dame Nature, 'a gorgeous idyll upon canvas ... So bright and true are his colours, and so correct is his drawing, that the audience is at once thrown into raptures of applause. It is, in fact, the triumph of refined realism.' The Abode was a sunny landscape, peopled by fruits, represented by 'charming young ladies'. A huge silver filigree vase rose through a trap, with living female caryatids supporting it, and it revolved slowly, displaying paintings of fruit on one side and flowers on the other. Charles Brew painted 'Endymion's Dream', a mythological vision. A crescent moon descended from a deep blue sky dotted with stars and planets. On it reposed the shepherd Endymion, enjoying the visions conjured up for him by Diana. 'The audience perhaps did not understand all this as well as they had done the luscious fruits and gorgeous flowers of Dame Nature's

Happy Valley.' Nevertheless, 'the tableau of "the Dream" completely "brought down the house"'. Blanchard thought the pantomime 'beautifully got up'.[29]

Once again Blanchard provided the Princess' pantomime, working in collaboration with Greenwood as The Brothers Grinn. The show was *Little Goody Two-Shoes and Tom, Tom, the Piper's Son, or Harlequin the Old Woman, the Pig, and the Silver Penny*. It opens with a view of the Exhausted Fountains of Amusement where Amusement, about to become the victim of the Demon Gloom, displays to Tradition and Public Taste the 'departed glories of those theatres not doing pantomime': Covent-Garden (Dion Boucicault and Lord Dundreary), the Alhambra (*King Carrot*), the Lyceum (*Charles the First*), the Queen's Theatre (*Cromwell*) and the Cremorne Gardens 'where no dancing is allowed'. There are passing allusions to current topics. The scene changes to the Palace of Imagination where there is, said *The Times* (27 December 1872), 'a grand ballet with the most brilliant effects'. *The Era* (29 December 1872) called it 'a masterpiece of Terpsichore'. Then the scene changes to King Harum Scarum's palace in the land of Hurri Scurri. He laments to his councillors the taciturnity of his younger son, Prince Niddi Neddie. No toys or amusements can please him. The King offers a reward of three millions to anyone who will cure him of his melancholy. But his chief councillor tells him it is impossible to raise the money. The King replies: 'You dunce, put tuppence on the income Tax, you've got the sum at once. Next year you will have a surplus; strike the tuppence off and earn the nation's gratitude.' 'This allusion to our National Exchequer was received with much laughter', reported *The Times*. An old beggar is introduced at court, and reveals to the King that his son is in love, and she discloses to him the object of his affections by means of a transparency. The King cannot believe that so young a child as his son can be in love, except through incantation, and the old woman is doomed to be ducked in a pond as a witch. But the young prince catches a glimpse of Little Goody Two-Shoes and dances with delight. We are next introduced to the village school, presided over by Goody Two-Shoes. She is carried off to Fairyland where Fairy Affable assures her of protection and eventual marriage to the prince. Tom the Piper's son who stole the pig and ran away is in love with Dolly Daisy and appeals to Goody, who persuades Fairy Affable to favour their suit. The two couples are eventually united.

The Era declared:

Never was a Pantomime more splendidly produced. All the resources of the artists in the different lines necessary for the production seem to have been ransacked to make this Pantomime the best. The Transformation scene is one of unsurpassed splendour. Trees of the most gorgeous description, illumined by varicoloured lights, are grouped around an elegant fountain of real water, the full height of the stage, and fairy forms are seen in all the branches of the trees. This is the crowning achievement of the evening, and eclipses in taste and elegance the many exquisite scenes which precede it.

These included the Mushroom Valley in the Land of the Little People and the Elfin Factory in Fairyland, 'productive of great amusement by the band of little people it exhibits dressed as blacksmiths'; the Wild Thyme Bank, with a distant view of Harum Scarum Castle; the enchanted cottage of Goody Two-Shoes; and Cloudland, leading to the Retreat of the Water Fairies in the Coral Cave.

There was praise for almost everyone involved, starting with Miss Kate Logan as Goody, 'the very Goody of our Childhood', a young girl performer ('and where Mr Chatterton picks up his marvellously clever children is a mystery'):

> The costumes, from designs by Mr Alfred Maltby, by Mr S. May, and Miss Gauthier, deserve unbounded praise, nothing having ever been hitherto shown that can excel them. The machinery, which was without a hitch, is by Mr Warton, and the elegant properties are by Mr Hassett. The music is composed and selected by Mr W.H. Montgomery, and comprises all the well-known songs of the day. Having spoken so highly of the scenery it is but fair to say it is designed and painted by Mr F. Lloyds, assisted by Messrs Perkins and Leitch. The comic scenes and ballet are invented and arranged by Mr John Cormack, whose name is sufficient guarantee of their excellence. The Opening is invented by the Brothers Grinn, and right well have they performed their part. The whole Pantomime is produced under the able direction of Mr F. Villiers.

The Times pronounced it 'a great success'.

The Era (29 December 1873) began its review of the 1873 Drury Lane pantomime with an encomium on Blanchard.

> For nearly a quarter of a century has Mr Blanchard furnished the Christmas annual for the old house. It would be a pleasant task to calculate how many little ones' hearts have been made merry by this wizard during that period; how many of mature years have found the cares of business lightened by the offshoots from his busy pen; how many going down the hill of life have found their way made pleasanter by recollections of the enjoyment his brilliant fancy and lively imagination have afforded ... It was once the fashion to sneer at Pantomimes; but there was no Blanchard in those days.

For *Jack in the Box or Harlequin Little Tom Tucker* the house was full and the gallery provided a vocal accompaniment to the music, led this time by an 'enthusiastic gentleman' who stood up and conducted them.

The pantomime opens in the village of Gotham where the 'three wise men' are constructing a bowl in which to go to sea. Prince Felix of the Fortunate Isles arrives, disguised as Tom Tucker, a travelling artisan. He sings a song with a moral:

> If in lives of honest labour
> All men do their best, I'm sure

Every man must do good to his neighbour
Till all are better off than before.

Cockalorum, King of Cockaigne, arrives on a royal progress and declares that he will give the hand of his daughter, Princess Poppet in marriage to whoever will give her wealth and lands and common sense. Prince Felix, who already loves her, determines to seek fairy help. He discovers that every 100 years a Fairy Fair is held on Midsummer Eve on Gotham Common. He comes to the aid of an old woman who turns into Elfina, Queen of the Fairies. Mushrooms spring up and turn into stalls, presided over by fairies. Prince Felix receives a Jack in the Box from one and out of it pops an elf who will do his bidding. He turns up at court and offers the Jack in the Box as a present. Princess Poppet accepts it but is too proud to marry a mere artisan. Jack in the Box promises to cure her of her conceit. Jack reduces the King, Princess, Tom and the royal court to child-sized nursery rhyme characters (Princess as Bo-Peep, King as Little Jack Horner, etc.) and removes them all to Buttercup Green on Nursery Island. There Princess Poppet learns her lesson – patience, economy, industriousness, humility – leading Tom Tucker to say:

Why, thus endowed, you'd lead a useful life,
And I would marry had I such a wife.

There follows the Reformation, Restoration, Reconciliation and Transformation as Jack in the Box returns them to their normal size and identities and they return to the Golden Land of Plenty and the Harvest Home of the Fairies. Prince and Princess are united. Intriguingly three of King Cockaigne's ministers were made up to look like Prime Minister William Gladstone, Home Secretary Robert Lowe and Tory leader Benjamin Disraeli, all of whom had distinct appearances: 'The likenesses being immediately recognized and eliciting a roar of applause,' said The Era.

At the Fairy Fair there was a grand ballet danced by 100 dancers and when the main characters were turned into children, there was a children's ballet with the dancers as buttercups and daisies. The Times (27 December 1873) noted that:

of all the brilliant 'introductions' appertaining to the pantomimes produced under the management of Mr F.B. Chatterton, the 'introduction' to Jack in the Box is perhaps the most effective. Its comic force is not remarkable, but the splendour of its choreographic displays could not be surpassed. Dances by Coryphées, dances by children follow each other in quick succession, and one of them does credit to the inventive talent of Mr John Cormack. The 'Fairies Fancy Fair' reveals to the London public something never before seen – namely, the entire depth of the Drury-lane stage, and the eye is carried through a series of glittering stalls to an apparently interminable distance. The 'transformation scene' is one of the most felicitous products of Mr Beverley's fancy, being not only beautiful, but original.

The Era was lost for words: 'The huge mushrooms are in an instant changed into the golden canopied stalls of the Fairies' Fancy Fair, a scene which defies description, and which will, we venture to say, become the talk of the town.' The fairies of the fair were:

> in all the colours of the rainbow, and in all sorts of combinations of those colours, but all so tastefully chosen, and so skilfully blended, as to form one grand and harmonious whole, delighting the eye, bewildering the brain, and exacting admiration of the most cordial character.

When the characters were turned into children, the girls playing Tom Tucker and Bo-Peep, Miss Amalia and Miss Violet Cameron:

> made quite a hit, and gained some of the loudest applause heard during the evening. Their lovemaking was charming; their singing elicited an overwhelming encore; and their dancing gained a similar compliment. One of the prettiest and freshest things we have seen for a long time came next, in the shape of a ballet of buttercups and daisies. The real flowers hardly ever danced more gaily in the wind than did the little folk who filled the stage, and once more proved how cleverly they had been trained'.

The Era was particularly impressed by Fred Evans as Jack in the Box, a role which gave him:

> an opportunity for the display of his agility, of which he certainly fully avails himself. He pops up traps, darts down traps, whirls round and round the stage, turns somersaults, and seemingly knocks himself about in a manner which would do serious injury to the anatomy of mortals possessed of less elastic frames. Here let us at once say that Mr Evans has never been seen to greater advantage than in this character. How hard he works only those who see him can tell; but there can be no doubt that his really wonderful performance pleased as much as it astonished all present.

The Era concluded that *Jack in the Box* was 'one of the most brilliantly successful Pantomimes ever placed on the Drury-lane boards', with praise all round for Beverley's scene-painting, W.C. Levey's music, Cormack's choreography and Edward Stirling's stage management.

Puss in Boots (20 December 1873) at the Crystal Palace departed from the norm by opening ahead of Boxing Day and being performed in the afternoon. It was part of a varied bill of fare which included a Christmas fair which stretched down both aisles and a display of stuffed animals. The building, said *The Times* (22 December 1873), was 'decorated with banners, flags, wreaths, and shrubs, a gigantic Christmas tree stands at the north end, and a pantomime [the *pièce de résistance* of the day according to *The Daily News*] ... may be seen in the afternoon in the theatre opposite the Handel Orchestra.' It attracted a large family attendance.

Blanchard provided a novel variation on the familiar story. The curtain rises on 'an antique kitchen in the old manor-house' which is turned by Dame Trot into a refuge for wandering and destitute cats. The important ceremony of naming a new kitten is proceeded with; but at the height of the festivities the spiteful witch Vixeria rises from the earth and carries off 'the little stranger'. Now it so happens that Love watches over the interests of cats and the fairies determine that he who treats a kitten properly shall have the benefit of a magic spell. Before Love retires there is a ballet in a 'pretty scene' called the 'Opening of the Valentine'. The kitten falls into the hands of the hero Josselin who is the youngest of three brothers and who, having displeased his wealthy father by attachment to 'domestic pets', is cut off from his inheritance. The kitten quickly arrives at cat's estate, and, being endowed with the power of speech and provided with a pair of boots, serves Josselin as valet. The news is brought to the dark witches' glen by a hawk, when the terrible Ogre, Fee-Fo-Fum, is raised by the malignant Vixeria for the purpose of getting rid of both the kitten and his master. Meanwhile the charm begins to work in Josselin's favour. The King of Brittany, with his retinue, passes through a part of Normandy, where the pastoral scenes of the pantomime are laid, on a hunting expedition. Princess Prettyface falls in love with Josselin, and His Majesty approves of the union. The dreadful Ogre proceeds to fulfil his mission; but Puss, accompanied by his master, courageously enters the castle, cajoles him into assuming a variety of shapes by questioning his power to do so, and at last, when he appears as a mouse, pounces upon and destroys him. Therewith the hand of the Princess is promised to Josselin. The transformation scene, 'effectively designed and painted by Mr Charles Brew', represented a little fairy hovering in mid air and waving her silver wand over the head of a sleeping child, who thereby gets a glimpse of fairyland. 'There is always something striking or poetical in the transformation scene at Sydenham,' said *The Times*.

The Times review concluded: 'This pantomime bears comparison with the most successful of its predecessors. It is written with humour and refinement, is put upon the stage with much splendour, and is supported by an efficient and well-disciplined company.' *The Times* singled out for praise George Conquest as the Ogre, saying that he 'has many opportunities to display his peculiar talents. He assumes different shapes with wonderful celerity and completeness. As the Ogre, he wears a huge head ... which is made to wink, roll its eyes, thrust out its tongue, and do other surprising things.' Josselin was played by Miss Caroline Parkes, 'one of the most vivacious and refined burlesque actresses of our time'. Male performers played Dame Trot and Fairy Vixeria and Master Conquest played Puss. *The Daily News* (22 December 1873) also praised Conquest, noting that:

with the assistance of a mask which he manages and grimaces with in the most horrible natural and repulsively attractive manner, he becomes a giant one moment, and a dwarf or a lion the next, to the wonder and delight of the vast audience. It is almost needless to add that everything he did … was hailed with shouts of applause.

The 'clever' acting of Caroline Parkes was also praised.

The Daily News complimented the scenery painted by Frederick Fenton. The pastoral scene – 'quite a French landscape – with a real windmill in the distance, and mild peasants coming in slow boats along a sluggish river with their corn to be ground' – was described as 'beautiful'. 'The Abode of Love', 'a scene upon which Mr Fenton has lavished all his taste and fancy', was:

> a wonderful fairy picture, dotted all over with personified 'Doubts and Hopes', 'Fancies and Glances', oscillating in a rose-coloured atmosphere in positions of suspended fascination, and all looking as beautiful as their own good looks and an abundance of complementary muslin and spangles can make them.

'The Abode of Love was the first great scenic success of the day, and the ballet with which it terminated was most favourably received.' The transformation scene was:

> a marvel of fanciful conception and skilful execution, of light, colour and sparkle. The audience were astonished as well as charmed, and the whole tableau was universally pronounced to be one of the most perfect of its kind that had ever been produced.

The Daily News noted that the harlequinade:

> went off with great fire, and being very properly kept free of political and other allusions which children don't understand, was vociferously applauded by the boys and girls. The words of the pantomime, which are by Mr E.L. Blanchard, are not unworthy of his experienced hand; and the music by Mr Oscar Barrett, is very creditable to a young and rising musician. The working of the piece was admirably efficient for a first representation,

thanks to the general manager, Isaac Wilkinson.

The Stage (26 December 1873) said:

> Mr Blanchard is undoubtedly the writer of Pantomime *facile princeps*. His *Puss in Boots* … put all productions of the kind in the shade; and if this is to be taken as a specimen, then is Pantomime soaring into the region of high art. We should like to know very much whence Mr Blanchard derives his novel information respecting the concerns of Fairyland. He appears to have made acquaintance with the prettiest, and the pertest, and the most talkative and the most fanciful; and they seem to have admitted him to secrets always denied to ordinary mortals. Else how is it that, with his *Puss in Boots* he takes us into such marvellous regions – that he tells us of wonders which we know not of – that he delights us with a peep at things which we have certainly hinted at in dreams, which have never come before us in our waking moments?

The Times (28 December 1874) noted that compared with twenty years before when there was 'the entire crushing out of pantomimes by burlesques' there had been a 'sudden increase of pantomime in the principal dramatic district of our capital [i.e., the West End]. In the suburbs pantomime has flourished for a long succession of years, but now the West End is catching up, with Drury Lane as ever pre-eminent.' It reported that the latest pantomime, *Aladdin or Harlequin and the Wonderful Lamp* 'surpassed anything' previously attempted by F.B. Chatterton. But the *I.L.N.* (2 January 1875) noted the restricted nature of the subjects: 'The modern pantomimist appears to care little for novelty of subject or title; rather he seems to delight in investing the undying old with fancies ever new.'

Aladdin opens in a street in Canton where the African magician Abanazar appears with his slave Kazrac, seeking the assistance of an innocent youth to help retrieve the magic lamp. The narrative then follows closely the script for his 1865 Covent Garden *Aladdin*. The transformation scene this time takes them all to the land of Fan-ta-see, illuminated by the rays of the lamp.

The Times ascribed the success of the show in great measure to the presence of the Vokes Family, who had been absent from England for the previous two years and therefore had not graced the year before's pantomime. Fred played Abanazar, Fawdon, Kazrac, Victoria, Aladdin, Rosina, Badroulbadour ('ravishingly bewitching' thought the *I.S.D.N.*) and Jessie, the Genius of the Lamp.

> Never perhaps have their varied abilities been displayed to greater advantage than in the pantomime under notice, and never, perhaps, has Mr F. Vokes more astonished an audience by the agility of his movements and the broad humour of his 'business'. The Family were received very cordially, and at the end of the opening had to repeat a characteristic dance and then appear in a body to acknowledge applause from all parts of the house.

Each member of the family was cheered on first appearance. 'The cheer which greeted Fred Vokes was quite deafening,' said the *I.S.D.N.* (2 January 1875). *The Era* (31 January 1875) declared *Aladdin* 'another decided hit for the Chatterton regime', and attributed it to the 'intrinsic merits of the production itself … and … the presence of the now world-famous Vokes family, the talented members of which play so prominent a part in it'. The critic praised 'Fred Vokes' legs which have reduced grotesque dancing to an art and his mobile pigtail which signalled various changes of emotion'; found the singing, dancing and acting of Victoria and Rosina as Aladdin and the Princess 'inimitable'; and said Jessie as the Genius of the Lamp proved that 'her grace and ability as a dancer have in no degree diminished'. Fawdon Vokes as Kazrac never spoke but proved 'thoroughly efficient' in all he did. Beverley's name was 'a guarantee for the beauty of the scenery' and the Flying Palace, which refused to fly on Boxing Night, 'now makes its aerial journey without interruption.' There was the usual ballet, here of fairies representing precious stones. William Beverley, said *The Times*, had 'painted in his best style' the interior of the cavern, the garden of jewels, the exterior of Aladdin's palace, and above all, the 'bright region of Fan-ta-See'. The critic in rather a backhanded compliment noted: 'Writing is a subordinate feature in pantomime, but those who listened attentively must have felt that the old story was retold with force and many touches of humour by Mr E.L. Blanchard.' The *I.S.D.N.* thought 'attractive though it is, by reason of the Vokes's grotesque dancing, and Beverly's scenery, *Aladdin* lacks much of that mirth-moving quality which made *Aladdin* at the Gaiety so popular.' Blanchard wrote of it 'very different from what I intended. I experience my usual disappointment. Comic business seems to be execrable'.[30]

The Crystal Palace pantomime for 1874 was *Cinderella or Harlequin and the Little Glass Slipper, the Magic Pumpkin, and the Butterflies' Ball and Grasshoppers' Feast*, opening on 22 December 1874 and running in the afternoons. It begins in the Cabinet of Crotchets full of children representing different musical instruments and owing fealty to Harmonia. Ballerina, the Spirit of Dancing, appears and debates with Harmonia the relative merits of music and dancing: 'An excellent opportunity for some sly hits at the influence of music on dramatic art,' said *The Era* (27 December 1874). But they eventually agree to co-operate in telling the story of Cinderella. So the Spirits of Music dance away to the Dell of the Dragon Flies which is protected by:

> an admirably painted curtain or gateway representing a gorgeous dragon fly of most abnormal size. Directly the monster dragon fly is raised aloft a coloured army of butterflies and moths, ranging from the gorgeous emperor to the ordinary sulphur, is seen hovering over banks of wild flowers, and from under each butterfly wing, peeps some entrancing fairy.

A butterfly enters to explain how it would have been destroyed but for a young girl (Cinderella) who saved it. The fairies agree to do something for her and perform a ballet in honour of the returned butterfly. The Grand Butterfly ballet follows, 'tastily coloured, gold-covered, and silver-spangled'. When the ballet concludes, a hunting horn is heard and Prince Felix enters the fairy glade with his tutor Bigwiggo and a crowd of attendants in comic masks. Eating, drinking and practical joking follows until they fall asleep and the Prince in Titania's Bower dreams of his ideal Princess Cinderella. Awakened by Bigwiggo, the Prince determines to find his ideal and proclaims a ball. Baron Pumpolino and his daughters Thisbe and Clotilda are invited but Cinderella is left behind. Her Fairy Godmother appears, turning rats, mice, pumpkin and lizards into footmen, coachmen, coach and horses. She gives her the glass slippers and warns her to leave by midnight. A dance of children dressed as cards precedes her arrival. She dances with the Prince and flees at midnight. The

Prince searches for and finds the wearer of the glass slipper. But the show is not yet over. Having impressed on young girls the importance of punctuality, the Fairy Goody-Goody seeks to show that the course of true love never does run smooth. So the transformation is a separate allegory, 'Fairy's Wedding'. A Prince is expelled from the Elfin Court by a beautiful fairy for having dared to make love to her. Eventually she relents, but the Prince cannot be found. She quits the palace to live in seclusion. One moonlit night, a dewdrop, falling from a fern leaf, alights on a mushroom bank and discovers the fairy's retreat. The dewdrop, turning into a fairy, promises to find the Prince and despatches an army of dewdrops who return with the Prince, bound by a garland of roses, and lead him to the Bridal Bower of Orange Blossoms and Forget-me-Nots, where the Prince can be married to the Fairy in the Land of Purity and Truth.

The harlequinade followed, 'busy and bustling and invented by Mr Harry Payne'; 'One of the funniest and jolliest of the season', according to the *I.S.D.N.* (2 January 1875). *The Era* (27 December 1874) thought it 'amusing and when the tricks are in good working order this will be one of the most welcome portions of the entertainment.' It consisted of scenes set at Temple Bar, the Gardens at the Brown Bear and a well-known street in the Metropolis. It did not commence until nearly 6.00 p.m. after a 2.30 p.m. start for the show, worrying *The Daily News*: 'It will not be expedient to have two great crowds rushing to the trains at such an advanced hour of the evening'.

The Times (23 December 1874) thought the transformation scene had been 'realized with great splendour by Mr Brew' and the pantomime 'well-acted' by Miss Caroline Parkes as the Prince (who 'as before, is not less refined than vivacious'), and the rest of the cast.

The Daily News (23 December 1874) said 'there is the usual allegorical opening which nobody understood, and in which animated big fiddles and exceedingly lively kettledrums discussed the merits of various sorts of entertainments, and at last decided upon making *Cinderella* ... the subject of this year's pantomime.' The dragon fly ballet, with the demoiselles Elliott proving themselves 'splendid dancers' was 'the first decided success of the day'. W.H. Payne (as the Baron) provided good fun in his dressing scene in the kitchen and in trying to get partners for his elder daughters at the ball. The transformations of coach and coachmen 'raised the laughter of the children to a climax of hilarity'. The grand transformation, 'The Fairy Wedding' would 'hardly be exceeded in beauty by any of its town competitors.'

On this tableau the Crystal Palace management had concentrated all its scenic resources, and Mr Brew, the artist, all his taste, his skill, and his originality. The audience were perfectly dazzled with the splendour and beauty of the stage, and cheer upon cheer rolled from the back of the Handel orchestra down to the vert footlights.

The transformation scene was 'so novel … in design, so perfect in execution, so exceptionally splendid in its general effect' that the audience insisted that Mr Brew take a bow, which he did. The *I.S.D.N.* called it 'superlatively good'. Of the acting, W.H. Payne 'ably represented the pompous old Baron' and his son Fred as Pedro the valet also 'made an excellent grotesque.' As the Prince, Caroline Parkes, 'quite recovered from her unfortunate Crystal Palace accident of last year' reported *The Era*:

> never looked better, nor acted with more fire and spirit, and her reception was enthusiastic. Bouquets were thrown upon the stage, the graceful Prince picked them up and pressed them to his heart, and the audience cheered as if the little episode was an entire novelty in theatrical affairs.

Of the three scenes of the harlequinade, *The Daily News* noted, 'they were all crammed with the jokes of the period, diversified by assaults on the police, which the little boys somehow relish more than any dramatic, melodramatic, or pantomimic entertainment that could be set before them.'

The Era commented on the accuracy of the depictions of butterflies and grasshoppers, 'thanks to Mr Wilson, the eminent naturalist of the Crystal Palace', suggesting an educational impulse. But it also added that:

> Mr E.L. Blanchard has invested the old nursery legend with a spell of fairyland which has not hitherto belonged to it. It seems to us, who know the legend of 'Cinderella' so well, that it has been entranced by Oberon and enjoyed a Midsummer Night's Dream … over all the romance is cast a graceful and poetical charm which comes fresh and new, and sweet and pleasant, like the scent of the country to a tired Londoner, or the sight of spring after a dreary winter.

In the Grand Transformation 'Fairy's Wedding':

> Mr Charles Brew has succeeded beyond success, and given a series of delicious pictures, which will be valued in the noble gallery of stage scenes. The Mushroom Glade, the discovery of the Lost Fairy asleep, and caressed by Endymion, the dewdrop fairies, glistening with all the purity and freshness of Spring, are, however, merely subordinate to the superb effect of the entrancing bouquet of orange blossoms and forget-me-nots. Before the last grand picture of triumph is discovered a curtain of pendant orange blossoms drops from the very skies. There is sunlight between each bloom, and, as the flowers hang, they are successively illuminated by the thousand rays of the rainbow. Now they are silver, now emerald green, now blue, now purple, now kissed by a sunset and now bathed in gold. We question if a more superb scene has ever been presented. We forget the point-lace scene of the Lyceum and the glories of the Island of Jewels and the King of the Peacocks. Nothing could be better. …. Over all, and above all, is the master-

hand of the artist, Mr Charles Brew, who in the final *tableau* has achieved quite a masterpiece of drawing and a crowning '*coup*' of stage decoration. ... Other delightful scenes were painted by Mr F. Fenton and H. Emden. The beautiful dresses were designed by Mr and Mrs Stinchcombe, and the properties by Mr Lightfoot. The lime-light and gas effects deserve special mention on this occasion ... Gas has seldom been so cleverly used with a view to stage effect. To the great intelligence and taste of Mr Oscar Barrett the charming selection and arrangement of the music is due, and ... M. Espinosa is responsible for the clever dancing.

Mr Wilkinson the manager was praised for his liberality in staging the show and T.H. Friend, 'the able stage manager' for directing.

Robert Reece had provided the 1873 Princess' pantomime, *Little Puss in Boots* but for 1874 F.B. Chatterton turned back to the Brothers Grinn, and Blanchard collaborated with Greenwood to write *Beauty and the Beast or Gog and Magog, the Butterfly Prince and the Realm of Flowers*, which opened ahead of Boxing Day on 23 December 1874, ran until after midnight and attracted, according to *The Era* (27 December 1874), 'a tolerably large audience', implying it would have got more on Boxing Day. The traditional tale was faithfully followed with an original framing story. The clock of Guildhall tolls out the last hours of the dying year and the Guildhall appears, 'bright in the winter moonlight' and safe under the wardship of Gog and Magog, gentle giants who bewail the fate they see in store for their ancient corporation. But before they have got far in their lamentations, the window of the Hall opens and down in a flood of light, to the 'good old tune' of 'Ninety-five', Happy New Year appears, singing 'I'm Seventy-five, I'm Seventy-five' and assuring everyone that if they will be good to her, she will be good to them. Briefly she reviews the year that has gone, touching on the principal topics 'likely to commend themselves to a Christmas audience', among them 'the great victory' of Epping Forest (a reference to the defeat of the Great Eastern Railway's plan to run a railway line through Epping Forest). In this she is assisted by the Spirit of Improvement and Twelfth Night and as each subject is treated of, its embodied representative takes a bow, thus 'poor old' Temple Bar, 'very shaky', Father Thames, 'much be-weeded', and the 'dislodged Lion of Northumberland House, glass in eye, and tail cocked jauntily under left arm'. Last comes Old Father Time, equipped with scythe and hour-glass, and after some merry stanzas as to what he has been doing and seeing in 1874, he drives off the Giants at the point of scythe, and the scene changes to the 'Grand Palace of Improvement in the Realms of Progress', which, after we have been introduced to the Four Seasons, the New Year's attendants, in its turn gives place to the 'Rose Palace in the Garden of the Flowers'. Princess Rosebud is in love with Flutterwing, Prince of the Butterflies, and despite the sensible advice of Nightshade, allows her feelings to get the better of her discretion. She is preparing to fly with him when the Rose Queen Centifolia appears. Prince Flutterwing is surrounded by a guard of cockchafers, a body of wasps appear to protect Queen and Princess, and Aconite and Poppy imprison the prince in fetters of flowers and despoil him of his pretty wings. The Queen then transforms him into a beast, to remain thus until Beauty's love will release him. Palace, garden, Queen and Princess disappear and the story proper begins outside the country house of Eastern merchant Okriki. There we meet the merchant, his modest and beautiful daughter Zemira (Beauty) and her vain and proud sisters Maimoune and Zobeide. News of a panic in the city dictates Okriki's immediate departure and he asks what the daughter would like as presents. A bracelet, a brooch and ten silk dresses says one; a set of diamonds and a seal skin coat says the other. Beauty asks for a rose. Okriki sets off and arrives at the beast's Palace in the Zoological Gardens where food and drink magically appears but when Okriki plucks a rose, the beast appears and offers to spare his life, if he produces a beautiful maiden to marry him. He provides a magic ring to transport Okriki home at once. There Okriki puts the proposition to the daughters. Only Beauty agrees to go, and she falls for the Beast who is transformed back into Prince Flutterwing. Snow and frost melt away before a blaze of light and splendour and the Abode of the Seasons appears with the nuptial bower of Beauty and the transformation.

The Times (28 December 1874) praised the dances: 'There were the celebrated Hungarian dancers, Herr Holzer and Signora Spinza', the former of whom 'obtains considerable applause for his active representation of the supposed manners and customs of a Red Indian on the warpath'. There is a 'very tasteful "ballet of flowers", in which colouring, grouping, and general arrangement is as pretty a thing as we could wish to see.' It was arranged by John Cormack. The chief honours of the evening, thought The Times, went to George Belmore as Okriki, described as 'amusing and exhibits with equal skill and equal comicality the various passions of fear, hope, and grief', and Miss Kate Vaughan, 'a very pleasing and sprightly personification of Beauty'. The Era (27 December 1874) seconded The Times' verdict, with Belmore called 'very amusing' and Kate Vaughan praised:

> she looks the character ... But she has something besides good looks to recommend her. Her acting is full of *chic* without vulgarity; she speaks her lines admirably ... she sings well ... while finally her dancing was singularly graceful. Indeed, throughout she captivated all eyes, and, we imagine, many hearts.

The Era also praised 'The Abode of the Seasons', 'where beauties animate and inanimate are scattered with a liberal hand, and where floral charms are in keen competition with female loveliness'. The scene reflected 'the highest credit' on Mr F. Lloyds, who was called by the audience to take a bow and greeted with 'general acclamation'. The Times praised his depiction of Okriki's bedroom ('a capital scene and a very faithful picture of an Eastern interior').

There were only two scenes in the harlequinade: the first the emporiums of a music-seller and a theatrical costumier and the second haunted houses, with a view of the river, which provided appropriate settings for the knockabout, 'rough and tumble fun of the usual variety', *The Era* called it.

Chatterton, having in 1874 taken over the Adelphi, now introduced an innovation, a pantomime with a mixed cast of children and adults, performed in the afternoons and 'written expressly for the amusement of children'. This was *Harlequin the Children in the Wood, Old Father Aesop, Cock Robin, and Jenny Wren* by the Brothers Grinn (Blanchard and Greenwood). It was, said *The Era* (27 December 1874), produced by Chatterton 'with great taste and liberality' and was 'a regular old-fashioned Pantomime, as entertaining to the old folks as to the young ones'. *The Times* (28 December 1874) said it was:

> one of those furious mixtures of many stories which are peculiar to Christmas time, and to that time alone. Splendidly defiant in their annihilation of all time and space, abounding in the most delicious anachronisms, they laugh to scorn the accepted traditions of our childhood, dressing out the old familiar forms and faces in garments so new, and of such fantastic cut, that had we time for any other feeling than those of wonder and delight, we might at times be well-nigh tempted to regret the ruthless shattering of so many cherished idols.

The pantomime opens in the Abode of Aesop in Fableland. The old sage enters, accompanied by his servants, bearing banners inscribed with the names of his most popular fables. Aesop then sings a song to the effect that what human nature was of old it is today, and at the conclusion of the song, the Fairy Mistletoe arrives to urge him to descend to Earth and visit England, 'the land of freedom'. While Aesop is boasting of the peace of his animal subjects, and complaining that children only read his fables without learning their moral, acquiring thereby false theories of Natural History, Little Mag, 'the tittle-tattler of the feathered race' (Miss Katie Logan, dressed as a magpie and acting, said *The Times*, in a role 'somewhat analogous to the Chorus of the Greek Drama') appears to tell of the rivalry between Cock Robin and Cock Sparrow for the hand of Jenny Wren and the approaching marriage of Cock Robin and Jenny. So they all depart for the village of Wren's Nest, arriving in time to find Cock Robin dead, killed by Sparrow. Miss Logan recites 'Death and Burial of Cock Robin' and each of the characters comes forward to perform their part 'with melancholy solemnity'. Aesop, owning himself mistaken in his estimate of animal virtues, agrees to protect the two children of the story, who are favourites with the Fairies. The scene ends with a ballet and the setting shifts to Hoppergollup House in the neighbourhood of Ware, the authors having moved the location of the story from Norfolk to Hertfordshire. There the children, Willie and Alice Goodchild, reside with their wicked uncle Sir Gabriel Grimwood, under the care of their governess Barbara Allen, who has a sweetheart, Walter Trueheart, a young soldier. Sir Gabriel wishes to dispose of the children to gain their wealth and he determines to advertise for someone to do it. Sir Gabriel surprises Barbara and Walter making love and throws Walter out. The scene changes to 'Deep Jack(y) Hole in a Dark Swim on the New River', where Daddy Jacky sings 'Ten Little Niggers' and each of the characters in the song comes forward to meet his fate. Daddy Jacky, having disposed of his numerous offspring, is recruited as one of two cut-throats to murder the children. The other is Walter in disguise. Willie and Alice are induced by oranges and lemons to go for a walk. But Sir Gabriel, having had a heavy supper and much liquor, retires to bed and experiences a nightmare. It is a dream trial before the Court of Fairy Queen's Bench parodying the famous dream trial in *The Bells*, which in 1871 had electrified audiences and made Henry Irving an overnight star. Little Mag has summoned Mother Bunch and Dame Trot, friends of the children, after they protected the latter's cat Tommy, plus 'all the other antique ladies what ever figured in nursery rhyme.' Evidence against Sir Gabriel is given by the Bells of London, who make their appearance singing their lines from the nursery rhyme 'Oranges and Lemons': 'You owe me five farthings etc.'. The dream converts Sir Gabriel and he repents, but too late. The children and their guides have reached 'Robin Redbreast's Retreat in the Wilds of Where' where Jacky and Walter fight as the latter tries to protect the children. Walter vanquishes Jacky who fights in the garb of an Ashantee and drives him off after capturing his umbrella which Jacky shrewdly surmises will be sent to South Kensington, to the Victoria and Albert Museum. This is a topical reference to the Ashanti war of 1874 in which Sir Garnet Wolseley defeated The Ashanti, destroying their capital and royal palace. The children cry themselves to sleep, the wilds disappear and they are transported to the Home of the Nereids and the transformation takes place.

The 'Who Killed Cock Robin?' sequence – of which *The Times* said: 'Why these characters should here appear, and what purpose they are to serve we confess ourselves unable to explain; we only know that they do well what they are expected to do, that is, make us laugh, and what better service could we ask?' – ended with a grand ballet in the Kingdom of Birds. *The Era* reported that it took place:

> in a sort of golden aviary, the gilt columns rising in a circular shape to a variegated dome, while in front steps in a pyramidal form give opportunities for the fairy birds to perform some hopping *pas* … that are not only novel, but effective, and displayed to their best advantage the bright and manifold colours of the ladies' dresses, which were made of an infinite number of small pieces of silk, to represent, as nearly as may be, the coverings of the feathered race. Perhaps the illusion was not carried very far, but at all events the effect was elegant and charming.

The Era also praised the scene-painting of Frederick Lloyds, especially the Home of the Nereids:

> First, the stage shows *Figurantes* placed above a gilded terrace, but this soon descends through traps, and a number of gelatine curtains, cut in serpentine strips and of varied and brilliant colours, are slowly raised one by one, each change throwing a more beautiful tint upon the scene. Meanwhile, at the wings and at the centre of the stage, fairies stand before pearl shells; while, on each side of the latter, others group themselves in sea coral, and high up at the back *figurantes* depend from seaweed, or are posed upon the crests of fountains. The *tableau* must be seen to be appreciated.

The Era concluded: 'The piece was very well acted, the ladies being especially good'. Katie Logan, who *The Times* calls 'a wonderful little lady', is also praised by *The Era*: 'Little Katie Logan's songs and dances gave delight to everybody, obtaining encores for both, especially for a dance in the fifth scene. She gave her lines, too, with great point and intelligence.' Among the men, James Fawn as Sir Gabriel received the accolades: 'His imitation of Irving, being much applauded, ... and his dancing received rapturous encores'. *The Times* reported that the Irving imitations were 'greeted with good-humoured recognition without ever transgressing the bounds of good taste or propriety.'

   The Era review praised the costumes ('elegant and rich, and quite in conformity with the suggestions recently made by the Lord Chamberlain'), machinery ('We have rarely seen machinery work so smoothly on a first night'), and John Cormack for the ballets and harlequinade. Overall it was pronounced a success. Blanchard recorded after seeing it, 'goes off well.'[31]

   Jack in Wonderland or the Magic Beanstalk, the Great Giant, and the Merry Pranks of the Good Little People was the 1875 Crystal Palace pantomime, 'expressly written for the Palace by Mr E.L. Blanchard and ... produced under the company's management, on the great stage of the centre transept' reported *The Daily News*. *The Times* (28 December 1875) reporting on the previous day at the Palace, recorded attendance by 47,005 people. The pantomime was only part of a total Christmas experience. The Palace was lighted up by long rows of jets of flame and decked with flags and greenery. The naves were crowded with stalls selling Christmas gifts. There were performances by a military band, the Bernard troupe of minstrels, a Russian comic ballet choreographed by Espinosa, a gymnastic display by the Midget Hanlons, swings in the grounds, a dwarf, Admiral Tom Trump, holding receptions in the concert room, and an exhibition of some 'cleverly modelled Japanese comic groups, never before shown in this country', while the aquarium and the Pompeii display also drew visitors. The pantomime began at 2.30 p.m. and played to 12,000 people, 'perhaps the largest numbers that can observe at one time a theatrical performance on any modern stage.' Sixty policemen were deployed to keep the crowds in order and barriers were set up for the duration of the pantomime performance. *The Era* (22 December 1875) noted:

> 'Jack and the Beanstalk' is the foundation upon which Mr Blanchard has built up his pleasant fancies, and the adventures of that hero, told in the graceful lyric fashion with which the author elevates pantomime to the region of the fairy tale, are blended with a host of scenes and incidents not only fascinating in themselves but affording additional interest owing to the many allusions to contemporary events, such as the Arctic exploration, the journey of the Prince of Wales to India, etc.

It was in fact a reworking of the 1859–60 Drury Lane pantomime, *Jack and the Beanstalk*. The pantomime opens with a glimpse into the Crystal Palace Almanac, and while Zadkiel, Whittaker and Old Moore are arguing about the relative merits of their almanacs, they discuss the unpredictable changeability of the weather. A 'pleasant fairy', The Weather appears – she takes the form of a woman because like women, the weather is changeable. She is attended by Heat, Cold, Snow, Hail, Mist, Rain and Dew, all played by children. Weather then summons the months, who appear with representations of the notable events of each. They enter successively as they are alluded to in a specially composed song sung by Weather: January with Twelfth Night and Plough Monday; February with St Valentine's Day, Shrove Tuesday and 'Hare-Hunting ends'; March with St David's, St Patrick's and Lady Days; April with All Fools' Day and Easter Monday; May with Whit Monday; June with the Longest Day; July with St Swithin's Day; August with the Dog Days; September with St Partridge and Michaelmas Days; October with 'Pheasant Shooting begins' and St Crispin; November with Guy Fawkes Day and Lord Mayor's Day; December with the Shortest Day. Zadkiel suggests a pantomime to cheer up the winter, whatever the weather. Weather offers them as subjects the inhabitants of Jack Land: Jack the Giantkiller, Jack Horner, Jack and Jill (a conceit Blanchard had used before). Zadkiel recommends Jack and the Beanstalk. The narrative was the same as the 1859 version and structured month by month from January to May. However, the story changes once Jack climbs the beanstalk. He finds himself at the North Pole, in, said *The Daily News*, 'a scene that would do credit to the imagination of Jules Verne'. Jack and an attendant, a 'goblin squire', the Scarlet Runner, play pranks on the icebergs with polar bears and walruses, 'their gambols highly delighted the younger portion of the audience.' The Arctic was in the news with the imminent departure of the 1875–6 British Arctic Expedition under George Nares. Jack and the Scarlet Runner 'are transported thence to India and in front of a gorgeous palace the stage is filled with a host of characters suggestive of the reception of the Prince of Wales.' The Prince of Wales' official visit to India had been the great royal highlight of 1874. 'This happy idea', said *The Era*:

is carried out in a manner worthy of the event itself. There is a grand Indian ballet, with dances by Nautch girls, and a shawl dance, arranged with great taste and skill by M. Espinosa, who, as Scarlet Runner ... figures prominently throughout the Opening. The shawl dance enables a group of *coryphées* to twine and intertwine with undulating motion, making a pretty and fanciful picture, while as a contrast there are palm trees, elephants, camels etc. The Midget Hanlon *troupe* do excellent service in this scene. Made up as monkeys, they climb the trees with wonderful agility, leap from branch to branch, tumble over head and heels, and gambol in the most approve monkey fashion. A group of Ethiopian minstrels – Bernard's *troupe* of Christy's – sing and dance in this scene, the conclusion of which is really splendid, the stage being filled with gaily-dressed figures, a good notion being that a number of natives carrying flags, inscribed with words 'Tell mama we are happy!' – a significant message for the Prince of Wales to carry home to the Queen, and one which we trust would be echoed by the natives in reality.

From India they proceed to the Giant's castle where the Giant's head filled the whole of the stage. 'It is wonderfully well painted. The mouth opens and shuts, the eyelids move, and the Giant's enormous moustache twirls with a most ferocious expression of defiance.' His snores were produced by a fog horn. His Baby filled half the stage. The Fairy of the Harp gives Jack the sword of Caradoc with which he despatches the Baby and beheads the Giant. The Giant's castle falls. Jack's sweetheart Rose appears to be united with Jack and in time for the transformation.

The transformation, as in the previous year, highlighted an entirely new and different legend from the main narrative. A little girl, named Gretchen, is given a fairy godmother at her christening by the intervention of fortune. When she learns that her godmother is a fairy, she realizes why she has become the good and thoughtful child everyone says she is. On her birthday, she determines to leave a posy of wild flowers for her godmother and goes at twilight to collect the choicest wild flowers from a glade. The fairy godmother appears and is so charmed that as a birthday reward, she conveys Gretchen for a short time to the abode of King Pleasantseye, himself a flower in the land of remembrance. This transformation was, said *The Era*:

> invented and painted by Mr Charles Brew, and certainly does credit to his imaginative powers and his abilities as an artist ... The groups are beautifully blended and the light most harmoniously arranged. This scene alone would make the Crystal Palace Pantomime successful, to say nothing of the highly effective scenes in the Arctic Regions and the Indian *tableaux*.

The ERA also commented: 'Nothing could possibly be in better taste than the music, selected, arranged and composed by Mr Oscar Barrett, who also conducted with great skill. Some of the choicest fragments from operas, popular ballads, Music Hall airs, and dance music were blended admirably.'

The harlequinade was arranged by James Doughty who played Clown and whose performing dogs were a feature of the sequence, which also included the Suez Canal, a Bow-Wow Pie Shop and Quiet Lodgings, before the finale at the Home of the Fairies.

As to the acting, Caroline Parkes as Jack 'with dance and song, and smartly delivered dialogue, greatly enhanced its effect. Miss Parkes has rarely, if ever, been seen to greater advantage. Unfortunately Miss Manetti as the Fairy Weather had recourse to the prompter.' T.H. Friend directed and stage managed and played Goody Grayshoes. M. Espinosa 'did good service as the Scarlet Runner and in arranging the ballet.' *The Times* critic claimed not to have heard much of the dialogue or the music, apart from the foghorn.

In 1873 a great new pleasure palace and amusement grounds had opened in north London to rival the attraction of the Crystal Palace – Alexandra Palace. It had almost immediately been burned down in a disastrous fire. But rebuilt and reopened in 1875, it commissioned a pantomime from the Brothers Grinn. Due to open on 22 December, *Harlequin Yellow Dwarf or the King of the Golden Mines* had to be postponed until 24 December when George Conquest, playing the title role, 'twisted his spine.' The chief attractions were a doll show and the pantomime. *The Times* (28 December 1875) estimated that it received between 30,000 and 50,000 visitors during the day.

The pantomime opens in the Silver Hall of Icicles in Jack Frost's Winter Palace near the North Pole and lit by the aurora borealis. Shortest Day, Jolly Time, Good Cheer and Jack Frost discuss the events of the year. These include the passing of the Merchant Shipping Bill, thanks to the efforts of the campaigning MP Samuel Plimsoll; the swimming of the English Channel by Captain Webb; the performance of Shakespeare in Italian by the great tragedian Salvini; the absconding while on bail of Alexander Collie who was accused of defrauding the London and Westminster Bank, among others, of £500,000; and the citing of *The Times* and *The Daily News* for breach of privilege in publishing a letter from the Honduran Minister in Paris to the Chairman of the Foreign Loans Committee. To cheer everyone up, they decide to propose a pantomime.

The icy scene melts into the golden Temples of Indian Fairyland where allusions are made to the Prince of Wales' visit to India, which is still a major event in the public consciousness. Little Great Britain appears ('To civilise the world I daily labour: Take my own part: don't quarrel with my neighbour') and calls forth the Bright Fancies of the East for a grand ballet. Little Great Britain promises the royal visitors will be protected and two sailors appear and dance a hornpipe: 'While they protect it, Britain's flag unfurled should safe be seen to go right through the world.'

The story of the pantomime begins in an Orange Grove with a withered tree, which contains the Yellow Dwarf. First as the tree, then as an owl and finally as himself, the Dwarf coerces Princess Allfair into agreeing to be his bride. At the Reception Hall of King Marmalade's Palace, the Dwarf appears to claim his bride but the King intends the Princess for Meliodorus, the King of the Golden Mines. The Dwarf carries her off, the scene ending with an imitation of Grand Opera – sung to the tune of an aria from *Lucretia Borgia*. The King of the Golden Mines follows to the Steel Castle of the Yellow Dwarf where he is helped by Magnet, a sprite, and the Desert Fairy. The King and the Dwarf engage in a tremendous struggle in the Cobweb Cave and the Spider's Glen, ending with the Dwarf killed. The Good Fairy unites the lovers and then comes the grand transformation, the Glow-worm Glade or the Fairy Forest leading to the Desert Fairy's Home. The harlequinade with scenes in a toymaker's and a quiet suburban lodgings followed provided by the Lauri family, and also featuring Nat Emmett and his performing goats, the skating of the Brothers Guida, and Adonis the 'African Miniature Man' before the grand finale in the Realm of Bliss.

The Era (2 January 1876) was dazzled by the performance of George Conquest as the Dwarf, his rapid changes, transformations and leaps. 'As an example of grotesque pantomime art of the most original and remarkable character, Mr Conquest's performance as the Tree, the Owl and the Demon Dwarf will be talked of as the most extraordinary pantomime effect of the season.'

The Golden Temples of Indian Fairyland were described as:

a scene by Mr William Brew and Henri Nedmé, one of the most brilliant pantomimic achievements we have witnessed this season. This Indian scene is really one of the most exquisite spectacles ever placed upon the stage; and not only is it remarkable for scenic effects, but the brilliant ballet introduced brings upon the stage such a host of gaily dressed and animated groups that we very much doubt whether the real Indian spectacle the Prince of Wales has witnessed would not look tame and dull by comparison with that of the Alexandra. Elephants and other animals covered with gay trappings, attended by slaves fancifully costumed, and carrying banners with all sorts of quaint and picturesque devices, occupy the background, while in the centre of the picture there is a splendid ballet, the dancers having been admirably drilled by M. Espinosa, who invented and arranged the ballet with his customary imaginative grace. The groups have been so well trained, and pass through a variety of difficult evolutions with so much grace and correctness, that the entire scene is one of the greatest successes of the Pantomime, and naturally gains most enthusiastic applause.

The Daily News (25 December 1875) called it 'exceedingly pretty'.

The grand transformation scene, the Glow-worm Glade or the Fairy Forest leading to the Desert Fairy's Home, was the work of Messrs Soames and J. Johnstone. It represented 'a host of ferns illuminated by many coloured lights contrasting brilliantly with the elaborate changes that follow, leading up to a grand scene composed of roseate bowers, fairy-like maidens, festoons of flowers enclosing the graceful groups, and gorgeous cloud scenery filling up the picture.' *The Daily News* called it 'a spectacle which for brilliancy and beauty can hardly be surpassed.'

The Era records the pantomime being received with 'rapturous applause' and praised the energy of all the performers, Miss Laura Conquest as Little Great Britain ('charming') and Carry Nelson as the King of the Golden Mines ('playing … with great spirit, singing and dancing gaily') along with George Conquest. *The Era* also praised 'the good work' done by scenic artists Brew, Soames, Johnstone and Nedmé, composer Oscar Barrett, choreographer Espinosa, and Auguste and co. 'whose splendid dresses enhanced the brilliancy of the Pantomime immensely.' George Conquest directed as well as starring. Blanchard saw it on 12 February, writing: 'George Conquest very clever; the story completely spoiled.'[32]

By Christmas 1875 *The Times* (28 December 1875) was reporting that in Central London, only Covent Garden and Drury Lane produced pantomimes, though they were plentiful in the suburbs. But *The Era* (2 January 1876) rejoiced that 'The masses who assemble in front to witness the wonders of the fairy world presented on the stage carry away with them remembrance of scenic splendour and wholesome merriment which will serve to freshen the brain, brighten the mind, and gladden the heart for many a month to come.' The Drury Lane pantomime was *Dick Whittington and His Cat or Harlequin Lord Mayor of London*. The gallery was less noisy than usual, apparently missing the man who had unofficially conducted them for the past two years, but eventually the singing, clapping, dropping of orange peel on the pit and roars of approval for the national anthem got them in the right spirit.

The pantomime opens on May Day in Cheapside with the lads and lasses singing the madrigal 'Now is the month of Maying' and carrying garlands and baskets of daisies, buttercups, primroses, violets and cowslips. They are intent on electing a Queen of the May but they are ordered back to work by the surly mercer Master Hugh Fitzwarren. The lasses return and crown Alice Fitzwarren Queen of the May. Then Dick Whittington and his cat Tommy turn up, having walked from Gloucestershire. Fitzwarren takes on Dick to work for him. Dick and the Cat both get into trouble with Fitzwarren's Cook and leave. Whittington goes to sleep and the sound of Bow Bells are heard and the choral strain: 'Turn again Whittington-thrice Lord Mayor of London'. The Fairy Bluebell and the elves dance around them. Then Fitzwarren and co. appear in pursuit, as Tommy the Cat has stolen the meat from the kitchen. But Alice intercedes for them and Dick and Tom are taken back. They all set sail on a trading voyage to Zanzibar, there the Sultan offers ten sacks of gold to whoever will rid his palace of a plague of rats. Tom does so and is rewarded. The substitution of Zanzibar for the traditional destination of Morocca can be explained by topicality: the official visit to Britain of the Sultan of Zanzibar in the summer of 1875. They all end up back in the Belfry of Bow Bells where there is a grand procession in honour of Tom, who marries a white cat, and Whittington and Alice are united.

The Vokeses once again received great praise: Fred as Hugh Fitzwarren, Victoria as Dick, Rosina as Alice, Fawdon as Tom the Cat and Jessie as Fairy Bluebell. *The Times* thought the honours of the evening went to Walter Fawdon Vokes as Tommy, 'who was throughout the life and soul of the pantomime, and in appearance and behaviour reflected great credit on Mr Vokes' knowledge of natural and pantomimic history.' *The Era* distributed praise equally, noting of the family, 'we have never known them to work more energetically, nor with greater success'. Fred Vokes was made up as an old man in a white wig, nevertheless:

> his dancing was, as usual, of an extraordinary description, his long and nimble legs seeming capable of all sorts of grotesque gyrations, and appearing most to delight the spectators when they went flying over the heads of the ladies who joined their owner in the dance. Old Fitzwarren on board ship and coming to grief in his endeavours to climb the rigging provoked the most uproarious merriment.

Rosina Vokes 'took all hearts by storm as Alice Fitzwarren. Her pretty face, her appreciation of fun, her expressive singing, her remarkable quick and clever powers as a dancer, entitle her to our warmest commendation.' Victoria Vokes 'was exactly suited for the role of Dick Whittington, entered upon her task with her wonted spirit and vivacity, and apparently enjoyed the fun quite as much as the audience her efforts were delighting.' Jessie as Fairy Bluebell 'was fully equal to the requirements of her part, and for her grace as a dancer we have the warmest commendation.' Fawdon Vokes 'contributed not a little to the fun as the Cat. The disguise was capital, the movements were comical by reason of their very truthfulness, while the antics he played, and the mischievous tricks of which he was guilty, furnished great fun, and provoked continued merriment.'

There were two major transformation scenes, one on the voyage to Zanzibar when the ship sinks and the other, the finale, the Blossoming of the Bell Flowers. Beverley was, as usual, called by the audience to take a bow. Blanchard saw it on 27 December 1875 and reported 'goes off well.'[33]

The 1876–7 pantomime was *Harlequin and the Forty Thieves*, a tale not previously done at Drury Lane. *The Times* (27 December 1876) observed that 'the national theatre' as it habitually called Drury Lane, was 'crowded to excess in every part. The spectacle it presents during this time may be accepted as an illustration both of the vitality and of the influence exercised in English life by traditional usage.' Blanchard's 'book' was 'characterized by much graceful humour and facility of versification. Upon these attractions he seems content to rely, the dialogue being singularly free from those allusions to passing events which elsewhere are awaited with so much eagerness, and applauded with so much energy.' *Forty Thieves* was pronounced very similar to Blanchard's previous annuals – 'a light travestie, unmixed with extraneous matter, of a familiar story, and designed to afford frequent opportunities of introducing whimsical acting and imposing scenery and dresses.'

Earlier *The Times* had observed: 'Different styles of entertainment come and go, but pantomime, with its odd though not incongruous mixture of poetry and broad humour, appears like Swedenborg's fabled angels, to acquire new vigour as the years pass away.'

The Era (31 December 1876) noted that 'Mr Blanchard always puts some meaning into his work, and invariably upsets the theory that, in order to be amusing and funny, it is also necessary to be stupid. Even in the names he gives to things and places bright fancy plays a part.'

The pantomime opens in the marketplace of Bagdad. Abdallah, the captain of the forty thieves, and his lieutenant Hassarac enter, disguised as merchants. At a signal from the former the forty thieves separate themselves from the crowd, arrange themselves in a semi-circle and break into a dance. Ali Baba, whose poor stall is seen in striking contrast with the imposing dwelling of his rich brother Cassim, enters with his precocious son Ganem. Trade is so bad that he resolves to go into the forest and fell trees. Meanwhile he asks Cassim and his shrewish wife Cogia Baba for financial assistance, but they both refuse, Cogia expressing her surprise that such nuisances as poor people had ever been invented. Their attendant Morgiana, however, offers her necklace to the needy trader and Ganem promptly falls in love with her. The forty thieves relieve the traders of their purses and join in the general dance with which the scene ends.

The scene changes to the Divan of the Genii, where the chief peri Eureka endows Morgiana with the necessary attributes to bring the thieves to justice, and she is transformed from a poor drudge into a graceful, courageous, shrewd and high-minded young woman. Ali Baba and Ganem repair to the Date Tree Grove and after 'a very diverting scene, in which', said *The Times*, 'by some ingenious mechanism their donkey is made to wink, snort, thrust out its tongue, and otherwise display something like human intelligence – a thing certainly worth seeing', Ali Baba and Ganem are lured by a dragon fly to the enchanted cavern in the depths of the forest. Eureka and her attendant fairies are first seen grouped among the trees but then disappear. The Forty Thieves arrive, laden with plunder, and Ali Baba and Ganem, hidden in the trees, hear the magic words to open the cavern. They then use these words themselves and remove the treasure. Cassim and Cogia, having lost their way in the forest after a picnic, witness the discovery of the treasure and seek to claim some for themselves. But Abdallah appears, chases Cassim and cuts him in two. Back in Bagdad, Ali Baba and Ganem are now living in splendour with Cogia, an impoverished widow, as their maid. Abdallah devises a plan to retrieve his wealth. Disguised as a merchant, he induces Ali Baba to take charge of forty oil jars, in which the thieves are concealed. Morgiana discovers the plot and pours boiling oil in on the thieves. Abdallah repents and decides to spend his money setting up a new Cooperative Bank. Cassim, sewn up by Morgiana, is brought back to life. Ganem and Morgiana marry. The transformation scene transports them all to the Peri's Palace.

Once again the Vokes Family starred: Fred as Ali Baba, Rosina as Ganem, Victoria as Morgiana, Jessie as Abdallah and Fawdon as his henchman Hassacrac. *The Times* noted that the Vokes Family, 'admirable both as pantomimists and singers', held the principal parts and 'all the scenes in which they appear pass off amid roars of laughter and applause.' *The Era* reported:

> Every member of the Vokes family worked with a will to add life to the piece, and the most gratifying success attended their efforts, Miss Rosina, as usual, being full of mischief, vivacity, and fun; Miss Victoria, adding the charms of sweet vocalisation to the other attractions of her part, especially noticeable being her interpretation of a song and dance with tambourine, composed expressly by Miss Julia Woolf. Miss Jessie looked and played in most bewitching fashion. Mr Fred proved that the elasticity of his legs is great as ever, and that he has not yet lost the art of passing them over the heads of his sisters; while the melodramatic nonsense was heartily welcome. The whole family made an immense hit in the dance which immediately preceded the Transformation, and in response to a tremendous outburst of cheering it was repeated.

William Beverley was in charge of the scenery and now under exclusive contract to Drury Lane. *The Times* noted that he 'rarely produces anything which does not leave an agreeable impression on the mind. On this occasion he painted in his best style the market place of Bagdad and the Divan of the Genii.' The grand ballet occurred in the Divan of the Genii where the peris with the aid of fans, feathers and flowers 'realised the poet's idea of a "garden of girls".' Karl Meyder's music, which according to the book of words, was 'largely derived from Ancient Oriental sources, with Modern Music Hall melodies', was well-received. Blanchard does not record in his diary when he saw it.

Blanchard remained in the Orient for the 1876 pantomime at Crystal Palace, *Sindbad the Sailor or Harlequin and the Fairies of the Diamond Valley*. It was credited to the Brothers Grinn, Blanchard and Greenwood, and was once again performed in the afternoons from 21 December onwards. Charles Wyndham was now in charge of producing the pantomime and the Brothers Grinn had produced a very free version of the legend. The opening scene is the seaport and slave-market of Bassorah. The King of Dahomey's Turkish High Admiral Toffy-Woffy arrives for the purpose of purchasing slaves. Fatima is put up for sale by her wicked uncle. Despite opposition from Sindbad, the high Admiral succeeds in carrying off the prize. In the second scene, Sindbad, accompanied by the faithful Ali, follows the ship in a small boat only to be captured by the High Admiral and sentenced to death. A pirate ship attacks; Fatima is carried off; and the Admiral's ship, riddled with shot, goes down in an undulating sea. Sindbad and Ali, having reached the shore in a raft, are made welcome at the Summer Abode of the Diamond Queen, where Sindbad's head is nearly turned by the splendour and beauty around him. But he never wavers in his devotion to Fatima. Sindbad and Ali dispose of the Old Man of the Sea. Meanwhile Fatima is recaptured from the pirates by the High Admiral, Sindbad and Ali reach the Diamond Valley and are carried off in 'a great spectacular effect' by the Roc. After a scene on the river of the Island of Pygmies Sindbad and Ali arrive at the Palace of the King of Dahomey. The King, despite having a score of wives, wants Fatima, but her purchase price is £2,000. The King does not have it but is confident that if he starts a grand Dahomean loan 'the English will take it up with avidity'. Sindbad, deposited in the vicinity by the Roc, concerts a plan for Fatima's escape with the King's twenty wives and the King is prevailed upon to resign her to Sindbad. The transformation scene told the story of Echo and Narcissus. The production was notable for several *coups de théâtre*. *The Stage* (24 December 1876) reported:

> When the huge ship sails from Bassorah, by an ingenious contrivance the town glides away, leaving the ship in mid-ocean. It is a masterpiece of scenic effect and arrangement, and it was greeted, as it deserved to be by enthusiastic applause ... and then a scene of the most novel description completely takes the spectators by surprise. A pirate vessel appears in sight, sailing across the stage in grand style, filled with fierce-looking fellows, who make an attack upon the other ships. There is a slashing sea fight and the unfortunate vessel from Bassorah sinks, the illusion being carried further by the appearance of a raft in the distance upon which a couple of the crew have escaped. A more realistic incident we have never seen attempted, and certainly we never saw anything of the kind so effectively represented. The scene has all the animation and vividness of reality.

The Times (23 December 1876) proclaimed the scenery by Julian Hicks, Frederick Fenton and Charles Brew and the dresses 'both appropriate and pretty', the acting 'generally good', with special praise for Mr Le Vite's Ali and Miss Edith Bruce's Sindbad, 'the one for his broad humour, and the other for her unflagging vivacity.' The transformation scene of Charles Brew 'would alone repay the visitor for his trouble.'

The Daily News (22 December 1876) declared *Sindbad the Sailor*:

> may be pronounced to be the most brilliant and best mounted Christmas piece yet produced at the Crystal Palace. The scenery, by Messrs Brew, J. Hicks and Fenton, is

very beautiful, notably Mr Brew's transformation scene ... For this the manager, Mr Wyndham, and the artist, Mr Brew, had both the honour of a call. Next to it we may place the panorama of the enchanted valley, which the Roc obligingly enables Sindbad to see; and, thirdly, the voyage of the ship, ... managed with great ingenuity and novelty of mechanical contrivances. The actors and actresses are all new, and all established themselves at once in the good opinion of the audience.

The Era (31 December 1876) concluded:

The 'Brothers Grinn' have done their work capitally, as usual, and have told the story of Sindbad the Sailor with humorous perception and poetical grace. Mr Julian Hicks and Mr Fenton have outdone all their previous efforts, and the allegorical *tableau* of Mr ... Brew ... is in itself a poem, and one of the most fanciful scenic displays ever placed before the public. The descriptions of the scenic effects at the Wagnerian Festival at Bayreuth must pale before such a triumph of poeticized mythology as this. The artists, specially engaged by Mr Charles Wyndham to do particular justice to this year's Pantomime, are not behindhand in assisting the liberal designs of the Directors and the artistic skill of the scenic artists. Miss Edith Bruce and Miss Bella Goodall both do excellent work, and the ballet, arranged by Miss Barbara Morgan, is once more a welcome and important feature. Nor should any record of an entirely successful Pantomime at Sydenham be complete without special mention of the music of Mr Oscar H. Barrett, an original and charming composer, who for many years has kept up the high-art tone of Crystal Palace music in an entertainment generally supposed to be so completely unartistic as a Pantomime. At any rate, Mr Barrett studies to relieve the holiday amusement from the slightest suspicion of vulgarity.

What The Daily News called 'the slight concluding harlequinade' included scenes of Trafalgar Square, London in Winter, Charing Cross Station and the Westminster Clock. The Times noted that 'Mr Augustus Harris, as stage manager, is to be congratulated on the general effectiveness with which this excellent but by no means easily-produced pantomime is worked.' Barrett's score included the market chorus from Auber's opera Masaniello, the rondo of Beethoven's violin concerto arranged as a Dance for Owls ('a bit of musical ingenuity such as few would have hit upon and worked out so cleverly') and the introduction to the Third Act of Lohengrin, 'mixed up with other music ... one way of bringing the "music of the future" down to popular comprehension.' There was also a grand march of the pygmy army with the King riding on an ostrich, a hornpipe danced by the Lord Admiral, and a shawl dance in the harem. The Stage concluded that the Crystal Palace pantomime was 'in every way a brilliant success'.

Complaints in the press about unsuitable material contained in pantomimes being witnessed by children multiplied. The Era (23 December 1866), for instance, suggested that producers eliminate 'those elements of slang and coarseness which are so often made the substitutes for wit and humour. There ought to be no line heard by a child on the stage which it could not repeat with safety in a drawing-room.' To meet these demands, F.B. Chatterton came up with a variation on the traditional pantomime – a pantomime for children performed entirely by children (18 of them). He turned to his regular collaborators, Blanchard for the script and John Cormack for the choreography, and staged it at the Adelphi, with scenery by Frederick Lloyds and music by Edwin Ellis.

Blanchard adapted his 1862–3 Drury Lane script, *Little Goody Two-Shoes and her Sweetheart Little Boy Blue*, for a show which opened on 23 December 1876, initially performed only at matinees starting at 2.30 p.m. but from February added to the evening programme. It lasted two and a half hours and according to *The Times* (27 December 1876) 'leaves nothing to be desired.' *The Times* thought Blanchard had:

> made it in itself almost a fairy play, it is so full of pretty thoughts, graceful sentiment, and poetry. Surely the little characters he has created and the fairies he has called into being must people his fertile brain, and we might almost suppose that they come before him in his dreams.

The acting of the children was praised: 'They act and sing and dance with a delicious freshness, and a smile and a laugh which come as they only can from children.' There was praise too for Edwin Ellis' music and John Cormack's arrangement of the ballet and 'general business'. *The Times* concluded, 'Mr Chatterton has given us a delightful novelty, unique in its entirety.'

The Era (24 December 1876) reported that the pantomime was a total success:

> Never did we hear more genuine laughter or more enthusiastic applause. *Little Goody Two Shoes* will be the talk of the town. Everybody will be asking 'Have you seen the children's Pantomime at the Adelphi?' ... Sometimes the visitors could not applaud for laughter, sometimes they applauded just to give themselves a rest when their sides ached. The reception of *Little Goody Two Shoes* has hardly been equalled in our remembrance. It was one continuous roar of merriment and approbation that did one's very heart good to hear.

The Opening was thoroughly enjoyed but it was surpassed by the harlequinade:

> If the entire performance of the Opening elicited our heartiest approval, greater praise, if possible, must be given to the harlequinade. Nothing could be more whimsically comic, nothing could be in better taste, nothing could be better carried out in every way. It was absolutely marvellous to witness how thoroughly these tiny pantomimists entered into their work ... As for Master Bertie Coote, the Clown, he is a comic genius of positively

wonderful ability. To see his merry grin as he plays his pantomimical pranks, to hear his singing of 'Hot Codlins' and 'Tippetywitchet', to watch his grotesque antics, and, more than all, to note the astonishing coolness with which he enters into the business of the scene, is one of the most complete theatrical successes we have ever witnessed.

When the audience called for Chatterton at the end, he came forward to take a bow, leading Bertie Coote by the hand.

Little Goody Two-Shoes received rave reviews all round and ran for over 150 performances. Blanchard, who evidently saw it in rehearsal, declared himself 'much delighted' with the production.[34] Chatterton was so encouraged by this success that he mounted another all-child pantomime, scripted by Blanchard, *Little Red Riding Hood*, in the summer and autumn of 1877. Many of the cast of *Goody Two-Shoes* returned, notably Bertie Coote, giving another notable comic performance. *The Era* (12 August 1877) was as taken with it as it had been with *Little Goody-Two Shoes*:

Everybody knows the story of 'Little Red Riding Hood', but everybody does not know it so happily treated as it has been in this instance. Therefore everybody must go and have a peep at Mr Stafford Hall's picturesque village in Normandy, with which at the Adelphi it opens. There everybody will see ... the miniature dairy maids with their milking-pails; the miniature serving men labouring beneath their miniature sacks of flower, and the prettily-dressed peasants making merry and joining in song and dance. They will see how prettily Little Red Riding Hood and the bold young villager Bonbon make love; how bravely the last-named defies the wicked Baron Malvoisin of the Chateau Loup, who cherishes evil designs against the scarlet-cloaked heroine of the story; how the good fairy Pomona, who has undertaken to watch over the fortunes and the misfortunes of our favourite, calls to her presence a host of 'fruit fairies' ... who dance and group in style that reflects high credit on Mr John Cormack; how a country lane near the abode of Hokey-Pokey, the Old Man of the Hill, is crowded with lads and lasses ... who are evidently resolved on keeping holiday; how Corneygrain, their master, having come to scoff, remains to sing and to dance; and how, with the remaining well-known incidents of the story fancifully and amusingly illustrated, we are taken to the Fairy Palace of Pomona, a beautiful scene sure to call forth the admiration of all who see it.

Robin Hood and his Merry Little Men followed for Christmas 1877 and the children's pantomimes might have continued had not Chatterton been forced to give up the Adelphi in 1878. Lewis Carroll, for one, adored the shows, seeing *Little Goody Two-Shoes* twice, *Little Red Riding Hood* twice and *Robin Hood* no fewer than six times.[35]

For the 1877–8 Christmas season the Drury Lane pantomime was *Harlequin and the White Cat*. *The Times* (27 December 1877) noted:

Wherever the pantomime may lose favour, at Drury Lane it holds its ground tenaciously, without the least sign of going out of fashion. For this class of entertainment Old Drury has long been famous, if not pre-eminent; and the piece produced last night was, on the whole, one calculated to maintain the high reputation of the house.

Of Blanchard's script, *The Times* observed:

of this production it is only fair to say that, although its author has furnished the holyday pieces at this theatre for the last 28 years, and generally with marked success, it exhibits no falling off in dramatic skill and power. As in most plays of its kind, the mere plot is a very subordinate element, the chief interest being derived from the spectacular effects, the broad humour, the graceful or grotesque dances and the sentimental or comic music which it is made the vehicle of introducing; and it must be admitted that in this case Mr Blanchard has made good use of each of these important accessories. If the dialogue is not particularly sparkling, nor the puns with which it is interspersed above the average in merit, the piece happily does not depend for its success on adjuncts as to which holyday audiences are proverbially indulgent, and its reception last night was certainly very favourable.

The pantomime opens in the courtyard of the hunting chateau and country palace of Queen Mytymama of Nevernoverre who is celebrating the eighteenth birthday of her daughter, Princess Blanchette. The Queen has previously been tricked into promising the bad fairy Violenta the hand of Blanchette for her son Psycho, the goblin dwarf. The festivities are also attended by King Colorado and his three sons, Prince Natty the Neat, Prince Nectar the Nimble and Prince Tremor the Nervous, the first of whom the Princess and her mother regard as an appropriate suitor. But the Fairy and the goblin appear to claim his bride and when the Queen resists, they turn the Princess into a white cat and carry her off. At the Lake of Water Lilies, a group of good fairies resolve to befriend the Princess and the three princes who have gone in search of her. The three princes and the Queen pass through the Wood of Enchantment searching for the lost Princess. They are harassed by Psycho and overtaken by a fierce storm. They find refuge at the Cats School of Cookery where the cats prepare food, repelling a plague of rats conjured up by Psycho. They move on to a levee at the Mother of Pearl Pavilion at the Cats' Castle where there is a cats' concert and a cats' dance and where Prince Natty dances with the White Cat, who tells him that the spell can only be broken if he cuts off her head. This takes place off stage. But back at King Colorado's palace, Natty appears with the restored Blanchette. Colorado promises to abdicate in favour of whichever of his sons presents him with something to amuse him in retirement. Natty gives him a tiny dog enclosed in an acorn and wins the throne. Prince Tremor defeats Psycho in single combat, demonstrating his courage, and Psycho disappears. The good fairy Myosotis (Forget-me-Not) declares Violenta beaten and she retires to foreign parts. The wedding of Prince and Princess is attended with the bestowal of gifts by the fairies.

The Era (30 December 1877) noted that The White Cat only two years before had 'furnished materials for one of the most dismal failures in the annals of things theatrical.' This was the production at the Queen's Theatre in December 1875. An English version of a French play, which had run for some 500 nights in Paris, it closed at the Queen's after only eight days. The Times (6 December 1875) said that the adaptors:

> have been careful to omit from their work anything which might offend the nicer ears of an English audience; with equal care have they obliterated whatever elements of · laughter the original may have contained ... The whole piece is dull from beginning to end ... there is about the stage and the people on the stage a prevailing air of dinginess.

This was not the case at Drury Lane where the Vokes Family were on top form, Fred as Prince Tremor, his wife Bella as Princess Blanchette, Victoria as Prince Natty, Jessie as Prince Nectar and Fawdon as Psycho. They contributed to the major highlights which included 'a coming of age in the golden time', illustrated 'In a very pretty fashion'. Then in a 'remarkably attractive scene', the Lake of Water Lilies and Fairy Grove by Moonlight, 'which must be pronounced one of Mr William Beverly's very best efforts', there was the 'F.B.C. [Fairy Ballet Chorus] performed by the corps de ballet, headed by the well-known première danseuse Mdlle Pitteri,

> who secured by the grace of her movements some of the loudest applause heard during the evening. The dances and groupings by the members of the corps de ballet reflected the continued skill of Mr John Cormack, who had contrived a marvellous coup d'oeil for the termination of the saltatory revels, the mirrors carried by the dancers suddenly taking the form of blazing suns and producing an effect which may not inaptly ... be compared to that of an unexpected and brilliant display of fireworks.

During the storm, the three Princes performed a comic umbrella dance which brought the house down and had to be repeated. The Cats School of Cookery was 'a capital scene, full of life, bustle and mirth-moving antics. After the action is resolved, the entire Vokes Family join in a dance before the transformation scene, the presentation of gifts and distribution of the wedding cake.' The Times said 'this is a most gorgeous and dazzling scene, in which Mr William Beverley certainly equals, if he does not indeed surpass all his previous triumphs.'

The Brothers Grinn transferred their skills from Crystal Palace to Alexandra Palace in 1877 with St George and the Dragon or Harlequin the Seven Champions of Christendom. The first scene, Mother Bunch's Bookcase in Baby Land, has Mother Bunch, Mother Shipton, Mother Glass, Mother Goose, Mother Hubbard and Mother Redcap discussing with Holyday and her daughter Half-Holyday the best method of recreation. Holyday and Half-Holyday reject the old crones' doctrine of 'all work and no play' and select a pantomime for recreation, debating the subjects, among them Cleopatra's Needle (which had arrived in England in 1877), the Colorado beetle (detected in Germany in 1877 and prompting the Destructive Insect Bill to prevent its arrival in England) and Mr Pongo, who all make an appearance, and finally select the story of St George and the Dragon. The next scene in Holyday's home has Easter, Midsummer, Michaelmas, Christmas and all the national holidays, including Twelfth Day, Shrove Tuesday, All Fool's Day, May Day and Guy Fawkes Day, holding a carnival which ends in a grand ballet. In the third scene, St George, living as an anchorite in a hermitage cell, feeds his friendly frog, raven and snake and rejects a bevy of beauties who invade his solitude. But the other champions of Christendom, St Denis of France, St Patrick of Ireland, St David of Wales, St Andrew of Scotland, St James of Spain and St Anthony of Italy, turn up and persuade him to join the ladies in keeping a rustic fête on St Valentine's Day, though he bets St Patrick a hundred pounds that he will regret it. The next scene has the rustic fête at the Village of Laughing Water where after the dancing and celebration, St Valentine sends a missive to George who vows 'Through fire and water I will my love pursue.' First he has to go to the Enchanted Cavern of the witch Kalyba, who is smitten with him, to gain her wand and his sword Excalibur. George proceeds to the court of King Ptolemy the Perplexed of Egypt where a Dragon has been devouring all the virgins. There Pendragon, son and envoy of the Dragon, arrives to claim Ptolemy's daughter Princess Sabra as his next meal. George, now in love with Sabra, travels through Frog Land to the Dragon's Haunt, kills him and returns to the Palace to claim his bride.

The Times (27 December 1877) noted that 'the claim of Alexandra Palace, young as the enterprise is, to a foremost rank among metropolitan places of entertainment on Bank Holidays and other like festive occasions is being still energetically asserted.' Among the attractions were the International Sweetmeat Fair, featuring Cleopatra's Needle in pink sugar and whose centre piece was an enormous 'twelfth cake', 50 feet wide and 4 feet high, surmounted by lifesize figures including Marshal MacMahon, Gladstone, Disraeli and Osman Pasha, with Father Christmas in their midst. Each child visitor received a free bag of sweets. At the east end of the Palace was a giant Christmas tree, loaded with toys, trinkets and trifles and surrounded by fairy tale scenes such as Jack and Jill and Little Red Riding Hood. There was also a display of dolls. But the pantomime – three hours long – was the principal attraction and ran every afternoon. The Times recorded that it was greeted with 'boundless applause'. The Daily News (24 December 1877) recorded it as 'one of the best ever seen on any stage', but The Era (30 December 1877) recalled several hitches with the scenery, though not enough to cause major delays.

The scenery by Henry Emden was praised by all the critics. The Era claimed that the pantomime's success owed much to Emden, 'whose picturesque pencil has embellished the Pantomime as few Pantomimes have ever been illustrated, and to whose graceful fancy is due one of the most charming Transformation scenes imaginable'. Particularly notable was his English landscape for the St Valentine's Day fete:

> We do not exaggerate when we say that this example of English landscape would shame half the landscapes hung on the walls of our picture galleries. We see the pretty old village at sunrise, and no praise can be too great for the skill with which nature has been simulated. The sun rises gradually, and as it ascends the clouds in every direction are tinted with its glowing beams. The glow of the roseate morn bathes the fairy-like valley, the distant hills, the old church, the trickling stream (real water), the overhanging trees, and the quaint gables of the cottages becoming each moment richer in colour. Nothing in the way of stage illusion was ever managed or carried out with greater completeness, for to make the effect absolutely complete we hear the very birds sing in the branches of the trees to greet the opening morn ... In this scene, there is also a village fête, with old English sports and pastimes, exceedingly well done.

Emden was called forth to take a bow, which he did. He was called again after the transformation scene, Vertumna and the Swallows. *The Era* praised:

> the brilliant changes and novel effects of this charming fancy, and, remembering how full it was of mechanical contrivances, as well as pictorial splendour, we could but admire the smoothness with which everything moved. The pretty young ladies suspended in the air, and groups of swallows with their pretty wings outspread, contrasting so beautifully with the glow of colour in all directions, formed a scene which, *blasé* as we are to Pantomimic effects, gave us unqualified pleasure. What better test could there be of the power of an artist than his management of colour, and Mr Emden has contrived some really magical combinations.

The Daily News called it 'a marvellous achievement' and *The Times*, 'a masterpiece of scenic art'.

The Daily News recalled 'There are several beautiful ballets, one of the most effective being a javelin dance, full of dazzling situations, at the Court of Ptolemy.' It praised John Lauri for his 'careful training' of the ballet corps. *The Times* praised the grand ballet at Holyday's Home, calling it 'pretty' and noting that the *première danseuse* Mdlle Luna was encored. *The Era* called the ballet 'charming'.

The Era observed that 'The admirable arrangements of the Opening and the completeness of the entire representation ... certainly places an additional feather in the professional cap of Mr T.H. Friend, the Stage-manager, whose labours must have been arduous in the extreme.' Miss Susie Vaughan was proclaimed 'a right merry, genial, sparkling, reckless, handsome St George ... She rattled through the Pantomime with a dash and animation, worthily representing the character of the hero.' Linda Verner played Princess Sabra 'with charming grace and considerable vocal skill' and her song 'She haunts me like a dream' was 'enthusiastically encored.'

The harlequinade, noted *The Era*, was 'short, but lively and bustling', with Fred Payne (who had played Pendragon in the Opening) 'the perfection of a sprightly Harlequin', while Harry Payne 'delighted all who saw him by his facetiousness as Clown'. 'The dresses, decorations, and paraphernalia of the piece are costly, tasteful and ingenious, and frequent and hearty applause testified to the satisfaction of the audience,' said *The Daily News*.

There was another children's pantomime at the Adelphi. This time Blanchard adapted his Drury Lane script from 1858–9, *Robin Hood*. *Robin Hood and His Merry Little Men*, opened on 22 December 1877, with music by Edwin Ellis, choreography by John Cormack and scene-painting by Stafford Hall. *The Times* (27 December 1877) noted that as the audience was children, 'Political jokes and lampoons are naturally banished from the book of such a pantomime.' It opens in Sherwood Forest with an indignation meeting at the Lover's Well and Fairy Grotto by starlight held by the fairies to protest against the enclosure of the forest threatened by the Sheriff of Nottingham. It is proposed and accepted unanimously that the Enclosure Act should be opposed and that Robin Hood should be protected by the Fairy Queen from imprisonment for contempt by the Master of the Rolls. After the fairies, the heroes and heroines of the ballads enter, Robin complaining of depression in trade, and that the groceries he steals are all adulterated nowadays. Maid Marian sings 'My Own Blue-Bell', Will Scarlett bears in a fat buck shot in the King's Forest, then comes Will Stukeley, Allan-a-Dale, Much the Miller's Son, the Pindar of Wakefield, Friar Tuck and stout Little John. They hold up the butcher on his way to Nottingham and Robin goes disguised in his place to sell American beef. 'Glorious news' he exclaims to the circle of buyers, 'beef is down again', and exhibits at his stall placards bearing the inscriptions 'Home-made sausages, only 1d. a pound', and 'premier legs of mutton, only 2d. a pound'. The outlaws participate in old English sports and pastimes. Robin is discovered by the Sheriff but blows his horn and his merry men come to his rescue. The sheriff pursues him to the woods, encounters a drunken Friar Tuck and fines him five shillings, and is about to arrest Robin when the Fairy Sylvia intervenes and conveys them all to her enchanted grotto, where they are transformed into the characters of the harlequinade. The show was 'vigorously applauded' by its child-audience. *The Era* (24 December 1876) said: 'It is a treat to sit out an entertainment admirably stage-managed and going off with the neatness and precision of clock-work.' Once again Bertie Coote stood out among the juvenile performers. But there was praise all round for the singing, dancing and clowning of the 'Lilliputian' performers.

In 1878 the Brothers Grinn provided the pantomime for the Royal Aquarium Theatre, Westminster. It was *Aladdin and His Wonderful Lamp or The Flying Palace and Big Ben of Westminster*, the location of the theatre inspiring the inclusion of Big Ben who summons up the fairies Aquaria and Novelty to ask for a subject for the pantomime. They provide the subject of Aladdin and at a fairy conference in the Maze of Illusion discuss its appeal with Mischief, Jollity, Variety and Laughter who add their suggestions. The familiar elements of the story are then performed with the Widow Ching Mustapha (James Fawn) pressed by the School Board to send Aladdin to school when he would rather play. He is inveigled by his wicked uncle, the magician Abanazar (Charles Collette) ('wonderfully amusing' in his parody of melodramatic acting styles) into searching for the lamp. But the loudest applause was received by Paul Martinetti as the magician's slave Kazrac for his 'fantastic dancing' and 'remarkable pantomime powers'. The transformation scene, taking inspiration from the theatre's name, was set in a marine aquarium. *The Era* (29 December 1878) reported:

> From a bed of sea anemones, clustering around caverns of coral, the sea nymphs rise through transparent waters and strange and curious objects of the ocean depths disport themselves, until the combination of colour and form is complete. The audience was entranced and called for the artist Mr Perkins to take a bow.

In addition to the comedy, there was a 'graceful ballet' and generally excellent scenery and costumes. *The Era* concluded that 'the refined tone of the production makes it eminently suitable for the recreation of ladies and juvenile visitors.' *The Times* (27 December 1878), generally agreeing, added 'a good proportion of pretty faces greatly assisted the agreeable affect of the performance.'

For 1878–9 Drury Lane's offering was the familiar fairy story, *Cinderella or Harlequin and the Glass Slipper*, a tale much retold but not previously done at Drury Lane, thought *The Times* (27 December 1878). While paying tribute to the 'playful fancy and facile versification' of Blanchard, it noted that the success of the pantomime was not entirely due to this, indeed that the dialogue was sometimes less than sparkling and the puns with which it was littered not above the average. It was the accessories that lifted it to success, and these included Beverley's scenery, the 'rich and varied costumes' of Carl Wilhelm, Cormack's choreography and the 'spirited' music of Karl Meyder. *The Times* noted that when the doors opened at 6.30, 400 people crowded in, 'noisy but eminently goodhumoured'. The opening farce, Henry Spicer's *His Novice*, virtually played in dumb show as the dialogue was drowned out by the talk and the showers of orange peel. *The Era* (29 December 1878) noted that the audience joined in music hall songs and demanded encores of 'Rule Britannia' and 'God Save the Queen'.

The pantomime opens in a Woody Glen and Mountain Pass in the Black Forest at Sunset, where Baron Pumpernickel and his servant Kobold are hunting boars, but the boars end up hunting them. They meet Prince Amabel, also in search of sport. But he falls asleep and Iris, the Spirit of the Rainbow, contrives to make him dream of Cinderella. He falls in love with her and determines to give a ball to find the beauty. The second scene is in the glass factory of the Fairy Slipper in the Basaltic Valley, where the glass goblins make the glass slippers at Iris' instruction and there is a 'grand prismatic ballet' of 100 dancers. In the garden of the Baron's castle the ugly sisters, Vixena the spiteful and Pavonia the proud, ill-treat Cinderella and when the invitation to the ball arrives, exclude her. Cinderella dances the Lancers with the mop and broom but ends up in tears by the fireside. Iris turns up and aided by Kobold, who produces a pumpkin, white mice, rats, lizards and a cabbage, turns them into coach, horses, footmen and bouquet, and clothes Cinderella in fine raiment and glass slippers. Guests arrive at the Palace and in the illuminated ball-room, Cinderella causes a sensation. She dances with the Prince, flees at midnight, but is eventually found and united with the Prince. The grand transformation is the 'Assemblage of the Hours'.

The Vokes Family filled the leading roles: Fred as the Baron, Fawdon as Kobold, Jessie as Prince Amabel, Victoria as Cinderella. Fred was praised by *The Era* for his customary eccentric dancing. Also, 'his fright in the first scene and his nervous agitation, produced through the worrying of a pet poodle during his process of shaving, were very comically depicted and many a roar of laughter must be placed to his account.' Fawdon Vokes was 'remarkable for his activity. He spared himself not a jot in order to add to the fun.' Jessie played with 'archness and commendable grace' as the Prince. Victoria was 'the very life of the piece, singing and dancing her way straight into the hearts of those before her.' Master Cullen as Azor the poodle performed pranks that induced roars of laughter. The grand ballet was praised and at the end there was a vocal and terpsichorean fandango composed especially for the Vokes Family by Frederick Clay, in which they all joined.

The opening scene of the woody glen and mountain pass was, thought *The Era*, 'a capital picture, reflecting great credit on Mr Wm. Beverley'. *The Times* thought the illuminated Ball Room 'splendid' and that the transformation, 'a brilliant combination of colours irradiating numberless fairy forms', defied description – 'so beautiful and so bewildering in its loveliness' that Beverley and Chatterton were called to take a bow. *The Times* thought the pantomime flowed with 'a style which is light and agreable, and which has the merit of being free from all taint of vulgarity.' However, it was overtaken by disaster. Blanchard saw it on 26 December and reports 'goes off all right; grand house.'[36] Then to his astonishment, passing the theatre on 4 February he saw large notices announcing the theatre's closure.[37] Chatterton had run out of money and a proposal to keep going with the company on half salary was rejected by the Vokeses, precipitating closure. The notice that went up declared 'owing to a combination of unforeseen circumstance, the theatre is unavoidably closed for the present.' Blanchard retired to his home 'to ruminate over my losses.'

Chatterton had always relied on the success of the pantomime to bail him out but in 1879 this recourse failed. He laid the blame squarely on the Vokeses, telling actor-manager John Coleman:

> For the first time during my management of the Lane the pantomime was a miserable failure. The cause was not far to seek. There was a certain troupe of pantomimists whom, for years, I had made the all-absorbing feature of my Christmas fare. For years I had kept them on, continually increasing salaries, until at length they became paramount. Their ability was unquestionable; but the truth is, they were played out, and their attraction was over.[38]

The truth is that Chatterton's financial situation had become too precarious. According to Edward Stirling, the Drury Lane stage manager, he owed £36,000 when the crash came.[39] He admitted to having borrowed money at 'usurious interest'.[40] William Beverley wrote indignantly to *The Daily News* (15 February 1879) implicitly denouncing the Vokes Family for demanding their 'pound of flesh' and claiming that the other staff would have been willing to carry on at reduced salaries until Chatterton could recoup his finances. But the Vokes' action had resulted in the whole staff being put out of work, and Chatterton losing the lease of Drury Lane.

In an article entitled 'The Drury Lane Disaster' in *The Theatre*, critic Clement Scott attributed the closure of the theatre three weeks before the end of *Cinderella's* advertised run to:

> the selfishness of Mr Vokes in refusing to consent to the reduction of his own and his sisters' salaries which had become necessary. The cruelty of thus allowing hundreds of poor *employés* to be thrown out of their expected work has been commented upon; the opinion has been freely expressed in print that some arrangement ought to have been come to by which the premature close of the season might be averted, and the manager has in several quarters been spoken of as a much ill-used man.

On the view expressed in several journals that the closure was due to the 'lack of attractiveness' in *Cinderella*, Scott said that the pantomime:

> had been kindly treated by the whole of the press, and had been regarded by the public as fairly successful. It was not perhaps so prettily told as some of Mr E.L. Blanchard's versions of nursery legends, but its 'book' was a work of art beside those of its rivals. It was not mounted with any great elaboration or brilliance of scenic effect; indeed, some of its 'effects' were … open to the charge of dinginess and meanness. But on the other

hand, the absence of meaningless spectacular display was felt by many to be relief, especially as the illustration was appropriate and adequate to all the real requirements of the piece. Moreover, the company engaged included a family of clever and popular artists who are the leading representatives of the modern pantomimic school, excelling as they do in the various kinds of 'business' now added to pantomime pure and simple.

However, he concluded that even if the pantomime had continued it would probably not have averted the manager's bankruptcy, given the spectacular failure of his autumn production of *The Winter's Tale* and the reported level of his debts (£40,000).

No man could have striven more courageously or by more varied means to make it pay than has Mr Chatterton. He has tried everything, from Shakespere to Mr Andrew Halliday, and he has in his misfortune only followed the road trodden by plenty of bankrupt Drury Lane managers before him.

The Chatterton regime was at an end and the future for Blanchard and the Theatre was uncertain.

Whether the Vokes Family were quite as played out as Chatterton suggested is open to question. *Bluebeard*, in which they starred for Harris after he took over Drury Lane, elicited from *The Times* (27 October 1879) the verdict that the acting throughout was 'excellent', many of the songs and dances were encored and the leading performers were called several times to take a bow.

What is remarkable in the light of Chatterton's subsequent comments about them is that when he transferred to Covent Garden to produce the pantomime *Valentine and Orson or Harlequin and the Magic Shield* by Frank Burnand, he immediately engaged the Vokes Family and Drury Lane veterans William Beverley as scene-painter and John Cormack as ballet-master. *The Times* (28 December 1880) praised the pantomime for its 'elaborate painting and splendour' and the performance of the Vokes Family: 'Their dancing is as ever of the lightest, the wildest and yet most finished in character.' But the pantomime fell victim to the weather. Chatterton recalled:

Our pantomime there made a great mark, and we should doubtless have done big business had it not been for the dreadful snow-storm which ruined half the managers in town and country. Doubtless you remember: half a dozen West End theatres were closed at a moment's notice in consequence of the streets being impassible.[41]

The Vokes Family were absent from West End pantomime for the next two years, returning in *Little Red Riding Hood* at Her Majesty's Theatre. It had something of the feel of a comeback both for them and for 'the traditional pantomime'. *The Times* (27 December 1883) rhapsodized that it had been produced with 'scrupulous regard for pantomime tradition in the treatment of fable' and 'marvellous fertility of resource in the matter of episode and spectacular display'. The critic argued that the artistic level attained by *Little Red Riding Hood* and *Cinderella* at Drury Lane would be:

> satisfactory to those who have deplored the corruption of Boxing-day morals through the influence of the music hall. Here, and at Drury Lane, the youthful spectator is at once transported from a prosaic world into the realm of fancy and kept there while the librettist, the scene-painter, the stage-carpenter and the stage manager combine to awe and dazzle him with alternate doses of the supernatural, the grotesque, the mysterious and the beautiful.

The Era (29 December 1883) reported:

> Mr Fred Vokes ... accomplished feats astonishing even his oldest admirers ... [he] has lost nothing of his striking ability as a dancer and pantomimist, while he has certainly gained new power as a burlesque actor ... Miss Jessie Vokes ... made a very amusing schoolmistress ... As for Miss Victoria Vokes, she was the very life and soul, the central figure of the pantomime, the moving spirit of all. Never have we seen her so full of fun and energy.

But it was virtually their last hurrah. Rosina had left the troupe in 1877 when she married. Jessie, who had been 'a great favourite' of Blanchard, died on 4 August 1884 aged only thirty-three and Fred died on 3 June 1888 aged forty-two. Meanwhile Augustus Harris saw off his rivals. Covent Garden ceased producing Christmas pantomimes after 1882 and Her Majesty's did not return with another pantomime in 1884.

The Chatterton era had been Blanchard's heyday. He had, in the eyes of critics and public alike, brought the genre to a peak of perfection. So much so that his services were sought not only at Drury Lane but at Covent Garden, Sadler's Wells, the Crystal Palace, Astley's and the Princess' Theatre among others. Year after year reviewers would deliver encomiums on his work. The *I.L.N.* (31 December 1864) reported:

> For many years this theatre has subsisted on the production of pantomime, the success of which has been so uniform as to ensure the management from loss in regard to the speculation. The Christmas six weeks provide for the entire year. Much of this success is justly due to Mr E.L. Blanchard, whose elegant introductions have been models of composition, judiciously written in the style of Pope's 'Rape of the Lock'. His couplets are carefully manipulated, and the wit and humour which they convey are equally suited to the ear of the refined adult as to the capacity of the politely-educated child. In structure his introductions are uniformly admirable, and the whole is conducted with such judgement and tact that the writer achieves a triumph with as much certainty as if he were stating a mathematical demonstration ... As usual Mr Blanchard has aimed not

only at amusement but instruction; and, notwithstanding the number of broad grins, which produced prodigious effect on the first night among the audience, there were some sententious lines which compelled the most laughter-loving to look grave for a moment and reflect. These lights and shadows in the dialogue are as delightful as they are artistic. Frequently it is scientific, and sometimes even of yet more profundity.

The Era (1 January 1865) echoed this opinion:

The ... accomplished writer has won for himself a reputation of which any literary man may be proud; and in the [field of pantomime] one of his greatest characteristics has always been, and still is, a careful avoidance of slang, disguised or undisguised. In these days of very free parodied and strongly seasoned burlesque dialogue, such a creditable determination is difficult to carry out, but this year the great excellence to which we have alluded is as perceptible as ever. It is something now-a-days to feel assured that some particular author's principles will, on this point, remain inflexible, notwithstanding the velocity with which the current of popular taste may run in the contrary and more unworthy direction. Mr Blanchard may congratulate himself on his fame and credit being now so firmly established that he can afford to take up this decisive attitude.

Reviewing *Number Nip*, *The Era* (30 December 1866) declared in the same vein:

We hear this or that illustrious person spoken of as 'the people's friend', but E.L. Blanchard may emphatically be called 'the children's friend', for he has a way of treating old nursery fables and legends peculiar to himself, and exactly calculated to amuse Young England, without, at the same time, inculcating the slightest lesson in slang and vulgarity. The genial rhymes of this compiler of so many Christmas Annuals have the true ring of simplicity, and never, in the faintest degree, offend the most delicate susceptibilities. As times go now this is a proud distinction to boast of, for burlesque and every description of 'fast' expressions go, too frequently, hand in hand. It is some comfort to miss unpleasantly familiar 'coves' and 'blokes' and 'fivers' and such refinements. In Mr E.L. Blanchard's writings there is always a wholesome spirit of satire none the less pungent from being expressed in language of a different order from that indicated above.

In years to come, the era of Blanchard's predominance would be looked back on as the 'golden age' of pantomime. But this was not due to Blanchard alone. For years he was part of a team which functioned productively and harmoniously and which gave visual, musical, mechanical and choreographic life to the products of his poetic imagination. Blanchard's diaries reveal that he counted many of these regular coadjutors as dear personal friends. Reviewing the Drury Lane production of *Faw, Fee, Fo, Fum*, *The Era* (27 December 1867) paid tribute to the other members of the team:

It is not easy for one who has an intimate knowledge of the skill and labour required to produce a Pantomime to find words which will convey an adequate idea of the merit which is due to Mr William Beverley for his charming scenery, so tasteful, so elegant, and so fairylike, involving so much thought, invention and painful labour; to Mr Edward Stirling, for his days and nights of toil in arranging the elaborate business, his watchful generalship in marshalling the forces at night, so that all may go smoothly before the eye and ear of the spectator; to that mysterious but able designer Dykwynkyn (the Tycoon of the Theatrical world, who is heard and known by his works, but never seen), for his quaint masks and grotesque dresses; to Mr J.H. Tully, for his well-selected and always spiritedly played music; and not least to Mr J. Cormack, for his cleverly arranged dances and groupings in the Opening, and his capital comic business and dancing in the harlequinade. We can but say that all acquitted themselves to the best purpose and effect, and that their combined efforts, furnished for their difficult task by the liberality of Mr Chatterton, than whom there is no more enterprising manager in London, they have produced a Pantomime which is in all respects worthy of the historic boards of 'Old Drury'.

It was an arrangement that suited Blanchard well and enabled him to do his best work. It would all be very different under Augustus Harris.

10

Sir Augustus Harris
and the Battle for Pantomime

By the 1870s the nature of pantomime was changing, with the role of the harlequinade increasingly curtailed, prose replacing the rhyming couplets and most significantly the interjection into the stories of music hall comedians and their acts. Augustus Harris Senior (1825–73), who for twenty-seven years was associated with the stage and general management of Covent Garden, was retrospectively accused of beginning the 'vulgarization' of the pantomime and specifically introducing music hall performers into West End pantomime. The key date was said to be 1871, when music hall star G.H. Macdermott appeared in *Bluebeard* at Covent Garden. Soon music hall performers (among them James Fawn, Herbert Campbell and Harry Nicholls) were performing in pantomimes in both the West End and the East End. It was Harris' son, Augustus Harris Junior, who set the seal on this development after he took over Drury Lane in 1879. So from the 1870s battle was joined for the soul of pantomime and the purity of fairyland. This battle took both theatrical and practical forms.

It was after a hiatus of eight months that the lease of Drury Lane was awarded to the ambitious, enterprising Augustus Harris Junior (1852–96), then only twenty-seven. He began his regime at Drury Lane with a production of *Henry V* on 6 November 1879. He at once applied to Blanchard for a pantomime script. But Blanchard was extremely wary of Harris, knowing his style from previous productions, and rather than write a new one, he offered him an old script of *Bluebeard* which he had written with T.L. Greenwood under their regular pseudonym of The Brothers Grinn. It was extensively revised without credit by the experienced pantomime writer Horace Lennard, who became Harris' literary adviser. Seeing it for the first time on 12 January 1880, Blanchard notes in his diary 'find the text set at nought as usual.'[1] Evidently so little of Blanchard's original remained that when some years later Harris revived the production at Glasgow and at the Crystal Palace, Lennard's name alone appeared as author.[2] This was an ominous development for Blanchard.

Harris had his own very clear ideas of how pantomime should be produced and ensured their implementation by taking over direction of the show himself. He dispensed with the curtain-raiser which had been a regular feature of earlier Drury Lane regimes. He truncated the harlequinade. He concentrated on spectacle, in particular lavish processions and dance sequences, and he introduced music hall stars as a regular and integral feature of his shows, which every year got longer and more lavish. Slapstick and spectacle was his recipe for success.[3]

The Times (27 December 1879) recognized the distinctive Harris formula when it reported that Bluebeard, which had been given an Oriental setting, had been put upon the stage 'on a scale of great magnificence' and that 'scenic display and burlesque humour are its two leading characteristics, every incident in the familiar story being treated entirely from this double point of view.' For the spectacle, The Times observed that 'the lessee ... wisely enlisted the services of at least five of our most talented scene-painters.' The reviewer went on to praise Henry Emden's seashore by moonlight ('beautiful'), Frederick Fenton's cave of mystery ('exquisite'), William Telbin's Grand Ottoman Apartment ('gorgeous') and pronounced Telbin's transformation scene 'Winter and Summer', 'one of Mr Telbin's masterpieces ... dazzling and gorgeous ... difficult for any other artists to equal.'

The comedy and dancing were in the hands of the Vokes Family for the last time. Harris, who confided in a friend that he 'dreaded the tyranny of the Vokeses', was determined to be rid of them but for the moment was stuck with them.[4] There was no indication of any decline in their abilities. The Times declared the acting throughout 'excellent' and noted that many of the songs and dances were encored and the leading performers called several times to take bows.

The Era (28 December 1879) thought Fred Vokes 'made a study of Blue Beard, and although there was as much fun extracted from the part as possible, he really ... worked up the climax of the story into a condition approaching the tragic.' Victoria Vokes was 'a remarkably good Fatima ... and sang the music allotted to her, including a new waltz composed by Mr [Ferdinand] Wallerstein, with good effect.' Miss Jessie Vokes was 'satisfactory as Selim, as was Mrs Fred Vokes as Sister Anne', Fawdon Vokes got 'a good deal of fun out of Shacabac' who had an alarm bell on his hat. The Era thought the one great feature which ensured its success was 'fun'. 'No one can see that scene in which Blue Beard and his servant are in a boat without laughing boisterously; the same is the case with the hobby-horses, while the property elephant is always causing entertainment.' It achieved eighty-one performances.

For 1880–1, Blanchard was back with a new script, Mother Goose and the Enchanted Beauty, which was basically Sleeping Beauty with Mother Goose acting as the Fairy Godmother. *The Times* (28 December 1880) noted approvingly that Blanchard, 'while providing many scenes into which the comic "business" expected in a pantomime can be introduced, has preserved enough of the romantic side of this charming story to please those among his audience for whom fairies and witches and sprites and magicians are still half realities.'

Dance continued to be a principal element of the shows. But Harris had succeeded in dispensing with the services of the Vokeses. He had discovered a young male dancer, Fred Storey, who could duplicate Fred Vokes' style of eccentric dancing and cast him as Rifum Tifum, a pretender to the throne. He brought in the children of the National Training School for Dancing under its formidable principal, Madame Katti Lanner, to dance ballets arranged by the new choreographer John D'Auban, who was playing the Grand Chamberlain. A visit by the christening guests to the Lowther Arcade and Mother Goose's Model Farm was the signal for a ballet of toys, dolls, white rabbits and punchinellos, so gracefully done it had to be encored. The passage of time between 1680 and 1780, 'The Flight of Time', was illustrated by hours, days, weeks, months and years being marked by a clock with a living pendulum and a Grand Ballet of Stars with the dancers 'in glittering array and with spear-crowned heads'. When Prince Florizel, in his search for the Sleeping Princess, reached the Valley of a Thousand Charms, child shepherds and shepherdesses attired after Watteau performed 'a very pretty and very picturesque' ballet which, said *The Era* (1 January 1881), was greeted with 'much applause'.

The visual effects were very much to the fore. *The Era* reported 'The scenery throughout is absolutely beyond reproach and reflects immense credit on the artists', who were William Telbin, Henry Cuthbert and Henry Emden. Telbin had been specially engaged to paint a grand panorama illustrating Prince Florizel's journey. *The Era* was particularly impressed by the Royal Nursery, 'a capital scene, which will be the joy of every little boy and girl who sees it. The walls are just as the walls of every nursery should be if we had our way, for every panel tells a nursery tale.' These were Humpty Dumpty, Little Jack Horner, Old Mother Hubbard, Puss in Boots, Dick Whittington, Jack the Giant Killer and Red Riding Hood. The grand transformation, Love's Fountain, painted by Henry Emden, featured a fountain 'from which spring Cupids without number, armed with their bows and arrows, and prepared to make us love them. It is a scene of dazzling beauty and on the opening night called forth a tempest of applause,' said *The Era*. Henry Emden and Augustus Harris were called out by the audience to take a bow. It achieved ninety-seven performances.

Ominously, however, William Yardley, reviewing the pantomime in *The Theatre*, while declaring: 'I have personally never seen anything better in pantomime than the Toy Scene – Mother Goose's Farm in Lowther Arcade', nevertheless noted 'the music hall element largely prevails in this cast – in fact the only true pantomimist amongst them is Mr John D'Auban.' The popular music hall double act, Arthur Roberts and James Fawn, were among the 'turns' populating the supporting cast.[5]

1881–2 saw *Robinson Crusoe* at Drury Lane. *The Times* (27 December 1881) declared 'the popular verdict of last night will certainly place *Robinson Crusoe* in the first rank among the almost numberless pantomimic successes recorded in the annals of "Old Drury"', a view entirely endorsed by *The Era* (31 December 1881). Indeed Harris had to announce extra Thursday morning performances to meet the demand for seats. *The Era* reported that the show combined 'great good taste' and 'a lavish expenditure' previously unknown at Drury Lane and resulting in fourteen elaborate scenes. *The Era* thought Blanchard's script 'marked by all the wit and grace and fancy and kind feeling that have characterised his Christmas productions in the past', a comment entirely at odds with his despairing diary entry about the bastardization of his script (see below). Oscar Barrett's score was pronounced 'music of an order certainly superior to that usually associated with the pantomime.' There was the usual quota of ballets, choreographed by John D'Auban, and notable, thought *The Era*, 'for an array of feminine beauty and for great choreographic skill'. On Will Atkins' ship, a crew of children, coached by Madame Katti Lanner, danced a hornpipe which was encored. The shipwreck scene which followed was 'very realistic and very exciting'. Spectators followed the ship to the bottom of the sea and witnessed the ballet of silver fishes. It took place:

> among the coral branches and the other curious and beautiful things that lie 'full fathoms five', and it fairly dazzles us by its brilliancy, the effect here being greatly enhanced by the use of the new patent lime-light apparatus, manufactured for the pantomime by Messrs. Allen and Co. of Cardiff.

On Crusoe's island, there was a grand Indian ballet,

> which is likely to become the talk of the town. Curious looking people arrive upon all sorts of animals, including elephants, alligators, ostriches, turtles and giraffes. The stage is very soon crowded by a glittering throng, and the eye becomes fairly dazed and the brain bewildered in the attempt to take in all the wondrous paraphernalia of this marvellous spectacle ... We can safely say that in the history of Drury-lane pantomime nothing so splendid has been witnessed.

The climactic procession featured representatives of all the city livery companies, showing the distinctive characteristics of all the London trades, a sequence so spectacular that Harris was called forth to take a bow. The supernatural spirits of good and evil were represented by *Youth*, cross-referencing Harris' autumn melodrama, and *Vice* ('because you're "Youth" and called a moral play. I don't like moral plays that good have done, and so intend to stop your further run').

The scenery, in the hands of Julian Hicks, Henry Emden, J.W. Hall, Walter Hann, J. Ryan and Brioschi, was, said *The Era*, 'all of a very beautiful and artistic character' and the wedding cake transformation scene resulted in its painter, Emden, being called to take a bow. *The Times* singled out for praise Emden's novel panorama of the Thames, showing both sides of the river ('a decided pictorial triumph') and Julian Hicks' scene of the picturesque streets of Old London.

The performances were universally praised but there was an even greater music hall presence than before, to the apparent delight and approval of the audience. Arthur Roberts played Mrs Crusoe but *The Era* assured its readers, he played the part 'without the slightest approach to vulgarity. His make-up for the character is splendid, and his acting throughout is in the true spirit of burlesque.' James Fawn, his music hall partner, as next-door neighbour Timothy Lovage was pronounced 'thoroughly diverting'. He and Roberts had a topical duet which was encored. Harry Nicholls played Will Atkins as a parody of a melodrama villain. 'One of the funniest things in the piece' thought *The Era*, 'is a burlesque of a "Minstrel" sand dance, given by Messrs. Roberts, Fawn, and Nicholls and it results in general laughter and enthusiastic plaudits.' Mr G. LeClerq 'the droll little "Nigger" from the music halls', played the Cannibal King Hoity-Toity ('very funnily'). The Friday of Charles Lauri Jr was 'wonderful. His rope climbing, his somersaults, his grotesque dancing, his general activity, and his never-tiring pranks astonish as much as they amuse.' One hundred and twenty-two performances were given.

In the 1882–3 pantomime *Sindbad*, Blanchard's thirtieth and Harris' third, the young impresario over-reached himself. *The Times* (27 December 1882) noted that the subject of Sindbad the Sailor, though previously told by pantomime librettists, 'has never probably been illustrated with such a wealth of mechanical and scenic effects as on the present occasion.'

The Times encapsulated the extent to which the Harris regime transformed the familiar story:

> To such an extent ... has the 'gorgeous East' been laid under contribution that the story is frequently lost sight of altogether, a great part of the action being taken up with the domestic and business arrangements of Kibosh Pasha, an Eastern slave-dealer, with whose niece Sindbad is in love and with the experiences of the youthful Khedive of Egypt, who travels in search of adventure under the guidance of a rascally tutor. But the familiar incidents of Sindbad's landing upon an island which proves to be a whale's back, and of his being carried out of the Diamond Valley in the talons of the Roc, are reproduced with tolerable accuracy upon the stage. The whale is an enormous creature of canvas, which disports itself in a sea of green muslin, snapping a pair of enormous jaws and lashing the water with its tail. In the Diamond Valley – a sombre scene glittering with jewels – the roc descends vertically with outspread wings, which extend over more than

half the stage, and bears off Sindbad without apparent effort. These scenes, however, are dwarfed in interest and picturesqueness by a grand panoramic sea view, as Sindbad starts upon his travels, and by a procession of the Kings and Queens of England ... together with a review of the troops returned from Egypt. The latter scene, in fact, outdoes in magnificence the transformation scene itself.

The explicit background to the pantomime was the recent military campaign in Egypt, resulting in the British victory at Tel-el-Kebir and the suppression of the nationalist revolt.

But the pantomime did not go smoothly. It was hissed and booed, because there was a succession of hitches and delays and confusions 'which cropped up in many of the scenes.' They slowed down the show so much that Scene Twelve, in which a giant and giantess at dinner cut into a pie containing Sindbad and other characters, was cut from the running order. *The Era* (30 December 1882) recalled that the good-natured audience had 'its patience and its temper sorely tried.' What added insult to injury was that many of them had paid an extra charge to be admitted early. *The Times* reported that 'the mechanical arrangements worked so badly ... as to endanger the success of the pantomime.'

The Era expressed sympathy with Harris, who had gone to 'vast expense' in order to outshine all previous efforts and had erred only in trying to do too much. But he had also erred in packing the cast with music hall stars, all of whose specialist turns had to be accommodated. *The Era* noted that 'there was so much talent that there was not room for the employment of it all.'

The journalist J.B. Booth commented that in the early days of Harris' regime at the Lane, things were conducted in a happy-go-lucky fashion in a belief that it would be 'alright on the night'. The result of this was *Sindbad the Sailor*:

Nobody who saw it will ever forget the first night of ... *Sindbad the Sailor*. Several of the scenes had never been set when the curtain rose on that memorable performance, and some of the elaborate mechanical effects had never been tested. So, after the big bird which was to carry off Sindbad, refused to fly, and the great whale lay flabbily immovable on the stage, Harris had to come forward in the famous Inverness cape over his dress clothes, to ask the indulgence of the audience. The gallery 'god's' comment became historic. 'Ladies and gentlemen' pleaded the impresario, 'this is the heaviest pantomime I have ever produced –'.

'By God, it is Gus!' roared 'the god'.

And then Charles Lauri, who played the part of a poodle, frisked about in the canvas waves, to draw attention from the carpenters who were dissecting the great whale, and as soon as there was room in front of it, a cloth was dropped, so that the comedians, Arthur Roberts, Jimmy Fawn, Harry Nicholls, and Herbert Campbell could 'gag' while the leviathan was being removed piecemeal.[6]

The Era found Blanchard's book 'as complete with wit and poetry and fancy as at any time during the past thirty years, but although Sindbad is not dropped altogether … his story is' and *The Times* noted 'the fairy element is not conspicuous in the pantomime.'

Blanchard hated it, writing in his diary: 'Hardly anything done as I had intended, or spoken as I had written; the music hall element crushing out the rest, and the good old fairy tales never to be again illustrated as they should be.'[7] Arthur Roberts, in nautical dress and a bald wig, played the comical Ali and sang 'The Winkle and the Whale' ('droll humour') and the cook Koolinari was played by James Fawn in drag. Herbert Campbell played Kabob the young Khedive and Harry Nicholls, Professor Hankipanki, his sinister tutor. Fawn, Campbell and Roberts did not have 'the scope that should have been given them.' Charles Lauri as the Poodle, 'won plenty of favour, so natural were his movements, the spectators becoming greatly excited when this poodle, escaping from his keepers, went at a gallop right round the front of the house, by the ledge of the first circle, and the supports of the second, making a pretence of falling into the pit when mid-way on his journey.'

It achieved 104 performances but the general verdict shared by the *I.L.N.* and the *I.S.D.N.* among others was that Harris had tried to pack in too much and lost sight of the story. But there was as ever praise for the visuals, in particular Henry Emden's sea panorama and the Christmas transformation featuring 'the very largest and very handsomest "Father Christmas" yet born.' Similarly the dancing attracted approval. The Persian Ballet in the market place was praised. The minuet ballet in the Bridal Bower 'very properly calls forth vociferous applause' and a ballet of children with their dolls was 'one of the most attractive and successful features of the pantomime'. The children, trained by Katti Lanner, produced a flight of cupids at the end of Act 5 and a Children's Dance in the Seraglio in Act 7.

The criticisms of *Sindbad* seem to have induced a change of heart in Harris, manifested in his 1883–4 production of *Cinderella*. *The Times* (27 December 1883) noted approvingly, 'the happy idea has been acted upon of eliminating to a great extent the sordid music-hall element which had mixed itself up with the amusements of Boxing Day and of keeping the fairy tale to the region of fancy to which it belongs.' Blanchard was praised for keeping faithfully to the familiar story.

William Beverley had been summoned back to join the team of scenic artists, Henry Emden, William Telbin, William Perkins and T.W. Grieve. *The Times* thought that the fairy conclave in Henry Emden's moonlit glen, enhanced by the 'most effective' fairy ballet, formed 'a beautiful scenic effect'. Beverley painted the illuminated palace gardens and the transformation scene, the Home of Light and Love; 'At first it is beautiful in its simplicity. Later it becomes dazzling in its brilliancy.' But it was somewhat eclipsed by the pageant, a procession of the famous figures from fairy tale and nursery rhyme, which *The Times* thought 'gorgeous, to be compared only with last year's famous procession of all the kings and queens of England', and of more interest to the young than last year's. *The Era* praised it as 'an army of unsurpassed and unsurpassable magnificence' which sent 'the onlookers frantic with delight', and led to calls for Augustus Harris who appeared hand-in-hand with his brother Charles, the stage manager, to take a bow.

The cast was praised by *The Era* (29 December 1883): 'Kate Vaughan as Cinderella delighted all present by her beauty and grace. She danced as only she can dance, and the only room for complaint was found in the fact that she did not dance enough.' Fred Storey as the Baron 'found favour with the audience through the medium of his legs, which are long and nimble, and which he uses in fashion extraordinary.' Harry Nicholls and Herbert Campbell 'proved diverting as the ugly sisters, and their topical duets are sure to be popular features of the pantomime.' Kate Sullivan was 'the best fairy godmother we have yet encountered.' George Lupino, 'admirably dressed, made a most active and energetic impersonator of Ignoramus, Spirit of Mischief.'

The Era concluded that 'at no previous period has so much care and attention been paid to the brilliancy and tastefulness of the decorative accessories. Costumes and scenery have now reached a degree of excellence of design and elaborateness of execution never anticipated even a quarter of a century ago.' Sadly Blanchard makes no mention in his diary of having seen it, perhaps due to the ill-health to which he was increasingly prone.

In 1884–5 there was only one pantomime in the West End, Drury Lane's *Whittington and His Cat*, written by E.L. Blanchard. It contained the note: 'This libretto is subject to alterations from time to time for the introduction of topical allusions.' But *The Era* (27 December 1884) declared Mr Blanchard's 'fanciful pen always wielded in the best possible taste' had 'followed his customary practise of keeping pretty faithful to the legend which, in pantomime, is sometimes … widely departed from.' *The Times* (27 December 1884) thought that there was nothing in the pantomime to 'indicate any decay or falling-off in the glories of this species of entertainment', declaring 'the traditions of Boxing Day at the "National Theatre" are upheld and fortified with an amount of scenic display which, to employ the strongest form of comparison available, Mr Augustus Harris has never surpassed.' The keynote of the show it saw as a blend of spectacle ('gorgeous scenery and fantastic pageants') and fun ('sprightly and humorous acting'), but added 'what may be called the dramatic interest of the story is necessarily to a great extent submerged in a vast and ever-changing panorama of civic and barbaric splendour.'

The usual forces were deployed by Harris to secure success. The scenery was painted by W.R. Beverley, Henry Emden, W.B. Spong and J. Ryan. *The Era* reported: 'There is really not a bit of painting upon which the eye of the spectator may not rest without delight.' The ballets were arranged by Katti Lanner and the incidental dances by John D'Auban. Costumes 'tasteful, costly and elegant' according to *The Era* were designed by Alfred Thompson, Arthur Fredericks and Carl Wilhelm. Emden painted the Abode of the Man in the Moon, the Cats' School Playground and Kittengarten near the Mountains, Fitzwarren's Universal Emporium, Highgate Hill, A Garret in London, Old London (background to the grand procession) and the transformation scene 'The Four Elements'. Beverley painted the seascape and the Emperor's Palace, Ryan painted the London Docks and 'On the Road to Highgate' and Spong, The Emperor's Pavilion. *The Era* (27 December 1884) praised 'the pretty view of Highgate-hill by sunlight and moonlight', with its ballet of glow worms and Mdlle Aenea flying in as Robin Goodfellow; 'the capitally painted cloth' of London docks by Ryan; the storm and wreck, 'One of the most realistic stage storms and stage wrecks that have come under our notice in an experience of years, and reflect great credit on Mr Beverley'; and the grand transformation scene, 'a thing of beauty, and is likely to be a joy for ever.'

There were two grand processions. The Lord Mayor's show represented all the livery companies, with their emblems and trains of heralds, pages and knights. 'The manager considers it the grandest and most complete pageant ever attempted behind the footlights and we do not think the manager far wrong,' said *The Era*. But it also praised the Oriental procession and ballet for the wedding in Morocco, with a succession of heralds, pages, fanbearers, wise men, warriors of the river in blue, warriors of the cliff in yellow, warriors of the valley in red, high priests, the noble guards in gold and silver, and then a ballet to entertain bride and groom. Its beauty, according to *The Era*, defied description. The audiences called for Augustus Harris and his brother and assistant Charles during the two processions to take a bow. *The Times* said of the Lord Mayor's show that 'It forms a brilliant spectacle filling the whole depth of the stage, and will be a feast of wonderment and delight to a simple-minded public for months to come.' The Wedding Procession was 'a barbaric pageant on the grandest scale, hundreds of male and female courtiers in the showiest costumes being artistically grouped upon the stage.'

The Era thought that the role of Dick 'could not possibly have a brighter or better exponent' than Fanny Leslie. Kate Munroe 'a most charming Alice Fitzwarren, dressing the part admirably, acting most winningly, and in one scene particularly getting some well deserved compliments for her sweet rendering of the old song called "The Nightingale's Trill".' 'The best stage cat we know' was Charles Lauri Jr. Harry Nicholls as the apprentice Tom Idle and Herbert Campbell as Eliza the Cook were 'useful' but did not get many chances to shine. Their topical duet was, however, deemed sure to become popular. Blanchard pronounced it 'a very long and brilliant spectacle'.[8]

The 1885–6 Drury Lane pantomime was another Oriental extravaganza, *Aladdin*. *The Times* (28 December 1885) noted:

The pantomimes, 'invented, arranged and produced' by Mr Augustus Harris, are all so resplendent and so bewildering in their magnitude that there seems at first blush to be little to choose between one and another as there is between the monster audiences that assemble regularly on Boxing-night within the walls of Drury-lane. There is a magnificent sameness about the whole thing – spectacle, story, audience and all – that for the moment overwhelms and crushes us. Who can say that if the same pantomime were given year after year, with only a change of name, it would not, like some sermons, escape detection? Mr Augustus Harris evidently strives, rightly or wrongly, however, after freshness of incident and spectacular effect, and *Aladdin*, which is the latest product of his vast nursery-tale factory, will be seen once we get rid of its dazzling effect and come to examine it in detail to be full of new ideas, all grafted with great dexterity upon the meagre story of the 'Arabian Nights', and all fitting in appropriately with a grand spectacular scheme. There is, we suppose, no dramatic motive in a pantomime, but if one had to be found for *Aladdin* it would be this – that the rubbing of the magic lamp is employed less for the advancement of the hero's fortune than for the systematic development of a series of stupendous *tableaux* such as the Persian chronicler could never in his most enraptured moments have dreamt of.

The Era (2 January 1886) noted:

One thing struck us forcibly before the rising of the curtain. It was neither a ginger-beer bottle nor a piece of orange peel, for Mr Harris has educated his gods up to a civilized level, and nearly all of the rough humour – that is, the humour of the roughs – which characterised Boxing Night in times gone by and kept ladies away has disappeared.

But the gallery still joined in the songs, familiar from the music hall, all stood for the National Anthem and all joined in 'Rule Britannia'.

This *Aladdin* had far more political references than usual, as *The Times* noted that:

Political troubles are rife in the Celestial City; the Emperor is having a bad time, his difficulties oddly enough, bearing some resemblance to those which have afflicted recent Governments in this country with respect to revenue and taxation. The fair trade craze has also laid hold of his subjects who sing –

'We've got no work to do-o-o,
We've got no work to do-o-o,
For Frenchmen, Germans, Dutch, and Yanks,
Are Taking all our screw.'

This is not in the book of words and was evidently added later in line with the practice regarding topicality. The context here is the putting up of taxes by

Gladstone's government, at a time of recession, unemployment and labour unrest. *Aladdin* opens in the Magician's Observatory where Abanazar, who, in a departure from the usual narrative, is already in love with Princess Badroulbadour, is scheming to get hold of the magic lamp in order to win the wealth that will bring him the Princess. But the Emperor of China and his Prime Minister arrive to say they are beset by troubles and want to know what the stars foretell. The people are demonstrating, claiming to be 'underpaid and overtaxed'. Abanazar predicts that all will be well as long as the Emperor's blue china dog is never broken. The Prime Minister (if the sketch in the book of words is accurate) is made up to resemble Gladstone (with the letters G.O.M. embroidered on his collar). Abanazar summons Kazrac, the slave of the ring. Kazrac tells him they need a brave boy to get the lamp and the ring transports them to Peking, where Widow Twankay keeps a newspaper shop. He gets the ring by casting into his cauldron:

Votes for the London School Board. What they teaches.
A bundle of parliamentary speeches,
Act passed in Parliament, 'Redistribution
of Seats' and also forms of Constitution.
A photograph of 'Jumbo', and, what more is,
Great promises of Liberals and Tories,
And not forgetting Radical and Whig.

He discovers that Aladdin is in love with the Princess, pretends to be his uncle and offers to make him rich enough to win her. The Prime Minister now makes a proclamation that in view of the fact that the Treasury is low in funds, a duty is being imposed on 'those things like Opium, Spirits, all that money brings.' Also, the hand of the Princess will be given to whoever brings most money into the Treasury. The people riot, rejecting the taxes, demanding the abdication of the Emperor and surrounding the Princess when she appears with her retinue. Aladdin knocks down the leader of the mob. The Princess promises to intervene with her father and plead their case. The Emperor appears and havers about the taxes and the mob demand 'Down with the Emperor and all the blessed lot, Down with the Emperor; Oh, let him have it hot.'

Aladdin courts the Princess, after saving her from the mob, but the Emperor orders his arrest for daring to approach her. Aladdin finds the lamp and has a Palace built. It is built by a team of British workmen, as Aladdin says: 'May I suggest, as Labour yields enjoyment, That British workmen here should find employment. None better can you get, search where you will.' Emperor, Princess and company arrive and are impressed, though the Emperor demands he pay his tax arrears on the building. Abanazar tricks the Princess into handing over the lamp and uses it to transport Princess and Palace to Africa. Aladdin summons the slave of the ring to transport him after it. They arrive at the Palace with a view of the Egyptian Pyramids. Aladdin disguises himself as a wine merchant, drugs Abanazar and rescues the Princess.

The two high points in this pantomime were the 'Dream of Fair Women' procession and the building of the Palace. Although, as *The Times* reported, rumour had suggested the procession of fair women would stretch from Eve to Mrs Langtry, in fact, preceded by Venus borne by Cupids, the line of beauties stretched from Semiramis, Queen of Babylon, 'borne by a Babylonian bull and soothed with music from Rossini's opera', via Helen of Troy, Lady Godiva, Nell Gwynne and Madame de Pompadour to the Empress Josephine; followed by the heroines of fairy lore such as Sleeping Beauty and the Fair One with the Golden Locks. This was followed by a ballet representing the riches of the earth which *The Times* called 'magnificent'. *The Era* said:

> no adequate description can be given. We look, we admire, and we are bewildered. There is no jewel that is not represented ... They fairly fill the vast stage. They are of all sizes and all colours, and yet by a triumph of stage management they are so arranged as to make up a grand harmonious whole. The brilliancy is enhanced by the aid of the electric lights which some of them carry; but resplendent as the whole scene is Mr Harris is not content, until with the assistance of Madame Katti Lanner, he has filled up the picture with the fruits and flowers of the earth, represented by a troop of juvenile dancers, the well-trained pupils of the lady named. The eyes of the spectators on Saturday night were dazzled by the blaze of splendour, and were moved to enthusiasm that did not subside until the Messrs. Harris and Madame Lanner had appeared at the footlights. Nothing grander or more costly had been seen on the stage of Drury-lane.

The second highpoint was the building of Aladdin's palace by a team of miniature British workmen, played by the children of Madame Lanner's National School:

> Madame Lanner's pupils are again to the fore here, and disguised as navvies, hod-carriers, brick-layers, plumbers, carpenters, carters commanding beautiful little ponies, stonemasons etc., they do loyal suit and service to their master, whose name is writ large as 'Gusarris, Builder and Decorator', upon the hoarding which at the commencement they set up. When the dinner bell rings they lay down their implements and welcome their wives with their mid-day meals. Each wife has a perambulator, and each perambulator bears a baby, which is forthwith kissed and cuddled. For the British workman in this instance has a soul above dinner, and he takes advantage of the temporary lull in building operations to enjoy a dance with the 'missis'. There are more gorgeous scenes than this in the production, as we have shown, but there is none more animated and interesting, and we venture to predict that it will become the favourite with all the good little boys and girls who during the season will be taken to see the pantomime at Drury-lane.

The Times agreed, noting that all the boys and girls were aged ten or under, saying: 'No scene in any recent pantomime ... has equalled this for interest.'

Harris had assembled his usual team: Oscar Barrett as composer and conductor, costume design by Wilhelm, ballets choreographed by Madame Katti Lanner, 'A Dream of Fair Women' realized from sketches by costume designer Alfred Thompson, and scenery by Beverley, Perkins and Emden. Emden painted the Magician's Observatory, the market place in Peking, the gallery leading to the royal baths, the interior of the royal baths, the entrance to the mystic cave and the enchanted cavern of the wonderful lamp. Beverley painted the background to the procession of fair women and the transformation scene 'Aladdin's Golden Dream', and unusually Wilhelm designed Widow Twankay's Shop, Widow Twankay's shop beautified, the swamp of the dismal demon, the fertile plains with lake in the distance and the flying palace, which were executed by Hicks and Perkins. Of the transformation scene, *The Era* reported: 'Mr William Beverley has supplied the Drury-lane stage with another gorgeous example of his unrivalled genius as the scenic artist.' The audience called for Harris again at this point. *The Times* reported:

> the mechanical arrangements of the stage could scarcely be more complete or more admirably designed, from the spectacular point of view, and infinite pains must have been bestowed upon the numerous processions and ballets, some of which are sustained by toddling little babies of three or four, who would, perhaps be better in bed, if they had beds to go to.

Of the cast, *The Era* pronounced the company 'a strong one' but opined that 'the most was not made of the abilities of the artistes.' Grace Huntley as Aladdin 'was satisfactory so far as it went. But through no fault of hers, it did not go far enough.' A similar remark applied to Kate and Nelly Leamar as Princess Badroulbadour and Widow Twankay's maid Che-Kee. All of them could sing and dance but got few opportunities. Charles Lauri was wasted as Kazrac, being given no opportunities for his agile capers. 'The only hit in the performance was made by Mr Harry Nicholls, who was genuinely comical as the Widow Twankay and whose imitation of the dancing of a well-known burlesque actress gave rise to immense enthusiasm and to much merriment.' *The Times* agreed that 'acting ... is of little account in a production which is almost wholly spectacular.' But Harry Nicholls and Herbert Campbell (as Abanazar) were praised for doing 'much to enliven the course of the story by their grotesque business and their topical songs.' *The Era* concluded: 'Splendour is all very well in its way, and is very welcome, but it is not everything. We would willingly spare some of it for the sake of an increase in pantomimic fun.'

The Drury Lane pantomime stayed in the Orient for the 1886–7 season with a new version of *Forty Thieves*. It opens in the Seventh Heaven of Mahomet with the famous Arabian Knights, including Sindbad, attended by houris, who dance before them. Then Aladdin arrives, with a message from Augustus Druriolanus. Last year's Oriental extravaganza was such a success, he wants another Eastern story and would like a version of Ali Baba and the Forty Thieves. Referring directly to what had become the lavish Harris tradition, Aladdin declares:

He'll pay for a new set; it is his whim!
What is the cost of Forty Thieves for him?
Mere Nothing! And besides, I don't mind bettin' you
That ev'ry thief will have a splendid retinue!

As Aladdin had predicted, forty thieves were not enough for Harris; each thief was provided with his own retinue and this was the cue for a grand procession. It was, according to *The Era* (1 January 1887):

the first great scene of the production, dazzling all eyes, and fully justifying the reports that have been circulated respecting the enormous and extravagant expenditure that Mr Harris had incurred in his resolve to put into the shade all former pantomime glories. . . . On they come, a glittering throng from the cavern entrance, through which is seen the resplendent moon with only the tiniest cloud to heighten its beauty; down both sides of the rocky cave they march clothed in shining armour or in cloaks made of the most costly material and supplying a wealth of harmonious colour. Their shields, their head pieces, their swords, their crescent wands, their battle axes dazzle by their brilliancy, and presently, by way of contrast to so much beauty, there follow gigantic guards wearing masks that are really wonderful in their ugliness. And now the stage is crowded; the effect is as bewildering as it is delightful, and when there have been grandly sung a chorus of welcome to the chief and a splendid finale borrowed from *The Huguenots*, and prophetic of Cassim's fate, the walls of the old house ring with the enthusiastic plaudits which bring Mr Harris to the footlights to receive congratulations upon the success of a spectacle which is simply wondrous in its magnificence.

The finale was a celebration of Queen Victoria's Golden Jubilee.

Comedy setpieces included the interaction of a troupe of monkeys (played by Katti Lanner's juvenile dancers) and the donkey outside the robbers' cave. *The Times* (28 December 1886) reported:

The cave is surrounded by a troupe of monkeys, of which the clever pantomimist, Mr Paul Martinetti, is the chief, and as Ali Baba and party possess an accomplished donkey in Mr Charles Lauri Junior, there is an abundance of comic relief to the dramatic aspect of the invasion of the robbers' den.

Of the monkeys and donkey, *The Era* said:

> The greater part of the fun on Boxing Night was furnished by Messrs. Charles Lauri, Jun., and Paul Martinetti, the former as Ali's donkey and the latter as a monkey. The antics of these creatures created roars of laughter, and they supplied some excitement, too, for they took a run round the front of the first circle, somewhat startling the occupants of the private boxes and of the foremost seats.

Then there was the 'New Club' of the Forty Thieves, celebrating contemporary club life.

There was the usual complement of child dancing. *The Era* reported:

> In the banqueting room of Cogia's mansion ... we get what is sure to be one of the most popular features of the production. This is a dance by Madame Katti Lanner's juveniles, who, being ordered to prepare for bed, strip to their nightgowns, and pave the way for slumber with a pillow fight. The business of this dance – the pretty polka 'Tres Gai', composed by Mr Chas. Coote – is well conceived and most admirably carried out, and it very properly secured some of the loudest applause heard during the evening and a hearty call for the lady who has once more shown that as a trainer of children in saltatory skill she has no superior. There occurred here an incident which, though trifling, moved the whole house to sympathy.

The *I.L.N.* (1 January 1887) reported that one little girl burst into tears when she could not unfasten 'an obstinate button'. This changed to smiles at 'the hearty encouragement of the audience'.

Harry Nicholls and Herbert Campbell as Ali Baba and Cogia were the leading comic team. 'They are droll, as usual, and we have no doubt they will be droller still as the season advances.' They had a topical duet, 'Not Really', which dealt with 'such ticklish subjects as the Grand Old Man (Gladstone), the Salvation Army and certain recent proceedings in the Divorce Courts'. Robert Pateman's Cassim was 'a most able performance, his comic terror in the scene of his capture by the thieves being in the Robsonian style which makes it somewhat difficult to tell where the comical leaves off and the tragical begins.' Constance Gilchrist was 'a pretty and graceful Morgiana' and Edith Bruce, 'a captivating Ganem'. *The Times* singled out Nicholls and Campbell and Connie Gilchrist for praise. *The Era* concluded by pronouncing *The Forty Thieves* 'the most sumptuous pantomime (Drury-lane) has ever known.'

Ferdinand Wallerstein had taken over as composer-conductor, Oscar Barrett having moved to the Crystal Palace to create his own pantomimes. Harris employed his usual team of scene-painters who garnered their customary praise. Henry Emden painted the opening scene in paradise, the bazaar, the depths of the forest and entrance to the mystic cavern, the banqueting room in Ali Baba's Palace and the courtyard of the Palace. William Beverley painted the interior of the robbers' cave.

William Perkins painted the 'interior of Ali's 'umble 'ome' and the exterior of Cassim's private house. J. Ryan painted the 'New Club' and William Telbin the exterior of Ali's Palace and the ruined Indian Temple. T.W. Grieve and Leolyn Hart had provided, said *The Era*, 'splendid artistic assistance'. The costumes were designed by Carl Wilhelm – 'Marvellously dazzling', said the *I.L.N.* But the pantomime did not conclude until 1.00 a.m. following the two-scene harlequinade.

The 1887–8 pantomime was *Puss in Boots*, credited still to Blanchard, but the pantomimes had since 1881 been bearing the credit: 'invented, arranged and produced by Augustus Harris', leaving little doubt as to whose vision is being realized. *The Era* (31 December 1887) noted that the pantomime had been written by 'that Drury-lane enchanter Mr E.L. Blanchard' and was based on the 'simple and kindly' legend recorded by Charles Perrault. But the critic then added:

> what the legend is, and whence it came, are things of little moment at Drury-lane, when it is to be regarded, first and foremost, if not entirely, as a pretext for gorgeous spectacle. Considered, then, in the light of gorgeous spectacle, *Puss in Boots* ... may be said at once to resolve itself into a couple of scenes, than which nothing more splendid can ever have been seen on the pantomime stage.

The Times (27 December 1887) concurred and described the two key scenes as 'veritable dreams of beauty'. The first was the royal palace. *The Times* described it:

> This inner court into which we are introduced is a dazzling structure of marble, with high raised galleries, lofty columns and a grand staircase down which a dozen people can walk abreast. Chambermaids, prettily dressed in gowns of the most delicate tints of yellow and blue, first trip down the staircase, and shortly afterwards, heralded by trumpeters clad in gorgeous tabards, the whole Court, in uniforms which could only be described by exhausting the catalogue of colours, make their way slowly into the court, which is almost completely filled with the brilliant throng. Upon the staircase remains a large body of retainers in slashed doublets and trunk hose of sheeny white sparkling with silver; and from the arches of the galleries above, gaily bedight attendants view the scene below.

The second was the procession scene, taking place in the castle, once of the ogre and now of the Marquis of Carabas:

> A hall of noble dimensions is seen filled with warriors in complete armour. Some of them are mounted, but the majority are foot soldiers, who go through some regular evolutions, brandishing their halberts. When their drill is over the hall is yet further enlarged by the removal of tapestry at the back and swarming down a lofty flight of steps countless warriors in gold and silver mail deploy before the audience, and are in their turn followed by knights accompanied by their squires and standard bearers. The entire stage in its

length and breadth is filled with glittering metal, nodding plumes, and fluttering pennons which rival in colour the whole tribe of butterflies, and when the trumpets blow the effect of this display is not only beautiful but stirring also.

The Era declared: 'Though armour has frequently been used on the stage for decorative purposes, nothing approaching the present lavish display has ever been attempted before.' After both scenes Harris was forced to come forward and take a bow.

Of the previous scene, *The Era* noted that the processions were attired in

rich brocades and satins, silk and fur, fashioned after the picturesque costume of the Emperor Maximilian period, familiar to us all on the canvases of Sir James Linton. Sumptuous as are the trappings of this superbly apparelled crowd, the effect produced by the scene is one rather of taste than of richness, so skilfully are the colours blended, and so artfully has the designer of the dresses, Mr Wilhelm, availed himself of neutral, in preference to primary, tints.

Wilhelm had designed the entire palace scene which had then been painted by William Perkins.

Again a team of artists did the scene-painting. Henry Emden painted the den of the demon lawyer, 'a pleasant scene of upland country studded with innumerable windmills in full sail', the barn where Jocelyn and Puss sleep, the Giant Ogre's stronghold, the pavilion of chivalry and the bridal toilet. T.E. Ryan did Love's Labyrinth and an interior of the Palace, and William Perkins, the Princess' Boudoir, the interior of the mill and the court of the Palace (to Wilhelm's design). The two great scene-painters Beverley and Telbin did one major scene each, Beverley the panorama taking in the park, the vineyard and the hayfield and Telbin, 'The Golden Honeymoon' transformation scene, a forest glade with a placid lake beyond bathed in the golden glow of a summer afternoon. But *The Times* noted that it was, after all the spectacle and sumptuousness, greeted coldly by the audience because of its simplicity, though the critic praised it as a piece of art.

Madame Katti Lanner devised the ballet scenes, which included 'a graceful ballet of "Dreamland"' while Puss and Jocelyn slept, a ballet of children in the palace undressing their dolls and rocking them to sleep in their cradles which led to Madame Lanner being called forth for an ovation, a ballet of haymakers, and a dance by the disappointed suitors, which *The Era* thought largely redundant.

The Times recorded that:

After the scenic effects of the pantomime what pleased the people most was the music, which has been arranged by Mr Walter Slaughter. There are many tuneful airs and captivating choruses, some of which are already popular, while others among them are fairly certain to become so. The libretto contains many graceful verses and some really pretty lyrics, such as that in which the suitors for the hand of the Princess assert their claims.

The Era said of Slaughter's score, 'where it is original is tuneful and appropriate, and, where it is not original, has been selected with skill from the current music hall repertory of the day.'

The Times thought:

> In the performance there is less mere clownery than is often seen in extravaganza, and last night there would have been less still if it had not been necessary to fill in some of the intervals which inevitably occur when highly elaborate scenery is presented for the first time ... the performers all did their work with a will.

Herbert Campbell and Harry Nicholls as the King and Queen, said The Era, 'will develop their drollery which on Monday night ... had only attained to conspicuously modest dimensions'. But Lily Wadman as the hero Jocelyn was 'a bright and vivacious actress, and, what is here even more important, a songstress of really first-rate excellence'. The songs 'liberally allotted to her in this pantomime furnish one of its most agreeable elements'. Letty Lind as Princess Sweetarte, the critic thought, needed to be given more chances to display her dancing talents. Charles Lauri Jr as the cat was already a popular performer but his 'clever make-up and wonderfully realistic antics' greatly enlivened the show. These Era comments suggest that the performers tended to be overwhelmed by the spectacle, though they would build up their parts as the run went on. Even The Era admitted that towards the end 'the eye begins to weary of the dazzling spectacle.' But it congratulated Harris on 'having scored another brilliant success.' Blanchard recorded in his diary for 26 December 1887: 'We go to Drury Lane to see Puss in Boots, brilliantly placed on stage, but to me very dull and dreary.'[9]

Of the opening night of Puss in Boots on 26 December 1887, the end of the year of the Golden Jubilee, The Stage (30 December 1887) reported:

> On Monday night after the orchestra had successfully waded through all the comic songs of the day they attacked the various National airs amid the greatest enthusiasm, which culminated when our own National Anthem, 'God save the Queen' was reached. Upon the first note the entire audience stood up – and what an audience it was! From the gallery, where ragged boys in short-sleeves perspired and strained that they might see all that was to be seen, down to the rich and well-clad ladies in the stalls, all were intent upon doing honour to the occasion, and joining heartily in the inspiring strains, the conductor meanwhile facing and leading the audience. Upon the conclusion three cheers were given, and then all settled down for the business of the evening.

The last Blanchard pantomime at Drury Lane was *Babes in the Wood* (1888–9). He had been ailing for some years and his health by the end of 1888 was seriously undermined (he was to die on 4 September 1889). For this production, he was credited for the first time as co-author with Augustus Harris and Harry Nicholls. He had evidently resurrected his script for the 1872–3 pantomime *The Children in the Wood* which had starred the Vokes Family. But the show as staged bore little relation to it. *The Times* (27 December 1888) said 'Although a nursery tale is *de rigueur* as the basis of every well-regulated pantomime considerable violence, we fear, is done to nursery tradition in the matter of treatment' and thought 'the best read youngster will have some difficulty in following it.' This version blended the traditional story of the Babes with Robin Hood and the Merry Men and the nursery rhyme 'Who Killed Cock Robin.' Blanchard attended the pantomime on Boxing Day and recorded that his wife was too ill to go, missing Boxing Night for the first time in fifteen years. He does not say what he thought of it.[10]

The Times (27 December 1888) reported:

When Leigh Hunt complained some 50 year ago that the 'comic opening' of the pantomime was extending beyond a mere introduction he little dreamt of such a development of plot and spectacle as was witnessed last night at Drury Lane in Mr Augustus Harris's new version of *The Babes in the Wood*, a picturesque but long introductory story – whirling ballets, changing views, interiors and exteriors, and a dramatic action conducted by a formidable cast of speaking characters, and half-an-hour at most of the pranks of clown and pantaloon, harlequin and columbine, such are the component elements of the latest and most elaborate Drury Lane spectacle. The fact is pantomime has for some years been in a transition state, and we are now within a measurable distance of the time when the so-called 'opening' will elbow the harlequinade out of the theatre altogether. Mr Harry Payne, the venerable clown of Old Drury, took his cue late last night and his professional greeting of 'A Muddy Christmas and a Sloppy New Year' was the signal for two-thirds of the house to make their way to the doors. This is truly a revolutionary state of things. It is needless to bewail it, however. No ancient institution is perishing. The harlequinade in its present form dates no further back than the days of Grimaldi [i.e. 1806–23], who invented the buttered slide, the sausage shop, the red-hot poker, and all the customary business of the spotted and bespangled clown, together with his very garb. Sorry business it generally is for the most part, and its almost total disappearance is not to be regretted when it makes for spectacle of so gorgeous and artistic a character as that with which Mr Augustus Harris has learnt to fill his enormous stage.

The babes, Bertie and Cissy, were played by adults, Herbert Campbell (in an Eton jacket) and Harry Nicholls (in a pinafore). They live with their wicked aunt and uncle, the Baron and Baroness. When their father is reported dead, the baron and baroness decide to get rid of them to claim their inheritance. The children are handed over to two robbers but the good-hearted one spares them. Eventually they are rescued by Robin and Marian and taken home for the transformation. In the forest the babes encounter a woodsman made up like Mr Gladstone and anxious to explain his Irish policy, but they pass rapidly on. His appearance was greeted by 'volleys of groans'.

The spectacular set pieces in the pantomime were the grand procession and ballet of toys and the birds' paradise when robins covered up the sleeping babes. *The Era* wrote of the procession of toys and games:

> There are Dutch dolls endowed with life, but having all the Dutch doll's woodenness ... there were toy soldiers, like those with which some of us frightened our anxious mammas in our eagerness to lick the paint off. There were kites and cricket-bats, and all the cards of all the suits and shuttlecocks; chessmen hobnobbed with tennis players; baby dolls fraternised with big ones, and when the whole crowd with its wondrous variety of colour, was set in motion the effect was truly remarkable ... The drollest and cleverest feature of this scene was beyond question the living marionette dance by the Henderson and Stanley Quartet who really seemed to be worked by strings, and when not worked to be an inanimate as puppets.

Madame Katti Lanner, who devised the ballet of the toys, was called upon to take a bow.

The bird ballet was equally praised. *The Times* called it 'one of the happiest discoveries ever made in that line [i.e., Drury lane spectacle]':

> From a woodland scene in which the robins are seen covering with leaves the sleeping ... babes, we are suddenly translated into what the programme calls a Birds' Paradise. All sorts of birds are here in their most resplendent plumage – green, pink, gray, and yellow cockatoos, innumerable parrots, kingfishers, birds of paradise, in short every ornithological variety that can lend colour to the scene, with a magnificent robin in the person of Mdlle. Aenea, the flying dancer who, by means of an invisible wire, vaults gracefully from one side of the stage to the other. Among the many picturesque concomitants of the Drury Lane version of the story of the wonderful babes, this bird ballet must be awarded the palm for beauty.

The Era said it was 'a scene that in beauty and richness surpasses all that even Mr Augustus Harris has done ... With the eyes bewildered and the senses enchanted by all the brilliancy and all the beauty that are here the keenest observer begins to scorn detail and to take delight in one grand, harmonious whole.' It was a 'triumph for Mr Harris, who was called and enthusiastically cheered; for Mr T.E. Ryan, who painted the scene, and for Wilhelm, who designed the dresses, and for all who had a hand in giving them shape.'

As always, Harris employed a team of top scene-painters. The opening scene was 'a beautiful moonlit glen' in which Robin Hood and his merry men discussed the mystery of who killed cock robin. This was the first of two scenes painted by 'Herr Kautsky of the Vienna Opera House'. The second was the moving panorama of the forest through which the babes passed, 'reflecting the highest credit on Herr Kautsky', said *The Era*. Julian Hicks painted the Palace of Games for the procession of toys. F. Taylor painted the poverty-stricken garret housing the Baron, Baroness and babes. William Perkins painted a glade in Sherwood forest, the nursery of the babes, the entrance hall of the baronial mansion; R. Caney painted 'The Deepest Recesses of the Forest' and Henry Emden, the grand transformation scene 'Hail! Smiling Morn', thought by *The Era* to be 'a most artistic piece of work'.

The Times praised the staging, particularly the fight between the two robbers done as a parody of the prize ring; the groupings of Robin Hood and the outlaws; and the contortions of Dezano, 'the man serpent' in the shadows of the forest. Walter Slaughter provided and conducted the score.

The cast was again made up of music hall favourites: Herbert Campbell and Harry Nicholls as the Babes were proclaimed very funny, particularly in the scenes where they objected to being washed and in the transformation scene when they appeared as classical beauties. Dan Leno, making his first Drury appearances as the Baroness, was very well received, 'his quaint dancing being especially diverting.' Victor Stevens as the Baron was 'amusing and energetic'. Charles Lauri played their poodle; 'the best dog ever seen on the stage, a dog that can talk, laugh, cry, howl, steal, dance, turn somersaults, and jump through hoops.' Harriet Vernon was 'a handsome and dashing Robin Hood'.

The death of Blanchard marked the end of an era, the era of the classic mid-Victorian pantomime. Ailing for much of the 1880s, he did not have the energy to fight Harris. But he clung on until the bitter end, proud of his record as the 'Drury Lane enchanter'. Harris acidly dubbed him 'the Old Man of the Sea' but conscious of the publicity value of his name, continued to pay him for his scripts. But Blanchard's diaries record his increasing distress at the way in which his scripts were adulterated and distorted to accommodate the music hall favourites.

Whereas Blanchard regularly recorded of the pantomime productions in the pre-Harris years 'goes off well' or 'goes off very well', from the start of the Harris regime he was unhappy. On 19 December 1881 he wrote:

> Look over the ghastly proofs of my Drury annual [*Robinson Crusoe*], in which I find my smooth and pointed lines are turned into ragged prose and arrant nonsense. Consider the payment made to me as an equivalent for the harm done to my literary reputation, and shall henceforth look upon it in that light alone.[11]

On 26 December 1882 he wrote of *Sindbad* at Drury Lane:

> though exquisitely got up it is a very dreary music-hall entertainment; and for the
> misprinting and grossly interpolated book I am in no way responsible. It is deservedly
> hissed at various portions – hardly anything there as I had intended, or spoken as I had
> written; the music hall element crushing out the rest, and the good old fairy tales never to
> be again illustrated as they should be.[12]

On 26 December 1885 he wrote: 'To Drury Lane to see *Aladdin*. The panto. not at all
following the text I have written ... it is more dazzling than funny, and I get very
weary of the gagging of the music-hall people.'[13] So it goes on until the final
despairing entry on 21 December 1888: 'Go through the distasteful librettos of *Babes
in the Wood* giving Augustus Harris permission to use my name in consideration that
he uses some lines of my old annual of seventeen years ago.'[14] So just as his first
pantomime for Harris had been a revival of an old script, so too was his last one. It
seems that leading Drury Lane comedian Harry Nicholls had rewritten both *Dick
Whittington* (1884) and *Aladdin* (1885) without credit, and the joint credit to
Blanchard, Harris and Nicholls on *Babes in the Wood* reflected what had become the
reality.

William Beverley, the great painter of pantomime fairyland, died the same year as
Blanchard, on 17 May 1889, aged seventy-eight. Asked in his *Sunday Times*
interview what were his views about the state of pantomime in 1885, he said:

> Well on that subject I had better not speak. For sixteen years I had the entire
> management of the productions at Drury Lane, and then pantomime was quite a
> different thing to what it is now. They are certainly more gorgeous spectacles now, and
> perhaps that is what people want. Years ago we would never have dreamed of spending
> the enormous sums that Mr Augustus Harris spends on his pantomimes. We looked
> formerly upon pantomime as belonging in a way to the 'legitimate drama', but then we
> endeavoured to tell the simple fairy story in the simple yet adequate manner.

He was perhaps being more guarded than he might have been off the record, as he
was still getting work from Harris. But he evidently shared Blanchard's dislike of the
latest developments.

The distance that Drury Lane pantomimes under Harris travelled from
Blanchard's ideals is indicated by the review in *The Athenaeum* (31 December
1892) of *Little Bo-Peep, Little Red Riding Hood and Hop O' My Thumb*:

> By the all but exclusive employment of music-hall 'artistes' the action gains in spirit, but
> loses in delicacy and charm. Pretence to poetry or grace of sentiment is no longer made.
> What is worse, the stories in which childhood delighted are vulgarized. To see Little Red
> Riding Hood or Little Bo-Peep presented by a young lady with the pronounced style of
> the music-hall, to hear her talk of nothing but kissing and hugging, and to watch Little

Boy Blue tipping a knowing wink to his sweetheart for the time being, is nothing short of desecration. So, Sir Augustus! Most lavish of caterers, most skilful of organizers, most inspired of managers, leave our children their fairy tales.

George Augustus Sala, journalist and author, one time scene-painter and writer of pantomime scripts, launched a ferocious attack on the modern pantomime, 'The Nemesis of Pantomime' in *Belgravia* (5 January 1875). He began with the proposition that 'the modern entertainment known as a Pantomime is altogether false to its name, traditions, and original scope and purport, and is therefore a sham.' He did not doubt that the children enjoyed them ('the noise, the glitter, the horseplay, the coloured fires, infinitely delight them ... Childhood is easily pleased'). But the grown-ups who claimed to like the pantomime, he divided into the excusables and the inexcusables. The excusables were the parents and benevolent uncles who:

> are only fostering an amiable delusion, and pretend to be wonderfully stricken by the beauty of the scenery, the splendour of the dresses, and the ingenuity of the transformations, and to be mightily tickled by the dreary tomfoolery of Mr Clown and his colleagues, simply because they hold that it is a right and proper thing to be gratified with anything which gives gratification to the little ones.

The inexcusables, 'humbugs, without a shadow of apology for their impostures, are the young women who go in their finery to be seen and envied by other young ladies and admired by all the young men.' He complained that the old linkage of opening and harlequinade had been lost, that the opening, 'to serve the purposes of spectacular display' was now spun out 'to an inordinate length; while the "comic business", owing to the lack of good clowns and pantaloons, is reduced to a minimum of two or three scenes.' So conscious, he claimed, were modern managers of 'the stupidity of the "comic business" that they have taken to interpolating into the harlequinade a spectacle, procession or ballet, performed entirely by children.' The opening, formerly a mere farce, brief, simple and funny, 'has now swollen into a lengthy burlesque extravaganza, crammed with bad songs, wretched jokes, and boisterous and vulgar "breakdowns", the whole, however, enlivened by well-grouped ballets and scenery, costumes, and appointments of extraordinary magnificence.' But he argued that the opening 'should be a thoroughly moral and even religious entertainment' like the old miracle or mystery plays. It should highlight the conflict between good and evil and the eventual triumph of good. 'The idea and the meaning have been in recent days utterly ignored both by pantomime writers, managers and spectators, and it is fully time that pantomimes should cease in their idiocy and impertinence to annoy and mislead the world.'[15]

The critic W.J. Lawrence in an article ironically entitled 'The Progress of Pantomime' and published in *The Gentleman's Magazine*, surveyed the history of the genre, concluding sadly: 'The genuine Christmas pantomime as founded by Rich and Grimaldi, has no longer an abiding place on English soil.' In a comprehensive indictment of the present, he attributed this state of affairs to the dearth of clowns following the retirement of Grimaldi; the popularity of burlesques which had 'continued to annihilate the simple taste which had hitherto obtained at the patent theatres for a thoroughly sober treatment of fairy lore'; the 'dominating influence of extravaganza' which expanded the opening at the expense of the harlequinade; 'that terrible managerial Frankenstein, the modern "Transformation Scene"' which severed the opening from the harlequinade; the sudden and unnecessary reduction of the once great variety of subjects to a handful, of which Robinson Crusoe, Blue Beard, Cinderella and Dick Whittington 'were the most in demand', plus the 'silly' expedient of merging two or three pantomime subjects thus 'irrevocably marring for the rising generation the intrinsic beauty of many a cherished fable'; and the injection of music hall performers whose presence meant that 'sensitivity, delicacy, artistic harmony – all were annihilated in one fell swoop.' He acknowledged, however, the impossibility of going back to the past by citing the case of Dion Boucicault's pantomime *Lady Bird or Harlequin Lord Dundreary* at the Theatre Royal, Westminster, in December 1862, done almost entirely in dumb-show, which was greeted enthusiastically by nostalgic critics but boycotted by the public.[16]

There was a battle underway for the soul of pantomime. At one level it was fought out in the journals and newspapers. One of the champions of traditional pantomime was John Ruskin. Ruskin, who was devoted to fairy tales and to children, approvingly referred to the 'Arcadias of Pantomime', seeing them as representations of an ideal or idealized world.[17] He compared church and pantomime: 'These two theatrical entertainments where the imaginative congregations still retain some true notions of the value of human and beautiful things ... also they retain some just notion of the truth, in moral things.'[18]

He evidently saw these values in Blanchard's pantomimes *Jack in the Box* and *The Dragon of Wantley*, which he saw respectively on 22 January 1874 and 18 January 1871. He said in *Fors Clavigera* that *Jack in the Box* had 'everything I want people to have always got for them, for a little while' – namely the combination of scenic beauty and moral instruction.[19]

Ali Baba and the Forty Thieves at Covent Garden, which he saw in 1867, had the opposite effect. He denounced it in a letter to the *Pall Mall Gazette* (1 March 1867) published under the heading 'The Corruption of Modern Pleasure'. This pantomime, written by Gilbert A'Beckett, subordinated the fairy tale elements of the story to contemporary references. Its dialogue was spattered with allusions to such modern phenomena as the Derby, cabs, water rates and Cod Liver Oil. The thieves' cave was an up-to-date London club complete with billiard tables and the Forty Thieves were played by cigar-smoking, scantily clad girls. Ruskin was appalled, regarding it as a desecration of womanhood and a betrayal of the fairy tale pantomime.[20] Blanchard shared Ruskin's distaste, writing in his diary after a visit to Covent Garden that the story was 'coarsely treated – all legs and limelight.'[21] Unsurprisingly the show was produced by Augustus Harris Senior, the pioneer of pantomime 'vulgarization'.

The Theatre, where controversies relating to the drama were regularly argued out, returned periodically to the subject of the pantomime. In 'A Plea for Pantomime' in 1879, the journalist W. Davenport Adams launched the first of his series of critiques. He conceded that pantomimes had qualities: they invariably yielded profits that could finance the 'more elevating but less popular' fare managers may wish to mount; they appealed to children; they yielded 'a certain amount of innocent gratification to the ordinary playgoer … being bright and lively, – bright with pretty scenery and gorgeous dresses, and lively with excruciating puns and "catching music".' But he wanted to make them better. He wanted the subjects of the scripts to be 'clear and simple' and treated 'simply and clearly'. Most pantomimes took their stories from popular nursery stories and 'many of them follow out those stories with a fair amount of regularity and strictness.' Blanchard was notable for sticking strictly to the original narrative and Adams wished more writers followed his 'admirable example'. 'Too often, pantomimes are a mere farrago of mingled narratives, a perfect hotchpotch of muddled themes and characters'. He wanted a minimum of topical allusion, 'an absence of vulgar ditties', not interruption by speciality acts (acrobats or 'wonderful dogs'). He wanted legitimate artists and not music hall stars in the cast. Since the shows were directed at children:

> we should have no such coarseness of action or such vulgarity of speech as we have too often at the present day; pantomimes would not be given up to horse-play and tawdriness, as they are too often at this moment; the fun would then be genuine and the sentiment pure … the eye would be gratified by all that was chaste, the ear by all that was harmonious. The whole performance would be one which, whilst it refreshed the jaded intellects of the seniors, would fill with beauty the unstained imagination of the young.[22]

Adams returned to the subject in 1882 in an article for The Theatre called 'The Decline of Pantomime'. In defence of pantomime, he repeated his previous comments that it supplied the monetary surplus to allow managers to produce legitimate drama throughout the year. It provided much employment for people. But there were problems. With a few exceptions like the Britannia and the Grecian which produced an original story every year, the range of subjects had narrowed and this had led to monotony. But the familiar tales were 'falsified and transmogrified; they are, in too many instances, vulgarised as well.' The vulgarization of the genre was due to the music hall element.

It is ... to the music-hall element that we owe the main portion of that impropriety of word, gesture, and 'business' which makes so much of our pantomimes unsuited to the youthful ear and eye – and not only unsuited to the youthful ear and eye, but unpleasant to all people, of whatever age, who possess good taste and feeling.

He arued that the music hall artists:

bring with them not only their songs, which, when offensive in their wording, are sometimes made doubly dangerous by their tunefulness; not only their dances, which are usually vulgar when they are not inane; but their style and manner and 'gags', which are generally the most deplorable of all.

In addition, under the influence of burlesque, pantomime was being filled with men dressed as women and women dressed as men, with the aim of making 'as great a display as possible of the female form'. 'A man in woman's clothes cannot but be more or less vulgar, and a woman in male attire ... cannot but appear indelicate.' The virtual semi-nudity of the ballet dancers was 'utterly and thoroughly gratuitous'. There was now no link between opening and harlequinade, the latter reduced to a deservedly small item, due to 'its triteness and lack of interest'.[23]

In his book, *The Pantomimes and All About Them* (1881), rather incongruously dedicated to Augustus Harris, whom many held responsible for the deterioration of the much-loved form, Leopold Wagner began by complaining:

There was a time, alas! When Pantomime was something very different to the now-a-day entertainment of that name, which has been described as 'a mass of insane absurdity and senseless incongruity', a time when reason and fanciful invention were called into requisition, to produce results as dignified as they were pleasing. Those were the days when visiting the theatre during the coldest nights of January might be regarded as a real treat; when the Pantomime was built upon a story or legend, intelligible to the merest child; when genuine delight was depicted on every countenance; when the jokes were new and practical; when acting was in earnest, and singing rendered with due regard to vocal harmony; when knockabout niggers, clog dancers, gymnasts, contortionists, Whitechapel songsters, and other music hall 'novelties' were not considered indispensable for success; and when pageants and processions, realistic representations of farm-yards with their live stock, cataracts of real water, and extravagant ballet scenes, with the lime-light directed upon an array of palpably naked thighs, which decency should require to be covered with skirts – were as yet unheard of.[24]

The journalist Charles Dickens Jr writing in *The Theatre* 'On the Decadence of Pantomime' complained: 'The simple fact is that the pantomime of to-day is not only not pantomime at all, but has no connection whatever with it.' He recalled the simplicity and individuality of pantomime 50 years before when it was done by gesture and without dialogue, and in which the harlequinade and its characters were dominant. He recalled the Vestris extravaganza with its 'beautiful' final scenes by William Beverley that led managers to compete in visual extravagance. Even when dialogue came in – and the earliest one he could recall as a verbal pantomime was in 1857 – they had a coherent story, outstanding clowning, and often 'the delightful and never-to-be forgotten Vokes family – the nimble and humorous Fred, the charming Victoria ... and the irresistible Rosina'. Pantomime at that time was still 'bright, and lively, and amusing, as well as sufficiently showy and splendid'. But then came the deluge. 'The floodgates of the music hall opened and all that was agreeable about "the grand comic Christmas pantomime" was promptly and effectually drowned out.' And then began the period of 'hopeless, inane, and offensive vulgarity all over the country' which, he admitted, had been 'highly remunerative to performers and managers alike'. He concluded sadly: 'The old English pantomime is dead'.[25]

Augustus Harris hit back, robustly defending the deployment of spectacle in the theatre in an article, 'Spectacle', in *The Magazine of Art* in 1889. He rejected the calls for the revival of the old harlequinade, dismissing it as visually wretched and recalling:

Three weeks were considered a long time to give to the preparation of the Christmas entertainment; old spangled dresses were looked out and 'dodged up'; a few pairs of flats and a couple of set scenes were painted new; some elaborate tricks were made for the harlequinade, the majority of which, not working on the first night, were cut out on the second. A popular clown, with a veteran to assist him as pantaloon, one of the 'ballet gentlemen' from the opera house dressed like harlequin, and one of the 'front row' of the ballet as columbine, were supposed to be good enough to attract our forefathers to the pantomime ... The dear old ladies and gentlemen who now insist that this class of performance should be played to-day, because it met with the approval of their generation, forget that the School Board was not invented when they were young. Whereas in the olden times a pantomime ran a few weeks, it now runs so many months. In some of our provincial towns the harlequinade is now dispensed with, and in all others reduced to the smallest limits. As in London so in the provinces, the appearance of the clown is the signal for departure.

So for Harris the key to theatrical change was the increased level of education of the audience. He argued that it was not sufficient just to spend money.

A spectacular theatre must be ... the trysting-place of all the arts. The work itself must be a labour of love, of perseverance, and of pluck; the co-operation of the most accomplished masters of the various arts should be secured ... It is, indeed, a question whether all the exquisite colourings and delightful combinations are fully appreciated, except by a small and highly-cultivated minority. Why, then, many ask, take the trouble to do the thing properly if not appreciated? Why not follow the old Boucicaultian managerial axiom, 'never try to educate your audience'? Because the minority is fast becoming the majority, thanks to the march of education ... the liberal expenditure of money in itself has little to do with an artistic result, but Art is a very extravagant and lavish mistress ... those who talk so much of the lover of art whilst producing very little that is artistic, are generally those who are either unable or unwilling to make such financial sacrifices at the shrine of the goddess as she demands.

Harris is defending his lavish pantomimes in terms of art and education, almost a Ruskinian position, paradoxically for someone who traditionalists accused of vulgarizing and undermining the form.[26]

The first pantomime of the post-Blanchard era was *Jack and the Beanstalk or Harlequin and the Midwinter Night's Dream* (1889–90), scripted now by Augustus Harris, who produced, and Harry Nicholls, the principal Drury Lane comedian who played the King. Harris stuck to his tried and tested formula. The pantomime opens with a parody of *A Midsummer Night's Dream*. Oberon and Titania are quarrelling about the desire of Princess Diamond Duckz to marry Jack the milkman. Titania approves and Oberon does not. The Princess is carried off by the Giant Gorgibuster and Jack has to climb the beanstalk to rescue her. Climbing to Cloudland, he finds the heroes and heroines of Shakespeare's plays held prisoner and frees them. Jack rescues the Princess, returns to earth and overcomes the Giant who resigns the Princess to him. Oberon and Titania are reconciled. Jack and the Princess will marry on Mount Olympus.

The Era (28 December 1889) declared of Harris: 'His eleventh pantomime as a display of grandeur is fully equal to its predecessors ... Mr Harris has given his artistic taste and wonderful skill in organisation full play at the same time, "crowning the edifice" with expenditure of the most lavish kind.' The reviewer said 'there are three grand scenes ... either of which would in bygone days have made the fortune of a manager.' There was the old English market where Jack brought his mother's cow to sell:

What a beautiful scene that was with the whole of the stage occupied by animated groups of figures; not dull automatons, but lively personages every one of them, and dressed in the daintiest manner. There were dances and choruses of last century, holiday makers in costumes as rich and tasteful as costly material and elegant designs could make them, and the movement and gaiety of the scene could not be praised too highly.

Then there was the Shakespearean procession ('What a feast there was for admirers of the national poet'). Twenty-one plays were represented:

by appropriate and picturesque scenes glowing with colour and harmony of effect, and frequently rendered by the performers with exquisite taste ... This was the scene in the

Giant's Library where piles of gigantic volumes, representing the genius and learning of past centuries are arranged so as to form a flight of gigantic steps, down which, to the echoes of a brilliant festival march, come the representative figures of the various plays, pausing a moment before the footlights to give with the requisite action some principal scene of the play. The groups had all been arranged by Mr Harris himself, and the costumes could not have been more perfect in design or costlier in material.

But even this was topped by the procession of the gods and goddesses of Olympus.

As a feast for the eye, and a most wonderful realisation of the splendour and grace of Greek mythology, nothing like the festival of gods and goddesses of Olympus *has* ever been seen on any stage. The mythical figures of the Greek poets stand before us in classical garb, and in costumes in which the utmost artistic beauty has been displayed. The loveliest designs are contrasted ... Description is baffled in attempting to describe this gorgeous scene, in which the beautiful dances are such an interesting feature, Madame Katti Lanner having displayed the utmost refinement of taste in the arrangement. Mr Harris was called for and warmly greeted in this wonderfully beautiful scene, the most brilliant and most perfectly planned that has ever been presented on the stage of Old Drury.

The Times (27 December 1889) complained:

there is just a little danger of pantomime at Drury-lane becoming 'groovy' [by which it meant samey]. The grand processions, in particular which have been the crowning feature of the performance for some years past, wear, inevitably, a close resemblance to each other. Still, considering their undeniable grandeur, this does not matter in the least, at all events, to the younger spectators.

The Stage (3 January 1890) praised Oberon's Bower, 'a lovely woodland scene by Kautsky. Here dog roses and wild convolvuli waited on their fairy sovereigns; mushrooms and brilliant toadstools were the umbrella bearers; whitewinged moths fluttered around, and hung high in mid-air were beauteous fays'. It praised the Shakespearean procession ('exquisite pictures') and the scene on Mount Olympus:

The grand procession of gods and goddesses of Ancient Mythology will live in the annals of Old Drury as the most gorgeous, yet tasteful, pageant that has ever graced its boards. Iris and her rainbow-tinted attendants, Venus and her white-robed vestals, Jupiter in imperial purple, and his consort in cerulean blue, Cupid with his rose-crowned cupidons, Neptune with his merman and maid, delicate Aurora and black Proserpine, stately Minerva and chaste Diana, the Graces and the weird Fates, Mercury the fleet-footed, and Mars the warlike, godlike Apollo and his priest and devotees, all file before us, preceded by guards in all the wealth of gold and silver armour, and by minstrels and ladies in shining robes; till from the fair temple that forms the background, the whole depth of the stage is filled with a blaze of splendour that dazzles the eye and makes one almost believe in the wondrous tales of the Arabian nights.

It took the place of the transformation and the harlequinade (two scenes only) began straight afterwards.

The comedy was in the capable hands of Harry Nicholls, Herbert Campbell and Dan Leno. Nicholls played the King, Henry the Bounder, as an amorous penniless swell, who spends his time at the club, the lodge, the smoking concert and the Gaiety Theatre, and who is first seen coming home with the milk unable to pay his cabman and trying to find the keyhole. ('Very funny business' thought *The Era*.) Herbert Campbell played Queen Fanny the Flirt, who is constantly nagging the King, is 'arrayed in the most fantastic feminine costume' and 'acts with comic effect in all the scenes with the King'. Dan Leno had 'a most amusing character as Jack's Mother, and his song so often disturbed by amorous cats was very diverting. Mr Dan Leno's dances must be seen to be believed. They are electrical.' George Conquest Jr played the Giant 'and entered into the humour of his part perfectly'. He was made up with a shock of red hair, scowling forehead and great blinking eyes. *The Stage* reported of Leno that 'with his fantastic dances, his song recalling the fond memories of "Number One" of her departed husbands, and his general ludicrous behaviour and very clever business, caused roars of laughter'. There was, said *The Stage*, 'excellent comic business' in the market scene caused by the cow and its keeper (played by the brothers Fred and Joseph Griffiths respectively). 'Tremendous fun', said *The Era*.

The Times noted:

It is worthy of remark that, despite the recent agitation against the employment of children, the juvenile ballets at Drury Lane remain pretty much the same as before. There are more children, perhaps, of medium growth than formerly, but there are also many toddling mites of extremely tender years, a whole battalion of little Cupids, with bows and arrows, figuring in the mythological scene.

The Stage called Katti Lanner's ballets 'exquisite'. *The Era* said the scenery of Dayes, Caney, Kautsky and Perkins 'enhanced the attractions of the pantomime.' *The Stage* concluded: 'When after a night or two the comic business in the opening has been worked up, *Jack and the Beanstalk* will not only be as gorgeous a pantomime as has been seen but may long claim to being one of the most amusing.'

For the Christmas pantomime of 1890–1, Augustus Harris had a change of co-writer. His new collaborator was William Yardley. Yardley (1849–1900) was a very different figure from Blanchard. Son of the Chief Justice of Bombay, educated at Rugby and Trinity College, Cambridge, he was described by Lord Harris as 'one of the finest amateur batsmen England ever produced'. He qualified for the bar, but devoted his time to the theatre. Having acted in amateur pantomime under the direction of John Hollingshead, manager of the Gaiety Theatre, he embarked on a career writing burlesques for the Gaiety, usually in collaboration, and achieving considerable success with *Herne the Hunted* (1881) (co-written with Robert Reece), *Very Little Hamlet* (1884), *The Vicar of Wide Awake Field* (1885) and *Little Jack Sheppard* (1885) (the last two co-written with H.P. Stephens). There were also a succession of comedy plays and comic operas. Alongside this authorial activity, he was drama critic as 'Bill of the Play' for *The Sporting Times*, known as 'The Pink 'Un'.[27] In 1890 he collaborated with Harris on *Beauty and the Beast*. *The Times* (27 December 1890) noted that 'It contains far better matter than is usual in pantomime' and that for this production the familiar story had been combined with *Cinderella* but 'the two stories have been brought into harmony with such rare skill that long before the end of the piece it is impossible to avoid the thought that memory has played one a trick in suggesting that the stories are distinct.' The *I.S.D.N.* (3 January 1891) echoed *The Times* in declaring that Yardley, 'who is Mr Blanchard's successor as author of the "opening" is to be congratulated upon the neat and straightforward way in which he has accomplished a task less easy than is the case in a story more rich and varied in incident than is the legend of the Beast and his fair sweetheart.'

The show opens in Pandemonium where the Bogey Man and his imps, Envy, Hatred, Malice, Dyspepsia, Misanthropy, Inebriety, Indolence and Spite plot. The new young King, King Courage, is pronounced 'far too virtuous' as he is granting everything his subjects ask: abolition of taxes, the opening of all public spaces to the poor and a four-hour working day. It is when the King refuses to stop doing good that he is turned into a Beast. Fairy Rosebud intervenes to say the spell will be reversed if someone falls in love with him. The two elder daughters of merchant Lombard Streete become the ugly sisters and Beauty the equivalent of Cinderella. She goes to the ball in disguise and the King falls in love with her. The familiar story of 'Beauty and the Beast' takes over, when the beast is transformed by Beauty's love and the pantomime ends with a grand procession of viands and the wedding breakfast.

The Era (1 January 1891) reported that every seat and every bit of standing room was taken long before the curtain rose and that the audience joined in vigorously with the national anthem and 'Rule Britannia'. There was a major hitch on the opening night when the panorama of the road to the port of Hungerford unfolded too slowly and there was a delay with getting the ship, 'so heavy that it had been necessary to move it upon tramway lines', upon the stage. It then rocked back and forth, making the passengers seasick and causing Streete to say 'This berth will be the death of me.' But it was all accepted with good humour by the audience, and according to the *I.S.D.N.* the pantomime was 'unanimously hailed as an artistic triumph and a popular success.'

The visuals, the ballet and the scenery were highly praised. The *I.S.D.N.* thought:

Something very like perfection is attained in the appropriate display of the Royal Ballroom wherein King Courage falls in love with Beauty. The lighting of the stage by huge chandeliers, the variety of rich and brilliant costume designed by Messrs. Edel and Russell, the kaleidoscopic changes of harmonious colouring, together with the dance itself, (a *pas de neuf* designed and arranged by John D'Auban) combine to make this one of the most memorable of pantomimic episodes.

This scene utilized the whole depth of the stage, with a fountain in the centre, a balcony full of courtiers on the right, noble statues at the back, and from the 'masked heads of the attendants ranged on either side sprung candelabra'. *The Times* thought the Ballroom scene 'emphatically pretty; but among many scenes of beauty which were displayed it was not the very best.' It preferred the grand ballet of roses in the Beast's rose garden, 'in which the dancers were attired in dresses conveying an exact representation of such roses as General Jacqueminot, Provence, Duke of Edinburgh, and William Allan Richardson', calling it 'emphatically one of the most beautiful things that has ever been put on the stage.' *The Era* noted that the spectacle built and built as the end approached. In the grand hall of the Beast's palace where the King awaits Beauty's return, 'we get the grand spectacular display always looked for in a pantomime produced by Mr Augustus Harris. The hall itself is built on lines of loveliness. The ceiling is gay with garlands' and there is a grand staircase, down which process dancers, Amazons in glittering armour and brightly coloured cloaks, damsels with fans springing from their shoulders and 'a bevy of juveniles quaintly clad and a troupe of Indian dancers with cymbals and glittering scimitars and snake dancers practising their curious calling.' After Beauty gives her consent to wed the Beast, there is a 'grand procession of viands' with knives, forks and spoons, fish and flesh and fowl, plum puddings and fruits and ices, and 'a very suggestive box of pills that brings up the rear.' A giant wedding cake made up the transformation scene, some delay attending its appearance on opening night.

Of the performers, *The Era* thought 'The most liberal contributors of fun ... were Messrs. Herbert Campbell and Harry Nicholls, and the Brothers Griffiths.' Campbell and Nicholls played the Ugly Sisters. 'Their appearance alone was provocative of great laughter, which got to a general and gigantic roar in the scene where the massive ladies were discovered mounted on their tandem tricycles.' There was a topical duet, 'I don't think it's ever been done.' Nicholls burlesqued 'the dancing in what we may call the Kate Vaughan and Letty Lind school.' The Griffiths Brothers played the two donkeys 'and a more comical pair of donkeys has never been known.' Their refusal to be harnessed, their unhappiness at being winched aboard ship and their sea-sickness during the voyage all evoked gales of laughter. Dan Leno as Lombard Streete was 'full of drollery, and prepared in speech, song, dance or "business" to increase the fun and add to the merriment'. Vesta Tilley made a 'handsome and dashing King' and 'a capital specimen of what pantomimic work should be was furnished by Mr John D'Auban as the Beast': 'A very terrible Beast' thought *The Times*, 'black-faced, shaggy-haired, claw-footed, and in every way uncouth.'

The *I.S.D.N.* found Nicholls and Campbell 'mirth-provoking'. 'Men in women's clothes have of course often been decidedly offensive upon the stage, but there is, happily, nothing vulgar in the management of their petticoats by these two comedians'. It found Nicholls' dance imitation 'not only amusing, but often really pleasing to the eye.' But it thought Leno's drunk act in the rose garden a mistake.

Scenery was by Caney, Kautsky, Ryan and Perkins and earned particular praise for the painting of the grand hall of the Beast's Palace. *The Times* thought they had 'excelled themselves' there. The music by the conductor P. Bucalossi was, thought *The Times*, 'pleasant and well-suited to the occasion'. The *I.S.D.N.* agreed that the music was 'melodious and pleasing' yet lacked 'the *verve* and character needed on an occasion like this.' Harris was called forth to take a bow.

He achieved something of a coup by casting music hall star Belle Bilton as Beauty. The choice of subject and this casting reflected a desire to cash in on a society scandal. In 1889 Belle Bilton had secretly married Lord Dunlo, son and heir of the Earl of Clancarty. Clancarty pressured his son to petition for divorce on the grounds of her adultery. But in the summer of 1890 Lord Dunlo asserted his wife's innocence and the proceedings were terminated. The popular press were on the side of the young lovers and Harris abandoned the planned production of *Dick Whittington* and put on *Beauty and the Beast*, casting Belle (billed in the programme as Lady Dunlo) as Beauty. There was a torrent of ready-made publicity. It mattered little that the *I.S.D.N.* reported that 'her acting is in all senses of the word indifferent, whilst her vocal and terpsichorean accomplishments are below rather than above the average.' It proved to be Belle's final stage appearance as on the sudden death of her father-in-law in 1891, she became the Countess of Clancarty and although never received at court, was popular with tenants and neighbours of the family in Ireland.[28] She bore the Earl five children before dying in 1906, at the age of thirty-six. The double act on the halls that Belle performed with her sister Flo was directly parodied by Campbell and Nicholls in their duet 'The Sisters Frillings', to general delight. *Beauty and the Beast* achieved 149 performances.

For 1891–2 Harry Nicholls was back as co-writer with Harris and again there was a subject merger for *Humpty Dumpty, or Harlequin the Yellow Dwarf and the Fair One with the Gold Locks*. Since the nursery rhyme of *Humpty Dumpty* contains only a situation rather than a narrative, the authors provided one by appropriating the story of the Yellow Dwarf and mixing in the *Queen of Hearts* nursery rhyme for good

Pantomime Posters

The posters for Drury Lane distilled the elegance and grace associated with the pantomimes of Augustus Harris and Arthur Collins.

25. Jack and the Beanstalk *at Drury Lane in 1889*

26. Cinderella *at Drury Lane in 1895*

27. The Forty Thieves *at Drury Lane in 1898*

measure. In this version, the King and Queen of Hearts have a beautiful daughter, Princess All-Fair whose hand is sought by both handsome King Dulcimar of the Gold Mines and Humpty Dumpty. Humpty first appears as an egg, has a fall from a wall, shattering the shell, and emerges as a malignant dwarf, who had adopted the egg shell as a disguise. The King's guards on hobby horses fail to reconstruct the shell. So Humpty as himself and aided by his aunt, the Desert Fairy Oltatina, will pursue the goal of marrying All-Fair. The problem is that All-Fair does not want to marry but prefers to play with her dolls. The Queen of Hearts and the Knave prepare some medicated tarts which they plan to use to quell the monsters guarding the Orange Grove, so that they can acquire a sprig of orange blossom to feed to the Princess. It will cause her to fall in love with the first man she sees. But the Desert Fairy causes the Knave to eat the tarts and fall asleep. Humpty disperses the monsters and hearing of the Queen's plan, gives her a fifteen foot long sprig of orange blossom, intending to be the first man All-Fair sees. However, she sees Dulcimar first, falls for him and is on the point of being married when Humpty Dumpty carries her off to his Steel Castle. Dulcimar besieges the castle with an army of wooden toy soldiers, defeats the dwarf's army and when Humpty prepares to abandon Oltatina and flee disguised as a ballet dancer she seizes him and hands him over to his enemies. Dulcimar and All-Fair are reunited. The grand transformation was a 'dream of bliss'.

The pantomime lasted four and a half hours but, said *The Era* (2 January 1892):

for brilliancy and fun [it] has hardly been equalled, and certainly has not been surpassed, in the history of pantomime at Drury Lane under the liberal, energetic, and enterprising direction of Sir Augustus Harris, who may be said to have raised these Christmas productions almost to the level of the fine arts.

The Times (28 December 1891) agreed, saying 'for splendour of display, for harmonious conception, and for abundance of entertaining incident [it] may fairly claim to be superior to any of its predecessors'. Pointing out that given its length, it:

depended for success upon resolute enterprise, careful organization, and the matchless power of providing spectacular effects, for which the well-known lessee and manager of Drury Lane is famous, the result was a complete triumph. Never has a more consistent and intelligible pantomime been placed upon the stage; seldom, if ever, has a display of equal intricacy and brilliance been unfolded without a hitch or impediment of any kind from start to finish.

The *I.S.D.N.* (2 January 1892) said:

There cannot be the slightest doubt this year as to the triumphant success of the pantomime at Drury Lane – a success the more noteworthy and creditable by reason of the exceptionally high standard of excellence which Sir Augustus Harris has set before himself in his previous Christmas production. The prolonged 'Oh!' of admiration caused by the magnificence of the appointment and the beauty of the scenery is broken at due intervals by the outbursts of laughter which are after all the best tribute to the practical efficiency of pantomimic achievement.

For the first time for many years members of the royal family attended the opening night. The royal box was occupied by the Princess of Wales, the Duke of Clarence, the Duke and Duchess of Fife, and the two youngest daughters of the Prince of Wales. The audience rose with cheers to acknowledge their entrance, and were not inhibited by this royal presence. *The Era* noted:

A Boxing Night audience at the national theatre has often been described. That of the Boxing Night of a week ago was very much like its predecessors in its elasticity, and its endurance of tight squeezing: in its good temper: in its love of noise, and in its readiness to shout itself hoarse upon the slightest provocation in an orchestral suggestion of a music hall chorus.

'With wonderful gusto', they joined in the choruses of such music hall favourites as 'Hi-tiddley-hi-ti', 'Knock 'em in the Old Kent Road' and 'Pretty little mermaids at the bottom of the sea'.

The Era noted that there were 'four special features by which the Drury-lane pantomime of Christmas, 1891, will be remembered': the Dolls' at-Home, the grand ballet in the scene of The Orange Grove, the procession of Nations in honour of the wedding of King Dulcimar and Princess All-Fair and the 'introduction in the person of "Little Tich" of the drollest dwarf ever seen on the Drury-lane stage.' The dolls, summoned from the toy shops in the Lowther Arcade by Princess All-Fair, came in every shape and form, male and female, black and white, stiff-legged and elastic-limbed, dressed and undressed, and:

> most imposing of all, a gathering of giant baby dolls in long – about twelve feet long – garments and becoming hoods, from which escape their flaxen curls and great big blue eyes that stare the spectators out of countenance. Never was known such a remarkable doll collection. At rest they made a wonderful show, but when they begin to dance the effect is altogether beyond description.

The same sequence featured a much-praised Japanese fan-dance executed by John and Emma D'Auban: 'One of the cleverest terpsichorean exhibitions of the evening', the *I.S.D.N.* called it.

The Era reported:

> The scene in the Orange Grove is sure to be voted enchantingly effective by reason of the floral divertissement, with its startling electric effects. The dancers carry lily or aurum boughs in their hands, and similar flowers decorate their dresses. While they dance the foliage over their heads is suddenly brilliantly illuminated, and in an instant each lily on their costume is converted into an electric lamp. A prettier or more startling spectacle could not be conceived, and acclamation loud and long is fairly compelled.

The Times called the ballet 'really exquisite'.

The highlight of the wedding scene was the procession of Nations. The *I.S.D.N.* said it:

> stands quite alone in the sumptuous glory of its colouring as designed by Mr Percy Anderson. No description can do any sort of justice either to the hues or the fabrics of the raiment here allotted to the representatives of four-and-twenty nationalities, all assembled for All-Fair's wedding.

The Times had a go at describing. The countries represented were India, Arabia, Dalmatia, Tartary, Cochin-China, Persia, Egypt, Lapland, Japan, Montenegro, Portugal, China, Timbuctoo, Italy, Greece, Holland, Germany, Austria, Russia, Turkey, America, Spain, France and England. According to *The Times*:

> the most pleasing costumes of all were the amber silk and fur of the Tartar maidens, the creamy robes and plumed headdresses of Cochin China, the white and fur of the Laps,

the embroidered purple of the Japanese damsels, the terra cotta stamped with gold of China, the classic-bordered tunics of the Greek girls, the sombre plumes and mantillas of the Spanish senoritas and the gorgeous red of the English. Very piquant were the Americans in stars and stripes.

The girls danced a *pas de deux*, arranged by John D'Auban. Then Princess All-Fair appeared, in white raiment trimmed with orange blossom, with a 'train of enormous expanse borne behind her.' *The Times* said: 'This was the climax and the lessee's triumph. For completeness, for splendour, for harmony of colour the scene had never been surpassed.' Harris was called upon twice to take a bow after this. *The Era*, however, noted that Germany and Russia had been booed, America, cheered, and that 'the pit and gallery reserved their loudest applause for their noble selves as represented by England.'

The *I.S.D.N.* said: 'The company engaged for the interpretation is one of such all-round strength as has seldom been paralleled even under this enterprising management.' *The Times*, however, had some criticisms. 'The absence of Mr Harry Nicholls from the cast was distinctly felt.' Nicholls, perhaps feeling himself upstaged by Dan Leno, had migrated to the Adelphi. There was a shortage of topical allusions and 'in some of the actors, lack of vocal power'. *The Times* also thought the opening scene of a chorus of caterwauling cats bordered on dullness. However, Herbert Campbell and Dan Leno as the broadly cockney King and Queen of Hearts were deemed 'excellent in their way'. There were some notable comic scenes: a burlesque boxing match between Dulcimar and Humpty, a kitchen scene 'opening with a chorus of *chefs* and some funny business by Buttons (Mr Tom Pleon)', (making a guest appearance from *Cinderella*) and:

> a witty but vulgar song by Dulcimar, entitled 'What a difference in the morning', containing allusions to false hair, false teeth and other refinements of civilization. Then came the making of the tarts, during which Mr Dan Leno, as Queen and chief cook, was excellent. It ended with the rapid conversion of the kitchen table into a steam engine having plates for wheels, frying-pan for driving wheel, broomstick for lever, a top boot for funnel, a bonnet box for safety valve, and roasting screen for boiler. On this the Queen and Knave started for the Orange Grove.

The Era praised Campbell and Dan Leno who:

> worked hard from start to finish, and were responsible for much hilarity. A sly bit of humour was brought into scene eight. The Queen has received her distinguished guests, representative of all the nations under the sun, and has shaken hands with each in turn. The reception over, Her Majesty brings in soap and water, and proceeds to wash her hands.

Fanny Leslie played King Dulcimar 'in very animated style' and was 'applauded in her song called "In the morning" and admired for her nimble dancing.'

Campbell and Leno now became an established pantomime team. They made a wonderfully grotesque pair: Campbell, nineteen stone and possessed of a distinctive and much imitated voice with a metallic intonation, and Leno, five feet three in height, skeletally thin, with high arched eyebrows and wide mouth. J. Hickory Wood, who subsequently wrote Drury Lane pantomimes, recalled their partnership in his biography of Leno, identifying their performances as the King and Queen of Hearts as the beginning of their partnership:

> As the King and Queen of Hearts, they pervaded the pantomime together, Herbert's calm stolidity contrasting finely with Dan's 'verve' and 'go', while Dan's excitable methods made Herbert appear to be the most abnormally and comically placid monarch ever seen upon the stage. It was an ideal partnership and was then and there perpetuated only to be broken by death.

Hickory Wood, who had observed Leno at first hand, perfectly captured the nature of his approach to his characters:

> To Dan Leno, a pantomime character was a real character; a character is to be carefully studied and thought out as that of the emotionally complex nature of a heroine in a problem play. His pantomime queens, for example, with all their absurd extravagance, yet contrived to convey some subtle suggestion of regality. An impossible queen, we say, of course; but still a queen ... His studies of women in a humble walk of life were entirely different. His gait, his manner, his expression were altered, and all his dignity had vanished. He was homely, discursive, and confidential, not to say occasionally aggressive ... when I saw him playing these kind of parts, the impression he left on my mind was ... as the picture of what Dan Leno would have been if he had actually been that particular woman. No comedian playing female parts has ever differentiated his studies of the sex so much as Dan Leno did.[29]

While conceding the strength of the cast, the I.S.D.N. was rather more critical. It thought that rather than Harry Nicholls, 'we could better have spared Mr Herbert Campbell, whose humour is more vigorous than refined, but whose King of Hearts seems nevertheless, quite to the taste of the audience.' Dan Leno, however, was 'really very diverting'. Marie Lloyd danced vigorously and sang tunefully and showed 'a certain piquant charm which she might use to still more advantage if she would modify the breadth of style that she has cultivated for the delectation of her exacting audience.' Fanny Leslie was thought 'lacking precisely in that quality of charm which just saves Miss Lloyd.' The critic is evidently hinting here at vulgarization of the pantomime by the music hall incursion, a point underlined in the comment on the script: 'The book ... is all, or almost all, that a pantomime libretto ought to be, falling short only in those congruities of fairy lore which the late E.L. Blanchard used to observe so religiously in his Boxing Day productions.'

But there was general praise for the scene-painting of Messrs Caney, Kautsky, Joseph Harker and Perkins, the costume designs of Percy Anderson and Edel, the choreography of John D'Auban, the music composed and conducted by John Crook and the stage management of Arthur Collins. The show ran for 147 performances.

Humpty Dumpty marked the arrival of two of the best-loved music hall stars in Drury Lane pantomime – Little Tich and Marie Lloyd. Little Tich (real name Harry Relph) was only four feet six inches tall but deployed his size to great comic effect in acrobatic dancing and gymnastic contortions which invariably convulsed audiences. In 1889–90 he appeared in the pantomime *Babes in the Wood* at the Prince's Theatre, Manchester, in the supporting role of Bantam, page to the wicked Baron, and literally stole the show. His performance became 'a talking-point in Manchester and word of it reached London.' This was significant, as according to comedian Harry Randall, 'there was nothing in London – outside of Drury Lane – to compare with the Prince's pantomimes' which were 'a household word in Manchester'.[30] Tich returned for the 1890–1 pantomime *Little Bo-Peep* and his Toddlekins was again a sensation. In between these shows he established himself securely as a 'bright particular star' at one of London's leading music halls, the Pavilion.[31] Inevitably Harris and Drury Lane beckoned. His signing almost certainly dictated the choice of story for *Humpty Dumpty*. Tich did not disappoint. *The Era* declared him as:

> easily the first in favour among the artistes engaged ... He has a funny little body, funny little legs, a funny little face, and a funny big smile that stretches right away from the footlights to the topmost gallery, and on Saturday night ... Humpty-Dumpty kept the house in a roar, now in nautical costume, now in sporting garb, now in a Scotch rig-out, and now – most comical of all – as a ballet girl with a *pas seul* that would send a hypochondriac into fits of merriment.

The *I.S.D.N.* agreed, 'the chief individual triumph is that ... of "Little Tich". This small performer has a genuine notion of eccentric comedy, and his drolleries are of the greatest service.'

Marie Lloyd as Princess All-Fair scored a hit with her song 'Whacky, whack, whack', about the School Board which was encored and 'with much "kicking up behind and before" seemed to give immense satisfaction to the gods, who cheered her to the echo,' said *The Era*. The infant Compton MacKenzie was taken to see the show and was 'greatly surprised' to see that Marie Lloyd's high kicks displayed her long amber silk drawers.[32]

The 1892–3 pantomime was *Little Bo-Peep, Little Red Riding Hood and Hop O' My Thumb*, written by Augustus Harris and Wilton Jones. The curtain rose at 8.00 p.m. and came down at midnight, a four hour show. It was generally agreed that Harris had equalled or even surpassed his previous efforts. 'A triumph of thoughtful organization and magnificent spectacle', *The Times* called it. 'As complete, as varied and as opulent a spectacle as the pantomime-style has ever had on show', thought the *I.S.D.N.*[33]

The script contrived to merge three traditional pantomime stories and involve a host of nursery rhyme characters. It begins with Daddy and Goody Thumb trying to abandon their seven children in the wood but being disconcerted by their reappearance. In the village of Happy Arcadia, Red Riding Hood is instructed by ageing spinster Dame Mary Quite Contrary to visit her grandmother and plans to use this to have a rendezvous with her suitor Little Boy Blue. Little Bo-Peep appears and is courted by Prince Poppetty and Dame Mary is wooed by the penniless Squire Oofless who is seeking his long lost child as well as a wealthy marriage. All three couples arrange to meet in Glow-Worm Glen. In the wood, Daddy and Goody try once more to lose their children. Mr and Mrs Wolf plot the capture of Red Riding Hood. The Squire makes advances to Bo-Peep and is rejected. She meets with the Prince. The Wolf tries to carry off Red Riding Hood but she is saved by the good fairies Ariel and Elfinella. She has a secret meeting with Boy Blue, who is too poor to contemplate marriage. Bo-Peep turns out to be the long lost daughter of the Squire. Daddy and Goody are captured by the Ogre Fee-Fo-Fum and prepared for roasting, but are rescued by Hop O' My Thumb. The Wolves stage the impersonation of Granny but are foiled. At the Palace, all the couples are united and the transformation 'The Language of Flowers' takes place.

The Era reported:

> There are four separate scenic effects, each one of which would have made its inventor famous in the old days – a ballet of Watteau shepherds and shepherdesses, a ballet of sports and games, a glow-worm ballet – in which the electric light is used with delicious effect – and then an orgie [sic] of serpentine dancers, leading up to a great pageant of fairy lore.

The ballet takes place in the village of Arcadia:

> Mr Perkins has painted a lovely landscape, bathed in warm sunlight, and hither troop Watteau shepherds and shepherdesses, with their pipes and panniers, their crooks and posies, till the stage looks like a little world of Dresden China brought to life and imbued with exquisite grace by Mr John D'Auban, a pretty embodiment of 'tea-cup times, of hoop and hood, or when the patch was worn'.

The village scene concludes with a ballet of sports and games. *The Era* said:

> There never was such an effective array of stage properties – so admirably realistic and so picturesque. A troop of sportsmen in Highland tweeds pop at imaginary game, gigantic

boxing gloves pummel each other lustily, a group of pretty girls trip across the stage with punt poles slipping through their fingers in the most approved style for showing buxom bosoms and well-shaped arms, skaters glide by, jockeys win and lose fanciful races, huntsmen in pink mingle with Dianas in smart riding habits, tennis players with their rackets talk with yachtsmen in bright blue, great cricket bats stalk solemnly across the stage, large footballs move in a mysterious way, billiard balls wink insidiously with 'quaint enamelled eyes', cyclists vie with skaters, fishermen mingle with dancers – the whole arsenal of British sport is there, reproduced with extraordinary effect and vraisemblance. There is nothing appeals to your Britisher like sport, and the audience was demonstrative in its delight.

The glow-worm ballet consisted of a troop of wood nymphs emerging from the recesses of the forest:

bearing in their hands tremulous sprays of electric light, with five or six glow-lights at the end of each spray. As they dance on the darkened stage their undulating lights group and divide in kaleidoscopic illumination with exquisite effect. Probably the electric light – that now-popular adjunct of stage illusion – has never been used so ingeniously and so admirably arranged.

The Times called it 'exquisitely pretty'. There was also general praise for Karl Kautsky's moving panorama of woodland landscape – 'really beautiful', said the *I.S.D.N.*

The grand spectacle came at the end in 'The Grand Hall of a Million Mirrors in the Prince's Palace'. *The Times* described it:

All the sides and back of the spacious stage were literally walled with mirrors, above was silvered tracery, and the mirrors were divided by gilded pillars, from which the electric light flashed and sparkled. In this scintillating hall ... innumerable persons in the most gorgeous dresses were already standing when, before the procession which was to follow, came a concerted skirt dance and then a species of serpentine skirt dance, the performers in which manipulated skirts of immense length with great dexterity. Those skirts were alike in having a border of gold at the bottom, in passing from dark to light shade from waist to hem; for the rest they were red, blue and purple, and exceedingly pleasing.

The procession was of characters and scenes from twenty-eight nursery rhymes (*The Era* said it was thirty-nine; *The Stage*, thirty). *The Era* said:

each is really a miniature show in itself, complete, and, we doubt not, as accurate as possible in every detail. The children shrieked with delight as they recognised one old friend after another ... It is a gorgeous pageant, a splendid masque of fable and folk lore, a liberal education in the art of the stage and the archaeology of the nursery ... when the curtain fell on this stupendous scene there was a great outburst of enthusiasm.

Harris was called forward to take a bow.

The spectacle was combined with comedy and song, performed by a virtually all-star cast of music hall favourites: among them Dan Leno and Herbert Campbell played Daddy and Goody Thumb; Marie Lloyd, Little Red Riding Hood; Marie Loftus, Little Bo-Peep; Little Tich, Hop O' My Thumb; and Ada Blanche, Little Boy Blue. There were several sequences of vintage knockabout. In the opening scene, Daddy and Goody Thumb, frustrated in their bid to lose their children, birch them, pass them through a mangle and put them to bed. Hop O' My Thumb (Little Tich), bathed by Herbert Campbell, discards his baby bottle and asks for brandy and soda. The Ogre's Kitchen also provided opportunity for much merriment. The giant and giantess (played by H.M. Clifford and E.S. Gofton) 'make love with elephantine finesse that is extremely funny', said *The Era*, and the scene climaxed with Leno and Campbell strung up to roast. 'The antics and grimaces, their philosophical remarks on the horrors of their situation, are followed with shrieks of laughter.' The *I.S.D.N.* thought 'The proceedings in nursery and kitchen and bedroom are just of the kind, which youthful lovers of pantomime enjoy much better than dazzling processions and brilliant ballets', and picked out Little Tich:

> The cleverest of the acting is that of Little Tich, who, from his stature and miniature personality is exceptionally well-fitted to the *role* of Hop O' My Thumb and who makes one of the hits of the evening by his skilful burlesque of skirt-dancing. But the dashing dance and song of Miss Loftus and Miss Lloyd as well as the comic vocalism and 'business' of Messrs. Leno and Campbell also contribute largely to the general success, whilst as Dame Mary Mr Arthur Williams contrives to make quite the most of scant opportunities.

The scenery of William Perkins, Robert Caney, Kautsky and Jackson was declared by *The Stage* to be 'always good and appropriate and at some points superb'. There were some criticisms. The *I.S.D.N.* thought it was too long and the script lacked the grace and refinement that was looked for 'especially where the entertainment of our children is concerned.' It complained that the heroes and heroines of nursery rhyme had been turned into 'mere modern mashers and girls of the period' and thought 'the fault is traceable partly to the tone of Mr Wilton Jones's dialogue, which has a distinctly cockney twang in its humour as in its verse, and partly to the methods of the clever music-hall ladies entrusted with the impersonation of the chief *dramatis personae*.' *The Era* thought the script lacking in coherence, elegant verse and ingenious punning, attributing this failure directly to Wilton Jones. The *I.S.D.N.* (31 December 1892) said:

Someone should tell Sir Augustus Harris how very far his 'book of words' falls short of what the occasion requires. Life [at Drury Lane] would be tolerable if it were not for its humour. The humour of this Pantomime is of the roughest cockney texture. In our over-plus of literature there must surely be someone who can write a really brilliant pantomime book; but it is clearly not Sir Augustus Harris, nor his colleague, Mr Wilton Jones.

Wilton Jones had been writing burlesques, extravaganzas and pantomimes in the provinces (Leeds, Liverpool, Manchester, Newcastle) since 1874 and *Little Bo-Peep* was his first London venture. However, although the show ran for 138 performances, Harris did not retain his services and the remainder of his pantomime writing career took him to East End and South London theatres, the Standard, the Pavilion and the Surrey. Marie Lloyd added to the perceived vulgarity by improvising a comic sequence in which, preparing to retire for the night, she searched under the bed for the chamber pot.

Harry Nicholls was back as co-writer of the pantomime, *Robinson Crusoe* in 1893–4. *The Times* (27 December 1893) noted approvingly:

One advantage of this story is to be found in the fact that it is full of incident, so that the framers of the pantomime are not compelled, as has happened often of late years, to mingle half-a-dozen fairy tales or more in order to fill up the time. From beginning to end the pantomime of *Robinson Crusoe* deals with Defoe's tale of ever-living interest, overlaid with whimsicalities and drolleries, interlarded with music-hall songs and every manner of amusing absurdity, but still the original story capable of being recognized by schoolboys less intelligent than him of whom Macaulay dreamed.

The pantomime opens near a public house adjoining the docks at Hull where there are a crowd of dock labourers, apparently on strike, who on being told that the public will support them, proceed – in a play on words – to loot the public house. This probably refers back to the great 1889 London dock strike, a key event in the history of trade unionism but evidently disapproved of by Harris. Robinson Crusoe wants to marry Polly Perkins but is too poor and determines to go abroad to make his fortune. Villainous Will Atkins and his pirates seek to kidnap Polly and are foiled by Robinson. He sails but is wrecked and cast upon on a desert island. Atkins tries again to abduct Polly but abducts Mrs Crusoe by mistake. Polly organizes a relief expedition to find Robinson, his whereabouts having been reported in the evening papers. Robinson meets Man Friday on the island and discovers he learned English from a missionary before eating him. The Cannibal Queen falls in love with Friday. Friday's father is captured by the Cannibal King to serve as dinner. Robinson rescues him by use of a Gatling Gun. The relief expedition arrives and Robinson and Polly are reunited, and everyone sails for England.

The Era (30 December 1893), noting that '"colossal" is the only word which accurately described Sir Augustus Harris' pantomime at Drury-lane', added:

> Drury-lane pantomime is, emphatically, not a children's entertainment. It is a magnificent show, in which the ripe and critical senses of the adult are strained to the utmost to estimate such almost bewildering beauty and splendour ... if the sense did not ache with the ecstacy created by the beautiful scenery and dazzling spectacle of *Robinson Crusoe*, it was not the fault of Sir Augustus Harris, who certainly spared no expense likely to produce such a result.

The *I.S.D.N.* (30 December 1893) complained that so much effort had been spent getting the climactic procession right that the rest of the show had suffered inadequate preparation.

> We do not remember a pantomime at Drury Lane where the telling of the story has dragged so sadly, where the fun has appeared to be so unrehearsed, and where the words have been so haltingly spoken as was the case in *Robinson Crusoe* on the opening night. Much of this has no doubt already been remedied; but the fault of irrelevant tomfoolery and tedious, aimless 'business' will not be completely corrected until a good many of the performers have been sternly reminded that they should learn the lines set down for them and should say very little else.

The chief offenders were W. and S. Poluski playing the Captain and the Mate and making the characters 'terribly tiresome', and Messrs Leclerc and Ben Brown as the King and Queen of the Cannibals. The imperfections may have been due to the absence of Harris through illness during the latter stages of rehearsals and his non-appearance on the opening night for the same reason.

The Era dismissed the book:

> who cares, nowadays, about the 'book' of a Drury-lane pantomime? All that we know, all that we care to know, is that celebrated music-hall artistes have been engaged to fill the principal parts of the piece. Whether they are funny on the first night makes little difference later on. We know, from long experience, that, given the mime of genius the droll dialogue must follow as the night the day ... why should the music hall artist who is placed in the cast of a pantomime learn his or her part? After a week or so most of the author's lines will be found to have disappeared, and to have been replaced by 'gag' of the very best quality, and what is better than the gag of a really clever comedian.

The critic thought the great music hall stars were hampered by the libretto but given time to rewrite their lines, the pantomime would become 'one of the funniest as it is already the most gorgeous' pantomime in London.

The reviews as ever emphasized the setpieces and the spectacle. There was the shipwreck ('one of the very best stage shipwrecks we have ever seen,' said *The Era*), followed by a fish ballet at the bottom of the sea ('full of colour and exquisite taste', said *The Stage*). There was a ballet of savages on the island – 'a most picturesque ballet – weird and attractive, the wonderful blending of colours reflecting praise on all concerned in its performance', said *The Stage* (28 December 1893). The transformation scene featured the House of Industry; 'a dazzling dream of delight in which bees, honey and electric light, combined to ravish the enraptured beholder' (*The Era*). The pantomime proper concluded with a 'History of England in Twenty Minutes', a procession of the Kings and Queens of England: William the Conqueror landing at Hastings, William II borne away slain by Tyrrel's arrow, Henry I dying of his gluttony and Rosamond of the Queen's poison, Richard I leaving for the Crusades, King John forced to sign Magna Carta, Edward I displaying his baby son to the Welsh, Edward III pardoning the burghers of Calais at the intercession of Queen Philippa, the assassination of Wat Tyler, the follies and submission of Prince Hal, Richard III and the Princes in the Tower, Henry VIII meeting Ann Boleyn in front of Hampton Court Palace, Edward VI being relieved of the tedium of study by a step dance by the Blue Coat Boys, Charles II merrymaking. 'The remaining periods were merged in the magnificent stage picture with which the procession concluded. At the very back sat Queen Victoria on her throne.' *The Era* said: 'As an education in costume, the "History of England in Twenty Minutes" is very valuable; as a simple spectacle it is artistic, elaborate and astonishing.'

The Times recorded that 'Some of the tableaux ... were of a high order of merit' and singled out:

> the Conqueror, stumbling as he landed on the English coast, seized two handfuls of sand. The tragedy of Rosamond's bower was presented in a very striking fashion; so was the signature of the great Charter, and the dresses in the Tudor period, with its dramatic incidents such as Raleigh's coat were gorgeous in the extreme.

Also Charles II and his ladies was deemed 'one of the best of the historical scenes'. However, *The Times* thought it would have been wise to have omitted the preparations for the execution of Charles I as in poor taste.

The Era praised the music hall stars on parade: Herbert Campbell as Will Atkins, Dan Leno's Mrs Crusoe, Marie Lloyd's Polly Perkins ('Her songs are encored and her Polly is adored'), Ada Blanche as Crusoe ('the life and soul of the pantomime') and Little Tich as Man Friday ('surely the most original rendering of the part ever seen upon the pantomime stage'). The Jee family scored as Crusoe's various animals. But *The Times* complained that Tich had not blacked up, unlike the Cannibal King and Queen and Old Friday, Man Friday's father. *The Times* said of Campbell that as Atkins made up to resemble an old-style melodrama villain he was 'full of quips as ever and amusingly grotesque in appearance' and Leno as Mrs Crusoe 'from beginning to end the funniest person on the stage'. But the critic concluded that the show was 'not quite so good as some of its predecessors'. The *I.S.D.N.* thought 'The jokes of the book, and the pantomime business pure and simple, do not strike us as being so good as usual; but on the other hand, as we have said, the spectacular display of the show is calculated to beat even the record of its predecessors here.' The costumes (Percy Anderson), the scene-painting (Messrs Caney, Ryan, Harker, Glendinning and Perkins), the choreography (John D'Auban) and the music (J.M. Glover) garnered general praise.

One of the problems Harris faced was that for the first time he had a formidable rival in the West End, putting forward a very different kind of pantomime, *Cinderella*, devised, produced and scored by Oscar Barrett. The mixed reviews for *Robinson Crusoe* contrasted with the ecstatic welcome *Cinderella* received. For once Harris found himself eclipsed. *Robinson Crusoe* ran for only 116 performances. According to Jimmy Glover, Harris lost £18,000 on the pantomime – other sources put the loss at £30,000.[34] But there were also problems with the cast. Little Tich announced his intention of withdrawing from Drury Lane pantomime. He told a reporter that he had less opportunity to make a hit as a solo performer:

> now that a pantomime is principally spectacular. In the provinces they still stick to the old-fashioned lines and give the principal characters a chance, but it seems to me that nowadays in London our performances serve only as a peg to hang processions and ballets on.

But he also asked for £100 a week, which is what Marie Lloyd earned in *Robinson Crusoe*, and Harris flatly refused to pay.[35] So Little Tich retreated to Manchester and never again appeared in a London pantomime.[36] Marie Lloyd, whose ad-libbed antics made her a target for charges of vulgarity, also departed the Drury Lane pantomime team. Christmas 1894 saw her playing principal boy in *Pretty Bo-Peep, Little Boy Blue and the Merry Old Woman Who Lived in a Shoe* at the Shakespeare Theatre, Liverpool.

The battle for the soul of pantomime was not just fought out in the pages of the periodical press. It took practical form in the production rivalry between Augustus Harris and Oscar Barrett. According to the writer H.G. Hibbert, Barrett was 'the one man who gave Harris furiously to think', the only rival whose success he feared and envied.[37]

Now largely forgotten and featured neither in the *D.N.B.* nor *Who's Who*, Barrett (1847–1941) was one of the giants of pantomime production. A musician and the son of a musician, he began his career playing in the orchestra of the Grecian Theatre in the East End of London. From there he toured the provinces for several years, becoming the first musical director of the Tyne Theatre, Newcastle. In 1870 he returned to London and the Grecian as composer-conductor.

Barrett became deeply imbued with the ethos and style of the traditional pantomime associated with the names of George Conquest and E.L. Blanchard. From 1870 to 1879 he was musical director and composer in residence at the Grecian Theatre, renowned for its pantomimes starring and produced by George Conquest. The editor of *Entr'acte* wrote of Conquest in 1903: 'I am inclined to surmise that he was responsible for much of Mr Oscar Barrett's stage education.'[38] After Conquest gave up his management of the Grecian, Barrett left too and *The Era* (1 January 1881) noted of the 1880 pantomime production *King Frolic* 'the much to be regretted absence of Mr Barrett.' Barrett also composed and conducted the music for the Blanchard pantomimes at the Crystal Palace: *Puss in Boots* (1873), *Cinderella* (1874), *Jack in Wonderland* (1875) and *Sindbad the Sailor* (1876). *The Era* reported of *Cinderella* (27 December 1874): 'To the great intelligence and taste of Mr Oscar Barrett the charming selection and arrangement of the music is due.' Other composers took over after Blanchard stopped writing the Crystal Palace pantomimes.

Of Barrett's music for the Crystal Palace pantomime *Sindbad the Sailor*, *The Era* (24 December 1876) wrote:

> Nor should any record of Sydenham be complete without special mention of the music of Mr Oscar H. Barrett, an original and charming composer, who for many years has kept up the high-art tone of Crystal Palace music in an entertainment generally supposed to be so completely unartistic as Pantomime. At any rate, Mr Barrett studies to relieve the holiday amusement from the slightest suspicion of vulgarity.

Barrett went to work for Harris as composer-conductor at Drury Lane in 1881–2, working on *Robinson Crusoe* and every annual pantomime until *Aladdin* in 1885–6. Barrett immediately changed the nature of the scores for the shows, which had habitually involved arrangements of current music hall favourites. *The Era* (30 December 1882), reviewing the 1882–3 *Sindbad the Sailor*, noted: 'Mr Oscar Barrett believes not in music-hall music. So this one of the old sources of enjoyment for humbler patrons of pantomimes at "The Lane" is ruthlessly cut off.' Reviewing the 1883–4 *Cinderella* at Drury Lane, *The Era* (29 December 1883) noted that the once rowdy Drury Lane audience had become staid and respectable and attributed this in part to the effect of Barrett's music:

> Mr Oscar Barrett has so educated the gods up to a taste for superior music that they now prefer to listen to the strains of his splendid orchestra rather than to the sounds of their own hoarse voices. Thus there is no bawling of vulgar choruses, and although, at the outset of the action, there was a little noise, good temper prevailed, and there was nothing that could be called disorder between the opening scene and the transformation.

However, by the time of *Aladdin* (1885–6), *The Era* (2 January 1886) reported that Barrett had included some music hall songs in his score, 'not un-mindful of holiday requirements'. Had Harris, one wonders, prevailed on him in this matter? For it is not without significance that this was Barrett's last Drury Lane pantomime for Harris. Next year, 1886–7, Ferdinand Wallerstein had taken over as composer and conductor for *The Forty Thieves*.

At the same time as he was producing the pantomimes at Drury Lane, Harris also for several years produced the annual Christmas pantomime at the Crystal Palace. Barrett also composed and conducted the music for those shows. This was made possible by the fact that the Crystal Palace pantomimes were performed in the afternoon and Drury Lane in the evening. Harris' production of *Jack and the Beanstalk* (1884–5) produced the comment from *The Era* (27 December 1884) that Barrett's music was 'as good as pantomime music can well be'. For Harris' *Cinderella* (1884–5), *The Era* (26 December 1885) reported that the 'excellent music' had been composed by Barrett who 'conducted with his customary skill and earnestness'.

In 1886–7 Barrett took over the production of the annual Crystal Palace pantomime and from then until 1894–5 he invented, produced and composed the music for the shows: *Red Riding Hood* (1886–7), *Robinson Crusoe* (1887–8), *Cinderella* (1888–9), *Aladdin* (1889–90), *Whittington and His Cat* (1890–1), *The Forty Thieves* (1891–2), *Babes in the Wood and Bold Robin Hood* (1892–3), *Jack and the Beanstalk* (1893–4) and *Bluebeard* (1894–5). Bringing together some of the top pantomime talents – choreographer and dance-mistress Madame Katti Lanner, 'the good genius of Ballet' as *The Stage* (31 December 1891) called her, Carl Wilhelm, the master costumier, and a team of painters that included Frederick Fenton and Henry Emden – Barrett created a succession of productions that regularly attracted critical encomia for their taste, elegance and beauty. Conceived as matinee performances, they were aimed specifically at children and family audiences. What most appealed to the critics was their traditional nature and freedom from what was perceived as the vulgarity that had accompanied the music hall invasion and the creation of lavish and often overwhelming processions which were the hallmarks of Augustus Harris.

The *I.S.D.N.* (28 December 1888), reviewing *Cinderella*, highlighted the show's freedom from the taint of music hall:

> It is worthy of special remark that in the new version of *Cinderella* … a departure of an important kind has been made from the plans ordinarily adopted in pantomimes during recent years. Instead of a host of the latest music hall songs and topical and political allusions, we have in the Crystal Palace *Cinderella* a humourous and at the same time a delightfully fresh and fanciful story, giving the fullest *scope* for the talents of the excellent performers, and keeping closely throughout to the original plot. It is Mr Oscar Barrett's desire in producing his pantomime this year to have one which children could follow, understand and appreciate. Consequently there is an entire absence of slang, music hall

ditties and political 'gags'. The admirable taste of Mr Oscar Barrett has led him to select the choicest music from modern operas etc. And in scenic splendour few pantomimes of the season will bear comparison with that of the Crystal Palace.

The Stage (3 January 1890) and The *I.S.D.N.* (4 January 1890), reviewing *Aladdin*, pointed to a welcome absence of 'ostentatious pageantry' – a direct knock at Harris. Tastefulness was a recurrent refrain of the reviews. 'Good taste everywhere prevails', said *The Era* (29 December 1894) of *Bluebeard*.

When he took his celebrated Lyceum production of *Cinderella* to New York, Barrett expounded his production philosophy in an interview with *The New York Times* (23 April 1894):

> For the last fifty years, the pantomime, as we continue to call it, has been a mere vehicle for spectacular effects and variety business. Even now, in the usual pantomime, no effort is made to go beyond this. The story from which the spectacle takes its name is not followed in any particular ... Now it has always been my desire to break away from this, which I call a defect in the English pantomime. I have always had the feeling, and kept it constantly before my mind, that, while giving myself every opportunity for spectacular display, I must make all the spectacle fall in naturally with the story. Even the ballets, instead of being side issues, belong to the dramatic action of the piece. We have in England ... what are called 'topical songs'. These I eschew entirely. My idea is that all the songs of the comedian must be in harmony with the character he presents and have a direct bearing on the story. I consider that we can do with ... our pantomime, from an art point of view, as much as, or even more than, can be done with a Shakespearean play, and for this reason. It calls into requisition the composer and the scenic artists, and gives the latter more liberty than he has in an ordinary play, where he is confined to certain limits in his work. The work of the costumer, and, in fact, every element of the spectacular, can be utilized to a far greater extent in our Christmas pantomimes than in any other form of entertainment.

Barrett revealed that he would rather have called his shows 'fairy extravaganzas' but if they were advertised as such, no-one would come. So he retained the name of pantomime, justifying it by the inclusion at the end of a harlequinade. The harlequinade, interestingly, was cut for the New York production, as America had no tradition of pantomime. He also revealed that he had produced forty-seven pantomimes over the previous fifteen years, two or three each year, and in one year, four.

His first Crystal Palace show, *Red Riding Hood*, had been scripted by Charles Daly. The *I.S.D.N.* (1 January 1887) reported: 'Nothing could be better than the music of Mr Barrett and the scenery of Mr Fenton.' The ballets were 'very attractive' and a distinctive feature was a children's choir singing nursery songs. But the critic found the script 'moderate indeed' and overly complicated. *The Stage* (31 December 1886) thought 'the whole *mise-en-scène* so beautiful that *Red Riding Hood* at the Crystal Palace may rank as one of the best produced this season' and praised Barrett's music for its range, something unique in pantomime music. For the next show and all the rest of the Crystal Palace pantomimes, Charles Daly was replaced by Horace Lennard as writer.

Barrett's second show, *Robinson Crusoe*, was a revival of H.J. Byron's 1860 pantomime, suitably updated by Horace Lennard. The *I.S.D.N.* (31 December 1887) praised the 'winsome music, dainty ballets and many excellent stage pictures'. *The Stage* (30 December 1887) praised the 'total absence' of coarse humour and the music hall element, and thought the scenery and dresses 'exquisitely beautiful'. The critics in general admired the undersea ballet which included a shrimps' polka danced by juveniles and a striking procession of richly garbed Indian troops mounted on giraffes and tortoises, ostriches and crocodiles.

The *I.S.D.N.* (4 January 1890) recognized Barrett's achievement of his aim when it called *Aladdin and His Wonderful Lamp* 'one of the greatest Sydenham successes – a graceful fairy extravaganza more than a pantomime, boasting a capital book and mounted by Mr Barrett without regard to cost.' The ballet of the Willow Pattern Plate was one of the show's highlights.

Similarly when *Whittington and His Cat* appeared as the next Crystal Palace pantomime, *The Era* (27 December 1890) took the opportunity to praise Barrett:

The untiring energy, good judgement, ripe experience and musicianly skill of Mr Oscar Barrett, backed up by a very liberal, and we may say lavish, expenditure on the part of the directorate, have provided the Crystal Palace this year with another pantomime that for beauty and general excellence will favourably compare with all that have gone before, and that certainly will be hard to beat. Mr Barrett is, before all things else, a musician, and while taking care to be never dull, is at the same time determined to be never vulgar. The most cultured ear may listen to the airs and concerted pieces with which he has embellished *Dick Whittington* with the certainty of getting keen enjoyment, and of never being offended, and it may safely be said that *Whittington and his Cat* combines the attractiveness of a comic opera with all the fun looked for by the juveniles in a pantomime production.

When *The Forty Thieves* appeared, *The Stage* (31 December 18091) reported:

the pantomime at the Palace is invariably one of the most artistic out of London or in it. This year it is that once again, and a funny pantomime too; a combination always devoutly to be wished, yet rarely to be seen. The achievement of it at Sydenham is, of course, chiefly due to Mr Oscar Barrett, who is quite a master of modern pantomime ...

here there is much that is beautiful, something that is magnificent; nothing that is garish and tawdry.

On *Babes in the Wood*, *The Era* (31 December 1892) praised the 'refinement, beauty and ... good honest fun without a trace of vulgarity.' On *Jack and the Beanstalk*, *The Era* (30 December 1893) reported: 'The Crystal Palace is always expected to be something superior in artistic and terpsichorean qualities, and this year Mr Oscar Barrett has excelled himself in these directions.' Of *Bluebeard*, *The Stage* (27 December 1894) said, 'the grace and beauty of *Bluebeard* have surely never been excelled in the long and famous history of pantomime at the Crystal Palace' and said that Barrett and Lennard had turned the annual Christmas show 'into a really homogeneous art work'. The *I.S.D.N.* (29 December 1894) had wondered if Barrett's venture into the West End might take the edge off his commitment to the Crystal Palace but 'Nothing of the kind, however, is to be observed ... the pantomime of 1894–5 may be safely pronounced equal if not superior to any of its predecessors.' But it was to be the last of Barrett's Palace pantomimes as his energies were now diverted to the West End. The circus replaced the pantomime as the Christmas attraction at the Crystal Palace.

Barrett's first West End pantomime was *Dick Whittington and His Cat* at the Olympic in 1892–3. Barrett brought to the Olympic his Crystal Palace team of scriptwriter Horace Lennard, set painter Henry Emden, choreographer Katti Lanner and costume designer Carl Wilhelm. Barrett himself devised, composed and produced the show. *The Times* (27 December 1892) welcomed it:

> Those who like pantomime of the old type, those who are fond of ballet, those to whom a gorgeous theatrical spectacle possesses attraction, and that class ... who enjoy a hearty laugh will all be pleased with the pantomime at the New Olympic ... No expense or labour has been spared in the production of the piece, either in respect of scenery or dresses, and Mr Horace Lennard's libretto is smart and often amusing. There is too less of the mere horseplay which used to be so wearisome a feature of old-fashioned pantomime.

The Era (31 December 1892) called it 'an exquisitely artistic entertainment' and praised the absence of puns from the script. *The Stage* (29 December 1892) reported that it had no variety 'turns' in it, but was a winning combination of 'a clearly told story of fun and fancy', 'popular and graceful music', rustic scenes of 'singular delicacy', 'rollicking humour' and 'gorgeous pageant'. It had notable performances from Victor Stevens (as the 'hideous' cook Eliza, who believed every man she met was in love with her), 'who did as much or more than anyone else to make the pantomime a conspicuous success,' said *The Times*, and Charles Lauri, whose 'skill and agility' as the Cat impressed *The Times*. The only criticism by *The Stage* and *The Era* was the topical allusions to Mr Gladstone and the government and the Salvation Army, which they thought would go down better with provincial than with London audiences. But Barrett and Lennard were called to take a bow and Madame Lanner (whose ballets were 'some of the best she has ever arranged' thought *The Era*) was called twice. The ballets included a maypole dance, done with 'much refinement and taste', a delicate dance of flowers on Highgate Hill and the Blue Ballet at the Palace of the Emperor of Morocco which was long remembered.[39]

But the pantomime almost never happened. The journalist Chance Newton recalled that at the dress rehearsal of *Dick Whittington* on Christmas Eve, the Olympic stage hands went on strike:

> Barrett, a man always much honoured and always trusted by all who knew him, tried in every way he could to pacify the strikers, but all in vain. I remember that there were hints abroad of this mutiny having been engineered by a rival manager who resented Barrett's intrusion from the musical directorial chair into theatrical management, and especially into the pantomime side thereof.

Could it have been Harris, one wonders? However, disaster was averted when Henry Irving, actor-manager at the Lyceum, heard what was going on and loaned Barrett his master carpenter and stage staff, who worked all night to set up the show for the Boxing Day opening. Newton added: 'A while ago my old friend Oscar wrote me an enthusiastic letter confirming all these details.'[40] It ran for 120 performances.

It was at Irving's Lyceum the next year that Barrett was to achieve his greatest pantomime success – *Cinderella*. Irving and Ellen Terry were away touring in America. So the Lyceum staged its first pantomime for twenty-five years. The *I.L.N.* (30 December 1893) said:

> Old time-honoured Drury will have a serious rival this year in the delightfully artistic and uniformly gorgeous setting given to the fairy story of 'Cinderella' by Mr Oscar Barrett. It is open to doubt if the London stage has ever seen any Christmas play of the kind conceived and executed in such faultless taste. It is hardly fair to call this dainty and charming 'Cinderella' a pantomime, for the modern pantomime is associated in the public mind with rough-and-tumble fun, wild dances, and music-hall songs. Nothing of the kind is found at the Lyceum ... Mr Oscar Barrett has out of the legend of 'Cinderella' extracted a fairy opera beautiful to behold and delightful to listen to ... No one should miss 'Cinderella' at the Lyceum.

In almost every respect this was an old-fashioned or traditional pantomime but one which aspired to the highest standards of taste and quality. Where Harris filled his cast with music hall performers, Barrett hired actors and singers for some of the leading roles. Where Drury Lane scores were largely composed of music hall songs, Barrett, who composed and arranged the score himself, went to Mendelssohn,

Weber and Edward German for appropriate melodies. He returned directly to Perrault for the substance of the story. *The Era* (30 December 1893) was enchanted. Viewing it, said *The Era*, audiences felt 'a new era of pantomime was about to begin': 'clever acting that concedes nothing to the vulgar phase of public taste', 'a coherent story, told with fancy and humour', and scene-painting and costume design of the highest standard. This was ensured by engaging top designer Carl Wilhelm, Irving's chief scene-painter Hawes Craven and Madame Katti Lanner as choreographer. Barrett also introduced a fifteen-minute intermission half-way through, a unique development. *The Era* said:

> Mr Horace Lennard, the author of the Lyceum 'book', has the imagination of a poet and he has the technique of the stage at his finger ends. He has told the story of Cinderella in neat rhymes, with here and there a humorous incongruity and here and there a dainty lyric.

The scene-painting of Henry Emden, Pritchard Barrett and Hawes Craven was praised, in particular the King's Wood as painted by Craven:

> What a scene it is – Mr Hawes Craven at his best. The King's Wood is the very paradise of verdure. The sun has kissed it with so much ardour that it has become red and brown and all the lovely tints of autumn. Here presently there is danced a ballet of autumn leaves, birch and beech and oak and elm mingling and intermingling. We are in the heart of splendid Kent.

It rhapsodized:

> Really one might take every single constituent of Mr Oscar Barrett's pantomime and write an essay on it – all the music ranging from grave to gay, from lively to severe; the dresses so quaint, so picturesque; the scenery a perfect picture-gallery of landscape and architectural design, the dances so novel and so graceful.

Critics agreed that Barrett had totally upheld the reputation for taste and refinement that the Lyceum enjoyed under the management of Sir Henry Irving. Interestingly the ugly sisters were played by Victor Stevens and Fred Emney as caricatured 'New Women'; Thisbe had been to Girton and could 'jabber Latin and Greek' and was acquainted with 'the drama of disease' (Ibsen), while Clorinda declared: 'In my manners I am mannish; I can smoke a cigarette; I can wear a stand-up colour; and I sometimes make a bet.' William Archer, writing in *The World* on 3 January 1894, wrote that Barrett:

> has certainly produced by far the prettiest and most entertaining pantomime we have seen for many a year. If it has anything like the success it deserves, he will be encouraged to follow it up, others will tread in his footsteps, and we shall indeed have a new epoch in

pantomime – an epoch of beauty, refinement, and, if not precisely wit, at least of reason and coherence.

He saw it as carrying the art of Christmas spectacle back to the days of Vestris, Planché and the Lyceum of his youth.[41]

The actress Ellaline Terriss in her first pantomime scored a personal triumph – 'an absolutely ideal Cinderella' the *I.L.N.* called her – and she recalled the experience in her autobiography, where she paid tribute to Barrett:

> It was a magnificent experience for me to work under the production of Oscar Barrett. He knew all there was to know about pantomime. He had produced them in the great provincial cities – and at the Crystal Palace ... But now he was coming into the West End. His method was to lay great stress on the story and he knew how to tell those tales in a manner which appealed to children and adults alike. He never forgot that pantomimes were really supposed to be for children and he also never forgot that unless you pleased the grown-ups as well, you would not have a financial success. He knew that the children expected – or rather demanded – that he should tell them the well-loved stories in the form that they knew them, otherwise they lost interest, their attention wandered, they would pester their parents, guardians and relatives with questions, and nobody would be pleased. He knew that the story was of prime importance and that the telling of it demanded a formula pleasing to all. He knew the formula all right ... Oscar Barrett made a point of never including a scene which had nothing to do with the plot. He did not allow his comedians to dominate the story or the stage – or be given a lot of scenes wherein they could exploit their own particular brand of entertainment or personality. They had to be funny, of course, but they had to be in the picture. I am certain that is a good principle and wish more pantomime producers of today would adopt it. They would find it helped. He determined to make *Cinderella* the loveliest production London had ever seen and to give it a glittering cast as well. He engaged Victor Stevens, Fred Emney ... Clara Jecks, a grand comedienne, Alice Brookes, and Kate Chard as his Principal boy – Prince Felix, not Prince Charming for once ... He had a Cat, however, and what a cat! No less a person than Charles Lauri, a wonderful animal impersonator who used to run round the front of the dress circle, to the wonder of the children, and who had no rival ... He had two prima ballerinas, Louie Loveday and Mlle Zanfretta, one of the finest dancers of her day and afterwards famous in the Empire Ballets.

Writing many years later, she could still recall the impact of the show:

> many of the scenes in that pantomime had a magical, dreamlike beauty. The audience sat enraptured whilst drifts of girls dressed as autumn leaves spun gracefully across that big stage, as if driven by the wind, in an autumnal ballet. They applauded vigorously the Grand Bal Champêtre in the grounds of the Royal Palace, a scene of glitter, splendour

and brilliance. The Transformation Scene, in which a wild storm broke over the stage, blotting out the summer, held them spellbound. The glowing sunlit scene became wild tumult and confusion – it seemed as if real magic was at work. And at the end, the enthusiasm was just amazing. Family parties stood on their seats, clapping, and cheering. We took call after call. They just would not stop and they went on applauding long after the lights had gone up and the band departed. It took a very long time before the auditorium could be cleared. Next morning there was what is now called a 'rave' Press.[42]

Running for 126 performances and exceeding the Drury Lane pantomime's run, the production was so successful that Barrett took it to New York where it played triumphantly for ten weeks.

As *The Sketch* (2 January 1895) openly suggested, Harris had learned the lesson of Barrett's success at the Lyceum. For his 1894–5 pantomime *Dick Whittington, The Times* (27 December 1894) observed: 'By those who esteem the "music-hall element" of pantomime to have been overdone in past years, the present pantomime will be regarded as a step in the right direction. There is certainly very little music-hall entertainment of the distinctive type in it.' Harris had also brought in Cecil Raleigh and Henry Hamilton, the authors of the autumn melodrama, to collaborate with him on the script. *The Times* observed:

> The whole story is knit together with an eye to dramatic effect which one would expect from the skilful authors of *The Derby Winner*, but which is less common in pantomime librettos than it ought to be; and the copious incidental business … is in most cases the appropriate outcome of the scene – another welcome detail.

One novelty was shifting the scene of the cat destroying the rats from Morocco, where it was conventionally set, to China, in part to capitalize on interest aroused by the Chinese–Japanese War, which also inspired an attack on Dick's ship by Japanese warriors. The *I.L.N.* (5 January 1895) suggested that Harris had intended a production of *Aladdin* and designed his Chinese scenes for it, but getting wind of a rival production of *Aladdin* switched subjects but retained its Chinese setting. There was indeed a rival production of *Aladdin*, at the Standard and scripted by Wilton Jones, so the *I.L.N.* could well be right. The result of the changes led *The Era* (29 December 1894) to declare the show, 'decidedly the best that Sir Augustus Harris has produced – the most artistic, the most effective, and the most refined.' The familiar elements of the story were all there. Dick Whittington works at Alderman Fitzwarren's emporium and is in love with Alice. Idle Jack and Eliza the Cook accuse him of robbing the till. He departs in disgrace, but asleep at Highgate Hill, is urged by the bells to turn back and seek his fortune. He sails with his Cat in search of fortune, arrives in China, rids the country of rats, and returns in time to save Alice from marrying to save her father from ruin. He and Alice are united, Idle

Jack is forced to marry the Cook and it all ends with the spectacle of the Lord Mayor's show. *The Stage* (3 January 1895) called *Dick Whittington*:

the best ever seen within the halls of Old Drury ... Its description in the programme is carried out to the letter, it is 'poetic, fantastic and funny' and it may be added gorgeous beyond the wildest dreams of ordinary managers, crowded with beautiful dresses and beautiful faces, and containing an amount of talent rarely, if ever brought together in one entertainment. And with all this the stage management is wonderfully well done.

The show was interspersed with the customary ballets and spectacles. While Dick was asleep at Highgate Hill, there was a 'delicately beautiful ballet of wild flowers'. *The Era* (29 December 1894) recorded:

Poppies, corn-flowers, lilies of the valley and bluebells are borne by fairies suitably attired. The art of the designer has been shown by the artistic manner in which the natural hues of the blossoms have been toned down and idealised with due regard for general effect. The dresses of the fairies are exquisite, with chrome and lemon yellows being introduced with delicious results. The ballet is one of the best things in the pantomime, and its quiet and unobtrusive beauty deserves our most cordial welcome.

The culminating point of the pantomime was the Feast of Lanterns in a setting with an ornamental bridge, two large green porcelain dragons, a semi-circle of nodding dummy mandarins and festoons of shaded electric lamps. Of the Lord Mayor's show finale *The Era* said, 'the blare of bands, the sheen of silver and gold, the glitter and glow of various costumes, and the ponderous panoply of horses in armour, and of those which drag in certain stately triumphal cars, make this scene almost overpowering in its radiance and richness.' Ada Blanche as Dick was 'excellent throughout – never over-acting, never flagging' and Dan Leno, 'irresistible' as Idle Jack. Herbert Campbell played Eliza the Cook 'with a sedateness and decorum which are admirable.' There were the usual compliments to Carlo Coppi for the ballets, John D'Auban for the special dances, Caney, Perkins, Ryan, Harker and Bruce Smith for scene-painting, J.M. Glover for music, Comelli, Edel and Bresche for costumes. *The Times* recorded that 'the pantomime as a whole was received with the vociferous applause which is unquestionably its due' and Harris was called forward three times to take a bow. The pantomime ran for 123 performances.

But once again Drury Lane had formidable competition from Oscar Barrett at the Lyceum with his pantomime *Santa Claus*. *The Times* (27 December 1894) said:

Exquisite is the epithet, by no means otiose, which ought to express the unanimous verdict of those who had the good fortune to be present at the first performance of the Christmas pantomime at the Lyceum last evening. It needs hardly to be said that Mr Oscar Barrett and Mr Horace Lennard are answerable respectively beforehand for, and to be credited afterwards with, music and libretto; and thus much having been written, it is all but superfluous to add that the music is delightful of its kind and full of sweetly melodious passages, that the words are appropriate and sometimes witty, and that the sequence of the plot is quite as regular and orderly as anything that any pantomime-goer, young or old, has any right to expect. Beyond that, these musical pantomimes of Mr Oscar Barrett are noteworthy as a rule for rigorous exclusion of the features which are familiar at the music hall, for avoidance of pomp and display for the purpose of display and pomp only, and for a tone of subdued and restrained refinement. The recent traditions of the theatre, in short, dominate the house, and even a Boxing-night audience, albeit enthusiastic, never breaks out into roistering merriment.

The titular figure of Santa Claus was only there really to introduce and conclude the selection of the traditional story, which merged *Babes in the Wood* and the story of Robin Hood and Maid Marian. Victor Stevens contributed another of his caricatures of the 'New Woman' in his comic governess, Miss Evadne Newfangle, which became one of the most popular characters in the pantomime.

Apart from the consistent good taste and charm commented on by all the critics, there was a patriotic episode. Santa Claus appeared to the sleeping children and gave them a vision of the Temple of Knowledge with a pageant of the letters of the alphabet, 'very novel and ingenious': A stood for Admiral with attendant sailors, 'symbolical of England's supremacy of the sea', E represented electricity, and V stood for the Queen. *The Era* reported:

and then a strange, impressive thing occurred. The vast audience rose to its feet, and the Lyceum Theatre rang again with the strains of what Mr Gilbert called 'the infernal National Anthem'. But there are times when the said National Anthem acquires a wondrous dignity and pathos; when it thrills the heart of every Englishman. Mr Barrett may be congratulated on a most ingenious effect.

Another innovation was the transformation scene, divided into four separate episodes in which Santa Claus and the Babes made their way through Dreamland, Poppyland, Snowland and Loveland, 'a lovely series of floral designs'.

The Stage (3 January 1895) declared *Santa Claus* 'a worthy successor to the gorgeous *Cinderella* of last season, and children of all growths may once more thank this amiable and popular gentleman for an entertainment full of charm and free from any trace of vulgarity'. It ran for only fifty-eight performances, presumably because Irving required the Lyceum for his own productions.

Significantly Harris chose *Cinderella* for the 1895–6 pantomime, the same subject with which Barrett had triumphed two years earlier. *The Times* (27 December 1895) approvingly began its review by saying 'the mot d'ordre at Drury Lane this year is refinement' and suggested that Harris had gone back to the fairy extravaganza of the

Planché period. It noted that 'the variety element' which had threatened to overwhelm all the other elements had been 'almost entirely suppressed'. Herbert Campbell as the Baron had only one topical song and Dan Leno as the Baroness a couple.

> For the rest we are in fairyland or on the borders thereof, and it will be a matter of surprise to many how ornate, bright and dramatic the familiar tale can become which set out with all the scenic resources of Drury Lane, and yet maintained within the legitimate bounds of extravaganza.

Clear evidence of the change was the casting of two female performers, Sophie Larkin and Emily Miller as the ugly sisters, roles that would previously have been played by Campbell and Leno. *The Era* (28 December 1895) agreed with *The Times*, calling *Cinderella*:

> undoubtedly the most beautiful and refined pantomime that Sir Augustus Harris has ever given us. The whole production is permeated by the artistic spirit, and, while as much or more money appears to have been lavished on the mounting and dressing of the 'annual' as on any of its popular predecessors, the generous and judicious outlay has been directed by an earnest desire to charm and delight rather than to dazzle and astound.

Harris also for the first time dispensed with his trademark processions. But he retained spectacle of a particularly charming kind. The pantomime opened in Toyland with a giant version of a toy train arriving to discharge its passengers, a set of toys, heading for Noah's Ark. There were a series of marches and dances among the toys until the Spirit of Pantomime arrived to select the subject of the Christmas show. Later there was a spectacular scene of 'light and beauty' in Fairyland where Cinderella received her dress and carriage (here an 'electronically lighted automotor' with the obligatory Shetland ponies trotting behind) and footmen for the ball from a gaggle of fairies. The big set pieces were the ball and the marriage of Cinderella and the Prince. *The Times* noted approvingly of the ball: 'A wondrous composition of colour, especially when the dazzling cohorts of the ballet engage in the giddy dance', with the wedding as 'the crowning effort of Drury Lane *mise-en-scène*'. It employed delicate tints rather than primary colours, floating fairies, a heart and anchor as electric emblems and '1896' in diamond-like letters in the centre of the stage as the Prince led forth Cinderella. *The Era* said: 'This scene certainly beats anything that has ever been seen at Old Drury.'

The Era found Dan Leno 'simply irresistible' as the Baroness:

> His performance is not a caricature but a genuine, if highly eccentric, impersonation. He works up the role with many little delicate and effective touches of gesture and facial play, and his dances are things to be remembered. Few that have seen it are likely to

forget the spectacle of the Baroness' entry into the Ballroom, mincing and bowing superbly to the assembled guests.

Campbell, said *The Era*, 'looks the sturdy, solid bourgeois Baron to the life, and the passive resistance he offers to the attacks of his waspish little wife are most diverting.' Isa Bowman, thought *The Times*, made a 'singularly sweet, gentle and engaging Cinderella', evidently seeking to duplicate Ellaline Terriss' success in Barrett's production. Ada Blanche was a 'dashing Prince, acting with ease and spirit, and doing her very best with the musical numbers allotted to her.'

The script was by Harris, Raleigh and Arthur Sturgess and when Harris was called forward to take a bow, he brought his co-authors with him. *The Stage* (2 January 1896) said:

Refinement, grace and elegance are the prevailing features of Sir Augustus Harris' seventeenth pantomime ... this statement need not imply that it is destitute of fun, far from it. There is abundance of humour, but it is of a more refined nature than that to which holiday playgoers have for a long time been accustomed; this is a step in the right direction worthy of all commendation ... Sir Augustus Harris has adorned [the story] with great elegance of costume, superb scenery, beautiful music and elaborate properties.

There was praise for Comelli and Alias for the costumes, Carey, Kautsky, Schweizer, Harker, Ryan and Bruce Smith for the scene-painting, Jimmy Glover for the music, Carlo Coppi for the ballets and John D'Auban for the specialist dance. It ran for 179 performances.

Harris' rival, Oscar Barrett, produced *Robinson Crusoe* at the Lyceum, though only in the afternoons and achieving sixty-nine performances. The *I.L.N.* (4 January 1896) expressed reservations:

In choosing 'Robinson Crusoe' for the subject of his pantomime, Mr Oscar Barrett has not given himself such scope for poetic treatment as upon former occasions. Consequently there may perhaps be some slight sense of disappointment to many. However, the old tale has been cleverly retold by Mr Horace Lennard, and the result is an entertainment more than commonly dramatic and enlivened by many scenes of happy humour. The beautiful has not been neglected – far from such being the case, the barbaric ballet on the savage island is extraordinary in the richness of its harmonious tones. The costumes may not represent Herr Wilhelm in his most original mood, but they well show his quite matchless gift for combining colours. A great feature of the pantomime is Mr Charles Lauri, who, as Friday, is exceedingly comic in gestures and grimaces, and remarkably expressive.

Other critics were more enthusiastic. *The Times* (27 December 1895) thought it 'wholly successful'. It also praised Charles Lauri for his Man Friday which:

compels universal admiration by a performance which is simply incapable of improvement. The extraordinary activity which he shows in struggling with his cannibal captors, the wild savagery of his yells, the representation of abject and shivering terror which he gives when Crusoe (very nervously) fires his gun and disperses the savages, his expression of his thoughts by dumb-show, and his wonderful barbarian language go together to make a performance which is no common order of excellence.

He also disguised himself as a monkey, allowing him to display 'his marvellous powers of rendering animal character and mimicking the ways of animals.' *The Era* (28 December 1895) thought Fred Storey made 'a most remarkable impression' as King Hullaballoo of the cannibals. 'His majesty is not a Christy Minstrel monarch, but a very weird and dreadful savage ... he plays King Hullaballoo with as much care and dramatic intensity as though he were playing King Lear – which, of course, has been the method of the greatest burlesque actors.' Victor Stevens as Mrs Crusoe kept up the running theme of satirizing the Trilby craze, to the amusement of all, but his humour was 'always free from suggestiveness or vulgarity', thought *The Stage* (2 January 1896). *The Era* concluded the pantomime was 'picturesque, interesting, amusing and wholesome'. It found Horace Lennard's book 'compact, intelligent and really versified' leaving nothing to be desired. The *I.S.D.N.* (4 January 1896) said 'Mr Barrett's present venture is perhaps somewhat more conventional than were its predecessors, and it has in particular little of the dainty charm which characterised his *Cinderella* here a couple of years ago', but concluded that it was 'as attractive an entertainment of its kind as any one need wish.' *The Stage* (2 January 1896) thought it 'a complete success', adding:

Mr Barrett is a good friend to the children and has done much to make pantomime what it should be for them, a source of wonder, amazing delight and pure fun. With him will lie the credit of banishing the crude banalities that have so often kept people from permitting their little ones to visit what should be a child's rational pleasure. From dainty grace and fairy sentiment he gives the little ones a familiar child's story, clearly told and with plenty of fun ... Here there are no irrelevant introductions, no futile wanderings, the story is unfolded as it should be dramatically, and fortunately it is well rendered in the same vein.

Barrett's selection, arrangement and composition of music resulted in something that was 'more of the character of high-class comic opera than of the customary pantomime arrangements'.

The reviews suggest that Harris had succeeded in out-Barretting Barrett. But it was his last triumph. He died on 22 June 1896 at the early age of forty-four, leaving

Drury Lane leaderless. For a year his widow and her brother carried on, assisted by Arthur Collins. But for the pantomime they called in none other than Oscar Barrett, who put on *Aladdin*. To produce it, Barrett effectively merged his Lyceum operation with the Drury Lane setup. Barrett directed and composed and arranged the score; Arthur Sturgess and Horace Lennard wrote the script and Carl Wilhelm designed the costumes; Katti Lanner choreographed the ballets, John D'Auban and son arranged the incidental dances; and scenery was painted by Henry Emden, Joseph Harker, Pritchard Barrett, William Telbin and Robert Caney, while the Drury Lane regulars starred. But it failed to be the triumph that might have been expected. All the critics agreed that it was far too long and too slow. The *I.L.N.* (2 January 1897) reported that it had all:

> the raw material of a big success ... a succession of scenic effects, impressive or charming, as the case may be; a blaze of beautiful dresses and graceful figures; a popular story, somewhat freshly treated; a cast of exceeding strength and variety, and, withal, a musical accompaniment of exceptional skill and interest.

But fatally 'the performance dragged and flagged'. It was 10.30 p.m. before the half-time intermission was reached, at which point Aladdin had only just got hold of the lamp. *The Times* (28 December 1896) noted:

> Only the traditional good humour of a Boxing-night house saved the pantomime from open failure. Those dreary three hours of preamble, at the close of which many people left the theatre, thinking that the end had arrived and wondering, no doubt, what had become of the details of the famous legend.

The *I.S.D.N.* (2 January 1897), complaining that it was over-long, under-rehearsed and failed to achieve a balance between 'the dainty refinement which was the keynote of Mr Barrett's achievements at the Lyceum, and the massive magnificence associated with spectacle at Drury Lane', compared it to 'a Christmas pudding manufactured of excellent and correct ingredients but insufficiently stirred, and boiled for too short a time.' On the positive side, the critic praised Barrett's score ('the music of *Aladdin*, in its varied borrowings from the operatic and variety stage is distinctly the happiest that we have ever heard chosen for this form of entertainment'). The classical composers utilized included Grieg, Gounod and Wagner. The critic praised the leading performers: Dan Leno as Widow Twankay ('extremely droll'), Herbert Campbell as Abanazar, Ada Blanche as Aladdin ('the brightest and most bustling of Burlesque princes') and the 'incomparable conjuring of Mr [Paul] Cinquevalli' as the Slave of the Lamp. *The Times* was much more critical:

the 'note of refinement', which has characterised Mr Oscar Barrett's previous productions at the Lyceum and elsewhere may be carried too far. It may be carried not only to the verge of dullness, but beyond, as when Aladdin and his Princess are transformed into a sentimental couple, who sing to each other in the vein of *The Bohemian Girl*. The essence of a pantomime is drollery. Much of *Aladdin*, however, consists of libretto after the manner of the poet Bunn, without the support of appropriate music, and literally it may be said that the first and last joke of Part No.1 was Mr Dan Leno's appearance in petticoats as the Widow Twankay.

The Times complained about the absence of a topical song and topical references. Some of the novel elements (Abanazar being an Egyptian mummy resuscitated in the interior of the Great Pyramid, Widow Twankay running a laundry manned by society ladies and the finale in the Hotel Cecil on the embankment whither the characters have been magically transported) all earned positive comment. So did the ballets which marked Aladdin's victory over the dragon guarding the lamp and his wedding in the palace of ivory and pearl. Sets and costumes were praised. All the critics expressed their confidence that it had all the elements necessary for success and that after drastic pruning and compression would succeed. It ran for 138 performances but the initial critical impression had been damning.

In 1897 Barrett's original Drury Lane production of *Aladdin*, utilizing his staging, book and music, was put on at the Theatre Royal, Manchester. Reviewing the original London production, *The Manchester Guardian* (28 December 1896) called Barrett the only rival to the late Sir Augustus Harris as a pantomime producer and described the show as 'a pantomime of undiminished splendour and considerable grace and charm to boot'. Of the Manchester staging, produced by Napier Barry, *The Guardian* (28 December 1897) said: 'For colour and glitter and graceful fancy, one remembers nothing finer in a Manchester pantomime.' The other Manchester papers agreed.

But management of Drury Lane passed to Arthur Collins and he immediately returned to the successful Harris formula. The creative partnership with Barrett was dissolved and the Barrett personnel eliminated. *The Babes in the Wood* was the 1897–8 pantomime. Collins collaborated with Arthur Sturgess on the script, music was composed and arranged by Jimmy Glover, ballets by Carlo Coppi and John D'Auban, costumes designed by Comelli, scenery provided by Henry Emden, Kautsky, Perkins, Caney, Ryan, McCleery, Julian Hicks and Bruce Smith. Dan Leno, Herbert Campbell and Ada Blanche starred. The pantomime's reception was rapturous.

The Era (1 January 1898) said:

There can have been few men more contented than Arthur Collins as midnight struck on Monday. When in the early autumn friends congratulated him on his succession to the vacant throne at Drury-lane, he knew that he had but begun his arduous task. 'Tis much to gain so proud a position; 'tis more to fortify and to maintain it against every onslaught of criticism and incision of jealousy. The young manager would be tried 'very high', as the sporting men say, first with melodrama, then with pantomime. Now he has emerged triumphant from the ordeal. *The White Heather* was a great success; the pantomime . . . is a great success – so is the capacity of the new director made manifest.

The *I.S.D.N.* (1 January 1898) put it more succinctly: '*Le Roi est mort; vive le Roi*', adding:

We can no longer cheer poor Sir Augustus Harris for a triumph of the season scored at Drury Lane. Hurrah! then, for Mr Arthur Collins in his successful effort to follow in the footsteps of his late master in the art of spectacular pantomime. *The Babes in the Wood* is, if the honest truth be told, wholly indistinguishable as regards any of its prominent characteristics from any one of its typical predecessors.

The Times (28 December 1897), however, disagreed:

The typical pantomime of the Augustus Harris *regime* is no more. Gone those glittering processions and the regal pomp that combined the attractions of a military review and a jubilee. In their place a new sort of pantomime has arisen which, on the whole, has much more affinity with musical comedy of the Arthur Roberts stamp than with the conventional fare furnished at Drury Lane on Boxing Night; and doubtless the novelty will be welcomed by the general public as warmly as it was by last night's holiday crowd.

But the critic had forgotten that Harris had himself moved away from that earlier model in his last pantomime, although this production did take that development further.

The Stage (30 December 1897) declared of *The Babes in the Wood*: 'It is a dream of beautiful and dainty women, magnificent costumes, artistically conceived and delightfully painted scenery, and a harmony of exquisite colouring in grouping, never surpassed.' But it added:

To the critical it might be pointed out that Mr Sturgess or Mr Collins . . . has treated the poetical possibilities of the pretty subject laid under tax with a somewhat unsympathetic hand, and that, having entirely perverted the time-honoured story, he has failed to impart much humour as compensation.

But the critic confessed that judging by the reception of the piece, the critical view was in a minority. 'As it stands, *The Babes in the Wood* is a great and glorious spectacle, and as such should be the talk of London and the attraction of the provinces.'

The pantomime opens in the nursery where sleeping children are tormented by the Spirit of Indigestion and the birch-wielding Spirit of Castigation, until the Spirit of Youth arrives to promise them the delights of pantomime at Drury Lane and nurses escort them away to see *Babes in the Wood*. The villain, Baron Banbury Cross, runs a bookmaking business but cannot pay off his debts and is besieged by his customers. He fobs them off temporarily with blank cheques, but they return for their money. He learns by telegram that his brother has died, leaving him his two most precious treasures. They turn out to be the babes, Reggie and Chrissie, played by Dan Leno and Herbert Campbell. They arrive and wreck the turf commission office. The Baron hands them over to be educated by the bluestocking Miss Gertie Girton in her school, while he goes to court to seek to overturn the will.

The hero, Prince Paragon, is performed as a parody of the Kaiser, singing:

> I'm the autocratic ruler of the nation,
> Don't cherknow? Don't cherknow? Don't cherknow?
> A military chappy I am,
> And you shall see how snappy I am,
> When they say my last new costume fits too tight,
> And I'm rude to my grandmotherly relation.

The *I.S.D.N.* thought it 'A very tasteless attack upon the German Emperor'. Having exhausted every pleasure, he seeks a new sensation. It is suggested he tries love and he immediately falls for Marian, the Baron's daughter who turns up with her father at court.

At Gertie Girton's school, Reggie and Chrissie perform a scene from *Hamlet*, the Prince turns up to present the prizes and the Baron asks him to deprive the children of their fortune. Urged on by Marian, the Prince refuses, and so the Baron denies him permission to marry Marian. The children bombard the Baron with books.

At a country fair, very realistic with roundabouts, shooting galleries, circus shows and steam whistles, the Baron recruits ruffians Bill and Will to kill the babes. In the woods, the ruffians fight each other when Will develops a conscience about killing the children. The children wander off, their wanderings illustrated by a panorama by Kautsky pronounced by *The Era* (1 January 1898) to be of 'exquisite beauty'. They encounter giants, dwarfs and frogs, and they finally fall asleep in the land of orchids where there is a fairy ballet. *The Stage* (30 December 1897) recorded that:

> beautiful flowers of every known hue fill the place until the entire scene resembles a bouquet of pretty fairies, clad in choice bloom, that constantly varies in its arrangement of colour. It is a wonderful scene, the equal of which has never been known, and the vast audience, roused to applause from the commencement of the first ballet movement here, was worked up to such a pitch of enthusiasm that the old theatre echoed again and

again with a whirlwind of applause only stayed when Mr Collins had appeared before the act drop, for the scene was the concluding one of the first act of the pantomime.

The Times agreed that the orchid ballet was 'one of the most beautiful spectacles that have ever filled this capacious stage', particularly with the 'graceful aerial ballet of the well-known Grigolati troop' added to the evolutions of the *corps de ballet*.

This effectively ended the traditional story of the Babes, for in part two, they are found magically grown up, leading an exciting and fashionable life on the town in what was essentially a musical comedy, set at the club, the race track and the babes' flat. Prince Paragon has been brought to the verge of ruin by the Baron but when the Baron tries a final card-sharping swindle he is exposed. The Prince retrieves his fortune when Reggie rides his horse Toastrack to victory. The pantomime ends with the coronation of Prince Paragon, now united with Marian, and the coming of age of the babes. There was general praise for music, costumes, ballets and scenery. Of the performers, Dan Leno and Herbert Campbell were praised. *The Stage* thought Leno 'superbly funny' as the boy Reggie in Eton jacket and short trousers and as 'the broken-down adult, with all the exaggerated airs of a swell' – 'he kept the house in roars of laughter.' Campbell in golden ringlets and pinafore also 'made a laughable figure as Chrissie, a well-favoured and plump child, and sang all his songs with that energy and go for which he is so much admired.' There was praise too for Ada Blanche as Prince Paragon. 'With but little to do, Miss Ada Blanche again proves her right to be considered the best principal boy on the stage. There are a snap and finish about all she does that make her portrayal of the Prince a right welcome one.' Alice Barnett, late of the Savoy, 'caused some merriment' as Gertie Girton. As always critics thought it would benefit from cutting, that it was too long, and that some of the performances would improve as the run went on. Most people left before the harlequinade commenced at midnight. It achieved 135 performances.

Barrett once again challenged Drury Lane, this time from the stage of the Garrick Theatre, with a revival of his greatest hit, *Cinderella*, without Ellaline Terriss but with the same scenario structure and Horace Lennard's lyrics, although new dialogue was provided by Geoffrey Thorn. Barrett's concept remained the same as before. *The Stage* (30 December 1897) said:

This, the prettiest of the cluster of childhood's dear romances, Mr Oscar Barrett once again makes, beyond all things, an enchanting appeal to the eye and the ear. The stage seems a vision of fair faces, a flower land of lovely hues, a maze of witching dances, haunted ever by the sweetest of sweet sounds known to a fairy pantomime.

Barrett's usual team were on hand (Hawes Craven, Pritchard Barrett and Henry Emden for scene-painting, Katti Lanner for ballets, Carl Wilhelm for costumes and music arranged and composed by Barrett himself). The ball – the climax of the show for *The Times* (28 December 1897) – became a history of dance with a classical dance followed by a pastoral dance, then a Florentine pavane, a Spanish bolero, an Indian nautch dance, a saraband, a gavotte and a Japanese dance, culminating in a grand waltz with all the dancers on stage. The score by Barrett blended classical melodies (Delibes, Schubert, Weber, Mendelssohn and German) with music hall favourites. There was praise too for the woodland ballet of the leaves, the wood pigeons and the fox. Altogether, *The Era* (1 January 1898) praised 'a series of stage pictures distinguished by delicate taste and artistic beauty of a high order of merit.'

The *I.L.N.* (1 January 1898) entered a note of dissent, complaining of too many mixed elements where one had expected 'a fairy tale pure and simple', an over-elaborate staging which 'clogged' the narrow stage of the Garrick and that 'the fancy of the fairy tale becomes rather lost in the rollicking low comedy of the ugly sisters.' But the ugly sisters, Thisbe and Clorinda, played by Harry Nicholls and John Le Hay, were impersonating characters present in the 1893 version, satires of 'The New Woman': Thisbe, a self-consciously academic Girton girl, a bluestocking in an academic gown decorated with algebraic symbols, and Clorinda, a muscular mannish girl who has taken a bodybuilding course with Eugene Sandow. The *I.S.D.N.* (1 January 1898) specifically said 'Both comedians deserve praise for avoiding all the vulgarity formerly associated with the humours of men in petticoats.' Several critics thought it too long and felt some of the humour rather hit and miss – a parody of the Chinese-American play *The First Born* fell flat, as not enough people had seen the original. On the script, *The Stage* remarked:

> Mr Thorn loves a pun, and he will go far for an example ... On the other hand, he is sparing of topical allusions and references – a reticence, for which, in this old world story, we should be loath to blame him. The book apart, *Cinderella* remains all it was, and more. Fancy, colour, music and the skilled arts of the stage conspire to make it a kaleidoscope of delight.

The *I.L.N.* (1 January 1898) praised the opening as 'much more dainty in taste and tender in feeling than the average production of its order'. But it pointed out that Barrett had been hampered somewhat in his staging by the 'comparatively narrow limits of the Garrick stage', though noting that this had not prevented him achieving some 'charming scenic effects, notably in Mr Hawes Craven's delightful autumn wood and in a *bal champêtre* upon a most extensive scale'. It ran for eighty-six performances.

The 1898–9 Drury Lane pantomime was *The Forty Thieves*, written by Arthur Sturgess and Arthur Collins. It provoked *The Stage* (29 December 1898) to comment that 'it is a great and magnificent spectacular production, one scene of which has never been equalled for its gorgeous splendour and beautiful effect.' But the critic went on to complain that it was too long and in need of cutting, and to quarrel with its description as 'a children's pantomime', claiming it was more like a modern musical comedy and that children could not be expected to appreciate jokes about relations between the crowned heads of Europe, for example, or transporting the characters to a London pub. The opening night was also unfortunate in that the actress playing Morgiana, Amelia Stone, was obviously ailing and had to be replaced at half time by Maud Fowler and in that one of the male performers did not know his lines.

The Times (27 December 1898) was less censorious, seeing merit in the London section of the show:

> Though Christmas pantomime is the stronghold of tradition, Mr Arthur Collins has taught us to look for an infusion of novelty into its composition at Drury Lane, and The Forty Thieves ... is not in this respect disappointing.

Ali Baba and his household decamp to London with their wealth. The Forty Thieves follow them there and it is in London that Morgiana pours boiling oil on the thieves in their forty barrels, which have been ordered as beer for the Red Lion public house, of which Ali Baba is the licensee. The Times thought 'there seems no reason why the entire *personnel* of nursery literature should not in turn be made to visit London. Their up-to-date adventures in the metropolis might be trusted to add a little piquancy to the original legend, as, indeed, happens, in the present instance.'

The pantomime was divided into two parts, broken by an interval. Part one told the familiar story of Ali Baba and part two had them transported to London, for scenes in up-to-date bachelor flats, Regent's Park, the Zoo and Newgate Jail, as well as the Red Lion pub. The visit to the Zoo provided the opportunity for topical satire as among the visitors audiences would recognize Lord Salisbury, Joseph Chamberlain, John Burns, General Kitchener, Captain Dreyfus, Emile Zola, Colonel Esterhazy and W.G. Grace.

The central comic characters were Dan Leno as Abdallah, leader of the Forty Thieves, and Herbert Campbell as his faithful female companion Zuleika. They developed their parts, thought The Times, 'with all the humorous extravagance at their command'. Leno, in fierce moustaches and an abnormal red-feathered hat, and with 'a preposterous property mare', scored a comic hit with his mock troubadour serenade, and Campbell created hilarity by his first entrance in a Salvationist bonnet, burlesquing Edna May in the musical comedy The Belle of New York.

The visual highlight was the porcelain ballet. The I.L.N. (31 December 1898) reported:

> No spectacle so gorgeous and aesthetically perfect as the Porcelain Ballet has been presented at the Lane within ordinary memory. Conceive a series of steps reaching almost to the summit of the stage, over which runs a cascade of real water, illuminated by

a constantly revolving and ever-changing mass of electric lights underneath. Imagine before this background troop after troop of dancers representing every tint of porcelain, Oriental, and all the many varieties ranging in colour from silver, light blue, and pink, to purple and black, and concluding with a magnificent display of the delicate hues of Dresden china; and then fancy, amid such a dazzling scene of beauty, the graceful motions (in old-gold costumes) of the Grigolatis, Aerial dancers, and so you will have complete a stage-picture that baffles description.

The Times thought the 'attractiveness of *The Forty Thieves*' considerably enhanced by the music, 'original and selected', by J.M. Glover. 'Most of the popular airs of the day are caught up in the score, and there is a stirring march for Abdallah's band which is used as sort of *leit-motiv*.' But after the brilliant transformation scene by Bruce Smith, 'Love's Golden Bridge', there was 'a small and restricted harlequinade of the old-fashioned sort, a concession to tradition which, owing to the lateness of the performance, few of the general public last night thought fit to wait for.' It ran for 130 performances.

The Oscar Barrett competition was this year staged at the Adelphi, its first pantomime for many years. It was *Dick Whittington*, written by Horace Lennard and scored, produced and conducted by Oscar Barrett. But there was evidently some concern that Barrett had been compelled to dilute his poetic fancies by the nature of the Adelphi audience. *The Stage* (29 December 1898) praised the team of Lennard and Barrett: 'Mr Lennard has humour, fancy, invention, and also the art of turning a versicle as neatly and finely as any practitioner ... Mr Barrett is a musician to his finger-tips, with a "record" of sweet and scholarly strains in pantomime.' But the critic then added: 'No doubt in this they have not been quite all that they were ... The Adelphi audience like their fare well seasoned; and Messrs. Lennard and Barrett have, to some extent, served the pantomime to this palate', Lennard including knockabout for the comedians and Barrett music hall songs in his score. The *I.L.N.* (31 December 1898) was even more forthright:

Gay music, pretty costumes, pleasant scenery, and a capable company – all these essentials Mr Oscar Barrett has secured for his Adelphi production ... And, yet, somehow, he seems to have fallen between the two stools of poetic fancy and music-hall vulgarity. There are here pretty pageants: fourteenth-century Cheapside and Oriental Morocco; there are garish processions; a Lord Mayor's show and a barbaric ballet. And yet the City Companies in silks and satins, and the Eastern Court in the boldest of colour harmonies, scarcely atone for a certain lack of vitality and variety. Mr Barrett, in fact, allows his entertainment occasionally to grow dull. There is a plethora of sentimental ditties and tedious songs from the 'halls'; his comedians grow tiresome ... a child is put to sing a silly naval ballad ... Mr Barrett should make up his mind which 'Dick Whittington' is to be: a fairy tale or a music-hall farce; and should determine – as his choice seems for the latter – to breathe into his first Adelphi pantomime more riotous and spontaneous mirth. The pretty show must be made a merrier one.

The Times (27 December 1898), on the other hand, thought it Barrett's best pantomime to date and likely to delight both children and adults, concluding that 'for spirit, fun, and beauty of scene and music *Dick Whittington* leaves little to be desired.' Barrett and Lennard both took bows before a cheering audience on the opening night. It achieved a run of eighty-eight performances.

Max Beerbohm in *The Saturday Review* (31 December 1898), however, took Barrett to task, complaining that he thought that with his *Cinderella*, Barrett:

> had inaugurated a new era in pantomime – or rather that he had reinaugurated an old era, with certain chaste improvements. I was wrong. The experiment seems to have been abandoned, for *Dick Whittington* at The Adelphi has been done very differently from *Cinderella*. Erst an apostle of Refinement, Mr Barrett now truckles to the 'giddy vulgar', and his new pantomime is tarred all over ... with the brush of the music-halls. A sad surrender is Mr Barrett's, and none, I am sure, deplores it as bitterly as he. For him, who in his day has sounded the depths of Refinement, it must indeed be terrible to sit nightly in the conductor's chair, face to face with so much that he despises utterly.

The Drury Lane offering for 1899–1900 was *Jack and the Beanstalk*, produced by Arthur Collins, written by Collins and Arthur Sturgess and scored by Jimmy Glover. Despite freezing weather, the theatre was 'full to overflowing' – the audience included the Lord Chancellor in a Box. Once again opening night was hit by disaster. The popular Australian principal boy, Nellie Stewart, playing Jack, lost her voice and could not go on. *The Stage* (28 December 1899) reported:

> This was an irreparable breach, and though Miss Millie Lowell stepped into it on the first night with remarkable and admirable address, it was of course impossible to make the deficiency entirely good. Miss Lowell not only could not sing much of the music, but was frequently uncertain of her lines; hence the frequency of the prompter's voice, the missing of cues, and the hesitation of attack begotten of this untoward state of things.

This time there were no musical comedy scenes but a straightforward re-telling of the old story. *The Stage* approved:

> Thin the story is, yet there is a certain amount of continuity about it; and, instead of the irrelevant 'musichally' characteristics of some former years, the comic scenes, of which there are plenty, grow largely out of the action. Songs, apropos of nothing, feats and tricks thrust in for their own sake, humour of the 'turn' order – are all ... conspicuous by their absence. The use of topical references is sparing. The writing might, perhaps, be better.

But the visual splendour compensated for the lack of literary finesse.

Scene rolls back scene, and with each the wonder grows … There are scenes of pastoral beauty, scenes of market animation, scenes of faerie, scenes of the monstrous and grotesque in giantland, scenes of ballet and music, scenes processional, scenes emblematical – scenes vividly imagined and not less dextrously wrought out by the brushes of Bruce Smith, W. Perkins, McCleery, R. Caney, H. Emden, W. Cross and W. Harford, by the designer's art of M. Comelli, and by the terpsichorean masteries of Sig. Carlo Coppi and Mr John D'Auban. Thus music, too, reaches a high level. Much of it is original; all of it is scored with an ability of which Mr J.M. Glover has often given the proofs; and the finale to the first part, the great Harmony scene in which sound finally becomes almost co-equal with sight, is far and away beyond the average ambitions of pantomime music. *Jack and the Beanstalk*, in short, is a decisive stride forward. It is beautiful, it is gaily melodious, it is funny, and it has a thousand ingenuities, from the very biggest and best giant that ever widened a child's eyes to a tiny property pea, or from a flight of fairies to the issuing of a miniature British Army from Blunderbore's waistcoat pocket.

This last reference is to the giant rechristened Blunderboer, who is made up to resemble the typical Boer of caricature, and after whose downfall there emerges from his pocket a miniature army, all played by children, some riding small ponies, and dressed as soldiers, some in scarlet, some in khaki, bluejackets with a machine gun, and Australian lancers. There was considerable enthusiasm when they raised their helmets on their rifles and sang 'Rule Britannia'. 'One of the most popular features of the pantomime', *The Stage* called it.

The comedy was in the hands of Dan Leno as Dame Trot, Herbert Campbell as Bobbie, Jack's brother, and Johnny Danvers as King Ratatat. *The Stage* thought them poorly served by their songs but given plenty of comic scenes: 'Rarely has the provision of comic scenes for the comedians been ampler.' *The Times* (27 December 1899) noted: 'Their humour may not be refined – it is not meant to be – but it is exhilarating and infectious and it was particularly noticeable that it made the children laugh last night.'

The Times noted that:

the set-pieces or ballets, the scenes in which the stage is crowded with gorgeously-attired persons and flashing light, and blazing colour, are not of quite the same character as the imposing processions which used to be characteristic of Drury Lane in the days when Sir Augustus Harris reigned; but they are perhaps none the less pleasing on that account.

The first of them was the Vegetable Ballet ('quite funny', thought *The Times*) in which children dressed as leeks danced to the music of 'Men of Harlech', as potatoes and carrots to Irish tunes, and so forth, ending with a 'pretty dance of girls with head-pieces of broccoli'. But the concluding ballet of the first half, the Land of Harmony, when Jack has climbed high enough to hear 'the music of the spheres' was 'the best of the spectacles'. As *The Stage* described it:

> The stage extends far back, creating a shimmery vista: Gradually shining bands emerge and thread a rhythmic way forward. Slowly they mass on the stage in their soft greens, salmons, heliotropes, and other lovely tints, backed by warriors in silver mail. Trumpets are blown, instruments are held aloft, and all break into song and into dance to the strains of harp and mandolin. Then a flying figure speeds from the stage, into the auditorium, back and forth, throwing flowers; Little drummers, green and gold-clad, troop on; then girls, in blue and yellow, clashing tambourines and dancing; finally, litter-borne, come representatives of Tragedy and Comedy, with the sudden sparkle of a thousand lights and the uprise of radiant forms in the air. The huge audience has sat entranced at this scintillating spectacle, so variously composed.

It was at this point that Collins was called forth to take his bow.

The transformation scene by Bruce Smith was 'The End of the Century' and had dancers attired as modern inventions and their development, 'chiefly in locomotion and wireless telegraphy', and an apotheosis in gold, silver and copper of the coinage, with a flood of electric light, song, music and gliding figures in the air: 'It is all very elaborate and gorgeous.' The pantomime did not finish until after midnight, with a single scene harlequinade. It achieved 141 performances.

This year Oscar Barrett had no competing pantomime in London. He had given up the unequal struggle and retreated to the provinces where his kind of show was still in demand. In the 1895–6 season, he grossed £28,568 for the three pantomimes he staged in London, Edinburgh and Birmingham.[43] In May 1903 Barrett succeeded Robert Courtneidge as manager of the Theatre Royal and Prince's Theatre, Manchester, holding the position until 1905 and producing the 1903 pantomimes at both theatres, *Bold Robin Hood* at the Theatre Royal and *The Forty Thieves* at the Prince's.

For 1900–1, there was again only one West End pantomime, *The Sleeping Beauty and the Beast*, a merger of the two fairy stories *Sleeping Beauty* and *Beauty and the Beast* made by Arthur Collins and a new writer, J. Hickory Wood, who worked closely with Dan Leno and would become his first biographer. *The Times* (27 December 1900) thought that the show 'abounds in honest fun ... None of it is vulgar fun, for, though music-hall art has not been wholly ignored – that would be too much to expect – its baser elements have been rigorously excluded.' *The Stage* (27 December 1900) praised Wood for departing from tradition in certain respects: 'He reduces his punning to the minimum, and this minimum is of the best.' It was written largely in prose which enabled Wood to 'give a dramatic force and conciseness to much of the dialogue, the want of which often hampers the best efforts of pantomime actor and actress. With one or two exceptions ... the book is free from the slightest error in taste.' The exceptions related to satire on the French government when after the King and Queen awake from their hundred years sleep, they find the country turned into a republic presided over by a stage Frenchman President Kerekerray. *The Era* (29 December 1900) similarly urged the deletion of the anti-French satire as dangerous to international amity.

Dan Leno and Herbert Campbell as Queen Ravia and King Screwdolph of Perhapsburg, a pun on Queen Flavia and King Rudolf of the romantic stage hit *The Prisoner of Zenda*, excelled in a succession of comic set-pieces, a stay in a hydropathic establishment at Aix-and-Pains, an 'utterly absurd' game of golf, an accident in which their car falls to pieces and a bungled raid on the National Museum to steal the crown jewels. *The Era* noted that the pantomime had been 'remarkably well rehearsed'.

As always the beauties of the scene-painting were hymned, starting with Robert Caney's 'very dainty and fanciful' evocation of Fairyland. One highlight was 'an exquisite ballet', 'The Dream of the Year', for which Henry Emden provided 'the loveliest possible background'. *The Era* described it:

> The seasons, and even the months, are symbolised by detachments of superbly-attired dancers; and, in the background, appear pictures of the English landscape at different times of the year. Then, on the ground supplied by the tenderer tints, are thrown flecks of intense black when the Gringolatis, in swallow costumes, rise and fall in the air. As the whites and greys of winter replace the rich autumnal hues, vivid scarlets and vermilions harmonise with the glowing crimson of the holly berries. The exquisite art of this spectacle ... could scarcely be surpassed.

The other two big scenic pieces were entrusted to Bruce Smith. The transformation scene was entitled 'Beauty's Wedding Gifts'. *The Stage*, returning for a second visit, praised it (3 January 1901):

> To his transformation piece, with its delicate harmony of cream and gold, ungrudging praise can be given, although the impression it creates is somewhat discounted by the previous *tour de force*, the Enchanted Crystal Garden. In this scene the great feature, of course, is the Palace of Glass, specially constructed in Venice from the famous Salviati designs, and illuminated by no fewer than 2,500 electric lights in various colours, but in providing an adequate background for this dazzling spectacle Mr Bruce Smith has had good scope for his own particular art. The Salviati Palace, extensive as it is, with a sumptuous staircase and decorative fountains, leaves sufficient space on the stage for an elaborate ballet *divertissement* such as proclaims the skill of Messrs. Carlo Coppi and John D'Auban.

The Times reported: 'Mr Glover's music is not only tuneful (it is always that) but often ambitious, going so far as to borrow from *Tannhauser* and *Die Walküre*. Nor can there be two opinions about the colour-scheme and splendour of the costumes, designed by the incomparable Comelli.' On the opening night, the pantomime ran for five hours and the harlequinade was omitted. It later returned after cutting and compression in the pantomime and featured in two scenes with the inevitable whimsical Walker. It ran for 136 performances interrupted by four days closure in January after Queen Victoria died, bringing the Victorian Age to an end.

While the music hall element had never been banished and had become an integral part of the Victorian pantomime, the battle between Harris and Barrett for the soul of pantomime had ensured the survival of an element of the refinement and poetry which the defenders of traditionalism had so much valued in Blanchard's pantomimes. But Jimmy Glover, musical director at Drury Lane, writing in 1911, refuted the view of pessimists that pantomime was in decline:

> It is ridiculous for people to state that pantomime has declined; it has, however, changed, and increased its public ... Whatever the criticisms may be, the intent of the present pantomime provider has always been good. We live in an age of splendour, luxury and comfort. Therefore the best in spectacular display, in talent, in music, and interpretation is provided.[44]

It is clear that audiences loved them too and whatever the laments of traditionalists, the box-office had the final say. The Harris–Collins formula was the standard by which pantomimes elsewhere were judged.

Epilogue

In 1904 both Dan Leno and Herbert Campbell, the beloved stalwarts of Drury Lane pantomime, died. But Arthur Collins, who remained in charge at Drury Lane until 1924, continued with the proven formula, seeking to vary it in 1912 and 1915 by introducing a male principal boy, an innovation which did not find favour with the customers. However, the pre-eminence of Drury Lane came to an end in 1920. The Drury Lane management were unwilling to curtail the run of its romantic melodrama hit *The Garden of Allah* and so for the first time since 1848, there was no Christmas pantomime at Drury Lane. They tried to make up for it by reviving the 1919 Drury Lane *Cinderella* at Covent Garden, the first pantomime there since 1887. But it was not a success. Thereafter there were no more pantomimes for the remainder of Collins' tenure. Under his successors, Drury Lane became the home of the spectacular musical: in the 1920s the great imported Broadway shows such as *Rose Marie*, *The Desert Song*, *Show Boat* and *New Moon*; and in the 1930s, the musical spectaculars of Ivor Novello (*Glamorous Night*, *Careless Rapture*, *Crest of the Wave*, *The Dancing Years*). There were just three more pantomimes at Drury Lane: *Sleeping Beauty* (1929–30), *Jack and the Beanstalk* (1935) and *Babes in the Wood* (1938). After that, pantomime did not return to Drury Lane.

The torch of pantomime in the West End passed to the Lyceum, run by the Melville brothers, Walter and Frederick. Every year from 1910 to 1939 (except for 1917), the Melvilles produced a traditional Christmas pantomime, complete with rhyming couplets, a fairy ballet and even an attenuated harlequinade. It always made money. It only ended when the brothers died and the theatre was closed prior to demolition (which in the event never occurred). Thereafter pantomime was sporadically to be seen at the Coliseum, the Casino and the Hippodrome until the Palladium became the definitive London home of pantomime from 1948.

Pantomime continued and continues to do big business in the provinces and a succession of 'pantomime kings' – Julian Wylie, Tom Arnold, Francis Laidler and

Emile Littler among them – would send pantomime productions around the country, often producing dozens a year.

The old homes of pantomime like Drury Lane and Covent Garden, so familiar to the Victorians, ceased to produce pantomime or ceased to exist altogether. Three of the most celebrated suburban London pantomime houses were the Standard, Shoreditch, the Britannia, Hoxton and the Surrey, Lambeth. In a sign of the times, all three went over in the 1920s to showing films. The Standard and the Britannia were destroyed by enemy bombing in 1940 and the Surrey was pulled down in 1935.

By the time of World War II many of the characteristic features of Victorian pantomime had disappeared: the rhyming couplets, the introductory 'dark scene' with the demon king plotting mayhem, the topical duet, the transformation scene, the harlequinade. Even the female principal boy was an endangered species, though nothing could displace the dame. However, many of structural elements remained: spectacle, slapstick, local and topical allusion, the participation of much-loved performers, the insertion of popular songs. It remains an enduring and profitable part of the British theatrical scene.

Appendix: E.L. Blanchard's Annual Income

1849	£152.18 shillings	1870	£371.7s.
1850	£147.14s.6d	1871	£451.14s.
1851	£139.14s.	1872	£508.15s.
1852	£136.10s.	1873	£586
1853	£146.10s.	1874	£587.11s.
1854	£189	1875	£692.12s.9d
1855	£198.6s.	1876	£641.17s.6d
1856	£266	1877	£708.17s.
1857	£260.10s.	1878	£590.15s.
1858	£221	1879	no income recorded
1859	£246.10s.	1880	no income recorded
1860	£289	1881	no income recorded
1861	£284.10s.	1882	£452.0s.6d
1862	£311.2s.	1883	£521.4s.6d
1863	£370.18s.	1884	£603.6s.
1864	£491.2s.6d	1885	£545.16s.
1865	£441.8s.	1886	£520.18s.
1866	£289	1887	£400.9s.
1867	£283	1888	£350.3s.6d
1868	income not stated	1889	£200
1869	income not stated		

Notes

Chapter 1: Transformations

1. The fact that a successful pantomime was the key to economic success in the theatre has been confirmed by the research into nineteenth-century theatre finances by Tracy C. Davis in her comprehensive study, *The Economics of the British Stage 1800–1914*, Cambridge: Cambridge University Press, 2000, pp. 342–5.
2. Richard Schoch, *Queen Victoria and the Theatre of her Age*, Basingstoke: Palgrave, 2004, pp. 19, 47–8, 117.
3. Charles Dickens, *David Copperfield*, London: Odham's Press, n.d., p. 258.
4. Dutton Cook, *A Book of the Play*, London: Sampson Low, Marston, Searle and Rivington, 1881, p. 364.
5. Leigh Hunt, *The Tatler* (28 December 1831); Andrew Halliday, *Comical Fellows*, London: J.H. Thomson, 1863, p. 46; W. Davenport Adams, 'The Decline of Pantomime', *The Theatre* 5 (1882), pp. 85–90; Max Beerbohm, quoted in Derek Salberg, *Once Upon a Pantomime*, Luton: Cortney Publications, 1981, pp. 86–9.
6. J.R. Planché, *Recollections and Reflections*, London: Tinsley Brothers, 1872, vol. 2, pp. 72–3.
7. See, for example, Joseph Donohue, 'Burletta and Early Nineteenth Century Theatre', *Nineteenth Century Theatre Research* 1 (1973), pp. 29–51; P.T. Dircks, 'James Robinson Planché and the English Burletta Tradition', *Theatre Survey* 17 (1976), pp. 68–81; V.C. Clinton-Baddeley, *The Burlesque Tradition in the English Theatre after 1600*, London: Methuen, 1952, pp. 1–2, 108–9, 110, 113–114.
8. J.R. Planché, *Extravaganzas*, ed. by T.W. Dillon Croker and Stephen Tucker, London: Samuel French, 1879, vol. 2, p. 66.
9. W. Davenport Adams, *A Book of Burlesque*, London: Henry and Co., 1891, pp. v, 44, 72.
10. Dutton Cook, *A Book of the Play*, pp. 366–7.
11. Richard W. Schoch ed., *Victorian Theatrical Burlesques*, Aldershot: Ashgate, 2003, p. xxviii.
12. From the 1820s on Clarkson Stanfield at Drury Lane and John Henderson Grieve (joined later by his sons Thomas and William) at Covent Garden became famous for their pantomime panoramas and dioramas, see chapter 6.
13. Gerald Frow, *'Oh, Yes It Is' – A History of Pantomime*, London: BBC Books, 1985, p. 124.

411

14. J.R. Planché, 'Extravaganza and Spectacle', *Temple Bar* 3 (1861), p. 532.

15. Planché, *Recollections and Reflections* vol. 2, pp. 136–7.

16. Dutton Cook, *A Book of the Play*, p. 369.

17. Kate Flint, *The Victorians and the Visual Imagination*, Cambridge: Cambridge University Press, 2000, p. 1.

18. Richard D. Altick, *Paintings from Books*, Columbus: Ohio State University Press, 1985.

19. Michael Booth, *Victorian Spectacular Theatre 1850–1910*, London: Routledge and Kegan Paul, 1981, p. 8.

20. Booth, *Victorian Spectacular Theatre*, p. 3.

21. Michael Booth, 'New Technology in the Victorian Theatre', *Theatre Notebook* 46 (1992), p. 122. See also Russell Jackson, 'Victorian and Edwardian Stagecraft: Techniques and Issues' in Kerry Powell ed., *The Cambridge Companion to Victorian and Edwardian Theatre*, Cambridge: Cambridge University Press, 2004, pp. 52–69.

22. *Oxford Dictionary of National Biography*, 'William Roxby Beverly', Oxford: Oxford University Press, 2004, vol. 5, p. 602.

23. Planché, 'Extravaganza and Spectacle', pp. 530–2.

24. H.J. Byron, 'Pantomimical', *The Theatre*, n.s.1 (1878–9) p. 410.

25. Dutton Cook, *A Book of the Play*, p. 369.

26. H.G. Hibbert, *A Playgoer's Memories*, London: Grant Richards, 1920, pp. 201–2.

27. A.E. Wilson, *Pantomime Pageant*, London: Stanley Paul, 1946, p. 57.

28. Hibbert, *A Playgoer's Memories*, p. 198.

29. Harold J. Perkin, *The Origins of Modern English Society, 1780–1880*, London: Routledge, 1969, p. 280.

30. G.M. Young, *Portrait of an Age: Victorian England*, Oxford: Oxford University Press, 1977, p. 20.

31. Jane Moody, *Illegitimate Theatre in London, 1770–1840*, Cambridge: Cambridge University Press, 2000, p. 214.

32. Andrew McConnell Stott, *The Pantomime Life of Joseph Grimaldi*, Edinburgh: Canongate, 2009, p. xxv.

33. Vic Gatrell, *City of Laughter: Sex and Satire in Eighteenth-Century London*, London: Atlantic Books 2007, p. 33.

34. Gatrell, *City of Laughter*, p. 7.

35. Gatrell, *City of Laughter*, pp. 143–4.

36. John Russell Stephens, *The Censorship of English Drama 1824–1901*, Cambridge: Cambridge University Press, 1980.

37. Mikhail Bakhtin, *Rabelais and his World*, translated by Helen Iswolsky, Bloomington, Indiana: Indiana University Press, 1984, p. 5.

38. Bakhtin, *Rabelais and his World*, pp. 11–12.

39. Bakhtin, *Rabelais and his World*, p. 19.

40. J.M. Golby and A.W. Purdue, *The Civilisation of the Crowd: Popular Culture in England 1750–1900*, London: Batsford, 1984, p. 71.

41. Gatrell, *City of Laughter*, pp. 435, 453.

42. Ben Wilson, *Decency and Disorder: The Age of Cant, 1789–1837*, London: Faber and Faber, 2007, p. 356.

43. Asa Briggs, *The Age of Improvement 1783–1867*, London: Longman, 1959, pp. 1–2.

44. Young, *Portrait of an Age*, pp. 4–5.

45. See F.M.L. Thompson, *The Rise of Respectable Society*, London: Fontana, 1988; Perkin, *The Origins of Modern English Society*; Ian Bradley, *The Call to Seriousness*, London: Jonathan Cape, 1976.

46. Edward Bulwer-Lytton, *England and the English* (1833), reprint Chicago: University of Chicago Press, 1970, pp. 19–20.

47. Wilson, *Decency and Disorder*, pp. 356–85.

48. W.L. Burn, *The Age of Equipoise*, London: Allen and Unwin, 1964. See also Martin Hewitt ed., *An Age of Equipoise?: Reassessing Mid-Victorian Britain*, Aldershot: Ashgate, 2000.

49. Donald J. Gray, 'The Uses of Victorian Laughter', *Victorian Studies* 10 (December 1966), pp. 154–5, 158–9.

50. Roger B. Henkle, *Comedy and Culture: England 1820–1900*, Princeton: Princeton University Press, 1980, p. 185.

51. Henkle, *Comedy and Culture*, p. 350.

52. Bernard Porter, *The Absent-Minded Imperialists*, Oxford: Oxford University Press, 2004, p. 140.

53. Marty Gould, *Nineteenth-Century Theatre and the Imperial Encounter*, New York: Routledge, 2011, p. 7.

54. Geneviève Ward and Richard Whiteing, *Both Sides of the Curtain*, London: Cassell, 1918, p. 234.

55. W. Macqueen Pope, *Ghosts and Greasepaint*, London: Robert Hale, 1951, p. 281.

56. *The Fortnightly Review* 38 (November 1885), p. 634.

57. W. Macqueen Pope, *Theatre Royal, Drury Lane*, London: W.H. Allen, 1945, p. 286.

58. Gould, *Nineteenth-Century Theatre and the Imperial Encounter*, pp. 50–72.

59. *The Theatre*, n.s.1 (1883), p. 17.

60. Earl of Cromer, *Modern Egypt*, London: Macmillan, 1908, vol. 2, pp. 327–8; vol. 1, p. 149.

61. *The Theatre*, n.s.1 (1883), pp. 18, 20.

62. *The Theatre* 5 (1882), p. 87.

63. Alan Ruston, 'Richard Nelson Lee and the Victorian Pantomime in Great Britain', *Nineteenth Century Theatre Research* 11 (1983), pp. 105–17; Alan Ruston, 'Richard Nelson Lee and Nelson Lee Junior, Authors of Victorian Pantomime', *Nineteenth Century Theatre Research* 18 (1991), pp. 75–85.

64. *The Theatre* 5 (1882), p. 87.

65. David Mayer, 'The Sexuality of Pantomime', *Theatre Quarterly* 4 (1974), pp. 55–64.

66. David Pickering, *The Encyclopedia of Pantomime*, Andover: Gale Research International, 1993, p. 159.

67. Pickering, *The Encyclopedia of Pantomime*, p. 57.

68. Kathy Fletcher, 'Planché, Vestris and the Transvestite Role: Sexuality and Gender in Victorian Popular Theatre', *Nineteenth Century Theatre* 15 (1987), pp. 9–33.

69. Laurence Senelick, 'Boys and Girls Together: Subcultural Origins of Glamour Drag and Male Impersonation on the Nineteenth Century Stage' in Lesley Ferris ed., *Crossing the Stage*, London and New York: Routledge, 1993, pp. 81–2.

70. Peter Ackroyd, *Dressing Up*, New York: Simon and Schuster, 1979, p. 102.

71. Fred Willis, *A Book of London Yesterdays*, London: Phoenix House, 1960, p. 255.

72. Ernest Shepard, *Drawn from Memory*, quoted in Marah Gubar, *Artful Dodgers*, Oxford: Oxford University Press, 2009, p. 184.
73. Sharon Weltman, *Performing the Victorian*, Columbus: Ohio State University Press, 2007, pp. 19–37; Edwin M. Eigner, 'Imps, Dames and Principal Boys: Gender Confusion in the Nineteenth-Century Pantomime', *Browning Institute Studies* 17 (1989), pp. 65–74.

Chapter 2: Harlequinade

1. On the eighteenth-century evolution of the harlequinade, see M. Willson Disher, *Clowns and Pantomimes*, Boston and New York: Houghton Mifflin, 1925; Thelma Nicklaus, *Harlequin or the Rise and Fall of a Bergamask Rogue*, New York: George Braziller, 1956; Allardyce Nicoll, *The World of Harlequin*, Cambridge: Cambridge University Press, 1963; John O'Brien, *Harlequin Britain: Pantomime and Entertainment 1690–1760*, Baltimore: Johns Hopkins University Press, 2004.
2. David Mayer III, *Harlequin in His Element: The English Pantomime, 1806–1836*, Cambridge, Massachusetts: Harvard University Press, 1969, p. 2.
3. David Worrall, *Harlequin Empire: Race, Ethnicity and the Drama of the Popular Enlightenment*, London: Pickering and Chatto, 2007.
4. Mayer, *Harlequin in His Element*, p. 7.
5. On Victorian stage effects, see Percy Fitzgerald, *The World Behind the Scenes*, London: Chatto and Windus, 1881; Richard Southern, *Changeable Scenery*, London: Faber and Faber, 1952.
6. Andrew McConnell Stott, *The Pantomime Life of Joseph Grimaldi*, Edinburgh: Canongate, 2009, pp. xxv–xxvi.
7. On Victorian varieties of humour, see Donald Gray, 'The Uses of Victorian Laughter', *Victorian Studies* 10 (December 1966), pp. 145–76; Ronald Pearsall, *Collapse of Stout Party: Victorian Wit and Humour*, London: Weidenfeld and Nicolson, 1975.
8. Andrew Halliday, *Comical Fellows*, London: J.H. Thomson, 1863, p. 5.
9. Halliday, *Comical Fellows*, pp. 5–6.
10. Harry Stone ed., *Charles Dickens' Uncollected Writings from 'Household Words'*, Bloomington and London: Indiana University Press, 1968, vol. 2, p. 384.
11. Derek Salberg, *Once Upon a Pantomime*, Luton: Cortney Publications, 1981, pp. 76–89.
12. Quoted in Mayer, *Harlequin in His Element*, p. 69.
13. Halliday, *Comical Fellows*, p. 46.
14. Edwin M. Eigner, *The Dickens Pantomime*, Berkeley: University of California Press, 1989.
15. Clement Scott, *The Drama of Yesterday and Today*, London: Macmillan, 1899, vol. 2, p. 164.
16. Clement Scott and Cecil Howard eds, *The Life and Reminiscences of E.L. Blanchard*, London: Hutchinson, 1891, vol. 2, p. 579.
17. J.R. Planché, *Recollections and Reflections*, London: Tinsley Brothers, 1872, vol. 2, pp. 136–9.
18. On the Victorian Christmas, see J.A.R. Pimlott, *The Englishman's Christmas*, Hassocks: The Harvester Press, 1978; J.M. Golby and A.W. Purdue, *The Making of the Modern*

Christmas, London: B.T. Batsford, 1986; Mark Connelly, *Christmas: A Social History*, London: I.B.Tauris, 1999; Neil Armstrong, *Christmas in Nineteenth-Century England*, Manchester: Manchester University Press, 2010; Tara Moore, *Victorian Christmas in Print*, New York: Palgrave Macmillan, 2009.

19. D.J. Anderson, 'Harlequin in Extremis', *The Theatre* (1 March 1879), pp. 103–6.
20. W.J. Macqueen Pope, *Theatre Royal, Drury Lane*, London: W.H. Allen, 1945, p. 292.
21. A.E. Wilson, *The Lyceum*, London: Dennis Yates, 1952, pp. 162–3.
22. Wilson, *The Lyceum*, p. 163.

Chapter 3: Fairyland

1. Diane Purkiss, *Troublesome Things: a History of Fairies and Fairy Stories*, London: Allen Lane – the Penguin Press, 2000, p. 220.
2. On fairies and fairyland, see besides Purkiss, Carole G. Silver, *Strange and Secret Peoples: Fairies and Victorian Consciousness*, Oxford: Oxford University Press, 1999; Nicola Bown, *Fairies in Nineteenth-Century Art and Literature*, Cambridge: Cambridge University Press, 2006; Alison Packer, Stella Beddoe and Lianne Jarrett, *Fairies in Legend and the Arts*, London: Cameron and Tayleur, 1980.
3. On spiritualism, see in particular Ruth Brandon, *The Spiritualists: The Passion for the Occult in the Nineteenth and Twentieth Centuries*, London: Weidenfeld and Nicolson, 1983, and Janet Oppenheim, *The Other World: Spiritualism and Psychical Research in England, 1850–1914*, Cambridge: Cambridge University Press, 1985.
4. Brandon, *The Spiritualists*, p. 231.
5. Oppenheim, *The Other World*, p. 28.
6. Logie Barrow, *Independent Spirits: Spiritualism and English Plebeians, 1850–1910*, London: Routledge, 1986.
7. Bown, *Fairies*, p. 85.
8. E.T. Cook and Alexander Wedderburn eds, *The Complete Works of John Ruskin*, London: George Allen, 1903–1912, vol. 33, pp. 346–7.
9. Silver, *Strange and Secret Peoples*, p. 4.
10. Jack Zipes, *Fairy Tales as Myth/Myth as Fairy Tale*, Lexington: The University Press of Kentucky, 1994, p. 11.
11. Michael Slater ed., *Dickens' Journalism*, vol. 3, London: J.M. Dent, 1998, pp. 167–8.
12. Jack Zipes, *Fairy Tales and the Art of Subversion: The Classic Genre for Children and the Process of Civilization*, New York: Routledge, 1991, p. 26.
13. Zipes, *Fairy Tales and the Art of Subversion*, p. 37.
14. The Brothers Grimm, *The Complete Fairy Stories*, London: Vintage Books, 2007, introduction by Jack Zipes, p. xlii.
15. Zipes, *Fairy Tales and the Art of Subversion*, p. 81.
16. Jack Zipes ed., *Victorian Fairy Tales*, New York: Methuen, 1987, p. xvii.
17. Bruno Bettelheim, *The Uses of Enchantment: The Meaning and Importance of Fairy Tales*, Harmondsworth: Penguin, 1986, p. 5.
18. Bettelheim, *Uses of Enchantment*, p. 6.
19. Bettelheim, *Uses of Enchantment*, pp. 6–7.

20. Bettelheim, *Uses of Enchantment*, pp. 8–9.

21. Bettelheim, *Uses of Enchantment*, pp. 12–13.

22. Marie-Louise von Franz, *The Interpretation of Fairy Tales*, Boston, Massachusetts: Shambhala Publications, 1996, p. 1.

23. In Jane Martineau ed., *Victorian Fairy Painting*, London: Royal Academy of Arts/Merrell Holberton, 1997, p. 63.

24. Bown, *Fairies*, p. 70.

25. Richard Altick, *Paintings from Books*, Columbus: Ohio State University Press, 1985, p. 263.

26. Cook and Wedderburn, *Complete Works of John Ruskin*, vol. 33, p. 327.

27. Tracy C. Davis, 'What are Fairies For?' in Tracy C. Davis and Peter Holland eds, *The Performing Century*, Basingstoke: Palgrave Macmillan, 2007, pp. 32–3.

28. Dutton Cook, *Nights at the Play*, London: Chatto and Windus, 1883, p. 275.

29. See Gary Jay Williams, *Our Moonlight Revels: A Midsummer Night's Dream in the Theatre*, Iowa City: University of Iowa Press, 1997.

Chapter 4: James Robinson Planché and the Classical Extravaganza

1. Planché published an autobiography, *Recollections and Reflections*, 2 vols, London: Tinsley Brothers, 1872. The best recent work on him is contained in a series of unpublished American PhD dissertations: 'Clair Oliver Haugen, Covent Garden and the Lyceum Theatre under the Charles J. Mathewses', University of Wisconsin, 1968; Cleon Vernon Bennett, 'James Robinson Planché: Victorian Craftsman', University of Wisconsin, 1971; Kathy Fletcher, 'The Planché Extravaganzas as Victorian Popular Theatre', Indiana University, 1986; Jon Kenner Evans, 'James Robinson Planché and his Influence on Playwriting, Design and Staging in the Early Nineteenth-Century British Theatre', University of California, 1986. The best single work on the history of burlesque is John Alden Degen's unpublished dissertation, 'A History of Burlesque-Extravaganza in Nineteenth-Century England', Indiana University, 1977. Donald Roy published a critical edition of seven Planché plays with a brief biography of the author in *Plays by James Robinson Planché*, Cambridge: Cambridge University Press, 1986. The complete set of Planché's extravaganzas was published in *The Extravaganzas of J.R. Planché Esq.*, ed. by T. F. Dillon Croker and Stephen Tucker, 5 vols, London: Samuel French, 1879.

2. Clement Scott, *The Drama of Yesterday and Today*, vol. 2, London: Macmillan, 1899, p. 150.

3. John Hollingshead, *My Lifetime*, vol. 1, London: Sampson, Low, Marston and Co., 1895, p. 192.

4. *The Theatre* n.s. vol. 1 (1878–9), p. 414.

5. *The Theatre* n.s. vol. 2 (1880), pp. 95–9.

6. 'A Letter from London by a Railway Witness', *Blackwood's Magazine* 58 (August 1845), pp. 177–8.

7. Richard Hengist Horne, *The New Spirit of the Age* (1844), vol. 2, New York: Garland reprint, 1986, pp. 85, 91, 97.

8. J.R. Planché, 'Extravaganza and Spectacle', *Temple Bar* 3 (1861), pp. 524–32.

9. Planché, *Recollections and Reflections*, vol. 2, p. 43.

10. Planché, *Recollections and Reflections*, vol. 2, pp. 72–3.

11. J.R. Planché, *Extravaganzas*, ed. by T.W. Dillon Croker and Stephen Tucker, London: Samuel French, 1879, vol. 1, p. 13.

12. P.T. Dirks, 'James Robinson Planché and the English Burletta Tradition', *Theatre Survey* 17 (1976), pp. 68–81.

13. Andrew Halliday, *Comical Fellows*, London: J.H. Thomson, 1863, pp. 46–9.

14. Planché, *Extravaganzas*, vol. 4, pp. 89–90.

15. Planché, *Extravaganzas*, vol. 2, p. 65.

16. Planché, 'Extravaganza and Spectacle', p. 531.

17. Planché, 'Extravaganza and Spectacle', pp. 529–30.

18. Planché, 'Extravaganza and Spectacle', pp. 530, 532.

19. Planché, *Extravaganzas*, vol. 1, p. 39; Dougald MacMillan, 'Planché's Early Classical Burlesques', *Studies in Philology* 25 (1928), p. 341.

20. Planché, 'Extravaganza and Spectacle', p. 528.

21. Planché, *Recollections and Reflections*, vol. 1, pp. 179–80.

22. Planché, *Recollections and Reflections*, vol. 1, p. 190.

23. Planché, 'Extravaganza and Spectacle', p. 528.

24. Planché, 'Extravaganza and Spectacle', p. 528.

25. Planché, 'Extravaganza and Spectacle', p. 529.

26. William Appleton, *Madame Vestris and the London Stage*, New York: Columbia University Press, 1974, p. 169.

27. For an excellent analysis of the Robson extravaganzas, see Paul Buczkowski, 'J.R. Planché, Frederick Robson and the Fairy Extravaganza', *Marvels and Tales: Journal of Fairy-Tale Studies* 15 (2001), pp. 42–65.

28. Planché, *Recollections and Reflections*, vol. 2, p. 300.

29. Clifford John Williams, *Madame Vestris: A Theatrical Biography*, London: Sidgwick and Jackson, 1973, p. 160.

30. Appleton, *Madame Vestris*, p. 52.

31. Planché, *Recollections and Reflections*, vol. 1, p. 252.

32. Quoted in Buczkowski, 'J.R. Planché, Frederick Robson and the Fairy Extravaganza', p. 42.

33. Planché, *Recollections and Relections*, vol. 2, p. 22.

34. W. Davenport Adams, *A Book of Burlesque*, London: Henry and Co., 1891, p. 72.

35. Planché, *Extravaganzas*, vol. 3, p. 81.

36. Edith Hall and Fiona Macintosh, *Greek Tragedy in the British Theatre*, Oxford: Oxford University Press, 2005, p. 390.

37. Michael Booth, *English Plays of the Nineteenth Century*, vol. 5: *Pantomimes, Extravaganzas and Burlesques*, Oxford: Oxford University Press, 1976, p. 2.

38. Richard Schoch ed., *Victorian Theatrical Burlesques*, Aldershot: Ashgate, 2003, p. xxviii.

39. Christopher Stray, *Classics Transformed*, Oxford: Clarendon Press, 1998.

40. Schoch, *Victorian Theatrical Burlesques*, pp. xxxi–xxxii.

41. Schoch, *Victorian Theatrical Burlesques*, pp. xxxiii–xxxiv.

42. Planché, *Extravaganzas*, vol. 5, pp. 309–10.

Chapter 5: James Robinson Planché and the Fairy Extravaganza

1. J.R. Planché, *Extravaganzas*, ed. by T.F. Dillon Croker and Stephen Tucker, London: Samuel French, 1879, vol. 1, p. 207.
2. H. Barton Baker, *History of the London Stage and its Famous Players*, 1904, New York: Benjamin Blom, 1969 reprint, pp. 263–4.
3. William Appleton, *Madame Vestris and the London Stage*, New York: Columbia University Press, 1974, p. 142.
4. Planché, *Extravaganzas*, vol. 2, pp. 145–6.
5. Planché, *Extravaganzas*, vol. 2, p. 181.
6. Planché, *Extravaganzas*, vol. 2, p. 184.
7. Planché, *Extravaganzas*, vol. 3, pp. 312–13.
8. Planché, *Extravaganzas*, vol. 4, pp. 89–90.
9. Planché, *Extravaganzas*, vol. 4, p. 131.
10. Planché, *Recollections and Reflections*, London: Tinsley Brothers, 1872, vol. 2, p. 154.
11. Planché, *Recollections and Reflections*, vol. 2, p. 154.
12. Raymond Mander and Joe Mitchenson, *The Lost Theatres of London*, London: Rupert Hart-Davis, 1968, pp. 276–7.
13. Mollie Sands, *Robson of the Olympic*, London: Society for Theatre Research, 1979, has a detailed account of Robson's travesty and pantomime roles.
14. Sands, *Robson of the Olympic*, reproduces the painting of Robson as the Yellow Dwarf, plate 11, opposite p. 77.
15. Planché, *Extravaganzas*, vol. 5, pp. 149–50.
16. Sir Frank Burnand, *Records and Reminiscences*, London: Methuen, 1904, vol. 2, pp. 330–5.
17. Michael Slater ed., *Dickens' Journalism*, London: J.M. Dent, 1997, vol. 2, pp. 98–102.
18. Edith Hall and Fiona Macintosh, *Greek Tragedy and the British Theatre 1660–1914*, Oxford: Oxford University Press, 2005, pp. 391–429.
19. Planché, *Extravaganzas*, vol. 3, p. 7.
20. Stanley Wells, 'Shakespeare in Planché's Extravaganzas', *Shakespeare Survey* 16 (1963), p. 104.
21. Planché, *Extravaganzas*, vol. 5, p. 103.

Chapter 6: William Roxby Beverley and the Triumph of Scene-Painting

1. Martin Meisel, *Realizations: Narrative, Pictorial and Theatrical Arts in Nineteenth-Century England*, Princeton: Princeton University Press, 1983; Michael Booth, *Victorian Spectacular Theatre 1850–1910*, London: Routledge and Kegan Paul, 1981.
2. Sybil Rosenfeld, *Georgian Scene Painters and Scene Painting*, Cambridge: Cambridge University Press, 1981, p. 4.
3. Rosenfeld, *Georgian Scene Painters*, pp. 15–18.
4. Richard Schoch, *Shakespeare's Victorian Stage: Performing History in the Theatre of Charles Kean*, Cambridge: Cambridge University Press, 1998.
5. Sybil Rosenfeld, *A Short History of Scene Design in Great Britain*, Oxford: Basil Blackwell, 1973, p. 107. On panorama and diorama in pantomime, see Richard Altick, *The Shows of*

London, Cambridge, Massachusetts: Belknap Press, 1978, pp. 198–201; David Mayer III, *Harlequin in His Element: The English Pantomime, 1806–1836*, Cambridge, Massachusetts: Harvard University Press, 1969, pp. 70–4; Ralph Hyde, *Panoramania!*, London: Trefoil Publications, 1988, pp 131–5.

6. Rosenfeld, *Georgian Scene Painters*, p. 90.

7. *Theatrical Examiner*, 28 December 1823; *The Times*, 27 December 1823.

8. On Stanfield, see Pieter van der Merwe, *Clarkson Stanfield, 1793–1867: Seaman, Scene-Painter, Royal Academician*, Gateshead: Tyne and Wear County Council Museum, 1979.

9. E.T. Cook and Alexander Wedderburn eds, *The Works of John Ruskin*, London: George Allen, 1903, vol. 3, pp. 226, 390.

10. Helen Guiterman and Briony Llewellyn eds, *David Roberts*, Oxford: Phaidon Press, 1987, pp. 27–44.

11. Throughout his career the artist was variously referred to in print as Beverley and Beverly. Jennie Bisset informs me that the name is spelled Beverly on his tombstone. But during his lifetime the most common spelling of his surname in the press was Beverley, so I have adopted that spelling for my discussion while retaining the variants in quoted passages.

12. Cook and Wedderburn, *The Works of John Ruskin*, vol. 37, p. 34.

13. Katherine Newey and Jeffrey Richards, *John Ruskin and the Victorian Theatre*, Basingstoke: Palgrave Macmillan, 2010, p. 170.

14. Jeffrey Richards, 'Irving and his Scenic Artists' in Richard Foulkes ed., *Henry Irving: A Re-Evaluation*, Aldershot: Ashgate, 2008, pp. 111–12.

15. *The Gentleman's Magazine* 266 (June 1889), p. 611.

16. *The Gentleman's Magazine* 266, p. 609.

17. Frank L. Emanuel, 'William Roxby Beverley', *Walker's Quarterly* 2 (January 1921), p. 10.

18. *Oxford Dictionary of National Biography*, 'William Roxby Beverly', Oxford: Oxford University Press, 2004, vol. 5, pp. 600–2.

19. James Robinson Planché, *Extravaganzas*, vol. 3, London: Samuel French, 1879, pp. 183–4.

20. Alice Finkel, *Romantic Stages: Set and Costume Design in Victorian England*, Jefferson, North Carolina: McFarland, 1996, p. 165.

21. Percy Fitzgerald, *The World Behind the Scenes*, London: Chatto and Windus, 1881, p. 41.

22. *The Magazine of Art* 12 (January 1889), p. 45.

23. James Robinson Planché, *Recollections and Reflections*, London: Tinsley Brothers, 1872, p. 135.

24. John Forster and George Henry Lewes, *Dramatic Essays*, London: Walter Scott, 1896, pp. 225–8.

25. Michael Williams, *Some London Theatres Past and Present*, London: Sampson Low, Marston, Searle and Rivington, 1883, p. 168.

26. Russell Jackson, 'Victorian and Edwardian Stagecraft: Techniques and Issues' in Kerry Powell ed., *The Cambridge Companion to Victorian and Edwardian Theatre*, Cambridge: Cambridge University Press, 2004, pp. 53–4.

27. *The Sunday Times*, 8 March 1885.

Chapter 7: The Drury Lane Pantomime: the Creators

1. A.E. Wilson, *Christmas Pantomime*, London: George Allen and Unwin, 1934, p. 174.
2. Stanley Lupino, *From the Stocks to the Stars*, London: Hutchinson, 1934, p. 69.
3. Leopold Wagner, *The Pantomimes and All About Them*, London: John Heywood, 1881, pp. 32–3. The over-concentration on London has begun to be remedied. Jill Sullivan's excellent *The Politics of the Pantomime: Regional Identity in the Theatre 1860–1900*, Hatfield: University of Hertfordshire Press, 2011, examines the pantomime tradition in Nottingham, Birmingham and Manchester.
4. Wagner, *The Pantomimes and All About Them*, p. 31.
5. *The Theatre* n.s. vol. 1 (January 1883), p. 12.
6. Geneviève Ward and Richard Whiteing, *Both Sides of the Curtain*, London: Cassell, 1918, p. 223.
7. Errol Sherson, *London's Lost Theatres of the Nineteenth Century*, London: Cassell, 1918, p. 223.
8. Ward and Whiteing, *Both Sides of the Curtain*, p. 223; Edward Stirling, *Old Drury Lane*, London: Chatto and Windus, 1881, vol. 1, p. 266.
9. Edmund Yates, *Recollections and Experiences*, London: Richard Bentley and Son, 1885, p. 125.
10. A.E. Wilson, *The Lyceum*, London: Dennis Yates, 1952, p. 90.
11. Jim Davis and Victor Emeljanow, *Reflecting the Audience: London Theatregoing, 1840–1880*, Hatfield: University of Hertfordshire Press, 2001, p. 204.
12. *The Era*, 2 January, 1853.
13. Stirling, *Old Drury Lane*, vol. 1, p. 251.
14. Sherson, *London's Lost Theatres*, p. 74.
15. Stirling, *Old Drury Lane*, vol. 1, pp. 265–6.
16. Ward and Whiteing, *Both Sides of the Curtain*, p. 224.
17. Sherson, *London's Lost Theatres*, p. 74.
18. Ward and Whiteing, *Both Sides of the Curtain*, pp. 231–2.
19. John Coleman, *Players and Playwrights I Have Known*, London: Chatto and Windus, 1888, vol. 2, p. 386.
20. Coleman, *Players and Playwrights I Have Known*, vol. 2, p. 326.
21. Ward and Whiteing, *Both Sides of the Curtain*, p. 233.
22. Coleman, *Players and Playwrights I Have Known*, vol. 2, p. 327.
23. Coleman, *Players and Playwrights I Have Known*, vol. 2, p. 345.
24. Coleman, *Players and Playwrights I Have Known*, vol. 2, p. 346.
25. W.J. Macqueen Pope, *Theatre Royal, Drury Lane*, London: W.H. Allen, 1945, p. 282.
26. Coleman, *Players and Playwrights I Have Known*, vol. 2, pp. 358–9.
27. Coleman, *Players and Playwrights I Have Known*, vol. 2, p. 345.
28. Stirling, *Old Drury Lane*, vol. 1, p. 317.
29. Coleman, *Players and Playwrights I Have Known*, vol. 2, p. 386.
30. Macqueen Pope, *Theatre Royal, Drury Lane*, p. 285.
31. *The Dictionary of National Biography*, Compact Edition, Oxford: Oxford University Press, 1957, p. 2427.
32. Ward and Whiteing, *Both Sides of the Curtain*, p. 234.

33. *Dictionary of National Biography*, Compact Edition, p. 2427.

34. Ward and Whiteing, *Both Sides of the Curtain*, p. 235.

35. W. Macqueen Pope, *Ghosts and Greasepaint*, London: Robert Hale, 1951, p. 288.

36. Ward and Whiteing, *Both Sides of the Curtain*, p. 235.

37. Ward and Whiteing, *Both Sides of the Curtain*, pp. 235–6.

38. Macqueen Pope, *Ghosts and Greasepaint*, p. 291.

39. Ward and Whiteing, *Both Sides of the Curtain*, pp. 240–2.

40. *The Theatre* vol. 28 (July 1896), p. 8.

41. Augustus Harris, 'The National Theatre', *The Fortnightly Review* 38 (November 1885), pp. 630–6.

42. J.B. Booth, *The Days We Knew*, London: Werner Laurie, 1943, p. 110.

43. Macqueen Pope, *Ghosts and Greasepaint*, p.288.

44. *The Era*, 20 February 1897.

45. Macqueen Pope, *Theatre Royal, Drury Lane*, pp. 310–11.

46. Davis and Emeljanow, *Reflecting the Audience*, p. 226.

47. Davis and Emeljanow, *Reflecting the Audience*, p. 225.

48. James M. Glover, *Jimmy Glover – His Book*, London: Methuen, 1911, pp. 158–9.

49. Jim Davis, 'Boxing Day' in Tracy C. Davis and Peter Holland eds, *The Performing Century: Nineteenth-Century Theatre's History*, Basingstoke: Palgrave Macmillan, 2007, pp. 28–30.

50. Dawn Lewcock, 'Once Upon a Time: the Story of the Pantomime Audience' in Susan Kattwinkel ed., *Audience Participation*, Westport, Connecticut: Praeger, 2003, p. 142.

51. Clement Scott and Cecil Howard eds, *The Life and Reminiscences of E.L. Blanchard*, London: Hutchinson, 1891, vol. 2, pp. 599 (*The World*), 586 (*Judy*).

52. Scott and Howard, *Life and Reminiscences of Blanchard*, pp. 2, 3.

53. Scott and Howard, *Life and Reminiscences of Blanchard*, pp. v–xv.

54. *The Dictionary of National Biography*, Compact Edition, p. 2376.

55. Sir Francis Burnand, *Records and Reminiscences*, London: Methuen, 1904, vol. 1, pp. 377–8.

56. Burnand, *Records and Reminiscences*, vol. 2, pp. 113–17.

57. *The Era*, 14 September 1889.

58. Clement Scott, *The Drama of Yesterday and Today*, London: Macmillan, 1899, vol. 1, pp. 307–18. On Bohemia, see Christopher Kent, 'The Idea of Bohemia in Mid-Victorian England', *Queen's Quarterly* 80 (1973), pp. 360–9; Christopher Kent, 'British Bohemia and the Victorian Journalist', *Australasian Victorian Studies Journal* 6 (2000), pp. 25–35; Patrick Leahy, *The Punch Brotherhood: Table Talk and Print Culture in Mid-Victorian London*, London: the British Library, 2010.

59. Scott and Howard, *Life and Reminiscences of Blanchard*, p. 332.

60. Scott and Howard, *Life and Reminiscences of Blanchard*, pp. 404–5.

61. Scott and Howard, *Life and Reminiscences of Blanchard*, p. 52.

62. John Russell Stephens, *The Profession of the Playwright: British Theatre 1800–1900*, Cambridge: Cambridge University Press, 1992.

63. Scott and Howard, *Life and Reminiscences of Blanchard*, pp. 334, 114, 113, 104, 342, 408, 409.

64. Scott and Howard, *Life and Reminiscences of Blanchard*, pp. 37, 77, 130, 131, 138, 137, 158, 166, 168.

65. Scott and Howard, *Life and Reminiscences of Blanchard*, pp. 186, 199, 211, 213, 220, 315, 334, 391, 392, 405.

66. For full details of Blanchard's annual income, see the Appendix.

67. Scott and Howard, *Life and Reminiscences of Blanchard*, pp. 101, 127, 191, 234, 253, 255, 268.

68. Scott and Howard, *Life and Reminiscences of Blanchard*, pp. 103, 230, 233, 274, 276, 277, 287, 319–22, 353, 356, 376, 379, 380, 391, 394, 405.

69. Scott and Howard, *Life and Reminiscences of Blanchard*, pp. 295, 305.

70. Scott and Howard, *Life and Reminiscences of Blanchard*, p. 318; Edward Wakeling ed., *Lewis Carroll's Diaries*, Luton: The Lewis Carroll Society, 1999, vol. 5, p. 345.

71. H.G. Hibbert, *A Playgoer's Memories*, London: Grant Richards, 1920, pp. 101–2; Glover, *Jimmy Glover – His Book*, p. 145.

72. Glover, *Jimmy Glover – His Book*, pp. 145–6.

73. Glover, *Jimmy Glover – His Book*, p. 145.

74. Booth, *The Days We Knew*, p. 112.

75. Scott and Howard, *Life and Reminiscences of Blanchard*, pp. 140, 92, 133, 134, 136, 137, 140, 143, 208, 271.

76. Scott and Howard, *Life and Reminiscences of Blanchard*, pp. 333, 365.

77. Scott and Howard, *Life and Reminiscences of Blanchard*, pp. 232, 440, 529.

78. Sherson, *London's Lost Theatres*, p. 259.

79. Kurt Gänzl, *The British Musical Theatre*, London: Macmillan, 1986, vol. 1, pp. 337–9.

80. Scott and Howard, *Life and Reminiscences of Blanchard*, pp. 533, 553, 556, 567, 573, 579, 615, 639, v–xv.

81. Scott and Howard, *Life and Reminiscences of Blanchard*, pp. 183, 317, 612.

82. *Belgravia* 1 (1867), pp. 359–64.

83. I am grateful to Jennie Bisset for placing her unpublished research on Dykwynkyn at my disposal.

84. On D'Auban, see the unpublished PhD dissertation, *John D'Auban, Phantom of the Light Opera* by Kelly Pierce Boyd, Texas Women's University, Denton, 1999.

Chapter 8: E.L. Blanchard and the Drury Lane Pantomimes: The Smith Management

1. Anne Humpherys and Louis James ed., *G.W.M. Reynolds: Nineteenth-Century Fiction, Politics and the Press*, Aldershot: Ashgate, 2008, p. 4.

2. Jeffrey Richards and John M. MacKenzie, *The Railway Station: A Social History*, London: Faber, 2010, pp. 1–2.

3. Lynda Nead, *Victorian Babylon*, New Haven and London: Yale University Press, 2000, pp. 88–9.

4. *The Times*, 27 and 28 December 1848.

5. Clement Scott and Cecil Howard eds, *The Life and Reminiscences of E.L. Blanchard*, London: Hutchinson, 1891, vol. 1, p. 89.

6. Scott and Howard, *Life and Reminiscences of Blanchard*, vol. 1, p. 89.

7. Allardyce Nicoll, *A History of English Drama 1660–1900*, Cambridge: Cambridge University Press, 1967, vol. 5, p. 393.

8. Scott and Howard, *Life and Reminiscences of Blanchard*, vol. 1, p. 89.

9. Nicoll, *A History of English Drama*, vol. 5, p. 393.

10. Nicoll, *A History of English Drama*, vol. 5, p. 263.

11. John Coleman, *Memoirs of Samuel Phelps*, London: Remington, 1886, p. 218. Dennis Arundell makes no mention of the pantomimes in his history of the theatre, *The Story of Sadler's Wells 1803–1977*, Newton Abbot: David and Charles, 1978.

12. Scott and Howard, *Life and Reminiscences of Blanchard*, vol. 1, p. 49.

13. Scott and Howard, *Life and Reminiscences of Blanchard*, vol. 2, p. 486.

14. Scott and Howard, *Life and Reminiscences of Blanchard*, vol. 1, p. 98.

15. Scott and Howard, *Life and Reminiscences of Blanchard*, vol. 1, pp. 100–1.

16. Scott and Howard, *Life and Reminiscences of Blanchard*, vol. 1, p. 117.

17. Scott and Howard, *Life and Reminiscences of Blanchard*, vol. 1, pp. 116, 115.

18. Edward Stirling, *Old Drury Lane*, London: Chatto and Windus, 1881, vol. 1, p. 252.

19. Scott and Howard, *Life and Reminiscences of Blanchard*, vol. 1, p. 126.

20. Scott and Howard, *Life and Reminiscences of Blanchard*, vol. 1, pp. 126–7.

21. Scott and Howard, *Life and Reminiscences of Blanchard*, vol. 1, p. 148.

22. Scott and Howard, *Life and Reminiscences of Blanchard*, vol. 1, pp. 146, 149.

23. Scott and Howard, *Life and Reminiscences of Blanchard*, vol. 1, p. 168.

24. See also *The Era*, 27 December 1857; *The Standard*, 28 December 1857; *I.L.N.*, 2 January 1858.

25. Daniel R. Headrick, *Tools of Empire*, New York: Oxford University Press, 1981, p. 163.

26. Headrick, *Tools of Empire*, pp. 158–9.

27. Scott and Howard, *Life and Reminiscences of Blanchard*, vol. 1, pp. 186, 191, 188.

28. At the time the pantomime opened, it was not known that Havelock had died on 24 November 1857, two days before the award of a baronetcy. News of his death reached England on 7 January 1858.

29. See *The Era*, 2 January 1859; *I.L.N.*, 1 January 1859; *The Standard*, 28 December 1858.

30. Scott and Howard, *Life and Reminiscences of Blanchard*, vol. 1, pp. 206, 209, 212.

31. Jerry White, *London in the Nineteenth Century*, London: Jonathan Cape, 2007, pp. 50–5.

32. Scott and Howard, *Life and Reminiscences of Blanchard*, vol. 1, pp. 230, 234, 232.

33. Scott and Howard, *Life and Reminiscences of Blanchard*, vol. 1, p. 251.

34. Scott and Howard, *Life and Reminiscences of Blanchard*, vol. 1, pp. 255, 253, 252.

35. Scott and Howard, *Life and Reminiscences of Blanchard*, vol. 1, p. 243.

36. Scott and Howard, *Life and Reminiscences of Blanchard*, vol. 1, pp. 285, 292, 285.

37. Scott and Howard, *Life and Reminiscences of Blanchard*, vol. 1, pp. 247, 251, 253, 255.

38. Scott and Howard, *Life and Reminiscences of Blanchard*, vol. 1, pp. 266–8, 264–5.

Chapter 9: E.L. Blanchard and the Drury Lane Pantomimes: The Chatterton Management

1. Clement Scott and Cecil Howard eds, *The Life and Reminiscences of E.L. Blanchard*, London: Hutchinson, 1891, vol. 1, pp. 274–7.

2. Scott and Howard, *Life and Reminiscences of Blanchard*, vol. 1, p. 273.
3. Scott and Howard, *Life and Reminiscences of Blanchard*, vol. 1, pp. 274–6.
4. Scott and Howard, *Life and Reminiscences of Blanchard*, vol. 1, p. 287.
5. Scott and Howard, *Life and Reminiscences of Blanchard*, vol. 1, pp. 281, 286.
6. Scott and Howard, *Life and Reminiscences of Blanchard*, vol. 1, pp. 295, 303, 305.
7. Scott and Howard, *Life and Reminiscences of Blanchard*, vol. 1, pp. 303, 304, 307.
8. Scott and Howard, *Life and Reminiscences of Blanchard*, vol. 1, pp. 322, 334, 318, 334.
9. Scott and Howard, *Life and Reminiscences of Blanchard*, vol. 1, pp. 319–22.
10. Scott and Howard, *Life and Reminiscences of Blanchard*, vol. 1, p. 333.
11. Scott and Howard, *Life and Reminiscences of Blanchard*, vol. 2, pp. 353, 356.
12. Catherine Robson, *Men in Wonderland: The Lost Girlhood of the Victorian Gentleman*, Princeton: Princeton University Press, 2001, pp. 3–15, 94–128. See also George Boas, *The Cult of Childhood*, Dallas: Spring, 1966.
13. Anne Varty, *Children and Theatre in Victorian Britain*, Basingstoke: Palgrave Macmillan, 2008, p. 2.
14. James Kincaid, *Child-Loving: The Erotic Child and Victorian Culture*, New York: Routledge, 1992; Marah Gubar, 'The Drama of Precocity: Child Performers on the Victorian Stage' in Dennis Dennisoff ed., *The Nineteenth-Century Child and Consumer Culture*, Aldershot: Ashgate, 2008, pp. 64–78; Marah Gubar, *Artful Dodgers*, New York: Oxford University Press, 2009; Jim Davis, 'Freaks, Prodigies, and Marvellous Mimicry: Child Actors of Shakespeare on the Nineteenth-Century Stage', *Shakespeare* 2 (2006), pp. 179–93.
15. Varty, *Children and Theatre in Victorian Britain*; Ellen Barlee, *Pantomime Waifs*, London: Partridge, 1884.
16. *The Theatre* 26 (1895), pp. 368–9.
17. Jim Davis ed., *The Britannia Diaries of Frederick Wilton*, London: Society for Theatre Research, 1992, pp. 75–8.
18. Edward Wakeling ed., *Lewis Carroll's Diaries*, Luton: The Lewis Carroll Society, 1999, vol. 5, pp. 127, 128, 130, 136.
19. George R. Sims, *My Life*, London: Eveleigh Nash, 1917, p. 190.
20. T. Brown, *A History of the New York Stage from 1732 to 1901*, New York: Dodd, Mead and Co., 1903, vol. 2, p. 533.
21. H.G. Hibbert, *A Playgoer's Memories*, London: Grant Richards, 1920, p. 21.
22. Bruno Bettelheim, *The Uses of Enchantment: The Meaning and Importance of Fairy Tales*, Harmondsworth: Penguin, 1986, p. 10.
23. Scott and Howard, *Life and Reminiscences of Blanchard*, vol. 2, pp. 366–8.
24. Hibbert, *A Playgoer's Memories*, p. 102.
25. Scott and Howard, *Life and Reminiscences of Blanchard*, vol. 2, pp. 376, 379, 380.
26. Scott and Howard, *Life and Reminiscences of Blanchard*, vol. 2, pp. 390–4.
27. Scott and Howard, *Life and Reminiscences of Blanchard*, vol. 2, p. 405.
28. Scott and Howard, *Life and Reminiscences of Blanchard*, vol. 2, p. 419.
29. Scott and Howard, *Life and Reminiscences of Blanchard*, vol. 2, p. 421.
30. Scott and Howard, *Life and Reminiscences of Blanchard*, vol. 2, p. 445.
31. Scott and Howard, *Life and Reminiscences of Blanchard*, vol. 2, p. 445.
32. Scott and Howard, *Life and Reminiscences of Blanchard*, vol. 2, p. 455.

33. Scott and Howard, *Life and Reminiscences of Blanchard*, vol. 2, p. 454.

34. Scott and Howard, *Life and Reminiscences of Blanchard*, vol. 2, p. 463.

35. Richard Foulkes, *Lewis Carroll and the Victorian Stage*, Aldershot: Ashgate, 2005, pp. 156–9. On children's pantomimes, see Varty, *Children and Theatre in Victorian Britain*, pp. 86–92; Gubar, *Artful Dodgers*, pp. 184–9; and Foulkes, 'Lewis Carroll, E.L. Blanchard and Frank W. Green' in Jim Davis ed., *Victorian Pantomime*, Basingstoke: Palgrave Macmillan, 2010, pp. 54–69.

36. Scott and Howard, *Life and Reminiscences of Blanchard*, vol. 2, p. 481.

37. Scott and Howard, *Life and Reminiscences of Blanchard*, vol. 2, p. 483.

38. John Coleman, *Players and Playwrights I Have Known*, London: Chatto and Windus, 1888, vol. 2, p. 376.

39. Edward Stirling, *Old Drury Lane*, London: Chatto and Windus, 1881, vol. 1, p. 317.

40. *The Theatre* 2 (March 1879), pp. 78–81.

41. Coleman, *Players and Playwrights I Have Known*, vol. 2, p. 382.

Chapter 10: Sir Augustus Harris and the Battle for Pantomime

1. Clement Scott and Cecil Howard eds, *The Life and Reminiscences of E.L. Blanchard*, London: Hutchinson, 1891, vol. 2, p. 498.

2. J.B. Booth, *The Days We Knew*, London: Werner Laurie, 1943, p. 112.

3. The only full-length study of Harris and his pantomimes is the dissertation by Frederick Coggin,'The Pantomimes of Augustus Harris: Drury Lane, 1879–1895', Ohio State University, 1979. A full-length biography of Harris is long overdue.

4. H.G. Hibbert, *A Playgoer's Memories*, London: Grant Richards, 1920, p. 78.

5. *The Theatre* 3 (1881), p. 93.

6. Booth, *The Days We Knew*, p. 115.

7. Scott and Howard, *Life and Reminiscences of Blanchard*, vol. 2, pp. 541–2.

8. Scott and Howard, *Life and Reminiscences of Blanchard*, vol. 2, p. 567.

9. Scott and Howard, *Life and Reminiscences of Blanchard*, vol. 2, p. 614.

10. Scott and Howard, *Life and Reminiscences of Blanchard*, vol. 2, p. 629.

11. Scott and Howard, *Life and Reminiscences of Blanchard*, vol. 2, p. 528.

12. Scott and Howard, *Life and Reminiscences of Blanchard*, vol. 2, p. 542.

13. Scott and Howard, *Life and Reminiscences of Blanchard*, vol. 2, p. 578.

14. Scott and Howard, *Life and Reminiscences of Blanchard*, vol. 2, p. 629.

15. *Belgravia* 5 (January 1875), pp. 340–9.

16. *The Gentleman's Magazine* 261 (1886), pp. 544–5.

17. E.T. Cook and Alexander Wedderburn eds, *The Works of John Ruskin*, London: George Allen, 1903–12, vol. 27, p. 256.

18. Cook and Wedderburn, *Works of Ruskin*, vol. 28, p. 52.

19. Cook and Wedderburn, *Works of Ruskin*, vol. 28, p. 52.

20. Cook and Wedderburn, *Works of Ruskin*, vol. 17, pp. 333–8.

21. Scott and Howard, *Life and Reminiscences of Blanchard*, vol. 1, p. 335.

22. *The Theatre* n.s.2 (1879), pp. 24–8.

23. *The Theatre* 5 (1882), pp. 85–90.

24. Leopold Wagner, *The Pantomimes and All About Them*, London: John Heywood, 1881, p. 9.
25. *The Theatre* 27 (1896), pp. 21–5.
26. *The Magazine of Art* 12 (1889), pp. 109–13.
27. Grenville Simons, *William Yardley – Master of Bat and Burlesque*, Malvern: Wisteria Books, 1997.
28. Barry Anthony, *The King's Jester: The life of Dan Leno, Victorian Comic Genius*, London: I.B.Tauris, 2010, pp. 95–6.
29. J. Hickory Wood, *Dan Leno*, London: Methuen, 1905, pp. 119, 126.
30. Harry Randall, *Harry Randall, Old Time Comedian*, London: Sampson Low, Marston and Co., 1931, p. 127.
31. Mary Tich and Richard Findlater, *Little Tich, Giant of the Music Hall*, London: Elm Tree, 1979, pp. 40–3.
32. Midge Gillies, *Marie Lloyd, the One and Only*, London: Victor Gollancz, 1999, p. 56.
33. *The Times*, 31 December 1892; *I.S.D.N.*, 31 December 1892.
34. J.M. Glover, *Jimmy Glover and His Friends*, London: Chatto and Windus, 1913, p. 71.
35. Gillies, *Marie Lloyd*, p. 83.
36. Tich and Findlater, *Little Tich*, pp. 49–50.
37. Hibbert, *A Playgoer's Memories*, p. 79.
38. Frances Fleetwood, *Conquest*, London: W.H. Allen, 1953, p. 164.
39. Hibbert, *A Playgoer's Memories*, p. 79.
40. H. Chance Newton, *Cues and Curtain Calls*, London: John Lane, 1927, pp. 63–4.
41. William Archer, *The Theatrical World of 1894*, London: Walter Scott, 1895, p. 1.
42. Ellaline Terriss, *Just a Little Bit of String*, London: Hutchinson, p. 55.
43. Tracy C. Davis, *The Economics of the British Stage, 1800–1914*, Cambridge: Cambridge University Press, 2000, p. 344.
44. J.M. Glover, *Jimmy Glover: His Book*, London: Methuen, 1911, pp. 158, 161.

Titles Index

All theatres are in London unless otherwise stated. References to images are in *italics*.

General Index

All theatres are in London unless otherwise stated. References to images are in *italics*.